# AFRICANA

*Civil Rights*

An A-to-Z Reference of the
Movement that Changed America

William Edward Burghardt Du Bois

# Praise for the original *Africana*:

"Attractive and well-designed. . . .It is the first reference work I have encountered that is attractive enough and accessible enough to simply pick up, open to any page and start reading. . . . A major achievement."

*—The Los Angeles Times Book Review*

"For this accessible, fascinating volume, [Gates and Appiah] have commissioned and condensed more than 3000 articles by more than 400 scholars . . . Bursting with information and enhanced by contributions from its illustrious advisory board . . . this book belongs on every family's reference shelf. Du Bois himself could not have done better."

*—Starred Publisher's Weekly Review*

"A landmark achievement."

*—Publisher's Weekly Best Books 99*

"An informational jewel."

*—Emerge*

The editors have admirably fulfilled the dream of African American scholar and leader W.E.B. Du Bois, who worked for much of his life to create such a monument. Highly recommended reading for all."

*—Library Journal*

"The best one-volume reference book on Africa and the African diaspora now available . . . Excellent articles . . . remarkably up to date."

*—The Philadelphia Inquirer*

*Africana* holds a unique place among reference works by bridging the Atlantic in numerous ways . . . the strength of *Africana's* unique linkage of the African and African-American becomes evident in comparison to other reference works treating one or the other half of that whole . . . *Africana* includes unique entries not found in the African American Almanac (Gale, 1997), An African Biographical Dictionary (ABC-CLIO, 1994), Encyclopedia of African American Culture & History (Macmillan 1996) to cite but a few prominent examples."

*—Booklist*

"Imposing in its sheer mass, *Africana* . . . is a 2,096-page, single volume 'encyclopedia of the black world.' This is no overstatement, as the range of entries ably demonstrates."

*—Vibe*

"Complete, balanced, informative, and addictively fun to browse."

—*Boston Magazine*

"A source of information that would surely make Du Bois proud."

—*The Tampa Tribune*

"Editors Henry Louis Gates and Kwame Anthony Appiah fulfilled W.E.B. Du Bois' vision on an encyclopedia of African-based culture throughout the world. The scholarship is unassailable [and] the text is accessible and understandable."

—*The Seattle Times*

"An invaluable resource of the historical, social, and cultural lushness of a scattered and varied people . . . Deserve[s] a place in every library, in every heart."

—*The Miami Herald*

"Belongs in every student's library and school . . . A monumental record of the black experience."

—*The Baltimore Sun*

"As the second millennium ends and a third begins, a new landmark volume brings together the richness and history of African and African-American culture."

—*Beyond the Cover*

"A monumental reference work, brings the richness of African and African American culture out of the shadows and into the living rooms of families across America . . . Destined to have a major effect by filling a cultural void . . . *Africana* presents exacting scholarship in an accessible, entertaining and visually animated style . . . conveys the richness, variety, and sweep of the African and African American experience as no other project before it . . . A reference work of both range and depth that symbolically will reunite the richly varied strands of the African Diaspora."

—*The Portland Skanner*

"A long-awaited overview of the history of the peoples of Africa and the African diaspora."

—*Wall Street Journal*

"*Africana* will be a very useful tool, and may even set new standards and change attitudes about the African and African-American experience."

—*The New York Times Book Review*

# AFRICANA

*Civil Rights*

An A-to-Z Reference of the
Movement that Changed America

**Editors**

Kwame Anthony Appiah, *Princeton University*
Henry Louise Gates, Jr., *Harvard University*

RUNNING PRESS
PHILADELPHIA · LONDON

Library of Congress Cataloging-in-Publication Number 2004095744
ISBN 0-7624-1958-X

Cover design by Amanda Richmond
Interior design by Bob Anderson
Edited by Veronica Mixon, Diana Von Glahn, and Lindsay Powers
Typography: 9.5/11.5 Berling Roman

The entries in *Civil Rights: An A-to-Z Reference of the Movement that Changed America* originally appeared in Basic Civitas Books' *Africana: The Encyclopedia of the African and the African American Experience* © 1999 Kwame Anthony Appiah and Henry Louis Gates, Jr.

This book may be ordered by mail from the publisher.
Please include $2.50 for postage and handling.
**But try your bookstore first!**

Running Press Book Publishers
125 South Twenty-second Street
Philadelphia, Pennsylvania 19103-4399

Visit us on the web!
www.runningpress.com

*To the memory of William Edward Burghardt Du Bois
and in honor of Nelson Rolihlahla Mandela*

# Advisory Board

Wole Soyinka, Chair of the Advisory Board; *1986 Nobel Laureate in Literature*
Robert W. Woodruff Professor of the Arts, *Emory University*

Kofi Agawu, *Princeton University*
Sara S. Berry, *Johns Hopkins University*
Suzanne Preston Blier, *Harvard University*
Lawrence Bobo, *Harvard University*
Frederick Cooper, *University of Michigan at Ann Arbor*
Moore Crossey, *Yale University*
Selwyn R. Cudjoe, *Wellesley College*
Jacques d'Adesky, *Centros de Estudos Norte Americanos, Rio de Janeiro*
Howard Dodson, *Schomburg Center for Research in Black Culture*
Anani Dzidzienyo, *Brown University*
David Eltis, *Queens University*
Paul Gilroy, *University of London*
Jane Guyer, *Northwestern University*
Martin Hall, *University of Cape Town*
Stuart Hall, *The Open University, London*
Evelyn Brooks Higginbotham, *Harvard University*
Paulin J. Hountondji, *National University of Benin*
John Hunwick, *Northwestern University*
Abiola Irele, *Ohio State University*
Miriam Jiménez-Roman, *Independent Scholar*
Randall Kennedy, *Harvard Law School*
Jamaica Kincaid, *Harvard University*
Marvín Lewis, *University of Missouri at Columbia*
J. Lorand Matory, *Harvard University*
Ali A. Mazrui, *State University of New York at Binghamton*
Lucia Nagib, *Universidade Católica de São Paulo*
Nell Irvin Painter, *Princeton University*
Hans Panofsky, *Northwestern University*
Orlando Patterson, *Harvard University*
Arnold Rampersad, *Princeton University*
Thomas E. Skidmore, *Brown University*
Werner Sollors, *Harvard University*
Doris Sommer, *Harvard University*
Claude Steele, *Stanford University*
Cornel West, *Princeton University*
William Julius Wilson, *Harvard University*

# Table of Contents

# Introduction

Editor's Note on this Edition: *Civil Rights: An A-to-Z Reference of the Movement that Changed America* was abridged from *Africana: The Encyclopedia of the African and African American Experience*. Some of the entries are accompanied by all new photographs. Credit goes to Veronica Mixon for distilling the very best of the original *Africana* into this more portable, compact desk reference.

The history of how the original *Africana* came to be is a poignant story of faith, politics, and persistence despite what seemed, at times, like an insurmountable struggle. Kwame Anthony Appiah, and Henry Louis Gates, Jr., editors of that original edition, told the story in its introduction. We've chosen to reprint that introduction in this edition, to help you appreciate the struggle that gave birth to *Africana* and the editorial decisions that shaped it.

May the story hearten you as you advance toward your own dreams.

## How the original *Africana* Came to Be

Between 1909 and his death in 1963, W. E. B. Du Bois, the Harvard-trained historian, sociologist, journalist, and political activist, dreamed of editing an "Encyclopedia Africana." He envisioned a comprehensive compendium of 'scientific' knowledge about the history, cultures, and social institutions of people of African descent: of Africans in the Old World, African Americans in the New World, and persons of African descent who had risen to prominence in Europe, the Middle East, and Asia. Du Bois sought to publish nothing less than the equivalent of a black *Encyclopedia Britannica*, believing that such a broad assemblage of biography, interpretive essays, facts, and figures would do for the much denigrated black world of the twentieth century what Britannica and Denis Diderot's Encyclopédie had done for the European world of the eighteenth century.

These publications, which consolidated the scholarly knowledge accumulated by academics and intellectuals in the Age of Reason, served both as a tangible sign of the enlightened skepticism that characterized that era of scholarship, and as a basis upon which further scholarship could be constructed. These encyclopedias became monuments to "scientific" inquiry, bulwarks against superstition, myth, and what their authors viewed as the false solace of religious faith. An encyclopedia of the African diaspora in Du Bois's view would achieve these things for persons of African descent.

But a black encyclopedia would have an additional function. Its publication would, at least symbolically, unite the fragmented world of the African diaspora, a diaspora created by the European slave trade and the turn-of-the-century "scramble for Africa." Moreover, for Du Bois, marshalling the tools of "scientific knowledge," as he would put it in his landmark essay, "The Need for an Encyclopedia of the Negro" (1945), could also serve as a weapon in the war against racism: "There is need for young pupils and for mature students of a statement of the present condition of our knowledge concerning the darker races and especially concerning Negroes, which would make available our present scientific knowledge and set aside the vast accumulation of tradition and prejudice which makes such knowledge difficult now for the layman to obtain: A Vade mecum for American schools, editors, libraries, for Europeans inquiring into the race status here, for South Americans, and Africans."

The publication of such an encyclopedia, Du Bois continued, would establish "a base for further advance and further study" of "questions affecting the Negro race." An encyclopedia of the Negro, he reasoned, would establish both social policy and "social thought and discussion . . . upon a basis of accepted scientific conclusion."

Du Bois first announced his desire to edit an "Encyclopedia Africana" in a letter to Edward Wilmot Blyden, the Pan-Africanist intellectual, in Sierra Leone in 1909: "I am venturing to address you on the subject of a Negro Encyclopædia. In celebration of the 50th anniversary of the Emancipation of the American Negro, I am proposing to bring out an Encyclopedia Africana covering the chief points in the history and condition of the Negro race." Du Bois sent a similar letter to dozens of other scholars, white and black, including William James, Hugo Munsterberg, George Santayana, Albert Bushnell Hart (his professors at Harvard), President Charles William Eliot of Harvard, Sir Harry Johnston, Sir Flinders Petrie, Giuseppe Sergi, Franz Boas, J. E. Casely-Hayford, John Hope, Kelly Miller, Benjamin Brawley, Anna Jones, Richard Greener, Henry Ossawa Tanner, and several others, all of whom—with the sole exception of President Eliot—agreed to serve on his editorial board. Du Bois sought to create a board of "One Hundred Negro Americans, African and West Indian Scholars," as he put it in a letter, and a second board of white advisors. Du Bois, in other words, sought the collaboration of the very best scholars of what we would call today African Studies and African American Studies, as well as prominent American and European intellectuals such as James and Boas.

Nevertheless, as he put it to Blyden, "the real work I want done by Negroes." Du Bois, admitting that this plan was "still in embryo," created official stationery that projected a publication date of the first volume in 1913—"the Jubilee of Emancipation in America and the Tercentenary of the Landing of the Negro." The remaining four volumes would be published between 1913 and 1919.

Despite the nearly unanimous enthusiasm that greeted Du Bois's call for participation, he could not secure the necessary funding to mount the massive effort necessary to edit an encyclopedia of the black world. But he never abandoned the idea. At the height of the Great Depression, the idea would surface once again.

Anson Phelps Stokes, head of the Phelps-Stokes Association, a foundation dedicated to ameliorating race relations in America, called a meeting of

20 scholars and public figures at Howard University on November 7, 1931, to edit an "Encyclopedia of the Negro," a Pan-African encyclopedia similar to Du Bois's 1909 project. Incredibly, neither Du Bois nor Alain Locke, a Harvard trained Ph.D. in philosophy and the dean of the Harlem Renaissance, nor Carter G. Woodson (like Du Bois, a Harvard Ph.D. in history and the founder of the Association for the Study of Negro Life and History) was invited to attend. Du Bois protested, angrily, to Phelps Stokes. A second meeting was convened on January 9, 1932, at which Du Bois was unanimously elected editor-in-chief. Between 1932 and 1946, Du Bois would serve as "Editor-in-Chief" of the second incarnation of his project, now named "The Encyclopædia of the Negro," and housed at 200 West 135th Street in New York City.

Du Bois planned a four-volume encyclopedia, each volume comprising 500,000 words. Just as he had done in 1909, he secured the cooperation of an impressive array of scholars, including Charles Beard, Franz Boas, John R. Connors, Edith Abbott, Felix Frankfurter, Otto Klineburg, Carl Van Doren, H. L. Mencken, Roscoe Pound, Robert E. Park, Sidney Hook, Harold Laski, Broadus Mitchell, "and scores of others," as Du Bois put it in a letter to the historian Charles Wesley. Du Bois's "Encyclopedia of the Negro" would require a budget of $225,000. It would be written by a staff of between "25 and 100 persons" hired to be "research aides," to be located in editorial offices to be established in New York, Chicago, Atlanta, and New Orleans. They would prepare bibliographies, collect books and manuscripts, and gather and write "special data" and shorter entries. Black and white scholars, primarily located in Europe, America, and Africa, would write longer interpretive entries.

Du Bois tells us that his project was interrupted by the Depression for three years. But by 1935, he was actively engaged in its planning full-time, time made available by his forced resignation from his position as editor of *The Crisis* magazine, the official organ of the National Association for the Advancement of Colored People, which Du Bois had held since its first publication in 1910. Du Bois had written an editorial advocating the development of independent Negro social and economic institutions, since the goal posts of the Civil Rights Movement appeared to be receding. The NAACP's board of directors was outraged and demanded his resignation. Du Bois obliged. Du Bois sought funding virtually everywhere, including the Works Progress Administration and the Federal Writers' Project, to no avail, despite the fact that Phelps Stokes had pledged, on a matching basis, half of the needed funds. He continued to write to hundreds of scholars, soliciting their cooperation. E. Franklin Frazier, the great black sociologist, declined Du Bois's overture, citing in a letter dated November 7, 1936, the presence of too many "politicians," "statesmen," "big Negroes," and "whites of good will" on Du Bois's editorial board. Throw out the table of contents, fire the board of editors, replace them with scholars, Frazier wrote, and he would consider joining the project.

A few months before this exchange, Du Bois was viciously attacked by Carter G. Woodson in the black newspaper the *Baltimore Afro-American*.

On May 30, 1936, a page-one headline blared the news that Woodson "Calls Du Bois a Traitor if He Accepts Post," with a subtitle adding for good measure: "He Told Ofays, We'd Write Own History." Woodson charged that Du Bois had stolen the idea of The Encyclopedia of the Negro from him and that his project was doomed to failure because Du Bois was financed by, and his editorial board included, white people. Du Bois was embarrassed and sought to defend himself in letters to potential contributors and board members. Between his enemies at the NAACP and his intellectual rivals such as Woodson and Frazier, Du Bois faced an enormous amount of opposition to his encyclopedia project. In this swirl of controversy, in the midst of the Depression, funding appeared increasingly elusive.

Du Bois's assistant editor, Rayford Logan, like Du Bois, Woodson, and Charles Wesley a Harvard-trained Ph.D. in history, told a poignant story about the failure of this project to receive funding. By 1937, Du Bois had secured a pledge of $125,000 from the Phelps-Stokes Fund to proceed with his project—half of the funds needed to complete it. He applied to the Carnegie Corporation for the remaining half of his budget, with the strong endorsement of Phelps Stokes and the president of the General Education Board, a group of four or five private foundations that included the Rockefeller Foundation. So convinced was Du Bois that his project would finally be funded, that he invited Logan to wait with him for the telephone call that he had been promised immediately following the Carnegie board meeting. A bottle of vintage champagne sat chilling on Du Bois's desk in a silver bucket, two cut crystal champagne flutes resting nearby.

The phone never rang. Persuaded that Du Bois was far too "radical" to serve as a model of disinterested scholarship, and lobbied by Du Bois's intellectual enemies, such as the anthropologist Melville J. Herskovits, the Carnegie Corporation rejected the project.

Nevertheless, Du Bois stubbornly persisted, even publishing two putative "entries" from the Encyclopædia in Phylon magazine in 1940, one on Robert Russa Moton, the principal of Tuskegee Institute between 1915 and 1935, the other on Alexander Pushkin. He even was able to publish two editions, in 1945 and 1946, of a Preparatory Volume with Reference Lists and Reports of the Encyclopædia of the Negro. But the project itself never could secure adequate backing.

David Levering Lewis, Du Bois's biographer, tells us what happened to Du Bois's promised funding. The executive committee of the General Education Board rejected the proposal early in May 1937. "In his conference a few days later with Carnegie Corporation president Frederick Keppel, GEB's Jackson Davis paradoxically pleaded for favorable Carnegie consideration of the project. 'Dr. Du Bois is the most influential Negro in the United States,' Davis reminded Keppel. 'This project would keep him busy for the rest of his life.' Predictably, Carnegie declined. Within a remarkably short time, the study of the Negro (generously underwritten by the Carnegie Corporation) found a quite different direction under a Swedish scholar then unknown in the field of race relations, one whose understanding of American race problems was to be distinctly more psychological and less economic than was Du Bois's. . . . When the president of the Phelps Stokes Fund wrote Du Bois in 1944 at the time of the publication of *An American Dilemma:* [The Negro Problem and Modern Democracy] that 'there has been no one who has been quite so often quoted by [Gunnar] Myrdal than yourself,' Du Bois must have savored the irony."

Adding insult to injury, in 1948 the General Education Board, along with the Dodd Mead publishing company, approached Frederick Patterson, the president of Tuskegee Institute, to edit a new incarnation of the project, to be entitled *The Negro: An Encyclopedia.* Then in 1950, the historian Charles Wesley wrote to Du Bois, informing him that in the wake of Carter Woodson's death, the Association for the Study of Negro Life and History had decided to resurrect The Encyclopedia Africana project, reminding him of Woodson's claims to have conceived of it in 1921. Du Bois wished him well, but cautioned him in a postscript that "there is no such thing as a cheap encyclopedia." Everyone, it seemed, wanted to claim title to the encyclopedia, but no one wanted Du Bois to serve as its editor. For black scholars, Africana had become the Grail. Its publication, as Du Bois put it "would mark an epoch."

Long after Du Bois had abandoned all hope of realizing his great ambition, an offer of assistance would come quite unexpectedly from Africa. On September 26, 1960, Du Bois announced that Kwame Nkrumah, the president of the newly independent Republic of Ghana, had invited him to repatriate to Ghana, where he would serve as the editor-in-chief of *The Encyclopædia Africana.* Du Bois accepted, moving in 1961. On December 15, 1962, in his last public speech before his death on the eve of the March on Washington in August 1963, Du Bois addressed a conference assembled expressly to launch—at last—his great project.

He wanted to edit "an Encyclopædia Africana based in Africa and compiled by Africans," he announced, an encyclopedia that is "long overdue," referring no doubt to his previously frustrated attempts. "Yet," he continued with a certain grim satisfaction, "it is logical that such a work had to wait for independent Africans to carry it out [because] the encyclopedia is concerned with Africa as a whole." Citing his own introductory essay in the Preparatory Volume of 1945, Du Bois justified this project by railing against "present thought and action" that "are all too often guided by old and discarded theories of race and heredity, by misleading emphasis and silence of former histories." After all of these centuries of slavery and colonialism, on the eve of the independence of the Continent, "it is African scholars themselves who will create the ultimate Encyclopædia Africana." Eight months later Du Bois would be dead, and with him died his 54-year-old dream of shepherding a great black encyclopedia into print. Nevertheless, the Secretariat of the Encyclopædia Africana, based in Accra, Ghana, which Du Bois founded, eventually published three volumes of biographical dictionaries, in the late seventies and early eighties, and has recently announced plans to publish an encyclopedia about the African continent in 2009, which is welcome news.

We first became enamored of this project as students at the University of Cambridge. One of us, Henry Louis Gates, Jr., was a student of Wole Soyinka, the great playwright who in 1986 became the first African to receive the Nobel Prize for Literature. The other, Kwame Anthony Appiah, was an undergraduate studying philosophy. Though we came from very different backgrounds—rural West Virginia and urban Asante, in Ghana—we both already had, like Soyinka, a sense of the worlds of Africa and her diaspora as profoundly interconnected, even if, as we learned ourselves, there were risks of misunderstanding that arose from our different origins and experiences. The three of us represented three different places in the black world, and we vowed in 1973 to edit a Pan-African encyclopedia of the African diaspora, inspired by Du Bois's original objective formulated in 1909. Du Bois's later conception of the project was, we felt, too narrow in its scope, and too parochial in its stated desire to exclude the scholarly work of those who had not had the good fortune, by accident of birth, to have been born on the African continent. (Du Bois himself, had this rule been literally applied, would have been excluded from his own project!) Instead, we sought to edit a project that would produce a genuine compendium of "Africana."

Our own attempts to secure the necessary support were in vain too until four years ago when, first, Quincy Jones and Martin Payson, and then Sonny Mehta and Alberto Vitale at Random House, agreed to fund the preparation of a prototype of a CD-ROM encyclopedia of the African diaspora, to be edited by us, with Soyinka serving as the chair of an international and multiethnic board of editors. Two years later we secured the support for a 2-million-word encyclopedia from Frank Pearl, the CEO of a new publisher called Perseus Books, and from the Microsoft Corporation. Modifying the editorial structure that Du Bois planned to use to complete *The Encyclopædia of the Negro*, we deployed a staff of some three dozen writers and editors, and we solicited about 400 scholars to write longer, interpretive articles.

Du Bois's own idea, although he did not admit this, probably arose at least in part out of the publication of the Encyclopædia Judaica in 1907, as well as black encyclopedia antecedents such as James T. Holly, who published *The Afro-American Encyclopedia* in 1895, Alexander W. Wayman's *Cyclopedia of African Methodism* (1882), Charles O. Boothe's *The Cyclopedia of the Colored Baptists of Alabama* (1895), and Revels Adams's *Cyclopedia of African Methodism in Mississippi* (1902). Other unpublished projects patterned after Du Bois's 1909 proposal included Daniel Murray's monumental "Historical and Biographical Encyclopædia of the Colored Race Throughout the World," which was to have been published in 1912 in six volumes and, later, Edward Garrett's self-written "A Negro Encyclopedia," consisting of 4000 entries, and completed on the eve of World War II. Both encyclopedias exist in manuscript form, but tragically were never published.

All told, more than two dozen black encyclopedias have been published in the past century with limited distribution, but none has explored in a single compass both the African continent and the triumphs and the tragedies of Africa's people and their descendants around the globe.

That continent is where human prehistory begins. It was in Africa, as biologists now believe, that our species evolved, and so, in a literal sense, every modern human being is of African descent. Indeed, it was probably only about 100,000 years ago that the first members of our species left Africa, traveled across the Suez Peninsula, and set out on an adventure that would lead to the peopling of the whole earth.

It is important to emphasize that Africa has never been separate from the rest of the human world. There have been long periods and many cultures that knew nothing of life in Africa. For much of African history, even in Africa, most Africans were unaware of other peoples in their own continent, unaware, in fact, that they shared a continent at all (just as most people in Europe, Asia, Australasia, and the Americas would have been astonished to learn that they were Europeans, Asians, Australasians, or Americans!). But the Straits of Gibraltar and the Suez Peninsula were always bridges more than obstacles to travel; the Mediterranean was already a system of trade long before the founding of Rome; the Sahara Desert, which so many people imagine as an impenetrable barrier, has a network of trade routes older than the Roman Empire. Starting some 2,000 or so years ago, in the area of modern day Cameroon, Bantu-speaking migrants fanned out south and east into tropical Africa, taking with them the knowledge of iron smelting and new forms of agriculture. And so, when Greek and Arab travelers explored the East Coast of Africa in the first millennium C.E., or European explorers began to travel down the West African coast toward the equator in the fifteenth century, they were making direct contact with cultures with which their ancestors had very often been in remote and indirect contact all along.

The first European scholars to write about Africa in the modern period, which begins with the European Age of Discovery, knew very little of Africa's history. They did not know that their ancestors thousands of generations ago had also lived in Africa. If they had read Herodotus, they might have noticed his brief discussion of the civilizations of the upper Nile, and so they might have realized that Egypt was in touch with other African societies. However, it would probably not have occurred to them that, since those societies were also in touch with still others, Egypt was in touch with Central Africa as well. So they thought of much of Africa as being outside the human historical narrative they already knew.

These first scholars were also obviously struck by the physical differences between Africans and themselves—especially of skin color and hair—and by the differences between the customs back home and the ones the European explorers found on the Guinea coast. And so they thought of Africans as different in kind from themselves, wondering, sometimes, whether they were really also descendants of Adam and Eve.

Attitudes like these had already distorted Western understandings of Africa from the fifteenth century on. Worse yet, as the transatlantic slave trade developed, so did an increasingly negative set of ideas about African peoples and their capacities. It became normal to think of black Africans as inferior to Europeans, and many Europeans found in that inferiority a rationalization for the enslavement of Africans. As a result, much of the writing about Africans and about people of African descent in the New World was frankly derogatory. Because modern Africans were educated in European colonies, they too inherited a distorted and dismissive attitude toward Africa's past and African capacities, and one of the first tasks of modern African intellectuals has been to try to frame a sense of the world and our place in it that is freed from these sad legacies.

There have been many skirmishes in the battle to find a just representation of Africa and her peoples. But in the course of this century—and more especially in the last 30 or 40 years—a more objective knowledge of Africa has gradually emerged, both in Africa and elsewhere. Anthropologists began to describe the rich religious, artistic, and social life of African peoples. African historians have learned to interpret oral histories, passed down in Africa's many traditions, cross-checking them against archæological and documentary evidence to produce a rich picture of the African past. Economists and political scientists, literary critics and philosophers, scholars of almost every discipline in the social sciences and the humanities have contributed to this new knowledge, as have scholars on every continent, Africans prominent among them. Work in African American Studies has led to new understandings of the culture of slaves and of the role of people of African descent in shaping the New World's language, religion, agriculture, architecture, music, and art. As a result, it is now possible to comb through a great library of material on African history and on the peoples of Africa and her diaspora, and to offer, in a single volume, a compendium of facts and interpretations.

An encyclopedia cannot include everything that is known about its subject matter, even everything that is important. So we have had to make choices. (And, alas, some of the most interesting questions are as yet unanswered.) But we have sought to provide a broad range of information and so to represent the full range of Africa and her diaspora. About two-fifths of the text of the encyclopedia has to do exclusively, or almost so, with the African continent: the history of each of the modern nations of Africa and what happened within their territories before those nations developed; the names of ethnic groups, including some that were formerly empires and nations, and their histories; biographies of eminent African men and women; major cities and geographical features: rivers, mountains, lakes, deserts; forms of culture: art, literature, music, religion; and some of Africa's diverse plant and animal life. Another third deals mostly with Latin America and the Caribbean, focusing on the influence of African cultures and people of African descent in shaping those portions of the New World. Slightly less than a third of the material deals with North America in the same way. And the rest is material of cross-cultural significance or has to do with the African presence in Europe, Asia, or the rest of the world.

Our main focus has been on history—political and social—and on literature and the arts, including music, to which African and African American contributions have been especially notable in modern times. Our aim has been to give a sense of the wide diversity of peoples, cultures, and traditions that we know about in Africa in historical times, a feel for the environment in which that history was lived, and a broad outline of the contributions of people of African descent, especially in the Americas, but, more generally, around the world.

It is natural, faced with a compendium of this sort, to go looking first for what we know already and to be especially pleased with ourselves if we find something missing! But in setting out to make an encyclopedia in a single volume, we had to make choices all the time about what to include, and we did so in the light of our own best judgments, in consultation with many scholars from around the world. It has been one of the great satisfactions of compiling a work with so many colleagues with so many different specialized areas of knowledge, that we have been able to fill in some of our own many areas of ignorance. That, we believe, is the great pleasure of this new encyclopedia: it not only answers many questions that you knew you wanted to ask, it invites you to ask questions that you had not dreamed of asking. We hope you will find, as we have, that the answers to these unfamiliar questions are as amazing and as varied as Africa, her peoples, and their descendants all around the globe.

We mentioned earlier some of the many encyclopedias of various aspects of African and African American life that have been published in the past. The publication of *Africana: The Encyclopedia of the African and African American Experience* as a one-volume print edition aspires to belong in the grand tradition of encyclopedia editing by scholars interested in the black world on both sides of the Atlantic. It also relies upon the work of thousands of scholars who have sought to gather and to analyze, according to the highest scholarly standards, the lives and the worlds of black people everywhere. We acknowledge our indebtedness to these traditions of scholarly endeavor—more than a century old—to which we are heirs, by dedicating our encyclopedia to the monumental contribution of W. E. B. Du Bois.

*Kwame Anthony Appiah*
*Henry Louis Gates, Jr.*

# Acknowledgments

In addition to the contributors, who are acknowledged elsewhere in this book, the editors wish to express their profound gratitude to the following persons:

Sharon Adams, Rachel Antell, Bennett Ashley, Robbie Bach, Tim Bartlett, Craig Bartholomew, John Blassingame, William G. Bowen, Peggy Cooper Cafritz, Elizabeth Carduff, Albert Carnesale, Jamie Carter, Sheldon Cheek, Chin-lien Chen, Coureton C. Dalton, Karen C. C. Dalton, the late Charles T. Davis, Rafael de la Dehesa, John Donatich, David Du Bois, Joseph Duffy, Olawale Edun, Richard Ekman, Lynn Faitelson, Amy Finch, Henry Finder, Lisa Finder, Kerry Fishback, Susanne Freidberg, Elaine Froehlich, Tony Gleaton, Peter Glenshaw, Lisa Goldberg, Matthew Goldberg, Jaman Greene, Holly Hartman, Pete Higgins, Jessica Hochman, Chihiro Hosoe, Pat Jalbert, Mary Janisch, Quincy Jones, Paul Kahn, Leyla Keough, Jeremy Knowles, Joanne Kendall, Harry Lasker, Todd Lee, Krzysztof Lenk, Erroll McDonald, Jack McKeown, Della R. Mancuso, Nancy Maull, Sonny Mehta, Joel W. Motley III, Richard Newman, Peter Norton, Mark O'Malley, Jennifer Oppenheimer, Francisco Ortega, Martin Payson, Frank Pearl, Ben Penglase, Kevin Rabener, Toni Rosenberg, Daryl Roth, Michael Roy, Neil Rudenstine, Kelefa Sanneh, Carrie Seglin, Keith Senzel, Bill Smith, Wole Soyinka, Patti Stonesifer, Patricia Sullivan, Carol Thompson, Larry Thompson, Lucy Tinkcombe, Kate Tuttle, Charles Van Doren, Robert Vare, Michael Vazquez, Alberto Vitale, Sarah Von Dreele, Philippe Wamba, Carrie Mae Weems, and X Bonnie Woods.

# Contributors to the original *AFRICANA: The Encyclopedia of the African and African American Experience*

Rosanne Adderley, *Tulane University*
Marian Aguiar, *Amherst, Massachusetts*
Emmanuel Akyeampong, *Harvard University*
Suzanne Albulak, *Cambridge, Massachusetts*
Samir Amin, *Director of the Forum Tiers Monde, Dakar, Senegal*
George Reid Andrews, *University of Pittsburgh*
Abdullahi Ahmed An-Na'im, *Emory University*
Rachel Antell, *San Francisco, California*
Kwame Anthony Appiah, *Princeton University*
Jorge Arce, *Boston Conservatory of Music*
Alberto Arenas, *University of California at Berkeley*
Paul Austerlitz, *Brown University*
Karen Backstein, *City University of New York, College of Staten Island*
Anthony Badger, *University of Cambridge*
Lawrie Balfour, *Babson College*
Marlyse Baptista, *University of Georgia*
Robert Baum, *Iowa State University*
Stephen Behrendt, *Harvard University*
Patrick Bellegarde-Smith, *University of Wisconsin at Milwaukee*
Eric Bennett, *Iowa City, Iowa*
Suzanne Preston Blier, *Harvard University*
Juan Botero, *Former Executive Director, Instituto de Ciencia Politica, Bogota, Colombia*
Keith Boykin, *Washington, D.C.*
Esperanza Brizvela-Garcia, *London, England*
Diana DeG. Brown, *Bard College*
Eva Stahl Brown, *University of Texas at Austin*
Barbara Browning, *New York University*
Eric Brosch, *Cambridge, Massachusetts*
John Burdick, *Syracuse University*
Andrew Burton, *London, England*
Alida Cagidemetrio, *University of Udine, Italy*
Chloe Campbell, *London, England*
Sophia Cantave, *Tufts University*
Yvonne Captain, *George Washington University*
Judy Carney, *University of California at Los Angeles*
Vincent Carretta, *University of Maryland at College Park*
Clayborne Carson, *Editor, Martin Luther King, Jr., Papers Project, Stanford University*

Odile Cazenave, *University of Tennessee*
Alistair Chisholm, *London, England*
Jace Clayton, *Cambridge, Massachusetts*
Patricia Collins, *University of Cincinnati*
Nicola Cooney, *Harvard University*
Belinda Cooper, *New School for Social Research*
Frederick Cooper, *University of Michigan at Ann Arbor*
Juan Giusti Cordero, *Universidad de Puerto Rico*
Thomas Cripps, *Morgan State University*
Selwyn R. Cudjoe, *Wellesley College*
Carlos Dalmau, *San Juan, Puerto Rico*
Darién J. Davis, *Middlebury College*
James Davis, *Howard University*
Martha Swearington Davis, *University of California at Santa Barbara*
Cristobal Diaz-Ayala, *Independent Scholar*
Rafael Diaz-Diaz, *Pontificia Universidad Javeriana, Bogota, Colombia*
Quinton Dixie, *Indiana University*
Andrew Du Bois, *Cambridge, Massachusetts*
Christopher Dunn, *Tulane University*
Anani Dzidzienyo, *Brown University*
Jonathan Edwards, *Belmont, Massachusetts*
Roanne Edwards, *Arlington, Massachusetts*
Joy Elizondo, *Cambridge, Massachusetts*
Robert Fay, *Medford, Massachusetts*
Martine Fernández, *Berkeley, California*
Paul Finkelman, *Harvard Law School*
Victor Figueroa, *Harvard University*
Gerdes Fleurant, *University of California at Santa Barbara*
Juan Flores, *Hunter College and City College of New York Graduate Center*
Paul Foster, *Chicago, Illinois*
Baltasar Fra-Molinero, *Bates College*
Gregory Freeland, *California Lutheran University*
Susanne Freidberg, *Dartmouth College*
Nina Friedemann, *Pontifica Universidad Javeriana, Bogota, Colombia*
Rob Garrison, *Boston, Massachusetts*
Henry Louis Gates, *Jr., Harvard University*
John Gennari, *University of Virginia*
Danielle Georges, *New York, New York*
Peter Gerhard, *Independent Scholar*
Mark Gevisser, *Editor of Defiant Desire: Gay and Lesbian Lives
    in South Africa*
Patric V. Giesler, *Gustavus Adolphus College*
Peter Glenshaw, *Belmont, Massachusetts*
Matthew Goff, *Chicago, Illinois*
Flora González, *Emerson College*
Mayda Grano de Oro, *San Juan, Puerto Rico*

Sue Grant Lewis, *Harvard University*
Roderick Grierson, *Independent Scholar*
Barbara Grosh, *New York, New York*
Gerard Gryski, *Auburn University*
Betty Gubert, *Former Head of Reference, Schomburg Center for Research in Black Culture, New York Public Library*
Michelle Gueraldi, *San José, Costa Rica*
Stuart Hall, *The Open University, London*
Michael Hanchard, *Northwestern University*
Julia Harrington, *Banjul, The Gambia*
Elizabeth Heath, *San Francisco, California*
Andrew Hermann, *Former Literary Associate, Denver Center Theatre Company*
Evelyn Brooks Higginbotham, *Harvard University*
Jessica Hochman, *New York, New York*
Cynthia Hoehler-Fatton, *University of Virginia*
Peter Hudson, *Toronto, Canada*
Michelle Hunter, *Cambridge, Massachusetts*
Abiola Irele, *Ohio State University*
David P. Johnson, Jr., *Boston, Massachusetts*
Bill Johnson-González, *Cambridge, Massachusetts*
André Juste, *New York, New York*
Chuck Kapelke, *Boston, Massachusetts*
Ketu Katrak,University of California at Irvine
Robin Kelley, *New York University*
R. K. Kent, *University of California at Berkeley*
Leyla Keough, *Cambridge, Massachusetts*
Muhonjia Khaminwa, *Boston, Massachusetts*
David Kim, *Cambridge, Massachusetts*
Martha King, *New York, New York*
Franklin W. Knight, *Johns Hopkins University*
Peter Kolchin, *University of Delaware*
Corinne Kratz, *Emory University*
Modupe Labode, *Iowa State University*
Peter Lau, *New Brunswick, New Jersey*
Claudia Leal, *Former Assistant Director, Socioeconomic Area of the Biopacific Project, Bogota, Colombia*
René Lemarchand,University of Florida
W. T. Lhamon, Jr., *Florida State University*
Margit Liander, *Belmont, Massachusetts*
David Levering Lewis, *Rutgers University*
Marvin Lewis, *University of Missouri at Columbia*
Lorraine Anastasia Lezama, *Boston, Massachusetts*
Kevin MacDonald, *University of London*
Marcos Chor Maio, *Rio de Janeiro, Brazil*
Mahmood Mamdani, *University of Cape Town*

Lawrence Mamiya, *Vassar College*
Patrick Manning, *Northeastern University*
Peter Manuel, *John Jay College of Criminal Justice*
Dellita Martin-Ogunsola, *University of Alabama at Birmingham*
Waldo Martin, *University of California at Berkeley*
J. Lorand Matory, *Harvard University*
Felix V. Matos Rodriguez, *Northeastern University*
Marc Mazique, *Seattle, Washington*
José Mazzotti, *Harvard University*
Elizabeth McHenry, *New York University*
Jim Mendelsohn, *New York, New York*
Gabriel Mendes, *Annandale, New York*
Claudine Michel, *Wellesley College*
Georges Michel, *Military Academy of Haiti, Port-au-Prince, Haiti*
Gwendolyn Mikell, *Georgetown University*
Zebulon Miletsky, *Boston, Massachusetts*
Irene Monroe, *Harvard Divinity School*
Sally Falk Moore, *Harvard University*
Judith Morrison, *Inter-American Foundation at Arlington, Virginia*
Gerardo Mosquera, *Independent Scholar*
Luis Mott, *Federal University of Bahia, Brazil*
Salikoko S. Mufwene, *University of Chicago*
Edward Mullen, *University of Missouri at Columbia*
Kurt Mullen, *Seattle, Washington*
Stuart Munro-Hay, *Independent Scholar*
Aaron Myers, *Cambridge, Massachusetts*
Abdias do Nascimento, *Former Senator, Brazilian National Congress, Brasilia*
Ari Nave, *New York, New York*
Marcos Natalí, *University of Chicago*
Okey Ndibe, *Connecticut College*
Nick Nesbitt, *Miami University (Ohio)*
Richard Newman, *W. E. B. Du Bois Institute for Afro-American Research, Harvard University*
Liliana Obregón, *Harvard Law School*
Kathleen O'Connor, *Cambridge, Massachusetts*
Tejumola Olaniyan, *University of Virginia*
Mark O'Malley, *Cambridge, Massachusetts*
Yaa Pokua Afriyie Oppong, *London, England*
Carmen Oquendo-Villar, *Cambridge, Massachusetts*
Kenneth O'Reilly, *University of Alaska at Anchorage*
Carlos L. Orihuela, *University of Alabama at Birmingham*
Francisco Ortega, *Harvard University*
Juan Otero-Garabis, *Universidad de Puerto Rico*
Deborah Pacini Hernandez, *Brown University*
Carlos Parra, *Harvard University*
Ben Penglase, *Cambridge, Massachusetts*

Pedro Pérez-Sarduy, *London, England and Havana, Cuba*
Julio Cesar Pino, *Kent State University*
Donald Pollock, *State University of New York at Buffalo*
Angelina Pollak-Eltz, *Univesidad Catolice A. Bella*
Paulette Poujol-Oriol, *Port-au-Prince, Haiti*
Richard J. Powell, *Duke University*
Jean Muteba Rahier, *Florida International University*
João José Reis, *Federal University of Bahia, Brazil*
Carolyn Richardson Durham, *Texas Christian University*
Alonford James Robinson, Jr., *Washington, D.C.*
Lisa Clayton Robinson, *Washington, D.C.*
Sonia Labrador Rodrigués, *University of Texas at Austin*
Gordon Root, *Cambridge, Massachusetts*
Aninydo Roy, *Colby College*
Sarah Russell, *Cambridge, England*
Marveta Ryan, *Indiana University (Pennsylvania)*
Ali Osman Mohammad Salih, *University of Khartoum*
Lamine Sanneh, *Yale University*
Jalane Schmidt, *Cambridge, Massachusetts*
Charles Schmitz, *Sonoma State University*
Brooke Grundfest Schoepf, *Harvard University*
LaVerne M. Seales-Soley, *Canisius College*
James Clyde Sellman, *University of Massachussetts at Boston*
Thomas Skidmore, *Brown University*
James Smethurst, *University of North Florida*
Paulette Smith, *Tufts University*
Suzanne Smith, *George Mason University*
Barbara Solow, *Associate of the W. E. B. Du Bois Institute for Afro-American Research, Harvard University*
Doris Sommer, *Harvard University*
Thomas Stephens, *State University of New Jersey*
Jean Stubbs, *London, England and Havana, Cuba*
Patricia Sullivan, *Harvard University*
Carol Swain, *Princeton University*
Katherine Tate, *Univerity of California at Irvine*
Richard Taub, *University of Chicago*
April Taylor, *Boston, Massachusetts*
Christopher Tiné, *Cambridge, Massachusetts*
Richard Turits, *Princeton University*
Kate Tuttle, *Cambridge, Massachusetts*
Timothy Tyson, *University of Wisconsin*
Charles Van Doren, *Former Vice President/Editorial, Encyclopædia Britannica Inc.*
Alexandra Vega-Merino, *Harvard University*
Joëlle Vitiello, *Macalester College*
Peter Wade, *University of Manchester*

James W. St. G. Walker, *University of Waterloo*
Phillipe Wamba, *Cambridge, Massachusetts*
William E. Ward, *Harvard University*
Salim Washington, *Boston, Massachusetts*
Christopher Alan Waterman, *University of California at Los Angeles*
Richard Watts, *Tulane University*
Harold Weaver, *Independent Scholar*
Norman Weinstein, *State University of New York at New Paltz*
Amelia Weir, *New York, New York*
Tim Weiskel, *Harvard University*
Alan West, *Northern Illinois University*
Cornel West, *Princeton University*
Norman Whitten, *University of Illinois at Urbana*
Andre Willis, *Cambridge, Massachusetts*
Deborah Willis, *Center for African American History and Culture,*
  *Smithsonian Institution*
William Julius Wilson, *Harvard University*
Barbara Worley, *Cambridge, Massachusetts*
Eric Young, *Washington, D.C.*
Gary Zuk, *Auburn University*

## Abernathy, Ralph David

(b. March 11, 1926, Linden, Ala.; d. April 17, 1990, Atlanta, Ga.), American minister and civil rights leader who organized nonviolent resistance to segregation and succeeded Martin Luther King Jr. as president of the Southern Christian Leadership Conference (SCLC).

Ralph Abernathy was born on March 11, 1926, in Linden, Alabama, to William and Louivery Abernathy. He earned a B.S. from Alabama State College and was ordained a Baptist minister in 1948. In 1951 he received an M.A. in sociology and became pastor of the First Baptist Church in Montgomery, Alabama. He and Martin Luther King Jr. led the successful boycott of the Montgomery bus system in 1955, protesting segregated public transportation.

In 1957, Abernathy helped King found the Southern Christian Leadership Council (SCLC) to coordinate nonviolent resistance to segregation. After King's assassination in 1968, Abernathy served as SCLC president until he resigned in 1977.

## Abolitionism in the United States,

a major American reform movement that sought to eradicate slavery in the United States by means of a wide range of tactics and organizations; the antislavery crusade mobilized many African Americans and a small minority of whites, who saw their goal realized during the Civil War.

During the three decades that preceded the Civil War in the United States, abolitionism was a major factor in electoral politics. Most historians use the term *abolitionism* to refer to antislavery activism between the early 1830s, when William Lloyd Garrison began publishing the *Liberator,* and the Civil War. Historians also commonly distinguish abolitionism, a morally grounded and uncompromising social reform movement, from political antislavery—represented, for example, by the Free Soil and Republican parties—which advocated more limited political solutions, such as keeping slavery out of the western territories, and were more amenable to compromise.

Abolitionists played a key role in setting the terms of the debate over slavery and in making it a compelling moral issue. Yet abolitionists had remarkably little influence in the North. Very few Northerners were abolitionists, and many regarded abolitionists as dangerous fanatics. What made their case telling was the South's violent reaction. Extreme Southern responses appeared to confirm abolitionist warnings about a conspiratorial "Slave Power." By the 1850s, however, the escalating sectional conflict had largely taken on a momentum of its own, one that owed less and less to abolitionism.

Abolitionism was never a self-contained or singular movement. It encompassed a bewildering array of national, state, and local organizations, contradictory tactics, and clashing personalities. Abolitionists are commonly portrayed as benevolent white people deeply concerned with the well-being of enslaved blacks, epitomized by such activists as Garrison and Harriet Beecher Stowe, the author of *Uncle Tom's Cabin* (1852). In fact, a great number of abolitionists, including Frederick Douglass and Sojourner Truth, were African American. Free blacks in the North were stalwart in their dedication to the cause and provided a disproportionate share of the movement's financial support, including a large majority of the *Liberator's* early subscribers.

Whether black or white, most abolitionists found inspiration in two key strains of American thought: republicanism, the intellectual legacy of the American Revolution, and Protestant Christianity, especially an emotionally charged evangelicalism. Yet like their non-abolitionist contemporaries, many white abolitionists were convinced of the racial inferiority of blacks. Abolitionists acted forthrightly to correct what they perceived as a grievous wrong, but they could not wholly separate themselves from the assumptions and limitations of their time.

Although later observers have noted glaring inconsistencies and obvious shortcomings in abolitionists' efforts, it is more remarkable that so many were inspired to challenge an institution deeply entrenched in American society. During the nineteenth century reformers could rely upon familiar arguments in condemning slavery. That critical language, by and large, emerged during the preceding century. Opposition to slavery increased dramatically during the antebellum years, but its roots lay in the last half of the eighteenth century. During these years a number of individuals sought to transform slavery from an unquestioned part of the status quo to a significant problem. The principal challenge facing these eighteenth-century activists was arousing a conviction that slavery was wrong.

## The Society of Friends and Religious Opposition to Slavery in the Colonial Era

In the United States today human slavery is regarded not simply as wrong but as utterly indefensible and an affront to humanity. This powerful consensus makes it hard to appreciate the significance of taking an antislavery stance in the eighteenth century. It was not easy to come to abolitionist principles. Eighteenth- and early nineteenth-century abolitionists had to wrench themselves free of institutions and attitudes that had been accepted for centuries. The Bible, viewed by many as a compendium of social as well as religious truth, did not condemn slavery. The ancient Greek democracies and the Roman republic, which provided political inspiration during the revolutionary era, practiced and accepted slavery.

Although it is hard to imagine, white society did not see slavery as a moral or philosophical problem until a small number of outspoken individuals made it a problem. Beginning in the 1750s members of the Society of Friends, or Quakers, took the lead in challenging the institution. The most important Quaker antislavery activists were New Jersey Quaker John Woolman, author of the pamphlet *Some Considerations on the Keeping of Negroes* (1754), and Philadelphia Quaker Anthony Benezet. During the mid-eighteenth century Woolman traveled widely in British North America, appealing to Friends to free their slaves.

Woolman and other antislavery Friends were unique in basing their opposition to slavery on their sympathy for enslaved African Americans. In the nineteenth century Friends would be at the vanguard of a wide range of reforms aimed at bettering American society. During the eighteenth century, however, they turned their attention inward, focusing on their own religious society. In 1775 Benezet and Woolman played a leading role in founding the first American antislavery organization, the Pennsylvania Society for the Abolition of Slavery. After long discussion and debate, the Society of Friends reached consensus on the issue and became the first institution in the United States to condemn slavery as a moral wrong.

By 1784 every yearly Quaker meeting in the United States had forbidden its members to own slaves. In 1797 the Philadelphia Yearly Meeting resolved that members should be admitted "without regard to colour." At the time, this was truly a radical stance. In 1790 the Society of Friends presented Congress with the first petition calling for emancipation. Friends remained active in their opposition to slavery. But American Protestantism as a whole did little to challenge the institution until well into the nineteenth century.

## The American Revolution and the Problem of Slavery

During the eighteenth century the most significant opposition to slavery was secular rather than religious. The political discourse of American radicals emphasized the degradation of slavery and the need to defend liberty. Revolutionary agitators such as Samuel Adams warned that the British government aimed to "enslave" the American colonists. Patriots declared that liberty was a fundamental human quality and intrinsic to natural law. Patrick Henry of Virginia declaimed, "Give me liberty or give me death!"

Most patriot leaders did not linger on the contradiction of a slaveholder such as Thomas Jefferson proclaiming that liberty was an "unalienable right." But some extended their political principles more widely. In 1764, for example, Massachusetts lawyer James Otis Jr. asked, if all people were born free and equal, how could it be "right to enslave a man because he is black?" In 1773 Philadelphia patriot Dr. Benjamin Rush portrayed slavery as a "vice which degrades human nature."

In the North, revolutionary idealism resulted in a series of political challenges to the institution of slavery. During the war, African Americans in New Hampshire and Connecticut petitioned their respective state legislatures, unsuccessfully, for their freedom, using the language of republican liberty. Vermont, which had almost no slaves or African Americans, abolished slavery in 1777. In 1780 Pennsylvania followed suit. During the 1780s Massachusetts courts ruled that the commonwealth's 1780 constitution had, in effect, outlawed the institution. Between 1784 and 1804 the states of Rhode Island, Connecticut, New York, and New Jersey all adopted plans for gradual emancipation. The United States Constitution set a date of 1807 for cessation of the African slave trade.

Neither the Revolution nor the Constitution solved the problem of slavery in the United States. But perhaps just as important, they helped create the problem of slavery. During the colonial era, very few whites considered slavery to be a major social problem. During the first six decades of the nineteenth century, very few could deny that it was. The Revolution created the problem of slavery in two ways. First, having accepted liberty as a fundamental political tenet, Americans could no longer view slavery with equanimity. It became a troubling inconsistency in America's democratic society. In response, a number of states and territories organized abolition societies, including Rhode Island (1785), New York (1785), Illinois (1785), Delaware (1788), Maryland (1789), Connecticut (1790), and New Jersey (1793). In 1794 the American Convention of Abolition Societies was established in Philadelphia to unite the various state societies.

Second, once revolutionary idealism resulted in immediate or gradual emancipation throughout the North, slavery became an exclusively Southern institution. The debate over slavery now had potent sectional overtones, and it quickly emerged as the most divisive topic in national politics. At the start of the century, however, opponents of slavery had no intention of sharpening sectional controversy. Most early nineteenth-century abolitionists invoked moderation rather than militancy. They shared two key assumptions: that emancipation would be gradual, and that the freed slaves would not remain in the United States but should be colonized in Africa.

## Gradual Emancipation and Colonization

Prior to the 1830s most antislavery activists focused on gradual emancipation. Most of these activists were Southern whites, who thought that the institution would gradually whither away. Only black abolitionists, whose numbers were relatively few, demanded an immediate end to slavery. Most white—and a considerable number of black—opponents of slavery viewed colonization as intrinsic to any planned emancipation. In 1776, the year in which he wrote the Declaration of Independence, Thomas Jefferson also formulated a proposal for the African colonization of American blacks. Jefferson was a slaveholder who deplored slavery; yet he—like many other whites—believed in the absolute inferiority of blacks.

Jefferson was far from alone in concluding that the two groups could not live together beyond the constraints of slavery. For those who held such views, colonization seemed to offer a congenial solution: African Americans would be freed and returned to Africa—where, colonizationists insisted, they belonged—leaving the United States to whites. The most important advocate of colonization was the American Colonization Society (ACS), founded in 1816 by a group of Presbyterian ministers gathered in Washington, D.C. The ACS's initial goal was to encourage free blacks to immigrate to Africa.

The ACS attracted such illustrious supporters as former American presidents James Madison and James Monroe, Supreme Court justice John Marshall, and Kentucky senator and slaveholder Henry Clay. In 1821 the ACS purchased a colony for African American settlement. The colony, soon christened Liberia, was located south of Sierra Leone in West Africa. During the nineteenth century the ACS sent an estimated 12,000 to 20,000 African Americans to Africa.

One of the first prominent black advocates of colonization was the Massachusetts ship owner and Quaker Paul Cuffe. In 1815 he carried a group of African American settlers to Sierra Leone. Although most free blacks despised the ACS, Cuffe supported the organization. Other important black advocates of colonization were Martin Robison Delany, Alexander Crummell, and Rev. Henry Highland Garnet, who in the early 1850s was president of the newly formed African Civilization Society, an organization that advocated a black return to Africa.

African Americans as a whole remained aloof from colonization schemes, although many free blacks were active in assisting runaway slaves and in raising money for legal challenges to the enslavement of individual blacks. They also formed black organizations that combined antislavery activism and self-defense. For example, the New York Vigilance Committee, founded in 1835 by David Ruggles, helped more than 1,000 runaway slaves avoid being recaptured and returned to the South. Following passage of the Fugitive Slave Law of 1850, which made African Americans much more vulnerable to claims that they were runaway slaves and to kidnapping by so-called slave catchers, many free blacks moved to Canada. But in most cases, flight to Canada was a practical means of protection rather than an endorsement of emigration.

The high point of colonization was during the 1820s. In 1821 white abolitionist Benjamin Lundy, an advocate of colonization, began publishing *The Genius of Universal Emancipation*. Eight years later, a young William Lloyd Garrison joined him as an associate editor. But Garrison grew increasingly critical of Lundy on the issue of colonizing freed slaves, and in 1831 he began publishing his own radical antislavery journal, the *Liberator*, which was adamant in rejecting colonizationist arguments. Garrison's pro-slavery opponents and many of his one-time reform allies condemned him as an intemperate extremist. In the first issue of the *Liberator*, he met their chal-

lenges head on: "I am aware that many object to the severity of my language; but is there not cause for severity? I will be as harsh as truth, and as
uncompromising as justice. On this subject, I do not wish to think, or speak,
or write, with moderation . . . . I am in earnest—I will not excuse—I will not
retreat a single inch—AND I WILL BE HEARD." Garrison helped to usher
in a new era in abolitionism, but he was not alone in setting abolitionism on
a more radical tack.

## The Sources of Radical Abolitionism

Abolitionism in its radical form dates from about 1830. A series of developments at about this time served to discredit gradualist approaches to emancipation. Southerners became more adamant in defending slavery, and
antislavery activists became more radical in their attacks on the institution.
The radical approach to abolitionism is termed immediatism, as opposed to
gradualism. The term immediatism is usually associated with Garrison, but
black abolitionists had for years demanded an immediate end to slavery.

In 1829, two years before Garrison commenced the *Liberator*, black
abolitionist David Walker published a far more inflammatory work, *Walker's
Appeal . . . to the Colored Citizens of the World* (1829). Walker urged slaves
to rise up against their masters and take their freedom by force. In August
1831 Nat Turner instigated a slave revolt in Southampton County, Virginia,
that resulted in the deaths of 57 white men, women, and children and more
than 100 slaves. Southern whites charged that the "fanaticism" of Walker,
Garrison, and other immediatists was the direct cause of Turner's Rebellion.

Antislavery supporters were radicalized not only as a result of the
increasing vehemence of their proslavery opponents, but also because colonization was discredited as a viable option. The pro-slavery Virginian Thomas
R. Dew, who was later president of William and Mary College, played an
important part in this effort. During the winter of 1831–1832 the Virginia
legislature debated the question of abolishing slavery in the state through
gradual emancipation and colonization. Dew's report of those debates, published as the *Review of the Debate in the Virginia Legislature of 1831 and 1832*
(1832), argued persuasively that colonization was unworkable.

Dew used census figures to show that the growth of the black population outstripped the passenger-carrying capacity of the nation's merchant
fleet. Perhaps the most surprising aspect of the Virginia debates, which followed Turner's Rebellion by only a few months, was that they took place at
all. The legislators decided against ending slavery, but the vote (73–58) was
remarkably close. It would, however, be the last time that any Southern
state would voluntarily consider emancipation.

Radical abolitionists like Garrison also worked tirelessly to counter the
advocates of colonization. Garrison's widely distributed *Thoughts on African
Colonization* (1832) offered an uncompromising attack on the idea, in part
by citing blatantly racist and pro-slavery statements of various leading colonizationists. Although the idea of colonization continued to appeal to many
whites—Abraham Lincoln was for years a colonizationist—after 1830 it was
clearly embattled.

The most important source of the radicalizing of abolitionism was evangelical Protestantism. Beginning in the late 1790s, a major religious revival, the Second Great Awakening, had spread across the United States. The revival was based in evangelicalism, a fervent and intensely personal form of Christianity. Evangelicals viewed themselves and the world as being in a constant battle against the temptations of sin; yet evangelicalism was an optimistic faith. Both the individual and the larger society could be saved. Salvation required putting oneself in God's hands and trying to live by Jesus' example, but it also required the concerted efforts of the faithful. Evangelicals who righted society's wrongs were thus doing God's work on earth.

At the height of the Second Great Awakening, in the two decades after 1820, the United States entered an age of reform. Reformers took up a wide variety of social problems. They promoted temperance and discouraged prostitution. Some advocated women's rights; others proposed improvements in public education or in prison conditions. Aside from temperance, abolitionism was the principal focus for antebellum reformers. Not all evangelicals became abolitionists; nor were all abolitionists evangelicals, but during the 1830s and 1840s the effort to eradicate slavery took on a new energy and radicalism due to the many evangelicals who joined the crusade.

## Abolitionist Organizations and Activities

The new phase of abolitionism after 1830 unfolded through new antislavery institutions and new forms of activism. In 1832 Garrison and ten others formed the New England Anti-Slavery Society. In 1833 Garrison and two wealthy New York City businessmen and philanthropists, Arthur and Lewis Tappan, played key roles in establishing the American Anti-Slavery Society (AASS). Also in 1833 black and white women of Boston organized the interracial Boston Female Anti-Slavery Society, and women established a similarly constituted organization in Philadelphia. Many other local and state societies appeared during these years. By 1837 Massachusetts had 145 different antislavery societies; New York had 274; and Ohio, 214. Abolitionist sentiment was strongest in New England, New York, and their cultural hinterlands across the upper Midwest. By 1838 the AASS claimed nearly 250,000 members and 1350 affiliated societies.

During the 1830s antislavery societies effectively made slavery a social issue. They sent out massive mailings of antislavery literature, much of it directed to the South. In 1835 alone the AASS mailed 1.1 million abolitionist tracts. The campaign led President Andrew Jackson to propose legislation that would prohibit mailing antislavery literature. Slave narratives, former slaves' graphic, first-person accounts of their experiences under slavery, were an especially effective form of abolitionist propaganda. During the antebellum years, abolitionists published some 70 fugitive slave narratives, the most celebrated being Douglass's *Narrative of the Life of Frederick Douglass* (1845).

Abolitionist speakers also carried the antislavery message throughout the North. Other notable black abolitionist speakers were Sarah Mapps Dou-

Frederick Douglass began his career as an abolitionist orator in 1841. This photograph of the powerful speaker was made between 1847 and 1860. *CORBIS/Bettmann*

glass, William Wells Brown, William and Ellen Craft, and Frances Ellen Watkins Harper. These traveling orators were impassioned and willing to debate their opponents. They were also courageous—abolitionist views were not popular and could elicit hostile responses.

During the 1830s and 1840s abolitionists encountered almost as much resistance in the North as they did in the slaveholding South. Many Northerners feared not simply that the abolitionists would unsettle national politics and worsen sectional conflict, but also that, if successful, they would upset the North's racial balance as hordes of freed slaves fled the South to join the tiny number of free blacks already residing in the North. Anti-abolitionist mobs in the North attacked abolitionist speakers and destroyed abolitionist presses. In 1837, for example, abolitionist editor Elijah P. Lovejoy died defending his press against a mob in Alton, Illinois. Five years later, Frederick Douglass had his hand broken by a stone-throwing mob in Pendleton, Indiana. These mobs were by no means simply rowdies or social rabble. They were organized and often led, in the phrase of the time, by "gentlemen of property and standing."

The Depression of 1837–1843 seriously undermined the abolitionist campaign by reducing its financial resources and by drawing Northern attention to more pressing economic concerns. Almost as severe an impediment was the so-called Gag Rule, a procedural rule of the House of Representatives, adopted annually between 1836 and 1844, which automatically tabled any petition or letter on the subject of slavery. Yet the Gag Rule also provided abolitionists with a new tactic. Beginning in 1837 the AASS began mounting antislavery petition drives. By 1838 it had inundated Congress with more than 400,000 signatures. Abolitionists rightly pointed out that the Gag Rule violated their First Amendment right to petition their elected representatives. In this struggle, they gained many non-abolitionist allies, the most important of whom was Massachusetts representative and former president John Quincy Adams, who opposed the Gag Rule and in 1844 saw it defeated.

Frustrated by their political leaders' general reluctance to confront slavery, more and more abolitionists turned to direct action and civil disobedience. In 1832 Theodore Dwight Weld was forced out of Cincinnati's Lane Theological Seminary for encouraging students to debate the merits of colonization. In 1833 Weld began teaching at Oberlin College, which became a hotbed of abolitionist sentiment and was soon an important stop on the Underground Railroad.

The Underground Railroad, a secret network of activists who aided fugitive slaves in their journey to freedom, was the most important example of abolitionist direct action. A system for assisting escaped slaves existed as early as 1786, but the network did not spread throughout the North until after 1830. More than 3,200 individuals are known to have been active in the Underground Railroad, and they aided perhaps as many as 50,000 escaped slaves in their journey to freedom. Among the best known of those active in the Underground Railroad are Harriet Tubman and Indiana Quaker Levi Coffin. Douglass, Delany, Garnet, and many other African Americans were also involved. Following the passage of the federal Fugitive Slave Law of 1850, abolitionists became even more militant in their efforts to assist runaway slaves. In 1851, for example, a Boston mob rescued a fugitive slave from a U.S. marshal and helped him safely reach Canada.

## Abolitionist Divisions and Slavery in the Territories

Although historians disagree on its political impact, abolitionism unquestionably helped define slavery as a pressing moral problem. During the 1840s, however, internal and external developments decreased the movement's significance. In 1840 the AASS split into two factions. Garrison and his radical followers retained control over the original organization; the Tappan brothers, Weld, and their followers formed the more conservative American and Foreign Antislavery Society.

There were numerous other fallings-out among abolitionists in subsequent years. In 1843 Douglass, a Garrisonian advocate of nonviolence, prevented the publication of a fiery speech by Garnet that called for slave insurrection. Garrison relied on moral suasion as the means to gain emancipation. He dismissed politics and declined to vote, and he was convinced that nonviolence was the proper means of combating slavery. In 1851 Douglass decided that political action was essential to the antislavery struggle and that violence might be needed as well. During the 1850s a number of white abolitionists, including Theodore Parker and Thomas Wentworth Higginson, similarly concluded that to emancipate the slaves might require violent acts of resistance.

By the mid-1840s America's territorial expansion was far more important than abolitionists in shaping the debate over slavery. The Mexican-American War (1846–1848) brought the United States a vast new area of land, which since it lay south of the Missouri Compromise line of 36 degrees, 30 minutes, would be open to slavery. Slavery was already well established in Texas, a large part of this new territory, because of its mainly Southern settlers. The South, as a section, was eager for new land in which to expand its social and economic system. But the North was reluctant to see the extension of slavery into new territories because Northern whites feared being unable to compete with Southern plantation slavery and, in large measure, because of their racial prejudice. Rather than the moral appeals of abolitionism, it was the practical question of slavery in the territories that drove a wedge between the North and South.

The issue of slavery in the territories made political antislavery the dominant form of abolitionism from the mid-1840s to the Civil War. In 1839 the antislavery Liberty Party nominated former slaveholder and abolitionist James G. Birney as its first presidential candidate. In 1848 the Liberty Party dissolved and joined in forming the new Free Soil Party. In 1854 the Free Soil Party, along with many former Whigs, antislavery Northern Democrats, and supporters of the nativist American Party, created the Republican Party. For Free Soilers and Republicans, the primary issue was the non-extension of slavery, in other words, keeping slavery out of the western territories.

That issue lay at the heart of the most divisive political controversies of the era, including the Wilmot Proviso (1847), the Compromise of 1850, the Kansas-Nebraska Act (1854), and the Supreme Court's Dred Scott decision (1857). During these years, abolitionists increasingly found themselves in the position of reacting to outside developments, rather than setting an agenda of their own. Two important exceptions were Harriet Beecher Stowe and John Brown.

## Harriet Beecher Stowe, John Brown, and the Coming of the Civil War

It is difficult to imagine a greater contrast between two abolitionists than that between Stowe and Brown. Stowe was deeply committed to moral persuasion. Brown, in essence, was an antislavery terrorist who committed reprisal killings and organized attacks on federal government installations. Brown was one of the only abolitionists who left his mark with a gun; Stowe, a better representative of the crusade, made the pen her weapon of choice. Stowe's sentimental antislavery novel *Uncle Tom's Cabin* became the most popular novel of the nineteenth century.

*Uncle Tom's Cabin* was quickly adapted for the stage, and touring theatrical companies presented versions of the story throughout the North. The novel's characters were, to a considerable extent, unflattering stereotypes, and the theatrical performances relied upon the demeaning racial caricatures of nineteenth-century minstrelsy. Yet *Uncle Tom's Cabin* played a crucial part in turning Northerners against slavery and against the South. When he met Stowe during the Civil War, President Lincoln reportedly declared, "So this is the little woman who wrote the book that started this great war!"

In 1856 John Brown led four of his sons and two other followers on a murderous spree in Kansas that culminated in the execution-style killings of five unarmed pro-slavery Kansas settlers. Three years later, he masterminded a bloody, misguided raid on the federal armory at Harpers Ferry, Virginia. Brown secured financial backing from half a dozen New England and New York abolitionists and expected to instigate a massive slave uprising. Black abolitionists such as Garnet, Tubman, and Douglass admired Brown's zeal, but by the time he made his raid, they had all carefully distanced themselves from him. Neither did Virginia's slaves rise up in response to his raid. Within 36 hours, Brown and his surviving followers were captured.

During his trial and execution Brown remained calm and dignified. His demeanor won the admiration even of those Northerners who condemned his actions. Many Northerners regarded him as a principled martyr. By contrast, Southerners viewed Brown's Northern defenders—and the revelations of his abolitionist backers—as proof that the North was actively conspiring to subvert slavery. Northerners were equally convinced of the threat posed by a conspiratorial Southern "Slave Power" bent on extending its dominion over the entire nation, North as well as South.

With the 1860 election of Republican presidential candidate Abraham Lincoln, these suspicions provided the tripwires for secession and war. Abolitionists doggedly continued trying to influence events. Douglass and Delany advocated the enlisting of African American soldiers for the Union army. Even more momentous, Douglass was prominent in imploring Lincoln to transform the war from its limited goal of restoring the Union into a full-fledged crusade against slavery. Both goals were realized in 1863, when Lincoln signed the Emancipation Proclamation and the Union army began accepting black recruits. Yet each of these decisions reflected larger political consideration as much as abolitionist appeals.

By the start of the Civil War, abolitionists were increasingly marginal to unfolding events. Although they had speeded the process of emancipation, the actual demise of slavery did not come according to their plans. Nonetheless, the abolitionists made lasting historical contributions. They were notable for their principled advocacy of unpopular ideas. They also insisted that American political and religious principles should apply to all. In particular, they provided a powerful model for later social movements. From the nineteenth-century women's rights movement to the twentieth-century Civil Rights, gay rights, and anti-abortion or right-to-life movements, American reformers have drawn upon the idealism and, in many cases, the specific tactics that are a central part of the abolitionists' legacy.

North America

# Accommodationism in the United States,

a conciliatory approach to racial issues in the late nineteenth and early twentieth centuries that was personified by Booker Taliaferro Washington.

North America

# Affirmative Action,

policies used in the United States to increase opportunities for minorities by favoring them in hiring and promotion, college admissions, and the awarding of government contracts. Depending on the situation, "minorities" might include any underrepresented group, especially one defined by race, ethnicity, or gender. Generally, affirmative action has been undertaken by governments, businesses, or educational institutions to remedy the effects of past discrimination against a group, whether by a specific entity, such as a corporation, or by society as a whole.

Until the mid-1960s legal barriers prevented blacks and other racial minorities in the United States from entering many jobs and educational institutions. While women were rarely legally barred from jobs or education, many universities would not admit them and many employers would not hire them. The Civil Rights Act of 1964 prohibited discrimination in public accommodations and employment. A section of the act known as Title VII, which specifically banned discrimination in employment, laid the groundwork for the subsequent development of affirmative action. The Equal Employment Opportunity Commission (EEOC) created by the Civil Rights Act of 1964, and the Office of Federal Contract Compliance became important enforcement agencies for affirmative action.

The term *affirmative action* was first used by President Lyndon B. Johnson in a 1965 executive order. This order declared that federal contractors should "take affirmative action" to ensure that job applicants and employees "are treated without regard to their race, color, religion, sex, or national origin." While the original goal of the Civil Rights Movement had been "color-blind" laws, simply ending a long-standing policy of discrimination did not go far enough for many people. As President Johnson explained in a 1965 speech, "You do not take a person who for years has been hobbled by chains and . . . bring him up to the starting line of a race and then say, 'you are free to compete with all the others' and still justly believe that you have been completely fair."

President Richard Nixon was the first to implement federal policies designed to guarantee minority hiring. Responding to continuing racial inequalities in the work force, in 1969 the Nixon administration developed the Philadelphia Plan, requiring that contractors on federally assisted projects set specific goals for hiring minorities. Federal courts upheld this plan in 1970 and 1971.

## Controversy

From its beginnings in the United States in the mid-1960s, affirmative action has been highly controversial. Critics charge that affirmative action policies, which give preferential treatment to people based on their membership in a group, violate the principle that all individuals are equal under the law. These critics argue that it is unfair to discriminate against members of one group today to compensate for discrimination against other groups in the past. They regard affirmative action as a form of reverse discrimination that unfairly prevents whites and men from being hired and promoted.

Advocates of affirmative action respond that discrimination is, by definition, unfair treatment of people because they belong to a certain group. Therefore, effective remedies must systematically aid groups that have suffered from discrimination. Supporters contend that affirmative action policies are the only way to ensure an integrated society in which all segments of the population have an equal opportunity to share in jobs, education, and other benefits. They argue that numerical goals for hiring, promotions, and college admissions are necessary to integrate fields traditionally closed to women and minorities because of discrimination.

## Legislation and Supreme Court Rulings

The scope and limitations of affirmative action policy have been defined through a series of legislative initiatives and decisions by the Supreme Court of the United States. In *Griggs v. Duke Power* (1971) the Supreme Court held that Title VII bans "not only overt discrimination but also practices that are fair in form but discriminatory in operation." In order to avoid discrimination lawsuits under Title VII, public and private employers began to adopt hiring policies designed to recruit more minorities. The Equal Opportunity Act of 1972 expanded Title VII protections to educational institutions, leading to the extension of affirmative action to colleges and universities.

In later cases the Supreme Court upheld the constitutionality of affirmative action but placed some restrictions on its implementation. The Supreme Court's ruling in *Regents of the University of California v. Bakke* (1978) declared that it was unconstitutional for the medical school of the University of California at Davis to establish a rigid quota system by reserving a certain number of places in each class for minorities. However, the ruling upheld the right of schools to consider a variety of factors when evaluating applicants, including race, ethnicity, gender, and economic status. In *United Steelworkers v. Weber* (1979) the Court ruled that a short-term voluntary training program that gave preference to minorities was constitutional. The Court reasoned that a temporary program designed to remedy specific past discriminatory practices did not unduly restrict the advancement of whites. In *Fullilove v. Klutznick* (1980) the Supreme Court upheld a provision of the Public Works Employment Act of 1977, which provided a 10 percent "set-aside" for hiring minority contractors on federally funded public works projects. The majority of the justices believed that the Congress of the United States has special powers to remedy past and ongoing discrimination in the awarding of federal contracts.

Conservative justices appointed to the Supreme Court by Republican presidents in the 1980s and 1990s attempted to limit the scope of affirmative action. Although sharply divided on the issue, the Court has struck down a number of affirmative action programs as unfair or too broad in their application. In *Wygant v. Jackson Board of Education* (1986) the Supreme Court struck down a plan to protect minority teachers from layoffs at the expense of white teachers with greater seniority. In *Richmond v. J. A. Croson Co.* (1989) the Court rejected a local set-aside program for minority contractors, ruling that local governments do not have the same power as Congress to enact such programs. The Supreme Court's ruling in *Ward's Cove Packing Company v. Antonio* (1989) revised the standards established by the 1971 *Griggs* decision. The *Ward's Cove* decision required that employees filing discrimination lawsuits demonstrate that specific hiring practices had led to racial disparities in the workplace. Even if this could be shown, these hiring practices would still be legal if they served "legitimate employment goals of the employer."

These rulings did not signal the end of affirmative action. In *Metro*

*Broadcasting v. Federal Communications Commission* (1990) the Court upheld federal laws designed to increase the number of minority-owned radio and television stations. Meanwhile, Congress responded to a number of conservative rulings by the Supreme Court by passing the Civil Rights Act of 1991, which strengthened anti-discrimination laws and largely reversed the *Ward's Cove* decision.

## Recent Developments

In the 1990s affirmative action became a highly charged legal and political issue. In *Adarand Constructors v. Peña* (1995) the Supreme Court examined a federal statute that reserved "not less than 10 percent" of funds provided for highway construction for small businesses owned by "socially and economically disadvantaged individuals." The Court's majority opinion, written by Sandra Day O'Connor, overturned the statute and declared that even federal affirmative action programs are constitutional only when they are "narrowly tailored" to serve a "compelling government interest." In April 1998 a federal appeals court eliminated a Federal Communications Commission program designed to increase opportunities for minorities in broadcasting.

Affirmative action has been controversial in local politics as well. Under pressure from Governor Pete Wilson, the regents of the University of California voted in 1995 to end all affirmative action in hiring and admissions for the entire state university system. In 1996 the Fifth U.S. Circuit Court barred the University of Texas Law School from "any consideration of race or ethnicity" in its admissions decisions. Since these rulings have been enacted, both institutions have seen a dramatic drop not only in the admissions of black and Hispanic students but also in the number of minority applicants.

In 1996 voters in California endorsed Proposition 209, called the Civil Rights Initiative by its supporters, ending all state-sponsored affirmative action programs. At that time, commentators predicted a wave of similar state rulings barring race and gender preferences. However, efforts failed in Ohio, Colorado, and Florida to collect signatures for a similar ballot initiative. Bills modeled on Proposition 209 have been introduced in 13 state legislatures and none has been successful. In November 1997 Houston, Texas, voters defeated a ballot measure that would have repealed the city's race- and gender-based hiring programs.

With legislatures, the public, and the courts divided over the issue, the status of affirmative action remains uncertain.

North America

# Alexander, Sadie Tanner Mossell

(b. January 1, 1898, Philadelphia, Pa.; d. November 1, 1989, Philadelphia, Pa.), American lawyer and civil rights activist, the first African American woman to earn a Ph.D. in economics, and an important advocate for social justice.

Sadie Mossell Alexander was born in 1898 to a prominent black Philadelphia family. Her father, Aaron Mossell, was the first African American to receive a law degree from the University of Pennsylvania. Her grandfather, Benjamin Tucker Tanner, edited America's first black scholarly journal, the *A.M.E. Church Review*.

Mossell received her doctorate from the University of Pennsylvania in 1921. She worked as an actuary in North Carolina, then left to marry Raymond Pace Alexander, a graduate of Harvard Law School. With her husband's encouragement, Sadie Alexander returned to the University of Pennsylvania, earning her law degree in 1927. The two entered law practice together. Their civil rights work began in 1935, when they fought to end racial segregation in Philadelphia, Pennsylvania. The Alexanders visited segregated city theaters, hotels, and restaurants to demand rightful admittance under law, and agitated for the legal prosecution of violators.

Sadie Alexander worked to integrate the American military, and served on President Harry S. Truman's Commission to Study the Civil Rights of All Races and Faiths in 1946. In 1963 President John F. Kennedy appointed her to the Lawyers' Committee for Civil Rights under Law. She chaired President Jimmy Carter's White House Conference on Aging in 1979 and 1980. In addition to fulfilling these appointments, Sadie Alexander also maintained a private legal practice from 1959 through 1983, when she retired at the age of 85.

North America

# Amenia Conference of 1916,

**meeting of African American leaders, organized by W. E. B. Du Bois, which established the preeminence of the National Association for the Advancement of Colored People (NAACP) in the black movement.**

As a sign of respect for Booker T. Washington, who died in 1916, the NAACP canceled its annual meeting, despite the fact that his accommodationist views differed from the NAACP activist stance. To unify adherents of both approaches, NAACP leaders Du Bois and Joel E. Spingarn organized a conference, held August 24–26, 1916, at Spingarn's estate near Amenia, New York. The attendants agreed upon a "Unity Platform" written by Du Bois, which outlined goals of political freedom. While not entirely successful, the conference helped reconcile divergent factions under the auspices of the NAACP.

North America

# Amenia Conference of 1933,

**meeting organized by the National Association for the Advancement of Colored People (NAACP) to find solutions to the economic problems facing African Americans in the Great Depression.**

Joel E. Spingarn, president of the NAACP in 1932, called for a conference at his Troutbeck estate near Amenia, New York, which assembled black leaders to restructure the NAACP's civil rights platform to accommodate economic issues. The conference met August 18–22, 1933. It called for the NAACP to criticize the New Deal for not addressing blacks and to bring black and white workers into a new labor union alliance. The conference did not produce a plan for implementing its goals, and, while important symbolically, was essentially ineffective.

North America

## American Electoral Politics, Blacks in

In a 1965 article entitled "From Protest to Politics: The Future of the Civil Rights Movement," civil rights activist Bayard Rustin predicted that the 1965 Voting Rights Act would transform the Civil Rights Movement into formal, institutionalized party politics. Although the strategies and thrust of the movement would change, blacks, he argued, would still be engaged in a movement radically oriented toward social change. The new electoral phase of black politics would function as the "second stage" of the black Civil Rights Movement. Writing in the aftermath of the landslide election of President Lyndon B. Johnson in 1964, Rustin also predicted that an alliance between progressive groups, blacks, labor, and liberals would emerge within the Democratic Party and that conservatives would align themselves with the minority Republican Party.

Charlotta Bass, 1952 Progressive Party candidate for vice president, tells reporters that the United States should negotiate in Korea. *CORBIS/Bettmann-UPI*

David Dinkins, with his hand on the Bible, is sworn in as the first black mayor of New York City by Judge Fritz Alexander. New York Governor Mario Cuomo stands behind Dinkins. *CORBIS/Bettmann*

While Rustin had correctly predicted the electoral mobilization of blacks, his hope for a liberal majority, which would then work through the Democratic Party, never materialized. Blacks, indeed, are a growing part of the American electorate, casting 7 percent of the presidential vote in 1966 and 11 percent by 1996. During this same time frame, the number of black elected officials would skyrocket from an estimated 500 or so to 8,000 and more by 1993. And as Rustin expected, after the 1964 presidential election, the vast majority of blacks had become Democrats. Up until 1963 only 50 to 60 percent of blacks identified themselves as Democrats in surveys. As of 1996, over 80 percent of blacks called themselves Democrats.

Yet the massive entry of blacks into the American electorate has not, as Rustin had hoped, aided progressive politics, but rather coincided with and perhaps provoked the rise of conservative politics. Southern whites rallied to massively resist the implementation of the new civil rights laws, while Northern whites grew more conservative in response to the urban riots and black militancy and as race issues moved from the South to the North in the form of busing and affirmative action. With the exception of Jimmy Carter's one term as president from 1976 to 1980, Republicans would occupy the White House from 1968 until 1992. Rather than serve as an opposition party to the Republicans, Democrats strategically moved to the center ground of politics and abandoned the Left in an effort to win back votes. Thus by the 1980s, instead of belonging to a liberal-progressive coalition within the Democratic Party, as Rustin had predicted, blacks found themselves constituting a political minority, isolated and increasingly marginal within the Democratic Party and in national politics in general.

The conservatism that rebounded at the end of the Civil Rights Movement nevertheless ignited blacks politically. Since 1965 differences in black and white registration and turnout rates have diminished considerably. In 1984, during the conservative Reagan years, the gap between black and white voter registration rates was the smallest ever recorded—2.2 percentage points compared to 9.2 percentage points in 1968. In 1984 more blacks turned out to vote in a collective effort to defeat Ronald Reagan. Blacks' feelings of political efficacy grew especially during the early civil rights years, 1954 to 1962. Since 1964 Americans have become more distrustful of government and more skeptical of their ability to be heard and influence government. However, this loss of confidence in government was less apparent in the black community. Although blacks are still somewhat more likely than whites to feel that they have "no say in government" and that "government officials don't care," racial differences have diminished mostly because larger percentages of whites now distrust government and have less faith in their ability to influence government.

Black mobilization during the Reagan years was greatly facilitated by the Reverend Jesse Jackson's two bids for the presidency in 1984 and in 1988. The Jackson campaigns gave "voice" to black dissatisfaction with the rightward drift of the Democratic Party. Millions of blacks supported both his bids. His campaigns were structured as a bargaining vehicle for black Democratic voters. In the end, while they stimulated black interest in political campaigns and mobilized new black voters, Jackson's candidacies did not enhance the effectiveness of the black vote. The record-high black turnout in 1984 did not affect the outcome of the Reagan-Mondale presidential race, and some have argued that Jackson's bids may have exacerbated blacks' political problems, pushing blacks further into a marginal and politically impotent corner of the party and in national politics in general.

While blacks mobilized but remained outside the national political scene during the 1980s, in 1992 they became part of the governing coalition in Washington. Contrary to Rustin's expectations, rather than liberalizing American politics, the incorporation of blacks has moderated their politics. Blacks have not only moved away from intra-party insurgent politics, but their political views have become more conservative. A number of factors explain blacks' move away from insurgent politics within the party. First, Bill Clinton's election in 1992 and his support within the black community have moderated black politics at the national level. Clinton had an 87 percent approval rating among blacks in 1996, and those who strongly approved of Clinton's performance in the White House were most likely to think that a third Jackson bid for the presidency in 1996 would have been "a very bad idea." Second, Jesse Jackson did little to resurrect the ideological divisions in the party that he capitalized on in his 1984 and 1988 presidential bids. In fact, Jackson's 1996 convention speech differed radically from his past three speeches insofar as there was little of his own political agenda in it and little criticism of the party. This speech was pointedly directed toward unifying the party. Finally, the majority of blacks came to believe that the Republican Party was hostile to their group's interests during the Reagan years, and Newt Gingrich's leadership of the new Republican majority in the U.S. House of Representatives beginning in 1994 did little to erase this image of the GOP as anti-black. In fact, more blacks felt in 1996 that the Republican Party does not work hard on issues blacks care about than in 1984 during the Reagan administration. The Republican Party has apparently not profited from growing black political conservatism. Democratic identification among blacks remained as strong in 1996 as it had been in 1984.

Blacks have also become more politically conservative. This was evident as early as the late 1980s, as the percentage of blacks opposing the idea of a federally guaranteed job program quadrupled from 7 percent in 1972 to 28 percent in 1988. Black opposition to federal assistance for minorities and blacks shot up during this period as well, from 6 percent in 1970 to 26 percent in 1988. Data from a national telephone survey of blacks in 1996 showed that fewer blacks favored government assistance to blacks and minorities than had in 1984.

When asked whether federal spending on defense, crime, food stamps, and Medicare should be increased, decreased, or kept about the same, more blacks in 1996 said spending should be decreased except in the area of crime. On crime, 63 percent in 1996 said that spending should be increased, in contrast to 56 percent in 1984. The growth in the proportion of blacks favoring an expansion of federal efforts on crime corresponds with other attitudinal shifts in the black community. More blacks in 1996 than in 1984 viewed crime as the single most important problem in the black community relative to unemployment or discrimination. In 1996 a large plurality (40 percent) of blacks ranked crime first and unemployment and discrimination second and third, respectively. In 1984 only 17 percent had placed crime above the other two problems; crime, in fact, came in third for half of the sample.

One of the most striking pieces of evidence that blacks have become more conservative is reflected in their attitudes toward welfare. In 1984 nearly half of the blacks polled felt that spending on food stamps should be increased, while only 10 percent thought it should be decreased. Twelve years later, however, that near-majority

Congressman John Lewis speaks with the press from his Atlanta, Georgia, home in 1985.
*CORBIS/Flip Schulke*

was cut down to 28 percent, while a nearly matching proportion thought that funds for this program should be cut. There was a less dramatic but still significant drop in the proportion of blacks who felt that federal spending on Medicare should be increased. Whereas 78 percent of blacks thought more money should go to Medicare in 1984, only 68 percent did in 1996. As in the case of food stamps, most in the black community felt that the spending levels for Medicare should remain where they are.

Black attitudes on welfare reform in 1996 matched their attitudes on spending levels for welfare programs. A solid majority (67 percent) in the black community favored the new law limiting welfare receipts to five years of benefits over the course of a recipient's life; only 30 percent opposed it. Blacks were divided, however, on the family cap policy that states enacted under waivers from the Clinton administration. Under this new policy, welfare payments are not increased for welfare recipients who have additional children while on welfare. About half (48 percent) favored such a policy, while 46 percent opposed it.

The 1996 National Black Election Study established that blacks today remain highly race conscious, and increasingly so. A higher percentage of blacks in 1996 believed their individual fates were linked to that of their group. More blacks in 1996 than in 1984 reflected on the meaning of their identities as blacks in this country. In 1984 blacks in a national telephone survey were asked whether or not blacks in this country would ever achieve full social and economic equality. More than one-third (36 percent) said no, that blacks would never win equality with whites in this country. The ranks of the pessimists have increased; nearly half (49 percent) of those surveyed

in 1996 said that blacks are never going to obtain equality in this country. Finding blacks to be more race conscious in the 1990s than in the 1980s and yet more conservative is puzzling, given the strong impact of black solidarity in promoting political liberalism.

The political incorporation of blacks into mainstream politics represented one of the most important outcomes of the Civil Rights Movement. Yet although blacks remain strongly race conscious, the new electoral phase of black politics has not functioned as the second stage of the Civil Rights Movement as Rustin had hoped. Black voters have not been able to facilitate the rise of progressive politics; instead, their incorporation has

Richard Arrington, the first black mayor of Birmingham, Alabama, waves to supporters celebrating his 1983 election to a second term.
*UPI/CORBIS-Bettmann*

Harold Washington hugs a baby during his 1983 campaign for mayor of Chicago, Illinois. Washington was the first African American mayor of Chicago. *CORBIS/Jacques M. Chenet*

resulted in the moderation of their politics. This is not entirely unexpected, given the nature of the American political system, which favors compromise and moderation as opposed to conflict and ideological purity. The American political system tends to support interests that favor the status quo or those who believe in incremental change. As participants in such a system, blacks' policy views and their political behavior have accordingly moderated. Furthermore, blacks in 1996 were highly satisfied with the centrist policy representation in Washington after decades of conservative Republican rule. This is not to argue that the potential for radical progressive politics no longer exists in the black community. Race remains a dominant issue on the political landscape. Nevertheless, in order to mount such a movement, blacks would have to move beyond the form of electoral politics that currently exists in the United States.

## Africa

# Annan, Kofi

(b. April 8, 1938, Kumasi, Gold Coast [present-day Ghana]), secretary general of the United Nations (UN).

The first person from sub-Saharan Africa to head the United Nations, Kofi Annan is also the first secretary general to have risen through the ranks of that organization. A lifelong diplomat, Annan assumed the UN's top post in January 1997 to serve a term ending December 31, 2001. Annan impressed the international diplomatic community while serving as undersecretary general for peacekeeping, a job in which he coordinated efforts to help such

Secretary General Kofi Annan answers questions at a press conference at the United Nations in New York on March 13, 2002. On March 12 Annan unleashed his toughest criticism to date of Israel, appealing to it to end its "illegal occupation" of Palestinian lands and curb its attacks on civilians. *Reuters/CORBIS*

tortured areas as Rwanda, Somalia, and the former Yugoslavia. He began his term as secretary general under pressure to reform the large and economically troubled UN bureaucracy. Following his appointment, Annan pledged to improve the effectiveness of UN programs in poor countries, saying, "Economic development is not merely a matter of projects and statistics. It is, above all, a matter of people—real people with basic needs: food, clothing, shelter, and medical care."

Annan was born into one of Ghana's most prominent families. His father was both a hereditary chief of the Fante people and a high-ranking civil servant. Annan took advantage of the educational opportunities presented to him. After studying science and technology in Ghana, in 1959 he traveled to the United States to study at Macalester College in St. Paul, Minnesota. "It was an exciting period," says Annan. Two years earlier, Ghana had claimed its independence, and in America the Civil Rights Movement was gaining momentum. He graduated from Macalester in 1961 with a degree in economics, saying that his American years had taught him that "you [should] never walk into a situation and believe that you know better than the natives."

It was a lesson Annan would apply often during his diplomatic career. After graduate studies in economics in Geneva, Switzerland, Annan took his first UN job at the World Health Organization (WHO). After more than a decade of diplomatic work, he took a break to serve from 1974 to 1976 as director of the Ghana Tourist Development Company. Four years later, he received his first high-level UN post, as deputy director of administration and head of personnel at the office of the UN high commissioner for refugees. He worked there until 1983, when he became director of budget in the office of financial services. By 1990 he had risen to the office of assistant secretary general for program planning, budget, and finance.

Annan's 1993 appointment to the head of peacekeeping operations made him one of the UN's most visible and potentially controversial leaders. UN peacekeeping missions in Somalia and the former Yugoslavia had recently provoked widespread criticism and raised doubts about the agency's future. According to an American official quoted in the New York Times, Annan was "the only top official of the UN who came out of the Bosnia experience with dignity and without having harmed the organization or relations with any one of the great powers. That's what a great diplomat's about." He gained an international reputation not only for shrewd diplomacy but also for his candor and personal charm. When the United States publicly campaigned against a second term for then-secretary general Boutros Boutros-Ghali, it was Annan to whom the UN turned.

Given that Annan was expected to scale down the UN administration while simulta-neously making it more responsive to member nations, it is not surprising that he has faced criticism in the early years of his secretariat. In particular, his preference for coalition-building and compromise over quick decision-making irritated some in the United States government, whose support—and repayment of its massive UN debt—is seen by many as crucial for Annan's success. At the same time, other member nations accused Annan of currying favor with America, to which he replied that he would "devote the same attention to any country that pays 25 percent of the dues and owes $1.3 billion." Annan silenced many of his critics, however, by his successful resolution of the first major diplomatic test of his leadership. In February 1998 his negotiations with Iraqi president Saddam Hussein averted what looked like a very likely war, further burnishing Annan's reputation as a devoted peacemaker.

Annan, whose first marriage ended in divorce, lives in the secretary general's residence in New York City with his wife, Nane Annan, a Swedish lawyer-turned-artist. The couple have three children from previous marriages.

North America

# Antilynching Movement,
the effort in the United States from the late nineteenth to the mid-twentieth century to halt the extralegal killing by mob violence of alleged lawbreakers, particularly African Americans.

Arthur F. Raper, in his classic 1933 study *The Tragedy of Lynching*, found that lynching rates were "highest in the newer and more sparsely settled portions of the South" and that poorer counties contributed a disproportionate share of such incidents. This study helped to reinforce the common view that lynchings were the product of an economically marginal lower class. However, current scholarship emphasizes the direct complicity of the prosperous and socially prominent, who in most cases condoned if they did not in fact take part in such incidents. Lynching thus served to unite whites of different classes and reinforced the subordinate status not only of blacks but also of Southern white women, whose lives were circumscribed due to their supposed irresistibility to black rapists. Given such circumstances, it is not surprising that African Americans were the first to take initiative against these attacks.

The origins of the antilynching movement lie in the single-minded efforts of one individual, the black journalist and political activist Ida B. Wells-Barnett. Three years before her marriage to Ferdinand L. Barnett, Wells launched her antilynching crusade in 1892 after the killing of three black businessmen in her hometown of Memphis, Tennessee. Wells investigated the incident and concluded that the accusations of rape that served to justify the killings were baseless. The three men lost their lives, she declared, because they were in competition with white-owned businesses. Shortly after Wells's newspaper, the *Memphis Free Speech*, published her exposé, a white mob ransacked the newspaper's offices and destroyed the press.

Wells fled Memphis, taking a job with the *New York Age*, an African American newspaper in New York City, but she continued her antilynching campaign with undiminished zeal. In addition to newspaper stories, Wells wrote a number of pamphlets, including "Southern Horrors: Lynch Law in All Its Phases" (1892) and "A Red Record . . . Lynchings in the United States, 1892–1893–1894" (1895), which offered the first systematic statistical analysis of lynching in the United States. Her work attracted the attention of America's leading black activist, Frederick Douglass, and the aging agitator joined her in his last crusade. Douglass's "Lynch Law in the South" appeared in the July 1892 issue of the *North American Review*. A year later, in his capacity as commissioner for the Republic of Haiti's exhibit at the World Columbian Exhibition in Chicago, Douglass provided Wells with a desk in the Haitian pavilion from which to distribute thousands of copies of her latest antilynching pamphlet.

Over the years the antilynching movement had two main goals. It sought to shake the American public out of its passivity on the subject of lynching, and since Southern state courts would not punish the participants, it lobbied for legislation that would make lynching a federal crime. African Americans had some success with the former goal but found themselves stymied with respect to the latter. Thus in 1901 Ida B. Wells-Barnett met with President William McKinley and pressed for the passage of anti-lynching legislation. But McKinley provided no assistance, and his successor, Theodore Roosevelt, did no better.

In the early twentieth century, the National Association for the Advancement of Colored People (NAACP) emerged as the key antilynching organization. The NAACP attempted to keep national statistics on lynchings and investigated many specific incidents. It published pamphlets such as "Thirty Years of Lynching in the United States, 1889–1918" (1919) and a book-length study of the problem by future NAACP executive director Walter F. White, entitled *Rope and Faggot: A Biography of Judge Lynch* (1929). Federal antilynching legislation remained one of the NAACP's highest priorities, a goal it came close to achieving three times, in 1922, 1937, and 1940. Indeed during the New Deal of the 1930s such legislation seemed within grasp, but despite vigorous NAACP lobbying, neither Congress nor President Franklin D. Roosevelt proved willing to embrace such a measure, because of the opposition of Southern Democrats.

The NAACP was not the only organization that actively opposed lynching, nor did such opposition imply a particular political leaning. Liberals in the American Civil Liberties Union, Southern conservatives—black as well as white—in the Commission on Interracial Cooperation, and the radicals of the Communist Party of the United States of America (CPUSA) all played a role in the antilynching campaign. The CPUSA was particularly visible in these years, directly or through so-called Communist-front organizations in which it was the leading force. During the 1930s, for example, the Southern Negro Youth Congress, a broad-based coalition with strong Communist ties, organized antilynching protests as part of its civil rights activism. The CPUSA was also prominent in responding to a wave of lynchings that followed World War II.

Yet another source of antilynching activism was white, middle-class Southern women, as exemplified by Jessie Daniel Ames's Association of Southern Women for the Prevention of Lynching, founded in 1930. Ames sought to challenge the underlying rationale for lynching among Southern whites, distilled in South Carolina Democrat "Cotton Ed" Smith's remark in a 1935 Senate filibuster that lynching was necessary to preserve "the sanctity of our firesides and the virtue of our women." It was generally assumed that an accusation of rape lay behind virtually every Southern lynching of an African American. In fact, less than a fifth of all blacks lynched between 1889 and 1918 were accused of rape. Even when these incidents are combined with those lynchings that followed other alleged attacks on women, the total amounts to only 28 percent of all blacks lynched. The most common justification for lynching was the charge of murder, which was leveled in 36 percent of all lynchings of African Americans during this 30-year period.

The various antilynching organizations often squabbled and worked at cross-purposes. For example, Jessie Daniel Ames emphasized the need for educational approaches at the state and local levels rather than coercive federal legislation, contending that education alone could end the social acceptance of lynching. Ames thus stubbornly opposed the NAACP's legislative campaign, taking such behind-the-scenes actions as meeting with Eleanor Roosevelt in a fruitless effort to turn the First Lady against the NAACP strategy. Likewise when Paul Robeson, W. E. B. Du Bois, and white liberal Bartley Crum called in 1946 for an "American crusade against lynching," NAACP executive director Walter White opposed them because he feared it might produce a new Communist-front antilynching organization. The staunchly anticommunist White complained privately to Robeson that the gathering would duplicate ongoing NAACP efforts, and he refused to have any part in it.

By the 1950s, however, lynching was clearly on the wane. Part of the explanation for the decline lies in growing opposition to the practice, inside as well as outside the South. In particular, the Civil Rights Movement of the 1950s and 1960s both mobilized the Southern black population and secured the passage of important new federal legislation. Although no federal law addressed lynching per se, the Civil Rights Act of 1968 included provisions making it a federal offense to deprive individuals of their civil rights. Though not without deficiencies, the new federal law was successfully applied to racially motivated assaults. Moreover, in recent years Southern states have demonstrated a greater willingness to punish racially based killings. For example, more than three decades after the 1963 murder of black civil rights activist Medgar W. Evers, the state of Mississippi successfully convicted longtime suspect Byron De La Beckwith.

Yet changes in the law and its enforcement do not account for the marked drop in lynching that began much earlier. Indeed this decline seems less a product of antilynching activism than of profound changes taking place in Southern society. During the 1940s and 1950s migration shifted the center of the African American population from the South to the North and West. Urbanization, industrial growth, and the emergence of stronger institutions of government all served to make the South more and more like the rest of the nation. In 1955 there were only three lynchings in the entire United States, all of them in Mississippi, and the NAACP had already ceased to regard lynching as a high-priority issue.

# B

## Baker, Ella J.

(b. December 13, 1903, Norfolk, Va.; d. December 13, 1986, New York, N.Y.),
social justice activist who was instrumental in the founding the Student Nonviolent Coordinating Committee.

The granddaughter of slaves, Ella Baker began her career as an activist early. As a student at Shaw University in Raleigh, North Carolina, Baker challenged school policies that she found demeaning. After graduating from Shaw as class valedictorian in 1927, she moved to New York City.

Baker responded to the suffering she saw in Harlem during the Great Depression by joining a variety of political causes. In 1930 she joined the Young Negroes Cooperative League and was elected as its first national director a year later. The league, which was founded by writer George Schuyler, aimed to develop blacks' economic power through collective planning. Baker also became involved with several women's organizations and, as an employee of the Works Progress Administration, offered literacy and consumer education to workers while educating herself about radical politics.

The year 1940 marked the beginning of Baker's affiliation with the National Association for Advancement of Colored People (NAACP). After working as a field secretary, Baker served as director of branches from 1943 to 1946. Her efforts to expand the reach of the NAACP throughout the South helped create the grassroots network that provided a base for the Civil Rights Movement in the following decades. At the same time, Baker fought to make the NAACP itself more democratic by shifting the organization's emphasis away from legal battles and toward community-based activism. Although Baker resigned from the NAACP staff in 1946, she stayed on as a volunteer and, as the first woman to head the New York branch, led its fight to desegregate New York City public schools.

In 1956 Baker, Bayard Rustin, and Stanley Levison established In Friendship, an organization dedicated to raising money to support the Southern struggle. She moved to Atlanta the following year to organize Martin Luther King Jr.'s newly formed Southern Christian Leadership Conference (SCLC) and to run the Crusade for Citizenship, a voter registration campaign. Baker stayed at SCLC for two years, but she never accepted its policy of favoring strong central leadership over local, grassroots politics.

When a group of students in Greensboro, North Carolina, touched off a sit-in campaign, Baker left SCLC. Determined to assist the fledgling student movement, she took a job at the Young Women's Christian Association (YWCA). She invited sit-in leaders to attend a conference at Shaw University in April 1960. From that conference, the Student Nonviolent Coordinating Committee (SNCC) was born the following October. Unlike older civil rights groups, SNCC was a decentralized organization that stressed direct-action tactics and encouraged women, the young, and the poor to take leadership positions. Among SNCC's achievements was its role in founding the Mississippi Freedom Democratic Party. Baker was a key player in the party's attempt to replace the all-white delegation from Mississippi at the 1964 Democratic party convention.

Baker returned to New York in 1964 and fought for human rights until her death. Called an "unsung hero" of the Civil Rights Movement, Baker has inspired a range of political organizations, including the Black Panthers, Students for a Democratic Society, and feminist groups.

North America

# Barber, Jesse Max

(b. July 5, 1878, Blackstock, S.C.; d. Sept. 20, 1949, Philadelphia, Pa.), African American journalist, managing editor of *Voice of the Negro*, and radical thinker who argued for black civil rights.

Jesse Max Barber was the son of former slaves. He trained as a teacher in Columbia, South Carolina, at Benedict College. His literary career began as editor of the *University Journal* at Virginia Union University in Richmond, Virginia.

Immediately after his graduation from Virginia Union in 1903, Barber began a literary career as managing editor of a new black journal, *Voice of the Negro*, founded in Atlanta in January 1904. While *Voice* initially sought a moderate position between accommodationists and activists, Barber made the journal a progressive forum. He was known at the time as a politically aware, radical thinker who sided with his friend W. E. B. Du Bois against Booker T. Washington. Writers for *Voice* included Pauline Hopkins, Du Bois, Washington, Charles W. Chesnutt, and Paul Laurence Dunbar, as well as Barber. Barber used his journal to argue for black civil rights and to chronicle historical events so that, in his words, "it will become a kind of documentation for the coming generations."

Relocated to Chicago after the Atlanta race riots of September 1906,

*Voice* ceased publication in 1907. Barber subsequently entered the dentistry profession but remained committed to social activism, serving on the executive committee of the National Association for the Advancement of Colored People from 1919 to 1921. Barber continued his journalism and published in the magazine *Abbott's Monthly* between 1930 and 1933.

North America

# Barry, Marion Shepilov, Jr.

(b. March 6, 1936, Itta Bena, Miss.), four-time mayor of Washington, D.C., and founding member of the Student Nonviolent Coordinating Committee.

Marion Barry's 1994 election to a fourth term as mayor of Washington, D.C., three years after his conviction for cocaine possession, was yet another twist in the turbulent career of the sharecropper's son from the Mississippi Delta. Born near the small town of Itta Bena, he moved to Memphis, Tennessee, at the age of five and grew up amid poverty, segregation, and racism. Despite these circumstances, he excelled academically and became the first member of his family to attend college. At LeMoyne College, a racially mixed institution in Memphis, Barry joined the campus chapter of the National Association for the Advancement of Colored People (NAACP), becoming its president his senior year.

Barry received his bachelor's degree in chemistry in 1958, and that fall began postgraduate study at the historically black Fisk University in Nashville. He organized the campus's first NAACP chapter and helped stage nonviolent sit-ins at Nashville restaurants. At a Southern Christian Leadership Conference (SCLC) gathering in 1960, Barry first heard the Reverend Martin Luther King Jr. speak and was impressed by the "new kind of leadership" King offered. Shortly afterward, Barry helped found and became the first chairman of the Student Nonviolent Coordinating Committee (SNCC).

For the next several years, Barry continued to work for civil rights in the Deep South, abandoning his doctoral studies in 1964 to devote more time to SNCC. In 1965 Barry moved to Washington, D.C., where he organized a massive boycott of the city's transit system, and a year later founded the Free D.C. movement in an effort to gain political control for the city's residents, long ruled by Congress in a quasi-colonial system. Proclaiming that it was time for African Americans to concentrate on "economic and political power," in 1967 Barry resigned from SNCC and founded Youth Pride, a nonprofit organization devoted to finding jobs for young African Americans. After its initial success, he expanded into profit-making ventures with Pride Economic Enterprises.

Barry served three terms on the city's school board before running for city council in 1974. He served two terms on the council before running for mayor, an office that had, with the advent of home rule, increased in political and financial power. In 1978, still recuperating from a gunshot wound received when terrorists raided the city council building, Barry won a narrow victory, with many observers citing the support of white voters as the decisive factor. Barry depended on the loyalty of the city's black majority for his reelection in 1982, following a first term marred by fiscal disaster and increasing crime rates. Barry's second and third terms, despite some successes in economic growth and job creation, were characterized by scandal and accusations of wrongdoing, including rumors of illegal drug use.

In January 1990 FBI agents, after offering Barry crack cocaine, video-taped the mayor smoking the drug in the hotel room of a former girlfriend. Despite charges of entrapment, Barry was convicted of misdemeanor possession and sentenced to six months in prison. Following his release in 1991, Barry began his political comeback with reelection to the city council in 1992, this time representing the city's poorest neighborhoods. Two years later, crediting Narcotics Anonymous for his rehabilitation and invoking themes of redemption, Marion Barry defeated incumbent Sharon Pratt Kelly to win a fourth term as the city's mayor.

North America

# Bates, Daisy Lee Gatson

**(b. 1920, Huttig, Ark.), African American civil rights activist who coordinated the integration of Central High School in Little Rock, Arkansas.**

Daisy Lee Gatson Bates barely knew her parents. Her mother was killed by three white men after she resisted their sexual advances; her father left town, fearing reprisals if he sought to prosecute those responsible. Orlee and Susie Smith, friends of her parents, adopted her. In 1941 she married L. C. Bates, a journalist. They moved to Little Rock, Arkansas, and established a newspaper, the *Arkansas State Press*; it became the leading African American newspaper in the state and a powerful voice in the Civil Rights Movement.

It was as president of the Arkansas state conference of the National Association for the Advancement of Colored People that Bates coordinated the efforts to integrate Little Rock's public schools after the Supreme Court's *Brown v. Board of Education* decision outlawed segregated public schools in 1954. Nine African American students, the "Little Rock Nine," were admitted to Little Rock's Central High School for the 1957–1958 school year.

Violent white reaction to integration forced President Dwight D. Eisenhower to order 1,000 army paratroopers to Little Rock to restore order and protect the children. Bates was the students' leading advocate, escorting them safely to school until the crisis was resolved. She continued to serve the children, intervening with school officials during conflicts and accompanying parents to school meetings. In 1962 Bates published her memoir of the Little Rock crisis, *The Long Shadow of Little Rock*.

# Beasley, Delilah Isontium

(b. September 9, 1872, Cincinnati, Ohio; d. August 18, 1934, San Leandro, Calif.), African American journalist and historian, campaigned to stop the use of derogatory racial terms in newspapers and chronicled the presence of African Americans in California history.

Delilah Beasley was born on September 9, 1872, in Cincinnati, Ohio, to Margaret and Daniel Beasley. She began her career in journalism by writing for the *Cleveland Gazette* at the age of 12; by 15, she had a regular column in the *Cincinnati Enquirer's* Sunday issue. After her parents' deaths while she was still a teenager, Beasley had to find another full-time job to support herself, and she pursued a career as a trained masseuse. In 1910, after she followed a client to California, Beasley resumed her original interest in journalism.

Beasley wrote a weekly column for the Sunday *Oakland Tribune* called "Activities among Negroes" for the next 20 years. She spoke out against racial stereotyping and discrimination throughout her career. One of her most significant contributions to journalism was her campaign to stop the use in mainstream newspapers of such derogatory terms as "darky" and "nigger" to refer to African Americans.

Beasley also studied history informally at the University of California at Berkeley and by searching research archives and collecting oral histories across the state. In 1919 she published *The Negro Trail-Blazers of California*, which chronicled the presence of African Americans in California history.

Beasley was active in the Oakland community, and was a member of several organizations, including the National Association for the Advancement of Colored People (NAACP), the League of Nations Association of Northern California, and the League of Women Voters. Delilah Beasley died of heart disease in San Leandro, California on August 18, 1934.

# Belafonte, Harold George (Harry)

(b. March 1, 1927, New York, N.Y.), African American singer, actor, producer, and activist who has used his position as an entertainer to promote human rights worldwide.

Harry Belafonte may be best known to American audiences as the singer of the "Banana Boat Song" (known popularly as "Day-O"), but it is his commitment to political causes that inspired scholar Henry Louis Gates Jr.'s comment that "Harry Belafonte was radical long before it was chic and remained so long after it wasn't."

Harold George Belafonte was born in Harlem, New York, to West Indian parents. The family moved to Jamaica in 1935 but returned five

Harry Belafonte waves to Martin Luther King Jr. after walking in the 1965 Selma-to-Montgomery civil rights march. Actor Tony Perkins, behind Belafonte, was another of the celebrities who participated in the march. *UPI/CORBIS-Bettmann*

years later. Struggling with dyslexia, Belafonte dropped out of high school after the ninth grade and, at the age of 17, joined the U.S. Navy. Although the work was menial—scrubbing the decks of ships in port during World War II—naval service introduced Belafonte to African Americans who awakened Belafonte's political consciousness and introduced him to the works of radical black intellectual W. E. B. Du Bois.

In 1948 Belafonte settled in New York City and, after working a variety of odd jobs, found a calling in acting. As a member of the American Negro Theatre in Harlem, he earned his first leading role in *Juno and the Paycock* and met Paul Robeson, his hero, and Sidney Poitier, who became his lifelong friend.

Belafonte's performance as the only black member of the cast of John Murray Anderson's *Almanac* earned him a Tony award in 1953. A year later he starred with Dorothy Dandridge in *Carmen Jones*, a movie remake of Bizet's opera that brought widespread attention to Belafonte's sensual good looks. His other early films include *Island in the Sun* (1957) and *The World, the Flesh, and the Devil* (1959). In addition, for his work in "Tonight with Belafonte," in 1960 he became the first African American to receive an Emmy Award.

As Belafonte began to achieve success as an actor, he stumbled into the singing career that made him one of the most popular entertainers of the late 1950s. In 1949 a performance at an amateur night at the Royal Roost nightclub in New York led to an RCA recording contract. Belafonte's 1956 album *Calypso* became the first record to sell more than a million copies and started a craze for his husky voice and for the infectious rhythm of such songs as "Matilda," "Brown Skin Girl," and "Jamaica Farewell."

To critics who charged that a singer who had never visited Trinidad could not claim to know calypso, Belafonte offered no apologies. Not only did he make his version of Caribbean music accessible to a mainstream American audience but, in the dozens of albums that followed *Calypso*, he also performed songs such as "Cotton Fields" that conveyed the pain of the black African American experience.

Belafonte's appeal to white audiences did not, however, protect him from racial segregation. As a result, he refused to perform in the South from 1954 until 1961, and he became deeply involved in the Civil Rights Movement. In 1956 Belafonte met Martin Luther King Jr. in Montgomery, Alabama, and they quickly became close friends. Belafonte was also a friend of Attorney General Robert F. Kennedy and frequently served as a liaison between King and policymakers in Washington, D.C.

It was Belafonte who sent the money to bail King out of the Birmingham City Jail and who raised thousands of dollars to release other jailed protesters, financed the Freedom Rides, and supported voter-registration drives. He joined Bayard Rustin in leading the youth march for integrated schools from New York to Washington, D.C., in 1958 and helped to organize the March on Washington five years later.

Belafonte continues to use his power as an entertainer in the struggle for civil rights. His production company, Harbel, formed in 1959, produces movies and television shows by and about black Americans. Belafonte's idea for the hit song "We Are the World" generated more than 70 million dollars to fight famine in Ethiopia in 1985. Two years later he became the second American to be named UNICEF Goodwill Ambassador. A long-time antiapartheid activist, Belafonte recorded an album of South African music, *Paradise in Gazankulu*, in 1988 and chaired the welcoming committee for Nelson Mandela's visit to the United States in 1990.

North America

# Berry, Mary Frances
(b. February 17, 1938, Nashville, Tenn.), American historian, civil rights activist, attorney, and the first African American woman to chair the United States Commission on Civil Rights.

The second of three children born to George and Frances Berry, Mary Frances Berry grew up in Nashville, Tennessee, and experienced the racial discrimination of the segregated South. Economic struggle led her parents to send her and her older brother, George Jr., to an orphanage temporarily, a period Berry likened to a "horror story."

Despite her considerable intellect, Berry remained an indifferent student until gaining the attention and support of Minerva Hawkins, one of only three black teachers at Nashville's segregated Pearl High School. According to Berry, Hawkins exhorted her to develop her intellectual gifts, telling her that she could do "all the things I would have done if it had been possible for me." Thus heartened, Berry applied herself to her studies and gained a deep interest in a broad range of subjects. She attended Nashville's Fisk University, studying philosophy, history, and chemistry before transferring to Howard University in Washington, D.C. She earned a bachelor's degree in 1961 and a master's degree in history in 1962. She then pursued a Ph.D. at the University of Michigan, focusing on United States history, with a concentration on constitutional history.

After receiving a Ph.D. in 1966, Berry taught history at Central Michigan University while simultaneously attending the University of Michigan's law school. She later taught at Eastern Michigan University, then at the University of Maryland. After earning her law degree, Berry accepted a professorship at the University of Maryland and the University of Michigan—both full-time positions.

Berry quickly established her reputation as a first-rate scholar, producing such books as *Black Resistance/White Law: A History of Constitutional Racism* (1971), in which she explored how racism influenced interpretation of the U.S. Constitution; *Military Necessity and Civil Rights Policy: Black Citizenship and the Constitution, 1861–1868* (1977); *Stability, Security, and Continuity: Mr. Justice Burton and Decision-Making in the Supreme Court, 1945–1958* (1978); *Long Memory: The Black Experience in America* (co-authored with John W. Blassingame, 1982); *Why ERA Failed* (1986); and *The Politics of Parenthood: Child Care, Women's Rights, and the Myth of the Good Mother* (1993). She added to her reputation by publishing regularly in scholarly journals.

Berry has also enjoyed success as an educational administrator, first at the University of Maryland as its director of Afro-American Studies, and later as interim chairperson and provost of the Division of Behavioral and of the University of Colorado, the first African American woman to hold that post at a major research university. In 1980 she accepted a professorship at Howard University and later at the University of Pennsylvania, where she became the Geraldine R. Segal Professor of Social Thought and Professor of History.

Berry's most visible contribution has been in the arena of civil rights. In 1980 President Jimmy Carter appointed her to the U.S. Commission on Civil Rights, an independent agency that was created in 1957 to investigate discrimination. Berry's political views differed from those of President Ronald Reagan, who sought to fire her in 1984. Her characterization in the press of Reagan's intentions—that he wanted to transform the agency from a "watchdog of civil rights" to a "lapdog for the administration"—summed up their differences. It also signaled her willingness to fight the president, which she did, in court, successfully blocking Reagan's attempt to unseat her. She continued to serve on the commission and in 1992 was named its chair by President Bill Clinton.

Berry has also participated in other civil rights activism, most notably as a founding member of the Free South Africa Movement, which gained notoriety on Thanksgiving in 1984 by protesting apartheid at the South African Embassy.

North America

## Bethune, Mary McLeod

(b. July 10, 1875, near Mayesville, S.C.; d. May 18, 1955, Daytona Beach, Fla.), African American civil rights leader, educator, and government official who founded the National Council of Negro Women (NCNW) and Bethune-Cookman College, and who had significant influence in Franklin D. Roosevelt's New Deal government.

Mary McLeod was born July 10, 1875, near Mayesville, South Carolina. In 1885 she enrolled at Trinity Presbyterian Mission School. With the aid of her mentor, Emma Jane Wilson, she moved on to Scotia Seminary in 1888, a missionary school in Concord, North Carolina. There she was given a "head-heart-hand" education, which emphasized not only academic but reli-

Mary McLeod Bethune and W. E. B. Du Bois speak with Lincoln University president Horace Mann Bond after receiving the university's Alpha Medallion in 1950. *CORBIS/Bettman*

gious and vocational training as well. Because McLeod's dream was to become a missionary to Africa, she entered the missionary training school now known as Moody Bible Institute. After a year of study, she applied for service but was rejected because Presbyterian policy did not permit African Americans to serve in Africa.

Following this rejection McLeod began teaching, first at Haines Institute in Augusta, Georgia in 1896, and a year later at the Presbyterians' Kendall Institute in Sumter, North Carolina. In 1900 Bethune moved to Palatka, Florida where she established two schools. In 1904 she relocated to Daytona, Florida and opened the Daytona Educational and Industrial Institute. The Daytona Institute initially consisted of five African American girls in a rented house, but eventually the school expanded to include a farm, a high school, and a nursing school. After merging with Cookman Institute, the school became the coeducational Bethune-Cookman College in 1929 and reached the status of fully accredited college in 1943. Bethune's achievement as the school's founder and president won her the National Association for the Advancement of Colored People's prestigious Spingarn Medal in 1935.

Through the Daytona Institute, Bethune proved her abilities not only as an educator but also as an organizer, fundraiser, and as one adept at negotiating between black and white communities. She also employed these skills as president and founder of several black women's organizations, which culminated in her establishment of the National Council of Negro Women (NCNW) in 1935. By the end of her presidency in 1949, the NCNW had coordinated the activities of many black women's organizations, presenting a unified voice to the federal government to secure greater equity for African Americans in social welfare programs.

Bethune had significant influence in Franklin D. Roosevelt's New Deal government. From 1936 to 1945 Bethune held the informal position of the federal administration's "race leader at large," and she was one of the influential black leaders who organized the Federal Council on Negro Affairs, known as the Black Cabinet. Bethune also became the Director of Negro Affairs for the National Youth Administration, a title she held from 1939 to 1943. This made her the highest-ranking black woman in government at that time. As director she fought for racial equality in the distribution of funds to young people and she secured state and local government positions for African Americans.

In her work Bethune emphasized an internationalism that advocated the unity of humanity. In the early 1940s the United States House Committee on Un-American Activities labeled her a Communist, which damaged her reputation. Still, Bethune's support for civil rights was unfaltering: she participated in the New Negro Alliance's picket line in 1939 and she joined A. Philip Randolph's March on Washington Movement in 1941. Bethune was honored with awards for her work as a civil and women's rights leader throughout her life; she suffered a heart attack and died May 18, 1955.

# Black Codes in the United States,

legal statutes that curtailed the rights of African Americans during the early years of Reconstruction in the United States.

Similar in both character and content to the Slave Codes, Black Codes were instituted by Southern legislative bodies in 1865 and 1866 in order to eviscerate civil rights legislation of the Reconstruction and reestablish control over the 4 million newly emancipated African Americans. Just as the Slave Codes denied African Americans any legal status besides that of property, Black Codes defined the freed people as legally subordinate to whites.

Faced with a rapidly transformed political and economic structure in the postbellum South, states such as Mississippi and South Carolina began passing laws in 1865 to limit the freedom of African Americans in many ways. Laws were instituted forcing black men and women to work or face imprisonment. Often the result was that freed men and women returned to work for their former slave owners or on nearby plantations. The termination of a contract was made illegal for "any freedman, free Negro or mulatto" with the consequence, again, of imprisonment or hard labor.

In order to restrict the movement and resettlement of ex-slaves, laws forbade blacks to own or rent farmland. Ironically, African Americans were given the new status of being allowed *some* legal responsibility; this had been absent during slavery. The rights to marry each other, sue each other, and own minimal property were written into the Codes. The purpose of the Black Codes, however, was the maintenance of a white-dominated hierarchy after the Civil War.

In 1865 Alabama and Louisiana joined Mississippi and South Carolina in the creation of laws that were, in spirit, attempts to reenslave African Americans. By 1866 all the states of the former Confederacy, except North Carolina, had enacted laws that echoed the Slave Codes. These Southern states passed laws that permitted the imprisonment or hiring out of vagrants, with vagrancy defined as black persons who were unemployed or possessed no contract with a white employer. Further, children who were orphans, or whose parents were impoverished, were turned over to the state and forced into apprenticeships with white private businessmen. Statutes requiring African American skilled laborers and artisans to pay exorbitant licensing fees made it rare for freed people to be anything besides wage laborers. Outrage over this virtual reenslavement led Northern journalists in such newspapers as the *New York Times* and the *Chicago Tribune* to print protests.

An important aspect of the Black Codes was their unequal system of punishment. The codes sanctioned the whipping of black workers by white employers, and a minor offense such as stealing food could bring physical brutality and forced servitude. Blacks found "unlawfully assembling themselves together either in the day or nighttime" were subject to immediate imprisonment. Whites could rarely be held culpable for any crime that they committed against an African American. Thus, intimidation and attacks upon freed people by white individuals and groups such as the Ku Klux Klan were commonplace, and blacks had no form of legal redress for their mistreatment.

## North America

# Black Consciousness in the United States

One of the most important aspects of the Civil Rights (1945–1965) and Black Power (1966–1975) Movements, or simply put, the Movement, was the increasing awareness among contemporary Negroes of the centrality of a positive racial identity. "Black Consciousness" here refers to how and with what consequences peoples of African descent in the United States have defined themselves as a people.

Since the creation of the American nation, and especially since emancipation in the Civil War and Reconstruction years, each generation of Negroes has consistently endeavored to build upon the struggles of its forbears. Black Consciousness crystallizes this enduring sensibility of struggle—both failure and achievement. Consequently, it includes how they have collectively viewed their history and culture. Black Consciousness also reflects the relationship between Africans in Africa and those spread throughout the African diaspora, in this case African Americans in the United States.

*Black* succeeded *Negro* as the major term of self-definition during the Black Power years. In the late 1980s, in the aftermath of a smaller cultural nationalist moment, *African American* superseded *black* as a preferred term of self-reference. On the cusp of the twenty-first century, *black* and *African American* are often used synonymously. Historically, the group, or race, has encompassed both Africans and Africans mixed with other groups, notably Europeans and indigenous Americans. Stretching back to the arrival of Africans in America, the ongoing melding of a diversity of African peoples and experiences into a singular group and experience was a profound historical and cultural development. Variously defined as Negroes, coloreds, and blacks, most Africans in America by the nineteenth century were born in the United States. As a result, their consciousness as a unique people evolved simultaneously with the notion that they, like whites or Caucasians, were not only a race, but inherently American as well. These two allegiances—to the Negro race and the American nation—have decisively shaped Black Consciousness in its various modes.

While it is readily conceded today that there is no scientific or biological basis for the idea of race, the historical and cultural impact of race continues to be widespread and profound. Indeed, in the modern world, race is often seen as a basis for peoplehood or nationhood. The enduring black freedom struggle has exemplified this complicated—at bottom paradoxical—development. Blacks and their allies have fought to create a world where race does not matter. Unfortunately, in spite of their best efforts, race still matters. It continues to frame group consciousness and affect American life in large and small ways.

During the Movement it was not enough to replace the social, political, and economic structures of Jim Crow with a fully desegregated environment. Attitudes, behaviors, and institutions among all Americans had to reflect and build upon racial equality. Indeed, racial egalitarianism was seen as both interwoven with and fundamental to the Movement in its entirety. Basic to the struggle was the related assumption that true freedom and equality demanded that Negroes feel good about themselves, their culture, and their history.

Among Negroes themselves, the Southern, church-based, grassroots social movement between 1945 and 1965 revealed a growing sense of group affiliation and pride. The widespread Negro commitment during World War II to fight for democracy at home as well as abroad characterized this intensifying group-based spirit. Negro membership in the National Association for the Advancement of Colored People (NAACP), the major civil rights organization of the modern era, grew exponentially. Further evidence of the more assertive wartime Negro mentality was the 1941 March on Washington movement, led by A. Philip Randolph. Indeed, President Franklin Delano Roosevelt created the Fair Employment Practices Committee, intended to alleviate racial discrimination in wartime industrial employment, in order to prevent the threatened mass march on the capital.

The same increasingly assertive Negro mentality thus sustained the modern Negro freedom struggle, from the principal local campaigns like the Montgomery Bus Boycott (1955–1956) and the 1963 Birmingham campaign to the inspiring leadership of Martin Luther King Jr. and Ella Baker. That very struggle intensified an expanding group-based commitment to a culturally and historically rooted sense of separateness. That sense of Negro nationhood, of cultural uniqueness, of historical distinctiveness, increasingly contributed to a race-based brand of cultural nationalism that emphasized the importance of an affirmative Negro identity. Race pride and a full commitment to the ongoing Negro freedom struggle were absolutely imperative to that evolving identity.

The full spectrum of the historical experiences and cultural development of Negro Americans—from the period of enslavement to the present—had to be critically yet sympathetically comprehended. This resounding and ever-widening emphasis on truthful yet uplifting resolutions to questions of Negro identity, self-concept, and self-esteem abounded. Taking root and flowering in the soil of the revitalized freedom struggle, the growing awareness of the significance of the cultural dimension of that struggle gave added emphasis to the belief that the realization of Negro freedom was as much mental, emotional, and psychological as structural, material, and physical.

Black Power was the historical moment in which cultural nationalism assumed unprecedented urgency and impact. Blackness signified the need to create an ever more positive and empowering group identity, thus alleviating the negativity associated with past representations of group identity,

Negroness in particular. As revealed in the militant politics of community empowerment of the Oakland-based Black Panther Party and the valiant efforts to create independent black political parties, Black Consciousness was an aggressive escalation of the ongoing black freedom struggle. As reflected in practices such as African styles of dress, African-inflected naming practices, and the creation of Kwanzaa as an African-based alternative to Christmas, Black Consciousness meant acceptance of the Africanness of blacks, another important component of the liberation struggle. As captured in King's last effort—the Poor People's Campaign—and the growing awareness of economic justice as crucial to racial justice, Black Consciousness mirrored an increasingly challenging radical politics. Black Consciousness thus represented a desire for black self-definition and greater black autonomy over a black nation within a nation, or black communities. According to this perspective, black lives, black institutions, and black spirit necessitated a militant commitment to the interests of the group. Once blacks had achieved power commensurate with an equal and fair stake in the American dream and they were truly respected as a people, a realistic merger of Black Consciousness with American consciousness and Black Power with American Power might be possible. Regardless, the omnipresence of race as a factor in American life at the end of the twentieth century ensures the necessity and viability of Black Consciousness in the foreseeable future.

## North America

# "Black Manifesto,"

**declaration authored by American James Forman demanding reparations for African American enslavement and oppression.**

Service was disrupted at New York's Riverside Church on May 4, 1969, when black nationalist James Forman strode to the pulpit before a predominantly white congregation and demanded that white churches and synagogues pay $500 million in reparations for the history of black enslavement and oppression. With the Black Manifesto, Forman implicated white religious institutions in this history, citing the church as part of "the vast system of controls over black people and their minds."

The Black Manifesto was the product of an organized effort that had its origins a month earlier at the National Black Economic Development Conference (NBEDC). Frustrated by the slow progress of reform projects in minority communities, Forman led the NBEDC in drafting a statement demanding money for a Southern land bank, four television networks, and a black university. With the support of the League of Black Revolutionary Workers and Forman leading the way, the NBEDC organized a series of church disruptions to announce the demands.

Despite the short-lived nature of the demonstration and the lack of support by the Student Nonviolent Coordinating Committee (SNCC), the

Black Manifesto did raise a half a million dollars for African American projects. Ironically, very little of the money went to the NBEDC, which was under investigation by the FBI and Justice Department. Instead, the funds ended up with the very reform projects Forman had criticized. With the money it did receive, the NBEDC established the Detroit publishing house Black Star Publications.

North America
## Black Nationalism in the United States,
the set of beliefs or the political theory that African Americans should maintain social, economic, and political institutions separate and distinct from those of whites.

Black Nationalism, also known as black separatism, is a complex set of beliefs emphasizing the need for the cultural, political, and economic separation of African Americans from white society. Comparatively few African Americans have embraced thoroughgoing separatist philosophies. In his classic study *Negro Thought in America, 1880–1915*, August Meier noted that the general black attitude has been one of "essential ambivalence." On the other hand, nationalist assumptions inform the daily actions and choices of many African Americans.

Over the course of the nineteenth and twentieth centuries, Black Nationalists have agreed on two defining principles: black pride and racial separatism. Black Nationalism calls for black pride and seeks a unity that is racially based rather than one grounded in a specific African culture or ethnicity. Thus the basic outlook of Black Nationalism is premised upon Pan-Africanism. Historian Sterling Stuckey argued that this Pan-African perspective emerged as an unintended byproduct of the institution of slavery. Slaveholders deliberately mixed together slaves of diverse linguistic and tribal backgrounds in order to minimize their ability to communicate and make common cause. In response, African slaves were forced "to bridge ethnic differences and to form themselves into a single people to meet the challenge of a common foe . . . . "

Those espousing nationalist or separatist philosophies have envisioned nationalism in quite different ways. For some, Black Nationalism demanded a territorial base; for others, it required only separate institutions within American society. Some have perceived nationalism in strictly secular terms; others, as an extension of their religious beliefs. Black Nationalists also differ in the degree to which they identify with Africa and African culture.

During the late eighteenth and the nineteenth centuries African Americans showed an increased level of racial pride and solidarity. African American leaders sought to highlight black accomplishments. For example, black ship owner Paul Cuffe of Massachusetts hired only black seamen to crew his ships so as to demonstrate their ability to a skeptical world. Boston's free blacks made Crispus Attucks—the black seaman killed in the Boston Massacre—a symbol of the African American role in the American Revolution, and for decades they celebrated March 5 as Crispus Attucks Day.

Nineteenth-century free blacks established separate religious organizations, such as the Free African Society, founded in 1787 by Philadelphians Richard Allen and Absalom Jones, and Boston's African Meetinghouse. In 1816 Allen played a leading role in the formation of the African Methodist Episcopal Church (AME).

Black pride has also involved an insistence on distinctly black standards of beauty. Black Nationalist Marcus Garvey, founder of the Universal Negro Improvement Association (UNIA), deplored black acceptance of white standards of beauty, for example, in preferring straight hair or a lighter skin color. During the 1920s he refused to place advertisements for hair straighteners or purported skin whiteners in *Negro World*, the UNIA newspaper. In the 1960s Black Nationalists embraced the political slogan Black Power, but they also proclaimed that "black is beautiful."

In many respects Black Nationalism represented a response to the overt hostility of white society. During the antebellum era David Walker's *Appeal . . . to the Colored People of the World* (1829) epitomized the demand for a united black defense. According to Stuckey, Walker's trenchant arguments earned him recognition as the "father of Black Nationalist theory in America." During the 1850s Martin Delany and the Reverend Henry Highland Garnet emerged as the most forceful nationalists. In the late nineteenth century AME bishop Henry McNeal Turner gained prominence as a nationalist leader. Booker T. Washington did not endorse Black Nationalism, but at Tuskegee Institute he insisted on the need for black economic independence and self-help, views that many separatists found congenial.

The most consistent proponents of Black Nationalism were those who advocated emigration or colonization. Delany, Garnet, Turner, and Alexander Crummell all endorsed colonization and insisted that African Americans' greatest hope lay in the establishment of all-black settlements or colonies, most often planned for Africa. Emigration or colonization entailed blacks leaving the United States to establish an African American settlement abroad, often in the hope of creating an independent black state.

In 1815, for example, Paul Cuffe led a group of 38 African Americans to found a settlement in Sierra Leone, which the British government planned to use for the repatriation of slaves freed in its colonies. Free African Society founders Richard Allen and Absalom Jones endorsed Cuffe's plan. Garvey's UNIA was the most powerful back-to-Africa movement of the twentieth century. But emigrationists differed among themselves over an appropriate destination and, in the case of emigration to Africa, in their attitudes toward the African people with whom they intended to settle.

Advocates of emigration diverged sharply in their perceptions of African culture. Delany, for example, contended that African ethical values were inherently superior to those of European Christians, who appeared to be driven by an insatiable lust for power and material gain. Turner and Garnet justified a return to Africa in terms of the opportunity it provided in bringing what they felt were the benefits of Christianity and economic progress to "savage and backward" Africans. Others stressed the opportunity that colonization would offer to demonstrate the extent of African American accomplishment when unencumbered by racial discrimination and prejudice. Some envisioned a black colony as an African American homeland to which all African Americans should return—in much the same way that twentieth-century Zionists call upon Jews to return to Israel.

Black Nationalists seek racial separation but differ on the degree and nature of that separation. Some have sought a specific territory that could be reserved for and controlled by blacks. Others have advocated separate black social, religious, economic, or political institutions within the existing white society. Territorial nationalists have differed on an appropriate location. Those calling for a return to Africa have most commonly suggested the territories of such present-day West African nations as Liberia, Sierra Leone, and Nigeria.

Others proposed creating a separate black nation in the Americas, often viewing Haiti as a likely possibility. Still others believed that a part of the United States should be set aside as a separate black state. In the late 1920s white radicals of the Communist Party of the United States of America (CPUSA) viewed African Americans as an internal colony of American imperialism and demanded recognition for a Negro Nation that would be located within the Black Belt counties of Mississippi, Alabama, and Georgia.

Many African Americans implicitly acted on nationalist principles. In the 1870s, for example, black Exodusters fled the South to found all-black settlements in Kansas. African Americans established other all-black towns, including Eatonville, Florida, the childhood home of Zora Neale Hurston. Hurston and such prominent African Americans as Paul Robeson and W. E. B. Du Bois also expressed attitudes that at times resembled or drew upon Black Nationalism. Hurston's writing, notably *Their Eyes Were Watching God* (1938), portrayed a black world in which whites rarely intruded and mattered little.

Singer and activist Robeson was never a Black Nationalist, but he held views that were, to some extent, compatible with nationalism. He believed that African Americans were fundamentally African people and insisted that they must be "proud of being black." He believed that African peoples were more spiritually attuned and more community-oriented than their white American or European counterparts. He studied several African languages and worked to end Europe's colonial domination of the African continent. Yet Robeson rejected separatism and never abandoned his vision of a racially integrated society. Moreover, in all of his extensive travels, he never visited sub-Saharan Africa.

W. E. B. Du Bois—one of America's foremost black intellectuals and a leading figure in the founding of the National Association for the Advancement of Colored People (NAACP)—had strong ties to Africa. In 1919 he organized the first Pan-African Congress. During the 1920s he traveled to Africa. Yet for most of his life, Du Bois rejected Black Nationalism. In the

1920s he opposed Marcus Garvey and the UNIA. During the 1930s, as Du Bois grew more radical, he turned to socialism and internationalism rather than to Black Nationalism. But during the harsh anti-communism of the cold war era, Du Bois lost his faith in American society. In 1961 he abandoned the United States and settled in Ghana, where he died two years later, shortly after taking Ghanaian citizenship.

From the 1930s through the 1950s Black Nationalists maintained a low profile. In 1935 Garvey failed to resurrect the UNIA, despite the hardships that many blacks endured during the Great Depression. Apart from Elijah Muhammad, the Nation of Islam's relatively obscure leader, there was no Black Nationalist who could supplant Garvey. Although Hurston, Robeson, and Du Bois were significant figures, they were not principled separatists.

The decade of the 1960s, by contrast, was a high point for Black Nationalist thought. In some respects, it became a radical extension of the Civil Rights Movement. Many blacks grew impatient with the slow pace of change and broke with the movement's principles of passive nonviolence. The Student Nonviolent Coordinating Committee (SNCC) contributed an important expression of Black Nationalism through its slogan Black Power. SNCC leader Stokely Carmichael (Kwame Turé) and political scientist Charles Hamilton wrote Black Power (1967) to elaborate that slogan into a philosophy and political program.

In 1966 Bobby Seale and Huey Newton founded the Black Panther Party, which advocated militant self-defense and Black Nationalism. The Black Panther Party, like SNCC Black Power advocates, embraced a Black Nationalism that was primarily secular and political. By contrast, Nation of Islam leaders Elijah Muhammad and the charismatic Malcolm X grounded their goals of racial separation in religious precepts. Black Muslims sought to establish separate economic enterprises, finding a religious justification for a racially separate business life.

As of the late 1990s African American attitudes and beliefs continued to reveal the significance of Black Nationalism, although less as a political philosophy than as a cultural attitude. It is difficult to weigh this cultural impact, but its manifestations can be seen throughout African American society. For example, a growing number of black parents give their children African names. Since the 1970s African-style clothing has been a recurring feature in black fashion. Likewise, the celebration of Kwanzaa emphasizes African Americans' distinctly African heritage.

Kwanzaa, however, is not a traditional African celebration. It is an invented tradition that was developed and promoted by the Black Nationalist Maulana Ron Karenga. Contemporary rap music, while not embracing African culture, emphasizes themes of black pride. Finally, the ubiquitous presence of Malcolm X suggests how broadly Black Nationalism has been disseminated throughout black culture. But few would argue that Malcolm X posters or X insignias on caps or sweaters represent a coherent outlook or set of principles. At the dawn of the twenty-first century, the most telling assessment remains that of August Meier: African Americans continue to view Black Nationalism with an essential ambivalence.

North America

# Black Panther Party,

a militant black political organization originally known as the Black Panther Party for Self-Defense.

The Black Panther Party (BPP) was founded in Oakland, California, by Huey Newton and Bobby Seale in October 1966. Newton became the party's defense minister and Seale its chairman. The BPP advocated black self-defense and restructuring American society to make it more politically, economically, and socially equal.

Newton and Seale articulated their goals in a ten-point platform that demanded, among other items, full employment, exemption of black men from military service, and an end to police brutality. They summarized their demands in the final point: "We want land, bread, housing, education, clothing, justice, and peace." They adopted the black panther symbol from an independent political party established the previous year by black residents of Lowndes County, Alabama.

Both Newton and Seale were influenced by the black Muslim leader Malcolm X, who called on black people to defend themselves. They also supported the Black Power Movement, which stressed racial dignity and self-reliance. The BPP established patrols in black communities in order to monitor police activities and protect the residents from police brutality. The BPP affirmed the right of blacks to use violence to defend themselves and thus became an alternative to more moderate civil rights groups. Their militancy quickly attracted the support of many black residents of Oakland. Newton, who had studied law, objected strongly when police engaged in brutality, conducted illegal searches, and otherwise violated the civil rights of black citizens.

The BPP combined elements of socialism and Black Nationalism, insisting that if businesses and the government did not provide for full employment, the community should take over the means of production. It promoted the development of strong, black-controlled institutions, calling for blacks to work together to protect their rights and to improve their economic and social conditions. The BPP also emphasized class unity, criticizing the black middle class for acting against the interests of other, less fortunate blacks. The BPP welcomed alliances with white activists, such as the Students for a Democratic Society (SDS) and later the Weather Underground, because they believed that all revolutionaries who wanted to change United States society should unite across racial lines. This position differed from the views of many black organizations of the late 1960s, such as the Student Nonviolent Coordinating Committee (SNCC), which excluded white members after 1966.

The party first attracted attention in May 1967 when it protested a bill to outlaw carrying loaded weapons in public. Reporters quickly gathered around the contingent of protesters, who had marched on the California state capital in Sacramento armed with weapons and wearing the party's

Black Panther Party members at the Alameda County Courthouse in July 1968, as the murder trial of Panther leader Huey Newton begins. Newton was accused of killing an Oakland, California, policeman. *UPI/CORBIS-Bettmann*

distinctive black leather jackets and black berets. After Seale read a statement, police arrested him and 30 others. News coverage of the incident attracted new recruits and led to the formation of chapters outside the San Francisco Bay Area. The BPP grew throughout the late 1960s and eventually had chapters all around the country.

Among those arrested in Sacramento was Eldridge Cleaver, a former convict who had recently published a book of essays called *Soul on Ice* (1967). Cleaver's influence in the party increased when Newton was arrested in October 1967 and charged with murder in the death of an Oakland police officer. Cleaver was a powerful speaker who took the lead in building the Free Huey Movement to defend Newton.

As part of this effort, Cleaver and Seale contacted Stokely Carmichael, the former chairman of SNCC and a nationally known proponent of Black Power. Carmichael agreed to become Prime Minister of the party and speak at Free Huey rallies during February 1968. The Free Huey movement allowed the BPP to expand its following nationally, particularly after it recruited well-known figures such as Carmichael and other SNCC members. The campaign on behalf of Newton saved him from the death penalty, but in September 1968 he was convicted of voluntary manslaughter and sentenced to 2 to 15 years in prison. This conviction was appealed and was overturned in 1970 due to procedural errors.

The SNCC-Panther alliance began to disintegrate in the summer of 1968 for a variety of reasons. Carmichael and other SNCC representatives had hoped to guide the less experienced Panthers but soon found that Cleaver and Seale were forceful leaders who were not easily led. In addition, Carmichael wanted to end all ties with white activists because he believed that they stood in the way of black self-reliance and equality. He eventually broke with Panther leaders over the issue of white support. The BPP also had differences with followers of the southern California black nationalist Maulana Karenga, leader of a group called US. Panther leaders saw themselves as revolutionary nationalists who wanted all revolutionaries, regardless of race, to unite. They disparaged Karenga as a cultural nationalist who placed too much emphasis on racial unity. The escalating verbal battles between the two groups culminated in a gun battle in January 1969 at the University of California at Los Angeles that left two Panthers dead.

As racial tension increased around the country, the Federal Bureau of Investigation (FBI) blamed the Black Panthers for riots and other incidents of violence. The bureau launched a program called COINTELPRO (short for counterintelligence program) designed to disrupt efforts to unify black militant groups such as SNCC, BPP, and US. FBI agents sent anonymous threatening letters to Panthers, infiltrated the group with informers, and worked with local police to weaken the party. In December 1969 two Chicago leaders of the party, Fred Hampton and Mark Clark, were killed in a police raid. By the end of the decade, according to the party's attorney, 28 Panthers had been killed and many other members were either in jail or had been forced to leave the United States in order to avoid arrest. In 1970 Connecticut authorities began an unsuccessful effort to convict Seale and other Panthers of the murder of a Panther who was believed to have been a police informant. In New York, 21 Panthers were charged with plotting to assassinate police officers and blow up buildings. Chief of staff David Hilliard awaited trial on charges of threatening the life of President Richard Nixon. Cleaver left the United States for exile in Cuba to avoid returning to prison for parole violations.

After Newton's conviction was reversed, he sought to revive the party and reestablish his control by discouraging further police confrontations, calling instead for the development of survival programs in black communities to build support for the BPP. These programs provided free breakfasts for children, established free medical clinics, helped the homeless find housing, and gave away free clothing and food. In 1973 Seale also tried to build popular support for the party by running for mayor of Oakland. He was defeated but received over 40 percent of the vote.

This attempt to shift the direction of the party did not prevent further external attacks and internal conflicts, and the party continued to decline as a political force. Newton and Seale broke with Cleaver, who continued to support black revolution instead of community programs. Newton became debilitated by his increasing use of cocaine and other drugs, and in 1974 he fled to Cuba to avoid new criminal charges of drug use. In that same year, Seale resigned from the party.

After the departure of Newton and Seale, the party's new leader, Elaine Brown, continued to emphasize community service programs. These programs were frequently organized and run by black women, who were a majority in the party by the mid-1970s. By then most of the party's original leaders had left or had been expelled from the group. The BPP lost even more support after newspaper reports appeared describing the illicit activities of party leaders, including extortion schemes directed against Oakland merchants. By the end of the 1970s, weakened by external attacks, legal problems, and internal divisions, the BPP was no longer a political force.

North America

# Black Power,

**political movement expressing a new racial consciousness among blacks in the United States in the late 1960s. Black Power represented both a conclusion to the decade's Civil Rights Movement and a reaction against the racism that persisted despite the efforts of black activists during the early 1960s. Black Power was influential mainly in the late 1960s.**

The meaning of Black Power was debated vigorously while the movement was in progress. To some it represented blacks' insistence on racial dignity and self-reliance, which was usually interpreted as economic and political independence, as well as freedom from white authority.

These themes had been advanced most forcefully in the early 1960s by Malcolm X, the articulate and controversial black Muslim leader. He argued that blacks should focus on improving their own communities rather than striving for complete integration, and that blacks had the right to retaliate against violent assaults. The publication of *The Autobiography of Malcolm X* (1965) created further support for the idea of black self-determination and had a strong influence on the emerging leaders of the Black Power Movement.

Other interpreters of Black Power emphasized the cultural heritage of blacks, especially the African roots of black identity. This view encouraged study and celebration of black history and culture. In the late 1960s black college students requested curricula in black studies that explored their distinctive culture and history. Led by the cultural critic Harold Cruse and the poet Amiri Baraka, some black intellectuals called for a cultural-nationalist perspective on literature, art, and history in the belief that blacks had separate values and ways of living. Blacks often expressed a sense of cultural nationalism by wearing loose, bright-colored African garments, called dashikis, and the natural "Afro" hairstyle.

Still another view of Black Power called for a revolutionary political struggle to reject racism and imperialism in the United States, as well as throughout the world. This interpretation encouraged the unity of non-whites, including Hispanics and Asians, against their perceived oppressors. Revolutionary nationalists like Stokely Carmichael, later known as Kwame Turé, first advocated a worldwide Marxist revolution but later emphasized Pan-Africanism, the political and cultural unity of all people of African origins.

Black Power as a political idea originated with the Student Non-violent Coordinating Committee (SNCC) in the mid-1960s. By 1965 many SNCC workers, frustrated at Southern whites' continued resistance to black civil rights, believed that any future progress could come only through independent black political power. When that faction took over the organization in 1966, with Carmichael leading the way, whites were ejected from SNCC membership.

Widespread use of the term Black Power started in June of 1966 during a protest march through Mississippi begun by James Meredith, who had been the first black to attend the University of Mississippi. Meredith was wounded by a sniper during the march and had to be hospitalized. Leaders of several civil rights organizations, including Carmichael and Martin Luther King Jr., took up the march. Along the route, Carmichael and SNCC activists exhorted marchers by demanding,

Black activists give the Black Power salute at a rally for the Black Panther Party. The Black Power Movement, which emerged in the mid-1960s, encouraged black solidarity and self-reliance. *CORBIS/Flip Schulke*

"What do you want?" and then leading the response, "Black Power!"

The national media began to report on Black Power, which immediately drew condemnation from whites for its racially separatist message. Leaders of several black organizations, including the National Association for the Advancement of Colored People (NAACP), the National Urban League, and the Southern Christian Leadership Conference (SCLC), also denounced Black Power. As head of the SCLC, King, who many people viewed as the leader of blacks in the United States, voiced his disapproval of the threatening, anti-white message often associated with Black Power. While encouraging blacks to be proud of their race and to appreciate their heritage, King advised them to "avoid the error of building a distrust for all white people."

From 1966 to 1969 SNCC and the Congress of Racial Equality (CORE), a New York-based civil rights organization, were dominated by Black Power. In 1966 and 1967 Carmichael and his successor as chairman of SNCC, H. Rap Brown, became well known as national spokespeople for Black Power. Brown once said, "Violence is as American as apple pie." Such statements were condemned by many whites and some blacks as efforts to instigate racial division and violence.

Opposition to Black Power became much stronger in 1968 when the Black Panther Party, which had been founded in Oakland, California, in 1966, became the most prominent organization advocating Black Power. Black Panthers battled with police departments in several major American cities between 1968 and 1970, and several of the group's leaders were killed, imprisoned, or made fugitives from the police. The party split in 1972, with some of its leaders favoring peaceful means to achieve its goals and others still urging revolution. Although Black Power as a movement largely disappeared after 1970, the idea remained a powerful one in the consciousness of black Americans.

North America

# Blackwell, Unita

(b. March 18, 1933, Lula, Miss.), American civil rights activist and politician who advocated affordable housing for African Americans and became the first African American woman mayor in Mississippi.

Unita Blackwell, the daughter of sharecroppers, was born March 18, 1933, in Lula, Mississippi. Although she never attended high school, Blackwell eventually earned a master's degree in regional planning from the University of Massachusetts-Amherst. She began her civil rights work in the early 1960s in Mayersville, Mississippi. At that time she supported herself by chopping cotton for three dollars a day. When civil rights workers came to Mayersville encouraging voter registration among African Americans, Blackwell was one of the first to register. She was fired shortly thereafter for urging others to register.

Blackwell then began working for the Student Nonviolent Coordinating Committee (SNCC), registering voters, leading boycotts and protests, and initiating civil proceedings to stop discriminatory practices in the state. The most notable case was the landmark *Blackwell v. Board of Education* in 1965 and 1966, which furthered school desegregation. Blackwell was also a founding member of the Mississippi Freedom Democratic Party (MFDP), which protested the Democratic Party's seating of Mississippi's all-white delegation at the 1964 Democratic National Convention in Atlantic City, New Jersey.

Through her civil rights work, Blackwell became an expert on rural housing and development, about which she lectured and launched projects to gain home ownership for low-income families. In 1976 she worked successfully to incorporate the town of Mayersville. Later that year she was elected mayor, becoming the first African American woman mayor in Mississippi—in a town where she was formerly prohibited from voting. She held this position until 1993. After serving as a town alderman, she was reelected mayor of Mayersville in 1997. She was also elected chair of the National Conference of Black Mayors in 1989, and in 1992 received a MacArthur Foundation Fellowship.

## Blaxploitation Films,

popular film genre of the 1970s that depicted African American heroes defying an oppressive system.

In the early 1970s an American film genre began to crystallize from different elements in the American political and cultural scene. At the center of the new genre was a new kind of hero: a black, urban, poor male striking back at a system that had denied him basic rights and respect. Set in the dense urban landscape of black America, these films gave a vision of America different from the one typically portrayed by mainstream Hollywood cinema.

The term *blaxploitation* was first coined to describe Gordon Parks Jr.'s *Superfly* (1972). Two earlier films are frequently cited as forerunners of the genre: Melvin Van Peebles's *Sweet Sweetback's Baadasssss Song* (1971), and Gordon Parks Sr.'s *Shaft* (1971). Throughout the 1970s it is estimated that some 150 films were made within the blaxploitation genre.

Drawing upon both the mainstream marketability of action films and the growing Black Power Movement, blaxploitation films were popularly well-received, if not always critically acclaimed. In these films, the black hero fought back and won, often against overwhelming odds. Filled with fast-paced action, the plot usually involved a male hero, or antihero, who found it necessary to renounce the system and resort to violence. These films portrayed a virile black male sexuality that had been missing in both mainstream and African American cinema up to that point. A few films, such as *Coffy* (1973) with Pam Grier, featured female protagonists.

Blaxploitation films drew criticism for resorting to formulas and portraying unrealistic scenarios, and were actively opposed by a coalition that included the National Association for the Advancement of Colored People (NAACP). Many critics felt that the films were too simplistic to offer any kind of viable model for African American resistance to an oppressive system. Others noted that the character development, particularly of women, was limited. Some, such as black psychiatrist Alvin Poussaint, saw the films as dangerous for their glorification of criminal life and machismo, and as ultimately destructive to the black community.

For director Melvin Van Peebles, however, this was not the point. The blaxploitation film's attraction was that "the black audience finally gets a chance to see some of their own fantasies acted out—[it's] about rising out of the mud and kicking ass."

The films were oriented specifically toward black urban audiences, who made the blaxploitation film a lucrative business. Made on low budgets, the films were proven financial successes for the studios, with *Shaft* making more than $16 million for MGM. Inner-city youth imitated the fashions and hairstyles worn in the films, and soundtracks, such as Curtis Mayfield's score for *Superfly*, achieved wide popularity.

Although most critics place the term *blaxploitation* within the 1970s, the genre had a noted effect on later films. Major film studios continued to produce "against the odds" action-packed films. Later works by John Singleton and Mario Van Peebles, Melvin's son, were influenced by the political concerns of blaxploitation, and continued to portray African American life in the inner city.

North America

# Borders, William Holmes

(b. February 24, 1905, Macon, Ga.; d. November 23, 1993), minister and civil rights worker.

William Borders was the third generation of preachers in his family. He earned a B.A. from Morehouse College in Atlanta, Georgia in 1929; a B.D. from Garrett Theological Seminary in 1932; an M.A. from the University of Chicago in 1936; and an L.H.D. from Wilberforce University in 1962. From 1937 to 1988 he served as pastor of the Wheat Street Baptist Church in Atlanta, where he was a leader in the fight for civil rights.

In 1939 Borders helped integrate Atlanta's police department, and in 1945 he directed a campaign to obtain jobs as bus drivers for African Americans. In the early 1960s he chaired the Adult-Student Liaison Committee, which worked to desegregate Atlanta's hotels, lunch counters, and restaurants.

North America

# Boston, Massachusetts,

a city in the northeastern United States that, despite its long history of rejecting official racial discrimination, has nevertheless experienced great racial tension and distrust.

Boston has the contradictory nature of being racially progressive while at the same time being racially oppressive. It was a noted center of abolitionist activity during the antebellum period, yet white Bostonians also permitted segregation and other acts of exclusion of blacks. During the 1970s, when a judge ordered busing of students to integrate Boston's schools, racial tensions rose to the fore again.

Blacks first came to Boston in bondage in 1638, on the slave ship Desiré. Boston became a prominent port in the slave trade, although slavery never came close to reaching the proportions in Boston that it did in the American South. By 1700 an antislavery movement had begun in Boston, and in 1701 Boston's board of selectmen unsuccessfully attempted to create a bill to end slavery by hiring white servants in their place. Many slaves were allowed to purchase their own freedom, or were otherwise freed by their owners, especially when antislavery activist Samuel Sewall published *The Selling of Joseph* (1712), which was followed by numerous manumissions.

By 1752 blacks numbered 1,500, or 10 percent of the population, and a free black community was beginning to form in Boston's North End, then known as New Guinea. Some slaves had already achieved prominence, including poets Phillis Wheatley and Lucy Terry Prince and artist Scipio Moorhead.

The events surrounding the Revolutionary War created a wave of antislavery sentiment, and blacks made efforts to secure their own freedom. On March 5, 1770, Crispus Attucks, an escaped slave, was the first of five people killed by British soldiers in a protest that became known as the Boston Massacre. In 1773 Caesar Hendricks, a slave, sued his owner for "detaining him in slavery." An all-white jury sided with Hendricks and awarded him damages. Also in 1773, Boston's blacks unsuccessfully petitioned the Massachusetts legislature to abolish slavery. Finally, in 1783 Massachusetts abolished slavery and granted voting rights to blacks and Native Americans. Blacks, free and slave, fought in the Revolutionary War.

But the ending of slavery did not necessarily signify that blacks were accorded social equality. Many whites were determined to maintain the structures of racial segregation. As a result, Boston's blacks engaged in self-help activities to promote their own well-being. Prince Hall's creation of the African Masonic Lodge in 1787 was one of the most notable institutions to arise. Forty-four of Boston's blacks founded the African Society, a mutual benefit society, in 1796. In 1805 Rev. Thomas Paul helped to found the African Baptist Church, the first black church in the Northern states. Shortly after that, the African Meeting House was constructed. Completed in 1806, it was the only black-owned property in the city, and it quickly became the focal point of black social life.

During the 1830s Boston became the center of abolitionist activities in the United States through such publications as William Lloyd Garrison's influential the *Liberator*. In 1832 Boston's abolitionist organization, the Massachusetts General Colored Association, reorganized and became the New England Anti-Slavery Society. Even as a small segment of the white population agitated to improve blacks' social conditions, blacks still faced regular indignities, such as public insults and segregated facilities. Frederick Douglass, for example, was forced to sit in a Jim Crow car on a train that he boarded in his hometown of Lynn, Massachusetts. William C. Nell was forcibly removed from the Howard Theater in downtown Boston for refusing to sit in the Jim Crow section. And, although public schools were provided for black children, they were poorly funded, scholastically inferior, and often inconveniently located for blacks.

In the 1840s Benjamin Roberts, a black printer whose daughter Sarah walked past five white schools on the way to the "colored" school she attended, requested that Sarah be admitted to the school closest to her home. The Primary School Committee's refusal to admit Sarah to the whites-only school led Roberts to sue for admission. The Roberts' legal counsel was Charles Sumner, an abolitionist and future United States senator who argued that racially segregated schools were necessarily inferior and that racial segregation in education was unconstitutional and damaging. Though his arguments did not persuade Massachusetts's Chief Justice Lemuel Shaw, the arguments closely paralleled those of Thurgood Marshall in *Brown v. Board of Education of Topeka* more than 100 years later.

A wave of Irish immigration began during the 1840s, threatening the precarious economic position that blacks had occupied in Boston. Many of the Irish immigrants came with few skills, putting them in direct competition with blacks who had historically occupied unskilled labor positions. Blacks also felt pressure with regard to housing.

Blacks became increasingly militant, best exemplified by the reaction to the Fugitive Slave Act of 1850, which mandated that citizens aid federal agents who were attempting to capture runaway slaves. Abolitionist activity in the city was refueled. During the Civil War, abolitionist activity led to the enlistment of blacks and the creation of the Massachusetts Fifty-fourth Colored Infantry, which formed in Boston.

In the postwar years, blacks from the upper South migrated to Boston, recruited by factory owners or by relatives. The city's black population doubled within a decade, giving blacks greater political clout. In the latter half of the nineteenth century black Bostonians in the city's "old" Ward 9 elected 20 black candidates to public office, including the city council, the state legislature, and the school committee. In addition, by the end of the nineteenth century, Boston boasted several successful black-owned businesses, including the Eureka Cooperative Bank.

Despite these advances, Boston's blacks still suffered from racial discrimination. Most blacks worked in menial jobs for near-subsistence wages. Banks refused to extend loans to black applicants. Paradoxically, Boston took great pride in its abolitionist past, as evidenced in the erection of the Massachusetts Fifty-fourth Colored Infantry monument on the Boston Common in 1893.

Seventy percent of African Americans held employment in menial jobs in 1910. The settlement houses and social services organizations prevalent in urban America during this era came to Boston in the form of the South End House and the Robert Gould Shaw House. Boston experienced a new wave of immigration of blacks from the Caribbean and the African nation of Cape Verde; during the 1920s the city's black population grew sixfold. In large part, however, the Great Migration missed Boston, and blacks still faced housing and job discrimination despite protests from civil rights groups. World War II brought Southern and Midwestern black migrants in search of work in the war industries, continuing into the 1950s. Although blacks were becoming a considerable demographic presence, greater political power eluded them because of the imposition of at-large city council seats.

In the 1960s Civil Rights Movement leaders sought to evoke change in Boston by exposing the city's de facto school segregation and other inequalities. The Student Nonviolent Coordinating Committee (SNCC) and the Congress of Racial Equality established offices in the city to fight housing discrimination. In 1961 the Boston branch of the National Association for the Advancement of Colored People successfully sued the Boston Housing Authority, charging racial discrimination. This essentially signaled the end of segregated housing.

The move to desegregate Boston's public schools provides perhaps the most famous example of the reforming impulse of activist blacks and progressive whites in conflict with the white community's resistance to such change. During the 1960s Boston's blacks sought to integrate Boston's schools and were the driving force behind the Massachusetts Racial Imbalance Act of 1965, which was intended to end de facto segregation in Massachusetts. The issue played out over a protracted period of time.

Proponents of integration developed plans for what are now called magnet schools, in addition to proposing "metropolitanization," a kind of merger between school districts in the city proper and in outlying areas. Resistance to these and other progressive plans finally led judge W. Arthur Garrity to order the busing of black students from Boston's Roxbury neighborhood to predominantly white schools in South Boston in 1974. This plan, which was known as Phase I, was to be temporary until Garrity could devise a better one. The school board complied with the judge's orders, but the plan was flawed and, predictably, many of South Boston's white residents resisted. Their anger took the form of throwing stones, rotten eggs, and rotten tomatoes at buses and shouting at black students. Resistance continued throughout the year, but schools were finally integrated.

Blacks seemed to be making political headway in Boston. Black politician Mel King ran unsuccessfully for mayor in 1979 and 1983, but he was supported in both elections by blacks and whites, with increasingly strong showings. Other prominent black politicians in Boston included State Representative Byron Rushing and State Senator Dianne Wilkerson. Still, political power lay in the hands of the white majority. Boston experienced an immigration of African Americans and other nonwhites so that, by the 1990s, the nonwhite population reached approximately 40 percent. This numerical strength has not translated to political power, however, as such age-old political maneuvers as gerrymandering have diluted nonwhite political power. In addition, many of the modern immigrant population have no political power because they have not acquired United States citizenship.

African Americans are leaders in all areas of life in Boston—and include such figures as Rev. Eugene Rivers; the *Boston Globe* journalist Wil Haygood; Fletcher Wiley, former president of the Boston Chamber of Commerce; Charles Stith, ambassador to Tanzania; leading civil rights lawyer Margaret Burnham; Kenneth Guscott of Long Bay Management; and Bob Moses, founder of the Algebra Project.

# Brotherhood of Sleeping Car Porters,

the first successful African American trade union.

Founded in 1925 by A. Philip Randolph, the Brotherhood of Sleeping Car Porters (BSCP) was instrumental in securing better wages and hours for the porters of the Pullman Company, but its significance goes beyond such accomplishments. The BSCP became an integral part of the fight for fair employment practices in other industries and helped bring black workers into the realm of organized labor. Under Randolph's leadership, the BSCP was also a voice for civil rights, providing the philosophical seed that bore fruit in the 1963 March on Washington.

The Pullman Palace Car Company was established in 1867 to provide luxurious service to train passengers. By the 1920s the company was the largest employer of African Americans. According to historians, Pullman favored black men as porters not only because they could be paid less than white men, but because white customers enjoyed being waited upon by African Americans. Working for Pullman also provided the porters some degree of status, at least within their communities. Wearing immaculate uniforms rather than field denims, and traveling to distant cities, they were seen as sophisticated professionals.

Yet the porters, many of whom were college-educated men, faced demeaning conditions at work. Placed in a servile relationship to white customers, porters were also exploited by their employers. Pullman paid black workers less than whites and restricted the men to jobs as porters. (Black women worked for Pullman as maids and launderers, but were for the most part not represented by the BSCP, which according to historian Melinda Chateauvert was more concerned with black manhood than with gender equity.) That such work was considered desirable is evidence of how few opportunities were open to educated black men at the time. One Pullman porter killed in a 1923 train crash was ultimately identified by his Phi Beta Kappa key; it is unlikely that any of his white Dartmouth classmates shined shoes for a living.

The first step toward fighting inadequate pay and inhumane working conditions (which included being allowed to sleep only in three-hour stints in the smoking room off the men's bathroom) came in 1920 with the formation of the Pullman Porters and Maids Protective Association (PPMPA). In addition, an industry-wide black union, the Railway Men's Association, tried to attract porters to its cause. Pullman attempted to defuse labor organizing by creating the Employee Representation Plan (ERP, a company union), and offering modest wage increases. Although porter dissatisfaction simmered, efforts to organize were stalled until A. Philip Randolph, editor of the Messenger and a strong voice for economic equality, addressed a meeting of porters in 1925. Randolph urged porters to reject the ERP and form their own union, and several of the porters agreed—if Randolph would lead them.

Starting in 1925, with only about 1,900 members out of the nearly 10,000 porters, the union faced intimidation by the company as well as resistance by some workers who were satisfied with the ERP. In addition, Randolph and his organizers had to battle the black community's long-standing ambivalence toward labor unions. Historically excluded from white unions and the secure jobs they represented, many African Americans believed that they owed their allegiance to their employers, not to unions. Randolph's eloquence on behalf of the BSCP helped change attitudes, as did the support of the National Association for the Advancement of Colored People (NAACP). While Randolph led the public fight, lobbying federal courts and agencies, Chicago porter Milton Webster ran the daily administration of the union, which achieved its largest membership (4,623) in 1928. After a series of setbacks, the 1934 passage of the Railway Labor Act finally forced Pullman to recognize the Brotherhood.

After negotiating its first contract with Pullman in 1937, the BSCP continued to represent the porters for more than 40 years, merging with the Brotherhood of Railway and Airline Clerks in 1978. The Pullman era had long since passed, but the union's contributions extended beyond the railroad industry. As one member of the powerful BSCP Ladies Auxiliary (made up mostly of porters' wives) later said, the union "laid the foundation for the Civil Rights Movement in this country. It inspired black people by proving that they could organize and get results."

Randolph's national leadership led to an executive order banning discrimination in the defense industries (an order not strongly enforced), the establishment of the Fair Employment Practices Committee, and the desegregation of the United States armed forces. When Rosa Parks was arrested for refusing to give up her bus seat to a white man in 1955, it was BSCP member E. D. Nixon who helped organize the Montgomery bus boycott in protest. In 1963 A. Philip Randolph's 1941 call for a March on Washington was finally realized; the event brought the civil rights message to a worldwide audience.

North America

# Brown, Charlotte Hawkins

(b. June 11, 1883, Henderson, N.C.; d. 1961), American civic leader and educator who founded the Palmer Institute (a prep school for African Americans) and argued against lynching and in favor of interracial cooperation.

Charlotte Hawkins Brown was born Lottie Hawkins on June 11, 1883, in Henderson, North Carolina, to Caroline Frances Hawkins and Edmund H. Hight. In 1888, Caroline and her new husband, Nelson Willis, moved the family to Cambridge, Massachusetts, where they operated a boarding house for Harvard students and a laundry. Around the time she graduated from Cambridge English High School, Lottie changed her name to the more serious sounding Charlotte Eugenia. She attracted the interest and support of Alice Freeman Palmer, who financed her education at the State Normal School in Salem, Massachusetts.

In 1902 Hawkins founded the Alice Freeman Palmer Institute in Sedalia, North Carolina, in honor of her mentor. In 1911 Hawkins married Edmund S. Brown, who then taught at the Palmer Institute. The couple divorced in 1915. The Palmer Institute began as a vocational school, but its curriculum evolved until it was a strictly academic institution, considered one of the finest preparatory schools for African Americans in the United States.

In addition to running the Palmer Institute, Brown fought tirelessly for African American civil rights, lecturing in opposition to lynching and in favor of interracial cooperation. She helped to found the National Council of Negro Women, the North Carolina State Federation of Negro Women's Clubs, and the North Carolina Teachers Association. She was also on the national board of the Young Women's Christian Association.

Brown served as the president of the Palmer Institute for 50 years before retiring in 1952. Even in retirement, however, she continued to act as the school's financial director and was deeply involved on its board of directors until her death in 1961. Though financial problems forced the Palmer Institute to close in 1971, Brown's tremendous contribution to African American education did not go unheralded. In 1983 the Charlotte Hawkins Brown Historical Foundation was incorporated and established on the Palmer Institute's campus, North Carolina's first historic site honoring either an African American or a woman.

North America

# Brown, Hubert G. ("H. Rap")

**(b. October 4, 1943, Baton Rouge, La.), American writer and activist also known as Jamil al-Amin; outspoken advocate of Black Power, elected national chairman of the Student Nonviolent Coordinating Committee in 1967.**

Hubert "H. Rap" Brown was born October 4, 1943 in Baton Rouge, Louisiana. In 1962 he dropped out of Southern University to join the Nonviolent Action Group (NAG) at Howard University. In 1965 he became chairman of the NAG. Labeled an "extremist" by the media for his nationalist views, he was an outspoken advocate of Black Power. In May 1967, when Stokely Carmichael stepped down, he was elected national chairman of the Student Nonviolent Coordinating Committee (SNCC).

That same year, Brown was charged by the states of Maryland and Ohio with inciting violence. He was harassed by the police and targeted by the Counterintelligence Program of the Federal Bureau of Investigation (FBI). While under indictment, he was arrested for transporting weapons across state lines. He resigned as SNCC chairman in 1968 and later that year was sentenced to five years in prison on federal weapons charges.

Fearing for his life, Brown refused to appear at his trial in Maryland, and in 1970 was placed on the FBI's Ten Most Wanted List. He was captured in 1972 and spent the next four years in prison. While incarcerated, Brown converted to Islam, taking the name Jamil ("servant of Allah") al-Amin ("the trustworthy"). After his release, Brown moved to Atlanta, Georgia, where he is in charge of the Community Grocery Store and serves as imam (spiritual leader) to Muslim families in and around Atlanta.

North America

## *Brown v. Board of Education,*

the 1954 United States Supreme Court decision that overturned the "separate but equal" doctrine that, since 1896, had made racial segregation legal in public facilities.

On May 17, 1954, in the case of *Brown v. the Board of Education of Topeka*, the U.S. Supreme Court ended federally sanctioned racial segregation in the public schools by ruling unanimously that "separate educational facilities are inherently unequal." A groundbreaking case, *Brown* not only overturned the precedent of *Plessy v. Ferguson* (1896), which had declared "separate but equal facilities" constitutional, but also provided the legal foundation of the Civil Rights Movement of the 1960s. Although widely perceived as a revolutionary decision, Brown was in fact the culmination of changes both in the Court and in the strategies of integration's most powerful legal champion, the National Association for the Advancement of Colored People (NAACP).

The Supreme Court had become more liberal in the years since it decided *Plessy*, largely due to appointments by Democratic presidents Franklin D. Roosevelt and Harry S. Truman. Though still all-white, the Court had issued decisions in the 1930s and 1940s that rendered racial separation illegal in certain situations. In *Smith v. Allright* (1944), it declared segregated political primaries unconstitutional. Four years later, in *Shelly v. Kraemer* (1948), the Court ruled that states could not enforce racially restrictive real-estate covenants. Over the next few years, often in response to cases brought by the NAACP's Legal Defense and Educational Fund, the Court further chipped away at the legal basis for state-sanctioned segregation.

Pushing the Court to this point had taken the NAACP more than 40 years. Since its founding in 1909, the organization had legally challenged racial inequality. Although for many years NAACP lawyers did not attack segregation itself, they found fertile ground in the rampant inequity it had spawned. This was particularly true in education. In 1929, for instance, the state of Alabama spent $36 per white student and only $10 per black student in its public schools. Such imbalance was widespread in the Southern states, where black schoolchildren endured overcrowded classrooms, insufficient libraries, undertrained teachers, and a lack of indoor plumbing. The NAACP's strategy throughout the 1930s demanded only that local governments provide African American children with facilities equal to those enjoyed by white children. Basing its lawsuits on individual states' or counties' failures to conform to *Plessy*'s formula of "separate but equal" in public accommodations, the NAACP won nearly every case.

On the national level, though, the NAACP, led by its first full-time legal counsel, Charles H. Houston, chose to focus on graduate and professional rather than elementary education. By demanding equal facilities on the graduate level, Houston hoped to force states into a difficult decision: either build prohibitively expensive new black professional schools or allow qualified African Americans to enroll in previously all-white law, medical, and other graduate schools. In 1936 Houston won a significant victory when Maryland's Supreme Court ordered the segregated University of Maryland Law School to admit Donald Murray, an African American student, rather than send him out of state for his legal education. A similar case went to the U.S. Supreme Court in 1938: in *Missouri ex rel Gaines v. Canada*, a 6–2 majority found that the University of Missouri, by denying a black student admission to its law school—though it did create a separate black law school in a building that also housed a movie theatre and a hotel—had created an unfair "privilege . . . for white law students" that it did not extend to similarly qualified African Americans.

Along with Houston, another black lawyer began to shape the NAACP's legal policy in the late 1930s. Thurgood Marshall, who later became the first African American U.S. Supreme Court justice, worked with Houston on *Murray* and by 1939 had succeeded Houston as NAACP chief counsel. Marshall also set up the NAACP Legal Defense and Educational Fund. Over the following decade, Marshall brought to the Court two graduate education cases that set the stage for *Brown*. In *McLaurin v. Oklahoma*, the state's segregated graduate school of education had admitted a black student, 68-year-old George McLaurin, but had segregated him within the school, roping off a separate seating area and scheduling his lunch hour at a different time from that of his white classmates. *Sweatt v. Painter*, a Texas case, concerned the state's offer of a separate law school for black students. Unlike *Gaines*, this school would come close to parity with the white school, including access to its library and faculty. In both cases, Marshall argued that segregation itself was inherently unequal and that it denied African Americans their rights to equal protection under the Fourteenth Amendment to the Constitution.

The Supreme Court decided both cases in 1950, the year in which Charles Houston died. In these rulings, the Court stopped just short of overturning *Plessy*. Meanwhile, the NAACP was considering a new challenge to the nation's segregated elementary schools. Within the organization, this was controversial. The 1948 NAACP conference stated a clear policy against joining lawsuits that recognized "the validity of segregation statutes"—as all the earlier "equalization" cases had done. Tackling local cases involving unequal elementary schools seemed to many to be a step backward. But when five groups of plaintiffs approached the NAACP beginning in 1949, Marshall and his colleagues agreed to help.

The cases came from Kansas, South Carolina, Virginia, and Delaware,

Nettie Hunt hugs her daughter, Nikie, 3, on the steps of the Supreme Court building after the court announced its decision in *Brown* v. *Board of Education*. *CORBIS/Bettmann*

with a related case from the District of Columbia. Each was a class-action lawsuit involving state-imposed school segregation. In the Virginia case, a group of African American high school students had initiated the action themselves. Along with the South Carolina plaintiffs, they faced obvious and extreme inequity; even South Carolina's governor had promised to improve black schools. In the Kansas case, the black and white schools were roughly comparable, and the lawsuit provoked local black opposition, as some African American teachers feared losing their jobs. But with inequality conceded in the Southern cases and not at issue in Kansas, the NAACP could at last directly challenge the constitutionality of segregation.

NAACP lawyers presented each case before federal tribunals in their respective districts. Among the evidence they presented was that of academic experts like social psychologist Kenneth B. Clark, known as the "doll man," whose work with children demonstrated the damaging psychological effects of segregation. As expected, the tribunals relied on Supreme Court precedent—*Plessy*—and ruled with the defendants. But the opinions gave Marshall hope. Delaware chancellor Collins Seitz wrote, "I believe the 'separate but equal' doctrine in education should be rejected, but I also believe its rejection must come from [the Supreme] Court."

Now consolidated under the name *Brown v. Board of Education*, the five cases came before the Supreme Court in December 1952. The NAACP followed the same strategy that had brought success in *Sweatt* and *McLaurin*. Marshall and his colleagues wrote that states had no valid reason to impose segregation, that racial separation—no matter how equal the facilities—caused psychological damage to black children, and that "restrictions or distinctions based upon race or color" violated the equal protection clause of the Fourteenth Amendment. Lawyers for the states argued that *Plessy* was correct: as long as accommodations were "equal," segregation itself hurt no one. They predicted dire consequences for integrated education, particularly in a South accustomed to segregation.

Though a majority of the justices already favored the NAACP's clients, some feared issuing a ruling that might have to be implemented by force. They decided to have the cases reargued the following term. In the intervening time, Chief Justice Fred Vinson died and President Eisenhower replaced him with California governor Earl Warren, who used his political skills to negotiate a unanimous Court verdict for desegregation.

The opinion, written by Warren and read on May 17, 1954, was short and straightforward. It echoed Marshall's expert witnesses, stating that for African American schoolchildren, segregation "generates a feeling of inferiority as to their status in the community that may affect their hearts and minds in a way unlikely to ever be undone." Critics decried such emphasis on psychological and sociological evidence, but Chief Justice Warren later argued for the importance of contradicting *Plessy*, which had stated that African Americans themselves had imagined any "badge of inferiority" conferred by segregation. The decision went on to say that segregation had no valid purpose, was imposed to give blacks lower status, and was therefore unconstitutional based on the Fourteenth Amendment.

Despite victory in the nation's highest court, desegregation was not immediate, easy, or complete. A separate decision, known as *Brown II* (1955), set guidelines for dismantling segregation. But without deadlines—the opinion contained the infamous phrase "with all deliberate speed"—desegregation came slowly. Throughout the South, whites reacted violently to school integration. Crowds threw rocks at black grade-schoolers in Little Rock, Arkansas, in 1957, and in 1962 Alabama governor George Wallace blocked the door when the first African American students attempted to enter the state university. Throughout the 1960s and 1970s urban schools increasingly experienced de facto segregation as middle-class whites fled to the suburbs. New strategies to achieve integration, like busing, sparked renewed frustration, anger, and resentment on all sides. At present, many urban American schools are nearly all-black while many suburban schools are all-white; in some cases, these schools are as unequal as those before *Brown*. Despite such setbacks, however, the case, considered by many legal scholars the most significant of the twentieth century, brought racial integration to thousands of American schools and inspired the Civil Rights Movement of the 1960s.

North America

# Bunche, Ralph Johnson

(b. August 7, 1904, Detroit, Mich.; d. December 9, 1971, New York, N.Y.), American diplomat and political scientist who won the Nobel Peace Prize in 1950, the first black American so honored.

Ralph Bunche spent his early years with his parents in Detroit, Michigan, and Albuquerque, New Mexico. He attributed his achievements to the influence of his maternal grandmother, with whom he lived in Los Angeles, California, after he was orphaned at age 13. Lucy Johnson not only insisted that her grandson be self-reliant and proud of his race, but that he be a high school valedictorian and go to college.

Bunche enrolled at the University of California at Los Angeles and graduated summa cum laude in 1927. He went on to graduate school at Harvard University, where he became the first black American to earn a Ph.D. in political science from an American university and where he also won the prize for outstanding doctoral thesis in the social sciences in 1934. He conducted his postdoctoral research on African colonialism at Northwestern University, the London School of Economics, and the University of Cape Town, where he defied the South African government's objections to hosting a black scholar.

While still a graduate student, Bunche established himself as a professor and an activist for civil rights. In 1928 he joined the faculty of Howard University in Washington, D.C., where he founded and chaired the political science department. Bunche expressed his commitment to racial integration and to economic improvement for workers during his years at Howard by participating in civil rights protests and in the establishment of the National Negro Congress in 1936. From 1938 to 1940, Bunche collaborated with Swedish sociologist Gunnar Myrdal on the research for Myrdal's massive study of American race relations, *An American Dilemma: The Negro Problem and Modern Democracy* (1944).

After years as a scholar of international politics, Bunche assumed a more active role during World War II. In 1941 he left Howard and joined the Office of Strategic Services (the predecessor of the Central Intelligence Agency), where he specialized in African affairs. He moved to the State Department in 1944, and, as the first African American to run a departmental division of the federal government, continued to work on Africa and on colonial issues.

Bunche's association with the United Nations (UN) also began in 1944, when he participated in the Dumbarton Oaks Conference, which laid the groundwork for the UN Charter signed in San Francisco a year later. In 1946 Bunche went to work full-time for the UN at the request of the organization's first secretary-general, Trygve Lie. From 1947 to 1954 he served as the principal director of the Department of Trusteeship and Information from Non-Self-Governing Territories, a post that allowed him to assist with the process of decolonization.

Bunche first made his name as a peacemaker in 1949, when, defying all expectations, he negotiated the truce that ended the first Arab-Israeli War. Originally sent to Jerusalem in 1948 as the assistant to UN mediator Count Folke Bernadotte, Bunche stepped in when Bernadotte was assassinated and worked almost single-handedly to bring Israel and the Arab states to an agreement. For his efforts Bunche was awarded the Nobel Prize for Peace in 1950.

In 1955 Bunche was appointed UN undersecretary for special political affairs. In that capacity he oversaw UN peacekeeping operations in some of the most heated conflicts around the world. As director of UN activities in the Middle East during and after the Suez Crisis of 1956, he broadened the organization's peacekeeping role by creating the United Nations Emergency Force. He represented the UN during crises in the Republic of the Congo, Cyprus, India, Pakistan, and Yemen. His successor, Sir Brian Urquhart, described Bunche as "the original principal architect" of the concept of international peacekeeping.

Despite the demands of an international career that lasted until just before his death, Bunche fulfilled extensive academic and civil rights commitments at home. His contributions as a scholar were recognized in 1953, when Bunche was elected the first black president of the American Political Science Association. A long-time member of the board of the National Association for the Advancement of Colored People (NAACP), he was awarded the organization's Spingarn Medal in 1950. He acted as an unofficial adviser to several civil rights organizations and joined Martin Luther King Jr. in the 1965 Selma-to-Montgomery Voting Rights March. In 1963 President John F. Kennedy awarded Bunche the nation's highest civilian honor, the Medal of Freedom. Bunche died in New York City a year after his 1970 retirement from the UN.

# Carmichael, Stokely

(b. July 29, 1941, Port-of-Spain, Trinidad; d. November 15, 1998, Conakry, Guinea), activist and writer who inaugurated the Black Power Movement of the 1960s.

Stokely Carmichael was not the first to use the phrase "Black Power," but he made it famous. Critical of Martin Luther King Jr's. peaceful approach, Carmichael advanced a militant stand on civil rights as chairperson of the Student Nonviolent Coordinating Committee (SNCC) in the 1960s.

A native of Trinidad, Carmichael moved with his family to a mostly white neighborhood in the Bronx, New York, when he was 11. He graduated from Bronx High School of Science in 1960 and, four years later, from Howard University in Washington, D.C., with a bachelor's degree in philosophy.

Carmichael became involved in civil rights protests during his years at Howard. He participated in demonstrations staged by the Congress of Racial Equality, the Nonviolent Action Committee, and SNCC. He was arrested as a Freedom Rider in 1961 and served seven weeks in Parchman Penitentiary for violating Mississippi's segregation laws. Carmichael returned to the South after college and devoted himself to the organization of SNCC's black voter registration project in Lowndes County, Alabama. There, he also founded an independent political party called the Lowndes County Freedom Organization, which used the black panther as its symbol.

Carmichael became chairman of SNCC in 1966. He catapulted into the national spotlight in August of that year, when he ended a speech with a call for Black Power. Black Power became a rallying cry for black protests during the 1960s and 1970s, and it created a wedge between SNCC and more moderate civil rights groups. Although it is defined in many ways, Black Power emphasizes independent political and economic development by blacks as a necessary element of social change. Carmichael and political scientist Charles Hamilton elaborate on the concept in their book, *Black Power* (1967).

A 1967 world tour to publicize the black struggle in the United States brought Carmichael more controversy in Washington, D.C. His passport was revoked for visiting Cuba and, when he returned to the United States, he faced indictment for sedition; however, he was never prosecuted. The following year, he became Prime Minister of the Black Panther Party.

In 1969 Carmichael began to focus his political activity on Africa. Having left the Black Panthers, he went to work for the All-African People's Revolutionary Party in Ghana. In that same year, he and his wife, the South African singer Miriam Makeba, went to live in the African nation of Guinea. In 1978 Carmichael took the first name of his mentor, Kwame Nkrumah of Ghana and the last name of Ahmed Sékou Touré of Guinea to become Kwame Turé. He continued to travel and to lecture on U.S. imperialism, Pan-Africanism, and socialism until his death from cancer in November 1998. His second book, a collection of speeches and essays titled *Stokely Speaks*, appeared in 1971.

North America

# Chaney, James Earl

**(b. May 30, 1943, Meridian, Miss.; d. June 21, 1964, Miss.), African American civil rights activist who participated in and was killed during the massive voter registration and desegregation campaign in Mississippi called Freedom Summer.**

James Earl Chaney was born May 30, 1943 in Meridian, Mississippi, to Ben and Fannie Lee Chaney. In 1963 he joined the Congress of Racial Equality (CORE). A year later CORE united with the National Association for the Advancement of Colored People (NAACP) and the Student Nonviolent Coordinating Committee (SNCC) to form the Council of Federated Organizations (COFO). In 1964 COFO led a massive voter registration and desegregation campaign in Mississippi called Freedom Summer. As part of the Freedom Summer activities, Chaney was riding with two white activists in Mississippi when they were attacked and killed by the Ku Klux Klan on June 21, 1964.

North America

# Chavis, Benjamin Franklin, Jr. (Chavis Muhammad)

**(b. January 22, 1948, Oxford, N.C.), Nation of Islam minister who helped organize the Million Man March; former executive director of the National Association for the Advancement of Colored People (NAACP); and long-time civil rights organizer.**

Civil rights activist and former NAACP director Benjamin Chavis has said that "the struggle for freedom, the struggle for justice, was a part of my family roots even before I was born." Chavis, who grew up in North Carolina, became an NAACP member at age 12. At age 14 he joined the Southern Christian Leadership Conference (SCLC), and while in college at the University of North Carolina at Charlotte, he became the North Carolina SCLC coordinator. After his 1969 graduation he continued his civil rights work at the Washington office of the Commission for Racial Justice, an organization sponsored by the United Church of Christ, in which Chavis became an ordained minister.

In 1971 Chavis went to Wilmington, North Carolina, to help a student group protest discrimination. The action culminated in a week-long riot in which a black church was fired upon and a white grocery store burned down. Along with nine others, Chavis was convicted of arson and conspiracy in 1972. Although groups such as Amnesty International called the Wilmington Ten political prisoners, Chavis eventually served four years before his conviction was overturned by a federal court in 1980.

While in prison, Chavis began advanced theological study, and after his release, he was able to complete a doctorate at Howard University. In 1986 he became executive director of the Commission for Racial Justice, where he worked to publicize what he called "environmental racism"—the practice of locating hazardous dumps near minority neighborhoods. He held the position until leaving for the NAACP.

Chavis served as executive director of the NAACP from April 1993 to August 1994 in a tenure that was as controversial as it was brief. In an effort to expand membership, Chavis reached out to Nation of Islam leader Louis Farrakhan—for whom he went to work soon after leaving the NAACP—thus inspiring fear and worry among some NAACP members that the venerable institution would abandon its integrationist tradition in favor of a more militant, separatist identity. Chavis also attracted criticism for some of his other actions, such as hosting a "gang summit" in an effort to end black-on-black youth violence. Chavis was forced to resign after it was revealed that he had used NAACP funds to pay an out-of-court settlement in a sexual harassment case.

Chavis remained close to Farrakhan and other Nation of Islam leaders, and helped organize the 1995 Million Man March. Three years after his resignation from the NAACP Chavis joined the Nation of Islam, adopted the name Chavis Muhammad, and began a new career as a Muslim minister.

North America

# Chicago Riots of 1919,

**one of the largest American race riots during the Red Summer of 1919, inflamed by segregation and police discrimination.**

In July 1919, Chicago, Illinois, erupted in a race riot that left 23 blacks and 15 whites dead, 537 people injured, and over a million dollars of property damage. One of 25 race riots that swept through the country during the Red Summer of 1919, the conflict in Chicago was galvanized, as historian

Mounted police lead away an African American man during the Chicago riots of 1919. Labor and housing tensions were major causes of the violence. *CORBIS*

William M. Tuttle Jr. has pointed out, by "gut-level animosities" between the city's white and black residents, for whom competition for residential housing and good union jobs had inflamed racial tensions.

Between 1910 and 1920 the population of the "Black Belt" on the south side of Chicago had almost tripled, while the perimeter of the neighborhood had remained relatively the same. Under the pressure of the Great Migration north, the conditions and quality of inner-city living declined drastically, with the black newcomers facing a mortality rate twice that of whites. Meanwhile, middle-class African Americans were making their way into previously all-white neighborhoods. For many, leaving squalid, overcrowded ghettos and seeking better jobs was an expression of the pride and self-respect forged in the crucible of World War I. These upwardly mobile families were often targeted by community-organized white violence directed at keeping the lines of segregation intact. Between 1917 and 1919, 26 bombs exploded at black residences in Chicago's white neighborhoods.

Adding to the racial antipathy that led to the riots were historic conflicts over labor. For decades the mostly white unions representing workers in Chicago's stockyards had excluded black workers; denied membership, blacks had often allowed themselves to be used as replacement labor during strikes. Despite some positive movement toward integration of labor unions, by the summer of 1919, most white workers were unionized and most black workers were not, and attitudes of resentment and mistrust had hardened on both sides.

The spark that finally ignited this overheated atmosphere came on July 27, 1919, when a 17-year-old African American, Eugene Williams, swam over the invisible line of racial segregation at the 29th Street Beach. An angry mob of whites stoned him as he swam in, and Williams drowned. When the police were called in, they refused to arrest any of the whites who had been seen throwing stones, and instead arrested one African American. A fight broke out between a growing crowd of blacks on one side and the police and whites on the other. Soon the riot overflowed from the beach, sweeping out into the rest of the city.

Over the next week, violence raged through Chicago. White workingmen attacked their black counterparts as they entered the stockyards. On both sides of the color line, gangs of youth attacked those who crossed the lines of segregated neighborhoods. The damage to property was extensive, especially in black sections, with thousands of African Americans left homeless. In addition, in a summer already marked by an unprecedented number of strikes, many workers stayed home as the rioting continued, bringing some industries and services to a near standstill.

As the violence continued, Chicago mayor William H. Thompson asked Illinois governor Frank O. Lowden to mobilize the state militia, but for reasons that are still unclear did not deploy the 3,500 troops until July 30, when there had already been dozens of deaths and hundreds of casualties. Before then the Chicago police, overburdened and often racist themselves—seven black men had been shot by the police, but no whites—had been solely responsible for containing the violence. The killing was over by August 8, the day the militia were recalled. But despite calls for calm by African American organizations, including the National Urban League, the National Association for the Advancement of Colored People (NAACP), and the Negro YMCA, tensions—especially on the stockyard floor—remained.

In the wake of the rioting, Governor Lowden appointed the Chicago Commission on Race Relations. Its groundbreaking 1922 report, *The Negro in Chicago*, warned that segregation and discrimination in labor and housing would continue to prove fertile grounds for violence.

North America

# Chisholm, Shirley

**(b. November 20, 1924, Brooklyn, N.Y.), the first African American woman elected to the United States Congress and the first to campaign for the presidency, known for her incisive debating style and uncompromising integrity.**

Shirley Chisholm is widely considered one of the foremost female orators in the United States. With a character that she has described as "unbought and unbossed," Chisholm became known as a politician who refused to allow fellow politicians, including the male-dominated Congressional Black Caucus, to deter her from her goals. In 1969 her first statement as a congressperson before the United States House of Representatives reflected her commitment to prioritizing the needs of the disadvantaged, especially children: she proclaimed her intent to "vote no on every money bill that comes to the floor of this House that provides any funds for the Department of Defense." While Chisholm advocated for black civil rights, she regularly took up issues that concerned other people of color, such as Spanish-speaking migrants and Native Americans. She also delivered important speeches on the economic and political rights of women and fearlessly criticized the Nixon administration during the Vietnam War.

Shirley Anita St. Hill Chisholm was the oldest of four girls born to parents who had immigrated from the West Indies, and who barely subsisted on their wages from factory work and housecleaning. When Chisholm was three, her parents, who wanted a better life for their daughters, sent Shirley and her sisters to Barbados to be reared by their maternal grandmother. For Chisholm island life seemed like a paradise, and she received an excellent education in Barbados's British school system. At the age of ten she returned to Brooklyn, where she was an outstanding student. Later, at Brooklyn College, she majored in sociology and joined the debating society, an experience that would help shape her cut-and-thrust oratory style. She also served as a volunteer in the Brooklyn chapter of the National Urban League and in the National Association for the Advancement of Colored People, where she debated minority rights.

In 1949, after graduating from college, Chisholm attended evening classes at Columbia University, earning a master's degree in child education. Meanwhile, she taught at a Harlem nursery school, and later acted as supervisor of the largest nursery school network in New York. It was through administering to hundreds of children, most of them African American and Puerto Rican, that Chisholm learned the executive skills that served her so well in the political arena. In 1953, as a key member of the Seventeenth Assembly District Democratic Club, she waged a successful political campaign to elect an eminent black lawyer to the municipal court.

Chisholm's political career took off in 1964, when she won by a landslide her campaign for the New York State Assembly. As an assemblyperson (1965–1968), she authored legislation that instituted SEEK (Search for Education, Elevation, and Knowledge), a program that provided college funding to disadvantaged youths, and introduced the bill that secured unemployment insurance for domestics and daycare providers. In 1968 Chisholm won a seat in the United States House of Representatives, where she served on a number of committees, including Education and Labor, and campaigned for a higher minimum wage and federal funding for daycare facilities. She also secured federal grants for a number of Brooklyn-based enterprises that benefited disadvantaged communities. In 1972 she became the first African American woman to campaign for the presidency, running as "a candidate of the people." In doing so she paved the way for others like herself who, as she said in her autobiography, *The Good Fight*, "will feel themselves as capable of running for high political office as any wealthy, good-looking white male."

Since her retirement from Congress in 1982, Chisholm has remained active as a political figure, an educator, and a spokesperson for women's rights. She has held several university teaching positions. During the 1980s she was a critical asset to Jesse Jackson's campaigns for the presidency. She also created and currently chairs the increasingly powerful National Political Congress of Black Women, and has served on the Advisory Council of the National Organization for Women.

North America

# Civil Rights Congress,

**American civil rights organization dedicated to protecting the civil rights and liberties of African Americans and suspected communists.**

The Civil Rights Congress (CRC) was established in 1946 after three organizations closely associated with the Communist Party of America—the National Negro Congress, the International Labor Defense, and the National Federation for Constitutional Liberties—decided to merge. During its relatively brief existence, the CRC fought for the protection of civil rights and liberties of African Americans and suspected communists primarily through litigation, political agitation, and the mobilization of public sentiment. Communist leader and lawyer William Patterson served as executive secretary of the organization for the duration of its existence. At its peak the CRC had 10,000 members.

Like the National Association for the Advancement of Colored People (NAACP), the CRC pursued legal cases that challenged racism and political persecution, establishing a number of civil liberties rulings that expanded the rights of all Americans. It sought to repeal legislation designed to restrict dissent and silence left-wing opposition, such as the Smith Act (1940) and the McCarran Act (1950). In one of its first cases, the CRC defended Rosa Lee Ingram, a black tenant farmer who, together with two of her sons, was convicted and sentenced to death in 1947 for the murder of John Stratford, a white tenant farmer. As a result of the CRC's efforts, Ingram and her two sons were freed. In May 1951 the CRC provided legal representation and waged a public relations campaign to defend 11 Communist leaders convicted under the Smith Act.

At the height of the McCarthy period, in the mid-1950s, the CRC was itself investigated by various government entities, notably the House Committee on Un-American Activities and the Internal Revenue Service. In 1956 the Subversive Activities Control Board declared the CRC to be a "communist front," substantially controlled by the Communist Party of America. In that same year, the CRC was forced to close down because of the increased legal cost of the investigations and a decline in contributions.

# Civil Rights Movement

## The Reconstruction Era, 1865 to 1890s

The Civil Rights Movement had its roots in the constitutional amendments enacted during the Reconstruction era. The Thirteenth Amendment abolished slavery, the Fourteenth Amendment expanded the guarantees of federally protected citizenship rights, and the Fifteenth Amendment barred voting restrictions based on race. The Reconstruction amendments were, as civil rights lawyer Oliver Hill observed, "a second Bill of Rights" for black Americans.

Reconstruction radically altered social, political, and economic relationships in the South and in the nation. Former slaves participated in civic and political life throughout the South. Black elected officials served at all levels of government, from local offices to state legislatures and the United States Congress. During the early days of Reconstruction, state governments drew up new constitutions that implemented sweeping democratic reforms, including, for the first time in the South, a system of universal free public education.

Yet the meaning of freedom was vigorously contested in private and public life to the end of the nineteenth century. Newly enfranchised blacks understood citizenship to embody constitutionally protected rights, realized through political participation and ultimately secured by the federal government. They acted upon an expansive view of the democratic process through their participation in Republican Party politics and by exploring alliances with independent groups and, in some cases, the Democratic Party as well.

This vision competed with the Democratic Party's politics of "redemption," which promised the restoration of white hegemony and "home rule" for Southern states. As Democrats regained control of state governments throughout the South, the Ku Klux Klan and other vigilante groups sought to drive blacks from political life through a relentless campaign of fraud and violence. Black men continued to vote in large numbers, often going to the polls in groups, accompanied by family members.

By the late nineteenth century, however, reconciliation between the North and the South was nearly complete, and popular "scientific" theories about race favored white supremacist views. State governments controlled by Democrats drew up new constitutions and enacted a variety of laws that dramatically restricted suffrage in the South, virtually barring blacks from voting and vastly reducing the scope of government. A combination of municipal ordinances and local and state laws mandating racial segregation ultimately permeated all spheres of public life. The Supreme Court, in rulings such as *Plessy v. Ferguson* (1896), upheld the South's "new order," which essentially nullified the constitutional amendments enacted during Reconstruction.

## Black Protest During the Age of Jim Crow, 1900 to 1930s

By the dawn of the new century, government and politics had become, as one historian noted, "inaccessible and unaccountable to Americans who happened to be black." While the rudiments of citizenship expired, black protest against new laws segregating streetcars spontaneously erupted in locally organized boycotts in at least 25 Southern cities from 1900 to 1906. Some boycotts lasted as long as two years, but these protests failed to stem the tide of segregation. Meanwhile, lynching and other forms of anti-black violence and terrorism reinforced legal structures of white domination.

Black leaders and intellectuals continued to debate a broad range of political strategies. There was, for example, the accommodationism and self-help advanced by Booker T. Washington and others, the civil rights protests advocated by Ida B. Wells and W. E. B. Du Bois, and the nationalist and emigration movements promoted by leaders such as Henry McNeal Turner. These overlapping and sometimes contradictory approaches revealed the tensions and challenges inherent in what often was a daunting effort: how to build and sustain black communities amid the crushing environment of white racism while envisioning a way forward.

Yet traditions of freedom and citizenship, born in the crucible of Reconstruction, nurtured communities of resistance. African Americans continued to create strategies for social and political development through a separate public sphere. Black community life was dominated in large part by the church and shaped by other institutions such as fraternal organizations, schools, and newspapers. The black church focused the mobilization of community resources to provide educational and welfare services, leadership training, and organizational networks and served as a site of mass gatherings and meetings—a place, as Evelyn Brooks Higginbotham has written, "to critique and contest America's racial domination."

## The NAACP, World War I, and the "New Negro"

In 1905 W. E. B. Du Bois, William Monroe Trotter (1872–1934), and other black militants founded the Niagara Movement, an organization committed to securing full citizenship rights for African Americans. The Niagara Movement was short-lived but its goals were adopted by the National Association for the Advancement of Colored People (NAACP), founded in New York in 1909 by an interracial group of reformers and civil rights activists. White progressives dominated the early leadership of the NAACP. But the NAACP provided the primary organizational and institutional foundation from which the black struggle for civil rights was mounted over the next half century.

World War I and the Great Migration altered the political and social landscape of black America. Beginning in 1914, wartime industrial opportunities in the North sparked a massive movement of nearly 1.5 million black Southerners to Northern urban centers, a migration that continued through the 1920s. While racial discrimination and segregation restricted black opportunities in the North, black community life flourished in Northern cities, where African Americans enjoyed free access to the ballot. As their numbers increased, the black vote in the urban North gradually became a factor of national consequence.

The participation of African Americans in World War I, the war that promised to "make the world safe for democracy," stirred the aspirations of a new generation determined to "make democracy safe for the Negro." Returning veterans formed organizations such as the League for Democracy, which advocated political activism and self-defense, and joined in establishing new branches of the NAACP throughout the South. Others, like Charles Hamilton Houston, enrolled in law school, determined to fight racial injustice through the courts.

Whites responded with a campaign of anti-black violence that erupted in a series of lynchings and more than 25 race riots throughout the country during the summer of 1919. The worst riot was in Chicago. In many instances blacks fought back, in the spirit of Claude McKay's defiant poem "If We Must Die." Yet state repression, supported by federal surveillance, effectively quashed the incipient democratic political initiatives spawned by the war.

During the 1920s the New Negro movement stretched the parameters of racial consciousness and expression. Urban communities nurtured the outpouring of black cultural, literary, and musical creativity that flowered in the Harlem Renaissance. Beyond the literary salons and art galleries, Marcus Garvey and his Universal Negro Improvement Association represented the largest mass black organization in the United States, one that promoted black economic development and celebrated Africa and racial pride. While W. E. B. Du Bois and some others dismissed Garvey as little more than a fool, Charles Houston contended that Garvey surpassed most race leaders of his time, for he had "made a permanent contribution in teaching the simple dignity of being black."

Despite cultural and economic changes ushered in by migration and urbanization, the status of African Americans remained largely unchanged. Some 80 percent of African Americans still lived in the Southern United States in 1930, where they were racially segregated, politically disfranchised, and economically marginalized. The fate of nine young black men in the Scottsboro case of 1931 focused national and international attention on the fact that blacks in the South were completely beyond the protection of the law.

## Charles Houston and the Legal Campaign for Civil Rights

With the normal channels of political participation closed to the vast majority of black Americans, Charles Houston envisioned a unique role for black lawyers as "social engineers," prepared to "anticipate, guide, and interpret his group's advancement." Houston, a graduate of Harvard Law School, joined the faculty of Howard University Law School in 1924. He transformed Howard into a laboratory for the development of civil rights law and trained a generation of black lawyers to lead the assault on Jim Crow.

When Houston became chief legal counsel of the NAACP in the early 1930s, he and former student Thurgood Marshall began laying the ground-work for a protracted campaign against racial discrimination in education. For Houston and Marshall, litigation was a slow and deliberate process, tied to the development of community support and participation. Houston and Marshall traveled as much as 16,667 km (10,000 mi.) a year through the South, where they met with small and large groups, explaining the mechanics of the legal fight and its relationship to broader community con-cerns. An associate recalled that Houston's efforts in the South were fueled by his confidence in the capacity "within the black community and the Negro race to bring about change." During the 1930s Houston and Marshall implemented a major reorientation of the NAACP's program, focusing staff efforts on the expansion of black membership and the cultivation of local leadership and branches, especially in the South. In 1934 Houston wrote Walter White, then executive secretary of the NAACP: "The work of the next decade will have to be concentrated in the South."

## The New Deal and the World War II Era

While the South was the primary arena of the black freedom struggle, the nationalizing trends of the New Deal and World War II enhanced the possi-bilities for a broad legal and political challenge to the segregation system and made civil rights an issue of consequence throughout the country.

### Blacks and the Roosevelt Administration

The 1932 presidential election of Franklin D. Roosevelt in the depths of the Great Depression precipitated a sea of change in American politics. New Deal programs and legislation expanded the scope of federal power and redefined the role of government and politics in American life. Government relief and job programs, along with the legalization of labor unions, stirred the expectations of groups long on the margins of national politics—indus-trial workers, sharecroppers, and African Americans of all classes.

When Roosevelt was inaugurated in 1933, racial segregation reigned in the city of Washington and in the corridors of government. The Republican Party offered no more than token representation to black Americans, and white Southerners dominated the Democratic Party. During the 1920s the NAACP had carved out a presence in the nation's capital through its efforts to gain support for antilynching legislation; in 1930 an NAACP lobbying campaign had helped defeat the nomination of John J. Parker, a white Southern conservative, to the Supreme Court. But there were no secure avenues through which African Americans could influence or shape govern-ment policy.

The implementation of a national recovery program, however, promised to have immediate and long-term consequences for black Americans. As more established black leaders deliberated about how to respond to the flurry of New Deal legislation, Robert C. Weaver, a doctoral student at Harvard, and John P. Davis (1905–1973), a new graduate of Harvard Law School, acted to ensure that black interests were represented. In the summer of 1933 the two men returned to their hometown of Washington and established an office on Capitol Hill, where they fought successfully against the racial wage differential in the first recovery program. Their efforts led to the establishment of the Joint Committee on Economic Recovery, a group of more than a dozen black organizations that included the NAACP and the National Urban League (NUL). The committee lobbied for fair inclusion of African Americans in government-sponsored programs and publicized incidents and patterns of racial discrimination.

The NAACP and the black press, along with the Rosenwald Fund, successfully pressed for the appointment of black government officials to represent black interests from within the Roosevelt administration. Robert Weaver and William Hastie were among the first African Americans hired. Shortly after joining the Department of the Interior they integrated the lunchroom, sparking the reversal of the segregationist policies enacted by Woodrow Wilson. By 1935 black advisers were serving in many cabinet offices and New Deal agencies and had created an informal network commonly known as the Black Cabinet.

## Southern Blacks and the New Deal

The Democratic rhetoric of the New Deal, along with federal programs, dovetailed with the NAACP's expanded activity in the South, the growth of industrial unionism in the region, and pockets of student and Communist Party activism. Together, these developments revived the expansive view of citizenship and politics that had informed black and biracial politics in the Reconstruction era.

Despite their conservative nature, early New Deal programs stirred the stagnant economic relationships that had persisted in the South since the 1890s. Federal work relief and credit, along with federal legislation securing the rights of labor to unionize, implicitly threatened the culture of dependency that shaped race and class relations in the South. New Deal initiatives combined with the organizing efforts of a revitalized NAACP and radical labor groups—such as the International Labor Defense—to support a renewed interest in politics on the part of the South's disfranchised.

Early in 1934 a South Carolina peach grower complained that black women would not work in the fields while their husbands had jobs with the federal Civil Works Administration. In Arkansas black and white sharecroppers organized the Southern Tenant Farmers Union to demand federal enforcement of guarantees provided by the New Deal's Agricultural Adjustment Administration. Organized groups of black citizens in Georgia and South Carolina attempted to vote in the Democratic primary that barred blacks in 1934, seeking entry into Roosevelt's party. Peter Epps, an administrator for the Works Progress Administration in South Carolina, told an interviewer that blacks "talked more politics since Mister Roosevelt's been in than ever before."

Contemplating the impact of recent federal programs on black political consciousness, W. E. B. Du Bois noted that the government was attending to economic matters and furnishing jobs and food in the provincial South. The question bound to arise was, "How can this political instrument which is the federal government be used more widely and efficiently for the well-being of the mass of people?"

## New Deal Political Coalitions: Blacks, Labor and the Democratic Party

### The 1936 Election

While blacks were essentially barred from voting in the South, black voters in the North emerged as a pivotal group in the 1936 presidential campaign. Following a steady stream of migrations from the South during the 1920s, blacks in the North came to cast significant numbers of votes in key industrial states. They had been drifting away from the party of Lincoln, establishing a tentative allegiance to the Roosevelt administration. Yet Roosevelt's party was also the party of Southern segregationists.

While the Roosevelt administration had failed to endorse racially sensitive legislation, such as an antilynching bill, it made other gestures that appealed to black voters. Roosevelt presided over a Democratic National Convention that, for the first time, opened its doors to the equal participation of black reporters and the handful of black delegates in attendance, drawing a howl of protest from Southern delegates. Mary McLeod Bethune and other members of the Black Cabinet took part in a sophisticated campaign aimed at black voters. It included an extravagant multi-city celebration of the 73rd anniversary of the Emancipation Proclamation. Such actions reinforced the bonds woven by New Deal relief and jobs, ensuring Roosevelt's sweep of the black vote. "The amazing switch of this great group of voters is the real political sensation of the time," wrote a national political analyst.

The basis of Roosevelt's landslide victory in 1936 was a broad, class-based appeal, one that pledged an activist federal government committed to the "establishment of a democracy of opportunity for all people." African Americans, urban ethnic groups, industrial workers, and farmers responded, creating a new Democratic coalition that eclipsed the singular dominance of old-line Southern Democrats. For the next three decades the Democratic Party was a major site of the struggle waged to define a national policy on civil rights.

### Race and the Politics of New Deal Reform

The late 1930s and the early 1940s witnessed the emergence of new organizations that were dedicated to expanding economic and political democracy in the South and were prepared to challenge Jim Crow laws. In 1937 a group of black students established the Southern Negro Youth Congress (SNYC) in Richmond, Virginia, dedicated to organizing black industrial workers in the South. During the next decade, SNYC grew into a regional organization based in Birmingham; in addition to supporting the work of organized labor, SNYC activists sponsored voter education and registration efforts and leadership training, often through community-based cultural activities.

In 1938 Roosevelt issued the Report on the Economic Conditions of the South, which identified the region as "the Nation's number one economic problem." In response to that report several thousand black and white Southerners met in Birmingham, Alabama, in November 1938 and established the Southern Conference for Human Welfare (SCHW). At the founding of the SCHW, Birmingham police commissioner Eugene "Bull" Connor enforced segregated seating in the group's meeting hall. First Lady Eleanor Roosevelt responded by placing her chair on top of the hastily established line separating the two races. With the endorsement of the Roosevelt administration and the strong support of the Congress of Industrial Organizations (CIO), the SCHW launched a decade-long effort to expand political participation in the South.

Just weeks after Eleanor Roosevelt's dramatic gesture in Birmingham, the Supreme Court ruled that Lloyd L. Gaines be admitted to the University of Missouri Law School, giving the NAACP its first major victory in the campaign for equal education. Pauli Murray, whose application to the University of North Carolina had been rejected solely on the grounds of race, observed that *Gaines* was the "first major breach in the solid wall of segregated education since *Plessy*." It was," she wrote, "the beginning of the end."


## World War II

By the late 1930s the crusading spirit of the New Deal had been obscured by mobilization for war and the increasing power of conservatives in Washington. Still, the war experience broadened the possibilities for civil rights struggles. On the eve of America's entry into the war, Osceola McKaine, a South Carolina NAACP organizer, observed: "We are living in the midst of perhaps the greatest revolution within human experience. Nothing, no nation, will be as it was when the peace comes . . . . There is no such thing as the status quo."

The demographic, economic, and political changes unleashed by the war had far-reaching consequences for African Americans. As scholar Henry Louis Gates Jr. has written, World War II "did more to re-cement black American culture, which migration had fragmented, than did any single event or experience." For the nearly 1 million African Americans serving in the armed forces, the army became "a great cauldron, mixing the New Negro culture, which had developed since the migration of the twenties and thirties, and the Old Negro culture, the remnants of traditional rural black culture in the South." The massive movement of black Southerners to centers of defense production in the North marked one of the largest internal migrations in American history.

Black civil rights activism accelerated under the banner of the Double V campaign, a movement first promoted by the Pittsburgh Courier. Double V advocates combined the fight against fascism abroad with the struggle for racial equality and full democracy at home. When the president failed to respond to black demands for equal inclusion in the war effort, labor leader A. Philip Randolph promised to lead 10,000 black Americans in a march on Washington to compel federal action. At the eleventh hour Roosevelt issued Executive Order 8802, which prohibited discrimination in defense industries and federal agencies and created the president's Fair Employment Practices Committee (FEPC) to implement the law. It was the first federal agency since Reconstruction devoted to dealing with racial discrimination.

## The NAACP and the Southern Movement

During the war years, NAACP membership soared to nearly 400,000 nationally, and the rate of growth in the South surpassed that in all other regions. Having reported 18,000 members in the late 1930s, the NAACP claimed 156,000 members in the South by the war's end. Ella J. Baker, Southern field secretary for the NAACP, reported that the growth in membership brought a "new surge of identity" among black communities around the South. Through the organization of local branches and state conferences of the NAACP, Southern blacks created an infrastructure for sustained political struggle.

In the spring of 1944, the U.S. Supreme Court ruled in *Smith v. Allwright* that the all-white Democratic primary was unconstitutional. This ruling was the culmination of the NAACP's 20-year-long legal battle against the South's most effective legal means of barring blacks from political participation. "Once the Supreme Court opened the door in 1944," civil rights activist Palmer Weber recalled, "the NAACP charged into the whole registration and voting area very hard."

From 1944 to 1948 the NAACP, along with SNYC, the SCHW, and the CIO Political Action Committee (CIO-PAC), joined with other local and state groups to promote voter registration. When South Carolina Democrats continued to bar blacks from the party, black newspaperman John McCray and NAACP activist Osceola McKaine organized the South Carolina Progressive Democratic Party (PDP). The PDP sent a delegation to the 1944 Democratic National Convention in an unsuccessful effort to challenge old-guard Democrats for failing to open the state party to blacks. That fall the PDP ran its own slate of candidates. Black veterans, like Medgar Evers and Charles Evers in Mississippi, often took leading roles in voter registration efforts. In Birmingham black veterans marched in uniforms to the Jefferson County Court House to register to vote.

Henry Lee Moon, a journalist and a Southern field organizer for the CIO-PAC, reported: "Negro groups, sometimes in collaboration with labor and progressive groups, sometimes alone, are setting up schools to instruct new voters in the intricacies of registration, marking the ballot, and manipulating the voting machine." By the late 1940s the total number of registered black voters in the South approached 1 million; it had been estimated at 200,000 in 1940. The increases were most striking in South Carolina, where the number of black voters climbed from 3,500 to 50,000, and in Georgia, where the number rose from 20,000 to 118,000.

Southern whites met growing black political participation with terror and fraud. There were countless individual acts of violence against blacks who voted, as well as public campaigns on the part of candidates like Eugene Talmadge in Georgia and Theodore Bilbo in Mississippi, inviting whites to do what was necessary to keep blacks from the polls. In several cases black veterans were gunned down after voting. Publicly staged acts of violence against blacks increased during the 1946 primary season and included the execution-style murders of two black couples in Walton County, Georgia. There is evidence that Talmadge stole his gubernatorial win in 1946 and that the Justice Department had enough information to indict him. But the department chose not to pursue the matter.

## Postwar America: The Emergence of Civil Rights as a National Issue

Wartime experience and the growing power of the Northern black vote elevated the importance of civil rights in national politics. At the war's end, decolonization movements in Africa and Asia and the beginnings of the cold war between the United States and the Soviet Union heightened the rhetoric of freedom, democracy, and self-determination. In 1947, W. E. B. Du Bois sought unsuccessfully to enlist the United Nations in an international investigation of racial discrimination in the United States.

President Harry S. Truman responded to the call for civil rights reform by commissioning a review of racial discrimination, which resulted in a report that called for sweeping federal action against Jim Crow. Truman was reluctant to act in the face of strong Southern opposition. But a close 1948 presidential race in which victory in key Northern states hinged on the black vote compelled him to endorse a strong civil rights plank at the Democratic National Convention. Southerners left the convention in protest and ran their own candidate for president in 1948 on the States Rights Party ticket. Shortly after the convention, Truman issued an executive order desegregating the armed forces.

The confident Democratic initiatives of the 1930s and 1940s, however, were overwhelmed by two postwar political factors: (1) the cold war and the Truman administration's domestic loyalty-security program, which limited civil liberties; and (2) the acceleration of white Southern repression of any challenge to the Jim Crow system. Groups like SNYC and the SCHW became targets of government investigations. The Federal Bureau of Investigation (FBI) sought out suspected communists and fellow travelers, while a revived Ku Klux Klan terrorized blacks attempting to vote in the South and Southern civic leaders presided over fraudulent elections. Indeed, Charles

Houston wondered why the loudly proclaimed crusade to "lead the world to democracy" did not extend to the Southern United States. Why were free and fair elections in Eastern Europe of greater import to the U.S. government than open elections in Alabama and Mississippi?

## The Civil Rights Struggle in the 1950s

During the 1950s the struggle against Jim Crow in the South remained distant from national issues and concerns. After 1948 the Democratic Party placated its rebellious Southern wing while its civil rights agenda floundered. Meanwhile, whites responded to the steady migration of Southern blacks to Northern cities by extending patterns of racial segregation and black exclusion in housing, employment, and education.

The foundation of the Civil Rights Movement remained anchored in the cumulative gains of the NAACP legal campaign and its extensive network of branches. Southern NAACP leaders, however, faced an emboldened defense of the racial status quo. In 1951 the Christmas Day assassination of Harry T. Moore, a leading NAACP organizer in Florida, and his wife inaugurated a decade of white terrorism and state-sponsored repression that heightened in the aftermath of the *Brown* decision.

### *Brown v. Board of Education*

On May 17, 1954, the U.S. Supreme Court unanimously ruled in *Brown v. Board of Education* that the doctrine of separate but equal as applied to public education was unconstitutional. *Brown* marked the culmination of the NAACP's long legal battle; the Court had effectively reversed its 1896 decision in *Plessy v. Ferguson*, the cornerstone of the segregation system. By implication, state-mandated racial segregation in all areas of public life violated the Constitution.

However, the Court issued a separate ruling one year later concerning the enforcement of this momentous decision. Sympathetic to warnings of Southern white defiance, the Court allowed for a policy of gradual implementation that would, the opinion explained, be responsive to local conditions and problems. While calling for compliance "with all deliberate speed," the Court reflected the ambivalence of the justices, executive and congressional leadership, and the vast majority of Americans about dismantling racial segregation in the South. For most white Southerners, *Brown II* was a license to resist. During the next ten years, less than 1 percent of black children in the South attended "white" schools.

*Brown* was a major turning point in the struggle for civil rights, and it marked the beginning of the most celebrated chapter of the Civil Rights Movement. The decade that followed saw a heightening interplay between Southern blacks striving to realize the promise of *Brown* in the face of "massive resistance" by Southern whites and the equivocal response of the federal government, unfolding on an increasingly national and international stage.

## Emmett Till, Montgomery, and the Emergence of Martin Luther King Jr.

In August 1955, just three months after the court ruled in *Brown II*, 14-year-old Emmett Till was murdered in Money, Mississippi, for allegedly whistling at a white woman. Mamie Bradley, Till's mother, brought her son's body home to Chicago and insisted on an open casket so that all could see "what they did to my boy." *Jet* magazine's photograph of Till's badly mutilated body offered gruesome evidence of the terror that reigned in Mississippi, and it informed the consciousness of a new generation of young black people. The widely publicized trial and acquittal of Till's murderers confirmed what most already knew about the Southern system of racial injustice.

That December, Rosa Parks, a local NAACP leader in Montgomery, Alabama, refused to surrender her seat on a city bus to a white man. This action, and the mobilizing work of the Women's Political Council, sparked a boycott of Montgomery buses that lasted for 381 days. Local black leaders elected Martin Luther King Jr., the new 26-year-old minister of the Dexter Avenue Baptist Church, as head of the Montgomery Improvement Association (MIA), the organization that led the boycott and sued to end segregation on the buses. Hundreds of African Americans, mostly women, walked several miles to and from work each day; as one woman commented, "My feet is tired, but my soul is rested." This dignified protest contrasted with the city's efforts to intimidate the MIA leadership through indictments, injunction, and the bombing of King's house, and it attracted the attention of the national and international media.

By the time the Supreme Court struck down segregation on the buses in December 1956, King had become a seasoned leader of and eloquent spokesman for the emerging nonviolent movement. Early in 1957, King joined with other activist ministers and civil rights leaders like Bayard Rustin and Ella Baker to establish the Southern Christian Leadership Conference (SCLC); King was elected its president, and Baker became the first executive director. The SCLC served as an umbrella organization, linking church-based affiliates throughout the South in the nonviolent struggle for racial justice and to "redeem the soul of America."

## The NAACP, Little Rock, and School Desegregation

The fight for school integration had few supporters outside the black community. The NAACP aided parents who petitioned school boards to admit their children to the all-white schools, in compliance with the *Brown* decision, but the organization became the target of an extensive effort across the South to shut it down. In 1956 Alabama passed a state law effectively barring the NAACP from operating in that state; South Carolina barred NAACP members from state employment. Five other states enacted laws requiring the NAACP to register and to provide lists of members and contributors. While such state action was often unconstitutional, the burden was on local NAACP branches to spend scarce resources in fighting to over-

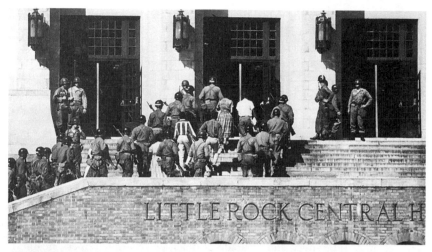

Escorted by United States troops, nine black students walk up the stairs to the main entrance of Central High School, Little Rock, Arkansas, on the first full day of integration, September 25, 1957. *CORBIS/Bettmann*

turn these laws. In the meantime, the White Citizens Council (WCC), founded in Sunflower County, Mississippi, in 1956, organized local businessmen and civic leaders throughout the South. WCC chapters used economic reprisals and manipulation of the law in an effort to intimidate and undermine civil rights activists and supporters.

Southern obstructionists met their first major setback in Little Rock, Arkansas. In 1957 a group of local parents, working with NAACP leader Daisy Bates, succeeded in winning a court order mandating the admission of black students to Central High School. Governor Orval Faubus employed the National Guard to block the admission of the nine young men and women selected to attend Central High. The governor's bold defiance of the federal courts compelled President Eisenhower, who was no supporter of school integration, to send in army troops and federalize the Arkansas National Guard in order to ensure peaceful compliance with the court order. After the school year ended, the governor closed the public schools to avoid further integration.

From 1957 to 1959 public schools in Virginia, Georgia, and Alabama closed rather than obey desegregation orders. In New Orleans, when public schools admitted four young black girls to the first grade, whites in the city rioted.

## The Right to Vote

### The Civil Rights Act of 1957 and Macon County, Alabama
While federal officials and the U.S. Congress sought to avoid the issue of racial integration, the Eisenhower administration—recognizing the possibility of wooing back Northern black voters to the Republican Party—was

sympathetic to extending protection of black voting rights in the South. In 1957 Attorney General Herbert Brownell introduced legislation that sought to provide federal protection of basic citizenship rights. The final bill, the first civil rights bill enacted since 1875, was trimmed to meet the opposition of Southern Democrats and lacked strong enforcement provisions. But the Civil Rights Act of 1957 did create a Civil Rights Division in the Justice Department, authorized to prosecute registrars who obstructed the right of blacks to vote. The bill also established the U.S. Civil Rights Commission as an independent agency charged with gathering facts about voting rights violations and other civil rights infringements.

In the fall of 1958, the new Civil Rights Commission sent investigators to Alabama to gather information on voter discrimination. The Tuskegee Civic Association (TCA), a black organization established in the early 1940s to encourage voter registration, shared its extensive records documenting voter discrimination. As a result, the commission held nationally televised hearings in Montgomery, and a parade of black witnesses—farmers, hospital technicians, and Tuskegee professors—described the deceptive and often bizarre devices used by registrars in Macon County to keep blacks from registering to vote.

While presenting the case before the Civil Rights Commission and the American public, TCA founder Charles Gomillion and several associates were also preparing their suit against the city of Tuskegee for redrawing the political boundaries of the town so that black voters would be excluded. In 1960 the Supreme Court ruled unanimously in favor of the TCA in *Gomillion v. Lightfoot*, a case that marked a major step in broadening federal review of state voting practices.

## Citizenship Schools and Black Voter Registration After Brown

Voter registration and education accelerated in communities around the South after the *Brown* decision. In 1957 Septima Clark (1898–1987), Bernice Robinson, and Esau Jenkins organized the Citizenship Schools program on South Carolina's Sea Islands, with the support of Highlander Folk School, one of the few politically active interracial organizations in the South. Over the next four years, the number of registered black voters on Johns Island tripled. The program was adapted in communities in Tennessee, Georgia, and Alabama.

In the mid-1950s in Mississippi, NAACP chapters and the Regional Council of Negro Leadership began a concerted effort to increase black voter registration. In 1954 just 4 percent of the state's eligible black voting-age population were registered. White reprisals were swift. Those attempting to vote risked losing their job and suffered other forms of economic intimidation. Leaders were often targets of physical violence. In 1955 George W. Lee, president of the NAACP branch in Belonzi, was gunned down by a mob of whites. That same year Lamar Smith, a political activist in Lincoln County, was assassinated in front of the courthouse in broad daylight. Several other leaders fled the state. Despite the efforts of a handful of organizers, including Amzie Moore, an NAACP leader in Cleveland, and Medgar Evers, political activity came to a standstill or was driven completely underground.

By the end of the decade the momentum for the kind of change that had seemed possible in the aftermath of *Brown* and the Montgomery bus boycott seemed remote in the face of hardening white resistance and the persistence of unchecked violence. Virginia Durr, a white civil rights activist in Montgomery, wrote plaintively to a friend in the North: "We have such a feeling here that we have been abandoned by the rest of the country and by the government and left to the tender mercies of the Ku Klux Klan and the White Citizens Council."

## Direct-Action Protests of the 1960s

On February 1, 1960, in Greensboro, North Carolina, 4 freshmen at Greensboro Agricultural and Technical College (A&T) sat at the "white" lunch counter in Woolworth's and asked to be served. The waitress refused; the young men waited, and left at the end of the day. The next day they were joined by 20 more students from A&T. Some white students from a local women's college "sat in" with black students on the third day. By the end of the week the "sit-ins" had spread to several other towns in the state, and students began targeting a broad range of public accommodations. By the end of February, sit-ins had been staged in towns and cities throughout the South.

The sit-ins inaugurated a direct-action mass protest movement that defied the racial and political boundaries of cold war America. In April 1960 young people who had participated in the sit-ins established the Student Nonviolent Coordinating Committee (SNCC) at a meeting convened by veteran activist Ella Baker. Working with rural Southern blacks, SNCC quickly became engaged in a movement for more fundamental social change—change that looked beyond the legalistic and legislative goals of the national NAACP and its white liberal allies. In particular, SNCC sought to empower black people at the local level.

Escalating black protest, along with fierce white resistance, invited more extensive coverage by the national press and tested the resolve of the president to enforce federal law. In the spring of 1961, the Congress of Racial Equality (CORE) initiated a "freedom ride" from Washington to the Deep South. The interracial group of freedom riders challenged the newly elected John F. Kennedy and his administration to enforce a 1960 Supreme Court ruling (*Boynton v. Virginia*) that banned segregation on interstate transportation. One bus was firebombed outside Birmingham; another rode into a savage mob assault at the bus station in Montgomery. In Jackson, riders were arrested, as one historian has noted, "on charges of traveling 'for the avowed purpose of inflaming public opinion.'" SNCC and CORE sent a steady flow of reinforcements, who filled the local and county jails to overflow. Attorney General Robert Kennedy finally directed the Interstate Commerce Commission to enforce regulations barring segregation in interstate terminals.

## Mississippi

During the early 1960s different groups and leaders experimented with a variety of tactics and strategies. SNCC and CORE organizers carved out a critical base as they fanned out across the South and established community-based projects to help support and sustain local organizing efforts around voting and mass protests against segregation.

In the summer of 1960 Robert P. Moses, a 26-year-old high school teacher from New York, traveled through Mississippi to recruit people for a SNCC conference to be held that fall. On the advice of Ella Baker, Moses sought out Amzie Moore, who told Moses about how white terrorism had crippled voter registration efforts in Mississippi. With Moore's encouragement, Moses and a team of SNCC workers returned the following summer prepared to live and organize in what was the poorest and arguably the most violently racist state in the nation.

The SNCC organizers joined with other civil rights activists in the state, including members of CORE, SCLC, and the NAACP, and created the Congress of Federated Organizations (COFO) to unify the efforts of all civil rights groups operating in Mississippi. Late in 1961 COFO's efforts won financial support from the newly established Voter Education Project, a foundation-based organization that Attorney General Robert Kennedy helped to establish. However, while the Kennedy administration, like the Eisenhower administration before it, was supportive of voter registration, it was not prepared to offer federal protection to those who sought to register—often in the face of violence, economic harassment, and, in some cases, death. The murder of Herbert Lee in 1961 and the beating and jailing of other voting rights activists had the desired effect. During 1962 and 1963, less than 4,000 black voters were added to the rolls, while 394,000 black adults in Mississippi remained unregistered.

The NAACP in Mississippi, under field director Medgar Evers, supported several desegregation efforts during this period. In 1962 NAACP lawyers secured a federal court order to gain the admission of the first African American to the University of Mississippi. Riots engulfed the campus on the eve of James Meredith's enrollment, claiming two lives and injuring hundreds of others. The Kennedy administration sent federal troops to restore order, and federal marshals remained on campus to protect Meredith.

The desegregation of Ole Miss encouraged Evers to revive the campaign against segregation in Jackson. SNCC workers offered training sessions for sit-ins. In the spring of 1963, students sat in at Woolworth's, attempted to gain admission to the public library and "whites-only" public parks, and organized protest marches in downtown Jackson. The demonstrators were beaten by police and arrested. On June 12, 1963, as he returned from a strategy meeting, Medgar Evers was gunned down in the driveway of his house.

## Martin Luther King Jr.: Emergence as a National Leader

Martin Luther King Jr., with his brilliant ability to articulate the ideals of the Southern movement to the nation at large, emerged as a national spokesman of the movement. King's eloquence was joined by his ability to bring media attention to flash points of peaceful black protesters and white racists. On occasion, the SCLC played a role in orchestrating these confrontations. Such tactics caused resentment on the part of young organizers laboring in communities over extended periods of time, beyond the glare of national attention. Indeed, the intervention of King and SCLC in Albany, Georgia, in 1962, the site of a major SNCC project, failed to achieve any concessions and probably undermined some of the organizing work that had been done. But Albany was a critical training ground for Birmingham, Alabama, which became a pivotal battleground in the Civil Rights Movement.

## Birmingham

In 1963 Birmingham was arguably the most segregated city in the nation and the most racially violent. During the previous six years, there had been 18 unsolved bombings in black communities, winning it the nickname "Bombingham." Police Commissioner Bull Connor was prepared to maintain the city's color line at all costs.

On the invitation of Fred Shuttlesworth, the leading civil rights activist in the city, King and the SCLC launched Project C (for "Confrontation") in Birmingham early in the spring of 1963. A boycott of downtown stores was launched at the peak of the Easter shopping season, protesting the stores' refusal to hire black clerks, and demonstrators protested the city's segregation laws in mass marches to City Hall. Bull Connor secured a federal court order barring the demonstrations, leading to the arrest of scores of protesters and of King and several other SCLC leaders. From his cell King penned his famous "Letter from a Birmingham Jail," in response to a group of liberal white clergy who criticized the protests as ill-timed and charged King and his associates with stirring up tensions between the races.

In his letter King distinguished the "type of constructive nonviolent tension that is necessary for growth . . . the type of tension in society that will help men rise from the dark depths of prejudice and racism to the majestic heights of understanding and brotherhood." With regard to the timing of the demonstrations, King acknowledged that he had "yet to engage in a direct-action campaign that was 'well-timed' in view of those who have not suffered unduly from the disease of segregation. For years now, I have heard the word 'Wait!' ring in the ear of every Negro with piercing familiarity. This 'Wait' has almost always meant 'Never.'"

Yet local black business leaders and some clergy were beginning to question the value of the demonstrations. With the jails full, spirits flagging, and bail money spent, they began pressuring King to call off the protests. At this juncture James Bevel, a veteran of the Nashville sit-in movement, suggested a strategy for reviving the protests: invite children to march. Bevel reasoned that children had fewer constraints than their parents did. Moreover, in King's words, exposing young people to the wrath of Connor's police force would "subpoena the conscience of the nation."

On May 2 children and young adults from age 6 to 18 gathered at the Sixteenth Street Baptist Church, the movement headquarters, and marched to downtown Birmingham. The police arrested more than 900 and carried them off to jail in paddy wagons and school buses. On the second day, more than 1,000 young people stayed out of school and assembled at the church to march. In an effort to abort the march, the police turned dogs and fire hoses on the demonstrators as they left the church. The pressure of the hoses, which was strong enough to strip the bark off trees, slammed children to the ground and sent others sailing over parked cars. As outrage spread through the black community, SCLC organizers struggled to keep blacks from retaliating.

With more than 2,000 people in jail, the marches were still growing larger. The next major confrontation with the police occurred several days later in downtown Birmingham. Once again the police turned attack dogs and fire hoses on the demonstrators. Television coverage of the brutal police assault on children shocked the nation, while photos and news reports quickly spread around the world.

With Birmingham on the brink of a full-scale race riot, city businesses began negotiating with King through a Kennedy administration intermediary. A tentative agreement to desegregate downtown stores and employ black clerks sparked a spate of bombings. With federal troops stationed on alert outside the city, Mayor Albert Boutwell finally ratified the agreement and repealed the city's segregation laws.

In the aftermath of Birmingham, mass demonstrations spread throughout the South, involving more than 100,000 people. With Birmingham, the Civil Rights Movement had irrevocably commanded the attention of the nation and the world, opening the possibility for decisive legislative action.

## The Kennedy Administration and Civil Rights

Birmingham marked a turning point for the Kennedy administration and its relationship to the Civil Rights Movement. Nearly three years earlier, the election of John F. Kennedy had raised the hopes of African Americans and their allies. The youthful Kennedy had actively courted black voters and brought vitality and a new vision to the presidency after eight years of Dwight Eisenhower. Yet the new administration faced the legislative reality of a Southern bloc that dominated key congressional committees whose support was critical to the success of the president's agenda.

The Justice Department, under Attorney General Robert Kennedy, pursued a more vigorous effort to enforce voting rights and school desegregation orders than the previous administration; but the jurisdiction of the Justice

A Birmingham policeman turns a fire hose on civil rights protesters taking part in a 1963 demonstration. *CORBIS*

Department was limited. In any event, Civil Rights was not a priority issue for the Kennedy administration during its early years, a time when the cold war loomed large in presidential deliberations. If anything, Kennedy was most inclined to placate and appease powerful Southern Democrats. He bowed to the wishes of Sen. James Eastland of Mississippi and other like-minded Southern senators when making appointments to the federal bench in the South, and appointed a number of arch segregationists. They stood in contrast to moderate Republican judges like Frank Johnson and Elbert Tuttle, Eisenhower appointees who actively enforced civil rights law.

By June 1963 Kennedy was prepared to align himself and his presidency with the struggle for civil rights. On June 12, the day that Governor George Wallace attempted, unsuccessfully, to block the entrance of two black students to the University of Alabama, Kennedy addressed the nation. In a televised speech he told Americans that they could no longer ask black citizens to "be content with the counsels of patience and delay." He pledged that he would urge Congress to act on "the proposition that race has no place in American life and law." Seven days later he requested legislation from Congress that would ban segregation in public facilities, broaden the powers of the Justice Department to enforce school integration, and extend federal protection of voting rights.

### The March on Washington

In response to the momentous events of the spring, veteran civil rights leader A. Philip Randolph broadened the agenda of a planned march on the nation's capital for jobs and equal opportunity. Other civil rights leaders joined with Randolph to orchestrate a mass gathering in Washington calling for passage of civil rights legislation, immediate integration of public schools in the South, and economic opportunity.

On August 28 an estimated quarter of a million people, black and white, from all parts of the nation assembled in front of the Lincoln Memorial in what was, at that time, the largest peacetime gathering in American history. The day culminated with Martin Luther King Jr.'s speech "I Have a Dream," in which he looked toward an America of racial harmony and justice. Writer James Baldwin remembered the feeling: "For a moment it almost seemed that we stood on a height and could see our inheritance . . . . " Malcolm X, who observed the march, commented to Bayard Rustin, "You know, this dream of King's is going to be a nightmare before it's over."

Less than a month after the March on Washington, the sense of foreboding articulated by Malcolm X overshadowed the euphoria of that extraordinary late summer day. On September 15 white terrorists dynamited the basement of Birmingham's Sixteenth Street Baptist Church during Sunday School, killing four young girls: Denise McNair and Cynthia Wesley, both 11 years old, and Carole Robertson and Addie Mae Collins, both 14. Dreading that the families would blame him for exposing the children to risk, King returned to Birmingham and presided over the funeral of the movement's youngest victims.

## The Movement at High Tide: 1964–1965

During 1964 and 1965, the accelerated momentum of the Civil Rights Movement was fueled by the escalation of organized protest activity in the South, particularly in Mississippi and Alabama, and by the commitment of President Lyndon Johnson to enact strong civil rights legislation.

### Civil Rights Act of 1964

The heightened expectations tied to the leadership of John F. Kennedy had been brutally aborted on November 22, 1963, when the president was assassinated in Dallas, Texas. Within days of assuming the office of the presidency, Lyndon Baines Johnson, in an address to a joint session of Congress, promised that Kennedy's commitment to civil rights would be carried forward and translated into action. As a Southerner, Johnson did not underestimate the opposition a strong civil rights bill would meet. But none knew the workings of the Congress better than this former majority leader of the U.S. Senate, and as a legislative strategist Johnson had no equal. Roy Wilkins, executive secretary of the NAACP, was struck by the contrast between Kennedy and Johnson. While Kennedy talked "about the art of the possible," Wilkins explained, "he didn't really know what was possible and what wasn't on Capitol Hill." Johnson, in comparison, "knew exactly what was possible, and how to get it."

Johnson orchestrated a "no holds barred" campaign for a civil rights bill, untainted by compromise. He enlisted the help of NAACP lobbyist

Clarence Mitchell and the formative Leadership Conference on Civil Rights (LCCR), a broad coalition of veteran lobbyists representing labor, church, and liberal groups. He held press conferences, directly enlisting the public in this great effort, and brought the full weight of his power and persuasive abilities to secure the votes of doubtful congressmen and senators. The civil rights bill passed the House on February 10, 1964, and, after much arm-twisting and ego stroking, it won Senate approval late in June. On July 2, 1964, Johnson signed the bill into law.

The Civil Rights Act of 1964 outlawed discrimination in public facilities and employment; authorized the attorney general to initiate suits to enforce school integration; and allowed for the withholding of federal funds to non-complying schools. While the legislation was directed specifically at removing the barriers to equal access and opportunity that affected African Americans, it vastly expanded the scope of federal protection of the rights of women and other minority groups who experienced discrimination. However, fearful that the issue of voting rights would sink the legislation, the president and his allies in Congress postponed action in that arena.

## Freedom Summer

In Mississippi, while efforts to register black voters stalled, the Congress of Federated Organizations launched Freedom Vote in the fall of 1963. More than 80,000 blacks participated in this mock election campaign and voted for unofficial Freedom Party candidates. The Freedom Vote enabled many black Mississippians who had never before voted to have the experience of casting a ballot, while demonstrating that despite white claims to the contrary, blacks were interested in voting. But it was clear that more aggressive action was needed. Bob Moses recalled that by the end of 1963, COFO organizers "were exhausted . . . . They were butting up against a stone wall, [with] no breakthroughs."

In an effort to revive a flagging movement, COFO launched the Summer Project in 1964, which brought hundreds of student volunteers, mostly white, into Mississippi to participate in a massive voter registration drive, with the expectation that the media would follow. White Mississippi prepared as if they were expecting an invasion. Freedom Summer, as it became known, was punctuated with violence and terrorism as well as the dramatic growth of black political participation—from the abduction and murder of three civil rights workers in June to the establishment of a new party, the Mississippi Freedom Democratic Party (MFDP). The MFDP sent a full delegation to the 1964 Democratic National Convention, challenging the seating of the delegation representing Mississippi's all-white party. The failure of the MFDP to win its challenge, and the way in which the president and key liberal Democrats attempted to undermine the challenge, left many disillusioned with the national Democratic Party. But the MFDP prepared the way for the expansion of black political enfranchisement in Mississippi and led to major revisions in the Democratic Party convention rules.

## Selma and the Voting Rights Act of 1965

After Lyndon Johnson's landslide win over Barry Goldwater in the 1964 presidential election, the Justice Department began preparing to develop legislation around voting rights. However, the Southern movement ensured that the issue moved to the top of the president's agenda; the final battleground was Selma, Alabama. SNCC organizers had been working with the Dallas County Voters League in Selma for nearly two years when Martin Luther King Jr. and the SCLC arrived in Selma in January 1965. King began a series of marches geared at bringing media attention to the violence and discrimination that barred blacks from the polls. After several police attacks on marchers and the murder of Jimmy Lee Jackson by a police officer, King planned to lead a march to Montgomery, the state capital, and petition Governor George Wallace directly. On March 7, as the marchers attempted to cross the Edmund Pettis Bridge, they were clubbed by police on horseback and driven back across the bridge. The scene flashed across the country on the nightly news. Bloody Sunday, as it was named, mobilized public opinion in support of federal legislation, and Johnson acted almost immediately.

The president introduced a comprehensive voting rights bill to Congress on March 15 with a speech that was televised across the nation. "Their cause must be our cause, too," Johnson said. "Because it's not just Negroes, but it's really all of us who must overcome the crippling legacy of bigotry and injustice." Borrowing the words of the movement's anthem, he concluded, "And, we shall overcome." Five days later, with federal troops and marshals standing by, King led marchers on the four-day-long march to Montgomery; 25,000 had joined by the time they reached the capital. On August 6, President Johnson signed the Voting Rights Act, which provided federal supervision of voter registration practices, effectively opening up the polls to African Americans throughout the South for the first time since the end of Reconstruction.

## Aftermath

The enactment of the Civil Rights Act of 1964 and the Voting Rights Act of 1965 reinforced the guarantees of full citizenship provided for in the Reconstruction amendments nearly a century earlier, and marked the end of the Jim Crow system in the South. The desegregation of public facilities was swiftly implemented, and the rapid increase in black voting had far-reaching consequences for politics in the South and the nation. With the enforcement powers of the federal government greatly enhanced, the desegregation of public schools proceeded steadily, though "white flight" and the proliferation of private schools often made integration an elusive goal.

The fall of Jim Crow in the South removed the most extreme manifestation of racial discrimination and inequality, only to reveal deeply entrenched patterns of racial discrimination woven deep into the fabric of national life. For African Americans segregated in Northern cities and locked into poverty, the gains of the Southern movement had little direct relevance. Five days after President Johnson signed the Voting Rights Act, black frustration erupted into nearly a week of rioting in the Watts section of Los Angeles; urban disturbances and rebellions followed in other cities over the next three years. In 1968 the National Committee on Civil Disorders (also known as the Kerner Commission), appointed by the president, described "a nation moving towards two societies—one black, one white, separate and unequal."

The Civil Rights Movement vastly expanded the parameters of American democracy and the guarantees of citizenship, while also raising new challenges in an ongoing struggle to advance racial and economic justice. Martin Luther King Jr. carried his efforts forward in very different settings: supporting challenges to residential discrimination in Chicago; protesting America's involvement in Vietnam; aiding striking garbage workers in Memphis; and developing plans for a Poor People's March on Washington, which went forward after his assassination in 1968. At the same time, the call for Black Power eclipsed the integrationist thrust of the early 1960s, focusing renewed attention on black political and economic empowerment, while heightened black consciousness and racial pride found expression in the cultural renaissance of the Black Arts Movement of the late 1960s and the 1970s.

North America

# Clark, Kenneth Bancroft

(b. July 24, 1914, Panama Canal Zone), African American psychologist, educator, and social activist whose research, in particular the "doll study," was crucial to the desegregation of public schools in the United States.

Kenneth Clark grew up with his mother in Harlem, where his childhood heroes included the poet Countee Cullen, who taught at his junior high school, and book collector Arthur Schomburg, who served as a curator at the 135th Street Branch of the New York Public Library. After attending integrated elementary and junior high schools, he graduated from New York's George Washington High School in 1931.

Clark distinguished himself as an undergraduate at Howard University, where he led demonstrations against segregation in Washington, D.C. While at Howard he met Mamie Phipps, who became his wife and closest intellectual collaborator. The Clarks then went to Columbia University to study psychology, and in 1940 Clark became the first black to receive a Ph.D. in psychology from Columbia. He joined the faculty of City College in New York City in 1942, becoming that college's first black permanent professor. He remained at City College until his retirement in 1975, but also served as a visiting professor at Columbia, the University of California, Berkeley, and Harvard.

Throughout his career Clark was committed to finding ways to use his expertise in the social sciences for the cause of racial justice. In the early

1950s he frequently served as an expert witness for the National Association for the Advancement of Colored People (NAACP) in its legal struggles against segregation. The work that earned him his greatest fame, however, was his research on the self-image of black children. Clark studied the responses of more than 200 black children who were given a choice of white or brown dolls. From his findings that the children showed a preference for the white dolls from as early as three years old, Clark concluded that segregation was psychologically damaging. This conclusion played a pivotal role in *Brown v. Board of Education*, the Supreme Court case that outlawed segregated education.

Although Clark fought for racial integration, his book *Dark Ghetto: Dilemmas of Social Power* (1965) was popular among Black Nationalists because it compared the situation of black citizens to that of colonized people. Clark's other writings include *Prejudice and Your Child* (1953), *Crisis in Urban Education* (1971), and *The Negro American* (1966), which he co-edited with Talcott Parsons. His televised interviews with James Baldwin, Malcolm X, and Martin Luther King Jr. were published in a book titled *The Negro Protest* in 1963.

In addition to his activities as a scholar, Clark was involved with a variety of community development programs and served as an adviser to local and national policymakers. In 1946 he and his wife founded the Northside Child Development Center in Harlem to serve the needs of emotionally disturbed children. He also played a key role in the establishment in 1962 of Harlem Youth Opportunities Unlimited, a program that influenced President Lyndon Johnson's War on Poverty program. And as the sole black member of the New York Board of Regents, he continued his fight against segregated education.

Clark's work for civil rights earned him the NAACP's Spingarn Medal in 1961. For his contributions to psychology, he was elected president of the American Psychological Association and received its Gold Medal award. After his retirement from City College as a professor emeritus, Clark organized a consulting firm that specializes in issues of racial policy.

North America

# Clark, Septima Poinsette

**(b. May 3, 1898, Charleston, S.C.; d. December 15, 1987, Charleston, S.C.), African American educator and civil rights activist.**

Septima Poinsette Clark's parents, Peter and Victoria Poinsette, instilled a sense of social responsibility in Clark that she demonstrated throughout her professional life. Between the years 1916 and 1954, in addition to her teaching career, she helped provide adult literacy training; improve living conditions for African Americans on Johns Island, South Carolina; change a law in Charleston that prohibited African American teachers from working in its segregated schools; and make African American teachers' salaries equal to those of white teachers. She earned a B.A. from Benedict College and an M.A. from Hampton Institute (now University).

Clark believed that literacy was an important component in gaining equality for African Americans, and at Highlander Folk School, a biracial training center for community activists in Tennessee, she developed citizenship schools, which taught adult literacy and basic life skills such as checkbook balancing and writing checks, and encouraged voter registration. In 1961 the program was transferred to the Southern Christian Leadership Conference. By 1970 the project boasted over 800 schools and over 100,000 graduates, who formed the grassroots of the Civil Rights Movement.

Clark retired in 1971 because she believed that long-term commitment to citizenship schools had waned. In 1979 President Jimmy Carter presented her with the Living Legacy award. In 1987 her second autobiography, *Ready from Within: Septima Clark and the Civil Rights Movement*, won the National Book Award.

North America

## Clayton, Eva

(b. September 16, 1934, Savannah, Ga.), Democratic member of the United States House of Representatives from North Carolina since 1993, and the first African American woman elected to Congress from North Carolina.

Eva Clayton was born in Savannah, Georgia. She received a bachelor's degree from Johnson C. Smith University in 1955 and a master's degree from North Carolina Central University in 1962. She worked as director of a civil rights organization called the Soul City Foundation before she began a four-year tenure as assistant secretary for community development in the North Carolina Department of Natural Resources and Community Development in 1976. She started a management and consulting firm in 1981. In 1982 she also joined the Warren County Board of Commissioners, which she chaired for eight years.

When long-time U.S. representative Walter Jones died in September 1992, Clayton won a close primary contest against his son, Walter Jones Jr., for the Democratic nomination to fill the seat in North Carolina's First Congressional District. Clayton easily defeated her Republican opponent in the general elections of 1992, 1994, and 1996.

The irregularly shaped First District is a primarily rural, "black-majority" district created in a 1992 reapportionment of North Carolina's voting districts. Rocky Mount, Fayetteville, and Wilson are the largest cities in the district. Fort Bragg and Pope Air Force Base are located in Cumberland County. Paper manufacturers and government agencies are important employers in the district.

Just after her term in Congress began, Clayton was elected head of the 1993 freshman Democratic class. She earned seats on both the Agriculture

Committee and the Small Business Committee. In the 105th Congress (1997–1999), she was ranking member of the Department of Operations, Nutrition, and Foreign Agriculture Subcommittee of the Agriculture Committee as well as the Budget Committee. She is also a member of the Congressional Black Caucus.

North America

## Cleaver, Eldridge Leroy

(b. August 31, 1935, Wabbaseka, Ark.; d. May 1, 1998, Pomona, Calif.), African American writer, political activist, and former minister of information for the Black Panther Party.

After growing up in Wabbaseka, Arkansas, and Los Angeles, California, Eldridge Cleaver spent much of his young adulthood in the California state penitentiary system. Convicted on drug and rape charges in 1953 and 1958, he used his prison time to broaden his education. During this time, Cleaver studied the teachings of the Nation of Islam and became a devoted supporter of Malcolm X. With the assassination of Malcolm X in 1965, Cleaver broke his ties to the Nation of Islam and sought to carry on the mission of Malcolm X's Organization of Afro-American Unity.

Paroled in 1966, Cleaver went to work as an editor and writer for *Ramparts* magazine. Soon after his introduction to Huey Newton and Bobby Seale, cofounders of the Black Panther Party, in Oakland, California, Cleaver joined the Panthers and became the party's minister of information. In this role, he called on black men to "pick up the gun" against the United States government.

The year 1968 was one of turning points for Cleaver. He established himself as a gifted essayist and cultural critic with the publication of *Soul on Ice*, a collection of prison writings that earned him the Martin Luther King Memorial Prize in 1970. Also in 1968, Cleaver was selected as the presidential candidate of the Peace and Freedom Party. After a shoot-out in Oakland that left Cleaver and a police officer wounded and 17-year-old Bobby Hutton dead, Cleaver was charged with assault and attempted murder. His parole was revoked. Believing his life was in danger, Cleaver fled the country in November 1968.

He spent the next seven years in Cuba, France, and Algeria with his wife, Kathleen Neal Cleaver. Still actively involved with the Panthers, Cleaver published essays in *Black Scholar, Ramparts*, and *The Black Panther*, and served as the head of the International Section of the Black Panther Party in Algeria. After visits to North Korea, North Vietnam, and the People's Republic of China, however, Cleaver became increasingly critical of Marxist governments. A deal with the FBI allowed him to return to the United States in 1975 with a sentence of more than one thousand hours of community service.

After returning to the United States, his commitments shifted toward conservative politics and fundamentalist Christianity. He describes this transformation in *Soul on Fire*, which appeared in 1978. Cleaver lectured on religion and politics in the 1980s and ran as an independent candidate for Ronald Dellums's seat in the House of Representatives in 1984. After dropping out of the congressional race, Cleaver ran for a seat on the Berkeley, California, City Council. His ongoing struggle with drugs became public in 1994, when Cleaver was arrested in Berkeley.

A varied and prolific writer, Cleaver authored numerous political pamphlets, short stories, and poetry. His books *Eldridge Cleaver: Post-Prison Writings and Speeches* and *Eldridge Cleaver's Black Papers* both appeared in 1969. *The Black Panther Leaders Speak: Huey P. Newton, Bobby Seale, Eldridge Cleaver,* and *Company Speak Out Through the Black Panther Party's Official Newspaper* was published seven years later.

North America

# Clement, Rufus Early

(b. June 6, 1900, Salisbury, N.C.; d. November 7, 1967, New York, N.Y.), first African American elected to office in the South since Reconstruction.

Rufus Clement was the son of George Clinton Clement, a bishop of the African Methodist Episcopal Church (AME). After graduating as valedictorian of Livingstone College in 1922, he taught there, eventually becoming a professor and dean. He earned a degree at Garrett Theological Seminary and a Ph.D. from Northwestern University.

In 1931 Clement became the first dean of the all-black branch of the University of Louisville. Six years later he was appointed president of Atlanta University. His history-making election to the Atlanta school board occurred in 1954. Through his participation in the Civil Rights Movement, Clement helped integrate public schools, fought for voting rights, and helped end segregation in downtown Atlanta.

North America

# Clyburn, James

(b. July 21, 1940, Sumter, S.C.), Democratic member of the United States House of Representatives from South Carolina since 1993; a civil rights activist since his youth.

James Enos Clyburn was born in Sumter, South Carolina, and received a bachelor's degree from South Carolina State College in 1962. Over the next decade, he worked as a teacher, ran a neighborhood youth organization, and headed the South Carolina Commission for Farm Workers. In 1974 he took over as the state's human affairs commissioner, a position he held until 1992. After two unsuccessful attempts while commissioner to win the statewide Democratic nomination for secretary of state, Clyburn ran for

South Carolina's redrawn Sixth Congressional District in 1992. Defending the strangely shaped Sixth District as a way of correcting past political discrimination against blacks, he won handily after the white Democratic incumbent, fearing a racially divisive campaign in the new black majority district, backed out of the election. This victory made Clyburn the first black since 1897 to represent South Carolina in the U.S. Congress.

The Sixth District, as created in 1992, was the poorest in the state, with nearly a fourth of its families living in poverty. The district's major crops include peanuts, tomatoes, and tobacco. Florence County, the most populous county in the district, is an important regional medical center and home to a major pharmaceutical research and development facility, as well as numerous manufacturing interests. Many district residents work outside the district in nearby military facilities.

In Congress, Clyburn served on the Transportation and Infrastructure Committee and the Veterans' Affairs Committee. He is also a member of the Congressional Black Caucus.

North America

# Cobb, William Montague

(b. October 12, 1904, Washington, D.C.; d. 1990), African American physician, anthropologist, and civil rights worker who was awarded Howard University's first distinguished professorship.

William Montague Cobb was the son of William Elmer and Alexzine Montague Cobb. After earning an A.B. from Amherst College in 1925, Cobb entered Howard University Medical School, graduating in 1929. He then earned a Ph.D. in anatomy and physical anthropology from Western Reserve University in 1932. He taught at Howard University from 1932 to 1973, chairing the Department of Anatomy from 1947 to 1969. He was awarded Howard's first distinguished professorship in 1969.

Cobb was an authority on physical anthropology and published over 600 related articles in professional journals. He contributed to E. V. Cowdry's *Problems of Aging: Biological and Medical Aspects*, Cunningham's *Manual of Practical Anatomy*, Gray's *Anatomy*, and Henry's *Anatomy*. He dispelled myths about African American biological inferiority in the American Journal of Physical Anthropology. In 1949 he was elected president of the Anthropological Society of Washington and in 1958 of the American Association of Physical Anthropologists, rare posts for African Americans at that time.

Cobb is also noted for his civil rights work. In the 1940s he represented the National Association for the Advancement of Colored People (NAACP) in support of a national health insurance bill. His Medical Care and the Plight of the Negro and Progress and Portents for the Negro in Medicine, published in 1947 and 1948, respectively, helped inform the American public about the detrimental effects discriminatory practices had on African American access to health care and jobs in the profession. Cobb helped desegregate Gallinger Hospital (now D.C. General), and in 1952 he worked to end the exclusion of African Americans in the all-white Medical Society of the District of Columbia. He served as NAACP president from 1976 to 1982.

North America
## Cone, James Hal
(b. August 5, 1938, Fordyce, Ark.), African American theologian who articulates a black theology of liberation.

In 1969, a year after the assassination of Martin Luther King Jr., James H. Cone published *Black Theology and Black Power*, a treatise that called liberation the center of the Christian Gospel, and the blackness expressed in black consciousness the only tool of liberation. This formulation of a uniquely black theology saw Jesus and the Bible as identified with the poor and exploited, and Black Power as divinely inspired resistance against racial oppression.

Cone's thesis drew upon his own deep involvement in the African Methodist Episcopal Church; the strength of the black Arkansas community in which he was nurtured; and the influence of Malcolm X's cultural critique of mainstream Christianity. The son of Lucille Cone, a homemaker, and Charlie Cone, a woodcutter, James Cone attended Philander Smith College, Garrett Theological Seminary, and Northwestern University. He taught at Adrian College, Philander Smith College, and, after the publication of Black Theology and Black Power, joined the faculty of Union Theological Seminary in New York. He was promoted to full professor in 1973, and was named Charles A. Briggs Professor of Systematic Theology in 1977.

Although he grew up in the tradition of Martin Luther King Jr., Cone continues to be strongly influenced by Malcolm X, who said, "I believe in a religion that believes in freedom." In Malcolm and Martin in America (1991), Cone argues that the two leaders were in fact moving closer to each other, as King became more radical and Malcolm more moderate. Cone's other publications include *A Black Theology of Liberation* (1970), *The Spirituals and the Blues* (1972), *The God of the Oppressed* (1975), and *For My People: Black Theology and the Black Church* (1984).

North America
## Congress, African Americans in
Of the more than 11,000 representatives who have served in the United States Congress since 1789, fewer than 100 have been African Americans, and most of these members entered the institution in two distinct waves. The first wave occurred in the Forty-first Congress (1869–1871), when three black members were elected. The number of black members of Con-

gress grew rapidly but peaked early in the Forty-fourth Congress (1875). After 1875 the presence of blacks in Congress was sporadic and dwindling. No blacks served during the Fiftieth Congress (1887–1889), three served during the Fifty-first (1889–1891), and between the Fifty-second and Fifty-sixth Congresses (1891–1901) there was only one black member per session. No blacks served in Congress between 1901 and 1929. The second wave of African American representation began in the late 1960s, and by 1970 nine blacks held congressional seats. In 1993 the number of blacks in Congress reached 40. As of 1998 that number had not been surpassed.

## The First Wave of Black Representatives

Black representatives first entered Congress after the end of the Civil War and the emancipation of the slaves. All of the newly elected representatives came from states with high black populations—the former slave states of the South. From 1870 to 1897 South Carolina (which is 59 percent black) elected eight blacks to the House. Mississippi (54 percent black) and Louisiana (50 percent black) each elected one black to the House. Mississippi also sent two blacks to the Senate. Five other states with sizable black populations—Alabama, Florida, Georgia, North Carolina, and Virginia—elected 20 black representatives among them. However, far fewer blacks served in Congress than one might expect considering the size of the total black population in the Southern states. For instance, four former slave states—Arkansas, Tennessee, Texas, and West Virginia—never elected any black representatives during the Reconstruction era despite very sizable black populations. What was true for congressional elections also applied to politics at the state level.

Most of the 22 blacks in Congress served on at least one committee. Six served on the Education and Labor Committee, four served on the Agriculture Committee, and four served on the Public Expenditures Committee. Blacks were also represented on the District of Columbia, Library of Congress, Manufactures, Mining, Militia, Pensions, and War Claims committees. However, there was only one black committee chairman, Sen. Blanche Bruce, who served on the minor Levees and Dikes of the Mississippi River Committee.

The first wave of black representatives sought both to advance national policies affecting their states and districts—policies related to public education and protective tariffs for local products, for example—and to deal with more specifically black issues such as the provision of relief for depositors of the failed Freedmen's Savings and Trust Company. They also worked for the interests of Native Americans. Their successes, however, were confined to procuring easily obtained political patronage appointments such as postmaster, customs inspector, and internal revenue agent for some of their constituents. According to Eric Foner's *Reconstruction, 1863–1877*, black representatives had few legislative accomplishments: most of their bills languished in committee.

A number of events and forces brought an end to Reconstruction and black representation in Congress: the Hayes-Tilden Compromise of 1877; late nineteenth-century Supreme Court decisions that negated the effect of the Fourteenth Amendment and the Civil Rights Act of 1875; intimidation of black voters by the Ku Klux Klan; and all the other concomitants of the return to power of the former Confederates and their allies. By the turn of the century black representation seemed about to end, even at the descriptive level. Only one black member remained in Congress in 1900: George White of North Carolina, who voluntarily left Congress the following year.

## The Second Wave of Black Representatives

The second wave of black electoral activity in the twentieth century began in 1928 with the election of Republican Oscar DePriest from an inner-city Chicago district. Like almost all the Reconstruction-era blacks before him, DePriest was elected from a district with a majority of black voters. After serving in the Seventy-third and Seventy-fourth Congresses (1929–1934), he was defeated in 1934 by Arthur Mitchell, the first black Democrat elected to Congress. More than five decades passed before another black Republican was elected to the House. In 1942, after eight years of service, Mitchell resigned, and William Dawson, another black Democrat, succeeded him. Two years later Adam Clayton Powell Jr. was elected congressman in Harlem, New York, and this meant that for the first time since 1891 there was more than one black representative in the House. In 1950 there was another breakthrough for black representation when Dawson gained enough seniority to become the first black to chair a standing committee, the Government Operations Committee. In 1960 Powell became chairman of the more important Education and Labor Committee. (Seven years later Powell was stripped of both his seniority and chairmanship after having been charged with an ethics violation.) Still another breakthrough came in 1966 when Edward W. Brooke was elected as a Republican senator from Massachusetts, a state whose population was less than 3 percent black. Brooke served until his defeat in 1978.

African American women were relative latecomers to Congress. The first woman to serve was Jeannette Rankin, elected to the House in 1916. Fifty-two years later Shirley Chisholm (D-N.Y.) became the first black woman to serve in the House. In 1992 Carol Moseley-Braun (D-Ill.) became the first black Democrat to serve in the Senate; she was also the first black woman senator and the fourth black senator. Unlike white women, who often followed their deceased husbands into office, black women did not use widowhood as a primary mode of entry into political life. All but one of the black women who served in Congress were highly educated, experienced politicians before they arrived on Capitol Hill. Rep. Shirley Chisholm had a master's degree from Columbia University and had served in the state assembly. Similarly, Rep. Barbara Jordan (D-Tex.) and Rep. Yvonne Burke (D-Calif.), both elected in 1972, had law degrees and had previously served in their state legislatures. In 1973 Cardiss Collins (D-Ill.), elected to replace her deceased husband, became the only black woman to have entered Congress through widowhood.

Regardless of their race or gender, black members of Congress are better educated and often come from higher-status jobs and backgrounds than most of their constituents. In the 105th Congress (1997–1999), for example, only 2 of 38 black members did not have at least a four-year degree. Fifteen held law degrees and had worked in the legal field; eleven held master's degrees; and one had a Ph.D. This level of educational attainment contrasts strikingly with that of the black population in general: in 1995 only about 14 percent of blacks aged 25 and older had received a bachelor's degree. Thus, twentieth-century blacks in Congress were similar in one respect to black representatives in the Reconstruction era—neither group reflected the typical makeup of the African American population at large. Many twentieth-century congressional blacks had already held political office, most often in state legislatures and city councils. Others had served as teachers or professors or had been business executives. However, such a disparity between representatives and the population they represent is not a major problem; few people would argue that politicians should personify their "average" constituent.

## The Creation of a Congressional Black Caucus

In 1971 the nine current black representatives established the Congressional Black Caucus (CBC). After much consideration the representatives decided that their effectiveness hinged on the creation of a formal organization with its own rules, by-laws, and chair. Caucus founders viewed the organization as a vehicle that would allow individual black representatives to coordinate their efforts on behalf of downtrodden Americans, particularly African Americans. The organization adopted as its official motto the statement that "Black People have no permanent friends, no permanent enemies, just permanent interests."

From the start the CBC challenged the distribution of power in the House. Caucus members would eventually win a number of key leadership positions and prestigious committee assignments. The group would also establish its own foundation for raising money, its own research group, and an important political action committee.

In 1992 the CBC's membership reached its highest level, comprising 38 representatives, one delegate, and one senator. Full membership in the group has always been restricted to African Americans, but in the mid-1980s the organization voted to allow white representatives who had acceptable voting records to join as associate members.

Because of its increased size and heightened media attention, the CBC became a major political player during the first term of the Clinton administration. The group had a major role in shaping and passing some of the legislation supported by the president. CBC members were heading key committees, and they held other leadership posts as well: nine were assistant whips, three served on the Democratic Steering and Policy Committee, and one was a deputy whip. The Clinton administration came to consult the CBC on all major political decisions in recognition of its increased stature. During this time the organization was more visible than it had ever been in its history and was a key factor in many of the important political debates that took place in Washington. It had become a powerful force on Capitol Hill, a development brought about largely by the personal influence of some of its individual members and by its ability to deliver a substantial bloc of votes.

As fate would have it, though, just when the organization appeared to be making a substantial difference in Congress, the Democrats lost both the House and the Senate. The 1994 elections profoundly changed the political environment in which the CBC had to operate, as the group's members were forced to negotiate with unsympathetic Republicans. Despite the CBC's assertion that "black people have no permanent friends," the caucus had never functioned as more than an extension of the Democratic Party. As an interest group within the minority party, the CBC was destined to become more marginalized than ever. Though it had four times as many members in 1994 as it did at its birth in 1971, in the wake of the Democrats' defeat the caucus exerted little power or influence. Many of the highest-ranking black Democrats resigned from Congress, giving up years of seniority that took decades to attain. When the Democrats regain control of the institution, black Democrats will not have the seniority to claim many of the key chairmanships. Greater institutional power for blacks in Congress will take decades to achieve.

North America

# Congressional Black Caucus,

**the coalition of black members of the United States Congress committed to promoting and protecting policies favorable to the African American community.**

The South African human rights activist Bishop Desmond Tutu once said, "Politics is the art of the possible." But for most of America's first 251 years, politics and political participation were reserved for whites only. African Americans were prohibited from voting and from holding political office and, since most were enslaved before 1865, were punished for participating in public protest. It was not until Reconstruction (1865–1877) and in 1870 the passage of the Fifteenth Amendment to the United States Constitution, giving black men the right to vote, that political participation by blacks became legal. Even then, it was weakened by officially sanctioned racial discrimination.

During Reconstruction 16 African Americans were elected to Congress and over 600 to state legislatures. But by 1877 many of the newly granted political rights were being rescinded by state officials. In the words of historian Eric Foner, "In illiteracy, malnutrition, inadequate housing, and a host of other burdens, blacks paid the highest price for the end of Reconstruction." It took 92 years for blacks to attain a measure of political representation in the U.S. Congress that was even close to nineteenth-century levels.

In 1969 the nine blacks then in Congress were isolated and powerless, unable to prevent passage of legislation detrimental to African Americans and other minorities. That year, Rep. Charles Diggs, a black Democrat from Michigan, formed the Democratic Select Committee, in the belief that a unified black voice could exert a measure of political influence in Congress. The committee investigated the murders of several Black Panther Party members in Chicago, Illinois, and defeated the nomination of conservative judge Clement Haynesworth to the Supreme Court. The potential strength of a collective black voice was immediately evident, and on June 18, 1971, at its first annual dinner, the Democratic Select Committee was reorganized as the Congressional Black Caucus (CBC), with Representative Diggs as its first chairperson.

Reactions to the CBC were immediate, as disapproval and opposition came from both blacks and whites. Black conservatives challenged the caucus's presumption in representing the entire black community. White liberals discounted the caucus's political effectiveness, and white conservatives labeled caucus members radicals and militants. During a trip to Africa, Vice President Spiro Agnew derogated the caucus by advising its members to take notice of the behavior of their African brethren, adding that they could "learn much" from them.

Despite the opposition, the CBC gained national attention in 1971 when its members presented President Richard Nixon with a list of 60 recommendations concerning foreign and domestic issues. In 1972 the caucus was one of the sponsors of the National Black Political Convention held in Gary, Indiana. That year, at the Democratic Party's national convention, the caucus drafted the Black Declaration of Independence, which urged the Democratic Party to commit itself to effecting complete racial equality. It also drafted the Black Bill of Rights, demanding, among other things, full employment and an end to subversive American military activity in Africa.

The caucus established the Congressional Black Caucus Foundation, a "nonprofit public policy, research, and educational institute," in 1976. Later that year, it formed the Congressional Black Caucus Graduate Intern Program to increase the number of African American professionals working for congressional committees. One year later, the caucus formed TransAfrica, an organization that lobbied on behalf of African interests. The caucus and TransAfrica, under the leadership of Randall Robinson, worked actively to secure economic sanctions against the apartheid regime in South Africa, to help build political stability in Haiti, and to establish a national holiday in honor of Martin Luther King Jr.

During its existence the Congressional Black Caucus was chaired by Reps. Charles Diggs (D-Mich.), Louis Stokes (D-Ohio), Ron Dellums (D-

Calif.), Charles Rangel (D-N.Y.), and Kweisi Mfume (D-Md.). As its membership grew, the caucus developed broad support among black state legislators, black businesses, and black academics. This support contributed to the unprecedented 1992 election of 40 African Americans to Congress. In 1993 Carol Moseley-Braun (D-Ill.) became the fourth African American, and the first African American woman, to be elected to the U.S. Senate.

Although the CBC was divided on issues like the 1993 North American Free Trade Agreement (NAFTA) and the organization's relationship with the Nation of Islam, it consistently provided a clear and unified African American voice on issues like crime, welfare, and housing. It stood at the forefront of African American leadership in the U.S. Congress for 24 years before it was stripped of federal funding in 1994. At its pinnacle, the caucus wielded considerable political influence over many of the most important issues affecting the black community, the nation, and the world. Although the CBC is no longer officially sponsored by Congress, its impact continues to be felt as its members remain actively involved in the formation of the nation's laws and policies.

North America

# Congress of Racial Equality,

American civil rights organization that pioneered the strategy of nonviolent direct action, especially the tactics of sit-ins, jail-ins, and freedom rides.

The Congress of Racial Equality (CORE) was founded in 1942 as the Committee of Racial Equality by an interracial group of students in Chicago. Many of these students were members of the Chicago branch of the Fellowship of Reconciliation (FOR), a pacifist organization seeking to change racist attitudes. The founders of CORE were deeply influenced by Mahatma Gandhi's teachings of nonviolent resistance.

CORE started as a nonhierarchical, decentralized organization funded entirely by the voluntary contributions of its members. The organization was initially co-led by white University of Chicago student George Houser and black student James Farmer. In 1942 CORE began protests against segregation in public accommodations by organizing sit-ins. It was also in 1942 that CORE expanded nationally. James Farmer traveled the country with Bayard Rustin, a field secretary with FOR, and recruited activists at FOR meetings. CORE's early growth consisted almost entirely of white middle-class college students from the Midwest.

From the beginning of its expansion, CORE experienced tension between local control and national leadership. The earliest affiliated chapters retained control of their own activities and funds. With a nonhierarchical system as the model of leadership, a national leadership over local chapters seemed contradictory to CORE's principles. Some early chapters were dominated by pacifists and focused on educational activities. Other chapters emphasized direct action protests, such as sit-ins. This tension has persisted throughout CORE's existence. Through sit-ins and picket lines, the group had some success in integrating Northern public facilities in the 1940s. With these successes it was decided that to have a national impact, it was necessary to strengthen the national organization. James Farmer became the first national director of CORE in 1943.

In April 1947 CORE sent eight white and eight black men into the upper South to test a Supreme Court ruling that declared segregation in interstate travel unconstitutional. CORE gained national attention for this Journey of Reconciliation when four of the riders were arrested in Chapel Hill, North Carolina, and three, including Bayard Rustin, were forced to work on a chain gang. In the aftermath of the 1954 *Brown v. Board of Education* decision, CORE was revived from several years of stagnation and decline. CORE provided the 1955 Montgomery Bus Boycott with its philosophical commitment to nonviolent direct action. As the Civil Rights Movement took hold, CORE focused its energy in the South.

CORE's move into the South forced the leadership to address the question of the organization's place within the black community. While whites remained prominent, black leaders were selected for high-profile positions. CORE remained committed to interracialism but no longer required that new chapters have an interracial membership, largely expecting little white support in the South. While middle-class college students predominated in the early years of the organization, increasingly the membership was made up of poorer and less educated blacks.

CORE provided guidance for action in the aftermath of the 1960 sit-in of four college students (who were not CORE members) at a Greensboro, North Carolina, lunch counter and subsequently became a nationally recognized civil rights organization. As a pioneer of the sit-in tactic, the organization offered support in Greensboro and organized sit-ins throughout the South. CORE members then developed the strategy of the jail-in, serving out their sentences for sit-ins rather than paying bail. In May 1961 CORE organized the Freedom Rides, modeled after their earlier Journey of Reconciliation. Near Birmingham, Alabama, a bus was firebombed and riders were beaten by a white mob. After this event CORE ended the rides; however, the Student Nonviolent Coordinating Committee (SNCC) resumed the rides in Mississippi. Some CORE officials resented SNCC for taking credit for the Freedom Rides, but CORE continued to locate field secretaries in key areas of the South to provide support for the riders.

By the end of 1961 CORE had 53 affiliated chapters, and they remained active in Southern civil rights activities for the next several years. CORE participated heavily in President John F. Kennedy's Voter Education Project (VEP) and also co-sponsored the 1963 March on Washington. In 1964 CORE participated in the Mississippi Freedom Summer project; two of the three activists killed that summer in an infamous case, James Chaney and Michael Schwerner, were members of CORE.

By 1963 CORE had already shifted attention to segregation in the North and West, where two-thirds of the organization's chapters were located. In an effort to build CORE's credibility as a black-protest organization, leadership in these Northern chapters had become almost entirely black. CORE's ideology and strategies increasingly were challenged by its changing membership. Many new members advocated militancy and believed that nonviolent methods of protest should be used only if they proved successful.

As the tactics were being questioned, so was the role of white members. In 1966 CORE endorsed the term Black Power, and by 1967 the word "multiracial" was no longer in the CORE constitution. Finally, in 1968, Roy Innis replaced Farmer as the national director, and Innis soon denied whites active membership in CORE and advocated Black Separatism.

Under Innis's leadership CORE took a conservative turn, lending its support to black capitalism and nationalism. In the 1970s Innis joined Southern whites in promoting separate schools rather than desegregation. James Farmer cut his ties to CORE in 1976, returning in the 1980s in a bid to remake CORE into a multiracial organization. Innis, however, remained firmly in leadership. In the 1990s CORE chapters engaged in little direct organization, but Innis remains one of the most prominent black conservatives in the United States.

North America

# Conyers, John F., Jr.

(b. May 16, 1929, Detroit, Mich.), Democratic member of the United States House of Representatives from Michigan since 1965.

John Conyers Jr. earned a bachelor's degree in 1957 and a law degree in 1958 from Wayne State University. He was a member of the Michigan National Guard from 1948 to 1952. In 1952 he joined the U.S. Army and fought in the Korean War. He was an assistant to U.S. Representative John Dingell from 1958 to 1961, and from 1961 to 1963 he worked for the Michigan Workmen's Compensation Department. In the 1964 Democratic primary for the newly created black-majority Fourteenth Congressional District in Michigan, Conyers won by only 108 votes on a platform of Jobs, Equality and Peace. He was one of only six black representatives in Congress. He ran for mayor of Detroit in 1989 and 1993 but lost decisively both times.

The Fourteenth District lies north of downtown Detroit. More than 500,000 district residents live in the city. The district takes in an economically depressed area with a high crime rate. Once a thriving community built around the auto industry, the district lost thousands of auto manufacturing jobs, and many residents who could afford to move left for the suburbs.

Conyers was the first black to chair the House Judiciary Committee, which is responsible for all crime and civil rights legislation. When the Republicans gained control of the House in the 104th Congress

(1995–1997), he became the ranking Democrat on the committee, a position he retained during the 105th Congress, which began in 1997.

## *Crisis, The*

**official publication of the National Association for the Advancement of Colored People (NAACP).**

*The Crisis* has been the official publication of the NAACP since 1910, and for its first quarter-century it also served as a public forum for the ideas of its first editor, noted black intellectual and civil rights activist W. E. B. Du Bois. The NAACP, founded in 1909, is an interracial organization that supports the struggles of people of color. Most of its original board members were white, and Du Bois's position as the editor of the *Crisis* made him the most powerful African American in the organization at that time. In turn, he established the *Crisis* as the most influential publication for African Americans during his tenure as editor.

Du Bois was first hired by the NAACP in June 1910 as its director of publicity and research. By September he had submitted a proposal to produce a monthly magazine that would document "very important happenings and movement in the world which bears on the great problem of interracial relations and especially those which affect the Negro-American." Du Bois intended the magazine's title, *The Crisis: A Record of the Darker Races*, to signify the current "critical time in the history of the advancement of men." The NAACP approved the proposal, a one-year line of credit, and hired Du Bois as editor. The first issue appeared in November 1910, 16 pages that sold for ten cents.

The magazine's standard departments included "Along the Color Line," which reported on politics, education, science, and art; "Along the Battle Line," which covered NAACP activities; "What to Read," which recommended recent books and articles; "Talks About Women," "Men of the Month," and features such as "Colored High Schools" and "American Negroes in College," which promoted race pride. the *Crisis* also became known for its inclusion of new literature by African Americans, including such landmarks as Langston Hughes's first published poem. In 1920 the *Crisis* was even briefly able to add a second publication, the *Brownies' Book*, intended for black children.

The inaugural issue of the *Crisis* sold 1,000 copies; within just over a year that figure had risen to 16,000, and the next year the paid circulation was at 30,000. Of those numbers, about 75 percent were sold to blacks, which showed that the *Crisis* reached a larger black audience in addition to the NAACP members who received the magazine as part of their membership.

Du Bois wrote many of the *Crisis*'s articles himself, but it was the editorial section where he—and by extension, the magazine—had the strongest impact. Du Bois used the editorial section to promote his ideas on whatever interested him, and in some cases, such as his famous 1919 essay protesting the racism black World War I veterans faced back home, they received national attention.

Predictably, Du Bois's strong opinions caused him problems throughout his tenure as editor. Du Bois's support of "social equality," including interracial marriage, was radical for his time, even for some of the progressive whites who supported the NAACP. Du Bois also openly criticized several African American institutions, including the black church, the black press, and black colleges whose governing bodies were predominantly white. These opinions caused controversy among some African American readers. Whenever Du Bois came under criticism from the NAACP's board of directors, he would claim censorship. Because he was the most prominent African American in the organization, he felt even more strongly that he should be allowed to state his views freely. His struggles with the board, combined with declining circulation, finally led to his resignation in 1934.

Without Du Bois the *Crisis* lost the singular voice that had brought it such recognition. But the magazine continued to serve as the NAACP's official publication and continued its focus on racism worldwide and the progress of efforts to fight it. Roy Wilkins succeeded Du Bois as editor, and Wilkins was followed in 1949 by James Ivy, who directed the magazine's coverage of the Civil Rights Movement over the next 20 years. Circulation had fallen from a high of 100,000 in 1918 to 10,000 when Du Bois left, but by the late 1980s it had risen again to 350,000. Even these numbers were not enough to keep the *Crisis* from suffering a financial setback in the winter of 1996, which forced it to cease publication for six months. But with its July 1997 issue the *New Crisis* reasserted its position as the "premier, crusading voice for civil rights," and "an honest forum for the politics, art and literature of human liberation."

North America

# Crosswaith, Frank Rudolph

(b. July 16, 1892, Fredericksted, St. Croix, Virgin Islands; d. 1965), African American labor organizer, political activist, and journalist who helped found the Harlem Labor Committee and the Negro Labor Committee.

Frank Crosswaith was born on St. Croix in the Danish West Indies (now the United States Virgin Islands) to William I. and Anne Eliza Crosswaith. He was educated at the University Preparatory School in Fredericksted and the Rand School of Social Science in New York. After graduating, he began his career in African American labor relations, becoming known as the Negro Debs because of his similarity to labor leader Eugene V. Debs.

A socialist, Crosswaith sought to ally African American workers with white workers under the banner of class. Thus, he opposed African American leaders who believed in racial alliance alone. In 1934 he helped found and then chaired the Harlem Labor Committee (HLC). He attempted to align the HLC with the American Federation of Labor (AF of L), which was then seeking African American members. This enabled African Americans to integrate unions that were previously closed to them.

In 1935 Crosswaith also helped found the integrated Negro Labor Committee, whose goals were to organize African American labor and highlight the common problems facing African American and white laborers. His zeal for equal employment opportunity was still evident at the March on Washington for Jobs and Freedom in 1963, at which he spoke.

Crosswaith's work in politics began in 1924 when he was vice chair of the American Labor Party during Robert LaFollette's presidential campaign. He lectured for the League for Industrial Democracy and the Socialist Party. He also edited the *Negro Labor News* for 12 years and co-wrote *True Freedom for Negro and White Workers* and *Discrimination Incorporated*.

# D

## Davis, Angela Yvonne

(b. Jan. 26, 1944, Birmingham, Ala.), African American political activist, philosopher, and educator whose imprisonment for murder generated worldwide protest.

Angela Davis was, in several ways, born into the heart of the civil rights struggle. Her family lived in the middle-class section of Birmingham, Alabama, that came to be known as Dynamite Hill because there were so many Ku Klux Klan bombings. Davis attended segregated schools where children were taught black history but at the same time were denied adequate school supplies and facilities. Her mother and grandmother encouraged Davis to fight for civil rights while she was still in elementary school. As a high school student, Davis helped organize interracial study groups that were broken up by the police.

When she was 15, Davis left Birmingham to attend the Elizabeth Irwin School in New York City. Teachers at the politically progressive school introduced Davis to the socialist ideas that informed her later activism. From 1961 to 1965 Davis attended Brandeis University in Waltham, Massachusetts, and graduated with honors. She spent her junior year in Paris, where her contact with Algerian students provided her with a global perspective on the struggle against colonialism and oppression. Her political commitments intensified in 1963, when four girls whom Davis had known were killed in the 16th Street Baptist Church bombing in Birmingham.

Davis began her doctoral studies in philosophy at the Johann Wolfgang von Goethe University in Frankfurt, Germany, but returned to the United States in 1967 when she decided that she could no longer stay away from the growing American racial conflict. She enrolled at the University of California at San Diego, where she continued to work with her undergraduate adviser, philosopher Herbert Marcuse. She earned her master's degree in philosophy in 1969, and within a year completed the requirements for the Ph.D., except for the dissertation.

While in graduate school Davis became increasingly politically active. At a workshop sponsored by the Student Nonviolent Coordinating Committee (SNCC), Davis met Frank and Kendra Alexander, both active members of SNCC, the Black Panthers, and the Communist party. Davis moved to Los Angeles to join the Alexanders in their work and in 1968 joined the Communist Party.

Davis was hired by the University of California at Los Angeles to teach philosophy in 1969. Despite the popularity of her courses and the positive recommendations of the faculty, she was fired by the state board of regents at the behest of Governor Ronald Reagan once her Communist affiliation became known. A court overturned the dismissal, but the regents refused to renew Davis's contract at the end of the 1969–1970 academic year.

Davis's political activities earned her international attention in 1970. Through the Black Panthers, Davis became an advocate for black political prisoners and spoke out in defense of the inmates known as the Soledad Brothers. After the killing of inmate George Jackson by guards at Soledad Prison, his younger brother, Jonathan, attempted to free another prisoner from a Marin County, California, courthouse by taking hostages. Four people were killed in the shoot-out that followed. The guns Jackson used belonged to Davis. Even though she was not at all near the courthouse at the time, she was charged with kidnapping, conspiracy, and murder. When Davis defied the arrest warrant and went into hiding, she was placed on the FBI's ten-most-wanted list. Her capture in a New York motel room and subsequent imprisonment inspired "Free Angela" rallies around the world.

An FBI poster lists Angela Davis among its ten most wanted fugitives after she went underground in 1970 to escape prosecution. Davis was eventually acquitted of all charges.
*CORBIS/Bettmann*

Davis spent 16 months in jail before being released on bail in 1972; she was later acquitted of all charges.

From the "Free Angela" movement, Davis and others established the National Alliance Against Racism and Political Repression. She ran for office in 1980 and 1984 as the Communist Party candidate for vice president, and she continues to lecture widely about social justice issues. Currently, Davis is a professor of the history of consciousness at the University of California at Santa Cruz. She is the author of several books, including *If They Come in the Morning* (1971), *Angela Davis: An Autobiography* (1974), *Women, Race, and Class* (1983), and *Women, Culture, and Politics* (1989).

North America

# Deacons for Defense and Justice,

a black organization established to protect civil rights workers against the Ku Klux Klan.

The Deacons for Defense and Justice, a group of African American men who were mostly veterans of World War II and the Korean War, organized in Jonesboro, Louisiana, on July 10, 1964. Their goal was to combat Ku Klux Klan violence against Congress of Racial Equality (CORE) volunteers who were participating in voter registration activities. Disciplined and secretive, the Deacons generally limited their activities to patrolling black neighborhoods and protecting mass meetings, CORE headquarters, and civil rights workers who were entering and leaving town. The Deacons accompanied marchers from Memphis, Tennessee, to Jackson, Mississippi, in the summer of 1966, during which Student Nonviolent Coordinating Committee (SNCC) leader Stokely Carmichael popularized the phrase Black Power.

The Deacons often inflated their membership numbers in order to appear more menacing to white extremists, and they once claimed to have 50 chapters throughout the South. The resulting picture painted by the national news media—thousands of armed and angry blacks involved in secret organizations that were spreading through the South—shocked many whites into speculating that the United States was heading for a race war. The membership claims of the Deacons attracted the notice of J. Edgar Hoover, director of the Federal Bureau of Investigation (FBI). During the investigation that Hoover ordered, and in which the organization cooperated, it came to light that the total membership was in the dozens, with only three chapters, all in Louisiana.

Ironically, as nonviolent civil rights activities were eclipsed in the later 1960s by the Black Power Movement, with its militant rhetoric and insinuations of racial violence, the Deacons' presence declined. By 1968 the Deacons for Defense and Justice had all but disappeared.

North America

# Du Bois, William Edward Burghardt (W. E. B.)

(b. February 23, 1868, Great Barrington, Mass.; d. August 27, 1963, Accra, Ghana), writer, social scientist, critic, and public intellectual; cofounder of the Niagara Movement, the National Association for the Advancement of Colored People (NAACP), and the Pan-African Congress; editor of the NAACP magazine, the *Crisis*.

Along with Frederick Douglass and Booker T. Washington, historians consider W. E. B. Du Bois one of the most influential African Americans before the Civil Rights Movement of the 1960s. Born only six years after emancipation, he was active well into his nineties. He died in 1963, on the eve of the March on Washington. Despite near-constant criticism for his often contradictory social and political opinions—he was accused, at various times, of elitism, communism, and black separatism—Du Bois remained throughout his long life black America's leading public intellectual.

Born in a small western Massachusetts town, Du Bois and his mother— his father had left the family when he was young—were among the few African American residents. Of his heritage, Du Bois wrote that it included "a flood of Negro blood, a strain of French, a bit of Dutch, but, Thank God! No 'Anglo-Saxon' . . . ." After an integrated grammar-school education, Du Bois attended the historically black Fisk University in Nashville, Tennessee, then Harvard University, from which he received a bachelor's degree in 1890. That fall Du Bois began graduate work in history at Harvard under the legendary professors George Santayana, William James, and Josiah Royce. Du Bois was especially influenced by Albert Bushnell Hart, one of the fathers of the new science of sociology. After two years at the University of Berlin (1892–1894), he received a Ph.D. from Harvard in 1895. His dissertation, "The Suppression of the African Slave-Trade to the United States of America, 1638–1870," was published in 1896 as the first volume in the *Harvard Historical Studies* series.

Despite exceptional credentials, discrimination left Du Bois with no options other than a job at Wilberforce College, a small black school in Ohio. Arriving in 1895, Du Bois left a year later with his wife, his former student Nina Gomer. They went to Philadelphia, where the University of Pennsylvania had invited Du Bois to conduct a sociological study of that city's black neighborhoods. The work led to *The Philadelphia Negro* (1899), which provided the model for a series of monographs he wrote while at Atlanta University, whose faculty he joined in 1897. As a young sociologist, he sought to "study [social problems] in the light of the best scientific research." But the persistence of segregation, discrimination, and lynching led Du Bois to feel increasingly that "one could not be a calm, cool, and detached scientist while Negroes were lynched, murdered, and starved . . . . "

In 1903 Du Bois published his first collection of essays, *The Souls of Black Folk*, which many have called the most important book ever written by an African American. In it he identified "the color line" as the twentieth century's central problem, and dismissed the accommodationism advocated by Booker T. Washington. "[When] Mr. Washington apologizes for injustice," Du Bois wrote, "does not rightly value the privilege and duty of voting, belittles the emasculating effects of caste distinctions, and opposes the higher training and ambition of our brighter minds . . . we must unceasingly and firmly oppose [him]." In 1905 Du Bois joined with William Monroe Trotter, militant editor of the black newspaper the *Boston Guardian*, in forming the Niagara Movement, a short-lived effort to secure full civil and political rights for African Americans. In its wake, Du Bois helped found the most influential civil rights organization of the twentieth century: the National Association for the Advancement of Colored People (NAACP).

Unlike the Niagara Movement, the NAACP was an interracial organization from the start. Its leadership was largely white; as director of publications and research, Du Bois was the only African American among its early officers. In 1910 Du Bois left Atlanta for the NAACP's New York City headquarters, where he founded the *Crisis*, the association's magazine. As editor he published the work of Langston Hughes, Countee Cullen, and other Harlem Renaissance literary lights as well as his own wide-ranging and provocative opinions. From 1910 until his resignation as editor in 1934, Du Bois's editorials revealed the continuing evolution of his political thought. Early calls for integration and an end to lynching hewed the NAACP line, while his pleas for African American participation in World War I brought scorn from more radical black voices. His insistence on absolute equality for "the talented tenth" of black intellectual elites coexisted uneasily with arguments for self-segregation and technical training for the black masses. Such shifting opinions, along with his sometimes haughty self-assurance, meant that—as one biographer has noted—Du Bois would always have "influence, not power."

Increasingly, Du Bois looked beyond American race relations to international economics and politics. In 1915 he wrote *The Negro*, a sociological examination of the African diaspora. In 1919 he helped organize the second Pan-African. Visiting Africa in the 1920s, he wrote that his chief question was whether "Negroes are to lead in the rise of Africa or whether they must always and everywhere follow the guidance of white folk."

Along with anti-imperialism, Du Bois also expressed interest in socialism, possibly in response to the disproportionate effect that the Great Depression was having on African Americans, as well as his favorable impressions of a visit to the Soviet Union in 1926. Meanwhile, starting with a new essay collection, *Darkwater: Voices from Within the Veil* (1920), Du Bois's writing became more militant and controversial, and conflicts with NAACP secretary Walter F. White led to Du Bois's resignation as editor of the *Crisis* in 1934.

Returning to Atlanta University, Du Bois continued to write weekly opinion columns in black newspapers, as well as books such as *Black Reconstruction in America* (1934); *Black Folk: Then and Now* (1939); and *Dusk of Dawn: An Autobiography of a Concept of Race* (1940). In 1939 he founded *Phylon*, a journal devoted to race and cultural issues, whose radical nature may have contributed to his forced resignation from Atlanta University in 1944. Then in his mid-seventies, Du Bois did not retire but instead rejoined the NAACP staff (although he did not resume editorship of the *Crisis*). Declaring that he would spend "the remaining years of [his] active life" in the fight against imperialism, Du Bois helped reorganize the Pan-African Congress, which in 1945 elected him its international president. In that same year he published *Color and Democracy: Colonies and Peace*, and in 1947 produced *The World and Africa*. Du Bois's outspoken criticism of American foreign policy and his involvement with the 1948 presidential campaign of Progressive Party candidate Henry Wallace led to his dismissal from the NAACP in the fall of 1948.

During the 1950s Du Bois's continuing work with the international peace movement and open expressions of sympathy for the Soviet Union drew the censure of the United States government and further isolated Du Bois from the civil rights mainstream. In 1951, at the height of the cold war, he was indicted under the Foreign Agents Registration Act of 1938. While he was acquitted of that charge, the Department of State refused to issue him a passport in 1952, barring him from foreign travel until 1958. Once the passport ban was lifted, Du Bois and his wife, the writer Shirley Graham Du Bois, traveled extensively, visiting England, France, Belgium, and Holland, as well as China and the Soviet Union, and much of the Eastern Bloc. On May 1, 1959, he was awarded the Lenin Peace Prize in Moscow. In 1960 Du Bois attended his friend Kwame Nkrumah's inauguration as the first president of Ghana; in the following year the Du Boises accepted Nkrumah's invitation to move there and work on the Encyclopaedia Africana, a project that was never completed. Du Bois died at the age of 95, six months after becoming a Ghanaian citizen.

# E

## Edelman, Marian Wright

(b. June 6, 1939, Bennettsville, S.C.), founder and president of the Children's Defense Fund, America's leading advocacy group for children.

Marian Wright Edelman was the youngest of Arthur and Maggie Wright's five children. When blacks in her hometown of Bennettsville, South Carolina, were forbidden to enter city parks, her father, a Baptist minister, built a park for black children behind his church. Edelman would later credit him with instilling in her an obligation to right wrongs. She attended Spelman College in Atlanta and spent her junior year in France, Switzerland, and Eastern Europe. Returning to Spelman in 1959, she helped organize protests for the nascent Civil Rights Movement. She graduated valedictorian the following year, then took a law degree from Yale.

By 1964 she was working as a lawyer in Mississippi, where volunteers for the Civil Rights Movement were jailed and often beaten on fabricated charges. In the course of representing them for the National Association for the Advancement of Colored People (NAACP), she became the first black woman to pass the bar in Mississippi. She also became a nationally recognized advocate for Head Start, a pre-kindergarten education program. This work brought her to Peter Edelman, an attorney and member of Sen. Robert Kennedy's staff, whom she married in 1968 and with whom she would have three children, Joshua, Jonah, and Ezra.

Relocated to Washington, D.C., Edelman started the Washington Research Project (WRP), which sought to discover how existing and proposed laws affected the poor. Over the next several years, the project evolved into the Children's Defense Fund (CDF). Meanwhile, Edelman directed Harvard University's Center for Law and Education in Cambridge, Massachusetts, and became the first black woman to serve on the board of directors of Yale University. When the CDF was incorporated in 1973, Edelman became its President. She returned to Washington in 1979 to direct the day-to-day operations of this increasingly influential advocacy group.

Edelman was aware that with more than half of black children being born out of wedlock, many of them to teenagers, future generations of blacks were assured of living in poverty. She also realized that because teenage pregnancy affected both whites and blacks, a campaign against it could attract broad support. In the early 1980s the CDF sponsored thousands of television, radio, and billboard advertisements counseling teenagers about the risks and costs of pregnancy. Careful to sidestep the controversial issue of abortion and focus instead on pregnancy prevention, the campaign proved popular. Observers widely agreed that it raised the public's awareness about teen pregnancy; its effect on the incidence of teenage sex and pregnancy, however, was less clear.

Edelman pursued other parts of CDF's agenda in Congress. With the slogan, "One dollar up front saves many dollars down the road," CDF won an increase in Medicaid coverage for poor children (1984); financial aid, albeit limited, for childcare (1990); and an increase in funding for Head Start (1992). By the late 1980s Edelman had gained a national reputation as "the children's crusader." The staff and budget of CDF grew correspondingly. Other CDF efforts have met with little or no success, including the attempt to secure medical insurance for every child and pregnant mother and to change the welfare reform bill of 1996—which the organization asserted would put millions of children into poverty.

North America

# Elaine, Arkansas, Race Riot of 1919,

a riot by white mobs that resulted in the deaths of 200 blacks and in the convictions of black union members. In a highly unusual step a federal court intervened against a racially biased Southern court and overturned the convictions.

In the summer of 1919 black sharecroppers and tenant farmers in Elaine, Arkansas, were angered by suspicions that they were being cheated by wealthy white land owners. Whites were accused of deliberately suppressing wages and undervaluing the price of cotton produced on black farms. A group of black farmers established the Progressive Farmers and Householders Union, and hired a white attorney to negotiate with white land owners for higher wages and better cotton prices.

On September 30 a group of white officials from the Missouri-Pacific Railroad set out to disrupt union activities by firing upon a group of blacks attending a union meeting. Union members returned fire, killing two whites. Word of the gunfight spread quickly, and soon hundreds of armed whites arrived in Elaine bent on revenge. The white mobs burned black homes and businesses. In response to the mayhem, federal troops targeted blacks who were trying to protect their possessions and defend their lives. Hundreds of blacks were arrested and many were forcibly held in the basements of the city's public schools.

Two hundred African Americans were killed in the riot and 67 African

Americans were indicted for inciting violence. A white mob gathered outside the courthouse as 12 black union members were convicted and sentenced to die. In 1921 the National Association for the Advancement of Colored People (NAACP) persuaded the Arkansas Supreme Court to reverse six of those convictions. The NAACP appealed the six remaining convictions to the U.S. Supreme Court; in 1923 the Court ruled that the Arkansas convictions had violated federal due process law. In January 1925 the remaining black union members were released, marking one of the first times that a federal court had intervened to reverse a racially biased Southern court.

Cross Cultural

# Environmental Racism: An Interpretation,

**the expression of racist assumptions in thought, action, or patterns of inaction, either in the formulation of environmental policy or the enforcement of environmental laws.**

The phrase *environmental racism* emerged in public usage to describe the circumstances surrounding a specific historical incident. In 1982 in North Carolina a plan was devised to collect 32,000 cubic yards of soil contaminated with polychlorinated biphenyls (PCBs) from 14 different locations throughout the state and to store it in a toxic waste facility in Warren County. The land chosen for the site had been owned predominantly by blacks since the time of slavery. It appeared to local residents that this site had been chosen not for its environmental suitability but rather because it was located in a poor, predominantly black, and politically powerless community.

State officials had not counted on the outrage or effectiveness of local citizens. Residents organized and protested the siting of the toxic dump, and more than 500 people were arrested in a large public demonstration protesting the implicit racism behind the choice of the Warren County location. The choice was considered a blatant example of the way in which communities of color are often doubly victimized in environmental matters: they are subjected to a disproportionate share of toxic pollutants and are also systematically excluded from decision-making processes affecting their own health and safety. Both the pattern of toxic dumping itself and the process of excluding communities of color from discussions of environmental policy came to be known as forms of environmental racism.

The citizens' demonstration against the Warren County dumping empowered other communities to examine their own circumstances. As communities of color across the United States and around the world have spoken up about similar patterns of environmental victimization and exclusion in decision-making processes, environmental racism has come to be understood as a pervasive and endemic feature of modern industrial society. Perhaps most important, it has become apparent that while individuals may express environmental racism in their assumptions or behavior from time to time, it is more common for environmental racism to manifest itself as a form of institutionalized racism. Institutional racism is a pattern of collective thought, action, or inaction characteristic of institutions like municipalities, state governments, private corporations, or national or international regulatory and enforcement agencies. Thus, individuals in management or decision-making positions in these institutions may not personally be racist, yet by acting to execute the established priorities of their institutions they may unwillingly or unwittingly perpetuate and extend patterns of environmental inequity and injustice—in short, they may propagate environmental racism.

Numerous studies since the 1982 Warren County incident provide further examples of environmental racism. At the request of Congressman Walter Fauntroy, the United States General Accounting Office conducted a study in 1983 of eight Southern states to examine the relation between the location of hazardous waste landfills and the racial and economic status of the surrounding communities. The results revealed a clear bias in the placement of the landfills: three of every four landfills were located near communities populated predominantly by minorities. In 1987 the Commission on Racial Justice of the United Church of Christ published a study titled "Toxic Wastes and Race in the United States," which pointed to the fact that 60 percent of black and Hispanic Americans live in communities with uncontrolled toxic waste sites.

In both urban and rural settings around the United States, communities of color and minorities have experienced levels of risk far higher than the norm in the society as a whole. Sociologist Robert Bullard has summarized the problem: "A growing body of studies clearly show that communities of color bear a disproportionate burden of pollution problems in the United States. Communities of color are adversely affected by industrial toxins, dirty air and drinking water, and the location of municipal landfills, incinerators, and hazardous waste treatment, disposal, and storage facilities."

Environmental racism is not confined only to the United States. Indeed, some of the most egregious examples of this elitist planning come from areas of the world formerly under colonial domination or currently subject to patterns of corporate exploitation with little or no governmental oversight or control. A striking example of this kind involves the Shell Oil Company's treatment of the Ogoni people of southeastern Nigeria. For more than a decade Shell's oil extraction practices polluted the Ogoni's land and water and damaged their health and welfare. In response, the Ogoni organized the Movement for the Survival of the Ogoni People (MOSOP), led by writer and activist Ken SaroWiwa. On November 10, 1995, SaroWiwa was executed by the Nigerian government on what many regarded as trumped-up charges despite the vocal objection of numerous social justice, environmental, and human rights organizations worldwide. In this instance both the Nigerian government and Shell Oil were considered responsible for the pattern of environmental racism in eastern Nigeria.

To combat specific cases of environmental racism as well as the institutional habits of thought, action, and inaction that work to perpetuate the problem, environmental justice, or "ecojustice," movements have emerged within the United States and around the world. In October 1991 the First National People of Color Environmental Leadership Summit, held in Washington, D.C., issued a formal declaration of the Principles of Environmental Justice, which clarified and publicly recognized the problem of environmental racism in America. Partially in response to this milestone declaration, in February 1994 President Bill Clinton issued Executive Order 12898 with a specific mandate for federal agencies: " . . . each Federal agency shall make achieving environmental justice part of its mission by identifying and addressing, as appropriate, disproportionately high and adverse human health or environmental effects of its programs, policies, and activities on minority populations and low-income populations in the United States . . . . "

Following the official governmental order, private environmental action groups and resource centers have begun to document instances of environmental injustice and help communities organize themselves to resist environmental racism. The Environmental Justice Resource Center (EJRC) of Clark Atlanta University, under the direction of Robert Bullard, has taken a leadership role in this respect, producing two editions of the important People of Color Environmental Groups Directory. In addition, the National Council of Churches has provided resources for its member groups to act on ecojustice issues, and the EcoJustice Network and the Working Group on Environmental Justice have created sites on the World Wide Web, providing public access to information about environmental justice and environmental racism.

---

Cross Cultural

# Eugenics,

**a scientific and social movement whose central tenet ascribes human behavior to genetic makeup and which supports social policies to maintain "racial hygiene."**

The philosophy behind the eugenics movement is that intelligence, health, and social behavior are determined solely by genetic makeup. Popular in the United States, England, and Germany from early in the twentieth century until World War II, eugenics dismisses the influence of social and economic factors on human behavior and advocates policies aimed at maintaining the "fitness" of a "superior" racial stock—that of white Anglo-Saxons.

British biologist Francis Galton coined the term *eugenics* in 1883 to describe his research on a trait he was convinced had been passed down through the generations of his own family—genius. Like other biologists of the time, Galton's interest in human heredity was piqued by the theories of species evolution outlined in Charles Darwin's classic treatise *On the Origin of the Species by Means of Natural Selection* (1859). Darwin's followers' application of his views to politics and economics, which has come to be known as social Darwinism, was the precursor to eugenics. Social Darwinists espoused a competitive model of species evolution summarized in the belief in "survival of the fittest." Because weaker, recessive genetic material would be naturally weeded out, the healthiness of a race would be ensured.

Social Darwinism's *laissez faire* attitude toward evolution distinguished it from the aggressive policies of the eugenics movement, which sought ways to intervene in human behavior to maintain "racial health." Eugenics aimed to institutionalize methods to ensure the continued "improvement" of the white race. Two branches of the field emerged to facilitate this, "positive" and "negative" eugenics. According to eugenicists, through positive eugenics, the stock of genetically healthy individuals would be improved and increased through selective breeding procedures. Negative eugenics was applied to unhealthy individuals. Through anti-miscegenation laws, curtailing immigration from countries considered to harbor weaker genetic material, forced sterilization, and mercy killings, negative eugenics would restrain the reproduction of the genetically unfit.

Early in the twentieth century the eugenics movement quickly gained public support in the United States, Germany, and Britain. The United States' first sterilization law was passed in 1907 in Indiana. Three years later, Charles Davenport, the doyen of the American eugenics movement, opened the Eugenics Record Office in Cold Spring Harbor, New York. Through the office, Davenport, a strong promoter of forced sterilization, meticulously reported on what he believed to be the intellectual degeneracy of the poor, criminals, and a range of ethnic and racial communities.

Numerous states enacted antimiscegenation and sterilization laws between 1911 and 1930. The infamous *Buck v. Bell* Supreme Court case of 1927, in which Justice Oliver Wendell Holmes authorized the sterilization of a Virginia woman on the grounds that "three generations of imbeciles" was enough, led to thousands of forced sterilizations across the country. The crowning moment of the U.S. eugenics movement was the passage of the Immigration and Restriction Act of 1924. Supported by a coalition of eugenicists and corporate interests concerned with American standards of "racial hygiene," it effectively barred immigration from Eastern European and Mediterranean countries by instituting drastically reduced quotas.

Eugenics has been largely discredited since World War II. The atrocities committed by the Nazis during the Holocaust forced a rethinking of eugenics policies. Contemporary geneticists now view human behavior as determined by a complex interaction of biological, social, and economic factors. Beliefs in the innate power of race in influencing human behavior have been debunked. The central tenets of eugenics still persist, however. The publication in 1994 of Richard J. Herrnstein and Charles Murray's controversial *The Bell Curve: Intelligence and Class Structure in American Life*, demonstrates the continued appeal of biological explanations of human behavior.

North America

## *Eyes on the Prize,*

award-winning PBS television series documenting the Civil Rights Movement from 1954 to 1965.

Following its release in 1987, *Eyes on the Prize* became the most celebrated documentary series in the history of public television. Many reviewers hailed the documentary as the finest depiction to date of the civil rights era. Carolyn Fluehr-Lobban of American Anthropologist wrote that what distinguishes the series from its predecessors "is not only its comprehensive grasp of the civil rights period, but its fair and equal representation of all of the signal events and the heroes and heroines of the Civil Rights Movement." The series won more than 20 awards, including the Peabody Award and the DuPont-Columbia Award, and has become a standard reference source in American libraries and schools.

Produced by African American Henry Hampton of Blackside, Inc., *Eyes on the Prize* comprises six one-hour television programs. It covers the 11 years between the landmark 1954 Supreme Court ruling to desegregate schools and, in 1965, the march from Selma to Montgomery and passage of the Voting Rights Act. Narrated by civil rights activist Julian Bond, the series combines archival films, newsreels, photographs, and interviews with those involved in the events. To accompany the series, Viking/Penguin published two guides for instructional use: *Eyes on the Prize: America's Civil Rights Years* by Juan Williams and *A Reader and Guide: Eyes on the Prize* edited by Clayborne Carson.

In 1990 Hampton produced *Eyes on the Prize II*, which chronicles the continuing civil rights struggles of African Americans from 1965 to 1985.

# Fair Employment Practices Committee

**(1941–1946), a short-lived United States federal agency charged with investigating and correcting discrimination in the defense and other industries, established in response to A. Philip Randolph's March on Washington Movement.**

Since the United States entered World War I in 1917, African Americans had protested both the segregation of the U.S. military and the rampant job discrimination in the war-powered defense industries. A number of black leaders, among them A. Philip Randolph—president of the Brotherhood of Sleeping Car Porters (BSCP), the first African American labor union—saw such inequities as symptomatic of the dismal economic situation most African Americans faced. Black workers, often the last hired and first fired, had been disproportionately affected by the Great Depression of the 1930s, and for most work remained an important issue. As the country prepared to enter World War II, Randolph spearheaded a movement that sought economic justice for African Americans.

Along with Walter White, secretary of the National Association for the Advancement of Colored People (NAACP), and T. Arnold Hill, of the National Urban League, Randolph asked President Franklin D. Roosevelt to end segregation in the armed forces and open wartime jobs to black workers. After a disappointing first meeting with Roosevelt in September 1940, Randolph began to plan what became known as the March on Washington Movement, issuing a call for a "March on Washington for jobs in national defense and equal integration in the fighting forces of the United States." Randolph wrote that the demonstration would "shake up official Washington," "gain respect for the Negro people," and build "self-respect among Negroes." With the help of BSCP members—who numbered around 10,000—Randolph sought to mobilize at least that many to march on July 1, 1941.

To avoid the embarrassing attention such a large demonstration would attract, Roosevelt met again with Randolph and White on June 18. This time, with the threat of the march—its size now predicted at 100,000 by

White—hanging over him, the president capitulated. On June 25 Roosevelt issued Executive Order 8802, which outlawed discrimination in "the employment of workers in defense industries or government" and provided for the creation of a Fair Employment Practices Committee (the FEPC, originally called the President's Committee on Fair Employment Practices). It did not, however, affect the position of blacks in the military, which was not desegregated until 1948.

The FEPC was responsible for enforcing the anti-discrimination law, and in so doing conducted investigations, gathered evidence, and reported abuses. It is not clear, however, exactly how effective the FEPC proved in curtailing government job discrimination, although the number of African Americans working for the federal government grew rapidly in the 1940s. Originally composed of two black and two white members, as the FEPC grew larger only white members were added. Milton Webster, vice president of the BSCP, and NAACP activists Clarence M. Mitchell Jr. and Charles H. Houston were among the African Americans who filled the perpetual two black slots on the FEPC.

The FEPC lost power throughout its brief existence, twice facing reorganization, and was disbanded in 1946. Despite its failure to become permanent—bills to establish a permanent FEPC failed to pass the U.S. Senate in 1946, 1950, and 1952—the FEPC inspired a host of state agencies. The March on Washington Movement that was directly responsible for its creation continued, and found new expression in the Civil Rights Movement of the 1960s, mostly notably in the landmark March on Washington of 1963.

North America
<hr>

# Farmer, James

**(b. January 12, 1920, Marshall, Tex.; d. July 9, 1999, Fredericksburg, Va.), educator, administrator, and founder of the Congress of Racial Equality (CORE).**

Raised in an environment that valued education and religious faith, James Farmer was an outstanding student. After skipping several grades in elementary school, at age 14 he entered Wiley College in Marshall, Texas (where his father, one of the few African American Ph.D.s in the South, had taught). Graduating in 1938, Farmer went on to Howard University's School of Religion. He graduated from Howard in 1941. Farmer opposed war in general, and more specifically objected to serving in the segregated armed forces. When the United States entered World War II later that year, he applied for conscientious objector status but found that he was deferred from the draft because he had a divinity degree.

Rather than become an ordained Methodist minister, Farmer, who told his father he would rather fight that church's policy of segregated congregations, chose to go to work for the Fellowship of Reconciliation (FOR). Farmer was FOR's secretary for race relations, helping the Quaker, pacifist organization craft its responses to such social ills as war, violence, bigotry, and poverty. It was a job that left Farmer, who was then living in Chicago, Illinois, enough time to begin forming his own approach to these issues—

one based less on FOR's religious pacifism than on the principle of nonviolent resistance.

Founded in 1942, Farmer's new group, CORE, was at first called the Committee on Racial Equality; the name was later changed to the Congress of Racial Equality. Using pacifist techniques borrowed from the Indian nationalist leader Mohandas K. Gandhi, CORE members sought to end racial segregation and discrimination by putting their bodies on the line. Some of CORE's first actions included restaurant sit-ins, in which African American and mixed-race groups tried to be served at various Chicago restaurants, where, despite civil rights statutes on the books in Illinois, many of the establishments still refused to serve black customers. CORE's sit-ins were so successful that they greatly influenced student activists nearly 20 years later.

In addition to sit-ins, stand-ins, and boycotts, CORE pioneered the technique called Freedom Rides. Starting in the late 1940s and most famously used in 1961, Freedom Rides tested the legality of segregation on interstate transportation in the South. Always risking violent retaliation and often enduring jail for their efforts, CORE members were specially trained to maintain a peaceful, nonviolent demeanor. Their work led to the desegregation of more than 100 Southern bus terminals.

CORE also worked with other civil rights groups on issues such as school desegregation, voter registration, and job training (most notably during 1964, known as Freedom Summer, when CORE collaborated with the Student Nonviolent Coordinating Committee [SNCC]). By the late 1960s, however, Farmer, seeing CORE drift away from its Gandhian roots, left the organization he had founded and had led for more than 20 years. Always an active writer and speaker, he continued to lecture publicly on civil rights and eventually took a teaching position at Lincoln University in Pennsylvania. In 1968 Farmer ran for the United States Congress on the Liberal Party ticket and was defeated by Shirley Chisholm, an African American running as a Democrat. He went to work for Republican president Richard M. Nixon's administration as assistant secretary of health, education, and welfare shortly thereafter.

In the years since retiring from politics (1971), Farmer served on many organizational boards, including the Coalition of American Public Employees. He also continued to teach and lecture widely. In 1985 he published his autobiography, titled *Lay Bare the Heart*, and in 1998 President Bill Clinton awarded him the Congressional Medal of Freedom. Farmer died a year later.

North America

## Farrakhan, Louis Abdul

(Louis Eugene Walcott; b. May 17, 1933, Bronx, N.Y.), African American religious leader, head of the Nation of Islam, a black religious organization in the United States that combines some of the practices and beliefs of Islam with a philosophy of black separatism.

Louis Farrakhan preaches the virtues of personal responsibility, especially for black men, and advocates black self-sufficiency. His message has appealed primarily to urban blacks, and draws on a long history of black nationalists who have called for black self-reliance in the face of economic injustice and white racism. His more inflammatory remarks have caused critics to claim that he has appealed to black racism and anti-Semitism to promote his views.

Born Louis Eugene Walcott in New York City, Farrakhan grew up in Boston, Massachusetts. He attended Winston-Salem Teacher's College in North Carolina, and worked as a nightclub singer in the early 1950s. In 1955 Malcolm X, a minister for the Nation of Islam, convinced Walcott to join the organization. Walcott dropped his last name and became known as Minister Louis X. The practice of dropping surnames is common among black Muslims, who often view them as names that were imposed on slaves and handed down over the years by white society. He later adopted the name Abdul Haleem Farrakhan and came to be known as Louis Farrakhan.

Farrakhan's speaking and singing abilities helped him to rise to prominence within the Nation of Islam, and he led the group's mosque in Boston, Massachusetts. In 1963 a split developed between Malcolm X and Elijah Muhammad, the leader of the Nation of Islam, and Malcolm X was suspended as a minister. Malcolm X had become increasingly dissatisfied with the group's failure to participate in the growing Civil Rights Movement, and Muhammad seemed threatened by the growing popularity of Malcolm X. Farrakhan sided with Muhammad in this dispute. In 1964 Malcolm X left the Nation of Islam and formed a new group, the Organization of Afro-American Unity (OAAU). Farrakhan publicly criticized Malcolm X for his break with the Nation of Islam. In 1965 Malcolm X was assassinated while addressing an OAAU rally in New York City. Three black Muslims were eventually convicted and jailed for the killing. While Farrakhan denied any connection with the shooting and never faced any charges related to Malcolm X's death, he later conceded that he had helped to create an atmosphere that may have induced others to carry out the assassination.

After the death of Malcolm X, Farrakhan became the head of a large mosque in Harlem, a neighborhood in New York City, and was the principal spokesperson for Muhammad. Farrakhan held high office in the Nation of Islam until Muhammad died in 1975. Muhammad's son, Wallace Muhammad, succeeded his father and asked Farrakhan to move to Chicago to assume a new national position. Wallace Muhammad downplayed Black Nationalism, admitted non-black members, and stressed strict Islamic beliefs and practices. Under Wallace Muhammad, the group's name changed to the World Community of Islam in the West, and later, to the American Muslim Mission.

In the late 1970s Farrakhan led a dissident faction within the organization that opposed any changes in the major beliefs and programs that had been instituted by Elijah Muhammad. In 1978 Farrakhan left Wallace Muhammad's organization and formed a new organization that assumed the original name, the Nation of Islam, and reasserted the principles of black separatism.

Farrakhan's public profile rose throughout the 1980s as he established new mosques, used radio appearances to increase his following in black communities, and was the featured speaker at events that often drew large crowds. His message of black self-reliance and mistrust of whites struck a responsive chord among young urban blacks, many of whom viewed Farrakhan as a courageous leader willing to confront a racist society. His followers praised his insistence that blacks assume moral and economic responsibility for themselves—that they avoid drugs and crime; that they provide for their children; that they stay in school and become involved in their communities.

Controversy surrounding the Nation of Islam also grew, primarily because Farrakhan attacked white society and voiced the anti-Semitism growing among some blacks in the inner cities. He was once quoted as calling Judaism a "gutter religion" and referred to German dictator Adolf Hitler, who was responsible for killing millions of Jews, as a great man. Farrakhan's controversial remarks on the radio and at press conferences were widely condemned by other black leaders.

In the 1990s Farrakhan continued his call for poor blacks to make stronger commitments to education and to their families. He also called on blacks to end black-on-black crime and to be less dependent on government welfare. In October 1995 Farrakhan organized the Million Man March in Washington, D.C. At the march, hundreds of thousands of black men vowed to renew their commitments to family, community, and personal responsibility. Although the march renewed criticism of Farrakhan's anti-Semitic statements and some black leaders refused to participate, it was widely regarded as a successful display of black solidarity. It helped Farrakhan move closer to the political mainstream, and some people also saw it as indicating the strength of his appeal to a significant segment of the black population.

In January 1996 Farrakhan made a 20-nation "world friendship tour" that included stops in Iran, Libya, and Iraq—all nations that the United States government regarded as pariah states run by dictators. On the tour Farrakhan repeatedly criticized the U.S. government, provoking condemnation by U.S. officials.

North America

# Feminism in the United States

"Shall it any longer be said of the daughters of Africa, they have no ambition, they have no force?" asked Maria W. Stewart in 1831. "By no means," she answered. "Let every female heart become united." Stewart's call for black women's unity, together with calls offered by other prominent nineteenth-century black feminists such as Sojourner Truth, Mary Ann Shadd Cary, Harriet Tubman, and Lucy C. Laney, marked the origins of black feminism in the United States. These nineteenth-century black women laid the intellectual and political cornerstone of black feminism, but African American women in the twentieth century brought black feminism as a political movement, and black feminist thought as its intellectual voice and vision, to full fruition.

## What Is Black Feminism?

Black feminism originated in the lived experiences that enslaved African women brought with them to the United States in the eighteenth and early nineteenth centuries. African women were socialized to be independent, self-reliant, and resourceful. While this African feminism was modified by slavery, being enslaved also encouraged black women to maintain these key elements of their African self-definitions as women.

Black feminism is the process of self-conscious struggle that empowers women and men to realize a humanistic vision of community. African American women's experiences with work and family during slavery and after emancipation led them to develop a specific perspective on the relationships between multiple types of oppression. Black women experienced not just racism but sexism, classism, and other forms of oppression. This struggle fostered a broader, more humanistic view of community that encouraged each person to develop his or her own individual, unique human potential. Such a community is based on notions of fairness, equality, and justice for all human beings, not just African American women. Black feminism's fundamental goal of creating a humanistic vision of community is more comprehensive than that of other social action movements. For example, unlike the women's movement in the United States, black feminism has not striven solely to secure equal rights for women and men, because gaining rights equal to those of black men would not necessarily lead to liberation for African American women. Instead, black feminism encompasses a comprehensive, anti-sexist, antiracist, and anti-elitist perspective on social change. Black feminism is a means for human empowerment rather than an end in and of itself.

## Core Themes in Black Feminism

Since its inception in the early 1800s black feminism has reflected a uniformity of theme and philosophical outlook. Despite differences of age, sexual orientation, ethnicity, and regional origin within the country, all black women share the universal experience of being African American women in a society that denigrates women of African descent. This commonality of experience suggests that certain characteristic themes will shape black women's thought and activism. Contemporary black feminist scholars' efforts to reclaim a long-standing yet suppressed black feminist intellectual tradition reveal black women's historical attention to four core themes: the legacy of struggle, the search for voice, the interdependence of thought and action, and the significance of empowerment in everyday life.

One core theme has been the legacy of struggle against racism, sexism, and social class exploitation. Despite heterogeneity within the community, this legacy has fostered a heightened consciousness among black women intellectuals about the importance of thinking inclusively about how race, class, and gender shape black women's lives. The legacy of struggle against racism, sexism, and classism is a common thread binding African American women regardless of historical era, age, social class, or sexual orientation.

This legacy of struggle and its resulting humanistic vision differentiate black feminism from historical expressions of white feminism in the United States. While middle-class white feminists condemn the restrictions of affluence, most black women struggle against the oppression of racism and poverty. As a result, black feminists' central concern has been the transformation of societal relations based on race, class, and gender.

The search for voice or the refusal of black women to remain silenced constitutes a second core theme of black feminism. In order to exploit black women, dominant groups have developed controlling images or stereotypes claiming that black women are inferior. Because they justify black women's oppression, four interrelated controlling images of black women—the mammy, the matriarch, the welfare mother, and the jezebel—reflect the dominant group's interest in maintaining black women's subordination. Challenging these stereotypes has been an essential part of the search for voice.

Black women's lives involve a series of negotiations aimed at reconciling the contradictions of their own internally defined images of self as black women with these controlling images. Much black feminist thought reflects this search for a self-defined voice that expresses a black feminist standpoint. Being labeled "black women" makes African American women especially visible and exposes them to the negative treatment afforded black women as a group. From their experiences black women have developed a unique vision and voice that many have used as a source of strength. The controlling images of black women are so negative that they require resistance if black women are to have any positive self-images. For African American women, the search for voice emerges from the struggle to reject controlling images and embrace knowledge that is essential to their survival.

Another core theme is the impossibility of separating intellectual inquiry from political activism. This theme of the interdependence of thought and action stresses the connections between black women's ideas and their actions. Historically, black feminism has merged the two forms of expression by espousing a both/and orientation that views thought and action as a part of the same process. This both/and orientation grows from black women's experiences living as both African Americans and women, and, in many cases, in poverty. It is this interrelationship between thought and action that allows black women to see the connections among concrete experiences with oppression, to develop a self-defined voice related to those experiences, and to enact the resistance that can follow.

The last core theme in black feminism is empowerment in the context of everyday life. Black feminism cannot challenge race, gender, and class oppression without empowering black women to take action in everyday life. Black feminist thought sees black women's oppression and their resistance to oppression as inextricably linked. Thus, oppression responds to human action. Black feminist thought views the world as a dynamic place where the goal is not merely to survive or fit in, but to experience ownership and accountability. The very existence of black feminism suggests that black women always have a choice and the power to act, no matter how bleak a situation may appear to be. It also shows that although the empowerment of individual black women is important, only collective action can effectively eradicate long-standing political, social, and economic inequalities.

Empowerment for African American women is achieved through a variety of methods. Empowerment occurs when a formerly silent black mother in the inner city complains to school officials about her child's treatment. Empowerment happens when black women take organized political action through churches, sororities, community advocacy groups, civil rights organizations, and unions. Black feminism can incorporate a variety of political strategies to bring about a more humanistic and just community. The program is not built into the philosophy itself. Instead, the adage "make a way out of no way" captures the range of strategies pursued by African American women to empower themselves and others.

Despite its overall consistency of thematic expression, black feminism has not been expressed in the same way across different historical periods. Black feminism in the twentieth century can be divided into three major periods: Laying the Foundation (1890–1920), when black women organized a national political movement and first articulated black feminist thought; Working for Change (1920–1960), when black women advanced the humanistic vision in black feminist thought primarily within African American communities; and Contemporary Black Feminism (1960–present), when black feminism as a political movement and black feminist thought as its intellectual voice emerge. Each period has its own specific set of historical issues, distinctive organizational and institutional locations, and a resulting unique expression of the core themes of black feminist thought.

## Laying the Foundation: 1890–1920

During the period from 1890 to 1920 African Americans organized on the national level, aiming to "live as we climb." The growth of Jim Crow segregation in schools, employment, political life, and public accommodations heralded deteriorating conditions in the South and fostered a mass migration of blacks to cities of the North. This increasing urbanization created African American communities that could support a range of ideas and organizations.

Politically, women struggled for suffrage and African Americans demanded political and civil rights, an end to the terrorism of lynching, and adequate standards of living. Spurred on by these catalysts, middle-class black women began to organize on a local level to undertake educational, philanthropic, and welfare activities. Black women's clubs were founded in a number of cities. The growth of black urban communities and the urgent needs of the poor gave rise to a national black women's club movement.

The National Federation of Afro-American Women was founded in 1896 and elected Margaret Murray Washington as its president. The National League of Colored Women was founded in Washington, D.C., in 1892. Together these two organizations represented more than 100 local black women's clubs. After their merger into the National Association of Colored Women (NACW) in 1896, Mary Church Terrell was elected president. The NACW became a unifying force, an authoritative voice in defense of black womanhood.

The black women's club movement was both an activist and intellectual endeavor. The leadership of the national organization worked not only to eliminate black women's oppression but also to produce analyses of that oppression. The work of these black feminist intellectuals was influenced by the four core themes of black feminism, particularly the merger of action and theory. The activities of early-twentieth-century black women such as Ida B. Wells, Fannie Barrier Williams, Mary Terrell, Anna Julia Cooper, and others illustrate that theme. These women produced analyses of subjects as diverse as the struggle for education, sexual politics and violence, race pride, racial prejudice, the importance of black women collectively defining black womanhood, and inclusion in white women's organizations. Since the vast majority of African American women in the early twentieth century were burdened both by long hours in either agricultural or domestic work and by shouldering the responsibilities of caring for families, they had little time to engage in either theorizing or organizing. The activities of the club women on behalf of all African American women, not just those of the middle class, remain noteworthy.

African American women in the black women's club movement did not identify themselves as black feminists. The concept shared by Wells, Terrell, and Cooper was much closer to Sojourner Truth's perspective—"I suppose I am about the only colored woman that goes about to speak for the rights of the colored women"—than to that of today's black feminists. Yet these women did construct and shape black feminism as a political movement and black feminist thought as its intellectual voice and vision.

To lay the foundation for black feminism, black women leaders challenged black women to reject the negative images of black womanhood so prominent in their times. Cooper, a black woman born into slavery and the recipient of an M.A. from Oberlin College in 1884 and a Ph.D. in Latin from the Sorbonne in Paris, spent the bulk of her life as an educator. In her book *A Voice from the South*, she described black women's legacy of struggle against racism and sexism by protesting black women's vulnerability to sexual violence: "I would beg . . . to add my plea for the Colored Girls of the South:—that large, bright, promising, fatally beautiful class . . . so full of promise and possibilities, yet so sure of destruction; often without a father to whom they dare apply the loving term, often without a stronger brother to espouse their cause and defend their honor with his life's blood; in the midst of pitfalls and snares, waylaid by the lower classes of white men, with no shelter, no protection."

Refusing to be silenced, Fannie Barrier Williams, the first black woman admitted to the Women's Club of Chicago and organizer of the first training school for black women in Chicago, championed the power of self-definition at the turn of the century, a period of heightened racial repression. Williams viewed the black woman not as a defenseless victim but as a strong-willed resistor: "As meanly as she is thought of, hindered as she is in all directions, she is always doing something of merit and credit that is not expected of her." She saw the black woman as "irrepressible. She is insulted, but she holds up her head; she is scorned, but she proudly demands respect . . . . The most interesting girl of this country is the Colored girl."

In their writings and teachings, early twentieth-century black feminists urged black women to forge their own self-definitions and to be independent and self-reliant. Through their actions in building a powerful national black women's club movement, they championed the utility of black women's relationships with one another in providing a community for black women's activism and self-determination. They analyzed why black women had such hard lives, and they empowered black women to make changes in their daily lives. This fusion of theory and activism is characteristic of black feminism, becoming the foundation on which subsequent black women were able to work for change.

## Working for Change: 1920–1960

The Great Depression, the New Deal, World War II, and the Civil Rights Movement all brought sweeping changes in African American community structures and corresponding shifts in the organizational bases for black feminism. Heightened *de jure* segregation in the South and *de facto* segregation in the North during this period meant that most African American women lived in highly segregated environments. Since the majority of black women worked in domestic service, their contact with white people, especially white women, afforded few opportunities for interracial interaction among equals. Until the resurgence of national organizing in the Civil Rights Movement of the 1960s, the decline of the black women's club movement in the 1920s left most black women with few options for participation in national political movements.

The period from 1920 to 1960 seemingly lacked a self-conscious black feminist movement that both identified itself as such and that explicitly advanced the core themes of black feminism. However, racism during the 1930s through the 1950s was so pervasive that black women advanced a black feminist agenda primarily through existing black organizations. High participation in the labor force coupled with substantial family responsibilities meant that most African American women during this period had little time or inclination to participate in organizations designed exclusively to address issues unique to black women. By far the largest number of African American women either worked within existing black organizations, such as churches or local self-help groups, or participated in black political movements to ensure that black women and men alike would be treated with dignity. Thus, while they lacked the overarching organizational structure of a strong, national black women's organization expressing a black women's position, black women undertook activism generally in the context of fostering local black community development.

Those women who engaged in political activities such as starting schools or organizations typically aimed at building black community institutions. While some organizations were designed to address issues unique to African American women, the majority aimed to serve both women and men. This choice does not make black women less feminist—instead, it represents the feminism inherent in black women's humanistic vision of community. Instead of just talking about inequality between women and men, these women built institutions based on black feminist principles. In keeping with the black feminist core theme of the fusion of theory and action, their feminism was embedded in their actions. By working on behalf of everyone, they were in effect working for black women.

Mary McLeod Bethune's work reflects the complexity of how black women of this period saw their special mission of working for black women. Elected president of NACW in 1924, Bethune continued efforts to acquire a federal antilynching bill, help rural women and those in industry, train clerks and typists, and support the rights of black women globally. Bethune's effort to build the Daytona School for Girls into the coeducational liberal arts school Bethune-Cookman College demonstrates her commitment to black community development and offers a glimpse of how many black women worked for change during this period. Still, Bethune's noteworthy influence on national politics foreshadowed the actions of black women in the contemporary period. Her life marks the transition from the foundation-laying activities of early twentieth-century black feminists to the broad-based activities characterizing contemporary black feminists.

Black women worked on behalf of the core themes of black feminist thought although they rarely described their work in these terms. Each core theme was woven through black women's political work and much of everyday life. For example, black women working in the Civil Rights Movement during the 1950s advanced the humanistic vision of community in black feminist thought. Women like Fannie Lou Hamer, Rosa Parks, Ella J. Baker, and Septima Clark were tireless workers for black community development. Since it came out of church groups, the movement was carried largely by women. Many rural black women showed extreme courage. "Dyin' is all right," said Mary Dora Jones, who was told that her house would be burned down if she continued to let civil rights workers stay there. "Ain't but one thing 'bout dyin'. That's make sho' you right, 'cause you gon' die anyway." A similar view was expressed by Hamer, the daughter of sharecroppers and a Mississippi civil rights activist: "The only thing they could do to me was kill me, and it seemed like they'd been trying to do that a little bit at a time ever since I could remember." Women like Jones and Hamer did not call themselves "black feminists"—this naming occurred in a later period—but they clearly lived the core themes of black feminism through their actions.

The search for voice and the refusal to be silenced pervade the words and actions of a range of women throughout this period. For example, Jones, Hamer, and numerous women in the civil rights struggle used their voices to challenge white racism. Other women fostered a black feminist agenda by refusing to be silenced, even within the context of black-controlled organizations. Black feminist activist Pauli Murray was president of the 1944 class at the Howard University School of Law. Since she was also the only woman, she did not receive the same privileges as her black male classmates. The discovery of this fact, remembers Murray, "aroused an incipient feminism in me long before I knew the meaning of the term 'feminism.'"

In other cases black women acquired wide-ranging influence within black organizations and used their status to advance women's issues. For example, in the 1920s Amy Jacques Garvey's women's page in the Negro World, the newspaper of the Universal Negro Improvement Association, took a strong women's rights position. As Paula Giddings notes, "while she held no specific office, it would have been hard to find anyone with greater influence in the UNIA, save for Marcus Garvey himself."

The refusal to be silenced was not confined to women in political movements. Zora Neale Hurston's work, especially her widely read 1937 novel, *Their Eyes Were Watching God*, aimed to give voice to black women's thought through fiction. By placing black women's issues in the center of their work, other black women writers of this period—including Ann Petry in *The Street* (1946), Gwendolyn Brooks in *Maud Martha* (1953), and Lorraine Hansberry in *A Raisin in the Sun* (1959)—explored a black woman's standpoint as something framed by both blackness and womanhood.

A black feminist emphasis on the importance of empowerment in the context of everyday life finds expression in multiple locations during this period. For example, Ella Baker, a major figure in the Civil Rights Movement who worked closely with students, believed that teaching people how to be self-reliant fosters more empowerment than teaching them how to follow. Baker recounts how she nurtured the empowerment of student civil rights workers: "I never intervened between the struggles if I could avoid it. Most of the youngsters had been trained to believe in or to follow adults if they could. I felt they ought to have a chance to learn to think things through and to make the decisions." Baker and Clark were particularly consistent in forwarding a humanistic vision of community through their leadership styles.

## Contemporary Black Feminism: 1960–Present

The fundamental distinguishing feature of contemporary black feminism is the self-conscious voicing of black feminist perspectives. Though turn-of-the-century black women laid the organizational framework of institutions and ideas on which subsequent black women built, until recently African American women neither called themselves black feminists nor identified what they were doing as working on behalf of black feminism. They worked on behalf of black women and advanced a black feminist agenda, but they refused to be categorized as solely advancing the special interests of any one group. In contrast, the contemporary period is characterized by the emergence of a broad-based movement that encompasses both traditional humanistic approaches and issues unique to black women. Contemporary black feminism embraces the key contributions of the two prior periods: articulating a black women's agenda and building an organizational base to advance core themes of black feminism. Contemporary black feminism expresses and gives voice to this long-standing, preexisting intellectual and political movement.

Contemporary black feminism advances the same core themes as its predecessors but does so from very different institutional locations and with a very different voice. Two major trends of the last 30 years fostered these changes. First, increasing social-class stratification among black women made more women available to think about and work on behalf of black feminist concerns. Black women graduated from high schools and colleges in record numbers, and they were no longer placed exclusively in domestic service jobs. Instead, they occupied previously unavailable positions, especially in academic institutions. The emergence of a sizable group of literate, middle-class black women meant that black feminist thought as the intellectual component of black feminism could be more readily advanced. This does not mean that only middle-class black women embrace black feminism. Rather, differential access to resources shapes black women's abilities to bring black feminism to voice.

Second, black women's growing sense of disenchantment with the racism in the women's movement and the sexism in the Civil Rights and Black Nationalist Movements led to a growing focus on black women's concerns. Specifically, black women in male-controlled nationalist organizations became increasingly unwilling to trade their silence for an ill-defined unity. Similarly, the narrow scope of the early phase of the contemporary women's movement—expressing the concerns of white middle-class women—held little appeal. African American women perceived that neither black organizations nor white feminist groups spoke fully for them. Thus emerged the need to develop a distinctive black feminist agenda that built on the core themes long guiding black women's actions yet simultaneously spoke to issues specific to African American women.

Contemporary black feminism dates to the efforts of numerous trailblazing African American women in the 1970s who stated black women's concerns as women. While these far-reaching efforts did not constitute a black feminist agenda per se, they did contain the powerful precursors of one. Toni Cade Bambara's publication of *The Black Woman: An Anthology* in 1970 marked the beginnings of a black feminist agenda. The black women in her anthology raise many issues still being explored today. For example, Frances Beale's article "Double Jeopardy: To Be Black and Female" provides a summary of race, class, and gender as interconnected oppressions. Several works of fiction also served to articulate black feminist thought. Ntozake Shange's 1975 choreopoem *For Colored Girls Who Have Considered Suicide/When the Rainbow Is Enuf*, Toni Morrison's 1970 novel *The Bluest Eye*, and Alice Walker's 1976 novel *Meridian* all raise issues specific to black women that have significance beyond black women. Echoing *Tomorrow's Tomorrow*—Joyce Ladner's groundbreaking 1972 study of black adolescent girls—social science researchers like Bonnie Thornton Dill, LaFrances Rodgers-Rose, and Cheryl Townsend Gilkes centered their work on the lives of African American women. Historians, including Jeanne Noble, Sharon Harley, Rosalyn Terborg-Penn, Darlene Clark Hine, and Elsa Barkley Brown, showed a willingness to ground their research in the lives and experiences of African American women. Paula Giddings's *When and Where I Enter: The Impact of Black Women on Race and Sex in America* (1984) provided an especially important synthesis of African American women's history. Political figures were increasingly willing to discuss their politics in the race-, class-, and gender-specific black feminist framework. For example, Shirley

Chisholm's 1970 autobiography, *Unbought and Unbossed*, resonates with the core themes of black feminist thought.

Many black writers and scholars took the ideas first expressed in these diverse sources during the 1970s and began to hone them into black feminist theory. During the 1980s African American women developed black feminist thought by emphasizing the unique concerns of African American women and explicitly exploring the core themes in black feminist thought. Noteworthy examples of important contemporary works include Angela Davis's 1981 book on African American women's political economy, *Women, Race and Class*; bell hooks's 1981 analysis of black women and feminism, *Ain't I a Woman*; the groundbreaking 1982 essay by the Combahee River Col lective, "A Black Feminist Statement"; Alice Walker's 1983 *In Search of Our Mothers' Gardens*; Barbara Smith's 1983 anthology of black women's writings, *Home Girls: A Black Feminist Anthology*, dealing with the overlooked issue of black lesbianism; Audre Lorde's important 1984 collection of essays, *Sister Outsider*; the works of black feminist literary critics, like Barbara Christian's 1985 *Black Feminist Criticism, Perspectives on Black Women Writers* and Hazel Carby's 1987 *Reconstructing Womanhood*; June Jordan's collections of political essays, *Civil Wars in 1981* and *On Call in 1985*; and Filomina Chioma Steady's 1987 essay "African Feminism: A Worldwide Perspective." These works spoke to black women inside and outside academia who were developing black feminist thought.

By the 1980s the many decades spent building black feminism as a political movement and expressing its vision through black feminist thought had grown into a broad-based black women's movement located in a variety of organizational settings and expressing various interpretations of black feminism. While they choose multiple strategies, African American women of all types typically ground their actions in the core themes of black feminism.

Contemporary black feminism finds a home in multiple organizational settings. First, many black women belong to and remain active in traditional black women's organizations such as churches, sororities, and black women's clubs and local organizations. Others remain active in organizations devoted to black community development such as the National Association for the Advancement of Colored People and the National Urban League.

Second, this period marks the formation of new black women's organizations. Some are housed within professional associations, such as the Association of Black Women Historians. Others represent black women organized to focus on specific issues. For example, the National Black Feminist Organization, founded in 1973, explicitly addressed the concerns of black women. The National Coalition of 100 Black Women, founded in 1981, focuses on voter registration and mobilization.

Third, black feminist intellectuals in academia have used their writings and teachings as vehicles for the spread of black feminism. *All the Women Are White, All the Blacks Are Men, But Some of Us Are Brave*, a 1982 anthology edited by Gloria T. Hull, Patricia Bell Scott, and Barbara Smith, was devoted to legitimizing black women's studies as a serious area of intellectual inquiry, and it offered a road map for black women academicians laboring to develop black feminist thought. Other works devoted to developing black women's studies and black feminist thought include *Black Womanist Ethics*, by Katie Geneva Cannon (1988); *Talking Back: Thinking Feminist, Thinking Black*, by bell hooks (1989); *Women, Culture, and Politics*, by Angela Davis (1989); *Black Feminist Thought: Knowledge, Consciousness and the Politics of Empowerment*, by Patricia Hill Collins (1990); and *Invisibility Blues*, by Michele Wallace (1990).

Fourth, black feminists have become actively involved in the women's movement and have begun to influence its purpose and direction. National women's organizations such as the National Organization for Women and the National Women's Studies Association are increasing efforts to grapple with race and class in their push for gender equality.

Fifth, black women who have acquired recognition or leadership positions in organizations and institutions that do not appear to be dealing directly with black women's issues have often used their positions to advance black feminist agendas. For example, during her tenure as the national head of Planned Parenthood, Faye Wattleton typically did not identify herself as being a black feminist but did advance programs perceived by many to be highly beneficial for black women. Bernice Johnson Reagon's work in African and African American culture at the Smithsonian Institution attends to black women as creators of culture. Marian Wright Edelman's founding and astute stewardship of the Children's Defense Fund, one of the most respected advocacy organizations in Washington, D.C., offers a similar example. Wattleton, Reagon, and Edelman tap a legacy of struggle wherein challenging the interconnectedness of race, class, and gender is a central tenet. Black women musicians like the five vocalists and one sign language interpreter in Sweet Honey in the Rock, as well as emerging black female rappers like Sister Souljah and Queen Latifah, demonstrate a willingness to raise their voices in song about black feminism.

Moreover, many black women who have been successfully elected to public office, such as Shirley Chisholm and Cardiss Collins, or who hold other governmental positions, such as Eleanor Holmes Norton, Mary Frances Berry, and Patricia Roberts Harris, have used their positions to advance a black women's vision of a humanistic community.

To an extent that they have not in prior periods, black feminism as a political movement and black feminist thought as its intellectual voice and vision find multiple expression in diverse organizational settings in the contemporary era. As the community of African American women has grown more heterogeneous, so has the expression of black feminism. Thus the foundation laid by early black feminists has supported and nurtured the complex and growing movement of today.

North America

# Fifteenth Amendment to the United States Constitution,

amendment ratified on March 30, 1870, that guaranteed African American men the right to vote.

The Fifteenth Amendment states that "the right of citizens of the United States to vote shall not be denied or abridged by the United States or by a State on account of race, color, or previous condition of servitude." The text also gives Congress the power to enforce the amendment. Although African Americans had been freed from slavery and made citizens after the Civil War by the Thirteenth and Fourteenth Amendments, Southern states used a variety of tactics, including violence, to keep blacks from voting, and even some Northern states had not given blacks the franchise. Radical Republicans in Congress proposed the Fifteenth Amendment to rectify this problem.

Most people, blacks and whites alike, believed that the franchise was the best assurance of progress and success for the freed people. Most whites felt that the right to participate in the political process was, in fact, all the nation owed the former slaves. But debate immediately arose over how strongly worded the amendment should be. Many Republicans feared that if the language was not strong, the South would keep blacks from voting through such indirect means as poll taxes and violence. Other Republicans, however, believed that all states—Northern and Southern—should have the right to keep illiterate citizens from voting. (Many Northerners feared the growing influence of foreign immigrants and wanted the literacy test to limit their

This 1870 lithograph celebrating the passage of the Fifteenth Amendment shows recently emancipated African Americans engaged in education, work, and political life. *CORBIS*

power.) The resulting compromise was the Fourteenth Amendment, which was ratified with the help of Reconstruction governments in the South, but which soon proved incapable of guaranteeing the franchise for blacks.

For a brief period during Reconstruction many African Americans voted, and some were elected to public office. In the late 1870s, however, enthusiasm for ensuring black equality waned in both the North and the Republican Party, and by 1877, when federal troops were withdrawn from the South, blacks were left to the power of whites committed to "redeeming" the South—that is, to restoring white supremacy. To quash the black vote, Southern states employed the poll tax, which poor blacks (and whites) were hard-pressed to pay; the literacy test, which uneducated blacks were ill-equipped to pass; confusing election procedures, which were not explained to blacks; and the grandfather clause, which allowed anyone whose father or grandfather had been registered to vote before the Fifteenth Amendment—in other words, almost any white man—to continue voting even if he could not pay the poll tax or pass the literacy test.

Where these methods failed, Southerners established whites-only voting in party primaries (which guaranteed election as the South became over-whelmingly Democratic) or gerrymandered electoral districts, thus diluting the strength of black voters. Most effective were intimidation and violence, including cross burnings, forced unemployment, imprisonment on trumped-up charges, house and church burnings, rape, beatings, and murder.

Not until the twentieth century would the Supreme Court invoke the Fifteenth Amendment in striking down state grandfather clauses and white primaries. But such changes had little effect on black voting: during World War II, only 5 percent of Southern blacks were registered to vote. Not until the Voting Rights Act of 1965 did discrimination in voting begin to end and did courts enforce the Fifteenth Amendment.

North America

# Forman, James

(b. October 4, 1928, Chicago, Ill.), civil rights activist who is credited with giving the Student Nonviolent Coordinating Committee (SNCC) a firm organizational base.

While reporting for the *Chicago Defender* in 1960, James Forman learned of black farmers in Tennessee who had been evicted by their white landlords for registering to vote. In support, Forman joined a program sponsored by the Congress of Racial Equality (CORE) that provided relief services to the displaced farmers. Later that year, he participated in Freedom Rides, in which blacks rode in buses throughout the South testing court-ordered inte-gration of public transportation. Forman then joined SNCC and began working for black civil rights full time.

Having served in the air force during the Korean War, Forman possessed more maturity and experience than most of the young members of SNCC. His organizational skills thrust him into a leadership role at the organizationally weak SNCC, where he directed fundraising and supervised staff. In 1964 he became SNCC's executive secretary, a post he held until 1966. In addition, Forman participated in many of SNCC's direct-action protests and helped organize voter registration drives in Alabama and Mississippi. Soon after the Freedom Summer of 1964, however, arguments over SNCC's direction, strategies, and tactics consumed the organization's leaders. Amid this debate in 1968 Forman left SNCC to seek economic development opportunities for black communities.

Forman published his memoir of the Civil Rights Movement, *The Making of Black Revolutionaries: A Personal Account,* in 1972; a new edition was published in 1997. He earned a master's degree in African and African-American Studies at Cornell University in 1980 and a Ph.D. from the Union of Experimental Colleges and Universities (in cooperation with the Institute for Policy Studies) in Washington, D.C., in 1982. He crystallized his studies in his 1984 book, *Self Determination: An Examination of the Question and Its Application to the African-American People.* Forman has been active in the fight to gain statehood for the District of Columbia.

North America

# Fourteenth Amendment to the United States Constitution,

amendment ratified on July 28, 1868, that was intended to guarantee the civil rights of African Americans.

During the Civil War the Thirteenth Amendment freed Southern slaves, but after the war most blacks in the segregated South were able to realize little of their new freedom. President Andrew Johnson, who wanted to accommodate the defeated Confederate states, was reluctant to press the South for black equality. As a result, Radical Republicans in Congress drafted and secured passage of the Fourteenth Amendment. Their intent was partly to guarantee black freedom as granted by the Thirteenth Amendment and partly to limit the power of the reconstructed South.

The Fourteenth Amendment contains five sections, the heart of which is Section 1 (discussed below). Section 2 guarantees that if black men (or other male citizens) are denied the right to vote, their state's representation in Congress will be reduced proportionately. Section 2 was motivated by Republicans' fears that although blacks were now considered fully in the apportionment of representation to Congress (previously black men counted for only three-fifths of a person for congressional apportionment), because they were too intimidated to vote, the white South might gain more representation in Congress as a result of freeing the slaves. In fact, the North's fears proved correct, but Section 2 was never enforced. Section 3 forbids former Confederate soldiers to hold political office, but enforcement of this ban also turned out to be short-lived. Section 4 absolves the United States government of responsibility for the war debt of the Confederate states. Section 5 gives Congress the power to enforce the amendment.

Section 1, historically the most important of the sections, is divided into four main clauses. The first clause, known as the citizenship clause, grants state and federal citizenship to "all persons born or naturalized in the United States" with the exception of Native Americans. The citizenship clause was intended to undo Supreme Court rulings such as *Dred Scott v. Sanford* (1857), in which the court held that neither slaves nor their descendants were citizens of the United States.

The second clause, known as the privileges and immunities clause, holds that no state shall "abridge the privileges or immunities" of citizens. This was an attempt to keep Southern states from passing racially discriminatory laws. The full potential of the clause was never realized, however, because the Supreme Court ruled in 1873 that only the rights of federal citizenship were protected by the clause. States, said the court, were free to restrict the rights of state citizenship as they saw fit. Because most matters of everyday life were governed by states, the practical effect of the ruling was that schooling, housing, employment, and other immediate concerns were ruled by discriminatory state laws; federal law protected mostly uncommon circumstances, such as life on the high seas.

The third clause of Section 1, the due process clause, holds that states shall not "deprive any person of life, liberty, or property without due process of the law." A restatement of a similar clause in the Fifth Amendment, it soon opened a debate among scholars and judges about whether the clause was meant to "incorporate" the Bill of Rights into the Fourteenth Amendment. In other words, was the clause an attempt to apply the protections of the Bill of Rights to the states instead of just to the federal government? (In *Barron v. Baltimore* [1833], the Supreme Court had ruled that the Bill of Rights did not apply to state laws.) The debate over the due process clause has never been resolved, but judges in the 1960s and 1970s used it to secure some rights for blacks and other minorities, including several rights related to desegregation.

A fourth and final clause, the equal protection clause, provided the framework for many anti-discrimination rulings. The clause holds that no state shall "deny to any person within its jurisdiction the equal protection of the laws." In the late nineteenth century the equal protection clause was routinely ignored by states and finally rendered useless by the Supreme Court in *Plessy v. Ferguson* (1896). In *Plessy* the court established its doctrine that facilities could be "separate but equal"—that segregation alone did not violate the equal protection clause. More than half a century later, however, the court relied on the equal protection clause to reverse *Plessy*. In *Brown v. Board of Education* (1954) the court argued that segregation was "inherently unequal" and therefore a violation of the Fourteenth Amendment. Thus rehabilitated, the equal protection clause provided the basis for desegregation of schools and housing as well as reapportionment of unfairly drawn congressional districts. The equal protection clause has also been used to guarantee the right to birth control devices and abortions.

# Frazier, Edward Franklin

(b. September 24, 1894, Baltimore, Md.; d. May 17, 1962, Washington, D.C.),
sociologist and activist famed for his pioneering studies of black families and
his critique of the black middle class.

Taught from an early age that education was the key to both personal success and social justice, E. Franklin Frazier used his learning as a weapon
during his lifelong battle against racial inequality. In a tribute to Frazier, the
Journal of Negro Education called him "a non-confomist, a protester, a
gadfly." He attacked the pretension of the black middle class, went to jail for
picketing D. W. Griffith's film *The Birth of a Nation*, and publicly defended
W. E. B. Du Bois and Paul Robeson although to do so meant that he risked
being branded a communist.

Frazier grew up in Baltimore, Maryland, and attended Howard University on scholarship. Shortly after graduating from Howard with honors in
1916, he began his career as a professor. Despite teaching commitments
throughout the 1920s and 1930s, he earned a master's degree from Clark
University in 1920 and a Ph.D. in sociology from the University of Chicago
in 1931. From 1929 until 1934 he taught at Fisk University in Nashville,
Tennessee. In 1934 he was hired as the chair of the sociology department at
Howard, where he remained until his retirement in 1959.

*The Negro Family in the United States* (1939), Frazier's first influential
book, discredited the idea that problems such as illegitimacy, divorce, and
desertion could be traced to biological or cultural defects. Instead, Frazier
demonstrated that problems within black communities mirrored the shortcomings of American society as a whole. In 1949 he published *The Negro in
the United States*, the first comprehensive textbook on black experiences.

Frazier's most controversial book, *Black Bourgeoisie*, appeared in 1957.
This study concluded that the black middle class had earned "status without
substance" and criticized affluent blacks for abandoning the cause of social
equality in the hope of becoming part of the American elite. Despite
charges of racial disloyalty, Frazier continued to write about class differences
within black communities in an effort to provide a systematic account of
American race relations. His other books include *The Free Negro Family*
(1932), *Race and Culture Contacts in the Modern World* (1957), *The Negro
Church in America* (1963), and *On Race Relations: Selected Writings* (1968).
Frazier's research extended beyond the United States to include studies of
race and culture in Brazil and the West Indies. Additionally, he was instrumental in the development of African studies in the United States.

Not content to restrict his activities to the university, Frazier was always
a public intellectual. After a race riot in 1935, the mayor of New York City
appointed him to conduct a survey for the Commission on Conditions in
Harlem. In 1944 the United Nations Educational, Scientific, and Cultural
Organization (UNESCO) named him an international authority on racial
issues. He was elected the first black president of the American Sociological

Association, served as president of the International Society for the Scientific Study of Race Relations, and was a founding member of the American Association for the Advancement of Science.

# Freedom Summer,

**a highly publicized campaign in the Deep South to register blacks to vote during the summer of 1964.**

During the summer of 1964, thousands of civil rights activists, many of them white college students from the North, descended on Mississippi and other Southern states to try to end the long-time political disfranchisement of African Americans in the region. Although black men had won the right to vote in 1870, thanks to the Fifteenth Amendment, for the next 100 years many were unable to exercise that right. White local and state officials systematically kept blacks from voting through formal methods, such as poll taxes and literacy tests, and through cruder methods of fear and intimidation, which included beatings and lynchings. The inability to vote was only one of many problems blacks encountered in the racist society around them, but the civil rights officials who decided to zero in on voter registration understood its crucial significance as well as the white supremacists did. An African American voting bloc would be able to effect social and political change.

Freedom Summer marked the climax of intensive voter-registration activities in the South that had started in 1961. Organizers chose to focus their efforts on Mississippi because of the state's particularly dismal voting-rights record: in 1962 only 6.7 percent of African Americans in the state were registered to vote, the lowest percentage in the country. The Freedom Summer campaign was organized by a coalition called the Mississippi Council of Federated Organizations, which included the Congress of Racial Equality (CORE), the National Association for the Advancement of Colored People (NAACP), and the Student Nonviolent Coordinating Committee (SNCC). SNCC volunteers, led by Robert Moses, played the largest role, providing 90 to 95 percent of the funding and 95 percent of the headquarters staff. By mobilizing volunteer white college students from the North to join them, the coalition scored a major public relations coup as hundreds of reporters came to Mississippi from around the country to cover the voter-registration campaign.

The organization of the Mississippi Freedom Democratic Party (MFDP) was a major focus of the summer program. More than 80,000 Mississippians joined the new party, which elected a slate of 68 delegates to the national Democratic Party convention in Atlantic City. The MFDP delegation challenged the seating of the delegates representing Mississippi's all-white Democratic Party. While the effort failed, it drew national attention, particularly through the dramatic televised appeal of MFDP delegate Fannie

Lou Hamer. The MFDP challenge also led to a ban on racially discriminatory delegations at future conventions.

Freedom Summer officials established 30 "Freedom Schools" in towns
throughout Mississippi to address the racial inequalities in Mississippi's educational system. Mississippi's black schools were invariably poorly funded,
and teachers had to use hand-me-down textbooks that offered a racist slant
on American history. Many of the white college students were assigned to
teach in these schools, whose curriculum included black history, the philosophy of the Civil Rights Movement, and leadership development in addition to remedial instruction in reading and arithmetic. The Freedom Schools
had hoped to draw at least 1,000 students that first summer and ended up
with 3,000. The schools became a model for future social programs like
Head Start and for alternative educational institutions.

Freedom Summer activists faced threats and harassment throughout
the campaign, not only from white supremacist groups, but from local residents and police. Freedom School buildings and the volunteers' homes
were frequent targets; 37 black churches and 30 black homes and businesses were firebombed or burned during that summer, and the cases often
went unsolved. More than 1,000 black and white volunteers were arrested,
and at least 80 were beaten by white mobs or racist police officers. But the
summer's most infamous act of violence was the murder of three young
civil rights workers, a black volunteer, James Chaney, and his white coworkers, Andrew Goodman and Michael Schwerner. On June 21, Chaney,
Goodman, and Schwerner set out to investigate a church bombing near
Philadelphia, Mississippi, but were arrested that afternoon and held for
several hours on alleged traffic violations. Their release from jail was the
last time they were seen alive before their badly decomposed bodies were
discovered under a nearby dam six weeks later. Goodman and Schwerner
had died from single gunshot wounds to the chest, and Chaney from a
savage beating.

The murders made headlines all over the country and provoked an outpouring of national support for the Civil Rights Movement. But many black
volunteers realized that because two of the victims were white, these murders were attracting much more attention than previous attacks in which
the victims had all been black, and this added to the growing resentment
they had already begun to feel toward the white volunteers. There was
growing dissension within SNCC's ranks over charges of white paternalism
and elitism. Black volunteers complained that the whites seemed to think
they had a natural claim on leadership roles, and that they treated the rural
blacks as though they were ignorant. There was also increasing hostility
from both black and white workers over the interracial romances that developed during the summer. Meanwhile, women volunteers of both races were
charging both the black and white men with sexist behavior. These conflicts
led to lasting divisions within SNCC, especially over the role of white volunteers. Some African American officials, such as Stokely Carmichael,
reacted by gravitating toward the all-black Black Power Movement, while
many white volunteers returned to their college campuses and became

involved in other forms of social activism, such as the antiwar and women's movements.

Despite the internal divisions, Freedom Summer left a positive legacy. The well-publicized voter registration drives brought national attention to the subject of black disfranchisement, and this eventually led to the 1965 Voting Rights Act, federal legislation that among other things outlawed the tactics that Southern states had used to prevent blacks from voting. Freedom Summer also instilled among African Americans a new consciousness and a new confidence in political action. As Fannie Lou Hamer later said, "Before the 1964 project there were people that wanted change, but they hadn't dared to come out. After 1964 people began moving. To me it's one of the greatest things that ever happened in Mississippi."

# G

## Garvey, Marcus Mosiah

(b. August 7, 1887, St. Ann's Bay, Jamaica; d. June 10, 1940, London, England), founder and leader of the Universal Negro Improvement Association, the largest organization dedicated to black economic self-determination and racial pride.

Photographs exist of Marcus Garvey in the full regal uniform that he wore during marches and rallies. These photographs are still sold on the streets of Harlem, where the Universal Negro Improvement Association (UNIA) had its headquarters in the years during and after World War I. Garvey, called a "black Moses" during his lifetime, created the largest African American organization, with hundreds of chapters across the world at its height. While Garvey is predominantly remembered as a back-to-Africa proponent, it is clear that the scope of his ideas and the UNIA's actions go beyond that characterization.

Marcus Garvey was born in St. Ann's Bay, Jamaica, to Marcus and Sarah Garvey. His father was a stonemason and the family did some subsistence farming. After leaving school at 14, he served as a printer's apprentice in his godfather's business. When he was 16 he moved to Kingston, where his political interests were sparked in the Jamaican anti-colonial and nationalist movement. He then moved to Costa Rica in search of work, and traveled through Central America and Europe until he settled in England in 1913. There he worked for Dusé Mohammed Ali on the successful Pan-African journal *Africa Times and Orient Review*.

In 1914 Garvey returned to Jamaica. On July 20 he began the UNIA in Kingston. Admittedly influenced by Booker T. Washington and his autobiographical *Up from Slavery*, Garvey wanted to create an industrial training school, much like Tuskegee. Garvey envisioned an organization dedicated to racial uplift, one that would "embrace the purpose of all black humanity." Disappointed with his limited success, Garvey went to New

York on March 23, 1916, planning to raise funds and lecture throughout the country. After delivering speeches around Canada and the United States, he returned to Harlem in 1917, where he became known for his street speeches. The UNIA headquarters, Liberty Hall, was reestablished in Harlem in May 1917.

The massive migration of black Southerners to Northern cities, triggered by the industrial demands of World War I, energized black urban life and stimulated racial consciousness, providing a vital outlet for the growth of Garvey's organization. At the same time, black participation in World War I, the war "to make the world safe for democracy," enticed black political aspirations. Wartime hopes, however, were quickly eclipsed by the racial violence and lynching that followed in the summer of 1919, underscoring the incongruity of America's democratic ideals and the determination of whites to maintain white supremacy.

Garvey's ideas particularly resonated with African Americans during the postwar period. At the core of Garvey's program was an emphasis on black economic self-reliance, black people's rights to political self-determination, and the founding of a black nation on the continent of Africa. Garvey's charismatic style, and the magnificent UNIA parades of uniformed corps of UNIA Black Cross nurses, legions, and other divisions, celebrated blackness and racial pride. Garvey urged black people to take control of their destiny: "There shall be no solution to this race problem until you yourselves strike the blow for liberty."

The UNIA movement won broad support in New York's black community, and Garvey quickly gained national and international prominence. Within a year UNIA chapters were created throughout the United States and in Central and South America, the West Indies, West Africa, England, and Canada. The UNIA created the Negro Factories Corporation in 1918, which supported the development of black-owned businesses, including a black doll factory, which employed more than a thousand African Americans. The UNIA also began publishing the *Negro World* weekly, which became the most widely distributed African diasporic publication.

Perhaps the largest endeavor of the UNIA was the Black Star Steamship Line, an enterprise intended to provide a means for African Americans to return to Africa while also enabling black people around the Atlantic to exchange goods and services. The company's three ships (one called the SS Frederick Douglass) were owned and operated by black people and made travel and trade possible between their United States, Caribbean, Central American, and African stops. The economically independent Black Star Line was a symbol of pride for blacks and seemed to attract more members to the UNIA.

In August 1920, 25,000 people attended the first UNIA convention in New York's Madison Square Garden. There, Garvey was elected president-general of the organization, and the Declaration of Rights of the Negro Peoples of the World was written. Members of the convention outlined the formal organization and leadership, calling for a commissioner of each chapter area. The document demanded that black schoolchildren should be taught African history. The convention produced an anthem—*The Universal*

*Ethiopian Anthem*—and red, black, and green became the colors of African peoples. Around this time, a UNIA leader was sent to Liberia to develop further Garvey's idea for a colony there.

As a result of large financial obligations and managerial errors, the Black Star Line failed in 1921 and ended operations. Constant criticism from the National Association for the Advancement of Colored People (NAACP) (most visibly from member W. E. B. Du Bois) and United States government opposition took its toll on the UNIA. Early in 1922 Garvey was indicted on mail fraud charges regarding the Black Star Line's stock sale. He was convicted and given a maximum prison sentence of five years by Judge Julian Mack, also an NAACP member. Garvey appealed and was defeated; he entered the Atlanta federal penitentiary.

Marcus Garvey, dressed in the uniform he adopted after the first UNIA convention elected him provisional president of Africa, rides in a parade. *CORBIS/Underwood & Underwood*

Garvey's second wife, Amy Jacques Garvey, led a national campaign for Garvey's release. During this time, she also edited and published two volumes of his speeches and writings titled *Philosophy and Opinions of Marcus Garvey* (1923 and 1925). The petition drive succeeded in winning Garvey's release after he had served nearly three years of his sentence. He was immediately deported to Jamaica and barred from entering the United States again. In Jamaica, Garvey held two more UNIA conventions. He also started two publications: *Black Man*, a monthly magazine, and *New Jamaican*. But controlling and leading the different international branches from Jamaica proved difficult. A core group in the United States continued to support Garvey; they published the *Negro World* into the 1930s. Garvey, however, turned to Jamaican politics. He lost a race for a colonial legislative council seat in 1930. He did, however, sit on the municipal council of Jamaica's capital.

Garvey moved to London in 1935. For the next few years he held annual conventions in Canada and continued to publish *Black Man*. After suffering a second stroke on June 10, 1940, Garvey died, having fathered two sons with Amy Jacques Garvey, Marcus Jr. and Julius. After his death, his leadership and significance continued to be influential and was recognized around the world. In the United States Garveyism was central to the development of the black consciousness and pride at the core of the twentieth-century freedom movement. The Jamaican Rastafarian movement and the United States Nation of Islam both grew out of and have been influenced by the UNIA. Jamaica named Garvey its first national hero.

## Granger, Lester Blackwell

**(b. September 16, 1896, Newport News, Va.; d. January 9, 1976, Alexandria, La.), African American civil rights leader and director of the National Urban League (NUL).**

The son of a doctor and a teacher, Lester Blackwell Granger grew up in Newark, New Jersey, and earned a bachelor's degree from Dartmouth College in 1918. He served as an artillery lieutenant during World War I (1914–1918), after which he taught school in the South. In 1922 he took a post at Ironsides, the state vocational school for African Americans in Bordentown, New Jersey, where he taught for most of the next 12 years. He became involved with the National Urban League, first as an educational secretary, then as a labor leader. In the 1930s he was instrumental in the Urban League's efforts to create trade unions for blacks.

In 1941 Granger became the league's executive director. Although a gradualist in combating racial discrimination, he pressed the United States government during World War II (1939–1945) to desegregate the armed forces and the defense industry. After the war he pressed the government to deny funding to racially discriminatory housing developments, and he helped black workers oppose discrimination in the labor movement. As the Civil Rights Movement gathered momentum in the late 1950s, Granger's critics called on him to accelerate his desegregation and anti-discrimination efforts and to use more aggressive tactics. Granger argued for a more moderate approach based on education and persuasion, and within the Urban League his view largely prevailed. He resigned from the league in 1961 and in 1962 taught at Dillard University in New Orleans.

## Great Depression,

**a massive economic collapse in the United States and throughout much of the world that had particularly serious consequences for African Americans.**

The Great Depression was a time of economic hardship throughout the United States that fell with particular severity on African Americans. But it also brought important political and social developments that in the years ahead would transform African American life. For blacks the Depression started long before the October 1929 stock market crash. During the 1920s Southern black farmers suffered the devastating impact of the boll weevil on their cotton harvests. They also faced a collapse in farm prices that followed World War I as President Woodrow Wilson lifted agricultural price supports and the government canceled wartime orders.

In one of the largest internal migrations in American history, which came to be known as the Great Migration, many African Americans abandoned farming and moved to cities in the North as well as the South. However, the low-wage jobs that they found in urban areas forced them to live in cramped low-rent districts that became black ghettos. The Great Migration also sharpened racial hostilities, as revealed in the unprecedented support given the Ku Klux Klan in the North. The formal onset of the Depression only made matters worse, economically as well as in race relations.

By 1932 roughly half of the black workers in New York, Chicago, Philadelphia, and Detroit were without jobs, and nearly one out of three African American families was receiving some form of public assistance. Moreover, the black unemployment rate greatly exceeded the white rate. In Pittsburgh during 1933, for example, 48 percent of black workers were unemployed; the comparable figure for whites was 31 percent. The number of lynchings of African Americans also rose—from 7 in 1929 to 20 in 1930 to 24 in 1933, the worst year of the economic collapse.

Blacks responded to hard times and heightened racial hostility with increased militancy. The National Association for the Advancement of Colored People (NAACP) struggled to secure a federal antilynching law. The Communist Party of the United States of America (CPUSA) also played an active role in fighting for black rights, for example, in the 1931 Scottsboro Case and the 1932 case of Angelo Herndon, a black Communist who led a protest of unemployed workers in Atlanta, Georgia. It was the driving force in the National Negro Congress (1936–1946) and in the Southern Negro Youth Congress (1937–1948). Other examples of Depression-era black radicalism include the Southern Tenant Farmers Union, founded in 1934, and the 1935 Harlem Riot.

On occasion white liberals actively supported black rights. The Congress of Industrial Organizations unionized thousands of black industrial workers in integrated unions such as the United Auto Workers and the United Steel Workers. In 1939 First Lady Eleanor Roosevelt helped arrange an Easter Sunday recital by famed black contralto Marian Anderson at Washington's Lincoln Memorial after the Daughters of the American Revolution refused her permission to appear at a concert hall owned by the organization. Moreover, President Franklin Roosevelt appointed an unprecedented number of black advisers, known collectively as the Black Cabinet, including William Hastie, Robert C. Weaver, and Mary McLeod Bethune.

But African Americans found themselves shortchanged by Roosevelt's New Deal. The National Recovery Administration permitted lower wages for blacks than for whites doing the same work. Racial discrimination was evident in the hiring and housing policies of the Tennessee Valley Authority (TVA) as well as in the segregated camps of the Civilian Conservation Corps. Many landowners, rather than share Agricultural Adjustment Administration subsidies with their black sharecroppers, had their tenants evicted and kept the entire payment for themselves.

Although a 1935 executive order banned discrimination in Works Progress Administration (WPA) projects, a subsequent cut in the WPA budget brought a sharp economic downturn, the so-called Roosevelt Recession, that jeopardized many black families. WPA policies were the subject of widespread protest, as seen in topical blues such as Casey Bill Weldon's *WPA Blues* (1936) and Porter Grainger's *Pink Slip Blues*, sung by Ida Cox in 1939. Furthermore, Roosevelt refused to endorse two key black political goals—a federal antilynching law and abolition of the poll tax.

Nonetheless, in 1936 African Americans rallied around Roosevelt and the New Deal. This support represented an electoral shift of historic proportions—for the first time since Emancipation a majority of black voters cast their ballots for the Democratic Party. On the other hand, this political support was not unquestioning, as a number of Depression-era black protests make clear. Paradoxically, the key protest of these years never took place. In 1941, as increased defense spending rapidly lifted the country out of depression, blacks found themselves almost wholly excluded from the new defense jobs. For example, the head of North American Aviation, then greatly expanding its work force, announced that blacks would only be considered for jobs "as janitors and other similar capacities."

African Americans answered with the first March on Washington, more than two decades before the better-known 1963 protest led by Rev. Martin Luther King Jr. The strategy behind the march foreshadowed that of the future Civil Rights Movement, particularly its use of large-scale direct-action protest in a powerfully symbolic setting, its focus on influencing the federal government, and its careful orchestration of national news coverage to multiply the impact of the planned demonstration.

The key forces behind the 1941 March on Washington were the Brotherhood of Sleeping Car Porters (a black labor union) and the Communist-led National Negro Congress. A. Philip Randolph, president of both organizations, proposed a gathering of at least 100,000 African Americans in the nation's capital to protest unfair defense industry hiring practices. Never had the capital faced such a massive demonstration, and a nervous Roosevelt wanted to prevent it altogether.

The result was a signal victory for Randolph. In June 1941 Roosevelt signed Executive Order 8802, prohibiting discrimination throughout the federal government as well as in defense work and establishing the Fair Employment Practices Committee to oversee the new policy. In response, Randolph called off the march, but he maintained his March on Washington organization to remind Roosevelt not to neglect black Americans.

North America

# Great Migration, The,

**mass movement by black Americans in the early twentieth century from the predominantly rural, segregated South to the urban North and West, where they sought greater economic, social, and political freedom.**

At the end of the Civil War (1861–1865) and the abolition of slavery, 91 percent of America's 5 million African Americans lived in the Southern states, roughly the same percentage as in 1790. Blacks made up 36 percent of the total Southern population (as compared with 3 percent of the total Northern population) and worked mostly as sharecroppers, tenant farmers, and domestic servants. Very few owned property. Most black farmers were heavily in debt and struggled to pay rents. Other forms of labor open to blacks were similarly low-paying and exploitative.

The Reconstruction era (1865–1877), which kept protective Union troops in the South and brought blacks the constitutional guarantee of full citizenship, raised hopes and expectations for better jobs and civil rights. A small but important minority of blacks found work in industries such as coal mining, timber, and railroads, and others received a limited education. As Reconstruction drew to a close, however, and with it the emergence of Northern dominance over Southern life, white legislatures in the South began to pass Jim Crow laws codifying state and local segregation and discrimination. Blacks, especially those attempting to exercise the franchise, were the victims of lynchings and other terrorism. Opportunities in school, work, and politics dwindled. Some blacks responded by migrating to Northern border states, especially Kansas. Their numbers, however, were limited to a few tens of thousands, and the migration was mostly to rural areas. In 1910, nearly 50 years after the war had ended slavery, 89 percent of all blacks remained in the South, and nearly 80 percent of those lived in rural areas.

Several events early in the second decade of the twentieth century coalesced to change black patterns of settlement. From 1913 to 1915 falling cotton prices brought on an economic depression that seriously hurt Southern farmers, both black and white. Just as they began to recover, they were struck by an overwhelming infestation of boll weevils, insects that destroyed much of the cotton crop between 1914 and 1917. In the Mississippi Valley, farmers suffered an additional plague: severe floods in 1915 ruined crops and homes, especially of blacks, who lived in disproportionate numbers in the valley's bottomlands. The few Southern blacks who had owned their own farms before 1910 were now largely reduced to sharecropping and tenant farming; most sharecroppers and tenant farmers, meanwhile, slid deeper into debt.

At the same time Northern industries were undergoing an economic boom, fueled in part by the start of World War I in Europe (1914–1918). The North and West were also experiencing a labor shortage: following several years of cheap labor from unlimited foreign immigration, Congress had now restricted the number of new immigrants. The labor shortage became even more acute as the United States entered the war in 1917. While wages in the South ranged from 50 cents to $2 a day, wages in the industrial North, expanded because of the war effort, ranged from $2 to $5 a day.

Southern blacks responded to these forces by filling Northern jobs by the hundreds of thousands. Between 1915 and 1920, from 500,000 to 1 million African Americans left the rural South for the urban North; several thousands more moved to the West. Others remained in the South but moved from the country to the city. On their arrival in the North, migrants found not just better wages but the freedom to vote, less exposure to white violence, and, sometimes, better schools for their children. Racism remained persistent, however. Discriminatory real estate practices forced blacks into ill-maintained and segregated housing, contributing to the rise of the urban black ghetto. Blacks were routinely excluded from labor unions, and many migrants were forced into menial jobs as butlers, waiters, and the like, or served as replacement workers ("scabs") during strikes by white unions.

The increased competition among blacks and whites for jobs and housing sparked race riots in dozens of Northern cities, including major white-on-black riots in East St. Louis in 1917 and Chicago in 1919. For blacks, the riots were an enduring reminder that white violence was not restricted to the states of Jim Crow. For the nation, the tensions caused by black migration made many people aware of what blacks had known for some time: the problems of race were an American, not only a Southern, phenomenon.

Despite the problems, migrants in the North wrote to family and friends in the South with stories of better living conditions, better jobs, and more freedom. Often they sent money and offered other help for the move. Prominent black newspapers such as the *Chicago Defender* and leading black aid societies such as the National Association of Colored Women proclaimed (often over-zealously) the virtues of the Promised Land, and helped newly arrived blacks find jobs. Northern companies, including meatpacking, automobile, and steel businesses, even sent agents to recruit blacks from the South.

In addition to the tide of unskilled laborers flowing out of the South, many of the few black mechanics, apprenticed workers, musicians, and professionals also left. Together with Northern skilled laborers, they made up a small new Northern black middle class, which established its own unions, social and fraternal orders, churches, and welfare services. The growth of this middle class during the 1920s was not without conflict. As wealthier blacks moved into better housing left by whites, poor blacks were left concentrated in overcrowded ghetto neighborhoods.

Southern states, which relied heavily on black agricultural, domestic, and sometimes industrial labor, tried to stop the population flow. Several state legislatures and city councils passed laws fining and jailing "vagrant" or "landless" blacks—that is, blacks who were traveling. They also fined and jailed Northern labor recruiters and Southern blacks who encouraged other blacks to move. In several states, the *Chicago Defender* was banned. Black people left in large numbers nonetheless. In addition to the hundreds of thousands who left before 1920, another 700,000 to 1,000,000 African Americans moved north and west in the 1920s.

The effect on Northern and western cities was dramatic. Detroit's black population, which was estimated at fewer than 6,000 before World War I, grew to more than 120,000 at the end of the 1920s. Chicago's black population grew from about 40,000 in 1910 to about 240,000 in 1930. New York's grew from 100,000 to 330,000. Western states, previously home to few blacks, received a smaller but still significant influx. In Los Angeles the population of 8,000 blacks in 1910 increased to almost 40,000 in 1930. By 1940, 23 percent of blacks in the United States were living in the North and West; black majorities in Louisiana, South Carolina, and Mississippi had come to an end. In the areas they left behind, several thousands of farm acres were reported idle, and many businesses in these areas were forced to close or slow down.

Widespread as the black exodus from the South was, black movement within the South was greater. The same forces of farm depression, industrialization, and wartime labor shortage that prompted many blacks to leave altogether prompted more blacks (as well as whites) to move from the Southern farm to the Southern city. Whereas blacks comprised at most 10 percent of some Northern cities in the 1920s, in the South they were routinely 25 to 50 percent of a city's population.

The Great Depression of the 1930s slowed the Great Migration, but the start of World War II (1939–1945) had similar effects on migration as the start of World War I. This time, a sagging farm economy, rapid economic growth, persistent Southern racism, and a national labor shortage were accompanied by mechanization of Southern farms and increasing gains in the Civil Rights Movement. However, as blacks again left *en masse*, they moved not just to the cities of the Northern Rust Belt, but increasingly to the cities of the West, especially Los Angeles, San Francisco, and San Diego. By 1960, at the end of the second wave of migration, 40 percent of the nation's blacks lived in the North and West, and nearly three-quarters of all American blacks lived in cities—the same percentage that had lived in rural areas at the start of the century.

For those who participated in it, and even for their children and grandchildren, the Great Migration continues to resonate as one of the most powerful stories of African American struggle and opportunity. Its impact can be seen in African American literature, music—particularly in the urban blues pioneered by such Southern transplants as John Lee Hooker—and visual arts, perhaps most notably in the paintings of Jacob Lawrence, whose Migration series explores the images and themes inspired by his parents' migration north.

North America

# Gregory, Richard Claxton "Dick"

(b. October 12, 1932, St. Louis, Mo.), African American comedian and civil rights activist whose social satire changed the way white Americans perceived African American comedians.

Dick Gregory entered the national comedy scene in 1961 when Chicago's Playboy Club booked him as a replacement for white comedian "Professor" Irwin Corey. Until then Gregory had worked mostly at small clubs with predominantly black audiences (he met his wife, Lillian Smith, at one such club). Such clubs paid comedians an average of $5 dollars per night; thus Gregory also held a day job as a postal employee. His tenure as a replacement for Corey was so successful—at one performance he won over an audience that included Southern white convention goers—that the Playboy Club offered him a contract extension from several weeks to three years. By 1962 Gregory had become a nationally known headline performer, selling out nightclubs, making numerous national television appearances, and recording popular comedy albums.

Gregory began performing comedy in the mid-1950s while serving in the army. Drafted in 1954 while attending Southern Illinois University at Carbondale on a track scholarship, he briefly returned to the university after his discharge in 1956, but left without a degree because he felt that the university "didn't want me to study, they wanted me to run." In the hopes of performing comedy professionally, he moved to Chicago, where he became part of a new generation of black comedians that included Nipsey Russell, Bill Cosby, and Godfrey Cambridge. These comedians broke with the minstrel tradition, which presented stereotypical black characters. Gregory, whose style was detached, ironic, and satirical, came to be called the "Black Mort Sahl" after the popular white social satirist. He drew on current events, especially racial issues, for much of his material: "Segregation is not all bad. Have you ever heard of a collision where the people in the back of the bus got hurt?"

From an early age Gregory demonstrated a strong sense of social justice. While a student at Sumner High School in St. Louis he led a march protesting segregated schools. Later, inspired by the work of leaders such as Dr. Martin Luther King Jr. and organizations such as the Student Nonviolent Coordinating Committee (SNCC), Gregory took part in the Civil Rights Movement and used his celebrity status to draw attention to such issues as segregation and disfranchisement. When local Mississippi governments stopped distributing federal food surpluses to poor blacks in areas where SNCC was encouraging voter registration, Gregory chartered a plane to bring in seven tons of food. He participated in SNCC's voter registration drives and in sit-ins to protest segregation, most notably at a restaurant franchise in downtown Atlanta, Georgia. Only later did Gregory disclose that he held stock in the chain.

Through the 1960s Gregory spent more time on social issues and less time on performing. He participated in marches and parades to support a range of causes, including opposition to the Vietnam War, world hunger, and drug abuse. In addition he fasted in protest more than 60 times, once in Iran, where he fasted and prayed in an effort to urge the Ayatollah Khomeini to release American embassy staff who had been taken hostage. The Iranian refusal to release the hostages did not decrease the depth of Gregory's commitment; he weighed only 44 kg (97 lbs) when he left Iran.

Gregory demonstrated his commitment to confronting the entrenched political powers by opposing Richard J. Daley in Chicago's 1966 mayoral election. He ran for president in 1968 as a write-in candidate for the Freedom and Peace Party, a splinter group of the Peace and Freedom Party, and received 1.5 million votes. Democratic candidate Hubert Humphrey lost the election to Republican Richard Nixon by 510,000 votes, and many believe Humphrey would have won had Gregory not run. After the assassinations of King, President John F. Kennedy, and Robert Kennedy, Gregory became increasingly convinced of the existence of political conspiracies. He wrote books such as *Code Name Zoro: The Murder of Martin Luther King Jr.* (1971) with Mark Lane, a conspiracy theorist whose ideas Gregory shared and espoused in numerous lectures.

Gregory's activism continued into the 1990s. In response to published allegations that the Central Intelligence Agency (CIA) had supplied cocaine to predominantly African American areas in Los Angeles, thus spurring the crack epidemic, Gregory protested at CIA headquarters and was arrested. In 1992 he began a program called Campaign for Human Dignity to fight crime in St. Louis neighborhoods.

In 1973, the year he released his comedy album *Caught in the Act*, Gregory moved with his family to Plymouth, Massachusetts, where he developed an interest in vegetarianism and became a nutritional consultant. In 1984 he founded Health Enterprises, Inc., a company that distributed weight loss products. In 1987 Gregory introduced the Slim-Safe Bahamian Diet, a powdered diet mix, which was immensely profitable. Economic losses caused in part by conflicts with his business partners led to his eviction from his home in 1992. Gregory remained active, however, and in 1996 returned to the stage in his critically acclaimed one-man show, *Dick Gregory Live!*

North America

# Guinier, Lani

**(b. April 19, 1950, New York, N.Y.), African American civil rights lawyer and a leading spokesperson on racial issues; in 1998 she became the first black woman to be appointed to a tenured professorship at Harvard Law School.**

In June 1993 civil rights lawyer Lani Guinier became the focus of a heated national debate. President Bill Clinton, who had nominated her to head the United States Justice Department's Civil Rights Division, abruptly withdrew his nomination. He did this after media critics, mostly from the political right, contended that Guinier's legal writings on racial and electoral issues were antidemocratic. She was a "hard-hitting extremist," according to a *New York Post* editorial.

Guinier's writings criticize the single-member, winner-takes-all local electoral system, in which black candidates are seldom elected except in majority black districts. Many voting-rights lawyers have advocated the creation of artificial black-majority districts in order to increase black representation in local government. Guinier, on the other hand, proposes a system she calls "proportionate interest representation," which is similar to the electoral systems of continental Europe and which allows for a more effective representation of diverse political interests.

Following the controversy over her nomination, civil rights leaders argued that the president and the media had misinterpreted her ideas.

Indeed, according to an article in the *New Yorker* (June 14, 1993), Guinier's writings "do not show her to be . . . a proponent of racial polarization, or an opponent of democratic norms. They do show her to be a provocative, interesting thinker, whose speculations could nourish what is a nascent debate [in the United States] about alternative electoral systems." Nonetheless, Guinier was not allowed to defend her writings before the Senate Judiciary Committee. She has since become one of the nation's leading spokespersons on racial and gender issues.

A graduate of Yale Law School, Guinier has had nearly two decades of experience in civil rights, including a key position in the U.S. Justice Department during the Carter administration. In 1996 she helped to found Commonplace, a nonprofit organization devoted to improving public discourse on racial issues. She has also published three books. She released *The Tyranny of the Majority* in 1994—a discussion of the pros and cons of fixed majority rule. In *Becoming Gentlemen: Women, Law School, and Institutional Change* (1997), she and her co-authors examine the difficulties experienced by women, people of color, and many non-Europeans in American law and graduate schools, and they fault the aggressive Socratic method of teaching that is prevalent in these institutions. *Lift Every Voice: Turning a Civil Rights Setback into a New Vision of Social Justice* (1998) has been described by the *New York Times* as "a detailed if defensive memoir of her nomination fight and its implications."

# Haley, Alexander Palmer (Alex)

(b. August 11, 1921, Ithaca, N.Y.; d. February 10, 1992, Seattle, Wash.), African American writer and journalist who authored two of the most influential books in the history of African American scholarship.

Alex Haley grew up in Henning, Tennessee, with maternal relatives who spent many hours telling family stories, some of which extended back to Africa. This exposure directed the course of much of Haley's work as an adult. Haley completed high school at age 15 and attended two years of college, but was uninspired by his studies and left school to join the United States Coast Guard, where he began writing to counteract the tedium of life at sea. When Haley retired from the service in 1959, he disembarked a mature, self-taught writer.

Haley settled in Greenwich Village, New York, determined to make his name as a journalist. After a period of hard work and obscurity, he broke into mainstream publications such as *Readers' Digest, Harper's,* and the *New York Times Magazine*. In 1962 he sold a Miles Davis interview to *Playboy* that began the magazine's famous interview series. Later that year *Playboy* commissioned Haley to interview Malcolm X, an assignment that led to Haley's first book, his ghostwritten *Autobiography of Malcolm X.*

*The Autobiography of Malcolm X* (1965) sold more than 5 million copies and changed the nation's opinion of the black nationalist leader. The book, which concludes with Malcolm X's reevaluation of the Nation of Islam, highlights the complexity, compassion, and humanity of a figure whose public image might otherwise have remained monolithic and negative. The assassination of Malcolm X in 1965 increased public interest, and Haley's book became required reading in many college courses.

Soon after the publication of *The Autobiography of Malcolm X*, Haley began research for a second contribution to African American literature. The half-fictive, half-factual epic *Roots* (1977), which traces Haley's own maternal lineage back to an enslaved West African named Kunta Kinte, captured the attention of the nation. Haley took 12 years to write and research Roots, consulting relatives, archives, and libraries as well as a tribal historian from Kunta Kinte's village. At one point Haley even attempted to relive the Middle Passage experience of enslaved Africans by sleeping in the hold of a transatlantic ship.

Roots sold more than 8.5 million copies, was translated into 26 languages, and won 271 different awards. The Pulitzer Prize and National Book Award committees honored its contribution to American history, and ABC turned it into an eight-part television series, of which 130 million Americans watched at least one episode. Roots not only touched blacks whose histories resembled Haley's but also whites who were confronted by America's tragic past.

In the wake of the Roots phenomenon, two different plaintiffs accused Haley of plagiarism. Haley disproved one of the claims but settled the other out of court, conceding that, given his extensive and often unannotated notetaking, he had accidentally used material from Harold Courlander's book The African (1968). Critics also questioned Haley's method of presenting fiction as fact. Haley, however, repeatedly defended his methods as a necessary way of tapping the emotional poignancy of his subject.

Haley's career peaked with Roots—despite a television sequel (Roots: The Next Generation, 1979), a second, similar book-and-television project (Queen: The Story of an American Family, 1992), and a television drama about race and childhood in the American South (Palmerstown U.S.A., 1980). These projects, along with a record called Alex Haley Speaks, which gave tips on constructing family genealogies, never achieved the success of Haley's second book. Haley worked on a long-delayed biography of Madam C. J. Walker that remained unfinished when he died from a heart attack in 1992.

North America

# Hamer, Fannie Lou

**(b. October 6, 1917, Montgomery County, Miss.; d. March 14, 1977, Ruleville, Miss.), African American civil rights activist who worked with the Student Non-violent Coordinating Committee (SNCC) to secure voting rights for blacks and helped form the Mississippi Freedom Democratic Party.**

The youngest of 20 children born to share-croppers Ella and Jim Townsend, Fannie Lou Hamer began helping her family pick cotton at age six, and left school to work full-time in the fields only six years later. Despite her relative lack of education, Hamer spoke often of her love of reading. Her childhood was spent in poverty; her family lived without heat or plumbing and often lacked nutritious food. Hamer suffered a lifelong limp because one of her legs was broken in infancy and never treated. In 1944, after many of her siblings had moved North, she married local farmhand Percy Hamer. The two moved to a small house on a cotton plantation near Ruleville, Mississippi.

In the summer of 1962 Hamer went to a mass meeting organized by the Student Nonviolent Coordinating Committee, which had recently begun organizing in the Mississippi Delta, where poor blacks lived in some of the worst conditions anywhere in the United States. SNCC and other civil rights groups hoped to register and educate many of the more than 400,000 African Americans in Mississippi who were being denied their constitutional right to vote by a variety of means, including voter registration tests, poll taxes, and violent reprisals for political activity. Following the meeting, Hamer went along with 17 others to attempt to register to vote in Indianola, the county seat. Facing the registration test, which was administered in such a way as to ensure that black people never passed, Hamer and the others failed.

Returning home, Hamer refused to promise her white boss that she would stop trying to vote; he fired her and threw her off the plantation where she had lived and worked for 18 years. "They kicked me off the plantation," she later told friends, "they set me free. It's the best thing that could happen. Now I can work for my people." Hamer joined SNCC as a field-worker, where she was soon seen by SNCC leader Robert Moses as a valuable asset because of her brilliant oratory and powerful singing. Hamer also became a living symbol of the dangers faced by civil rights workers after she was unfairly jailed and severely beaten in Winona, Mississippi (June 1963), while returning from citizenship classes. Eventually, due to the intervention of the FBI and the Justice Department, the jailers were tried for assaulting Hamer, but an all-white local jury later found the jailers not guilty.

In 1963 Hamer began working with the Council of Federated Organizations—a coalition of SNCC, the Congress of Racial Equality (CORE), and the National Association for the Advancement of Colored People (NAACP)—on what was called the Freedom Vote. The first statewide voting rights effort, Freedom Vote provided Mississippi's unregistered black citizens with "freedom ballots," with which 80,000 of the citizens cast votes. During the next year, in addition to her SNCC work during Freedom Summer (when thousands of college students came South to assist in voter education and registration), Hamer and others founded the Mississippi Freedom Democratic Party (MFDP) in an attempt to force the state's traditionally all-white, racist Democratic party to integrate. At the same time, Hamer launched her own run for Congress as the MFDP candidate. Although she did not win the primary (and probably did not expect to), her candidacy and work with the MFDP brought her to national attention. When the MFDP was rebuffed in its attempt to seat delegates at the 1964 Democratic National Convention, Hamer appeared on television to "question America" about its failure to provide equal justice for all.

Over the next several years Hamer began to see results from her efforts. In 1965 Congress passed the Voting Rights Act, which theoretically ensured the rights of African Americans to register and vote. By 1968 Mississippi's convention delegation was no longer all-white. And in 1968 a black man, Robert Clark, was elected to the state legislature: the first black state congressman since Reconstruction. Hamer continued her involvement in civil rights work, branching out to issues of poverty and economic justice. From 1969 to 1974 she ran the Freedom Farm, a cooperatively owned and operated farm that provided poor blacks with both food and jobs.

Both Howard University and Morehouse College awarded Hamer honorary degrees; her work was also recognized by the Congressional Black Caucus in 1976, and by her own hometown, Ruleville, shortly before her death. At Hamer's funeral, Andrew Young proclaimed that "[There is] no one in America [who] has not been influenced or inspired by Mrs. Hamer," and then he led the mourners in singing one of her trademark songs, "This little light of mine, / I'm gonna let it shine."

North America

# Harlem, New York,

**political and cultural center of black America in the twentieth century, best known as the major site of the literary and artistic "renaissance" of the 1920s and 1930s.**

Slaves to the Dutch West India Company, Africans built the first wagon road into Harlem in the seventeenth century, and in the next 200 years African slaves worked the Dutch and then English farms in Harlem. In 1790, 115 slaves were listed for the "Harlem Division," equal to one-third the population of the area.

But the evolution of Harlem into the political and cultural capital of black America is a twentieth-century phenomenon. Housing in Harlem, which was once a wealthy suburb of New York City, soared in value at the turn of the century, only to collapse beneath excessive real estate speculation in 1904 and 1905. Those years coincided with the completion of the Lenox Avenue subway line to lower Manhattan, facilitating the settlement of African Americans migrating from the South and the Caribbean in Harlem. Philip Payton's Afro-Am Realty Company leased large numbers of Harlem apartment houses from white owners and rented them to black tenants in neighborhoods that began at 135th Street east of Eighth Avenue and over the decades expanded east-west from Park to Amsterdam avenues and north-south from 155th Street to Central Park.

By 1930 the black population of New York had more than tripled, to 328,000 persons, 180,000 of whom lived in Harlem—two-thirds of all African Americans in New York City and 12 percent of the entire population. Between 1920 and 1930 the black population of Harlem increased by nearly 100,000 persons, developing middle- and upper-middle-class neighborhoods such as Striver's Row on West 139th Street.

The migration led to a political, cultural, and social community that was unprecedented in scope. The African Methodist Episcopal Zion Church, St. Philips' Protestant Episcopal Church, and Abyssinian Baptist Church moved north to Harlem. the *Amsterdam News* was founded in Harlem in 1919. The community also supported a vital literary and political life: by 1920 the trade union newspaper the *Messenger*, edited by A. Philip Randolph and Chandler Owen, was published in Harlem, as were the National Association for the Advancement of Colored People's (NAACP's) magazine the *Crisis*, edited by W. E. B. Du Bois and Jessie Fauset, and the National Urban League's magazine *Opportunity*, edited by Charles S. Johnson. Incipient political movements followed the establishment of a branch of the

NAACP in 1910 and Marcus Garvey's Universal Negro Improvement Association in 1916. Flamboyant and charismatic, Garvey promoted both a back-to-Africa drive and the first popular Black Nationalist Movement. Harlem also nurtured a socialist movement led by H. H. Harrison, W. A. Domingo, and A. Philip Randolph.

Especially in the 1920s Harlem fostered pioneering black intellectual and popular movements as well as a dynamic nightlife centered on nightclubs, impromptu apartment "buffet parties," and speakeasies. Many of Harlem's cultural venues developed at this time, ranging from the Lincoln and Apollo theaters to the Cotton Club, Smalls Paradise, and Savoy Ballroom. In popular dance Florence Mills was one of the most celebrated entertainers of the 1920s, while in tap, Bill "Bojangles" Robinson was called "the Mayor of Harlem." In vaudeville Bert Williams broke the color line. In drama Paul Robeson was an honored figure for both his acting and singing.

In 1925 Alain Locke filled an issue of *Survey Graphic* magazine with black literature, folklore, and art, declaring a "New Negro" renaissance to be guided by "forces and motives of [cultural] self determination." The renaissance was led by writers such as Jean Toomer, Langston Hughes, Countee Cullen, Claude McKay, Nella Larsen, and Zora Neale Hurston, and Harlem became its symbol. In art Aaron Douglas, Richmond Barthé, and (later) Jacob Lawrence launched their careers.

In music Harlem pianists such as Fats Waller and Willie "the Lion" Smith began one of the most storied traditions of jazz in the world. In the 1920s it included big bands led by Fletcher Henderson, Duke Ellington, and Chick

Not only the cultural and intellectual center of black life in the United States, Harlem has also served as a safe haven, a black community with strong connections among its inhabitants.
*CORBIS/Bettmann*

From Marcus Garvey's Universal Negro Improvement Association to the National Memorial African Bookstore, pictured here in 1964, Harlem has long served as home to movements and ideas stressing African American self-reliance and self-esteem. *UPI/CORBIS-Bettmann*

Webb and individual virtuosos such as Eubie Blake. Later, it included Charlie Parker, Bud Powell, Ornette Coleman, Thelonious Monk, and Miles Davis.

In the 1920s Harlem gained some political power and institutions. Arthur Schomburg's renowned collection of black literature and historical documents became a branch of the New York Public Library. Three years later Charles Fillmore was elected the first black district leader in New York City, and black physicians were admitted to the permanent staff of Harlem Hospital.

But such advances were modest. Harlem blacks owned less than 20 percent of Harlem's businesses in 1929, and the onset of the Depression quadrupled relief applications within two years. Blacks continued to be excluded from jobs, even in Harlem. The Communist Party and the Citizens' League for Fair Play organized a boycott of Harlem businesses that refused to hire blacks, but the boycott collapsed in 1934. A year later frustration erupted into a riot in which millions of dollars of property was damaged and 75 were arrested. By 1937 four African American district leaders were elected, and the Greater New York City Coordinating Committee for the Employment of Negroes was formed.

During World War II migration from the South and the Caribbean increased enormously, the direct result of the opening of defense industry jobs to blacks, for which the 1941 March on Washington—organized by A. Philip Randolph—was instrumental. But racism persisted, and an incident of police brutality in 1943 precipitated a riot in which six African Americans were killed and 185 were injured. In 1944, on the heels of widespread efforts to improve race relations, Adam Clayton Powell Jr. was elected to the United States Congress and Benjamin Davis replaced him on the City Council.

The 1940s and 1950s brought further political cohesion and literary expression. Hulan Jack was elected the first black borough president in 1953. Through the 1970s Harlem was home to heralded writers such as novelist Ralph Ellison, essayist James Baldwin, playwright Lorraine Hansberry, and poets Audre Lorde and Maya Angelou—many of them associated with the Harlem Writers Guild. Yet by 1960 middle-class flight from Harlem produced a ghetto in large sections of the community. Half of all housing units were unsound, and the infant mortality rate was nearly double that in the rest of the city. Under the leadership of Harlem Youth Opportunities Unlimited (HARYOU), organized by Kenneth B. Clark, Harlem tried to draw federal funding into the area to rebuild the community and create jobs. The effort was largely unsuccessful, and in 1964, when an off-duty police officer shot a black youth, a riot ensued. One person was killed, and 144 were injured; stores were looted for several days.

In the 1950s Malcolm X arrived to head the Harlem Mosque and soon created an independent religious and Black Nationalist Movement that declared itself ready to fight—"by any means necessary"—against white racism and violence toward African Americans. In 1965, however, Malcolm X was assassinated. His death made him a martyr for Black Nationalists even as his religious movement dissipated.

Percy Sutton was Manhattan borough president for 11 years beginning in 1966. In 1970 Charles Rangel was elected to the congressional seat vacated by Adam Clayton Powell Jr. By the late 1970s, however, de-industrialization and inflation led to widespread unemployment, while poverty, drugs, crime, and a deteriorating school system plagued the community for the next decade.

When, in 1989, Harlem's David Dinkins was elected mayor of New York, racial divisions briefly lessened and some parts of Harlem were revitalized. But Dinkins's defeat in the 1993 election cut short those efforts. In the more mercantilist environment of the late 1990s Harlem has turned to private development efforts by African Americans, such as the mall planned for 125th Street, as a means for rehabilitating an impoverished community.

# Harlem Riots of 1935,

**a New York City uprising caused by a combination of the disastrous economic effects of the Great Depression and job discrimination and police brutality.**

On March 19, 1935, a white Harlem store owner accused a dark-skinned Latino boy, Lino Rivera, of shoplifting a knife. After a scuffle, in which ten-year-old Rivera struck a store clerk, the police arrested him. Rumors about the arrest and the police's treatment of the boy in custody spread throughout Harlem. Some people believed that the police had beaten or killed Rivera. Incited by street corner speakers, people began to riot, first attacking the store where Rivera had been arrested. They caused an estimated $2 million worth of damage, mostly to white-owned property. By the riot's end, 3 black people were dead and more than 200 wounded.

The riot may have been set off by Rivera's arrest, but Harlem's African American residents were already tense with frustration about their dire social and economic conditions and their treatment at the hands of whites. The Great Depression was unusually hard on Harlem, particularly because white store owners, most of whose businesses were frequented by African Americans, refused to hire African Americans as clerks. In 1933 African Americans had picketed and boycotted such stores, but in 1935 the store owners obtained an injunction against the picketing. Many Harlemites insisted that the police enforced the injunction with brutality.

After the riot, New York mayor Fiorello La Guardia established the Mayor's Commission on Conditions in Harlem, a biracial commission headed by the African American sociologist E. Franklin Frazier to investigate and propose solutions. The commission's report, *The Negro in Harlem: A Report on Social and Economic Conditions Responsible for the Outbreak of March 19, 1935*, recommended anti-discrimination measures to be taken in city housing, relief agencies, the police department, and the hiring practices for municipal jobs. La Guardia appointed Alain Locke to implement the program and attempted to expand government services to Harlem, including public housing, facilities at Harlem Hospital, and special training for police. Conditions, however, remained tense throughout the decade and well into the 1940s.

# Harlem Riots of 1943,

**one of the first modern urban disturbances in which African Americans reacted violently to police brutality.**

Marjorie Polite, an African American woman, was arrested on August 1, 1943, for causing a disturbance at the Braddock Hotel in Harlem, a predominantly black section of New York. Robert Bandy, a black soldier in uniform, demanded that the police release Polite. Reports about what happened next differ, but witnesses said that Bandy either grabbed the arresting officer's nightstick or struck the police officer and ran. In any event, police shot and wounded the fleeing Bandy. A rumor soon circulated that the police had killed an African American soldier trying to protect his mother.

A crowd of approximately 3,000 African Americans, already frustrated by frequent police brutality, as well as housing and job discrimination, surrounded the Braddock, Sydenham Hospital, and the 28th police precinct, threatening the arresting officers. At approximately 10:30 p.m., the crowd began breaking windows and setting fires. Despite efforts by Mayor Fiorello La Guardia and prominent African Americans to convince the rioters to stop, the violence continued until dawn. Six African Americans were killed, 185 injured, and 500 arrested.

City officials and African American leaders attempted to minimize the racial aspects of the riot, but La Guardia convened the Emergency Conference for Interracial Unity, which was charged with suggesting ways to reduce racial tensions in New York. He also ordered the establishment of the Office of Price Administration in Harlem to investigate alleged price gouging, and reopened the Savoy Ballroom, a popular nightclub that city officials had closed—many African Americans believed—unfairly. La Guardia's evenhanded response to the initial violence and his prompt institution of reforms garnered him further esteem from a Harlem population that already supported him.

North America

# Harlem Riot of 1964,

**an urban rebellion resulting from African American protest of police brutality.**

At 10:30 p.m. on July 18, 1964, demonstrators rioted in Harlem to protest the fatal shooting of a 15-year-old African American, James Powell, by a white police officer. The protest, sponsored by the Congress of Racial Equality (CORE), began peacefully, but later protesters began hurling missiles and Molotov cocktails at police and roaming the streets with bottles and bricks. The rioting in Harlem continued for four nights before spreading to Brooklyn's Bedford-Stuyvesant neighborhood. In all, one person was killed, more than 100 people were injured, and hundreds were arrested. Although smaller than the uprisings in urban African American communities later in the decade (Watts, Detroit), the Harlem Riot anticipated these uprisings.

North America

# Hawkins, Edler Garnett

**(b. June 13, 1908, Bronx, N.Y.; d. December 18, 1977), minister and civil rights leader who led the Presbyterian Church's participation in the Civil Rights Movement.**

Born to Albert and Annie Lee Hawkins, Edler Garnett Hawkins received the bachelor of divinity degree from Union Theological Seminary in 1938.

Upon graduation he entered the ministry and was the first pastor of Saint Augustine Presbyterian Church in the Bronx.

In 1964 Hawkins became the first African American moderator of the General Assembly of the United Presbyterian Church, the denomination's highest office. As a member of the Presbyterian Interracial Council, he promoted his church's involvement in the Civil Rights Movement. In 1970 he retired from the pastorate to join the faculty of Princeton Theological Seminary as professor of black studies.

North America

# Hedgeman, Anna Arnold

**(b. July 5, 1899, Marshalltown, Iowa; d. January 17, 1990, New York, N.Y.), African American public servant and civil rights advocate.**

Though born in Iowa, Anna Arnold Hedgeman grew up in Anoka, Minnesota, and later attended Hamline University in St. Paul, where she was the first black student in the school's history. She received her B.A. in 1922, but after finding teaching opportunities for blacks scarce in the North, she began teaching at a Southern black school, Rust College in Holly Springs, Mississippi. Though impressed with the resilience and determination of students who confronted terrible poverty and discrimination, Hedgeman was deeply discouraged by the South's rampant racism and deep-rooted segregation, and she left Rust to work in a series of positions with the Young Women's Christian Association (YWCA) in several cities.

Hedgeman's long career in public service included positions as executive director of the National Council for a Permanent Fair Employment Practices Committee, in the Federal Security Agency, and in the New York City mayor's cabinet. Hedgeman was the only woman on the organizing committee of the 1963 March on Washington.

North America

# Highlander Folk School,

**an interracial adult education center in Mounteagle, Tennessee, where some of the most important figures of the Civil Rights Movement studied.**

In 1932 educator Myles Horton founded the Highlander Folk School. It was loosely modeled on Danish folk schools, which provided adult education, especially in history and government, to raise the consciousness of its students. Because of Horton's belief in education as an instrument for social change, Highlander offered leadership training courses to classes that were integrated in the segregated Tennessee of the 1930s, 1940s, and 1950s. Highlander focused on empowering ordinary citizens by teaching them the skills to organize and self-advocate. During the Great Depression, Highlander attempted to help the unemployed and impoverished in the nearby Cumberland Mountain communities. In the late 1930s and early 1940s Highlander worked with the southwide industrial union movement, and in the late 1940s it worked with the National Farmers Union. It is best known, however, for its association with the Civil Rights Movement. Civil rights leaders Martin Luther King Jr., Rosa Parks, Stokely Carmichael, Fannie Lou Hamer, Andrew Young, and Septima Clark all studied at Highlander.

Septima Clark became Highlander's director of education, and she developed the Highlander concept of Citizenship Schools, which proliferated in the South and provided instruction in everything from checkbook balancing to registering to vote to reading. But the main objective of the schools was to motivate its students to embrace political activism. As Horton said, students learned that they "couldn't read and write their way into freedom. They had to fight for that and they had to do it as part of a group, not as an individual."

Highlander's success in developing leaders within oppressed communities led to harassment, particularly from the Tennessee state government, which sought to close the school. In 1982 Highlander celebrated its 50th anniversary—confirming Horton's observation that "you can't padlock an idea."

North America
_____

# Hill, Anita Faye

**(b. July 30, 1956, Morris, Okla.), African American lawyer and educator known for her controversial role in the Senate confirmation hearings of United States Supreme Court nominee Clarence Thomas.**

Born July 30, 1956, in Morris, Oklahoma, to Irma and Albert Hill, Anita Hill became valedictorian of her high school class. She completed a Bachelor of Science degree in psychology at Oklahoma State in 1977 and was one of 11 black students out of 160 graduates of Yale Law School in 1980. Her first position as a lawyer was at Ward, Harkrader and Ross, a Washington, D.C., firm in 1981. Later that year she became assistant to Clarence Thomas, who was head of the Office of Civil Rights at the U.S. Department of Education. In 1982 she joined him when he became chairman of the Equal Employment Opportunity Commission (EEOC).

In 1983 Hill left this job to join the faculty of Oral Roberts University as a law professor. In 1986 she accepted a position at the University of Oklahoma and received tenure in 1991. In October 1991 Hill testified in the nationally televised Senate confirmation hearings for Thomas's nomination to the U.S. Supreme. Hill claimed Thomas had sexually harassed her while at the EEOC; Thomas denied the allegations. Despite Hill's assertions, Thomas was confirmed, but her testimony brought public awareness to the issue of sexual harassment and revitalized the feminist movement. Hill describes her professional relationship with Clarence Thomas and offers her account of the Thomas hearings in her book, *Speaking Truth to Power*, published in 1997.

In 1991 *Glamour* magazine honored Hill as Woman of the Year, and the National Coalition of 100 Black Women presented her with the Ida B. Wells Award.

# Hooks, Benjamin Lawrence

(b. January 31, 1925, Memphis, Tenn.), lawyer, minister, civil rights activist, and executive director of the National Association for the Advancement of Colored People (NAACP).

After graduating from Howard University in 1944 and from DePaul University with a law degree in 1948, Benjamin Hooks worked as a public defender and a Baptist minister, serving from 1956 into the mid-1990s as a pastor of Memphis's Middle Baptist Church.

Through his legal and ministerial work Hooks became a prominent figure in the Civil Rights Movement and sat on the board of directors of the Southern Christian Leadership Conference from its founding in 1957 until 1977. In 1965 he became the first African American to become a criminal court judge in Tennessee. He was also the first black to sit on the Federal Communications Commission.

In 1977 he became executive director of the National Association for the Advancement of Colored People (NAACP) and became chairman of the Leadership Council on Civil Rights (LCCR) as well. A nationally recognized leader and the first African American to address both the Republican and Democratic national conventions, Hooks turned the attention of the NAACP to issues including national health insurance, welfare, urban problems, and the environment. He left the NAACP in 1992 and the LCCR in 1994 to return to Middle Street Church as a full-time pastor.

# Hope, John

(b. June 21, 1868, Augusta, Ga.; d. February 20, 1936, Atlanta, Ga.), African American university president and civil rights leader who founded the Atlanta University consortium and dedicated his life to achieving racial equality by improving black education.

John Hope's mother, Mary Frances, was a freed slave and his father, James Hope, a Scot. He graduated with honors from Worcester Academy in 1890, and received a scholarship to Brown University, where he graduated, also with honors, in 1894. He married Lugenia Burns, a social worker from Chicago; they became parents of two sons.

Hope was a teacher in Nashville at Roger Williams College, where he taught Greek, Latin, and the natural sciences from 1894 to 1898. His career reflected his belief that African Americans could achieve equality through higher learning. In 1898 he moved to Atlanta Baptist College, which in 1913 was renamed Morehouse College, where he was professor of classics.

In 1906 Hope became Morehouse's president. He was the only university president to join W. E. B. Du Bois's militant Niagara Movement in 1906. During his years in Atlanta he became well acquainted with Du Bois and the two became lifelong friends.

In 1929 Hope founded the Atlanta University consortium, which affiliated Atlanta University, Morehouse College, Spelman College, and, later,
Clark University and Morris Brown College. Hope was the group's first
president. He also became president of the National Association of Teachers
in Colored Schools and honorary president of the Association for the Study
of Negro Life and History. He sat on the Advisory Board of the National
Association for the Advancement of Colored People (NAACP) and on the
Executive Committee of the Urban League of New York, and was a
member of Atlanta's Commission on Interracial Cooperation.

North America
## Houston, Charles Hamilton
(b. September 3, 1895, Washington, D.C.; d. April 22, 1950, Bethesda, Md.),
first chief counsel of the National Association for the Advancement of Colored
People (NAACP) and vice dean of Howard University Law School; helped craft
the legal groundwork and train lawyers for the Civil Rights Movement.

At Charles H. Houston's 1950 memorial service, his cousin, federal judge
William H. Hastie, eulogized him as "the Moses of our journey." Referring
to the hard-won victory against segregation, Houston's protégé and successor as NAACP chief counsel, Thurgood Marshall, described him as "the
engineer of it all." In his work at both the NAACP and at Howard University Law School, which, according to historian Richard Kluger, Houston
made into "a living laboratory where civil-rights law was invented," Houston
was one of the most influential American lawyers of the twentieth century.

Born in Washington, D.C., in 1895, the only child of William and Mary
Houston was raised in an atmosphere of racial and family pride. Houston
graduated from the M Street School, the most academically rigorous black
high school in the nation, and in 1911 entered Amherst College in Massachusetts. The only African American in the Amherst class of 1915, he
studied diligently and was elected to Phi Beta Kappa.

After college Houston returned to Washington, where he taught part-
time at Howard University until the United States entered World War I.
Determined to avoid the menial service to which most black soldiers were
subjected, Houston joined other black college men in pushing for a separate
officers' training school for African Americans. The War Department complied by establishing a camp in Des Moines, Iowa, to which Houston
reported in June 1917. He earned his commission as a second lieutenant
and was sent to France in 1918, where he saw no action but did experience
the racism that the segregated United States Army brought to Europe
during the war.

Houston returned home during the Red Summer of 1919, named for its
near-epidemic racial violence and lynchings. That fall he entered Harvard
Law School, determined to "study law and use my time fighting for men
who could not strike back." Houston excelled at Harvard. He was the first
black student elected to the prestigious *Law Review* and after graduating

was awarded a traveling scholarship for further study, which he spent in Madrid, Spain, completing his education in 1924.

Houston joined his father's law firm and began teaching evening classes at Howard University's law school. In 1929 Mordecai Johnson, Howard's first African American president, tapped Houston to revitalize the moribund institution, which had been denied accreditation by the American Bar Association. Houston closed Howard's legal night school, hired new faculty, coordinated guest lectures and workshops, and designed a curriculum aimed at his dream of "litigation against racism." He recruited bright young men throughout the South to attend the school, including future civil rights leaders Thurgood Marshall and Oliver W. Hill, telling them, "A lawyer's either a social engineer or he's a parasite." Due largely to Houston's boundless energy and exacting standards, the school was accredited in 1931.

Once he had established Howard as the nation's premier training ground for "capable and socially alert Negro lawyers," Houston was ready for a new challenge. He had served on the NAACP's Legal Committee and as informal adviser to NAACP secretary Walter White since the early 1930s. In 1934 he reluctantly agreed to assist in the defense of George Crawford, a black man accused of murder in Virginia, where African Americans were systematically excluded from jury duty. Houston lost the case (though the following year the Supreme Court of the United States ruled such jury discrimination unconstitutional) but saved Crawford from execution.

It was in the field of educational equality that Houston, who finally accepted White's invitation to become NAACP chief counsel in 1935, proved indispensable. With financial support from the Garland Fund (later called the American Fund for Public Service), the association commissioned the *Margold Report*, a rough blueprint for the fight. Houston agreed that education should be the primary battlefront, writing in a 1935 letter that "discrimination in education is symbolic of all the more drastic discriminations which Negroes suffer in American life." Reflecting Houston's understanding of political power and sensitivity to public opinion, his strategy differed from the *Margold Report* in its emphasis on gradual change and the building of legal precedent. He chose three primary targets: the different pay scales for black and white teachers; the disparity in transportation provided for black and white students; and the inequality in opportunity for graduate study at state-supported segregated institutions. It was the third approach that proved most successful, spawning the three Supreme Court cases that together provided the ammunition to topple *Plessy v. Ferguson*'s prescription for "separate but equal" accommodations.

The first, *Missouri* ex rel. *Gaines v. Canada*, involved Missouri's refusal to admit African American students to the state university's law school, offering applicants instead the choice of going out of state or attending a separate black law school yet to be established. The Court found in 1938 that such unequal provisions created an unfair "privilege . . . for white law students" that was denied African Americans. Though argued by Marshall, who had succeeded him as chief counsel, it was Houston's strategy and advice that helped win two cases in which inequality was less blatant.

*McLaurin v. Oklahoma* concerned a lone black student who was segregated within the state's graduate school of education; and in *Sweatt v. Painter*, Texas provided a separate black law school that shared some facilities with the white institution. In both cases, eventually decided in 1950, the year of Houston's death, the court edged closer to overturning *Plessy*, ruling that intangible effects of inequality could violate a plaintiff's right to equal protection under the Fourteenth Amendment.

His health poor, in 1938 Houston stepped down as NAACP chief counsel. But he continued fighting for racial justice, as his biographer Genna R. McNeil says, "on diverse fronts." Returning to Washington, where he had served on the district's board of education from 1933 to 1935, Houston rejoined his father's law firm and began to focus on economic inequality. Representing two railroad unions, he challenged discriminatory actions by government negotiators and contractors. In 1944 he was appointed to the Fair Employment Practices Committee (FEPC), from which he resigned in 1945 in protest over its imminent disbanding. Already hospitalized for exhaustion once before, Houston suffered a serious heart attack in 1948. He died two years later, leaving behind his second wife, Henrietta, and their only child, Charles Hamilton Houston Jr.

Friends and associates remembered him as hard-driving and brilliant, a perfectionist whose passion was submerged beneath a dignified demeanor ("Lose your temper, lose your case" was one of many aphorisms his law students heard). For his work on behalf of school desegregation (which ultimately prevailed in 1954's *Brown v. Board of Education*), the NAACP posthumously awarded him its Spingarn Medal. In 1958 Howard University renamed its main law school building after the man who had written to one of his students, "The most important thing . . . is that no Negro tolerate any ceiling on his ambitions or imagination."

North America

# Hudson, Hosea

(b. 1898, Wilkes County, Ga.; d. 1988, Gainesville, Fla.), American union leader and communist activist who was a voice for African American workers during the Great Depression.

As a youth Hosea Hudson worked with his family on the sharecropping land where they lived and was, therefore, unable to attend school. In 1917 he married and began share-cropping land separately from his family. After boll weevils destroyed his crops, he moved with his new family to Atlanta in 1923. The next year he settled in Birmingham, Alabama, where he began his career in iron molding.

Hudson soon engaged in informal attempts to better the treatment of African American workers. But it was not until 1931, when he joined the Communist Party of the U.S.A. (CPUSA), that he became a public voice for worker's rights. Fired within a year from the Stockham Foundry and forced to find work under pseudonyms, he nonetheless continued to fight the Great Depression's devastating effects on African American workers. During the 1930s he strengthened his ties to the CPUSA while simultaneously working for the government on the Works Progress Administration (WPA). He also founded the Right to Vote Club in the struggle for African American enfranchisement. From 1940 to 1947 Hudson was an official in the United Steel Workers Local and the Birmingham Industrial Union Council, but eventually was expelled from any involvement in the organizations as a result of his CPUSA membership.

Forced to conceal his identity from this period until 1956 due to widespread anticommunist sentiment, Hudson lived in Atlanta and New York City. After moving to Atlantic City, he remained a CPUSA liaison while working as a janitor. Rediscovered by the American left in the early 1980s, Hudson was given the key to the city of Birmingham for his civil rights work. He remained politically active until his death in 1988.

North America

# Hurley, Ruby

(b. November 7, 1909, Washington, D.C.; d. August 9, 1980, Atlanta, Ga.), civil rights leader who was the only full-time civil rights activist working in the Deep South in the 1950s.

Ruby Hurley began working in 1939 with the Washington chapter of the National Association for the Advancement of Colored People (NAACP). She became the National Youth Secretary of the NAACP in 1943, and during her tenure the number of youth councils and college chapters grew from 86 to more than 380.

Hurley transferred to Birmingham, Alabama, as regional secretary in 1951 in order to organize new NAACP branches throughout the South. One year later she became regional director. Hers was the NAACP's first full-time office in the Deep South. In 1955 she investigated the murders of Rev. George W. Lee and Lamar Smith, who were killed for participating in black voter registration drives in Mississippi. In the same year, with Medgar Evers, she investigated the murder of 14-year-old Emmett Till, traveling at personal risk, in disguise, to locate witnesses. She also helped register Autherine Lucy Foster, the first black student admitted at the University of Alabama.

When the NAACP was banned from operating in Alabama in 1956, Hurley relocated to Atlanta. There she became involved in disputes between the NAACP and the newer Student Nonviolent Coordinating Committee (SNCC) and the Southern Christian Leadership Conference (SCLC). She dedicated herself to defending the strategies of her generation of civil rights workers to the new generation of activists.

# I

## Inner Cities in the United States

commonly defined as urban ghettos or black ghettos; many white politicians and policy analysts portray the predominantly black inner city as the source of the nation's worst urban problems. To a great extent, however, the ills of the American city also reflect the consequences of suburbanization.

## Innis, Roy

(b. June 6, 1934, St. Croix, United States Virgin Islands), civil rights activist and promoter of black nationalism and separatism.

Roy Innis moved from the U.S. Virgin Islands to New York City with his mother in 1946. He served in the army for two years during the Korean War, before returning to City College of New York as a chemistry major. In 1963 he began a 25-year involvement with the Harlem chapter of the Congress of Racial Equality (CORE), an interracial, nonviolent civil rights organization. He was first elected chairman and became the associate national director in 1968.

Innis was also the coeditor and founder of the *Manhattan Tribune*. He gained national publicity in 1973 when he participated in a televised debate with Nobel physicist William Shockley on the topic of black genetic inferiority. Through his work, Innis promoted Black Power as well as black nationalism and separatism, and encouraged self-defense over nonviolence.

# J

## Jackson, George Lester

(b. September 23, 1941, Chicago, Ill.; d. August 21, 1971, San Quentin Prison, Calif.), African American anti-capitalist revolutionary whose prison writings served as a manifesto for New Left activists in the 1970s.

George Jackson grew up on the West Side of Chicago, the son of Lester Jackson, a postal worker, and Georgia Jackson. He was the second oldest of five children. Street smart and rebellious, Jackson had several run-ins with the law for petty crimes by the time he was ten. In 1956 his family moved to Los Angeles, where Jackson's troubles with the law continued, including several arrests for robbery. Paroled in June 1960 after serving time for a gas station holdup, Jackson was arrested later that year for a gas station robbery that netted $71. Due to his previous convictions, he received an indeterminate sentence of one year to life. He was 19 and remained in prison for the rest of his life.

While in prison, Jackson studied the writings of Karl Marx, Frantz Fanon, Mao Zedong, Fidel Castro, and others. He developed a critique of capitalism and racism that enabled him to see his criminal activity and his imprisonment within a political context. Jackson and several others organized study groups to help raise the political consciousness of African American prisoners. Jackson, who worked as a prison organizer for the Black Panther Party, aimed to channel the anger and rebellious spirit of African Americans toward political activism. His revolutionary philosophy cohered around a program of armed struggle directed at overthrowing the racist and imperialist establishment in the United States.

Over the years Jackson was repeatedly denied parole. Prison officials said that it was because of Jackson's disruptive behavior; Jackson and his supporters argued that it was due to his political activism.

On January 16, 1970, in response to the death of three black inmates, a white guard, John Mills, was killed in Soledad Prison. Jackson and two other black men, John Clutchette and Fleeta Drumgo, were accused of the murder. The facts of their alleged involvement have never been satisfactorily established. The three accused men became known as the Soledad Brothers and attracted international attention. *Soledad Brother: The Prison Letters of George Jackson* was published during this time and became a national bestseller. Many people protested that the Soledad Brothers were being framed due to their political activities. Angela Davis played a leading role in organizing support for their defense.

The trial dissolved into complete chaos on August 7, 1970, when Jonathon Jackson, younger brother of George, attempted to take over the courthouse and free the three accused. During the melee, Jonathon was shot to death, along with the judge and two of the inmates. A little more than a year later, on August 21, 1971, prison guards killed George Jackson. The official report said that Jackson was armed, that he had participated in a revolt, killing two white prisoners and three guards, and that he was attempting to escape. Supporters have noted several inconsistencies in the report and believe that prison authorities, fearful that Jackson had grown too powerful, set him up and murdered him.

North America

# Jackson, Jesse Louis

**(b. October 8, 1941, Greenville, S.C.), African American minister, founder of Operation PUSH and the National Rainbow Coalition, and twice candidate for president of the United States.**

One of America's best-known and most respected black leaders, Jesse Jackson appeared on the national scene following the 1968 assassination of his mentor, Martin Luther King Jr. In the years since, Jackson has continued to work for racial and economic justice, international peace, and empowerment of society's outsiders. With projects like Operation Breadbasket, Operation PUSH, and the Rainbow Coalition, as well as political action—particularly his candidacy for the Democratic nomination for president in 1984 and 1988—he has attracted fame, admiration, and criticism. For his work on behalf of racial and social justice, he has been awarded at least 40 honorary degrees, and for ten years he has been listed among the top ten men most admired by Americans. Despite all of Jackson's achievements, however, some commentators and biographers admit to a sense of disappointment because of what he has not accomplished.

Jackson was born to Helen Burns, an unwed teenaged mother, herself the child of an unwed teenaged mother. His childhood was marked by feelings of isolation and difference, according to his biographers. His biological father, Noah Robinson, was one of Greenville's most prosperous black citizens, while Jackson, along with his mother and grandmother, lived in relative poverty. Robinson's initial refusal to acknowledge Jackson (who took the name of his stepfather, Charles H. Jackson, upon being adopted by him in 1957) changed as Jesse grew into a promising athlete and scholar. Despite the material and emotional deprivations of Jackson's early life, one of his friends told biographer Marshall Frady, "Not only does Jesse believe in God, but Jesse believes God believes in him."

This self-assurance and sense of destiny was first tested at college. A football scholarship to the University of Illinois brought Jackson north in 1959, but after being denied the coveted quarterback position he returned south to the historically black North Carolina Agricultural and Technical State College. There he fulfilled his athletic and leadership potential, serving as the student body president as well as quarterback of the football team. It was also while he was at college that Jackson became involved in the Civil Rights Movement, first by protesting the whites-only local library system, then later by leading demonstrations against segregated restaurants, theaters, and hotels.

By the time Jackson graduated in 1964, he had decided to become a minister. Accepting a scholarship from the Chicago Theological Seminary, he returned to Illinois, this time with a family; he had married Jacqueline Brown the same year. In Chicago Jackson worked hard at his studies, and at first kept his distance from the local civil rights organizations, many of which were trying to recruit him as a potential leader. All that changed, according to Frady, when Jackson went to Selma, Alabama, in March 1965, to take part in a historic civil rights march led by Martin Luther King Jr., president of the Southern Christian Leadership Conference (SCLC). Leading a group of fellow divinity students, Jackson arrived in Selma, met King, and made himself noticed, as much for his obvious ambition as for his leadership skills.

Before long Jackson was working for SCLC. By 1966 he had left seminary to head the Chicago branch of Operation Breadbasket, an organization dedicated to improving the financial position of the black community; in 1967 he became its national chairman. Blessed with charm, energy, and a fiery oratorical style, Jackson soon found success and local fame as the man who pressured several large Chicago organizations into hiring more African Americans. Relations between Jackson and the SCLC leadership, which had been stormy at times due to competition among strong personalities, deteriorated further after King's assassination in April 1968. Accused by some of exaggerating his closeness to the slain civil rights hero, Jackson nevertheless quickly became a national figure, assumed by some to be King's natural heir. After the SCLC board selected Ralph David Abernathy as its next president, Jackson continued with the organization, even serving as mayor of the ill-fated antipoverty demonstration Resurrection City. In 1971 he left in order to begin a new project called Operation PUSH.

PUSH, which stands for People United to Serve Humanity, grew out of Operation Breadbasket and continued many of its themes, especially the theme of economic empowerment. Embellishing a line from one of King's speeches, Jackson provided PUSH with a catchy and compelling motto: "I Am Somebody." Jackson began attracting large and enthusiastic crowds to his weekly PUSH prayer meetings. As his influence and celebrity grew, so did his family, which soon included five children. With the addition of PUSH-Excel, a branch devoted to educational issues, and with a new emphasis on voter registration drives, Jackson became a powerful voice for minorities and the poor, appearing often in the national media and speaking on behalf of political candidates.

In 1983 Jackson declared himself a candidate for the presidential nomination of the Democratic Party. Emphasizing his compassion and fervor on behalf of the poor, the marginalized, and the downtrodden, he pledged to build a "rainbow coalition." Jackson had already been criticized for his support of the Palestinian Liberation Organization during a trip to North Africa and the Middle East in 1979. During the race for the 1984 election he faced renewed charges of anti-Semitism—for his association with the controversial Nation of Islam leader Louis Farrakhan and for his reference to New York City as Hymietown. Jackson apologized repeatedly for this remark and has since emphasized his distaste for all forms of bigotry, but the stigma remains.

Caught between the high expectations of the black community and the fear and indifference of the white mainstream, Jackson did not win the nomination in 1984. But he did amass far more delegates than anyone had predicted. In his speech before the Democratic Convention, his dramatic call to "Keep Hope Alive" electrified the crowd, and some commentators later called it the best political speech of the century. In 1986 Jackson founded the National Rainbow Coalition. Two years later he again sought the presidency and failed to be nominated, although this time he won several major primaries and, for a while, was the frontrunner. Although nominee Michael Dukakis did not ask him to be his running mate, despite that suggestion from several polls and advisors, Jackson worked hard to support the Democratic ticket, which eventually lost to George Bush and Dan Quayle. Beyond their simple success or failure, Jackson's presidential runs were significant: through them, he galvanized black voters, millions of whom he had helped to register prior to the election; he raised important social and racial issues on the national level; and, for the first time, he introduced the possibility that an African American could win the nation's highest office.

In the decade following the 1988 election, Jackson continued in leadership roles, although he has passed the political torch to his son, Jesse Jr., who is a congressman from Illinois. Despite the urging of supporters, Jackson chose not to run for mayor of Washington, D.C., where he and his family had moved in 1989. He left PUSH the same year. In 1990 he began serving as "statehood senator," a position created to lobby for statehood for the District of Columbia. Jackson also resumed the unaligned diplomacy he had begun in 1979 and that he had continued in 1983 when he had won the release of a black prisoner of war who was being detained in Syria. In 1991 Jackson's intervention was responsible for the release of hundreds of hostages being held by Iraqi president Saddam Hussein. In 1996 he returned to Chicago to resume leadership of PUSH. In 1999 Jackson once again assumed the role of roving ambassador and succeeded in securing from Slobadan Milosevic the release of three American soldiers taken prisoner on the border between Yugoslavia and Macedonia.

North America

# Jackson, Jimmy Lee

(b. December 1938, Marion, Ala.; d. February 26, 1965, Selma, Ala.), African American civil rights activist whose death at the hands of Alabama state troopers inspired the march from Selma to Montgomery.

Jimmy Lee Jackson, a pulpwood cutter, had recently become the youngest deacon in the history of St. James Baptist Church in Marion, Alabama, before becoming a martyr in the struggle for civil rights. Born and raised in Marion, Jackson began to advocate for voting rights for African Americans as a participant in a local right-to-vote movement, led by Albert Turner. On February 18, 1965, Jackson and his family attended a nighttime rally at Zion's Chapel Methodist Church, held to protest the jailing of one of the Southern Christian Leadership Conference (SCLC) leaders, James Orange. Upon leaving the church, the congregation was attacked by state troopers and local police. Inside a nearby café Jackson was beaten and shot in the stomach while attempting to protect his mother and grandfather. Taken first to Perry County Hospital, Jackson was transferred to the Negro Good Samaritan Hospital in Selma, where he died eight days later due to the gunshot wound.

Martin Luther King Jr. preached at Jackson's funeral on March 3, criticizing the federal government for failing to protect its own citizens while spending millions of dollars to fight a war in Vietnam. Jackson's death caused activists to galvanize plans for a march from Selma to the state house in Montgomery. More than 500 African Americans began the march on March 7, 1965, and were savagely beaten back by police, some of them on horseback. The brutal encounter, which became known as Bloody Sunday, was televised across the nation and was critical to securing national support for voting rights legislation.

North America

# Jackson, Joseph Harrison

(b. September 11, 1900, Rudyard, Miss.; d. August 18, 1990, Chicago, Ill.), African American Baptist leader who opposed Martin Luther King Jr. and the Civil Rights Movement.

As president of the 5-million-member National Baptist Convention U.S.A., Inc., from 1953 to 1982, Joseph H. Jackson was one of the most powerful black ministers of his day. Strongly opposed to the popular civil rights program and activity of Martin Luther King Jr., Jackson managed to continue his autocratic control of the denomination to which they both belonged. In

1960 Gardner C. Taylor, who was supportive of King, was elected to the presidency of the convention on a roll call vote, but Jackson refused to relinquish power. Consequently, King, Taylor, and other liberal activists withdrew to form the Progressive National Baptist Convention.

Born in Mississippi, Jackson attended Jackson College and Colgate-Rochester Divinity School. From 1922 to 1941 he served churches in Mississippi, Nebraska, and Pennsylvania. In 1941 he was called to Olivet Baptist Church in Chicago, Illinois, the largest black Baptist church in the country. In 1953 he was elected president of the convention, the governing body of thousands of autonomous congregations. He wrote several books, including a history of the convention.

Jackson eschewed political civil rights agitation in favor of black economic self-development, a position advocated by conservatives such as Booker T. Washington as well as radicals such as Marcus Garvey. In *Unholy Shadows and Freedom's Holy Light*, Jackson wrote, "Civil disobedience is a form of lawlessness and, is in reality, not far removed from open crime." Extending his idea of self-development, Jackson promoted African land development in Liberia. He died in 1990.

North America

# Jackson, Lillie Mae Carroll

**(b. May 25, 1889, Baltimore, Md.; d. July 5, 1975, Baltimore, Md.), long-time civil rights activist and Baltimore branch president of the National Association for the Advancement of Colored People (NAACP).**

One of the women who helped revitalize a flagging NAACP in the 1930s was its Baltimore branch president, Lillie May Jackson. Known as "fearless Lil," she became involved in the association after her daughter, Juanita Jackson Mitchell, founded the Baltimore Young People's Forum in 1931. In her advisory role to her daughter's group, Jackson helped campaign for economic justice and voter education and against lynching. In 1935, around the same time that NAACP president Walter White recruited her daughter to serve as its first youth director, Jackson took over the association's Baltimore branch. With the help of her friend and fellow Baltimorean Thurgood Marshall, she soon transformed it into one of the nation's most active branches.

Membership in the Baltimore branch swelled to 20,000 during Jackson's tenure as president, and under her leadership voter registration among the area's African Americans nearly doubled by the late 1940s. The branch also played a national role, fighting segregation in a series of lawsuits that included *Murray v. Maryland* (1936), an important precursor to 1954's *Brown v. Board of Education*. After *Brown* outlawed school segregation, Jackson proved instrumental in seeing that the verdict was enforced in her home state. Jackson retired from the NAACP in 1970 but continued to work for human rights in Baltimore through her own organization, Freedom House, which served the city's poor. She died in 1975 at age 86, survived by four children, ten grandchildren, and nine great-grandchildren.

North America

## Jackson, Luther Porter

**(b. 1892, Louisville, Ky.; d. April 20, 1950, Petersburg, Va.), African American historian of the black American South and advocate of black voting rights.**

Luther Porter Jackson was the ninth of 12 children born to Delilah and Edward Jackson, both former slaves. Inspired by his mother, who had become a schoolteacher after Emancipation, Jackson developed a keen interest in education. He earned bachelor's and master's degrees from Fisk University in Nashville, then taught at high schools and colleges in South Carolina and Kansas. By 1922 he was an instructor at the Virginia Normal and Industrial Institute (later Virginia State College) in Petersburg, where he spent the rest of his life.

Affected by the time he spent in South Carolina, Jackson published two studies about the education of Carolina blacks during the mid-1800s. He then focused almost exclusively on the history of black Virginians. Delving into courthouse records—wills, tax ledgers, marriage licenses, and property lists—he discovered previously unpublicized information about black life. The result was the pioneering Free Negro Labor and Property Holding in Virginia, 1830–1860, published in 1942.

Thereafter, Jackson published dozens of articles and books about the history of Virginia's blacks, prompting historian Carter G. Woodson to say of Jackson, "He knows more about Negro families in Virginia than any other man living." Along the way, Jackson received a full professorship from Virginia State and a doctoral degree from the University of Chicago.

Jackson was also a fervent supporter of black equality and an active fundraiser for the National Association for the Advancement of Colored People (NAACP). His Petersburg League of Negro Voters grew to become the Virginia Voters League, and his Petersburg Negro Business Association later became the Virginia Trade Association.

Not content with available data on black voters, he published yearly *The Voting Status of Negroes in Virginia*, and this effort, too, outgrew its beginnings: the Southern Regional Council commissioned him to conduct a larger study on voting rights, which was published in 1948 as the pamphlet *Race and Suffrage in the South since 1940*. Notorious for his long hours of work, Jackson died of a heart attack in 1950, his place secured as one of the most influential historians of Southern black life.

North America

## Jackson, Maynard Holbrook, Jr.

**(b. March 23, 1938, Dallas, Tex.), three-time mayor of Atlanta, Georgia, who helped bring the 1996 Olympic Games to the city.**

By the time he was sworn in as Atlanta's mayor in 1974, Maynard H. Jackson Jr. had already captured the youthful energy of the capital of the New South, a city known for its relatively harmonious racial politics and pro-business attitude. At 34, Jackson, a Democrat, was not only Atlanta's first black mayor, he was also its youngest. But he was already a political veteran, having worked at Emory University's Community Legal Services Center on grassroots issues such as housing litigation and legal services for the poor, and he came from a family long prominent in Atlanta's history.

After serving the maximum of two consecutive terms allowed by Atlanta's city charter, Jackson stepped aside in 1982 for the new mayor, Andrew Young, the former ambassador to the United Nations, whom Jackson had recruited to succeed him. In 1990 Jackson was elected for a third term, during which he worked to bring the Olympic Games to Atlanta. Capitalizing on the city's upbeat image, strong corporate community, and international appeal—financial magazines consistently rate it among the best cities for business—Jackson won approval from the International Olympic Committee to host the Olympic Games in 1996. In addition, the city hosted the 1992 Democratic National Convention, attracting attention as a vibrant, successful, predominantly black city. In part because of health problems (he underwent cardiac bypass surgery in 1992), Jackson did not run for another term as mayor, stepping down in 1994.

North America

# Jackson State Incident,

**anti-Vietnam demonstration that turned into a race riot in which two black youths were killed.**

On May 13, 1970, some 150 protesters gathered on the all-black campus of Jackson State College (now Jackson State University) in Mississippi to protest the Vietnam War. The crowd was in an angry mood, their hostility fueled by the killing of four white students at Kent State University by National Guardsmen nine days earlier, and by the racially motivated murder, two days before, of six African Americans in Augusta, Georgia. While some of the young black demonstrators were content to chant slogans, others burned police barricades and threw rocks and bottles at passing white motorists. Local officials alerted the National Guard, which arrived in force on the campus when the demonstrations recurred the following day. Later that night, in the face of escalating violence, members of the Jackson police department and the Mississippi Highway Patrol fired into the crowd and killed 2 black students, wounding 12 others.

The Jackson State Incident took place at the height of the anti-Vietnam protest era, when violence and unrest gripped many American college campuses. The events at Jackson State reflected not only the national antiwar sentiment of college students but long-simmering racial conflicts. Jackson State students were protesting both President Nixon's plans to invade Cambodia and the racism of local police.

Throughout the 1960s the campus at Jackson State had seethed with tensions, not only between the students and the city's police, but also between the students and the school's own black administrators, who feared the possibility of losing state funding because of the campus turmoil. The problems were exacerbated by the frequent harassment of white motorists by neighborhood toughs, whom city police often mistook for Jackson State students.

After the shootings in 1970, local politicians and law enforcement agents tried to pass the blame off on the students, claiming that a sniper had caused the deaths. Survivors and family members of the victims took the issue to court, but no local police or National Guardsman was ever indicted.

North America

# Jessye, Eva

(b. January 20, 1895, Coffeyville, Kans.; d. February 21, 1992, Ypsilanti, Mich.), African American choral director, composer, and educator, the first African American woman to gain international renown as a professional choral director.

A woman of many talents, Eva Jessye pursued a music career that spanned more than half a century and won her a reputation as "the dean of black female musicians." During the 1930s she gained international attention as director of the Eva Jessye Choir, which toured the United States and Europe and sang in the first production of George Gershwin's folk opera *Porgy and Bess* (1935). During the next three decades she led the choir in numerous revivals of the opera and in 1963 directed the choir for the historic March on Washington led by Martin Luther King Jr.

Jessye grew up in Coffeyville, Kansas, where, after the separation of her parents in 1898, she was reared by her grandmother and her mother's sisters. As a child she began singing, organized a girls' quartet, and, at age 12, helped composer Will Marion Cook copy music for his orchestra when he toured her hometown. At age 13 she began musical studies at Western University in Quindaro, Kansas. After earning a teaching certificate from Langston University in Oklahoma, she spent several years teaching music in Oklahoma schools, and in 1920 became the head of the music department at Morgan State College in Baltimore.

In 1922 Jessye moved to New York, where she studied privately with Will Marion Cook and the music theorist Percy Goetschius. Four years later she had established herself as director of the Original Dixie Jubilee Singers, later renamed the Eva Jessye Choir. In 1929 she went to Hollywood to train a choir to perform in the first black musical film, *Hallelujah* (1929, Metro-Goldwyn-Mayer), written and directed by King Vidor, and in 1934 she became choral director of Virgil Thompson's opera *Four Saints in Three Acts*. Achieving international fame as choral director of Gershwin's *Porgy and Bess*, she continued to tour with her choir for more than 40 years. A respected composer, she conducted her own music in both radio and stage performances and in 1972 directed her critically acclaimed folk oratorio *Paradise Lost and Regained* (composed in 1934) at the Washington Cathedral.

Jessye exerted considerable influence as a teacher. She held several teaching posts, lectured widely, and played an important role in the careers of such concert artists as Muriel Rahn, Andrew Frierson, and Lawrence Winters. In 1974 she established the Eva Jessye Collection of Afro-American Music at the University of Michigan in Ann Arbor, where she spent the last ten years of her life. She died of natural causes in Ypsilanti, Michigan, at age 97.

North America

# Jim Crow,

the system of laws and customs that enforced racial segregation and discrimination throughout the United States, especially the South, from the late nineteenth century to the 1960s.

African Americans living in the South during the first half of the twentieth century saw graphic reminders of their second-class citizenship everywhere. Signs reading "Whites Only" or "Colored" hung over drinking fountains and the doors to restrooms, restaurants, movie theaters, and other public places. Along with segregation, blacks, particularly in the South, faced discrimination in jobs and housing and were often denied their constitutional right to vote. Whether by law or by custom, all these obstacles to equal status went by the name Jim Crow.

Jim Crow was the name of a character in minstrelsy (in which white performers in blackface used African American stereotypes in their songs and dances); it is not clear how the term came to describe American segregation and discrimination. Jim Crow has its origins in a variety of sources, including the Black Codes imposed upon African Americans immediately after the Civil War and prewar racial segregation of railroad cars in the North. But it was not until after Radical Reconstruction ended in 1877 that Jim Crow was born.

Jim Crow grew slowly. In the last two decades of the nineteenth century many African Americans still enjoyed the rights granted in the Thirteenth, Fourteenth, and Fifteenth amendments, along with the 1875 Civil Rights Act. But according to historian C. Vann Woodward, by the late 1890s various factors had combined to create an environment in which white supremacy prevailed. These included the reconciliation of warring political factions in the South, the acquiescence of Northern white liberals, and the United States' military conquest of nonwhite peoples in the Philippines, Hawaii, and Cuba.

Some of the earliest Jim Crow legislation came from the transportation industry. An 1890 law in New Orleans requiring separate railroad cars for black and white passengers was soon followed by regulations in other cities and states. Such laws, ostensibly written to "protect" both races, were given federal support when the United States Supreme Court ruled in *Plessy v. Ferguson* (1896) that "separate but equal" accommodations on Louisiana's railroads were constitutional. The ruling led to legalized segregation in education, public parks, and libraries.

Other Jim Crow laws did not specifically mention race but were written and applied in ways that discriminated against African Americans. Literacy tests and poll taxes, administered with informal loopholes and trick questions, barred nearly all African Americans from voting. For example, though more than 130,000 blacks were registered to vote in Louisiana in 1896, only 1,342 were on the rolls in 1904.

Disfranchisement was often defended by invoking the mythology of Reconstruction, in which Southern whites claimed that unsophisticated black voters had been manipulated by Northern "carpetbaggers" who had moved south after the war. Jim Crow proponents also found ammunition in the incendiary propaganda of the Southern white press, which published sensational and exaggerated accounts of crimes committed by African Americans. As Woodward and other historians have pointed out, an atmosphere emerged of racist hysteria, which further fueled lynching, anti-black rioting, and the rise of the Ku Klux Klan. In addition, early twentieth-century trends in scholarship, including the pseudoscience of eugenics, lent respectability to the view that blacks were inherently inferior to whites.

Jim Crow extended to deny private as well as public, or civil, rights to African Americans. Businesses routinely refused to serve blacks, and many white homeowners would not rent or sell property to African Americans. A strict, unwritten code of behavior governed interracial interaction. Under Jim Crow etiquette, African Americans were denied all social forms of respect. Whites addressed even adult black men as "boy," and all blacks were expected to show deference to all whites. The combination of constant personal humiliation, dismal economic opportunities (sharecropping consigned most rural, Southern blacks to perpetual poverty), and inferior segregated education for their children prompted thousands of African Americans to leave the South in the Jim Crow era. Waves of exodus culminated in the Great Migration north in the 1920s, 1930s, and 1940s, but many African Americans found conditions in the North little better.

A combination of factors led to the dismantling of Jim Crow starting in the late 1940s. Attention attracted by Gunnar Myrdal's 1944 book *An American Dilemma* made Jim Crow a national embarrassment. After more than a decade of litigation, the legal work of the National Association for the Advancement of Colored People (NACCP) began to bear fruit. Supreme Court decisions in *Sweatt v. Painter* (1949) and *McLaurin v. Oklahoma* (1950) started to break down the separate but equal standard set by *Plessy* and finally outlawed state-sponsored segregation in 1954's *Brown v. Board of Education*. Violent resistance by some white Southerners was met by a growing Civil Rights Movement that used boycotts, sit-ins, marches, and other forms of nonviolent protest to achieve goals such as passage of the 1964 Civil Rights Act and 1965 Voting Rights Act. But despite victories against segregation and discrimination, African Americans continued to face unequal opportunities, and new approaches, such as the Black Power Movement, sought to repair the lasting damage of Jim Crow.

# Johnson, Eddie Bernice

(b. 1935, Waco, Tex.), Democratic member of the United States House of Representatives from Texas (1993– ).

Eddie Bernice Johnson was born in Waco, Texas. She received a bachelor's degree in 1955 from St. Mary's at Notre Dame and a nursing degree in 1967 from Texas Christian University. She worked as a nurse until being elected to the Texas House of Representatives in 1972. She earned a master's degree in public administration in 1976 from Southern Methodist University. Johnson left the Texas House in 1977 when President Jimmy Carter appointed her regional director of the Department of Health, Education, and Welfare (HEW). She worked at HEW until 1981, then started her own business consulting firm in Dallas.

In 1986 Johnson was elected to the Texas Senate. As chair of the Texas Senate subcommittee responsible for drawing congressional districts for 1992, she created the new Thirtieth Congressional District, which subsequently elected her to Congress in 1992. In 1994 federal judges ruled the district unconstitutional because it was minority-based and ordered the Texas legislature to redraw it. The redistricting was completed in August 1996 and in November 1996 Johnson was easily reelected.

The Thirtieth District is now located entirely within Dallas County and includes portions of the cities of Dallas and Irving. The city of Dallas is a center of banking, insurance, and medical care in the Southwest. Electronic Data Systems, a manufacturer of computer semiconducters, is a major employer. Irving is home to the Dallas-Fort Worth Airport.

In the 105th Congress (1997–1999), Johnson sat on the Science Committee and the Committee on Transportation and Infrastructure. She also served as secretary of the Congressional Black Caucus.

# Johnson, James Weldon

(b. June 17, 1871, Jacksonville, Fla.; d. June 26, 1938, Wiscasset, Maine), diplomat, poet, novelist, critic, composer, and the first African American executive secretary of the National Association for the Advancement of Colored People (NAACP).

Few leaders have combined such keen intelligence with such varied talents as did James Weldon Johnson, whom his biographer Robert Fleming called "truly the 'Renaissance man' of the Harlem Renaissance." A leading literary and political figure, Johnson was instrumental not only in the growth of the NAACP but also in the formation and nurturing of a distinctly African American artistic community. Poetry, song lyrics, fiction, history, and editorials flowed from his pen and made him one of the great men of African American letters.

Born in Jacksonville, Florida, in 1871, Johnson grew up in a cultured household. His mother, a schoolteacher, had been born free in Nassau, Bahamas, and had spent much of her childhood in New York City. His father worked as headwaiter at a Jacksonville resort restaurant but still found time to read Plutarch; he was a self-educated man who spoke and read Spanish and enjoyed philosophical discussions. Both James and his younger brother, John Rosamond Johnson, were given music lessons at an early age, and their mother read to them at night from Charles Dickens and other Victorian novelists. Early trips to the Bahamas and New York supplemented Johnson's cosmopolitan upbringing.

After completing his education in Jacksonsville, where the black schools went only to the eighth grade, Johnson enrolled in Atlanta University both for preparatory and university classes. He spent seven years there, learning Latin and Greek, studying public speaking, singing with the Glee Club, and writing poetry. Upon his graduation in 1894, he took a job as principal of his old grammar school, a position he held for nearly eight years. As principal he added a ninth and tenth grade and visited white schools in search of ideas for improving his students' education. While working full-time as a principal, in 1895 Johnson launched a newspaper, the *Daily American*, which, though it was published for only eight months, gave him an opportunity to use his literary talents in the service of racial justice. At the same time he learned the law by apprenticeship with a local attorney and passed the bar exam in 1898.

Johnson's brother Rosamond, who had received formal musical training in Boston, convinced Johnson to collaborate with him in writing songs. In 1900 the two wrote *Lift Ev'ry Voice and Sing*, the song that became known as the Negro national anthem. Two years later Johnson accompanied Rosamond to New York, where the brothers, along with Robert Cole, became a successful songwriting team. While there Johnson studied literature at Columbia University and met other African American artists such as Paul Laurence Dunbar and Will Marion Cook. In 1904 friends from Atlanta University invited Johnson to join the Colored Republican Club in New York, where his work for presidential candidate Theodore Roosevelt earned him a consulate post; he left for Puerto Cabello, Venezuela, in 1906.

Johnson's career as a diplomat lasted eight years, during which he served in both Venezuela and Nicaragua. With his excellent Spanish and elegant social manner, he became a popular figure in the racially diverse Latin American cities to which he was sent. Meanwhile, he continued to pursue literary work, beginning a novel that would eventually be titled *Autobiography of an Ex-Coloured Man* (published anonymously in 1912). In 1910 Johnson married the former Grace Nail, gaining companionship for the less enjoyable Nicaragua posting he began in 1909. When the Democrats regained the White House in 1914, Johnson resigned his consular duties, returned to New York, and turned his attention to literature.

He became a contributing editor at the *New York Age*, an African American weekly, writing sharp essays against racist violence, Jim Crow segregation, and the unequal treatment of blacks in the military. He also established a poetry section to showcase black literary talent. The political and the artistic realms were equally important and intertwined, Johnson argued, for "the world does not know that a race is great until that race produces great literature." To that end, Johnson not only continued to produce song lyrics and poetry (a collection, *Fifty Years and Other Poems*, came out in 1917) but also encouraged other African American writers to succeed.

Impressed with the multitalented young editor, the NAACP's Joel Spingarn and W. E. B. Du Bois asked Johnson to work with them. In 1916 he became the association's first field secretary, responsible for the formation of new branch offices throughout the country. While traveling in the South, Johnson recruited a young Atlantan, Walter White, who became one of the association's most important leaders. He also researched the lynchings and other racist violence that were beginning to increase in the years leading up to the Red Summer of 1919. Johnson himself had nearly suffered lynching when a group of white men saw him talking with a very fair-skinned black female journalist in 1901; only the woman's insistence that she herself was African American saved him. Upon visiting the site where a black man had been burned alive for a crime he believed the man could not have committed, Johnson realized, as he wrote in his autobiography, "that in large measure the race question involves the saving of black America's body and white America's soul."

Despite antilynching activities as varied as the Negro Silent Protest Parade in 1917 and the 1919 publication of *Thirty Years of Lynching* (the product of research by Johnson and White, among others), in 1922 the NAACP saw the defeat of the Dyer Bill, which would have made lynching a federal crime. Johnson had lobbied hard for its passage and was bitterly disappointed at its death by Southern Democratic filibuster and Northern Republican indifference. In his autobiography, though, he writes with characteristic optimism of the opportunity to make "the floors of Congress a forum in which [lynching was] discussed and brought home to the American people." While lynchings continued, their numbers did decrease dramatically following the public debate over the Dyer Bill.

In 1920 Johnson became NAACP secretary, the chief executive position within the association. His ten years in office were a decade of intense legal and organizational activity for the NAACP; for Johnson himself it also heralded a period of prodigious literary output. He edited three anthologies in the 1920s: *The Book of Negro American Poetry* (1922), *The Book of Negro American Spirituals* (1925), and *The Second Book of Negro American Spirituals* (1926). In addition, he published a second collection of poetry, *God's Trombones* (1927), and oversaw the republication, this time under his own name, of *Autobiography of an Ex-Coloured Man* (1927). After retiring from the NAACP in 1930, he published a work of social history, *Black Manhattan* (1930); a memoir, *Along This Way* (1933); and a collection of essays, *Black America, What Now?* (1934). A third poetry collection, *St. Peter Relates an Incident: Collected Poems* (1935), also appeared. In 1938, while vacationing in Maine, Johnson was killed in an automobile accident at age 67.

# Johnson, Mordecai Wyatt

(b. January 12, 1890, Paris, Tenn.; d. September 11, 1976, Washington, D.C.),
the first African American president of Howard University.

Mordecai Wyatt Johnson received a bachelor of arts degree from Atlanta
Baptist College (now Morehouse College) in 1911, after which he taught
several courses there, including English, history, and economics. He then
enrolled at the University of Chicago, where he took a second bachelor's
degree, in social sciences, in 1913. A third bachelor's degree, in divinity,
came from Rochester Theological Seminary three years later. For the next
several years he served as pastor of a Baptist church in Charleston, West
Virginia, and organized Charleston's first office of the National Association
for the Advancement of Colored People (NAACP). In the early 1920s he
returned to school, first at Harvard Divinity School, where he was awarded
a master's degree in theology in 1922, then at Howard University, where he
received a doctoral degree in theology in 1923. Supported by the Young
Men's Christian Association (YMCA), he traveled throughout the Southwest studying black schools and became a noted orator.

At the time the trustees of Howard faced growing pressure from faculty, alumni, and students to appoint a black president. In 1926 Johnson
received the trustees' unanimous nomination. As president, he advocated
academic freedom inside the university and civil rights outside. He also
proved adept in prying appropriations for Howard from the United States
Congress, a task that required steady diplomacy with often hostile
Southern Congressmen. In 1929 Johnson received the NAACP's Spingarn
Medal. He retired in 1960.

# Joint Center for Political and Economic Studies,

a powerful and respected public policy institute, or think tank, in the United
States specializing in political and economic issues affecting African Americans.

Initially sponsored by Howard University and the Metropolitan Applied
Research Center in 1969 and funded by a two-year $820,000 grant from the
Ford Foundation, the Washington, D.C.-based Joint Center has developed
into an independent nonprofit organization with an annual operating budget
of more than $6.5 million. Its original mission was to provide policy consul-
tants and political training to the new African American politicians who
were elected after the Voting Rights Act of 1965. But the Joint Center soon
began turning its attention to providing reliable reports and research about
the African American community to politicians and public policy analysts.

The Joint Center's research is highly sought after. During the 1984 presidential campaign, Jesse Jackson's campaign office relied heavily on its data.

Its research is also considered fair and accurate, as illustrated by a Mississippi voting rights lawsuit in which lawyers from both sides used the Joint Center's data to support their claims. In recent years the Joint Center has expanded its scope to provide economic analysis. President Eddie N. Williams, who took office in 1972, explains the shift this way: "Economic advancement must be the next big move in the life of African Americans. And the Joint Center must be as relevant to that movement as it has been to the black political movement in the community." In the late 1990s the Joint Center began planning a major conference for minority businesspeople to discuss United States economic policies, and publishing papers recommending African American job strategies for the twenty-first century.

North America

# Jordan, Barbara Charline

**(b. July 9, 1936, Houston, Tex.; d. January 17, 1996, Austin, Tex.), African American Texas state senator, United States congressperson, and educator, one of the foremost orators of the twentieth century.**

Barbara Jordan was a political pioneer of her time, the first African American since 1883, and the first woman ever, to be elected to the Texas state Senate and the first Southern black woman to serve in the U.S. Congress. A spellbinding orator, she may be best remembered for the speech she gave as a member of the House Judiciary Committee that in 1974 determined the impeachment of President Richard Nixon. She stated that although the U.S. Constitution's clause "We the people" had not originally included her as an African American and as a woman, she had faith in the Constitution and refused to be "an idle spectator" to its "subversion" by the president.

Jordan was reared and educated in one of Houston's predominantly black districts, the Fifth Ward. She was the youngest of three daughters born to Benjamin Jordan, a warehouse laborer and part-time minister, and Arlyne (Patten) Jordan, a former church orator. The Jordans focused their lives on the local Good Hope Baptist Church. Yet Barbara felt constrained by the Jordan family's strict religious principles, and developed a close relationship with her maternal grandfather, John Ed Patten, a former minister who no longer attended church. In 1919 Patten had been imprisoned for shooting a white policeman in self-defense. After his release he set up a junk business, traveling around Houston on a mule-drawn wagon. Jordan was inspired by Patten's courage and independence and each Sunday helped him sort his rags and scrap iron, which the two of them sold to Houston merchants. Until his death in the early 1950s, Patten remained Jordan's key supporter, encouraging her always to follow her heart.

Jordan attended Phillis Wheatley High School, where she was an exemplary student. As a member of the debate team she won numerous awards, including the national Usher's Oratorical Prize. In 1953, determined to be a lawyer, she enrolled in the historically black Texas Southern University

(TSU). She majored in government and, with the guidance of debating coach Tom Freeman, polished her oratorical skills. She also persuaded Freeman to include her in the all-male traveling debate team, despite his policy of never taking women on national tours.

College was a momentous time for Jordan. In *Brown v. Board of Education* (1954), the Supreme Court ended federal tolerance of segregation in U.S. educational institutions. Before *Brown v. Board of Education*, black debaters were customarily excluded from white debate contests; afterward, Jordan began traveling around the United States to debate white teams and became one of the first African Americans to tie white debaters from Harvard. Yet in Houston, most schools remained segregated. As Jordan said later: "I woke to the necessity that someone had to push integration along in a private way if it were ever going to happen." She wanted the best education possible in a non-segregated setting, and on Freeman's advice decided to attend Boston University Law School.

In 1956 Jordan found herself one of two black women in a freshman law class of 600. She again realized the abysmal consequences of segregated education, and felt she was "doing sixteen years of remedial work in thinking." Within months of graduating from law school, she returned to Houston, this time with an eye to a political career. In 1960 she volunteered on the Kennedy-Johnson campaign. Campaign coworkers soon noticed her talent for public speaking, and she was put on the speech-making circuit for the Harris County Democrats.

Despite her widespread popularity among Houston's black and Chicano communities, Jordan lost her first two attempts to win a seat on the Texas state Senate in 1962 and 1964. However, following passage of the Civil Rights Act of 1964, the Supreme Court required Southern states to reapportion their electoral districts, and in 1966 Jordan, running against a popular white liberal, won a state Senate seat by a two-to-one margin. During Jordan's six years in the Texas Senate, she consistently advocated for the working-class constituencies that she represented. She was instrumental in setting up the Texas Fair Employment Practices Commission; she introduced the first Texas minimum wage bill; and she sponsored much of the state's environmental legislation.

In 1972 Jordan was elected to the U.S. House of Representatives, where she became a member of the Judiciary Committee and won national recognition for her moving indictment of Richard Nixon during the Watergate hearings. As a congressperson, she was neither confrontational nor radical in her politics, believing that she could best bring about change for her fellow African Americans by working within the system. As Jordan said of herself: "I am neither a black politician nor a female politician, just a politician."

In 1976 Jordan gave the keynote address at the Democratic National Convention. Many commentators believed that in 1978 she would run for governor or for the U.S. Senate; she was also mentioned as a possible candidate for the U.S. Supreme Court.

But in 1979 Jordan retired from Congress. Afflicted with multiple sclerosis, a neuromuscular disease, she returned to Texas and taught public

policy at the University of Texas Lyndon B. Johnson School of Public
Affairs. Between 1978 and 1996, the year of her death, she continued to
devote herself to public service, acting as keynote speaker at the Democratic
National Convention in 1992 and subsequently as chair of the U.S. Commission on Immigration Reform.

The numerous awards Jordan received include the Eleanor Roosevelt
Humanities Award (1984) and more than 20 honorary doctorates from
leading U.S. universities.

North America

# Jordan, Vernon Eulion, Jr.

**(b. August 15, 1935, Atlanta, Ga.), African American lawyer, business executive,
former president of the National Urban League and United Negro College Fund,
and adviser to President Bill Clinton.**

One of the most powerful, well-connected lawyers in the United States,
Vernon Jordan has had a long, sometimes contradictory career. Few civil
rights spokespeople of his generation have attained the kind of corporate
and political influence Jordan has, an achievement enhanced by his position
as a top adviser to and close friend of President Bill Clinton. Yet some critics
have charged that the former National Association for the Advancement of
Colored People (NAACP) field secretary and Urban League president has
lost touch with his original goal, to improve the economic lives of African
Americans.

The middle son of a postal clerk and his wife, a caterer, Jordan was
deeply influenced by his mother's drive and business sense. As a child he
sometimes accompanied her to catering jobs, where he observed Atlanta's
white establishment, especially the Lawyer's Club. In an interview with the
*New York Times*, Jordan talked about admiring the way the men dressed,
spoke, and carried themselves. "I didn't necessarily like their views," he said,
"but I think I learned from them."

After graduating with honors from David T. Howard High School in
1953, Jordan went to DePauw University in Indiana. Though the only black
student in his class, Jordan excelled at DePauw, where he served in the student senate, won statewide honors in speaking contests, and played basketball. After college he went to law school at Howard University; he
graduated in 1960.

Jordan's early days as a lawyer in Atlanta were devoted to the cause of
civil rights. While working as a law clerk for a local black attorney, Jordan
helped organize the integration of the University of Georgia, personally
escorting student Charlayne Hunter (now journalist Charlayne Hunter-
Gault) past a hostile white crowd. In the following decade Jordan served as
Georgia field secretary for the NAACP, director of the Voter Education Project for the Southern Regional Council, head of the United Negro College
Fund, and a delegate to President Lyndon B. Johnson's White House Conference on Civil Rights.

Always more identified with mainstream groups within the Civil Rights Movement, in 1971 Jordan was named head of the National Urban League, one of the more conservative, established African American organizations. Under his leadership, the Urban League flourished. Jordan's experience in fundraising and with the business community helped him attract corporate sponsors, which allowed the organization to more than triple its budget and hire many more employees. At the same time Jordan joined the boards of many of the country's biggest corporations—including Xerox, American Express, and Dow Jones—where he was able to influence hiring policies and push for more jobs for blacks and women.

In 1981, following his recuperation from a May 29, 1980, shooting by a white supremacist, Jordan resigned from the Urban League to take a job with the Washington, D.C., office of Akin, Gump, Strauss, Hauer and Feld, an influential law and lobbying firm based in Dallas, Texas. This job, in addition to his membership in the corporate elite, and his long-standing friendship with President Bill Clinton, made Jordan one of Washington's most important power brokers. He has played a role in influencing the president's positions on foreign trade, budgetary issues, and affirmative action, as well as key decisions on personnel. In 1998 Jordan's friendship with the president brought him once again into the news, this time in connection with allegations that Clinton, while carrying on a sexual relationship with a White House intern, Monica S. Lewinsky, had obstructed justice by asking Jordan to find Lewinsky a job in exchange for her silence about the affair. A corps of Republican congressmen used Jordan's taped deposition in their 1999 impeachment trial against the president, which ended in his acquittal. Known for his charm, elegant clothing, and impeccable manners, Jordan is described by many, including the president, as "larger than life."

# Kerner Report,

**the 1968 report of a federal government commission that investigated urban riots in the United States.**

The Kerner Report was released after seven months of investigation by the National Advisory Commission on Civil Disorders and took its name from the commission chairman, Illinois governor Otto Kerner. President Lyndon B. Johnson appointed the commission on July 28, 1967, while rioting was still underway in Detroit, Michigan. The long, hot summers since 1965 had brought riots in the black sections of many major cities, including Los Angeles (1965), Chicago (1966), and Newark (1967). Johnson charged the commission with analyzing the specific triggers for the riots, the deeper causes of the worsening racial climate of the time, and potential remedies.

The commission presented its findings in 1968, concluding that urban violence reflected the profound frustration of inner-city blacks and that racism was deeply embedded in American society. The report's most famous passage warned that the United States was "moving toward two societies, one black, one white—separate and unequal." The commission marshaled evidence on an array of problems that fell with particular severity on African Americans, including not only overt discrimination but also chronic poverty, high unemployment, poor schools, inadequate housing, lack of access to health care, and systematic police bias and brutality.

The report recommended sweeping federal initiatives directed at improving educational and employment opportunities, housing, and public services in black urban neighborhoods and called for a "national system of income supplementation." Reverend Martin Luther King Jr. pronounced the report a "physician's warning of approaching death, with a prescription for life." By 1968, however, Richard M. Nixon had gained the presidency through a conservative white backlash that ensured that the Kerner Report's recommendations would be largely ignored.

# King, Coretta Scott

(b. April 27, 1927, Marion, Ala.), widow of the slain civil rights leader Martin Luther King Jr. who is world renowned for her devotion to furthering his ideals.

Long active in the fight for civil and human rights, Coretta Scott King has become an international icon for her efforts to promote nonviolent social change.

The second of three children of Obadiah and Bernice (McMurry) Scott, King grew up in rural Alabama, where she helped her family harvest cotton and tend to their farm. Her father hauled lumber for a white sawmill owner, a job that enabled him to purchase and operate his own sawmill. The local white community resented her father's success: vandals allegedly burned his sawmill, and the Scotts's house, to the ground. King was deeply shaken by her family's trials. She dreamed of moving to the North and diligently focused on her education, enrolling in a local private high school, where she pursued her talent for music. In 1945 she won a scholarship to Antioch College in Yellow Springs, Ohio. She studied music and elementary education and in 1948 debuted as a vocalist at the Second Baptist Church. Also while at Antioch, she performed in a program with Paul Robeson, the renowned African American singer and civil rights activist, who encouraged her to pursue advanced musical training.

In 1951 King entered the New England Conservatory of Music in

President Ronald Reagan signs the bill that established a national holiday in honor of Martin Luther King, Jr., as dignitaries including Vice President George Bush and King's widow, Coretta Scott King, look on. *CORBIS/Bettmann-UPI*

Boston on a scholarship. She struggled to support herself, living and working at a Beacon Hill boardinghouse. In 1953 she married Martin Luther King Jr., then a doctoral student in theology at Boston University. Her marriage to King was a pivotal point in her life: upon graduating from the conservatory, she returned with him to Montgomery, Alabama, where he worked as a pastor at Dexter Avenue Baptist Church. During the following years she reared their four children and stood by her husband at the forefront of the Civil Rights Movement. In 1962, following the King family's move to Atlanta, she taught voice lessons at Morris Brown College while continuing her civil rights work. Steadfastly loyal to her husband, she joined him in civil rights demonstrations throughout the South, led marches, spoke at rallies, and organized fundraising events at which she lectured and performed.

After the assassination of her husband in 1968, King continued to lead major demonstrations in support of striking workers and the poor, and organized marches to promote Dr. King's principles, such as the 20th anniversary March on Washington in 1983. In 1969, as a memorial to Dr. King, she founded the Atlanta-based Martin Luther King Jr. Center for Nonviolent Social Change, a center principally devoted to training people, especially students, in nonviolent social protest. Serving as the center's president and chief executive officer, she has maintained a high public profile both in the United States and abroad, and traveled through southern Africa to protest apartheid. In 1986 she prevailed in her campaign to establish a national holiday honoring Dr. King.

Since then she has continued to campaign worldwide for human rights, social justice, and urban renewal programs for disadvantaged communities.

North America

# King, Martin Luther, Jr.

(b. January 15, 1929, Atlanta, Ga.; d. April 4, 1968, Memphis, Tenn.), African American clergyman and Nobel Prize winner, one of the principal leaders of the American Civil Rights Movement and a prominent advocate of nonviolent protest. King's challenges to segregation and racial discrimination in the 1950s and 1960s helped convince many white Americans to support the cause of civil rights in the United States. After his assassination in 1968, King became a symbol of protest in the struggle for racial justice.

## Education and Early Life

Martin Luther King Jr. was born in Atlanta, Georgia, the eldest son of Martin Luther King Sr., a Baptist minister, and Alberta Williams King. His father served as pastor of a large Atlanta church, Ebenezer Baptist, which had been founded by Martin Luther King Jr.'s maternal grandfather. King Jr. was ordained as a Baptist minister at age 18.

King attended local segregated public schools, where he excelled. He entered nearby Morehouse College at age 15 and graduated with a bach-

The Dexter Avenue Baptist Church in Montgomery, Alabama, where Rev. Martin Luther King, Jr. was pastor from 1954 to 1960.
*CORBIS/Raymond Gehman*

elor's degree in sociology in 1948. After graduating with honors from Crozer Theological Seminary in Pennsylvania in 1951, he went to Boston University, where he earned a doctoral degree in systematic theology in 1955.

King's public-speaking abilities—which would become renowned as his stature grew in the Civil Rights Movement—developed slowly during his collegiate years. He won a second-place prize in a speech contest while an undergraduate at Morehouse, but received Cs in two public-speaking courses in his first year at Crozer. By the end of his third year at Crozer, however, professors were praising King for the powerful impression he made in public speeches and discussions.

Throughout his education King was exposed to influences that related Christian theology to the struggles of oppressed people. At Morehouse, Crozer, and Boston University, he studied the teachings on nonviolent protest of Indian leader Mohandas Gandhi. King also read and heard the sermons of white Protestant ministers who preached against American racism. Benjamin E. Mays, president of Morehouse and a leader in the national community of racially liberal clergymen, was especially important in shaping King's theological development.

While in Boston, King met Coretta Scott, a music student and native of Alabama. They were married in 1953 and would have four children. In 1954 King accepted his first pastorate at the Dexter Avenue Baptist Church in Montgomery, Alabama, a church with a well-educated congregation that had recently been led by a minister, Vernon Johns, who had protested against segregation.

## The Montgomery Bus Boycott

Montgomery's black community had long-standing grievances about the mistreatment of blacks on city buses. Many white bus drivers treated blacks rudely, often cursing and humiliating them by enforcing the city's segregation laws, which forced black riders to sit in the back of buses and give up their seats to white passengers on crowded buses. By the early 1950s Montgomery's blacks had discussed boycotting the buses in an effort to gain better treatment, but not necessarily to end segregation.

On December 1, 1955, Rosa Parks, a leading member of the local branch of the National Association for the Advancement of Colored People (NAACP), was ordered by a bus driver to give up her seat to a white passenger. When she refused, she was arrested and taken to jail. Local leaders of the NAACP, especially Edgar D. Nixon, recognized that the arrest of the popular and highly respected Parks was the event that could rally local blacks to a bus protest.

Nixon also believed that a citywide protest should be led by someone who could unify the community. Unlike Nixon and other leaders in Montgomery's black community, the recently arrived King had no enemies. Furthermore, Nixon saw King's public-speaking gift as a great asset in the battle for black civil rights in Montgomery. King was soon chosen as president of the Montgomery Improvement Association (MIA), the organization that directed the bus boycott.

The Montgomery bus boycott lasted for more than a year, demonstrating a new spirit of protest among Southern blacks. King's serious demeanor and consistent appeal to Christian brotherhood and American idealism made a positive impression on whites outside the South. Incidents of violence against black protesters, including the bombing of King's home, focused media attention on Montgomery. In February 1956 an attorney for the MIA filed a lawsuit in federal court seeking an injunction against Montgomery's segregated seating practices. The federal court ruled in favor of the MIA, ordering the city's buses to be desegregated, but the city government appealed the ruling to the United States Supreme Court. By November 1956, when the Supreme Court upheld the lower court decision, King was a national figure. His memoir of the bus boycott, *Stride Toward Freedom* (1958), gave a thoughtful account of that experience and further extended his national influence.

## Civil Rights Leadership

In 1957 King helped found the Southern Christian Leadership Conference (SCLC), an organization of black ministers and churches that aimed to challenge racial segregation. As SCLC's president, King became the organization's dominant personality and its primary intellectual influence. He was responsible for much of the organization's fundraising, which he frequently conducted in conjunction with preaching engagements in Northern churches.

SCLC sought to complement the NAACP's legal efforts to dismantle segregation through the courts, with King and other SCLC leaders protested discrimination through the use of nonviolent action such as marches, boycotts, and demonstrations. The violent responses that direct action provoked from some whites eventually forced the federal government to confront the issues of injustice and racism in the South.

King made strategic alliances with Northern whites that would bolster his success in influencing public opinion in the United States. Through

Bayard Rustin, a black civil rights and peace activist, King forged connections to older radical activists, many of them Jewish, who provided money and advice about strategy. King's closest advisor at times was Stanley Levison, a Jewish activist and former member of the American Communist Party. King also developed strong ties to white Protestant ministers in the North, with whom he shared theological and moral views.

In 1959 King visited India and worked out more clearly his understanding of Satyagraha, Gandhi's principle of nonviolent persuasion, which King had determined to use as his main instrument of social protest. The next year he gave up his pastorate in Montgomery to become co-pastor (with his father) of the Ebenezer Baptist Church in Atlanta.

## SCLC Protest Campaigns

In the early 1960s King led SCLC in a series of protest campaigns that gained national attention. The first was in 1961 in Albany, Georgia, where SCLC joined local demonstrations against segregated restaurants, hotels, transit, and housing. SCLC increased the size of the demonstrations in an effort to create so much dissent and disorder that local white officials would be forced to end segregation to restore normal business relations. The strategy did not work in Albany. During months of protests, Albany's police chief jailed hundreds of demonstrators without visible police violence. Eventually the protesters' energy, and the money to bail protesters out, ran out.

The strategy did work, however, in Birmingham, Alabama, when SCLC joined a local protest during the spring of 1963. The protest was led by SCLC member Fred Shuttlesworth, one of the ministers who had worked with King in 1957 in organizing SCLC. Shuttlesworth believed that the Birmingham police commissioner, Eugene "Bull" Connor, would meet protesters with violence. In May 1963 King and his SCLC staff escalated anti-segregation marches in Birmingham by encouraging teenagers and schoolchildren to join. Hundreds of singing children filled the streets of downtown Birmingham, angering Connor, who sent police officers with attack dogs and firefighters with high-pressure water hoses against the marchers. Scenes of young protesters being attacked by dogs and pinned against buildings by torrents of water from fire hoses were shown in newspapers and on televisions around the world.

During the demonstrations King was arrested and sent to jail. He wrote a letter from his jail cell to local clergymen who had criticized him for creating disorder in the city. His *Letter from Birmingham City Jail*, which argued that individuals had the moral right and responsibility to disobey unjust laws, was widely read at the time and added to King's standing as a moral leader.

National reaction to the Birmingham violence built support for the struggle for black civil rights. The demonstrations forced white leaders to negotiate an end to some forms of segregation in Birmingham. Even more important, the protests encouraged many Americans to support national legislation against segregation.

Martin Luther King Jr. (1929-1968) addresses a large crowd at a civil rights march in Washington, DC, 1963. *Hulton-Deutsch Collection/CORBIS*

### "I Have a Dream"

King and other black leaders organized the 1963 March on Washington, a massive protest in Washington, D.C., for jobs and civil rights. On August 28, 1963, King delivered the keynote address to an audience of more than 200,000 civil rights supporters. His "I Have a Dream" speech expressed the hopes of the Civil Rights Movement in oratory as moving as any in American history: "I have a dream that one day this nation will rise up and live out the true meaning of its creed: 'We hold these truths to be self-evident, that all men are created equal.' . . . I have a dream that my four little children will one day live in a nation where they will not be judged by the color of their skin but by the content of their character."

The speech and the march built on the Birmingham demonstrations to create the political momentum that resulted in the Civil Rights Act of 1964, which prohibited segregation in public accommodations as well as discrimination in education and employment. As a result of King's effectiveness as a leader of the American Civil Rights Movement and his highly visible moral stance, he was awarded the 1964 Nobel Prize for Peace.

President Lyndon B. Johnson shakes hands with Martin Luther King Jr. after signing the Civil Rights Act in 1964. *CORBIS/Bettmann*

## Selma Marches

In 1965 SCLC joined a voting-rights protest march that was planned to go from Selma, Alabama, to the state capital of Montgomery, more than 80 km (50 mi) away. The goal of the march was to draw national attention to the struggle for black voting rights in the state. Police beat and tear-gassed the marchers just outside Selma, and televised scenes of the violence, on the day that came to be known as Bloody Sunday, resulted in an outpouring of support to continue the march. SCLC petitioned for and received a federal court order barring police from interfering with a renewed march to Montgomery. Two weeks after Bloody Sunday, more than 3,000 people, including a core of 300 marchers who would make the entire trip, set out toward Montgomery. They arrived in Montgomery five days later, where King addressed a rally of more than 20,000 people in front of the capitol building.

The march created support for the Voting Rights Act of 1965, which President Lyndon Johnson signed into law in August. The act suspended (and amendments to the act later banned) the use of literacy tests and other voter qualification tests that had been used to prevent blacks from registering to vote.

After the Selma protests, King had fewer dramatic successes in his struggle for black civil rights. Many white Americans who had supported his work believed that the job was done. In many ways the nation's appetite for civil rights progress had been filled. King also lost support among white Americans when he joined the growing number of antiwar activists in 1965 and began to criticize publicly American foreign policy in Vietnam. King's outspoken opposition to the Vietnam War (1959–1975) also angered President Johnson. On the other hand, some of King's white supporters agreed with his criticisms of United States involvement in Vietnam so strongly that they shifted their activism from civil rights to the antiwar movement.

## Black Power

By the mid-1960s King's role as the leader of the Civil Rights Movement was questioned by many younger blacks. Activists such as Stokely Carmichael of the Student Nonviolent Coordinating Committee (SNCC) argued that King's nonviolent protest strategies and appeals to moral idealism were useless in the face of sustained violence by whites. Some also rejected the leadership of ministers. In addition, many SNCC organizers resented King, feeling that often they had put in the hard work of planning and organizing protests only to have the charismatic King arrive later and receive much of the credit. In 1966 the Black Power Movement, advocated most forcefully by Carmichael, captured the nation's attention and suggested that King's influence among blacks was waning. Black Power advocates looked more to the beliefs of the recently assassinated black Muslim leader, Malcolm X, whose insistence on black self-reliance and the right of blacks to defend themselves against violent attacks had been embraced by many African Americans.

With internal divisions beginning to divide the Civil Rights Movement, King shifted his focus to racial injustice in the North. Realizing that the economic difficulties of blacks in Northern cities had largely been ignored, SCLC broadened its civil rights agenda by focusing on issues related to black poverty. King established a headquarters in a Chicago apartment in 1966, using that as a base to organize protests against housing and employment discrimination in the city. Black Baptist ministers who disagreed with many of SCLC's tactics, especially the confrontational act of sending black protesters into all-white neighborhoods, publicly opposed King's efforts. The protests did not lead to significant gains and were often met with violent counter-demonstrations by whites, including neo-Nazis and members of the Ku Klux Klan, a secret terrorist organization that was opposed to integration.

During 1966 and 1967 King increasingly turned the focus of his civil rights activism throughout the country to economic issues. He began to argue for redistribution of the nation's economic wealth to overcome entrenched black poverty. In 1967 he began planning a Poor People's Campaign to pressure national lawmakers to address the issue of economic justice.

## Assassination

This emphasis on economic rights took King to Memphis, Tennessee, to support striking black garbage workers in the spring of 1968. He was assassinated in Memphis by a sniper on April 4. News of the assassination resulted in an outpouring of shock and anger throughout the nation and the world, prompting riots in more than 100 U.S. cities in the days following King's death. In 1969 James Earl Ray, an escaped white convict, pleaded guilty to the murder of King and was sentenced to 99 years in prison. Although over the years many investigators have suspected that Ray did not act alone, no accomplices have ever been identified.

After King's death, historians researching his life and career discovered that the Federal Bureau of Investigation (FBI) often tapped King's phone line and reported on his private life to the president and other government officials. The FBI's reason for invading his privacy was that King associated with Communists and other "radicals."

After his death, King came even more than during his lifetime to represent black courage and achievement, high moral leadership, and the ability of Americans to address and overcome racial divisions. Recollections of his criticisms of U.S. foreign policy and poverty faded, and his soaring rhetoric calling for racial justice and an integrated society became almost as familiar to subsequent generations of Americans as the Declaration of Independence.

King's historical importance was memorialized at the Martin Luther King Jr. Center for Social Justice, a research institute in Atlanta. Also in Atlanta is the Martin Luther King Jr. National Historic Site, which includes his birthplace, the Ebenezer Church, and the King Center, where his tomb is located. Perhaps the most important memorial is the national holiday in King's honor, designated by the Congress of the United States in 1983 and observed on the third Monday in January, a day that falls on or near King's birthday of January 15.

North America

# Kwanzaa,

**a holiday that African Americans celebrate during the final week of the year to reaffirm their African roots.**

Kwanzaa, Swahili for "first fruits," is a secular holiday. Maulana Karenga, current chairman of the Black Studies Department at California State University at Long Beach, introduced this holiday in 1966 at the height of the Black Power Movement in the United States. At that time he was a graduate student and the head of US (United Slaves), a Los Angeles-based Black Nationalist group committed to learning about African history and teaching it to African Americans. After formulating the holiday, Karenga and members of US traveled around the country to promote it. Since then, the number of African Americans who observe the holiday has dramatically increased. In 1996, 13 million African Americans in the United States and 5 million people of African descent in other parts of the world were estimated to have celebrated Kwanzaa. Although Karenga designed the holiday to "give a Black alternative to the existing holiday," many African Americans who celebrate Kwanzaa also celebrate Christmas.

An elaborate and symbolic table setting is a central part of the Kwanzaa celebration. First, African Americans place on a table one of two items—a mat made of straw or a Kente-patterned textile—which represents the African American heritage in the materials of traditional African culture. Celebrants then put a seven-pronged candleholder in the center of the mat. The candle-holder contains one central black candle that is flanked by three red and three green candles. Each candle stands for one of the seven principles Kwanzaa commemorates. Near the base of the candleholder, observers place a cup, which symbolizes the unity of all African peoples. Around these two centerpieces, vegetables, fruits, and nuts are arranged, which represent the yield of the first harvest.

The philosophical foundation of Kwanzaa is the seven principles collectively known as the Nguzo Saba. They include umoja (unity); kujichagulia (self-determination); ujima (collective work and responsibility); ujamaa (cooperative economics); nia (purpose); kuumba (creativity); and imani (faith). After researching cultures throughout the African continent, Karenga selected these Swahili-named principles because of their predominance in African history. The Nguzo Saba, according to Karenga, are the core principles "by which black people must live in order to begin to rescue and reconstruct [their] history and lives."

Each day before dinner celebrants light a candle and interpret its corresponding principle. In addition to explaining the principle and illustrating it through parables, African Americans discuss how to live according to the principle. After dinner, they blow out the candle. On the following day they light an additional candle along with the candle(s) from the preceding day(s), until the seventh day when all seven candles burn together.

While Kwanzaa's candle-lighting ritual tends to be solemn, the rest of the celebration is upbeat and festive. On each evening of the celebration, family and friends gather to eat and drink. A typical Kwanzaa feast may feature spicy oven-fried catfish or Creole chicken accompanied by a bean or rice dish, such as Hopping John or Jollof Rice, and completed by desserts such as fried candied sweet potatoes or sweet and tart lemon cake. All celebrants drink from the unity cup in reverence of their predecessors. They tell stories about their African ancestors, sing, and dance.

As part of the celebration family members exchange gifts of cultural significance, such as dashikis (African tunics). Another popular gift is a *Nia Umoja* figurine, also known as Kente Claus, which represents an ancient African storyteller. He wears a Kente cloth robe and has a neatly trimmed gray beard.

When he introduced Kwanzaa, Karenga urged that gifts as well as all decorations for the holiday be homemade, but in recent years there has been a proliferation of Kwanzaa merchandise. Since 1990 New York City has hosted an annual Kwanzaa Holiday Expo, which has attracted an increasing number of vendors. They sell publications such as cookbooks, how-to manuals, children's stories, and paraphernalia such as factory-made mats, mass-produced unity cups, and Taiwanese-made candleholders. Hallmark, which introduced a line of Kwanzaa greeting cards in 1992, is one of several major American corporations that market Kwanzaa-related merchandise.

Some African Americans have criticized the commercialization of Kwanzaa on the grounds that black-owned businesses are not the benefactors. Karenga argued that "We [African Americans] should be producing our own items for our own practice of the holiday." Other social critics have interpreted the commercialization of Kwanzaa as society's acknowledgment of the holiday's significance and the rising economic status of blacks. Even with this commercialization, Kwanzaa continues to be a cultural mainstay in the homes of many African Americans.

# L

## Labor Unions in the United States,

**the history of African Americans and organized labor, in which the attempt of black workers to unionize was met first with violent resistance and then began a slow process toward racial integration in the trade union movement.**

The relationship between African Americans and organized labor in the United States has been both empowering and troubled. Unions have traditionally given vulnerable workers protection through the strength of collective bargaining. Yet African American unionizing efforts consistently met with resistance from both employers and the existing unions, which were white. Black workers who attempted to organize faced not only losing their own jobs and being blacklisted, but also violent actions by the police, militia, and vigilante groups. Although barred from white unions, black workers were still regarded as strikebreakers when they attempted to work during strikes, or as "union-busters" when they worked for lower pay than the union wage.

The eventual decision to integrate white unions was both moral and pragmatic. As the number of black workers swelled in the industrial sector during the two World Wars and some of the immense group of agricultural workers attempted to organize, national labor federations saw the benefit of shoring up union ranks with these workers. But membership did not necessarily mean that blacks held power within the union, or even that the entire union and its affiliates were racially integrated. African Americans carried on the fight for the desegregation of "Jim Crow" unions through the Civil Rights Movement. The struggle continues for black representation in union leadership, union-secured grievance procedures to fight discrimination, and training for more highly skilled jobs.

The precursors of the labor unions that organized black workers existed as early as the antebellum period. These groups included benevolent societies, such as the New York African Society for Mutual Relief (1806); the

Negro Convention Movement, which held annual meetings of black leaders during the 1840s and 1850s; and groups that promoted worker unity and industrial education, such as the American League of Colored Laborers (1850). Black workers also formed collectives, such as the Association of Black Caulkers, founded in 1858 in Baltimore, to protect themselves from the mob violence of immigrants who felt threatened by black employment. These groups sometimes engaged in unofficial bargaining for wage increases, as did the black waiters of the Waiter Protective Association of New York in 1853.

The formal unionization of black workers from the period following the Civil War to the present has followed two basic imperatives: integration of large white unions and separate organization of black-only unions. Most of the later unions sought the added strength of affiliation with a white-dominated federation, since, in the words of labor leader Isaac Myers in 1868, "Labor organizations are the safeguard of the colored man, but for real success, separate organization is not the real answer."

In 1869 a group of black leaders traveled to a convention of the National Labor Union to lobby for the organization of black affiliates. Although they were recognized as a delegation, they were unsuccessful at introducing integration into the white union. To fill the gap of black-worker representation in the labor movement, 214 African American delegates met the same year to create a confederation of autonomous black local and state unions, the Colored National Labor Union, with headquarters in Washington, D.C.

In 1869 the Philadelphia-based Noble Order of the Knights of Labor became the first white labor union to organize black members actively. By 1886 they had enrolled 60,000 African American workers, predominantly in the South. Yet it was clear that African Americans were second-class citizens in the union when in 1887 the Knights abandoned the 9,000 black workers who had walked off the sugar plantations in Louisiana, thus leaving them open targets for militia and vigilante force.

Nevertheless, there were hopeful signs of a slow process of change as other unions integrated. Black workers still did not hold much power in integrated unions, but some African Americans made their way into the ranks of the leadership. In the 1890s African American miner Richard L. Davis became a member of the executive board of the United Mine Workers of American, a union in which more than half of the workers were black. He used the power of this position to fight against the segregation of the Southern affiliates and the exclusion of blacks from skilled jobs. Another African American labor leader, Benjamin H. Fletcher, organized the most powerful dockworkers' union in Philadelphia, the Marine Transport Workers Union, in 1913, as part of the socialist International Workers of the World's campaign to organize black workers.

As the Northern industrial centers bore the weight of a massive influx of black workers during the Great Migration north in the first half of the twentieth century, the distinction between unionized and non-unionized black workers became blurred in the growing climate of racial hatred.

Many whites feared that blacks would take their jobs. With a few exceptions, racial differences overwhelmed worker solidarity, and the race riots of the Red Summer of 1919 made clear the demarcation lines between black and white.

In the South, despite the fatal risk of organizing farm labor, blacks forged labor unions to gain some measure of personal and financial protection. These efforts led to tragedy in Elaine, Arkansas, where sharecroppers, tenant farmers, and laborers had banded together to form the Progressive Farmers and Household Union of America. White planters responded to the unionizing efforts with official and vigilante violence that left 100 blacks dead and destroyed the union. Twenty years later, the Southern Tenant Farmers' Union would reclaim some measure of success by achieving national recognition for a massive protest in which 1,700 evicted sharecroppers set up camp along Missouri's Highway 61.

The detrimental effects of the Great Depression were compounded for black workers, who were the first to be let go and the last to be hired. Desperate for work, many took nonunion jobs, undercutting the power of unions, while employed blacks faced animosity from unemployed white workers. Yet organizing efforts continued through the 1930s, gaining momentum in the latter part of the decade. After a long battle with the Pullman Company, A. Philip Randolph organized company porters into the Brotherhood of Sleeping Car Porters in 1928, and nine years later the Brotherhood became the first black affiliate of one of the most powerful unions of the era, the American Federation of Labor (AFL). Another prominent union, the Congress of Industrial Organizations (CIO), created in 1935, organized semiskilled and unskilled workers in mass-production industries with many black workers, such as steel, auto, rubber, and meatpacking.

Despite the relatively progressive stance of these federations, blacks still found themselves barred from most of the skilled jobs, and many affiliates remained segregated. A plan to march on Washington, D.C., pressured President Franklin Roosevelt into signing an order banning racial discrimination in war employment and created the Fair Employment Practices Committee.

The progressive measures that these unions had achieved in the 1930s lost ground during the cold war. The expulsion of so-called communist organizations effectively meant the removal of affiliates that had been at the forefront of the fight for black workers. The short-lived National Labor Conference for Negro Rights attempted to fill this gap in 1951, until it too fell victim to the McCarthy Era purges.

The 1950s and 1960s saw an alliance forged between the Civil Rights Movement and the labor movement, and some have called organized labor the staunchest institutional supporter of civil rights legislation. After an indictment of racist practices led by A. Philip Randolph, the newly merged AFL-CIO announced its support for the struggle for civil rights and its promise to organize without regard to race. Despite this promise, the union refused to take measures against affiliates practicing segregation and was accused of perpetuating racist practices.

In response black labor activists organized the Negro American Labor Council in 1960 to promote civil rights in the American labor movement. Randolph and the council initiated the famous 1963 March on Washington for Jobs and Freedom, where Martin Luther King Jr. gave his famous "I Have a Dream" speech. In 1964 the last segregated affiliate of the AFL-CIO integrated.

Local 1199: Drug, Hospital and Health Care Employees Union brought the labor movement to a new sector of black workers: the predominantly poor, black, and female workers of the voluntary hospitals. The union attracted support from prominent civil rights leaders, including King, since Local 1199 was, in the words of Malcolm X, "not afraid of upsetting the apple cart of those people who are running City Hall." In 1969 civil rights leaders rallied together for a massive protest in Charleston, South Carolina, for a labor dispute so contentious it ultimately led to federal mediation. The union's ultimate victory strengthened its ranks, and Local 1199 grew to a membership of more than 150,000 by the mid-1970s. More important, the shared struggle of the Charleston protest forged bonds between Southern civil rights leaders and those attempting to rework traditional unions to serve the needs of black workers.

Some African American workers, however, felt that their issues would forever be subsumed by white-dominated labor organizations. They sought a separate movement. With the rise of the Black Power Movement in the late 1960s, certain sectors of black labor became increasingly militant. In the automobile plants of the Northern industrial centers, a group of workers formed the League of Revolutionary Black Workers. Beginning with the idea that the issue of black labor was linked to a broader struggle for the decolonization of African Americans in a white supremacist society, this group connected organized labor to the ideologies of socialism and Black Power.

The leadership of large integrated unions such as the United Auto Workers responded to a perceived threat from radical elements by opening leadership positions to more moderate blacks and working with national black organizations. In the late 1960s national black organizations and labor unions worked together to develop several federally funded programs, including the Recruitment and Training Program (Workers Defense League), the Labor Education and Advancement Program (Urban League), and the Human Resources Development Institute (AFL-CIO). These programs brought blacks into apprenticeship programs in the 1970s, giving some workers a long-awaited upward mobility toward more highly skilled and better-paying jobs.

African American unemployment grew in the 1980s as a result of a national movement toward de-industrialization, an increased dependence on technology, and the shift of production out of the United States. Black workers were hit hard in the steel, auto, textile, and rubber industries as well as in the public sector, which had become the destination of more than half of the nation's black college graduates. In addition, unions had still not made inroads into the mostly non-unionized service sectors where many blacks were concentrated. Even so, by 1990, blacks were statistically more unionized than the rest of the work force.

Black participation in union leadership, affirmative action, protection from discrimination, and training for more highly skilled jobs (now high-tech jobs) have continued to be issues for the labor movement in the United States. Yet most proponents of organized labor still hold A. Philip Randolph's vision of worker solidarity across color lines: "The white and black workers . . . cannot be organized separately as the fingers on my hand. They must be organized altogether, as the fingers on my hand when they are doubled up in the form of a fist . . . If they are organized separately, they will not understand each other. They will fight each other, and if they fight each other, they will hate each other. And the employing class will profit from that condition."

North America

# Lampkin, Daisy Elizabeth Adams

(b. 1884?, Washington, D.C.?; d. March 10, 1965, Pittsburgh, Pa.), African American civil rights worker, newspaper executive, and national field secretary for the National Association for the Advancement of Colored People (NAACP).

Daisy Lampkin is best known for her work as national field secretary of the NAACP from 1935 to 1947. In addition to her NAACP service, she brought energy and passion to the *Pittsburgh Courier*, the nation's premier African American newspaper, as well as a host of clubs, organizations, and causes.

Historians are unsure of the date and place of Lampkin's birth, but it is known that she grew up in Reading, Pennsylvania, moved to Pittsburgh in 1909, and married William Lampkin in 1912. Around this time she became active in the Lucy Stone League, a women's suffrage organization, and in 1915 she became president of the Negro Women's Franchise League. By 1930, when she joined the NAACP as field secretary, she had been named vice president of the *Pittsburgh Courier* and had served as a delegate to the 1926 Republican National Convention.

Lampkin's work for the NAACP was legendary. Named national field secretary in 1935, she is credited with bringing in new members—and new money—at unprecedented rates with her finely honed fundraising, recruiting, and speaking talents. Along with Walter White, then the NAACP's national secretary, Lampkin was influential in engineering the defeat of a racist Supreme Court nominee and in convincing Thurgood Marshall, Roy Wilkins, and other future civil rights leaders to join the organization. Even after poor health forced her to step down from her post in 1947, Lampkin continued to work with the NAACP, serving on its board of directors. When she died in 1965, her obituary in the *Courier* dubbed her "Mrs. NAACP."

Lampkin was also active in the National Association of Colored Women, in which she served as vice president in the 1940s; the National Council of Negro Women, on whose board of directors she sat; and Delta Sigma Theta, an African American sorority. After her death, the state of Pennsylvania honored Lampkin for her wide-ranging devotion to humanitarian and political efforts by proclaiming her house a historic landmark.

# Lawson, James Morris

(b. September 22, 1928, Uniontown, Pa.), African American minister and civil rights leader who trained early civil rights activists in nonviolent resistance tactics.

Although he served as a low-profile leader of the Civil Rights Movement, James Lawson's influence was profound and lasting. He first made his mark on the civil rights struggle by teaching Indian activist Mohandas Gandhi's nonviolent civil disobedience techniques during the Nashville, Tennessee, sit-in demonstrations of 1960. Lawson, an ordained minister and pacifist who in the early 1950s had gone to prison rather than fight in the Korean War, had traveled to India as a missionary after his release and studied Gandhi's tactics firsthand. A divinity student at Vanderbilt University when the sit-ins began, he was dismissed from the school when he refused to accede to the university's demand that he discontinue his organizing activities. Lawson's willingness to accept expulsion from the seminary rather than cease his civil rights work moved its sympathetic faculty members to pressure the university to provide him with an alternative educational institution to attend. The university eventually capitulated, but by that time Lawson had transferred to Boston University, earning a bachelor of sacred theology degree in 1960.

Though not as visible as other civil rights leaders, Lawson was involved with many of the well-known civil rights organizations and demonstrations of the Freedom Movement. He was an adviser to the Student Nonviolent Coordinating Committee (SNCC) and authored the organization's statement of purpose while attending its initial conference in April 1960. He led the direct action projects of the Southern Christian Leadership Conference (SCLC), and he participated in the Freedom Rides, which were first sponsored by the Congress of Racial Equality (CORE). In 1968, while serving as a pastor in Memphis, Tennessee, he helped coordinate the garbage workers' strike, by which he hoped to highlight the lasting and adverse economic effects of segregation.

# Leadership Conference on Civil Rights,

an important American lobbying organization for civil rights legislation in the last half of the twentieth century.

The Leadership Conference on Civil Rights (LCCR) was formed in 1950 in response to the federal government's elimination of the Fair Employment Practices Committee (FEPC), an agency that had been created to end racially discriminatory hiring practices in the federal government. After failing to persuade the administration of President Harry S. Truman to revive the FEPC, Roy Wilkins and Arnold Aronson of the National Association for the Advancement of Colored People (NAACP) organized a conference in Washington, D.C., called the National Emergency Civil Rights Mobilization. Out of that conference, which was held on January 15, 1950, and was attended by 4,000 African Americans representing more than 100 civil rights groups, came The Leadership Conference on Civil Rights (LCCR), a broad coalition dedicated to lobbying Congress for the passage of civil rights laws and serving as an information clearinghouse for its member organizations.

The LCCR became a force in United States politics, mainly through the efforts of Clarence Mitchell, its chief strategist, who was seen so often roaming the halls of Congress that he became known as "the 101st Senator." The LCCR played a pivotal role in the passage of the Civil Rights Acts of 1957, 1960, and 1964 and the Voting Rights Act of 1965 and its extension in 1976. The organization expanded its scope in the 1960s and 1970s, working with other minority groups such as women's, Asian American, and Latino organizations.

North America

# Lewis, John

**(b. February 21, 1940, Troy, Ala.), African American civil rights leader and member of the United States House of Representatives.**

John Lewis was one of ten children born to sharecroppers in Pike County, Alabama. He graduated from high school and entered the American Baptist Theological Seminary in Nashville in 1957. After graduating in 1961, he enrolled at Fisk University, where he earned a Bachelor of Arts degree in 1967.

While a seminary student, Lewis participated in nonviolence workshops taught by civil rights activist James Lawson. Lawson was a member of the Fellowship of Reconciliation (FOR), an organization committed to pacifism, and he made Lewis a field secretary. Working with Septima Clark, director of the interracial adult education center Highlander Folk School, Lewis became a leader in the Nashville Student Movement. He participated in sit-ins at segregated lunch counters, became a founding member of the Student Nonviolent Coordinating Committee (SNCC) in 1960, and helped organize the Mississippi Freedom Summer in 1964.

During his tenure as national chairman of SNCC, Lewis delivered a powerful speech at the 1963 Civil Rights March on Washington, criticizing the federal government for its failure to protect the rights of African Americans. Two years later he marched with Dr. Martin Luther King Jr. from Selma to Montgomery, Alabama, in an effort to secure voting rights for African Americans. During the march a confrontation with police occurred, and Lewis was one of many beaten in what became known as Bloody Sunday.

John Lewis, chairman of the Student Nonviolent Coordinating Committee, and Hosea Williams of the Southern Christian Leadership Conference announce plans for demonstrations in Georgia in 1965. *CORBIS/Bettmann*

Lewis's commitment to nonviolence strained his relationship with SNCC when the organization grew more militant under the leadership of Stokely Carmichael. Lewis resigned from SNCC in 1966 to become director of the Atlanta-based Voter Education Project (VEP). Under Lewis's leadership the organization led voter registration drives and helped elect black politicians throughout the South. In 1976 President Jimmy Carter appointed Lewis to the staff of ACTION, a government agency responsible for coordinating volunteer activities.

After Carter's defeat in 1980, Lewis returned to Atlanta and won a seat on the Atlanta City Council. He served in this capacity until 1986, when he defeated his friend and fellow civil rights activist Julian Bond in the Democratic primary for Georgia's Fifth Congressional District seat, a position Lewis assumed when he defeated his Republican opponent later that year. In Congress, Lewis has served on the Committee on Interior and Insular Affairs, the Committee on Public Works and Transportation, and the House Ways and Means Committee.

North America

## Little Rock Crisis,

1957, an early crisis in the Civil Rights Movement that began in 1957 when whites in Little Rock, Arkansas, rioted in protest against the integration of Central High School; in so doing they—and Arkansas governor Orval Faubus— challenged the supremacy of the federal courts, and President Dwight D. Eisenhower reluctantly sent in United States troops to maintain order.

North America

## Los Angeles Riot of 1992,

one of the first major urban insurrections since the 1960s. This riot shocked many suburban Americans who had come to believe that the days of explosive racial tensions were behind them.

Like the Los Angeles Watts Riot of 1965, the 1992 rioting was sparked by an act of anti-black police brutality. On March 3, 1991, Los Angeles police officers stopped a car driven by a 34-year-old African American named Rodney King, who, they said, was speeding. According to the officers, King emerged from his automobile in an aggressive manner that suggested he might have been high on drugs. Before handcuffing King, the police delivered some 56 blows and kicks and a number of shocks from a stun gun to the fallen body of the suspect. A bystander captured the beating on videotape, and within two days the footage was being broadcast all over national television.

King brought charges of brutality against four of the policemen, and the officers, who claimed they had acted in self-defense, were tried before a predominantly white jury in a white middle-class suburb of Los Angeles. On April 29, 1992, all four men were acquitted. Within two and a half hours of the verdict, a crowd of furious protesters had gathered at the corner of Florence and Normandie streets in South Central Los Angeles, and through the next day and night the rioting exploded across 130 sq km (50 sq mi) of South Central. At the same time, smaller disturbances were erupting in San Francisco, Seattle, Atlanta, Pittsburgh, and other cities.

President George Bush called in 4,500 United States Army troops to quell the rioting, which ended on Friday, May 1. In three days of turbulence more than 50 people were killed, almost 400 injured, and about 17,000 arrested. The city incurred an estimated $1 billion worth of damage.

Unlike the race riots of the 1960s, the 1992 uprising resulted in considerable black-on-black violence as well as the looting of many black-owned shops. Korean shopkeepers were also prime targets of the rioters' rage, as one minority community attacked another. Writing about the riot in a 1992

Men try to salvage what they can from a South Central Los Angeles building burned during the 1992 riots. *CORBIS/Joseph Sohm; ChromoSohm, Inc.*

essay, "Learning to Talk of Race," the philosopher Cornel West suggested that "what we witnessed in Los Angeles was the consequence of a lethal linkage of economic decline, cultural decay, and political lethargy in American life. Race was the visible catalyst, not the underlying cause." In a 1992 interview with the *CovertAction Information Bulletin*, labor historian Mike Davis offered a similar opinion, calling the riot "a hybrid social revolt with three major dimensions. It was a revolutionary democratic protest characteristic of African-American history when demands for equal rights have been thwarted by the major institutions. It was also a major postmodern bread riot—an uprising of not just poor people but particularly of those strata of poor in southern California who've been most savagely affected by the recession [of the early 1990s]. Thirdly it was an interethnic conflict—particularly the systematic destroying and uprooting of Korean stores in the Black community." The 1992 riot represented a rude awakening for many Americans who had assumed that after two relatively quiet decades, the days of large-scale urban race riots had been put behind them.

# Los Angeles Watts Riot of 1965,

**the first major racially fueled rebellion of the 1960s, an event that foreshadowed the widespread urban violence of the latter half of the decade.**

With the arrest of a 21-year-old African American, Los Angeles' South Central neighborhood of Watts erupted into violence. On August 11, 1965, a Los Angeles police officer flagged down motorist Marquette Frye, whom he suspected of being intoxicated. When a crowd of onlookers began to taunt the policeman, a second officer was called in. According to eyewitness accounts, the second officer struck crowd members with his baton, and news of the act of police brutality soon spread throughout the neighborhood. The incident, combined with escalating racial tensions, overcrowding in the neighborhood, and a summer heat wave, sparked violence on a massive scale. Despite attempts the following day aimed at quelling anti-police sentiment, residents began looting and burning local stores. In the rioting, which lasted five days, more than 34 people died, at least 1,000 were wounded, and an estimated $200 million in property was destroyed. An estimated 35,000 African Americans took part in the riot, which required 16,000 National Guardsmen, county deputies, and city police to put down.

Although city officials initially blamed outside agitators for the insurrection, subsequent studies showed that most of the participants had lived in Watts all their lives. These studies also found that the protesters' anger was directed primarily at white shopkeepers in the neighborhood and at members of the all-white Los Angeles police force. The rioters left black churches, libraries, businesses, and private homes virtually untouched.

The Watts Riot was the first major lesson for the American public on the tinderbox volatility of segregated inner-city neighborhoods. The riot provided a sobering preview of the violent urban uprisings of the late 1960s and helped define several hard-core political camps: militant blacks applauded the spectacle of rage; moderates lamented the riot's senselessness and self-destructiveness; and conservative whites viewed the uprising as a symptom of the aggressive pace of civil rights legislation.

The Watts Riot changed California's political landscape and damaged a number of political careers, including that of Governor Edmund G. "Pat" Brown. The liberal Brown lost his office to challenger Ronald Reagan, in part because Reagan was able to pin the blame on the incumbent for the riot.

North America
_____

# Lowery, Joseph Echols

(b. October 6, 1924, Huntsville, Ala.), leader of the Southern Christian Leadership Conference (SCLC) from 1977 to 1997.

One of the founding members of the Southern Christian Leadership Conference in 1957, Joseph Lowery was part of a core group of ministers, including Martin Luther King Jr., Fred Shuttlesworth, and Ralph Abernathy, who were integral to the Civil Rights Movement of the 1960s. Yet it was not until 20 years later, when he became president of the SCLC, that Lowery gained celebrity as an outspoken leader who moved the desegregation organization fully into the international political arena.

Lowery brought a wealth of activist experience to his position as the president of the SCLC. Ordained by the United Methodist Church, he had used his ministry in Mobile, Alabama, from 1952 to 1961 to sponsor lower- and middle-class housing developments. He then became one of the central organizers for the SCLC in the Montgomery, Birmingham, and Selma, Alabama, desegregation campaigns. In 1962 he received national recognition as one of four ministers sued for libel over a *New York Times* advertisement exposing racism in the Montgomery city government. Lowery and the others were ultimately acquitted in a landmark Supreme Court ruling on libel that reversed an earlier Alabama court decision.

In 1977 Lowery, then a pastor of Central United Methodist Church in Atlanta, was elected president of the SCLC. The election was contentious, and supporters of incumbent Hosea Williams accused Lowery of wanting to create a "middle-class clique of blacks." Despite the original view of Lowery as part of the more moderate faction of the SCLC, he led the organization beyond traditional civil rights issues with an unflinching outspokenness.

Throughout the 1970s and 1980s Lowery was an active leader in both the national and international arenas. He vocally opposed apartheid in South Africa and in 1978 launched a protest against a Mississippi energy company buying coal from that country. He moved into the national spotlight in 1979, when he led a group of African American clergy to Lebanon to meet with Yasir Arafat, leader of the Palestinian Liberation Organization. Lowery called for the establishment of a Palestinian homeland recognized as a nation by Israel, and a reduction in United States aid to Israel. In the 1980s Lowery criticized U.S. policy in Central America and used the SCLC to assist Haitian refugees in seeking political asylum.

Lowery also maintained the traditional concerns of the SCLC. During the 1970s he directed marches to free the "Wilmington Ten," a group accused of conspiring to murder segregationists, and to free Tommie Lee Hines, a mentally retarded young black man accused of raping a white woman. Lowery revived the SCLC economic empowerment program Operation Breadbasket, which promoted support for black-owned businesses. During this time he also established Crusade for the Ballot, a campaign that carried on the drive for Southern black voter registration begun by the organization during the 1960s.

North America

# Lucy Foster, Autherine

(b. October 5, 1929, Shiloh, Ala.), African American civil rights activist who sued to integrate the University of Alabama.

Autherine Lucy Foster attended public schools in Alabama and did her undergraduate work at Selma University and Miles College in Birmingham. After her graduation in 1952, she and Pollie Myers, an activist for the National Association for the Advancement of Colored People (NAACP), applied to the University of Alabama. The two women were accepted but then rejected when the university learned that they were not white. With the backing of the NAACP, they went to court and successfully charged the university with racial discrimination. While Foster was re-accepted, the university rejected Myers again, claiming that a child she had had out of wedlock rendered her an unfit student.

Foster's enrollment at the University of Alabama was met with violent anti-integration demonstrations, burning crosses, and a rioting mob that pelted Lucy with rotting food and death threats. For this, Foster was suspended "for her own safety." Again Foster sued and won, but the decision was preempted by her expulsion on the grounds that she had maligned school officials by taking them to court. Lucy and the NAACP decided to drop the case.

For many years Foster had trouble finding work as a teacher because of the controversy. She and her husband, Hugh Foster, and their five children moved throughout the South, with Foster speaking on civil rights issues. She finally was hired for a teaching position in Birmingham in 1974. In 1988 Foster's expulsion was overturned by the University of Alabama and she enrolled there, receiving an M.A. in elementary education in 1992.

# Lynching,

mob execution, usually by hanging and often accompanied by torture, of alleged criminals, particularly African Americans.

Apart from slavery, lynching is perhaps the most horrific chapter in the history of African Americans. Although lynching, defined as execution without the due process of law, has been used against members of many different ethnicities, the vast majority of victims have been African American men, mostly in the Southern states, during a 50-year period following Reconstruction. Despite its stated justification—that lynching is merely a response to crime—in most cases victims had not been convicted, or even charged with, a specific crime. As historian W. Fitzhugh Brundage has noted, lynching was not only "a tragic symbol of race relations in the American South" but also "a powerful tool of intimidation." A constant and unpredictable threat, lynching was used to maintain the status quo of white superiority long after any legal distinction between the races remained.

Because of its unpredictability and extra-legal nature—black men knew that they could become victims at any time, for any reason—lynching cast a shadow greater than its 3,386 known black (mostly male) victims between 1882 and 1930. It is almost certain that these numbers are understated. Despite groundbreaking research into lynching by historians and sociologists, many cases were never recorded. Even those that were well documented rarely reveal the names of the perpetrators; as scholar Robert Zangrando points out, coroners' reports typically attributed the murder to "parties unknown," even though "lynchers' identities were seldom a secret."

More than an epidemic of racially targeted violence, lynching has become a symbol of the most disheartening aspects of American race relations. For many African Americans, there is no more potent reminder of their history of slavery, subjugation, and pain at the hands of white society. In music—most notably jazz singer Billie Holiday's *Strange Fruit*—literature, and painting, black artists have explored this brutal and complex crime. As many scholars have pointed out, lynching was directed not only at a particular victim, but at all black people.

## The History of Lynching

Lynching has its roots in the lawless early days of pre-Revolutionary America. Lacking an established system of courts, jails, and legal rights, mobs often attempted to maintain social order by executing alleged criminals. From its beginning, though, lynching was also a means of controlling people deemed marginal by society's mainstream. Although slaves were often beaten, whipped, and sometimes killed by white slaveholders, systematic violence against African Americans in the form of lynching was not prevalent before the Civil War and Emancipation.

In the five years that followed the Civil War (1861–1865), a series of constitutional amendments conferred several rights upon African Americans: freedom from slavery, legal recognition as United States citizens, and, for men, the right to vote. At this time Reconstruction—primarily an effort to reunite the country—began, and the federal government, dominated by Northern Republicans, maintained a presence in the South and established agencies to oversee the transition from slavery to freedom. But after their emancipation, blacks faced a threat of social violence. With white supremacy challenged throughout the South, many whites sought to protect their former status by threatening African Americans who exercised their new rights. Southern blacks, particularly political and religious leaders, became the targets of white violence. But as Republican resolve weakened, Reconstruction waned, and white Southern Democrats were able to engineer limits on state and federal rights for African Americans.

Incidents of lynching increased even as Reconstruction faltered. Although good statistics on lynching were not kept before 1882, historians believe that the numbers grew throughout the 1870s and 1880s, peaking around 1892, which saw 230 victims, 161 of them African American. From that year on, white victims of mob execution sharply and steadily decreased, while blacks in the South continued to be lynched in large numbers (for instance, in 1900, 106 African Americans were lynched, compared to 9 whites). From its frontier roots, when it took the place of legal law enforcement, lynching became almost entirely a Southern, racial phenomenon—in which, as historians have pointed out, mob execution was really about social control, not crime control.

With the rise in racially motivated mob execution, an antilynching movement was born. Its foremost voice was Ida B. Wells-Barnett, an African American who in the early 1890s published several influential pamphlets detailing the horrors of lynching. Her statement that many of the alleged rapes that led to lynchings were actually consensual interracial encounters caused Wells-Barnett to be vilified by Southern whites, and she was forced to flee her home city of Memphis on threat of lynching. Many of her potential supporters, middle-class black clubwomen, saw Wells-Barnett's bold and passionate rhetoric as unfeminine and supported her cautiously.

In 1909, when the National Association for the Advancement of Colored People (NAACP) was founded, an end to lynching was named as one of the organization's top priorities from the start. In 1917 the NAACP staged the Negro Silent Protest Parade in New York City to criticize the federal government's lack of commitment to ending lynching. The Dyer Bill, which would have made participating in a lynch mob a federal crime, was first introduced in 1918 by Leonidas Dyer, a white Republican congressman from Missouri. Over the next ten years, the NAACP, led by James Weldon Johnson and Walter White, lobbied heavily for its passage, which was repeatedly blocked by Southern Democrats in the Senate. Despite its legislative failure, the Dyer Bill debate allowed the NAACP to educate the white American public about the amount and severity of racial violence that was going unpunished.

The number of lynchings began to decrease in the twentieth century, especially during the 1920s; by the late 1930s the annual victim count was in the single digits. Although some African Americans were still lynched in the following decades, lynching was more or less ended by 1965. Historians have different explanations for the decline in lynching, among them increased public awareness, national pressure on the South, and the growing exodus of African Americans from the region in the Great Migration of the 1930s and 1940s.

## The Significance of Lynching

Starting in 1882, scholars at the Tuskegee Institute began collecting data on lynching, including documenting every known case of mob execution. Because of the availability of this detailed information, sociologists and historians have been able to study the phenomenon of lynching and to try to understand this most extreme form of racial violence.

Early theories about lynching emphasized the economic and political threats that African Americans posed to the superior status of poor whites in the period following the Civil War. Historians such as Arthur Raper suggested that lynch mobs were made up of marginalized white men who murdered black men out of fear and frustration. Most historians today recognize that lynchers were, in fact, as W. Fitzhugh Brundage says, not "isolated deviants" but instead "representative . . . members of society." In the collected testimony of some Southern sheriffs, jailers, and lawyers—typically the people most likely to be in a position to prevent lynching—several mention that they would release the prisoner to the mob after noticing several of the town's leading citizens among it.

Some historians have proposed a new interpretation of lynching, seeing it as a political and economic tool. Marxist historians have suggested, for instance, that rich white businessmen supported lynching, as it helped cement the racial hatred that could work to their advantage. Such scholars reasoned that without racism to divide poor blacks and whites from each other, workers on both sides of the color line could unite against their capitalist oppressors.

Although some scholarship, especially in the late nineteenth and early twentieth centuries, focused exclusively on lynching as an economic and political event, many historians now also consider social and psychological factors in mob executions. Historian Jacquelyn Dowd Hall, who has written about the antilynching movement, argues that lynching was intimately linked to white men's fears about black men's sexuality. While interracial sex was a staple of the prewar South (slaveholders regularly raped their female slaves), it was part of the white South's code of honor that white women must be protected from the supposed threat of black men. So, while less than 30 percent of the black lynching victims had even been accused of sexually assaulting white women, defenders of lynching continued to claim that the practice was necessary to prevent rape.

Lynching's basis in the sexual fears of white society would account, more than cotton prices or other economic reasons, for the extreme brutality with which many lynchings were carried out. It was not uncommon for lynching victims to be castrated. Many were burned alive. Other common tortures were to have their eyes gouged out, their fingers severed, or their teeth pulled out—with the white lynch mob taking home various body parts as souvenirs.

As antilynching activist Ida B. Wells-Barnett pointed out, the emphasis on rape as a justification for lynching only served to reinforce racist stereotypes of black men as sexual predators and to put them "beyond the pale of human sympathy." The sexual excuse for lynching helped perpetuate both the racial and gender inequalities in American society. Lynching reflected a value system that put white men at the top of a hierarchy, above both the white women lynching was said to protect and the black men it was meant to intimidate. In this system, black women's humanity was ignored—although their vulnerability to sexual assault by white men continued to remind black men that they could not protect their wives, mothers, sisters, and daughters. Historian Patricia Schechter says of Wells-Barnett's work that it proves that lynching was "both about sex and not about sex." That is, most lynchings were not directly the result of rape accusations, but all of them served to remind both whites and blacks, men and women, where they stood in Southern society.

## The Legacy of Lynching

Despite the end of lynching, African Americans continued to suffer from inferior legal status. Subject to discriminatory segregation under the South's Jim Crow laws, blacks were unable to choose freely where to work, live, eat, or go to school. Until the Civil Rights Movement of the 1960s, most Southern African Americans could not exercise their constitutional right to vote. If they no longer faced the threat of death at a hangman's noose, they were still vulnerable to being beaten, fired from their jobs, or arrested for whatever infractions a white person might accuse them.

Increasingly, the criminal justice system—which had been, in lynching days, an accused man's one hope for safety—began to seem another arena of unfairness. Still treated as second-class citizens, black men were often tried, convicted, and executed on shaky charges. Only a strong defense and nationwide publicity saved the defendants in the Scottsboro affair—young black men who had been accused of having sex with white women—from such a lynching-like fate. Many scholars have called this sort of unequal application of the death penalty "legal lynching."

# M

## Makeba, Miriam Zenzi

**(b. March 4, 1932, Prospect, South Africa), South African singer and political activist who helped introduce South African music to the world.**

Throughout her life and singing career, Miriam Makeba has used her voice, which journalist Michael A. Hiltzik described as having "the clarity of a Joan Baez with the timing and throaty authority of a Sarah Vaughan," to draw the attention of the world to the music of South Africa and to its oppressive system of racial separation, apartheid. Makeba became an indirect victim of South African policies at the age of 18 days when she began serving a six-month prison term with her mother for illegally selling traditional Swazi homemade beer as a result of economic necessity. For eight years Makeba attended the Kilmerton Training School in Pretoria, where she sang in the school choir. During her teenage years Makeba assisted her mother with the domestic work she did for white families.

She also pursued singing, and in 1950 joined an amateur Johannesburg group called the Cuban Brothers. In 1954 Makeba caught the notice of a successful professional South African group, the Black Manhattan Brothers, an 11-piece band that toured South Africa, Rhodesia (now Zimbabwe), and the Belgian Congo (now the Democratic Republic of the Congo). Makeba left the Manhattan Brothers in 1957 to become a member of a touring revue show, African Jazz and Variety; this stint led to a successful recording career in South Africa.

With her appearance in the semi-documentary, antiapartheid film *Come Back, Africa* (1959), Makeba, already a major star in southern Africa, drew the attention of international audiences. As a result she attended the premiere of *Come Back, Africa* at the 1959 Venice Film Festival in Italy.

After the festival Makeba traveled to London, where she met African American performer and civil rights activist Harry Belafonte, who had requested a private screening of the film. Struck by Makeba's mixture of traditional African rhythms and popular musical forms, Belafonte called the artist "the most revolutionary new talent to appear in any medium in the last decade" and became her sponsor and promoter in the United States. Through Belafonte, Makeba appeared on the Steve Allen Show, which led to performances in nightclubs around New York City and recordings of the music of South Africa. Some songs became hits in the United States, including *Patha Patha, Malaika,* and *The Click Song,* which earned Makeba the nickname of "the click-click girl."

Makeba's music also contained a political component—the denunciation of apartheid. Her criticism of the system earned Makeba the enmity of the South African government, which revoked her passport when she attempted to return for her mother's funeral in 1960. Makeba pressed the issue of apartheid, nevertheless. In 1963 she addressed a United Nations special committee on apartheid, characterizing South Africa as "a nightmare of police brutality and government terrorism" and demanding an international boycott of her homeland. In response, the South African government banned Makeba's music from South Africa.

Marriage to African American civil rights activist Stokely Carmichael (later Kwame Turé) derailed her career in the United States. Carmichael, who at the time was involved with the Black Panther Party and who had popularized the phrase "Black Power," was considered by many in mainstream society to be a revolutionary. The entertainment industry virtually blacklisted Makeba. According to one account, her record company never called her in to record again after the marriage. As Makeba said in her 1987 autobiography *Makeba: My Story,* "My concerts were being canceled left and right . . . . What does Stokely have to do with my singing?" She and Carmichael eventually moved to Guinea in West Africa.

Makeba's career continued outside the United States, however, and during the 1970s and 1980s she toured Europe, South America, and Africa and was a fixture on the jazz festival circuit, appearing regularly at the Montreux Jazz Festival, the Berlin Jazz Festival, and the Northsea Jazz Festival. In 1977 she traveled to Lagos, Nigeria, to serve as the unofficial South African representative at Festac, a Pan-African festival of arts and culture. In 1982 "Mother Africa," as she was known, reunited with South African trumpeter Hugh Masekela, to whom Makeba was married from 1964 to 1966.

Continuing her activism, in 1975 Makeba served a term as a United Nations delegate from Guinea. In addition, she was awarded the Dag Hammerskjöld Peace Prize in 1986. In 1987 American musician Paul Simon invited Makeba to perform on his Graceland tour, which reintroduced her to a United States audience, reigniting her career there.

In 1990 Makeba finally returned to South Africa. In 1991 she released *Eyes on Tomorrow,* which was recorded in a Johannesburg studio and featured such musical lights as Dizzy Gillespie, singer Nina Simone, and Masekela. That same year Makeba gave her first live performance in South Africa since her departure more than 30 years earlier. She has continued to record and tour.

# Malcolm X (Malcolm Little; later El-Hajj Malik El-Shabazz)

(b. May 19, 1925, Omaha, Nebr.; d. February 21, 1965, New York, N.Y.); a leading figure in the twentieth-century movement for black liberation in the United States, and arguably its most enduring symbol.

Malcolm X has been called many things: Pan-Africanist, father of Black Power, religious fanatic, closet conservative, incipient socialist, and a menace to society. The meaning of his public life—his politics and ideology—is contested in part because his entire body of work consists of a few dozen speeches and a collaborative autobiography whose veracity is often challenged. Gunned down three months before his fortieth birthday, Malcolm X's life was cut short just when his thinking had reached a critical juncture.

Malcolm's life is a Horatio Alger story with a twist. His is not a "rags to riches" tale, but a powerful narrative of self-transformation from petty hustler to internationally known political leader. The son of Louisa and Earl Little, who was a Baptist preacher active in Marcus Garvey's Universal Negro Improvement Association, Malcolm and his siblings experienced dramatic confrontations with racism from childhood. Hooded Klansmen burned their home in Lansing, Michigan; Earl Little was killed under mysterious circumstances; welfare agencies split up the children and eventually committed Louisa Little to a state mental institution; and Malcolm was forced to live in a detention home run by a racist white couple. By the eighth grade he left school, moved to Boston, Massachusetts, to live with his half-sister Ella, and discovered the underground world of African American hipsters.

Malcolm's entry into the masculine culture of the zoot suit, the "conked" (straightened) hair, and the lindy hop coincided with the outbreak of World War II, rising black militancy (symbolized in part by A. Philip Randolph's threatened March on Washington for racial and economic justice), and outbreaks of race riots in Detroit, Michigan, and other cities. Malcolm and his partners did not seem very "political" at the time, but they dodged the draft so as not to lose their lives over a "white man's war," and they avoided wage work whenever possible. His search for leisure and pleasure took him to Harlem, New York, where his primary sources of income derived from petty hustling, drug dealing, pimping, gambling, and viciously exploiting women. In 1946 his luck ran out; he was arrested for burglary and sentenced to ten years in prison.

Malcolm's downward descent took a U-turn in prison when he began studying the teachings of the Lost-Found Nation of Islam (NOI), the black Muslim group founded by Wallace D. Fard and led by Elijah Muhammad (Elijah Poole). Submitting to the discipline and guidance of the NOI, he became a voracious reader of the Koran and the Bible. He also immersed himself in works of literature and history at the prison library. Behind prison walls he quickly emerged as a powerful orator and brilliant rhetorician. He led the famous prison debating team that beat the Massachusetts Institute of Technology (M.I.T.), arguing against capital punishment by pointing out that English pickpockets often did their best work at public hangings! Upon his release in 1952 he renamed himself Malcolm X, symbolically repudiating the "white man's name."

As a devoted follower of Elijah Muhammad, Malcolm X rose quickly within the NOI ranks, serving as minister of Harlem's Temple No. 7 in 1954, and later ministering to temples in Detroit and Philadelphia, Pennsylvania. Through national speaking engagements and television appearances, and by establishing *Muhammad Speaks*—the NOI's first nationally distributed newspaper—Malcolm X put the Nation of Islam on the map. His sharp criticisms of civil rights leaders for advocating integration into white society instead of building black institutions and defending themselves from racist violence generated opposition from both conservatives and liberals. His opponents called him "violent," "fascist," and "racist." To those who claimed that the NOI undermined their efforts toward integration by preaching racial separatism, Malcolm responded, "It is not integration that Negroes in America want, it is human dignity."

Distinguishing Malcolm's early political and intellectual views from the teachings of Elijah Muhammad is not a simple matter. His role as minister was to preach the gospel of Islam according to Muhammad. He remained a staunch devotee of the Nation's strict moral codes and gender conventions. Although his own narrative suggests that he never entirely discarded his hustler's distrust of women, he married Betty Sanders (later Betty Shabazz) in 1958 and lived by NOI rules: men must lead, women must follow; the man's domain is the world, the woman's is the home.

On other issues, however, Malcolm showed signs of independence from the NOI line. During the mid-1950s, for example, he privately scoffed at Muhammad's interpretation of the genesis of the "white race" and seemed uncomfortable with the idea that all white people were literally devils. He was always careful to preface his remarks with "The honorable Elijah Muhammad teaches . . . . " More significant, Malcolm clearly disagreed with the NOI's policy of not participating in politics. He not only believed that political mobilization was indispensable but occasionally defied the rule by supporting boycotts and other forms of protest. In 1962, before he split with the NOI, Malcolm shared the podium with black, white, and Puerto Rican labor organizers in the left-wing, multiracial hospital workers' union in New York. He also began developing an independent Pan-Africanist and, in some respects, "Third World" political perspective during the 1950s, when anti-colonial wars and decolonization were pressing public issues. As early as 1954 Malcolm gave a speech comparing the situation in Vietnam with that of the Mau Mau Rebellion in colonial Kenya, framing both of these movements as uprisings of the "darker races" creating a "tidal wave" against United States and European imperialism. Indeed, Africa remained his primary political interest outside of black America. He toured Egypt, Sudan, Nigeria, and Ghana in 1959, well before his famous trip to Africa and the Middle East in 1964.

Although Malcolm tried to conceal his differences with Elijah Muhammad, tensions between them erupted. The tensions were exacerbated by the threat that Malcolm's popularity posed to Muhammad's leadership and by Malcolm's disillusionment with Elijah upon learning that the NOI's moral and spiritual leader had fathered children by former secretaries. The tensions became publicly visible when Muhammad silenced Malcolm for remarking after the assassination of President John F. Kennedy that it was a case of the "chickens coming home to roost." (Malcolm's point was that the federal government's inaction toward racist violence in the South had come back to strike the president.) When Malcolm learned that Muhammad had planned to have him assassinated, he decided to leave the NOI.

On March 8, 1964, he announced his resignation and formed the Muslim Mosque, Inc., an Islamic movement devoted to working in the political sphere and cooperating with civil rights leaders. That same year he made his first pilgrimage to Mecca and took a second tour of several African and Arab nations. The trip was apparently transformative. Upon his return he renamed himself El-Hajj Malik El-Shabazz, adopted from Sunni Islam, and announced that he had found the "true brotherhood" of man. He publicly acknowledged that whites were no longer devils, though he still remained a Black Nationalist and staunch believer in black self-determination and self-organization.

During the summer of 1964 he formed the Organization of Afro-American Unity (OAAU). Inspired by the Organization of African Unity (OAU), made up of independent African states, the OAAU's program combined advocacy for independent black institutions (e.g., schools and cultural centers) with support for black participation in mainstream politics, including electoral campaigns. Following the example of Paul Robeson and W. E. B. Du Bois, Malcolm planned in 1965 to submit to the United Nations a petition that documented human rights violations and acts of genocide against African Americans. His assassination at the Audubon Ballroom in New York—carried out by gunmen affiliated with the NOI—intervened, and the OAAU died soon after Malcolm was laid to rest.

Malcolm X speaks to a crowd at a prointegration rally in Harlem, New York, in May 1963.
*CORBIS/Bettmann*

Although Malcolm left no real institutional legacy, he did exert a notable impact on the Civil Rights Movement in the last year of his life. Black activists in the Congress of Racial Equality (CORE) and the Student Nonviolent Coordinating Committee (SNCC) who had heard him speak to organizers in Selma, Alabama, in February 1965 began to support some of his ideas, especially on armed self-defense, racial pride, and the creation of black-run institutions. He also gained a small following of radical Marxists, mostly Trotskyists in the Socialist Workers Party (SWP). Malcolm convinced some SWP members of the revolutionary potential of ordinary black ghetto dwellers, and he began to speak more critically of capitalism. Was Malcolm about to become a civil rights leader? Could he have launched a successful Pan-Africanist movement? Was he turning toward Marxism? Scholars and activists have debated these issues, but no firm answers are possible.

Ironically, Malcolm X made a bigger impact on black politics and culture dead than alive. The Watts Rebellion occurred and the Black Power Movement emerged just months after his death, and his ideas about community control, African liberation, and self-pride became widespread and influential. His autobiography, written with Alex Haley, became a movement standard. Malcolm's life story proved to the Black Panther Party, founded in 1966, that ex-criminals and hustlers could be turned into revolutionaries. And arguments in favor of armed self-defense—certainly not a new idea in African American communities—were renewed by Malcolm's narrative and the publication of his speeches. Even after the death of Martin Luther King Jr., when the civil rights leader was celebrated as an American hero by many blacks and whites, Malcolm's image loomed much larger in inner-city communities, especially among young males.

Despite the collapse or destruction of Black Nationalist organizations during the mid-1970s, Malcolm X continued to live through the folklore of submerged black urban youth cultures, making a huge comeback thanks to rap music, black-oriented bookstores, and Afrocentric street vendors. The 1980s were a ripe time for a hero like Malcolm X, as racism on college campuses increased, inner cities deteriorated, police brutality cases seemed to rise again, and young black men came to be seen as an "endangered species." Malcolm's uncompromising statements about racism, self-hatred, community empowerment, and his background as a "ghetto youth" made him the undisputed icon of the young.

The recirculation of Malcolm as icon during the late 1980s and the 1990s got its biggest boost from the commercial market-place, as retailers, publishers, and Hollywood cashed in on the popularity of hip hop music and culture. As Afrocentrism achieved respectability among black urban (and suburban) professionals, Malcolm's face and name became a central staple among the "Afro-Chic" products that made up their casual attire. The rush to purchase "X" paraphernalia affected not only African Americans but also suburban whites, Latinos, and Asian Americans, who were dubbed the X Generation and were fascinated with black youth cultures. Ad agencies boldly marketed "X" products without even mentioning Malcolm. "Malcolmania" reached its high point with the release of Spike Lee's cinematic rendering of Malcolm's autobiography in 1992. Following Lee's lead, retailers sold millions of dollars worth of "X" caps, T-shirts, medallions, and posters emblazoned with Malcolm's name, body, or words.

Not surprisingly, the selling of Malcolm X in the 1990s generated pointed debate among African Americans. Some argued that marketing Malcolm undermined his message, while others insisted that the circulation of his image has prompted young people to search out his ideas. Some utilized his emphasis on black community development to support a new African American entrepreneurialism, while others insisted on seeing him as a radical democrat devoted to social justice. His anti-imperialism has dropped out of public memory, whereas his misogyny has been ignored by his supporters and spotlighted by his detractors. However these disputes evolve, it appears that Malcolm X's place in U.S. history, and in the collective memory of African Americans, is secure. Ironically, some of his centrality can be attributed to the mutability of his own viewpoint. Because his ideas were constantly being renewed and rethought during his short career, Malcolm has become a sort of *tabula rasa*, or blank slate, on which people of different positions can write their own interpretation of his politics and legacy. Chuck D of the rap group Public Enemy and Supreme Court Justice Clarence Thomas can both declare Malcolm X their hero.

Africa

# Mandela, Nelson Rolihlahla

(b. July 18, 1918, Mvezo, South Africa), former president of South Africa, winner of the Nobel Peace Prize, and former head of the African National Congress.

The first black president of South Africa, Nelson Mandela became a worldwide symbol of resistance to the injustice of his country's apartheid system. Imprisoned for more than 27 years, and before that banned from all public activity and hounded by police for nearly a decade, Mandela led a struggle for freedom that mirrored that of his black countrymen. After his 1990 release from the Robben Island prison, his work to end apartheid won him the 1993 Nobel Peace Prize (which he shared with South African president F. W. De Klerk) and then the presidency itself a year later.

Mandela's father, Chief Henry Mandela, was a member of the Thembu people's royal lineage; his mother was one of the chief's four wives. Mandela grew up in Qunu, a small village in the Eastern Cape. At age seven he became the first member of his family to attend school. When his father died two years later, Nelson—the Christian name he had acquired at school—was sent to live with Chief Jongintaba Dalindyebo, the regent, or supreme leader, of the Thembu people. From the regent, Mandela said, he learned that "a leader . . . is like a shepherd. He stays behind the flock, letting the most nimble go on ahead, whereupon the others follow, not realizing that all along they are being directed from behind."

Mandela finished his secondary education at Healdtown, a missionary school where an emphasis on English traditions molded students into "Black

Former South African President Nelson Mandela smiles May 2, 2001, after a ceremony at Magdalene College, Cambridge, where he was made an honorary fellow. © Reuters/CORBIS

Englishmen." Only as a student at Fort Hare University did Mandela begin to question the injustices he and all black South Africans faced. Fort Hare was considered an oasis of black scholarship; it was also a training ground for future leaders (lawyer and antiapartheid activist Oliver Tambo was Mandela's classmate, and Freedom Charter originator Z. K. Matthews taught there). But a dispute with the adminstration over students' rights caused Mandela to leave Fort Hare in his second year; at the same time he broke with the regent rather than accept an arranged marriage.

Jobless when he arrived in Johannesburg in 1941, Mandela found work assisting a lawyer—a job arranged by activist Walter Sisulu—while finishing his bachelor's degree by correspondence from the University of South Africa. His political education continued as well, as he met members of the Communist Party of South Africa and, more important, the African National Congress (ANC). Of his decision to join the ANC in 1943, Mandela later wrote that he was motivated by "no epiphany, no singular revelation, no moment of truth, but a steady accumulation of a thousand slights." Soon afterward Mandela and a group of fellow ANC members, including Walter Sisulu and Oliver Tambo (with whom Mandela formed South Africa's first black-run law firm), founded the ANC Youth League.

Mandela also worked as the volunteer-in-chief of ANC's Campaign for the Defiance of Unjust Laws, in which about 9000 volunteers defied selected laws and consequently were imprisoned. As a result, the National Party government banned him from all public gatherings in 1952 and again from 1953 to 1955. When, in 1960, the government banned the ANC outright in the wake of the police massacre of demonstrators in Sharpeville township, Mandela and several thousand apartheid opponents were detained. A con-sistent voice for nonviolence, Mandela at this point decided that "it was wrong and immoral to subject [his] people to armed attacks by the state without offering them some kind of alternative." Consequently, in 1961 he went underground and he helped create the ANC's paramilitary wing Umkhonto we Sizwe (Spear of the Nation), which carried out acts of sabotage against the government. Captured in August

1962, Mandela was charged with traveling outside the country without a passport and inciting workers to strike. At his trial he acted as his own lawyer, arguing not that he was innocent but rather that the South African government had used the law "to impose a state of outlawry" upon him. Several months into his five-year sentence, Mandela was charged with treason and in 1964 was sentenced to life in prison without the possibility of parole.

Until 1982 Mandela was imprisoned on Robben Island, South Africa's most notorious prison, located just offshore from Cape Town. Initially he lived in a cell measuring seven by seven feet, could write and receive only one letter every six months, and was forced to break rocks in the prison yard for hours daily. By the early 1980s South Africa's apartheid government, faced with international sanctions, began to make gestures toward Mandela, its most famous political prisoner, including moving him to Pollsmoor Prison—a much less brutal environment than Robben Island—in 1982. The negotiations unfolded gradually over the next decade. In 1985 President P. W. Botha publicly stated that he would release Mandela provided he "rejected violence as a political instrument," a deal designed to alienate Mandela from other ANC leaders. Mandela rejected the offer. In 1988 he was transferred to a private facility at Victor Verster Prison, where talks continued in secret. F. W. De Klerk succeeded P. W. Botha as president in 1989, and within a few months he lifted the 30-year-long ban on the ANC. On February 2, 1990, he announced Mandela's release from prison.

Freedom brought new challenges. During his imprisonment Mandela's wife, Winnie Madikizela-Mandela (whom he had married in 1958 following the end of his first marriage), had been accused of crimes that included ordering the torture and murder of her enemies. In 1991 Mrs. Mandela was convicted of kidnapping and accessory to assault in the death of a Soweto teenager. The couple, who have two daughters (Mandela has three older children from his first marriage), separated in 1992.

Mandela succeeded Oliver Tambo as president of the ANC in 1992. In September 1992 he and De Klerk agreed on a framework within which to negotiate a transition to multiracial democratic rule. The Record of Understanding they signed in December 1993 provided for a new constitution and free elections to be held April 27, 1994. With black South Africans voting for the first time in their lives, the ANC won handily, and Mandela was inaugurated as president on May 10, 1994. Since assuming office he has earned a reputation as an international peacemaker, helping to mediate conflicts both in Africa and abroad. In addition, Mandela has worked to strengthen South Africa's economy by pursuing international trade agreements and foreign investment. In 1997 Mandela, who has always indicated that he would not run for reelection in 1999, stepped down as ANC leader and was succeeded by Thabo Mbeki. On his 80th birthday on July 18, 1998, Mandela married Graca Machel, the widow of Mozambican president Samora Machel. In September 1998 Mandela received the Congressional Gold Medal in a ceremony at the United States capitol. He was the first African to receive this award.

North America

# March on Washington, 1941,

a protest planned by A. Philip Randolph, who canceled the march after President Franklin D. Roosevelt established the Fair Employment Practices Committee to eliminate discrimination in World War II defense-industry hiring.

North America

# March on Washington, 1963,

a massive public demonstration that articulated the goals of the Civil Rights Movement.

The 1963 March on Washington attracted an estimated 250,000 people for a peaceful demonstration to promote civil rights and economic equality for African Americans. Participants walked down Constitution and Independence avenues, then—100 years after the Emancipation Proclamation was signed—gathered before the Lincoln Monument for speeches, songs, and prayer. Televised live to an audience of millions, the march provided dramatic moments, most memorably the Reverend Martin Luther King Jr.'s "I Have a Dream" speech.

Far larger than previous demonstrations for any cause, the march had an obvious impact, both on the passage of civil rights legislation and on nationwide public opinion. It proved the power of mass appeal and inspired imitators in the antiwar, feminist, and environmental movements. But the March on Washington in 1963 was more complex than the iconic images for which most Americans remember it. As the high point of the Civil Rights Movement, the march—and the integrationist, nonviolent, liberal form of protest it represented—was followed by more radical, militant, and race-conscious approaches.

The march was initiated by A. Philip Randolph, international president of the Brotherhood of Sleeping Car Porters, president of the Negro American Labor Council, and vice president of the AFL-CIO, and was sponsored by five of the largest civil rights organizations in the United States. Planning for the event was complicated by differences among members. Known in the press as "the big six," the major players were Randolph; Whitney Young, president of the National Urban League (NUL); Roy Wilkins, president of the National Association for the Advancement of Colored People (NAACP); James Farmer, founder and president of the Congress of Racial Equality (CORE); John Lewis, president of the Student Nonviolent Coordinating Committee (SNCC); and Martin Luther King Jr., founder and president of the Southern Christian Leadership Conference (SCLC). Bayard Rustin, a close associate of Randolph's and organizer of the first Freedom Ride in 1947, orchestrated and administered the details of the march.

It was Randolph who first conceived of a march on Washington. In 1941 his threat to assemble 100,000 African Americans in the capital helped convince President Franklin D. Roosevelt to sign an executive order banning discrimination in the defense industries and creating the Fair Employment

Leaders of the March on Washington for Jobs and Freedom link arms as they head down Constitution Avenue on August 28, 1963. *CORBIS*

Practices Committee. More than 20 years later, Randolph revived his idea. His primary interest, as always, was jobs—African Americans were disproportionately unemployed and underpaid. In a December 1962 meeting, Randolph and Rustin began planning the March on Washington for Jobs and Freedom.

While Randolph (and the NUL's Young) focused on jobs, the other groups centered on freedom. Both SNCC and CORE were organizing nonviolent protests against Jim Crow segregation and discrimination. In 1963 King's SCLC was waging a long campaign to desegregate Birmingham, Alabama. The violence Sheriff "Bull" Connor and his men visited upon peaceful demonstrators in Birmingham brought national attention to the issue of civil rights. As Rustin later said, credit for mobilizing the March on Washington could go to "Bull Connor, his police dogs, and his fire hoses."

By June, King had agreed to cooperate with Randolph on the march. The older, more conservative NAACP and NUL were still ambivalent. After winning Randolph's promise that the march would be a nonviolent, nonconfrontational event—a promise that dismayed the more militant CORE and SNCC leaders, who had also joined with Randolph—the NAACP's Wilkins pledged his support. In addition, white supporters such as labor leader Walter Reuther and Jewish, Catholic, and Presbyterian officials offered their help. The date was set for August 28, 1963.

Operating out of a tiny office in Harlem, Rustin and his staff had only two months to plan a massive mobilization. Money was raised by the sale of buttons for the march at 25 cents apiece, and thousands of people sent in small cash contributions. The staff tackled the difficult logistics of transportation, publicity, and the marchers' health and safety. Attention to detail was crucial, for the planners believed that anything other than a peaceful, well-organized demonstration would damage the cause for which they would march.

On August 28 the marchers arrived. They came in chartered buses and private cars, on trains and planes—one man even roller-skated to Washington from Chicago. By 11 o'clock in the morning, more than 200,000 had gathered by the Washington Monument, where the march was to begin. It was a diverse crowd: black and white, rich and poor, young and old, Hollywood stars and everyday people. Despite the fears that had prompted extraordinary precautions (including pre-signed executive orders authorizing military intervention in the case of rioting), those assembled marched peacefully to the Lincoln Monument.

After the national anthem and an invocation by Archbishop Patrick O'Boyle came the speeches. Although the official march goals included an endorsement of Kennedy's civil rights bill—in part because the administration had officially cooperated with the march—some of the most passionate speeches criticized the bill as incomplete. John Lewis, the 23-year-old president of SNCC, promised that without "meaningful legislation" blacks would "march through the South." (His original text, edited to avoid controversy, had continued, "through the heart of Dixie, the way Sherman did. We shall pursue our own scorched earth policy and burn Jim Crow to the ground nonviolently.") The speech written by CORE's James Farmer, imprisoned in Louisiana, was read by Floyd McKissick. Farmer said the fight for legal and economic equality would not stop "until the dogs stop biting us in the South and the rats stop biting us in the North." By the time Young and Wilkins spoke, the crowd was quieted by the heat. When Mahalia Jackson took the stage to sing *I've Been 'Buked and I've Been Scorned*, the crowd revived.

King, the last speaker of the day, was introduced by Randolph as "the moral leader of our nation." King's speech, eloquent on the page, was electrifying when delivered. With the passionate, poetic style he had honed at the altar, King stirred the audience and built to his reportedly extemporaneous "I have a dream" finale.

The rally concluded with Rustin's reading of the march's ten demands—which included not only passage of the civil rights bill but also school and housing desegregation, job training, and an increase in the minimum wage—and the marchers' pledge, followed by a benediction from Dr. Benjamin E. Mays, president of Morehouse College. The march ended at 4:20 in the afternoon, ten minutes ahead of schedule. As marchers returned to the buses that would take them home, the organizers met with President Kennedy, who encouraged them to continue with their work.

Although white racists decried it as a sentimental appeal to mainstream white America, the March on Washington was a success. It had been powerful yet peaceful and orderly beyond anyone's expectations, including those of the organizers themselves. Yet it was, according to most historians, the high tide of that phase of the Civil Rights Movement that looked to white support and government solutions. The bombing, just three weeks later, of the Sixteenth Street Baptist Church in Birmingham, Alabama, which resulted in the deaths of four young black girls, reminded African Americans of the depth and violence of segregationist America. Increasingly, young African Americans turned to the Black Power Movement or to the Nation of Islam (whose leader, Malcolm X, had criticized the march) in their search for freedom and strength.

North America

# Marshall, Thurgood

(b. July 2, 1908, Baltimore, Md.; d. January 24, 1993, Bethesda, Md.), first black United States Supreme Court justice, founder of the NAACP Legal Defense and Educational Fund; lawyer whose victory in *Brown v. Board of Education* (1954) outlawed segregation in American public life.

When Thurgood Marshall died in 1993, he was only the second justice to lie in state in the Supreme Court's chambers. Chief Justice Earl Warren, who had written the opinion in Marshall's most celebrated case, *Brown v. Board of Education*, was the other. This honor capped the outpouring of praise for the Court's first black justice, a man who, said one of his former law clerks, "would have had a place in American history before his appointment" to the Supreme Court.

Indeed, Marshall's tenure as chief counsel for the National Association for the Advancement of Colored People (NAACP) and founder of its Legal Defense and Educational Fund made him one of America's most influential and best-known lawyers. His 30 years of public service—first as a federal appeals court judge, then as America's first black solicitor general, and finally as the first black U.S. Supreme Court justice—came after he had already helped millions of African Americans exercise long-denied constitutional rights.

Marshall once said that his father told him, "If anyone calls you nigger, you not only have my permission to fight him, you got my orders." Both of Marshall's parents—William, who worked as a dining steward at an all-white private club, and Norma, a grade school teacher—instilled in their son racial pride and self-confidence. As a child, Marshall later recalled, he was a "hell-raiser," whose high school teacher punished him by sending him to the school's basement to read and copy passages from the United States Constitution. It was valuable training for the future lawyer, who claimed that by the time he graduated he could recite nearly the entire document by heart. From Baltimore's Douglass High School, Marshall entered Lincoln University in Oxford, Pennsylvania, where he won respect as a debater and graduated with honors in 1930.

Denied admission to the University of Maryland's all-white law school—an institution whose segregation he later challenged and defeated in *Murray v. Maryland* (1936)—Marshall entered the law school at Howard University.

There he met Charles H. Houston, the school's vice dean, who became the NAACP's first chief counsel and the first black man to win a case before the U.S. Supreme Court. Shortly after graduating magna cum laude in 1933, Marshall went to work for Houston at the NAACP, replacing him as chief counsel in 1938.

From Houston, Marshall absorbed the lesson that lawyers could be "social engineers." Since its inception in 1909 the NAACP had challenged racial inequality, winning many local cases involving inadequate segregated schools. But Marshall was the architect of a new strategy that increasingly attacked segregation itself. *Plessy v. Ferguson* (1896), a case involving segregated public railroads in Louisiana, had decreed segregation to be constitutional as long as facilities for both races were equal. In a series of cases concerning graduate education, Marshall and the NAACP began asking whether separate could ever be equal. Each victory—in Murray and other law school cases such as *Gaines v. Missouri* and *Sweatt v. Painter*—brought the Supreme Court closer to toppling *Plessy*'s "separate but equal" formula.

The case that finally ended legal segregation in America was *Brown v. Board of Education*. Drawing on psychological and sociological evidence, Marshall argued that the mere fact of racial separation, even without gross inequality, irrevocably harmed African American children. The Court unanimously agreed. In *Brown* (1954) and its companion decision, *Brown II* (1955), the Supreme Court outlawed state-imposed segregation and set guidelines for eradicating it, a process that was neither quick nor easy nor complete. But despite often violent resistance to desegregation, the constitutional impact of Marshall's victory in *Brown* was enormous and lasting.

Thurgood Marshall brought 32 cases before the Supreme Court; he won 29 of them. He had an even more impressive record as a judge for the U.S. Court of Appeals, a position to which President John F. Kennedy appointed him in 1961. Of the 112 opinions he wrote for that court, not one was overturned on appeal. In 1965 President Lyndon B. Johnson appointed Marshall solicitor general of the United States—in essence, the nation's chief counsel. Two years later Johnson nominated Marshall to fill the Supreme Court vacancy left by Justice Thomas C. Clark. The first African American to serve as solicitor general or a Supreme Court justice, Marshall said he hesitated to take on the roles, not wanting to abandon his friends in the Civil Rights Movement. But, he said, "when one has the opportunity to serve the Government, he should think twice before passing it up."

On the Court, Marshall wrote important majority opinions in *Bounds v. Smith* (1977), which defended prisoners' rights to legal assistance and libraries, and *Stanley v. Georgia* (1969), which protected the rights of individuals to possess pornography. His opinion in *Stanley* illustrates the common sense and clarity for which Marshall was famous: "If the First Amendment means anything, it means that the state has no business telling a man, sitting alone in his own house, what books he may read or what films he may watch." Known as the "great dissenter," he stood firmly for the rights of poor people and minorities and against the death penalty even as the Court grew more conservative in the 1980s. Marshall continued to fight for educational equality, writing a 63-page dissent in *San Antonio School Dis-*

Representing defendant Walter Lee Irvin, *third from left*, at his second trial for rape are, *left to right*, Paul C. Perkins, Jack Greenberg, New York attorney for the National Association for the Advancement of Colored People (NAACP), and Thurgood Marshall, chief counsel for the NAACP. *CORBIS/Bettmann*

*trict v. Rodriguez*, a 1973 case in which the majority decided that unequal funding of urban and suburban school districts, based on their disparate tax bases, was constitutional. Marshall disagreed, asserting "the right of every American to an equal start in life."

Gruff and sometimes intimidating from the bench, Marshall was known in private life as a warm man and a brilliant storyteller. When he announced his retirement in 1991, even his most conservative colleagues expressed their respect and affection for the 83-year-old justice. After Marshall's death in 1993, Paul Gewirtz, his former law clerk and a professor at Yale Law School, wrote in remembrance that Marshall, growing up among discrimination, segregation, and racist violence, "had the capacity to imagine a radically different world . . . the strength to sustain that image in the mind's eye and the heart's longing, and the courage and ability to make that imagined world real." Marshall himself, when asked by a reporter how he wished to be remembered, was characteristically plainspoken, saying, "He did the best he could with what he had."

North America

# Mays, Benjamin Elijah

(b. August 1, 1894, Ninety-Six, S.C.; d. March 28, 1984, Atlanta, Ga.), African American educator and Baptist minister.

Benjamin Mays was the son of Hezekiah and Louvenia Carter Mays, both former slaves. After attending Virginia Union University in Richmond, Virginia, he transferred to Bates College in Maine, where he earned a bachelor's degree in 1920. The following year he was ordained as a Baptist minister. He then attended the University of Chicago's Divinity School, earning a master's degree in 1925 and a Ph.D. ten years later. In 1934 Mays assumed the deanship of Howard University's school of religion, where he revitalized a moribund program. In six years under his administration, enrollment increased, the quality of the faculty improved, and the library grew. In addition, the school achieved the American Association of Theological Schools' highest rating.

In 1950 Mays became President of Morehouse College in Atlanta, Georgia; he served in that position until 1967. Although he enhanced the quality of the faculty and the campus at Morehouse, Mays valued even more his relationship with students, particularly with Martin Luther King Jr., who attended Morehouse from 1944 to 1948. Mays and King developed an almost father and son relationship. King later said that Mays was his "spiritual mentor and my intellectual father." Mays had encouraged King's civil rights activities, although critics attacked Mays's moderate views and his denunciation of such organizations as the Black Panther Party for Self-Defense.

In addition to his work in black higher education, Mays was a scholar of the Black Church, and together with Joseph W. Nicholson authored a survey of the Black Church in 12 cities, *The Negro's Church* (1933). In 1938 he published a study of how God figured in the lives of blacks, *The Negro's God as Reflected in His Literature*. Mays was also active in the National Baptist Convention and participated in a number of ecumenical groups, including the National Council of Churches and the World Council of Churches. Mays worked with these groups to facilitate interracial understanding and to promote a more active commitment to racial justice on the part of Christian churches.

After retiring from Morehouse in 1967, Mays was elected to the Atlanta Board of Education, becoming its president in 1970. In 1982, in recognition of his life of service to the African American community, the National Association for the Advancement of Colored People awarded Mays its highest honor, the Spingarn Medal. He died in Atlanta in 1984.

North America

## McKinney, Cynthia

(b. March 17, 1955, Atlanta, Ga.), Democratic member of the United States House of Representatives from Georgia (1993– ).

The first black woman elected to the House of Representatives from the state of Georgia, Cynthia McKinney was born in Atlanta, Georgia. She was the daughter of J. E. "Billy" McKinney, a civil rights activist and a member of the Georgia state legislature for more than 20 years. McKinney earned a bachelor's degree in international relations from the University of Southern California in 1978. She taught political science at various

Georgia colleges and universities and then received a master's degree in 1994 from Tufts University.

McKinney was elected to the Georgia House in 1989, where she served alongside her father. She was part of the state legislative committee that reorganized the state's voting districts in 1992 to create two new black-majority districts. In 1992 she was elected to represent one of these new districts—the primarily urban and Democratic 11th Congressional District of Georgia. In September 1994 a federal appeals court ruled that McKinney's district was unconstitutional. While the appeal was pending in the U.S. Supreme Court, the 1994 election continued with the existing boundaries and McKinney was reelected. In July 1995 the Supreme Court ruled that the 11th District must be redrawn. Resultant changes in district boundaries in 1995 placed her in the newly drawn Fourth District, from which she was reelected in 1996. In the 105th Congress (1997–1999), McKinney served on the International Relations Committee and the Banking and Financial Services Committee. She is a member of the Congressional Black Caucus.

North America

# Memphis, Tennessee,

**Southern American city just north of the Mississippi Delta that developed as a result of the cotton trade, hosted the first urban blues scene, and is home to one of the largest and poorest black populations in the South.**

A visitor to Memphis today can still discern the mark of cotton brokerage on the fronts of abandoned offices and warehouses; she can visit the National Civil Rights Museum at the Lorraine Motel, where Martin Luther King Jr. was assassinated; she can hear old and new blues on Beale Street, and eat barbecued pork ribs in the restaurant owned by blues singer B. B. King.

Memphis sits on a bluff overlooking the Mississippi River and was probably named for its geographical similarity to Memphis, Egypt, which flanks the Nile. Its proximity to the Mississippi River has played a key role in the city's 200-year history. In the antebellum period regional slave trading and cotton commerce centered on the riverside town. Even after the Civil War, the economy of Memphis depended on the transport and sale of cotton as well as other goods.

The geography of Memphis often caused serious problems for poor African Americans, whom whites pushed onto the least valuable land—swampy bayou that drains poorly and breeds tropical disease. The status of Memphis as a port town, however, has contributed to its bustling cultural milieu and its historic centrality to black music in the American South.

White people founded Memphis in 1819. Early black residents worked as domestic servants, artisans, or laborers in river commerce; most voted freely and lived as citizens. In 1834, however, the local government stripped blacks of their rights and in 1840 repealed a ban on the slave trade. Memphis became a center of slave trading and remained so until the Civil War, when the Union Army took the city in 1862.

During and after the war many African Americans gravitated to Memphis, filling the freed people's camps of the Union Army. Blacks often roused the hatred of white immigrants – Germans, Irish, and Italians—who competed for the same jobs and living quarters. The changing racial climate of Reconstruction encouraged some cooperation along class lines, and in the 1860s and 1870s blacks formed political coalitions with foreign-born whites. Yet the alliance was short-lived. Jim Crow laws and the *Plessy v. Ferguson* decision of the United States Supreme Court encouraged racism among lower-class whites.

Yellow fever epidemics in 1877 and 1878, caused by mosquito-infested Memphis swampland, hastened the deterioration of good relations between blacks and their white neighbors. Well-off whites, whose residency began in days of greater racial tolerance, fled the mosquito-infested neighborhoods; white immigrants from poor regions of Arkansas, Mississippi, and Tennessee replaced them, introducing a new, provincial racism. For African Americans, civil rights diminished and segregation proliferated as the century reached its end.

While the yellow fever epidemics hurt Memphis in many ways, they did spell some prosperity for entrepreneurial blacks. Robert Reed Church Sr., a local businessman, bought many properties that had been vacated during the late 1870s. Church accrued exceptional wealth from his saloons and real estate holdings, becoming one of the first African American millionaires. He returned much of his wealth to the black community, founding an auditorium and a park to facilitate social events and recreation.

Through the efforts of black clergy and other African American businessmen, Memphis blacks developed an economic community of their own. Beale Street, which stretched along the Memphis waterfront, soon came to symbolize African American independence in the Jim Crow era of racial violence and discrimination. Both honest businesses and seedy clubs lined the concourse, attracting black doctors, lawyers, gamblers, and blues musicians.

In fact, Beale Street became known as the home of the blues, when musician W. C. Handy arrived in 1908, introducing music of the Southern countryside, popularizing this new sound, and founding a company that published the first blues sheet music. Beale Street became a black haven in a racist city and state, attracting itinerant blues musicians such as Memphis Minnie and Robert Johnson. Historians Margaret McKee and Fred Chisenhall write, "On Beale you could find surcease from sorrow; on Beale you could forget for a shining moment the burden of being black and celebrate being black; on Beale you could be a man, your own man; on Beale you could be free." Although Beale Street suffered immensely during the Great Depression, it survived to produce master bluesmen after World War II. Performers such as B.B. King and Memphis Slim emerged from Beale Street clubs in the 1950s.

Memphis in the early twentieth century showcased black cultural prosperity, yet it also reflected the poor state of African American political life. Irish-American Edward H. "Boss" Crump dominated Memphis politics from the late 1920s until 1954. Although he never became mayor himself, Crump consolidated power and assembled a formidable political machine. All the while he maintained an ambivalent and paternalistic relationship with the black community of Memphis. He oversaw massive voter registration campaigns, enfranchising a large segment of the African American population. Yet in the single-party politics of Crump's Memphis, the power he bestowed on blacks served only his ends; and as a staunch segregationist, his generosity was predicated on the submissiveness of his black constituents.

Under the Crump administration few African Americans gained any political power. When Crump died in 1954, however, his self-serving registration drives ultimately set Memphis blacks ahead of blacks in other cities. In 1963 as many African Americans as whites were registered to vote, and throughout the 1950s and 1960s black candidates began to run for office. African American political victories came slowly. Blacks voters comprised a minority, and within that minority there was much competition. Furthermore, white candidates often ran for office using racist rhetoric. The most successful black politician of the era, Harold Ford, did not win his congressional seat until 1974. W. W. Herenton, the first black mayor of Memphis, won office only in 1987.

Despite the languor of conventional political channels in Memphis, the city played an active role in the Civil Rights Movement. Through the power of the church and the success of voter registration drives, blacks secured the vote. Through sit-ins and demonstrations, they gained access to segregated business and schools. One of the most tragic events of the Civil Rights Movement, the assassination of Martin Luther King Jr., occurred amid the strike of Memphis's predominantly black sanitation workers in 1968. After addressing a rally at Mason Temple, the city's largest black church, King was shot dead at the Lorraine Motel.

Census data in the 1990s showed that blacks in Memphis were among the poorest in the nation. Despite the success of black politicians, Memphis suffered from a limited economy. The city's dependence on service industries and commerce—instead of industry or new technology—left it with few well-paying jobs for blue-collar blacks.

North America

# Meredith, James H.

**(b. June 25, 1933, Kosciusko, Miss.), African American who in 1962 became the first black student to enroll at the University of Mississippi; this landmark event and the attention surrounding his 1966 "walk against fear" were central events of the Civil Rights Movement.**

While attending the all-black Jackson State University in Jackson, Mississippi, James Meredith applied to the all-white University of Mississippi. Rejected because he was black, he sued for admission, and after a series of appeals the university was ordered to admit him. Gov. Ross Barnett, with support of the state legislature, vowed to block Meredith. On September 30, 1962, federal marshals escorted Meredith to the Ole Miss campus in

Oxford, Mississippi. Approximately 3,000 whites rioted in protest. More than 23,000 United States troops restored order by the next morning. But two people had been killed and 160 injured. Meredith attended classes and graduated the following year.

After studying at Ibadan University in Nigeria and at the Columbia University School of Law, in 1966 Meredith returned to Mississippi to stage a 225-mile march from Memphis, Tennessee, to Jackson, Mississippi. By completing this "walk against fear," Meredith hoped to inspire blacks to vote in the upcoming primary elections. He was shot on the second day of his march and, although he was not seriously injured, was hospitalized and unable to complete the march. Major civil rights organizations, most notably the Southern Christian Leadership Conference (SCLC) and the Student Nonviolent Coordinating Committee (SNCC), started from the spot of the shooting and finished Meredith's march to Jackson. Significant was SNCC member Stokely Carmichael's use of the phrase "Black Power" during the march, which signaled a schism between moderate and militant civil rights groups.

In 1968 Meredith unsuccessfully tried to unseat Congressman Adam Clayton Powell Jr. He lectured about racial justice and published a memoir, *Three Years in Mississippi*, as well as numerous pamphlets and other publications. He also became active in several business ventures. In the late 1980s he allied himself with the Republican Party, serving in 1989 as a domestic policy adviser to conservative Southern senator Jesse Helms. In 1991 he endorsed former neo-Nazi and Ku Klux Klan Imperial Wizard David Duke in Duke's unsuccessful bid to become governor of Louisiana.

In 1995, once again living in Mississippi, Meredith began teaching literacy and standard English to African American boys and men, whose material and social progress, Meredith believed, had been stunted by their use of Black Vernacular English. Critics charged that Meredith's plan would do little more than undermine African American culture.

North America

# Mfume, Kweisi

**(b. October 24, 1948, Turners Station, Maryland), congressman, civil rights leader, and president of the National Association for the Advancement of Colored People (NAACP).**

The eldest of four children, Kweisi Mfume (born Frizzell Gray) was raised in a poor community just outside Baltimore, Maryland, by his mother and stepfather, Mary and Clifton Gray. After years of physical abuse, Mary Gray left her husband in 1960 and moved the family to a neighborhood closer to the city. Four years later she was diagnosed with cancer and within a short time learned that the disease was terminal. Mfume and his sisters were devastated by the news and suffered another traumatic blow when she died, literally, in the arms of her only son. In his autobiography, *No Free Ride*, Mfume recalls just how difficult it was losing his mother. After his mother's death, Mfume quit high school and began working to support his three sisters. Disillusioned, he also began hanging out on the streets, becoming a gang leader and fathering several illegitimate children.

Disappointed with his reckless lifestyle, Mfume made a decision to change his life when he was 22 years old. He earned a high school equivalency diploma and graduated magna cum laude from Morgan State University in 1976. In the early 1970s he began working as a disc jockey on local radio stations, where he developed an interest in politics. He changed his name from Frizzell Gray to Kweisi Mfume (which means "conquering son of kings" in the African language spoken by the Igbo) and in 1978 won a seat on the Baltimore City Council.

Mfume honed his political skills and in 1986 won the seat in the Seventh Congressional District vacated by the legendary black politician Parren J. Mitchell. Mfume served five terms in Congress, eventually becoming leader of the Congressional Black Caucus (CBC). On February 20, 1996, he left Congress to become president and chief executive officer of the National Association for the Advancement of Colored People (NAACP), the nation's oldest and largest civil rights organization. As president of the NAACP, Mfume has eliminated the organization's six-figure debt and has worked to revitalize its image among young African Americans.

North America

# Miami Riot of 1980,

**the first major American race riot since the Civil Rights Movement, an event that heightened American awareness of the volatility of neglected urban enclaves.**

Violence erupted in Dade County, Florida, on the night of May 17, 1980, when residents of Liberty City, a predominantly African American neighborhood, learned of the verdict in a case of white-on-black police brutality. Furious blacks threw bricks, rocks, and bottles at white suburban motorists who had to drive through Liberty City to reach a main Miami highway. Rumors of whites shooting children in retaliation fueled the violence. Black mobs attacked white derelicts and white motorists who tried to flee their damaged cars on foot.

Meanwhile, a nominally peaceful protest, sponsored by the National Association for the Advancement of Colored People (NAACP), failed to produce a speaker. Soon, the frustrated crowd joined in the violence, attacking the Dade County Department of Public Safety headquarters as well as local white-owned businesses.

Joining forces with Miami police, the National Guard restored order with roadblocks and guns. By the time the rioting ceased the following morning, 855 people had been arrested and $80 million of property damage had been incurred. In the skirmishes between blacks and white motorists, eight white people and ten African Americans had died.

The acquittal of five white policemen who had been accused of beating a black motorist to death sparked the violence. In December 1979, police officers had pursued an African American motorcyclist, Arthur McDuffie, in a high-speed chase. Although the officers claimed that the chase ended when McDuffie crashed his motorcycle and died, the coroner's report concluded otherwise. One of the pursuing officers cleared up the story, testifying that five of his fellow policemen had beaten McDuffie with their flashlights. According to his testimony, the officers murdered McDuffie after McDuffie forcefully resisted arrest. An all-white jury acquitted the officers after brief deliberation.

For the Miami police the McDuffie case was one incident in a history of unpunished malfeasance and neglected allegations. Stories—some verified, some not—of roadside sexual harassment, physical assault, and even murder tarnished the department's reputation. Because African Americans in Liberty City faced tough competition for jobs (due to a growing Cuban population) and a dwindling tax base (attributable to white flight to the suburbs), the community readily burst into violence on the conclusion of the McDuffie case.

The 1980 riot shattered the illusion that the racially motivated uprisings of the 1960s were a thing of the past. Like the Los Angeles Riot of 1992, the Miami conflagration awakened many suburban and middle-class Americans to the explosive potential of impoverished inner-city neighborhoods.

## North America

# Miscegenation,

**a term for sexual relations across racial lines; no longer in use because of its racist implications, the word was invented in 1863 for political purposes and was created from two Latin words: miscere (to mix) and genus (race).**

The word *miscegenation* was coined by two Democrats in the presidential election campaign of 1864 in an attempt to embarrass and discredit the Republican incumbent running for reelection, Abraham Lincoln. In an anonymous pamphlet that appeared in December 1863 entitled *Miscegenation: The Theory of the Blending of the Races Applied to the American White Man and Negro*, the authors played on white fears of interracial sex by pretending to issue a Republican-sponsored booklet advocating racial mixing and amalgamation. The real authors were David Goodman Croly, managing editor of *New York World*, a staunchly Democratic paper, and George Wakeman, a *World* reporter.

Sex across the color line was an obsession of white America, particularly the stereotype of black men's alleged craving for white women, and of believers in Anglo-Saxon "racial" superiority, who feared that "mongrelization" was degenerative. In fact, black-white sex existed from the beginning of the slave trade in the sixteenth century, virtually always on the initiative of Europeans, who held Africans in their total power. During the notorious Middle Passage between Africa and the New World, for example, black women and children were allowed mobility on board ship so that white sailors could have unlimited sexual access to them.

Sex played a role in the gradual differentiation of Africans from other indentured servants in Virginia, a process that culminated around 1700 in the unique North American phenomenon of chattel slavery, by which people were legally defined as property. The very first case in this sequence of events was a sexual one: in 1630 Hugh Davis was sentenced by the Virginia court to a whipping "for defiling his body in lying with a Negro." Even though it was a white man who was convicted and punished for the act, the case shows the early eroticization of racial differences.

The interracial sexual pattern in the antebellum South is clear: because slaves were property, like animals or objects, they had no rights, and all black women were sexually available to all white men. In addition, African American marriage and parenthood were not recognized in law, and there was no recourse for sexual abuse in the courts, government, church, or press. Virtually every plantation produced children of mixed race: the 1860 federal census classified 588,532 persons as mulattos. A minuscule number of white fathers recognized their children and provided for them; some parents encouraged the fairest skinned to run away and hide their racial identity by passing for white. Most mixed-blood slave children were simply worked and sold like all other slaves.

The white South combined the permissive sexual exploitation of black women by white men with a fanatic "protection" of white women from black men. In both cases, the ideology was that people of African descent were closer to nature and savagery, but the real reason was probably economic: legally, a child was slave or free depending on the status of the mother. All white women were free and nearly all black women were slaves.

The uniqueness of chattel slavery prohibited in North America (except for New Orleans) the emergence of mulattos as a distinct third group between black and white, as existed in the West Indies, Latin America, and South Africa. American slavery was race and color based, but it would have become weakened ideologically and economically if it had allowed any deviation from the one-drop rule, that is, the belief that any black ancestry made a person black.

Miscegenation was about marriage as well as sex, since sexual relationships were legitimized by marriage. Therefore, interracial marriage was prohibited, a law upheld by the United States Supreme Court in *Pace v. Alabama* (1883). That decision was not overturned until well after the modern Civil Rights Movement had begun, in *Loving v. Virginia* (1967), when 16 states still had laws prohibiting interracial marriage. Civil rights and voting rights were extended to African Americans before the right was granted both to whites and blacks to marry (and have legitimate sexual relationships) across the color line.

North America

# Mitchell, Clarence Maurice, Jr.

(b. March 8, 1911, Baltimore, Md.; d. March 18, 1984, Washington, D.C.), lobbyist to the United States Congress for the National Association for the Advancement of Colored People (NAACP).

Less visible than many of his NAACP colleagues, Clarence Mitchell nonetheless had a major impact on the lives of African Americans. Known as "the 101st Senator," the long-time NAACP lobbyist was instrumental in the passage of both the Civil Rights Act of 1964 and the Voting Rights Act of 1965, the two most significant successes of the Civil Rights Movement. Mitchell, a 1932 graduate of Lincoln University in Pennsylvania and the husband of Juanita Jackson Mitchell, an NAACP official, joined the NAACP staff following his work with the National Urban League and the Fair Employment Practices Committee (FEPC).

Formed in 1941 to eliminate employment discrimination, the FEPC was dissolved in 1946. While acting as the NAACP's labor secretary, Mitchell continued to fight for economic fair play, founding the National Council for a Permanent FEPC in 1949, and participating the following year in the Leadership Conference on Civil Rights, a group with representatives from more than 50 civil rights organizations. Mitchell began his legislative work as part of this struggle, quickly becoming the association's chief lobbyist, a position he held until his retirement in 1978. The veteran lobbyist became a lawyer himself in 1962, when he completed four years of night school at the University of Maryland Law School. In 1968 the NAACP awarded Mitchell the Spingarn Medal and in 1980 he was honored with the Presidential Medal of Freedom, the nation's highest nonmilitary decoration. After his death in 1984, the city of Baltimore, Maryland, renamed its courthouse after him.

North America

# Mitchell, Juanita Jackson

(b. January 2, 1913, Hot Springs, Ark.; d. July 7, 1992, Baltimore, Md.), civil rights lawyer; first African American woman admitted to the Maryland bar; and first national youth director of the National Association for the Advancement of Colored People (NAACP).

By the time Juanita J. Mitchell received her law degree in 1950, she had already spent nearly 20 years working for civil rights on the local and national levels. Born to racially conscious parents—her mother, Lillie Mae Carroll Jackson, was president of the state conference of NAACP branches—Mitchell earned a degree in education from the University of Pennsylvania in 1931. Upon graduation she returned to her native Baltimore to help African Americans struggling with both the economic devastation of the Great Depression and the persistence of lynching and other racist violence. Hoping to alleviate some of their suffering, Mitchell founded the City-Wide Young People's Forum of Baltimore in 1931 and served as its president until 1934. In 1935 Walter White, then executive secretary of the NAACP, recruited Jackson to head that organization's newly created youth program, a position she held until her 1938 marriage to Clarence M. Mitchell Jr.

After the birth of four sons, Mitchell entered law school at the University of Maryland, from which she graduated in 1950. That same year she became the first African American woman to be admitted to the bar in her state. As a lawyer, she continued the work she had begun as an organizer:

improving the lives of African Americans. She filed lawsuits that helped integrate public beaches and schools, represented students arrested during sit-ins in the 1960s, and continued to direct voter registration drives. By the time she died in 1992 at age 79, Mitchell had been recognized by the National Council of Negro Women—which she had helped found with Mary McLeod Bethune—the NAACP's Youth/College Division, and the Maryland Women's Hall of Fame.

North America

# Montgomery Bus Boycott,

the year-long protest in Montgomery, Alabama, that galvanized the American Civil Rights Movement and led to a 1956 United States Supreme Court decision declaring segregated seating on buses unconstitutional.

In December 1955, 42,000 black residents of Montgomery began a year-long boycott of city buses to protest racially segregated seating. After 381 days of taking taxis, carpooling, and walking the hostile streets of Montgomery, African Americans eventually won their fight to desegregate seating on public buses, not only in Montgomery, but throughout the United States.

The protest was first organized by the Women's Political Council as a one-day boycott to coincide with the trial of Rosa Parks, who had been arrested on December 2, 1955, for refusing to give up her seat to a white man on a segregated Montgomery bus. By the next morning, the council, led by JoAnn Robinson, had printed 52,000 fliers asking Montgomery blacks to stay off public buses on December 5, the day of the trial. Meanwhile, labor activist E. D. Nixon, who had bailed Parks out of jail, notified Ralph Abernathy, minister of the First Baptist Church, and Martin Luther King Jr., the new minister at Dexter Avenue Baptist Church, of her arrest. A group of about 50 black leaders and one white minister, Robert Graetz, gathered in the basement of King's church to endorse the boycott and begin planning a massive rally for the evening of the trial. Graetz offered his support from the pulpit of his predominantly white Lutheran church. The Montgomery Chapter of the National Association for the Advancement of Colored People (NAACP), which had been looking for a test case for segregation, began preparing for the legal challenge.

The issue of segregated seating had long been a source of resentment in Montgomery's black community. African Americans were forced to pay their fares at the front, and then re-board the bus at the back. They faced systematic harassment from white drivers, who sometimes pulled away before black passengers could re-board. On the bus blacks sat behind a mobile barrier dividing the races, and as the bus filled, the barrier was pushed backward to make room for white passengers. No black person could sit in the same row as a white, and whites had priority in this middle "no-man's land."

On the morning of Parks's trial, buses rumbled nearly empty through the streets of Montgomery. Police officers with shotguns roamed in search of imaginary "Negro goon squads" who they believed were forcing blacks to

An empty bus makes its rounds of the city during the Montgomery, Alabama, bus boycott in 1956.
*CORBIS/Bettmann-UPI*

stay off the buses. After Parks lost her case and was convicted of violating the segregated seating laws, black leaders met again to organize an extension of the bus boycott. To this end they formed the Montgomery Improvement Association (MIA) and elected King as its president. That evening, 7,000 blacks crowded into Holt Street Baptist Church, where King inspired the audience with his words: "There comes a time when people get tired of being trampled over by the iron feet of oppression."

With this speech, King was able to spark the black residents' collective outrage into a grassroots movement that would sustain the boycott. The Montgomery Bus Boycott followed King's credo of nonviolent resistance, even in the face of a police crackdown and attempts by white supremacists to undermine the protest. Montgomery police threatened to arrest taxi drivers giving discount rates to the black riders, and when the MIA arranged carpools, the police systematically harassed drivers, arresting them for allegedly going too fast or too slow. Meanwhile, the boycott leaders squared off at the bargaining table with the local officials. The MIA presented its modest demands for bus seating by race, with no mobile area, and "Negro routes" with black drivers. They were met with unconditional refusal.

Many white supremacists joined the White Citizen's Council, one of many racist citizens' organizations that would gain power throughout the South in the 1960s. Convinced that there was an outside mastermind of the movement, they focused their attention on terrorizing boycott leaders. Vigilante groups set off bombs at black homes and churches. In addition, there were several police sweeps, and twice King joined the other black protesters in Montgomery's crowded jails. In one attempt to sabotage the boycott, the *Montgomery Advertiser*, a white newspaper, planned to put out a false story that the boycott had ended. King and other leaders, warned in advance of the story, traveled late that night to the rural jook joints where black workers went to dance and drink. Thus forewarned, African Americans continued to stay off the local buses. Shortly after, the *Advertiser* announced that Montgomery was on the verge of a "full scale racial war."

Even as the protesters and black leaders were confronted with escalating violence, they maintained both nonviolent resistance and their exhausting day-to-day schedule without public transportation. At the same time the MIA moved ahead on the legal front. On February 1, 1956, shortly after a bomb went off in King's home, the MIA filed a federal suit against bus segregation in the names of four black women.

In the spring protesters led by E. D. Nixon turned the tables on the local government and caught the attention of the national press. Indicted under a statute that prohibited boycotts "without just cause or legal excuse," leaders presented themselves at the courthouse rather than waiting to be arrested. The national press came down to cover the scene of black leaders marching into the courthouse while hundreds cheered them on. As protesters walked to work through the summer of 1956, the issue of civil rights took center stage in the national consciousness. After the March trial of the MIA, King appeared on the cover of *Time* magazine and the *New York Times Magazine*.

In June a federal court ruled segregated seating unconstitutional, and the case went on appeal to the U.S. Supreme Court. Meanwhile, King and the MIA leadership went to the Montgomery court to try to stave off an injunction against the carpools. They were in court when they were handed a notice from the Associated Press wire announcing the Supreme Court decision that ruled segregated seating on public buses unconstitutional. King addressed a euphoric crowd that night, and over the next week, celebrities such as singer Mahalia Jackson and New York minister Gardner C. Taylor came to Montgomery to celebrate. On December 20, 1956, when the federal ruling took effect, an integrated group of boycott supporters, including King, Abernathy, Fred Gray, and Glenn Smiley, rode the city buses.

The Montgomery Bus Boycott had implications that reached far beyond the desegregation of public buses. The protest propelled the Civil Rights Movement into national consciousness and Martin Luther King Jr. into the public eye. In the words of King: "We have gained a new sense of dignity and destiny. We have discovered a new and powerful weapon—nonviolent resistance."

North America
_____

# Moody, Anne

(b. September 15, 1940, Centerville, Miss.), African American civil rights activist and writer.

The daughter of sharecroppers, Anne Moody was educated in the segregated schools of rural Mississippi and began her college career at Natchez Junior College on a basketball scholarship. She later transferred to Tougaloo College in Jackson, Mississippi, where she became active in the Civil Rights Movement.

From 1961 to 1963 Moody served as an organizer for the Congress of Racial Equality (CORE) in Mississippi, then considered to be the state with the most violent and most dangerous white resistance to civil rights activities in the South. She participated in direct action protests, including the first sit-in demonstration at a Woolworth's lunch counter in Jackson, Mississippi. In 1964, the same year she graduated from Tougaloo, she began fundraising for CORE. From 1964 to 1965 she also worked for Cornell University as its civil rights project coordinator. Her civil rights activities soon cooled, however, because of her frustration with the changing nature of the movement, in particular its shift toward Black Nationalism.

But Moody is best known for her autobiography, *Coming of Age in Mis-*

*sissippi* (1968), which received the Best Book of the Year Award from the National Library Association in 1969. One of the most widely read works to come out of the Civil Rights Movement, this moving book traces her life from the poverty and racism of the rural Mississippi Delta through her educational struggles and civil rights activities up to the 1963 March on Washington. In 1975 Moody published *Mr. Death*, a book of short stories.

North America

# Moore, Audley ("Queen Mother")

(b. July 27, 1898, New Iberia, La.; d. May 2, 1997, New York, N.Y.), American black nationalist and Harlem civil rights leader.

Born in rural Louisiana, Audley Moore and her family experienced the terror of racism in its most brutal form with the lynching of her paternal grandfather. Her parents died when Moore was in the fourth grade, and by the time she was 15 she had to raise and support herself and her two sisters as a hairdresser.

Her family's suffering and the racism she faced pushed Moore to political activism. In New Orleans she joined Marcus Garvey's militant Universal Negro Improvement Association, inspired by Garvey's Black Nationalism and pride in blacks' African heritage. Part of the Great Migration from the rural South to the urban North, Moore and her sisters moved to Harlem in the 1920s. Moore became a prominent organizer for the Communist Party, particularly in defense of the Scottsboro Boys, eight young men in Alabama who were wrongly convicted of rape and sentenced to death. Through the party, she fought on behalf of black tenants and for black political representation, but because of the racism she encountered within the party she eventually resigned.

Moore continued her political activity by fighting for education for the poor and becoming a leader in the movement demanding reparations from the federal government for the labor of blacks under slavery. She stated: "Ever since 1950, I've been on the trail fighting for reparations. They owe us more than they could ever pay. They stole our language, they stole our culture. They stole us from our mothers and fathers and took away our names from us. They worked us free of charge 18 hours a day, 7 days a week, under the lash, for centuries."

Moore promoted Pan-Africanism and was one of the founders of the Universal Association of Ethiopian Women. In 1972, on one of her many visits to Africa, she was honored by the Asante people of Ghana as "Queen Mother." In 1989 Moore was among the black women honored at the Corcoran Gallery of Art, where "I Have A Dream," an exhibition of one of these prominent women, was on display. Moore participated in the Million Man March in 1995.

In a life that spanned some six decades of activism, Moore exemplified Nelson Mandela's dictum, which she often referred to: "The struggle is my life."

# Moore, Harry Tyson

(b. November 17, 1905, Houston, Fla.; d. December 25, 1951, Mims, Fla.), teacher, political activist, and Florida state coordinator of the National Association for the Advancement of Colored People (NAACP), whose murder was never solved.

The victim of a bombing on Christmas night, Henry Tyson Moore was only 46 when he died, but in his short life he accomplished much. Trained as a schoolteacher, he worked for the Brevard County, Florida, school system from 1925 until 1946, when his NAACP-supported campaign to secure equal pay for African American teachers cost him his position as superintendent of the area's Negro High School. Following the loss of his job, Moore continued to work for the state branch of the NAACP, focusing not only on economic and educational equality but also on voter registration and the fair enforcement of laws. When in November 1951 a white sheriff shot two black handcuffed defendants, killing one, Moore demanded that the sheriff be indicted for murder.

On December 25 of that year, a bomb exploded under the bedroom of Moore's house, killing him instantly (his wife, Harriet, died a few days later). Neither local law enforcement nor the Federal Bureau of Investigation (FBI) was able to solve Moore's murder. Documents unveiled when Florida's governor reopened the case in 1991 reveal that the FBI's initial investigation focused solely on African American suspects, including all 600 people who attended Moore's funeral. To date, no one has been charged with the crime, which a 1952 editorial in *Nation* described as "part of a clear pattern of open force directed against the struggle of racial minorities to win full rights as citizens."

# Moore, Richard Benjamin

(b. August 9, 1893, Hastings, Christ Church, Barbados; d. August 18, 1978, Barbados), activist and intellectual who was a leading figure in black socialism and labor politics in the United States.

Richard Moore became a political activist when he immigrated to New York in 1901. He joined the Socialist Party in 1918 and became a member of the African Blood Brotherhood (ABB), a secret organization with ties both to Black Nationalism and the Communist Party USA.

In 1921 Moore left the Socialist Party because of its indifference to African American concerns. Soon after he joined the Workers Party, the Harlem branch of the Communist Party. In 1925 he was elected to the executive board and council of directors of the American Negro Labor Congress (ANLC), a national organization of black radicals, and became a contributing editor to the ANLC's the Negro Champion. In 1931 Moore became vice president of the International Labor Defense (ILD), which was

formed to resolve legal problems caused by labor disputes and racism.
Moore and the ILD became well known for defending the Scottsboro case,
in which nine black boys were sent to prison for raping two white girls,
although doctors determined that no rape had taken place.

Moore founded the Pathway Press and the Frederick Douglass Historical
and Cultural League in 1940. In 1942 he established the Frederick Douglass
Book Center, an Afro-American and Caribbean bookstore, which was a
well-known intellectual center in Harlem until it was burned in 1968. The
Communist Party expelled him in 1942 for his "Negro Nationalist way of
thinking."

Throughout his life Moore was dedicated to the independence of
Caribbean nations. He was invited by Barbados to participate in its independence celebration in 1966.

Moore fought ceaselessly to end racism. In 1960 he published *The Name
"Negro"—Its Origin and Evil Use*. He strongly promoted the term "Afro-
American," which, he felt, "proclaims at once our past continental heritage
and our present national status."

## North America

# Moses, Robert Parris

(b. January 23, 1935, New York, N.Y.), African American civil rights activist; first
Student Nonviolent Coordinating Committee (SNCC) worker in Mississippi.

Inspired by student sit-ins in 1960, 25-year-old Harvard Ph.D. candidate
and middle-school teacher Bob Moses left his New York teaching job to join
the Civil Rights Movement, where he led the effort of the Student Nonviolent Coordinating Committee (SNCC) to register black voters in Mississippi. Many civil rights workers had believed that Mississippi was too
dangerous a place to attempt to organize. His courage and stoicism made
Moses an almost mythical figure to other civil rights workers, who stood
amazed by stories such as the one in which a bloodied Moses accompanied
prospective black registrants to the county courthouse just minutes after
being beaten by whites.

Disturbed by competition between SNCC and other civil rights organizations in Mississippi, Moses helped found the Council of Federated Organizations (COFO), an umbrella organization that coordinated all of
Mississippi's civil rights organizations. As COFO's project director in September 1963, he developed the Freedom Vote, a mock gubernatorial election in which 80,000 blacks voted to protest their disfranchisement.
Encouraged by the turnout, COFO launched Freedom Summer the following year, a massive voter registration and education project. Later in
1964 Moses helped establish the Mississippi Freedom Democratic Party,
which challenged the all-white Mississippi Democratic delegation to the
Democratic National Convention.

In 1982, believing that math literacy was the key to modern citizenship,
just as literacy and voter registration had been the keys to citizenship in the
1960s, Moses founded the Algebra Project, a program in which students use

concrete examples from their lives to master abstract algebraic concepts. He brought the Algebra Project to the Mississippi Delta in 1992, thereby helping to empower a new generation of Mississippi blacks.

# MOVE,

**a counter-cultural organization founded in Philadelphia, Pennsylvania; its activities led to two controversial clashes with police in 1978 and 1985, resulting in the imprisonment or death of more than two dozen members.**

MOVE was founded in 1972 by Vincent Leaphart, an African American handyman. Leaphart believed that various problems plaguing American society, such as crime, substance abuse, and violence, grow out of humanity's growing alienation from the natural world through technology and various social institutions. He advocated a lifestyle based on the "principle of natural law," which involved observances such as eating only uncooked, unprocessed foods, living without electric heat, letting one's hair grow naturally, and rejecting "man's [corrupt] laws." Donald Glassey, a white leftist graduate student at the University of Pennsylvania, befriended Leaphart—who began calling himself John Africa—and collected his ideas into a manuscript called *The Guidelines*.

*The Guidelines* circulated throughout the Powelton Village section of Philadelphia, attracting a small number of disciples, mostly students from surrounding universities, relatives of John Africa, working-class folk from the community, and veterans of various radical groups, including the Black Panthers. Although the group's membership was predominantly African American and its activities often focused on racially charged issues such as police brutality against blacks, a few sympathizers and members like Glassey were white. All followers, emulating their leader, took "Africa" as their surname. The group was first named the Christian Movement for Life; John Africa eventually shortened the name of his new "family" to MOVE. Glassey purchased a house on North 33rd Street, and, although not all members lived there, the house became MOVE's communal residence.

MOVE's early activities included protests against city and school board policies, police brutality (rampant under law-and-order Mayor Frank Rizzo, 1971–1979), and pollution and other environmental abuses. They picketed the Philadelphia Zoo, comparing the caging of animals to the Jewish Holocaust and the treatment of blacks during times of slavery. Meanwhile, MOVE's neighbors on North 33rd Street had their own complaints: rats, rotting garbage, fecal odor, unclothed children, the 50 to 60 stray animals adopted by the "family," and increasingly violent arguments with group members (with MOVE usually gaining the upper hand). The complaints finally led to a court-ordered inspection that Rizzo hesitated to enforce, especially after he received reports that the organization was stockpiling food and weapons at the house in anticipation of an invasion.

After a politically embarrassing ten-month delay, Rizzo had a four-block area surrounding the MOVE house blockaded by police, cutting off all food, water, and supplies to the house. Supporters somehow smuggled provisions to the group. Three months later, on August 8, 1978, Rizzo sanctioned a police raid, during which five police officers and firefighters were wounded and one police officer was killed. One MOVE member, Delbert Africa, was beaten by police while he was trying to escape (local television news crews captured this beating on videotape). After the house was evacuated, it was immediately seized, condemned, and razed by the city. Rizzo blamed the group and a hostile media presence for the violence. The group briefly dispersed, with some members going underground to avoid various weapons and conspiracy charges, while others remained to work toward the release of members who had been detained after the 1978 showdown.

In 1980, after a controversial trial in which compelling evidence suggested that "friendly fire" may have been the cause of the officer's death, nine MOVE members (including Delbert Africa) were convicted of manslaughter charges stemming from the confrontation and were sentenced to terms of 30 to 100 years. The three police officers charged with beating Delbert Africa were acquitted in 1981 by a judge, before the case could go to a jury trial.

That same year John Africa returned to Philadelphia to face weapons and conspiracy charges and was acquitted. Soon after, the family regrouped and moved into a house at 6221 Osage Avenue. Nearly two years passed before problems with neighbors arose again. A community delegation appealed to the new city administration, now led by Philadelphia's first black mayor, Wilson Goode, who had been elected in November 1983. Goode, fearful of another deadly showdown, avoided any direct action against the group, and even delayed the arrests of several MOVE members for outstanding warrants. But he was eventually forced into action because of political pressure from the community and the media, and because of reports that bunker-like additions were being built around the house. He authorized a hastily planned raid on the MOVE house on May 13, 1985.

The police attempted to break into 6221 Osage Avenue from neighboring houses but failed. Then they dropped a bomb on the house from a helicopter, presumably in an effort to make an opening in the roof for tear gas. A fire started, but police intentionally allowed it to burn, hoping to disable the rooftop bunkers. The blaze soon grew wildly out of control, spreading to neighboring houses and adjoining city blocks. In the end, the fire had consumed 61 homes and killed 11 MOVE members, including John Africa and five children. Only two of the members in the house escaped the blaze: Ramona Africa, who was eventually imprisoned for seven years on conspiracy and riot charges, and Birdie Africa, a 13-year-old boy.

Two grand jury investigations—city-commissioned and independent—found that the decision to drop the bomb had been "unconscionable," and they exposed a police cover-up concerning the use of C-4, a military-grade explosive, in the bomb. But no criminal charges were ever filed against Goode, other city officials, or any of the police officers involved.

Wrongful death lawsuits by relatives of the deceased and by surviving MOVE members (including Ramona Africa, released in 1992) against the city have already led to nearly $5 million in damages, with more suits pending. There are at least three dozen active MOVE members either still in prison or living in the Philadelphia area.

North America
***

# Muhammad, Elijah (Elijah Poole)

(b. October 1897, Sandersville, Ga.; d. February 25, 1975, Chicago, Ill.), leader of the Nation of Islam; black separatist.

The sixth of seven children of William and Mariah Poole, Elijah was the favorite of his siblings, parents, and grandfather, and was perceived by them as being destined for greatness. It was his grandfather who named him after the biblical Elijah, and throughout his childhood he was teasingly referred to as "the Prophet."

Aside from sharecropping and working at a sawmill, William Poole pastored at two Baptist churches. Young Elijah was exposed to the ministry from a tender age. He took an avid interest in Christian theology, but his father's fire and brimstone sermons caused him to question what seemed like a dour intrepretation of spirituality. It was many years before he would break away from Christianity completely, and ironically it was his father who first introduced him to the Nation of Islam.

When he was around ten years old, he left school out of economic necessity and began chopping firewood with his sister. Until this point he had lived in relative shelter from the brutal racist practices of the region. This ended when he witnessed, as an adolescent, the lynching of an 18-year-old acquaintance. On another occasion, as he was walking home from work, a white man taunted him with the severed ears of a black person. The horror of these two incidents, he later recounted, made him ripe for black separatist ideology. "I had seen enough of the white man's brutality in Georgia to last me 26,000 years."

Elijah's youth and early adulthood were marked by a pattern of floating jobs and long periods of unemployment. In 1923, married with two children, he migrated to industrial Detroit. But even in the years before the Depression there was an economic downturn in many large cities. With the pressure of three more children to support and little prospect of work, he went through a period of listlessness and heavy drinking.

It was at this time that his father, on a spiritual quest of his own, started speaking to Elijah and his brothers about the Islamic movement. In 1931 Elijah attended his first Islamic meeting and met its leader, Wallace D. Fard. He became fully immersed in the movement, abandoning his "slave owner" surname. He was initially called Karriem, and later Muhammad. Within the year he became Fard's top assistant. As the Muslim movement grew more prominent in the black community, it became a target for government investigation, and Fard's leadership began to suffer. In 1933, in an attempt to remove himself from the negative spotlight, Fard named Muhammad Supreme Minister and gave him full administrative power.

Despite continual police hostility and subsequent relocation to Chicago, the Nation of Islam under Muhammad prospered and evolved. Rather than shunning the technology of Western culture, as Fard had encouraged, Muhammad invested in radios and modern farm equipment. In order for black separatism to succeed, he believed, total economic independence was crucial. In 1945 the Nation purchased 140 acres of farmland in Michigan. Two years later a Nation-owned grocery store, restaurant, and bakery opened in Chicago.

As the Nation's influence spread throughout various black communities around the United States, Muhammad began to live a more luxurious lifestyle that seemingly contradicted the Muslim creed of stringency and humility. He purchased cars and real estate and apparently had sexual liaisons with a number of young women in the movement. When Malcolm X was murdered after leaving the movement, there were many who believed that Muhammad's violent denunciation of his one-time protégé had instigated the assassination.

As a leader in the quest for black nationalism, Muhammad was, for a long time, considered a hostile force by the United States government. He served a jail sentence for draft evasion during World War II and was wired by the FBI for more than two decades. Nevertheless, by the time of his death in 1975, his conservative approach made him seem moderate compared to other radical groups of the Civil Rights era. His emphasis on black self-sufficiency rather than overthrow of the government made him an appealing ally to such local officials as Mayor Richard Daley, who in 1974 declared March 29 "Honorable Elijah Muhammad Day in Chicago."

North America

# Murphy, Carl

(b. January 17, 1889, Baltimore, Md.; d. February 26, 1967, Baltimore, Md.), publisher of the influential *Baltimore Afro-American*.

Carl Murphy's father, John Henry, began publishing the *Baltimore Afro-American* in 1892. Murphy graduated from Howard University in 1911, and then attended Harvard, where he received an M.A. in German in 1913.

After teaching German at Howard, Murphy resigned in 1918 to work for the *Baltimore Afro-American*. He assumed leadership of the newspaper when his father died in 1922, and retained that position until 1961. When he retired, the paper's circulation had risen to 200,000, and his company owned newspapers in several other cities.

Murphy served on the board of directors of the National Association for the Advancement of Colored People (NAACP) in 1931. In 1955 he received the NAACP's Spingarn Medal for his dedication to civil rights and education.

# N

## NAACP Legal Defense and Educational Fund,

**the major organization by which African Americans have, through law, achieved advances in civil rights in the twentieth century.**

Created in 1940 by the National Association for the Advancement of Colored People (NAACP), the NAACP Legal Defense and Educational Fund (LDF) pioneered the field of public interest law, using the courts to gain and expand civil rights for African Americans when other avenues were blocked. The LDF was most visible during the 1940s, when its first director, future Supreme Court justice Thurgood Marshall, led it in the fight against legal segregation in the South. Its victories laid the groundwork for, and inspired the participants in, the Civil Rights Movement. After overcoming legalized segregation in the courts, the LDF fought against the backlash of angry Southern state governments, several of which attempted to challenge the LDF's right to practice in their states. It worked to strengthen and protect those rights through the courts, by lobbying and providing scholarships to help African Americans attend law schools.

The LDF is most famous for arguing before the Supreme Court in 1954's landmark *Brown v. Board of Education of Topeka, Kansas*, which ended legal segregation in United States public education. *Brown*, however, marked the culmination of the strategy to desegregate public education. Since shortly after the end of Reconstruction (about 1877), the South had been a one-party region, dominated by the Democratic party and its white supremacist policies. Southern states were able to retain their segregationist policies because voters returned the same representatives, who gained seniority and influence in both houses of Congress and blocked any federal civil rights legislation proposed. In response, Charles Hamilton Houston—called the Moses of the Civil Rights Movement—developed in the mid-1930s, as head of the NAACP's legal department, the strategy that gained civil rights for blacks through the courts by indirectly attacking segregated public education. Houston believed that suing for greater African American participation in graduate schools would be less incendiary to segregationist whites than directly attacking public schools, because the number of people attending graduate programs at that time was low.

Houston aimed to force Southern states to strengthen black public schools or eliminate them by underscoring the high cost of maintaining two "separate but equal" school systems. The strategy proved effective by as early as 1938, when the NAACP's legal department successfully argued *Missouri ex rel. Gaines v. Canada*. The Court determined in *Gaines* that Missouri's proposal to provide financial aid so that Lloyd Gaines could attend an out-of-state law school while denying him admission to an in-state, whites-only law school was not equal treatment under the Constitution, and violated the Fourteenth Amendment.

The NAACP, because it lobbied and issued propaganda, was ineligible for non-profit status. Thus, its contributors could not deduct donations to the NAACP from their tax returns. In 1939 NAACP secretary (its highest position) Walter White attempted to attract contributors by creating a separate organization to administer the NAACP's charitable activities. On March 20, 1940, the NAACP created the LDF. Although created to be independent of the NAACP, the boards of directors for each organization were interlocked, and the LDF was largely guided by the same principles as the NAACP. Director-counsel Marshall, a former student of Houston's and an NAACP lawyer, continued the NAACP legal department's strategy at the LDF. With Marshall executing Houston's strategy, the LDF won a number of graduate school desegregation cases, including *Sipuel v. Board of Regents of the University of Oklahoma* (1948), *McLaurin v. Oklahoma State Regents* (1950), and *Sweatt v. Painter* (1950), all of which contributed to *Brown*, the final assault on segregated education.

Earl Warren, writing for the Court in *Brown*, worded the decision ambiguously, directing schools to desegregate "with all deliberate speed." Many Southern states emphasized the "deliberate" rather than the "speed," maneuvering to slow integration. The LDF, therefore, began concentrating on ensuring that states complied with *Brown*, as in *Cooper v. Aaron* (1958), in which the Court ordered the desegregation of the Little Rock, Arkansas, Central High School. The Supreme Court did not order complete school desegregation, however, until 1968, with *Green v. County School Board of New Kent County*.

*Brown* ended one era for the LDF and it began another era, as African Americans began to demand equal access to all public facilities and equal treatment before the law, and the protest moved from the courthouses to the streets. The LDF, which had set the agenda in the fight against legal segregation, now yielded to civil rights activists and organizations, representing their members when they were arrested for participating in sit-ins, protest marches, and rallies.

In addition to attempting to block integration, Southern governments reacted to *Brown* by attacking the NAACP and the LDF, which it saw as the catalysts of all the activism and protest. According to Jack Greenberg, an

LDF lawyer who became its director after Thurgood Marshall left in 1961, almost every Southern state "passed laws and started legislative investigations . . . to put the NAACP and the LDF out of business." South Carolina's legislature prohibited schools from hiring NAACP members. Arkansas, Florida, Georgia, Louisiana, North Carolina, Tennessee, Texas, and Virginia all followed suit. Virginia's attempt to outlaw the NAACP ended in *NAACP v. Button*, in which the Supreme Court ruled that the NAACP had a first amendment right to pursue public interest law.

Although the LDF, which fully separated from the NAACP because of threats to its tax-exempt status, is best known for its fight against school segregation, it also sought changes in other areas. In its earliest days, despite a small budget and the threat of violence posed by angry whites, LDF lawyers often traveled to small Southern towns to represent accused African Americans and make certain they received fair trials. Many of those local cases became Supreme Court cases, such as *Shepherd* and *Irvin v. Florida* (1950), in which the LDF successfully argued that a defendant must be tried in a bias-free venue. In *Smith v. Allwright* (1944), the Supreme Court ruled that primary elections excluding blacks were unconstitutional. *Morgan v. the Commonwealth of Virginia* outlawed segregated accommodations on interstate buses. In *Shelley v. Kraemer* (1948), the Court ruled that covenants prohibiting blacks from purchasing homes were unconstitutional.

In the late twentieth century the LDF's efforts continued in the courtroom and beyond. In court, it worked to end discrimination in employment, education, and in the criminal justice system. Among the issues it championed were fair employment practices, affirmative action in employment and education, and ending the death penalty, which its studies indicated was applied disproportionately to black defendants. It has also formed and strengthened coalitions of civil rights groups to monitor the enforcement of civil rights laws, report civil rights abuses, and inform the American public about areas of need. The LDF, with its lasting and profound influence, has successfully pioneered a style of civil rights law that numerous agencies have emulated, as seen in those agencies with the phrase "legal defense fund" in their titles.

North America

# Nabrit, James Madison, Jr.

(b. September 4, 1900, Atlanta, Ga.; d. December 27, 1997, Washington, D.C.), civil rights attorney and university president who became the first African American United States Delegate to the United Nations.

James Madison Nabrit Jr. was born to the Reverend James Madison Nabrit and his wife, Gertrude. He graduated from Morehouse College in 1923 and from Northwestern University Law School in 1927. In 1930 he moved to Houston, where he worked as a civil rights lawyer. Nabrit joined the faculty of Howard University Law School in 1936, where, in 1938 he taught the first formal civil rights course in any law school in the United States. While a teacher and administrator at Howard from 1936 to 1960, Nabrit was involved in numerous civil rights cases, including *Bolling v. Sharpe*, in which he and attorney George E. C. Hayes challenged segregation in the public schools of the District of Columbia. *Bolling* was ruled on by the Supreme Court in conjunction with *Brown v. Board of Education*, wherein the Court found segregation to be unconstitutional. In 1960 Nabrit became the president of Howard University, a post he retired from in 1969. He took a leave of absence from 1965 to 1967 to serve on the United States delegation to the United Nations. In 1966 President Lyndon Johnson appointed Nabrit to the second highest post in the U.S. mission, deputy to the chief delegate.

North America

# Nash, Diane Bevel

**(b. May 15, 1938, Chicago, Ill.), African American civil rights activist, a founder of the Student Nonviolent Coordinating Committee (SNCC), and one of the few female leaders of the Civil Rights Movement.**

Diane Nash attended Howard University and then transferred to Fisk University in Nashville, where she confronted Southern racial segregation and became active in the young Civil Rights Movement. She co-founded the Student Nonviolent Coordinating Committee (SNCC) in Raleigh, North Carolina, in April 1960. In February 1961 in Rock Hill, South Carolina, she was a member of the first group arrested for civil rights protest who refused to pay bail and remained in prison as a symbol of the plight of blacks in America.

Nash soon became SNCC's head of direct action. After marrying fellow civil rights activist James Bevel, taking his last name as her middle name, Nash moved to Georgia in 1962. There she worked with the Southern Christian Leadership Conference (SCLC), a civil rights organization led by Martin Luther King Jr., which coordinated civil rights activities. SCLC awarded Bevel and Nash the Rosa Parks Award in 1965.

North America

# National Association for the Advancement of Colored People,

**an interracial membership organization, founded in 1909, that is devoted to civil rights and racial justice.**

Founded February 12, 1909, the National Association for the Advancement of Colored People (NAACP) has been instrumental in improving the legal, educational, and economic lives of African Americans. Combining the white philanthropic support that characterized Booker T. Washington's accommodationist organizations with the call for racial justice delivered by

W. E. B. Du Bois's militant Niagara Movement, the NAACP forged a middle road of interracial cooperation. Throughout its existence it has worked primarily through the American legal system to fulfill its goals of full suffrage and other civil rights and an end to segregation and racial violence. Since the end of the Civil Rights Movement of the 1960s, however, the influence of the NAACP has waned, and it has suffered declining membership and a series of internal scandals.

The NAACP was formed in response to the 1908 race riot in Springfield, the capital of Illinois and the birthplace of President Abraham Lincoln. Appalled at the violence that was committed against blacks, a group of white liberals that included Mary Ovington White and Oswald Garrison Villard, both the descendants of abolitionists, issued a call for a meeting to discuss racial justice. Some 60 people, only 7 of whom were African American (including W. E. B. Du Bois, Ida B. Wells-Barnett, and Mary Church Terrell), signed the call, which was released on the centennial of Lincoln's birth. Echoing the focus of Du Bois's militant all-black Niagara Movement, the NAACP's stated goal was to secure for all people the rights guaranteed in the Thirteenth, Fourteenth, and Fifteenth Amendments to the United States Constitution, which promised an end to slavery, the equal protection of the law, and universal adult male suffrage.

The NAACP established its national office in New York City and named a board of directors as well as a president, Moorfield Storey, a white constitutional lawyer and former president of the American Bar Association (ABA). The only African American among the organization's executives, Du Bois was made director of publications and research, and in 1910 he established the official journal of the NAACP, the *Crisis*. With a strong emphasis on local organizing, by 1913 the NAACP had established branch offices in such cities as Boston, Kansas City, Washington, D.C., Detroit, and St. Louis.

A series of early court battles—including a victory against a discriminatory Oklahoma law that regulated voting by means of a grandfather clause (*Guinn v. United States*, 1910)—helped establish the NAACP's importance as a legal advocate, a role it would play with overwhelming success. The fledgling organization also learned to harness the power of publicity in its 1915 battle against D. W. Griffith's inflammatory *Birth of a Nation*, a movie that perpetuated demeaning stereotypes of African Americans and glorified the Ku Klux Klan.

With its membership growing rapidly—from around 9,000 in 1917 to around 90,000 in 1919—and with more than 300 local branches, the NAACP leadership soon included more African Americans. The writer and diplomat James Weldon Johnson became the association's first black secretary in 1920, and Louis T. Wright, a surgeon, was named the first black chairman of its board of directors in 1934; neither position was ever again held by a white person. Meanwhile, the *Crisis* became a voice of the Harlem Renaissance, as Du Bois published works by Langston Hughes, Countee Cullen, and other African American literary figures.

Throughout the 1920s the fight against lynching was among the associa-

The NAACP joined with civic and religious groups to organize the 1917 silent protest parade in Harlem. About 8000 African American men, women, and children marched down Fifth Avenue, silently bearing signs protesting the racist violence of the recent East St. Louis riot and the continuing scourge of lynching. Marchers questioned as well the bitter irony of the United States's entrance into World War I – a war meant to "make the world safe for democracy" – while the government continued to tolerate racial injustice at home. *CORBIS/Bettmann*

tion's top priorities. After early worries about its constitutionality, the NAACP strongly supported before the U.S. Congress the Dyer Bill, which would have punished those who participated in or failed to prosecute lynch mobs. Though Congress never passed the bill, or any other antilynching legislation, many credit the resulting public debate—fueled by the NAACP's report *Thirty Years of Lynching in the United States, 1889–1919*—with drastically decreasing the incidence of lynching.

When Johnson stepped down as secretary in 1930, he was succeeded by Walter F. White, who had been instrumental not only in his research on lynching (in part because, as a very fair-skinned African American, he had been able to infiltrate white groups) but also in his successful block of segregationist judge John J. Parker's nomination by President Herbert Hoover to the U.S. Supreme Court. Though some historians blame Du Bois's 1934 resignation on White, the new secretary presided over the NAACP's most productive period of legal advocacy. In 1930 the association commissioned the *Margold Report*, which became the basis for its successful drive to reverse the "separate but equal" doctrine that had governed public facilities since the *Plessy v. Ferguson* decision in 1896. In 1935 White recruited as NAACP chief counsel Charles H. Houston, the Howard University Law

School dean whose strategy on school-segregation cases paved the way for his protégé Thurgood Marshall to prevail in 1954's *Brown v. Board of Education*, the decision that overturned *Plessy*.

During the Great Depression of the 1930s, which was disproportionately disastrous for African Americans, the NAACP began to focus on economic justice. After years of tension with white labor unions, the association cooperated with the newly formed Congress of Industrial Organizations (CIO) in an effort to win jobs for black Americans. Walter White, a friend and adviser to First Lady Eleanor Roosevelt—who was sympathetic to civil rights—met with her often in attempts to convince President Franklin D. Roosevelt to outlaw job discrimination in the armed forces, defense industries (which were booming in anticipation of U.S. entry into World War II), and the agencies spawned by Roosevelt's New Deal legislation. Though this effort was not initially successful, when the NAACP backed labor leader A. Philip Randolph's March on Washington movement in 1941, Roosevelt agreed to open thousands of jobs to black workers and to set up a Fair Employment Practices Committee (FEPC) to ensure compliance.

Throughout the 1940s the NAACP saw enormous growth in its membership, claiming nearly half a million members by 1946. It continued to act as a legislative and legal advocate, pushing (albeit unsuccessfully) for a federal antilynching law and for an end to state-mandated segregation. By the 1950s the NAACP Legal Defense and Educational Fund, headed by Marshall, secured the second of these goals through *Brown v. Board of Education*, which outlawed segregation in public schools. The NAACP's Washington, D.C. bureau, led by lobbyist Clarence M. Mitchell Jr., helped advance not only integration of the armed forces in 1948 but also passage of the Civil Rights Acts of 1957, 1964, and 1968 as well as the Voting Rights Act of 1965.

Despite such dramatic courtroom and congressional victories, the implementation of civil rights was a slow, painful, and sometimes violent process. The unsolved 1951 murder of Harry T. Moore, an NAACP field secretary in Florida whose home was bombed on Christmas night, was just one of many crimes of retribution against the NAACP and its staff and members during the 1950s. Violence also met black children attempting to enter previously segregated schools in Little Rock, Arkansas, and other Southern cities, and throughout the South many African Americans were still denied the right to register and vote.

Arising out of frustration at the continuing lack of equality and justice, the Civil Rights Movement of the 1960s echoed the NAACP's moderate, integrationist goals, but leaders such as the Reverend Martin Luther King Jr. of the Southern Christian Leadership Conference (SCLC) felt that direct action was needed to obtain them. Though the NAACP was opposed to extralegal popular actions, many of its members, such as Mississippi field secretary Medgar Evers, participated in nonviolent demonstrations such as sit-ins to protest the persistence of Jim Crow segregation throughout the South. Although it was criticized for working exclusively within the system by pursuing legislative and judicial solutions, the NAACP did provide legal representation and aid to members of more militant protest groups.

Led by Roy Wilkins, who had succeeded Walter White as secretary in 1955 the NAACP cooperated with organizers A. Philip Randolph and Bayard Rustin in planning the 1963 March on Washington. With the passage of civil rights legislation the following year, the association had finally accomplished much of its historic legislative agenda. In the following years the NAACP began to diversify its goals and, in the eyes of many, to lose its focus. Rising urban poverty and crime, de facto racial segregation, and lingering job discrimination continued to afflict millions of African Americans. With its traditional interracial, integrationist approach, the NAACP found itself attracting fewer members, as many African Americans became sympathetic to more militant, even separatist, philosophies, such as the beliefs espoused by the Black Power Movement.

Wilkins retired as executive director in 1977 and was replaced by Benjamin L. Hooks, whose tenure witnessed the *Bakke* case (1978), in which a California court outlawed several aspects of affirmative action. At around the same time tensions between the executive director and the board of directors—tensions that had existed since the association's founding—escalated into open hostility that threatened to weaken the organization. With the 1993 selection of the Reverend Benjamin F. Chavis (now Chavis Muhammad) as director, new controversies arose. In an attempt to take the NAACP in new directions, Chavis offended many liberals by reaching out to Nation of Islam leader Louis Farrakhan. After using NAACP funds to settle a sexual harassment lawsuit, Chavis was forced to resign in 1995 and subsequently joined the Nation of Islam.

Now headed by Kweisi Mfume, former congressman and head of the Congressional Black Caucus, with Julian Bond acting as chairperson of the board, the NAACP has focused in recent years on economic development and educational programs for youth, while also continuing its role as legal advocate for civil rights issues. The organization currently has more than half a million members.

North America

# National Council of Negro Women,

influential African American women's organization founded by Mary McLeod Bethune.

The National Council of Negro Women (NCNW), one of the largest and most prominent black women's groups of the twentieth century, was the inspiration of civil rights and women's rights leader Mary McLeod Bethune. In 1924, after almost two decades of activism in clubs and organizations dedicated to black women's issues, Bethune became president of the National Association of Colored Women (NACW), then the country's leading association of African American women. But five years later, she was announcing her dream of creating a larger coalition of black women's groups, modeled after the mainstream National Council of Women. As Bethune wrote in a letter to her friend Mary Church Terrell, "Such an organization will, I believe, make for unity of opinion among Negro women who must do some thinking on public questions; it will ensure greater cooperation among women in varied lines of endeavor; and it will lift the ideals not only of the individual organizations, but of the organizations as a group."

After almost six years of planning, Bethune's vision was realized when the National Council of Negro Women held its founding meeting in Harlem on December 5, 1935. Several groups were initially hesitant about joining the NCNW—including Bethune's former organization, the NACW—because of fears that it might detract from the prestige or power of individual groups. But representatives from 29 groups, including religious, political, and professional organizations, sororities, and even the NACW, ultimately attended the founding meeting.

Members of the NCNW quickly began to speak out on issues they felt were important to African Americans in general and black women in particular. Their public insistence on opening more federal jobs to African Americans and their documentation of discriminatory hiring practices in government factories during World War II helped lead to the establishment of the national Fair Employment Practices Committee (FEPC). They also fought for integration of the military and desegregation of schools and other public facilities. In addition to their work for racial and social equality at home, the NCNW spoke out on international affairs. NCNW delegates were present at the founding of the United Nations (UN), and have since attended all UN proceedings as official observers. By the mid-1950s the council's 11 national departments included Archives and Museum, Citizenship Education, Education, Fine Arts, Human Relations, International Relations, Labor and Industry, Public Relations, Religious Education, Social Welfare, and Youth Conservation.

In 1957 Dorothy Height became the fourth president of the NCNW. Height has continued to hold that post for more than four decades, and under her administration the NCNW became a nonprofit organization, allowing it to receive grants from such sources as the Ford Foundation and the United States Department of Health, Education and Welfare. During the last 30 years the NCNW has sponsored such programs as Operation Sisters United, Youth Career Development, the Fannie Lou Hamer Day Care Centers, Project Woman Power, the NCNW Leadership Development Project, and the national Black Family Reunion celebrations. In 1975 a grant from the Agency for International Development enabled the NCNW to establish an international department, making it possible for African American women to coordinate their efforts with those of black women across the diaspora. The NCNW was instrumental in the founding of the National Archives for Black Women's History, and in 1974 Height and the NCNW were able to oversee the unveiling of the Bethune Memorial Statue in Washington, D.C., a long-overdue tribute to the organization's extraordinary founder.

# National League for the Protection of Colored Women,

an early twentieth-century organization, designed to aid African American women, that eventually became part of the National Urban League.

The National League for the Protection of Colored Women grew out of the Associations for the Protection of Negro Women, an organization founded by white social worker Frances Kellor in 1902 to help black women workers in New York. By the turn of the century many African Americans had started migrating to Northern cities from the South in search of economic opportunity, but 90 percent of urban black women found work only in low-paying domestic service jobs. Some agents had begun meeting black women travelers at train stations and docks and taking advantage of their precarious economic situation by coercing them into signing unfair contracts or encouraging them to engage in prostitution. The Associations for the Protection of Negro Women established travelers' aid networks in Baltimore, Washington, Richmond, and Savannah to prepare women passing through those cities for what they might find in the North. The organization also set up employment agencies in black neighborhoods and worked with the White Rose Mission, the Young Women's Christian Association, and other agencies to provide safe lodging houses for African American women.

The first affiliated branch of the Associations for the Protection of Negro Women was located in Philadelphia and was run by Mrs. S. W. Layten, a black activist. In 1906 the organization became the National League for the Protection of Colored Women, opening up additional branches in Baltimore, Washington, D.C., and Chicago, and extending its travelers' aid service to Memphis and Norfolk. In October 1911 the National League for the Protection of Colored Women merged with several other African American social welfare organizations to form the National League on Urban Conditions Among Negroes, which in turn became the National Urban League.

# National Negro Labor Council,

American organization that was formed in 1951 to promote the cause of black workers and was labeled a "Communist-front organization" by the House Committee on Un-American Activities.

In 1951 the National Negro Labor Council (NNLC) was established to end discrimination against blacks in hiring, in promotions, and within labor unions themselves. Within five years, however, the organization had succumbed to attacks by the United States House Committee on Un-American Activities (HUAC). The collapse of the NNLC indicates the extent to which cold-war, anticommunist hysteria in the United States pervaded the ranks of organized labor and undercut the fledgling movement to advance the cause of the black worker.

In the late 1940s one of the most powerful American unions, the Congress of Industrial Organizations (CIO), had purged from its ranks a number of affiliate unions because of alleged Communist leanings. Several of these affiliates had been the leading advocates within the CIO for racial equality, and had histories of promoting job opportunities and increased union representation for black workers. The expulsion of these affiliates left a dearth of black proponents in the labor movement.

In 1950, 900 predominantly black labor delegates from various unions met in Chicago to air the problems of African American workers, who faced discrimination not only on the job but also in their own unions as well. The next year 23 newly formed Negro Labor Councils, representing industrial centers around the country, forged a permanent vehicle of advocacy, the National Negro Labor Council.

Working under the guiding principle that "blacks would attain first-class citizenship only if black workers organized to fight for full economic opportunity," the NNLC also promised to fight police brutality and segregation of housing and public facilities. Local NLCs targeted large corporations such as the Ford Motor Company, Sears-Roebuck, and the Detroit Tigers to force fair hiring and promotion practices, while the national council pushed for fair employment practices clauses in union contracts. Throughout the 1950s the NNLC supported black workers in a number of important strikes, including those against International Harvester in Chicago (1952) and Louisiana sugar cane plantations (1953). In the well orchestrated "Let Freedom Crash the Gateway to the South" campaign of 1954, the NNLC anticipated hiring discrimination at a new General Electric plant in Louisville, Kentucky, and organized an extensive workers' training program. When the plant opened, it attempted to exclude blacks workers for lack of training, a common tactic of employment discrimination. The workers, with certificates from night classes to prove their qualifications, forced General Electric to reconsider. Despite the relatively successful outcome of these efforts, there was still firm resistance to reform in many industries. American Airlines, for example, refused to hire black pilots and stewardesses in spite of the national attention that the NNLC drew to the airline's discriminatory practices.

The NNLC became a highly visible force in the labor movement and attracted support from the likes of Paul Robeson. One of the key features of the NNLC was its links to progressive unions, to black-worker bastions of mainstream unions, such as Detroit's UAW Local 600, and to the unions that had been expelled from the CIO. These associations led to charges that the NNLC was controlled by the Communist Party—accusations that came from not only organized labor, but from African-American organizations themselves, including the National Association for the Advancement of Colored People (NAACP) and the National Urban League. In 1952 and again in 1956, the HUAC and the Subversive Activities Control Board charged the NNLC with being "a Communist-front organization." Although the

Communist Party may well have had some adherents within the ranks of the NNLC, the degree to which the party controlled the organization is open to debate. Unable to meet the legal costs of defending itself before HUAC, the organization voted to disband in 1956.

# National Urban League,

**an interracial social service organization that attempts to obtain full participation in American society for African Americans through lobbying, research, and direct social services.**

Unlike organizations such as the National Association for the Advancement of Colored People (NAACP), which has been judged by how successfully it has fought for blacks' civil and political rights, the National Urban League (NUL) has pursued less measurable goals. Since its founding in 1911, the organization has used the tools of scientific social work to offer programs to help African Americans. The NUL originally provided direct services to African Americans who had migrated from the rural South to Northern cities. Later in the century, as social conditions changed, the organization increased its scope. It undertook sociological research that disputed commonly held misconceptions about African American inferiority; began to lobby businesses, labor unions, and the government; and embraced direct protest during the Civil Rights Movement as a means of gaining greater social and economic participation for African Americans.

Vernon Jordan announces his resignation as president of the National Urban League in 1981, a year after he was wounded in an assassination attempt. *CORBIS/Bettmann*

At its inception the NUL modeled its social services on white charitable organizations of the day, such as settlement houses, charitable agencies, and immigrant aid societies, and adapted them to blacks' needs. As many African Americans moved north during the Great Migration, the NUL worked through local affiliates to help them adjust to urban life. The affiliates taught basic skills such as behavior, dress, sanitation, health, and homemaking. The

NUL also sponsored community centers, clinics, kindergartens, day care, and summer camps. League workers provided individual care to African Americans in a range of areas, including juvenile delinquency, truancy, and marital adjustment.

The Great Migration increased demands on the NUL, and the organization soon had affiliates in nearly every industrial city in the United States. The NUL began offering vocational training to immigrants, urging businesses to hire blacks and attempting to persuade unions such as the American Federation of Labor (AFL) to accept black members. The NUL achieved its primary aim of improving employment opportunities for blacks, but such gains were temporary: at the end of World War I returning soldiers put many blacks out of work again.

During the Great Depression the NUL broadened its scope still more under the leadership of Lester B. Granger. While continuing to offer vocational training and social services to urban blacks, the NUL sought to persuade the federal government to include blacks in President Franklin Roosevelt's New Deal programs. The organization lobbied the federal government to end discrimination in allocating government benefits. During World War II the NUL fought to desegregate wartime employment and the armed forces, supporting A. Philip Randolph's plan for a March on Washington. In exchange for Randolph's calling off the march, Roosevelt issued Executive Order (E.O.) 8802, which barred discrimination in defense industries and in federal agencies, and established the Fair Employment Practices Committee (FEPC), which was responsible for implementing E.O. 8802.

The NUL also sought to shape public and private opinion through its research. Its sociological studies—published independently and, from 1923 to 1949, in its journal, *Opportunity*—took an explicitly scientific approach to social problems. NUL leaders criticized the NAACP's journal, the *Crisis*, believing it to be too "subjective." *Opportunity* also published black writers and artists such as Gwendolyn Bennett, Langston Hughes, James Weldon Johnson, and Countee Cullen.

In the 1960s, under Whitney M. Young Jr., the NUL expanded its traditional social service approach by strengthening its commitment to civil rights. It embraced direct action, promoted community organization, and sponsored leadership development and voter education and registration projects. It helped organize two important events of the Civil Rights Movement: the March on Washington in 1963 and the Poor People's Campaign in 1968. Toward the end of the 1960s the NUL attempted to revitalize ghettos by calling for a domestic Marshall Plan.

Following Whitney Young's death in 1971, Vernon Jordan became president of the NUL. Jordan helped to begin programs in health, housing, education, and job training. In 1975 the NUL began to publish a journal, the *Urban League Review*, and began issuing an annual report, *The State of Black America*. In 1982 Jordan was succeeded by John Jacobs.

When the federal government cut social programs in the 1980s, the NUL responded by emphasizing self-help and seeking solutions to new and continuing problems facing African Americans, including high rates of teen pregnancy, families headed by single women, declining quality of public schools, and crime. Under Hugh Price, who became NUL president in 1994, the Urban League tackled the consequences of welfare "reform," the rollback of affirmative action programs, and the persistence of racial discrimination and exclusion in the workplace. A communications veteran, Price has been a strong national voice on behalf of economic opportunity and equality.

North America

# National Welfare Rights Organization,

**coalition of poor Americans, mostly black and mostly women, who demanded better welfare assistance from state governments and the federal government in the late 1960s and early 1970s.**

By the mid-1960s the Civil Rights Movement in the United States had achieved several of its basic political goals: blacks could vote, eat at integrated lunch counters, and send their children to integrated schools. Many activists, however, believed such gains were of little value as long as most blacks lived in poverty. Among these activists were several black women in Los Angeles, New York, and other cities who received Aid to Families with Dependent Children (AFDC, or welfare). Separately and somewhat spontaneously, they organized fellow welfare recipients to demand better benefits and treatment from welfare agencies.

To coordinate and spread their protests, George Wiley, a black chemistry professor and former worker for the Congress of Racial Equality (CORE), created the Poverty Rights Action Center in 1966. The following year the office evolved into the National Welfare Rights Organization (NWRO), with headquarters in Washington, D.C. With help from the NWRO, women receiving welfare gathered by the dozens or hundreds, went to the local welfare office, and demanded money for basic needs—such as clothes for school—that were not being met by their welfare benefits. If refused, they held a sit-in. The strategy won better benefits for large numbers of women. The NWRO, in turn, received valuable publicity and thousands of dollars from the antipoverty agencies of Lyndon Johnson's Great Society as well as from private donors.

In the late 1960s the NWRO held mass marches and rallies to publicize its demands, which now included livable grants for all welfare recipients, access to daycare, and programs for job training. Although these goals went mostly unmet, the NWRO did succeed in ending the intrusive investigations that were often a prerequisite for receiving benefits. Partly due to the NWRO and partly to the programs of the Great Society, many women previously reluctant to apply for welfare now did so, and were accepted. Others who had been denied relief earlier were finally accepted. Welfare rolls, with about 750,000 participants in 1960, were at 3 million by 1972.

The NWRO had a peak membership of about 100,000. As such, it was one of the first large-scale attempts by poor black women to take control of their political and economic future. However, while the women on welfare exercised great power locally, the NWRO's national staff, who were primarily white, male, and middle class, dominated many of the NWRO's important decisions. By the early 1970s relations between national and local offices had grown increasingly strained over the question of how much autonomy to give locals. That question, though, was eclipsed by a broad public backlash against welfare programs that emerged at the end of the 1960s. After 1970 the NWRO had few important successes; by 1972 it was badly in debt; and by the mid-1970s it was defunct.

North America

# Nation of Islam,
religious movement based on black separatism; founded around 1930 in Detroit, Michigan.

The Nation of Islam (NOI) was established in Detroit at the beginning of the Great Depression, by Wallace D. Fard, a door-to-door silk salesman. In addition to selling his wares, he spread his message of salvation and self-determination throughout Detroit's black neighborhoods. He held the first meetings in people's homes, but the movement soon grew big and Fard rented halls for his gatherings. Far from adhering to strict Islamic law, NOI under Fard was an eclectic mix of philosophy that borrowed from earlier black Muslim movements, Christian Scripture (largely to debunk Christianity), and Fard's Afrocentric interpretation of the story of Origin. The organization attracted many followers because of its angry rejection of white society.

Fard wrote two manuals, *The Secret Ritual of the Nation of Islam*, which is still used as a blueprint for oral instruction, and *Teaching for a Lost-Found Nation of Islam in a Mathematical Way*, written in a coded language that a select few are able to decipher. He also established the University of Islam, the Muslim Girls Training Corps—an instruction center that trained females to follow the tenets of proper Muslim womanhood—and the Fruit of Islam, a militaristic unit that served as Fard's bodyguard faction and enforced the Nation's laws.

When word reached white authorities that Fard was preaching about the Western "blue-eyed devil" whose civilization would soon perish, the Nation was deemed subversive. The hostile relationship between the movement and law enforcement (including ultimately the FBI) would continue for the next several decades. In 1931 Fard was investigated and detained by the Detroit police department for endorsing a sacrificial killing performed by a fringe member of the movement. There is no evidence to indicate that

Fard was involved in the murder. Despite the fact that the victim was black, the charge against Fard was exacerbated when authorities found a pamphlet in his possession calling for the annihilation of "white devils."

Fard apparently had the foresight to know that his presence in the Nation would potentially lead to its demise. In 1933, months before he was told to leave Detroit or face incarceration, Fard began preparing his young right-hand man, Elijah Muhammad, for leadership. Fard's departure and his replacement by Muhammad led to internal strife within the movement. The Nation of Islam splintered, and within a couple of years Muhammad's trusted circle, including his family, moved to Chicago. The Temple of Islam No. 2 was built and later became the national headquarters of the Nation.

Under Muhammad the Nation was able to put into practice the concept of black economic self-sufficiency, a premise that Fard had envisioned but never fully realized. Because of their highly disciplined lifestyle, Muslims were hired more readily than other blacks. A good portion of their salary went into the Nation's coffers. One decade later, in 1945, members had pooled enough earnings to invest in 57 hectares (140 acres) of farmland in rural Michigan. In subsequent years more than 100 temples flourished nationwide, and Muslim-owned bakeries, grocery stores, and other small businesses were opened in African American communities.

During its early days the NOI tended to attract Southerners who had migrated north and had little formal education. The appeal of the movement was not just self-sufficiency but the structured lifestyle, with its emphasis on marriage, family, strict diet, and hygiene. In particular, the

Benjamin Chavis, *right*, chats with Louis Farrakhan at the African American Leadership summit in Washington, D.C., in November 1995. *CORBIS/Jacques M. Chenet*

image of womanhood in the Nation of Islam was acclaimed for "purity, domesticity, and piety." Muhammad carried on Fard's program of providing female members with an education that included classes in nursing, gymnastics, cooking, sewing, child rearing, and the proper approach to gender relations. While its women seemed to be put on a pedestal, NOI has nevertheless been criticized over the years for being ambiguously caught between glorification and objectification of females.

By the 1950s NOI did begin to resemble a nation. Complete with its own national flag and anthem, militaristic marches and salutes, the movement was, in essence, a military theocracy. The structure and ritual, and the promise of salvation from the "grave"—the soulless, dog-eat-dog world outside the Nation—appealed to many poor blacks, particularly convicts in jail. One of those recruited from prison was a young man named Malcolm Little. Like all inductees into the movement, Little discarded his "slave" surname; he became known as Malcolm X. Recognized as a brilliant orator, Malcolm X quickly rose through the ranks of the Nation. He had arrived at an opportune time. The early rumblings of the Civil Rights Movement were beginning as a result of the government's failure to satisfy African American demands for equality. The Nation would soon be competing with other black movements for members. Malcolm's charisma and the advent of television brought the movement greater visibility than ever before. NOI actively began to recruit black, middle-class professionals. Not only was Muhammad interested in incorporating their skills for the betterment of the Nation, but he was also adamant that their expertise not be wasted in "the white man's world."

By the late 1950s NOI's separatist beliefs stood in contrast to the growing Civil Rights Movement, which sought integration. The primary focus of NOI was economic self-sufficiency, and by the early 1960s some, including Malcolm X, criticized the interest in financial gain and the money-and-wealth fixation among the upper ranks of the movement. In 1964, discontented with Muhammad's political philosophy and allegations that the leader had fathered several illegitimate children, Malcolm broke away from the Nation to form his own religious organization. One year later he was assassinated.

Critics of Muhammad claimed that his violent denunciation of Malcolm X in speeches and in the Nation's newspaper, *Muhammad Speaks*, incited the murder. The Nation has continued to prosper economically, but there has not been another surge in membership since the 1960s. In 1975, after Elijah Muhammad's death, his son Wallace Deen Muhammad was named supreme minister. However, two months into his leadership he declared that whites were no longer viewed as evil and would be allowed into the movement. This shift, as well as a move toward the more orthodox Sunni Islam, shocked and alienated a large group of followers. The Nation splintered into several alliances, and by 1978 national spokesman Louis Farrakhan led a group that resurrected the original Nation of Islam teachings of Black Nationalism and separatism.

Despite his controversial persona, Farrakhan in the 1990s has been credited with reaching out to non-Muslim black religious leaders and activists in order to effect positive change in inner cities. In 1995 he successfully orchestrated the Million Man March, an event that brought together many people and organizations of opposing political viewpoints.

There is no official information on the size of NOI membership as of 1998. Various sources estimate that it numbers between 10,000 and 100,000.

North America

# Negro American Labor Council,

AFL-CIO splinter group of black workers who organized in 1960 to pressure the federation to end discrimination in its affiliate unions, and who became a driving force behind the 1963 March on Washington.

In May 1960, after the AFL-CIO refused to impose sanctions against affiliate unions practicing discrimination, 75 African American trade unionists formed the Negro American Labor Council (NALC). Under the leadership of A. Philip Randolph, president of the Brotherhood of Sleeping Car Porters, the new organization set out to accelerate the unionization of black workers and to put blacks into positions of union leadership. The broader aim of the group was to end discrimination against blacks in hiring and promotion.

By 1961 membership in the NALC had swelled to 10,000 across the nation. That year Randolph presented a series of demands to the AFL-CIO Executive Council. Asserting that the status of black workers in the labor movement was that of "second class citizenship," he called on the federation to end discrimination within its ranks. This would require, he said, not only ending the color bar in affiliate unions and desegregating unions, but also placing African Americans on the AFL-CIO Executive Council and fighting to abolish barriers to employment training programs. The AFL-CIO's immediate response was to censure Randolph, and its officers charged that he himself had created the breach between blacks and labor with his accusations. At its fall convention, the federation passed a series of civil rights resolutions that vowed an end to discrimination in the union. The AFL-CIO refused to meet the NALC demands fully, however, and left the decision to desegregate a voluntary one for the affiliates.

In one of the group's most important achievements, Randolph and the NALC first envisioned a massive march on Washington to demand jobs. The movement led to the 1963 March on Washington for Jobs and Freedom, where Martin Luther King Jr. gave his famous "I Have a Dream" speech. The AFL-CIO refused to support the march publicly, but other powerful unions, such as the United Auto Workers, did put their force behind it. The 1963 March on Washington solidified alliances between the leaders of the NALC and those of the Civil Rights Movement, which was expanding rapidly in the South.

North America

# New Deal,

President Franklin Delano Roosevelt's domestic reform program of 1933–1941, which, though inconsistent in its treatment of African Americans, greatly strengthened black hopes for racial justice.

The New Deal, a reform effort unparalleled in American history, took shape during the troubled times of the Great Depression. It gave substance to President Franklin Delano Roosevelt's vague campaign promises to restore hope and revive the United States economy. When he took office in March 1933, Americans had already endured more than three years of the worst economic depression in the nation's history. African Americans, in particular, had suffered the brunt of the hardship. In the early 1930s nearly one in three African American families was receiving some form of public assistance, and roughly half the black workers in New York City, Chicago, Philadelphia, and Detroit were unemployed.

During his first hundred days in office, Roosevelt secured passage of a record number of programs, and he continued implementing domestic reforms until the onset of World War II. Temporary initiatives included the Works Progress Administration (WPA) and Public Works Administration (PWA), which created work projects for the unemployed, and the Federal Emergency Relief Administration (FERA), which offered federal assistance to individuals in need.

The New Deal also sought more far-reaching reforms. A wave of Great Depression-era bank failures led to the Federal Deposit Insurance Corporation (FDIC), which guaranteed bank deposits. The Securities Exchange Commission (SEC) was established to regulate the stock market, whose 1929 collapse had triggered the Great Depression. The Tennessee Valley Authority (TVA) and the Rural Electrification Authority (REA) were development projects aimed primarily at the South and the West. Roosevelt flirted briefly with national economic planning in the National Recovery Administration (NRA), but with the Social Security Administration (SSA) he left a lasting mark.

Although their need was particularly great, African Americans found themselves short-changed by Roosevelt's New Deal. The social security system, which excluded agricultural workers, had nothing to offer the South's black sharecroppers. Many Southern land-owners, rather than share Agricultural Adjustment Administration (AAA) subsidies with their sharecroppers as the enabling legislation intended, evicted their tenants and kept the entire payment for themselves. Overt racial discrimination was evident in the segregated camps of the Civilian Conservation Corps (CCC) and in the hiring and housing policies of the TVA. NRA guidelines permitted lower wages for blacks than for whites doing the same work. Although a 1935 executive order banned discrimination in WPA projects, a cut in the WPA budget in 1937 helped bring on the sharp downturn of 1937–1939, known as the Roosevelt Recession, which jeopardized many black families.

In general, the Roosevelt administration recognized blacks in ways that were more symbolic than substantive. Yet Roosevelt appointed an unprecedented number of African American advisers. His Federal Council on Negro Affairs, known informally as the Black Cabinet, included William H. Hastie, Robert C. Weaver, and Mary McLeod Bethune. In 1939 First Lady Eleanor Roosevelt played a prominent role in arranging an Easter Sunday recital by famed black contralto Marian Anderson at Washington's Lincoln Memorial after the Daughters of the American Revolution had refused to let Anderson perform at a concert hall owned by the organization.

Politically, the New Deal solidified Roosevelt's Democratic coalition into a force that dominated American politics for more than a generation, but for African Americans the political results were less clear. In Northern cities blacks achieved greater political influence. In the 1936 presidential election, they rallied around Roosevelt and the New Deal. Their support represented a political shift of historic proportions; Northern black voters became a cornerstone of the liberal-labor coalition that challenged the dominance of Southern conservatives in national politics. During the 1930s, however, most African Americans still lived in the South, where disfranchisement effectively deprived them of any political voice. Yet the New Deal had particularly important political consequences for Southern blacks.

The New Deal encouraged political activism among African Americans in the South. In 1934 groups of black citizens organized in South Carolina and Georgia to try to vote in whites-only Democratic primaries. In Arkansas a number of black and white sharecroppers formed the Southern Tenant Farmers Union to press the federal government to enforce protections written into the Agricultural Adjustment Act of 1933. Student activism in the 1930s and the growth of the industrial labor movement frequently facilitated interracial alliances in support of economic reform. During the New Deal era, the National Association for the Advancement of Colored People (NAACP) undertook major organizing drives among Southern blacks, building black membership, supporting voter registration efforts, and initiating the legal campaign against unequal education that laid the groundwork for the 1954 *Brown v. Board of Education* decision.

New Deal programs and policies often accommodated the racial status quo. But African Americans responded to the democratic rhetoric of the New Deal—and the unprecedented expansion of federal power it envisioned—in ways that created an atmosphere conducive to organizing and mobilizing for full citizenship rights. Indeed, the roots of the modern Civil Rights Movement can be traced to the black political activism of the New Deal era.

North America

# Nixon, Edgar Daniel

(b. July 12, 1899, Robinson Springs, Ala.; d. February 25, 1987, Montgomery, Ala.), African American civil rights leader and organizer of the Montgomery Bus Boycott.

E. D. Nixon's struggle to organize African Americans in Montgomery, Alabama, illustrated several sources of tension within the United States Civil Rights Movement: social class, the roles of the labor movement and the church, and older versus newer leadership. Nixon was the son of Wesley Nixon, a tenant farmer turned Primitive Baptist preacher, and Susan Chappell Nixon. Having little formal education, Nixon began to work full-time at age 13, and worked for 41 years as a Pullman car porter.

A supporter of African American labor union leader A. Philip Randolph, Nixon became president of the Brotherhood of Sleeping Car Porters Montgomery chapter in 1938. Despite white hostility, he also organized a registration drive for black voters in Montgomery.

When the middle-class Montgomery branch of the National Association for the Advancement of Colored People (NAACP) failed to support the 1943 voter registration drive actively, Nixon organized poorer African Americans to gain control of the local chapter, and he was elected its president in 1945 and 1946. After he became president of the state NAACP in 1947, the national NAACP leadership, embarrassed by Nixon's homespun demeanor and sixth-grade education, orchestrated his 1949 reelection defeat. The following year Nixon was also ousted from the presidency of the NAACP Montgomery chapter.

Nixon spearheaded a plan to challenge Montgomery's segregated public transportation system, and when Montgomery NAACP secretary Rosa L. Parks was arrested for refusing to relinquish her bus seat to a white patron, it was Nixon who posted her bail and called for a bus boycott. As treasurer of the Montgomery Improvement Association, organized to end discrimination on the buses, Nixon resented the association's president, the Reverend Dr. Martin Luther King Jr., who was associated with Montgomery's African American middle class, and who, Nixon believed, did not properly credit him and the masses of poor African Americans for the boycott's ultimate success.

Following a number of unsuccessful attempts to regain leadership roles, an embittered Nixon withdrew from public life.

North America

# Norton, Eleanor Holmes

(b. June 13, 1937, Washington, D.C.), District of Columbia delegate to the United States House of Representatives, first woman chair of the Equal Employment Opportunity Commission (EEOC).

Eleanor Holmes Norton has devoted much of her professional life to defending human rights and combating racial and gender discrimination. A graduate of Yale University Law School, in the 1960s Norton became active in the Civil Rights Movement, joining the Student Nonviolent Coordinating Committee (SNCC) and the Mississippi Freedom Democratic Party. From 1965 to 1970 she was a highly visible lawyer for the American Civil Liberties Union in New York City, where she specialized in controversial free speech cases. She represented Vietnam War protesters, Ku Klux Klan members, and politicians, most notably Alabama's segregationist Governor George Wallace, then a presidential candidate who had been denied a permit to hold a rally.

Norton's activist credentials led to her appointment as chair of the New York City's Human Rights Commission (HRC) in 1970, an agency charged with ending discriminatory practices in the workplace and schools. Her seven-year HRC record, which ranged from reforming workmen's compensation laws to helping women sportswriters gain access to the press box at hockey games, prompted then-President Jimmy Carter to appoint her chair of the EEOC in 1977, a post she held until 1981. Norton emphasized bureaucratic reform during her tenure at EEOC, cutting a 130,000-case backlog in half.

Despite the negative publicity surrounding her failure to file tax returns from 1982 to 1988, Norton was elected District of Columbia Delegate to the U.S. House of Representatives in 1990, where she waged an uphill battle to maintain the autonomy of the D.C. government.

## Operation Breadbasket,

**organization formed by the Southern Christian Leadership Conference (SCLC) and later led by Jesse Jackson that put pressure on corporations to hire blacks and support black businesses.**

In 1962 Operation Breadbasket was established by the SCLC to put "bread, money, and income into the baskets of black and poor people." With the mandate of improving the economic conditions of African Americans, Operation Breadbasket organized black consumers to press for jobs and to encourage and expand black-owned businesses. In its first campaign in Atlanta, Georgia, the organization won a commitment from local companies to create 5,000 jobs over the next five years.

After establishing affiliates in several Southern states, the organization expanded north. In 1966 Jesse Jackson, then a student at Chicago Theological Seminary, helped found the Chicago chapter, which directed protests at several dairy companies and supermarket chains to demand that they hire black workers and support black-owned businesses. Although the protesters were able to secure promises of employment for black workers from several major corporations, they had trouble ensuring compliance. The A&P supermarket, for example, promised 770 permanent jobs and 1,200 summer jobs in May 1967, but did not deliver until another protest was launched in 1970.

As Operation Breadbasket expanded across the country in 1967, Martin Luther King Jr. appointed Jackson to be its national director. From then on the group became increasingly identified with Jackson's high-profile leadership. Under Jackson, Operation Breadbasket took on a number of projects, among them a free breakfast program and the 1968 Poor People's Campaign in Washington, D.C. The organization also became a voice in local and national politics, opposing welfare cuts and supporting electoral candidates.

By 1971 the group had started to collapse under the weight of too many projects, too few resources, and charges of financial corruption. Some criticized Jackson for using Operation Breadbasket as his own personal power base in Chicago, Illinois, and faulted him for the failure of the group to act like a true national organization. That year Jackson left the SCLC, dissolving the Chicago chapter and forming Operation PUSH (People United to Save Humanity). Since then Operation Breadbasket has continued as a subsidiary operation of the SCLC but has never regained the momentum it had during the 1960s.

North America

# Operation PUSH,

**organization founded by Jesse Jackson in 1971 to promote economic security for black workers and businesses and to provide assistance to African American urban youth.**

Jesse Jackson left Operation Breadbasket, the economic arm of the Southern Christian Leadership Conference, in 1971 to found Operation People United to Save Humanity (PUSH). Like Operation Breadbasket, the new organization set its sights on strengthening the economic security of African Americans. Under Jackson's charismatic leadership, Operation PUSH organized boycotts for black consumers to press for minority employment and support for black-owned businesses.

Over the years Operation PUSH expanded its mission and focused on national issues like education and national politics. In the late 1970s Jackson brought national attention to the subject of minority education and raised money for an elementary school education program called PUSH for Excellence, or PUSH/EXCEL. Despite substantial federal and private support, the education program foundered because of poor administration. Following accusations of shady business alliances and embezzlement, the organization scaled down and, by the early 1980s, had reduced its agenda to consciousness-raising.

Operation PUSH, which was largely dependent on Jackson's powerful personality for its success, lost momentum when he left to run in the 1984 presidential election primaries. Jackson remained a spokesperson for the organization through the 1980s, however, keeping Operation PUSH afloat through his fundraising efforts. Returning to a more active role in 1991, Jackson turned the group toward the issues that had been a part of his election campaign, including the crises of acquired immune deficiency syndrome (AIDS) and urban violence. In 1993 Operation PUSH began a program in Chicago to promote education and employment opportunities for minority youth.

# P

## Pan-African Congress of 1919,

major international gathering to promote worldwide black unity, held in Paris in 1919.

African American activist and writer W. E. B. Du Bois organized the Pan-African Congress in order to bring together Africans and leaders of nations involved in the African diaspora, and to promote the cause of African independence. Du Bois insisted that the conference be held in Paris in 1919 during the proceedings of the Paris Peace Conference, soon after World War I. He wanted Germany's former colonies in eastern and southern Africa internationalized as the first step in gradual African self-determination. The Paris gathering followed a previous conference held in London in 1900, organized by Henry Sylvester Williams, a London barrister born in Trinidad.

The congress received considerable publicity, partly because of the cooperation of French Prime Minister Georges Clemenceau, who accepted its resolutions. The congress delegates did not advocate immediate independence for Africa. Instead they called for greater African participation in the affairs of the colonies and for the newly created League of Nations to undertake the protection and well-being of the African people. Individual resolutions called on the colonial powers to allow Africans to own land and participate in government, to tax and regulate companies operating in Africa in the interests of Africans' welfare, to ban forced labor and corporal punishment, and to safeguard Africans' religious and social freedom.

Blaise Diagne of Senegal, the first African to serve in the French Chamber of Deputies, delivered the keynote speech at the congress, which attracted 57 delegates. Despite the refusal of the United States and Great Britain to issue passports to some potential delegates, Americans constituted the most numerous contingent, with 16 delegates. Other nations represented were the French West Indies, 13; Haiti, 7; France, 7; Liberia, 3; and the Spanish colonies, 2. There was one delegate each from the Portuguese colonies, Santo Domingo, England, British Africa, French Africa, Algeria, Egypt, the Belgian Congo (now the Democratic Republic of the Congo), and Abyssinia (Ethiopia).

Prominent black Americans at the congress included Dr. Robert R. Moton, principal of the Tuskegee Institute; his secretary Nathan A. Hunt; and Lester A. Walton, managing editor of *New York Age*, a weekly black newspaper in New York. White support was welcome; liberal activists such as Charles Edward Russell and William English Walling of the National Association for the Advancement of Colored People (NAACP) attended.

To keep African solidarity alive, Du Bois was also instrumental in the convening of several subsequent gatherings. The second Pan-African Congress was held in three sessions in 1921 in London, Brussels, and Paris; a third congress was held in 1923 in London and Lisbon. In 1974—well after most African countries had achieved independence—the sixth Pan-African Congress was held in Dar es Salaam, Tanzania, and hosted by Tanzanian president Julius Nyerere. Attended by delegates from all over the world, including activists Owusu Sadaukai and Amiri Baraka, the gathering revealed a growing split between revolutionary Marxists and those delegates who supported African governments already in power.

Cross Cultural

# Pan-Africanism,

**a wide range of ideologies that are committed to common political or cultural projects for Africans and people of African descent.**

In its most straightforward version Pan-Africanism is the political project calling for the unification of all Africans into a single African state to which those in the African diaspora can return. In its vaguer, more cultural forms Pan-Africanism has pursued literary and artistic projects that bring together people in Africa and her diaspora.

## Main Trends

The Pan-Africanist Movement began in the nineteenth century among intellectuals of African descent in North America and the Caribbean who thought of themselves as members of a single, "Negro," race. In this they were merely following the mainstream of nineteenth-century thought in North America and Europe, which developed an increasingly strong focus on the idea that human beings were divided into races, each of which had its own distinctive spiritual, physical, and cultural character. As a result the earliest Pan-Africanists often limited their focus to sub-Saharan Africa: to the region, that is, whose population consists mostly of darker-skinned (or, as they would have said, "Negro") peoples. In this way they intentionally left out lighter-skinned North Africans, including the large majority who speak Arabic as their first language.

In the twentieth century this way of thinking of African identity in racial terms has been challenged. In particular, the intellectuals born in Africa who took over the movement's leadership in the period after the World War II developed a more geographical idea of African identity. The founders of the Organization of African Unity (OAU), such as Gamal Abdel Nasser of Egypt and Kwame Nkrumah of Ghana, for example, had a notion of Africa that was more straightforwardly continental. African unity for them was the unity of those who shared the African continent (though it continued to include, in some unspecified way, those whose ancestors had left the continent in the enforced exile of the slave trade).

Nevertheless, the movement's intellectual roots lie firmly in the racial understanding of Africa in the thought of the African American and Afro-Caribbean intellectuals who founded it. Because Pan-Africanism began as a movement in the New World, among the descendants of slave populations, and then spread back to Africa, it aimed to challenge anti-black racism on two fronts. On the one hand, it opposed racial domination in the diaspora; on the other, it challenged colonial domination, which almost always took a racial form, in Africa itself. The stresses and strains that have sometimes divided the movement have largely occurred where these two rather different goals have pulled it in different directions.

## Intellectual Origins

The idea of linking together the whole "Negro" race for political purposes was developed by a wide range of nineteenth-century, African American intellectuals. We can still speak of these nineteenth-century thinkers as Pan-Africanist, even though they did not use the term. Like Pan-Slavism in Eastern Europe and the forms of romantic nationalism that created modern Germany and Italy, early Pan-Africanism reflected a philosophical tradition, derived from the German philosopher Johann Gottfried Herder (1744–1803). In Herder's opinion, peoples (or, as they were often called, nations) such as the Slavs, Germans, and Italians, were the central actors of world history. He suggested that their identities were expressed largely in language, in literature, and in folk culture. And he thought that such nations were naturally drawn together by the desire to live together in states, with a shared language, culture, and traditions. The cultural oneness of a nation led naturally, in Herder's view, to political union.

The first black intellectual to apply this theory in a systematic way to people of African descent was W. E. B. Du Bois (1868–1963). In a lecture on "The Conservation of Races," published by the American Negro Academy in 1897, Du Bois used the word "Pan-Negroism." Du Bois was an African American who had studied as an undergraduate at Harvard with the philosopher William James. But in 1892 Du Bois had gone on to do graduate work at the Friedrich Wilhelm University in Berlin, and was, therefore, thoroughly familiar with the intellectual traditions of modern European nationalism, as well as with the philosophical tradition that began with Herder.

In "The Conservation of Races" Du Bois argued that "the history of the world is the history, not of individuals, but of groups, not of nations, but of races." (But he mentions Slavs, Teutons—that is, Germans—and the Romance race, indicating that, like so many other Western intellectuals of his day, he took real nations to *be* races.) He argued, too, that the differences among races were "spiritual, psychical, differences—undoubtedly based on the physical, but infinitely transcending them." And, finally, he insisted (in a manner strongly reminiscent of Herder) that each race was "striving . . . in its own way, to develop for civilization its particular message."

The problem for Pan-Negroism was how the Negro people were to deliver their message. Du Bois believed that African Americans (whom he called the "advance guard of the Negro people") were to play the leading role in that task. He thought that they were especially well-suited for this task because some of them, like Du Bois himself, had been exposed to the best modern education and the highest forms of knowledge.

Though Du Bois's formulation had roots in the theorists of European nationalism, he was also strongly influenced by a number of earlier African American thinkers, whose work we can understand most easily in the context of the broad nineteenth-century history of antislavery or "abolitionist" thought. The focus of attention for all the major black thinkers in the New World in the early nineteenth century was the abolition of slavery and of the slave trade. Since most people, both black and white, believed that racial hostility between blacks and whites was inevitable (this view was explicitly held, for example, by United States presidents Jefferson and Lincoln), one major preoccupation of some abolitionists concerned finding territories that could be inhabited by freed blacks. The colony of Sierra Leone was created in the late eighteenth century by British abolitionists, in part as a home for freed blacks and the black poor of England; the American Colonization Society played a similar role in the creation of Liberia in the 1820s. But other schemes were proposed to colonize parts of Latin America, the Caribbean, and the American western frontier.

All of these schemes, of course, presupposed that Africans (and their descendants in the New World) belonged naturally together in a political community, separated from other peoples. There were significant voices raised in protest against this assumption—notably that of the American ex-slave and abolitionist Frederick Douglass—and they were joined by many others after the United States formally recognized the citizenship of people of African descent in the post-Civil War amendments to the U.S. Constitution. But in the first half of the nineteenth century the majority view, among both black and white intellectuals, was that a home was needed for the Negroes if they were to be free.

Perhaps the most important black intellectual forerunners of Pan-Africanism were three men who addressed themselves to this situation: Martin R. Delany (1812–1885), Alexander Crummell (1822–1898), and Edward Wilmot Blyden (1832–1912). Martin R. Delany was born in the southern United States, but his family moved to Pennsylvania during his youth. He began a medical education at Harvard, but was forced to leave because white students would not work alongside him. Delany's contributions to the pre-history of Pan-Africanism begin with his own sense of a profound connection with Africa. He was proud that he was a "full-blooded Negro" and he named his children for—among others—Toussaint L'Ouverture (the black leader of the Haitian Revolution), Ramses II (the pharaoh of

Egypt), and Alexander Dumas (the French novelist of African ancestry). But he was also a powerful voice for black emigration from the United States, arguing in *The Condition, Elevation, Emigration and Destiny of the Colored People of the United States* (1852) that only in a country without white people could black people flourish. In that early work Delany did not make the obvious suggestion that blacks should "return" to Africa. This was not because he was against the idea but because, along with other leaders of the re-emigration movement, he believed that most African Americans (convinced by anti-Negro propaganda) were likely to see Africa as a very unattractive place to live. In his *Official Report of the Niger Valley Exploration Party* (1861), written after he had been to Africa, he wrote of the continent as "our fatherland" and argued that its regeneration required the development of a "national character." And he proposed the formula, "Africa for the African race and black men to rule them," which is one of the earliest formulations of a Pan-Africanist principle.

Alexander Crummell was born in New York and studied at Cambridge University in England. He was the first African American to do so and was an ordained Anglican clergyman. He was also the first African American intellectual to spend a significant amount of time in Liberia. (When Delany visited that country in 1859, he met Crummell, who by then had been there for two decades.) In *The Future of Africa* (1862), a collection of essays and lectures written while he was in Liberia, Crummell developed a vision of Africa as the motherland of the Negro race. In "The English Language in Liberia," based on a lecture given on Liberian independence day in 1860, he argued that African Americans who had been "exiled" in slavery to the New World had been given by divine providence "at least this one item of compensation, namely, the possession of the Anglo-Saxon tongue." Similarly he argued for the providential nature of the transmission of Christianity to Negro slaves, and that it was the duty of "free colored men" in America to convert their ancestral continent to Christianity.

In the essay "The Relations and Duties of Free Colored Men in America to Africa," he also expressed with great clarity the underlying racial basis of his understanding of Negro identity. There he defined a race as "a compact, homogeneous population of one blood ancestry and lineage," and argued that each race had certain "determinate proclivities," which manifested themselves in the behavior of its members. Crummell was, with Blyden, one of the founders of Liberia College (later the University of Liberia). Unlike Blyden, however, he did not become a permanent resident of Liberia, returning rather to the United States, where he continued to argue for the importance of an engagement with Africa on the part of blacks in the African diaspora. Crummell was the leading spirit in the foundation of the American Negro Academy, and was present at the meeting at which Du Bois first read "The Conservation of Races." He was also a significant influence on Du Bois, who included an essay about Crummell in his extremely influential volume *The Souls of Black Folk* (1903).

Edward Blyden was born in the West Indies but traveled to Liberia in 1850 under the auspices of the American Colonization Society and became a citizen of that country for the rest of his life. Like Crummell, he was a priest, and, as we have seen, they worked together in the early days of the University of Liberia. Blyden spoke many languages. His essays include quotations in the original languages from Dante and Virgil, and he studied Arabic in order to teach it at Liberia College. Later he became the Liberian ambassador to Queen Victoria.

In *Christianity, Islam and the Negro Race* (1887) Blyden expressed the conviction that underlies Du Bois's first explicit formulation of Pan-Africanism: "Among the conclusions to which study and research are conducting philosophers, none is clearer than this—that each of the races of mankind has a specific character and specific work." Blyden, like Crummell, had little respect for the traditional cultures of Africa. They shared the view that Christian blacks in the diaspora had a responsibility to convert their African cousins. But Blyden argued explicitly that what he called Africa's current "state of barbarism" did not reflect any innate deficiency in the Negro. "There is not a single mental or moral deficiency now existing among Africans," he said, " . . . to which we cannot find a parallel in the past history of Europe."

## The Pan-African Congresses

Pan-Africanism as an intellectual movement begins, then, in the work of Du Bois, Delany, Crummell, and Blyden. But its institutional history starts with Henry Sylvester Williams, a London barrister born in Trinidad. He planned to bring together people of the "African race" from around the world in 1897; and in July 1900, after a preliminary conference in 1899, such a gathering took place in London. (The actual word "Pan-Africanism" seems to have been coined either at this first Pan-African Congress or at the earlier planning conference.) There were four African representatives—one each from Ethiopia, Sierra Leone, Liberia, and the Gold Coast colony—and a dozen from North America (among them Du Bois); eleven representatives came from the West Indies, five from London. The conference opened with the clearly stated aim of allowing black people to discuss the condition of the black race around the world.

The First Pan-African Congress convened in Paris in February 1919; it was attended by 57 delegates from 15 countries. In 1921 Du Bois and others organized a second Pan-African Congress, which met in three sessions, in London, Brussels, and Paris, this time with representatives from French and Portuguese colonies in Africa as well. They issued a final declaration that insisted on the equality of the races, the diffusion of democracy, and the development of political institutions in the colonies. It also urged the "return" of Negroes to their own countries and urged the League of Nations to pay attention both to race relations in the industrialized world and the condition of workers in the colonies.

A third congress occurred in London in 1923 and continued, according to Du Bois, in Lisbon (though this appears to have been little more than an opportunity for Du Bois to talk to some people from the Portuguese colonies on his way from London to Liberia, where he was the official representative of the United States at the installation of the Liberian president). The Pan-African Congress movement then effectively disappeared until the fifth congress in Manchester in 1945, during which the baton was handed from the diaspora to the continent. Du Bois's contribution now lay in the shadow of that of figures such as Kwame Nkrumah, who was to be Ghana's first Prime Minister. (And, indeed, Du Bois was the only African American present.) The sixth Congress, held in 1974 in Dar es Salaam, was presided over by Tanzanian president Julius Nyerere.

During the period between World War I and World War II, in the heyday of the Pan-African Congress movement, the sentiment received a substantial practical boost from the growth of the Universal Negro Improvement Association (UNIA). Led by Marcus Garvey, a Jamaican immigrant to the United States, the UNIA became the largest black move-ment in the African diaspora. While the slogan of the movement was "Back to Africa," and Garvey did indeed plan a shipping line for the purpose, rela-tively few members of the organization actually left the New World for the Old. Nevertheless, Garvey's commitment to racial pride and to the celebra-tion of black historical achievement, and his concern to link the diaspora to the continent, make him an important figure in the movement's history.

One West-Indian-born intellectual did play an important role in plan-ning the 1945 Congress, namely George Padmore (1902–1959). (Padmore was a pseudonym: he was born Malcolm Nurse.) Padmore was a Trinidadian who had spent some time in the United States studying at Columbia Uni-versity and at Fisk (a university in Nashville, Tennessee, which Du Bois had also attended). He worked as a Communist Party organizer among students at Howard University in Washington, D.C. Later he spent time in Germany and in Russia, where he became in 1930 the head of the Negro Bureau of the Red International of labor unions. In the next few years he worked for communist organizations in Austria and Germany, moving to London in 1935. From then until his death in 1959 he was the leading theorist of Pan-Africanism, and was a close friend and adviser of Kwame Nkrumah. His *Pan-Africanism or Communism* (1956) is probably the most important state-ment of his position.

## Pan-Africanism Today

In the period after World War II African intellectuals were preoccupied with the question of independence. Once independence was attained, Pan-Africanism became an ideology through which relations among the newly independent states could be thought about. Pan-Africanist rhetoric con-tinues to be important in the language of the Organization of African Unity, which was founded in 1963.

In that same period black intellectuals in North America were taken up with questions of civil rights. There were always resonances between these two projects—Du Bois was involved in both throughout his long life, and died a citizen of Ghana; African diplomats sought to have civil rights ques-tions raised in the forum of the United Nations. But Pan-Africanism took philosophical form in the period leading up to Padmore's work, and its major theoretical works are those of Padmore and Du Bois.

# Parks, Rosa Louise McCauley

(b. February 4, 1913, Tuskegee, Ala.), African American civil rights activist,
often called the "Mother of the Civil Rights Movement"; her arrest for refusing
to give up her seat on a bus triggered the 1955–1956 Montgomery bus boycott
and set in motion the test case for the desegregation of public transportation.

On December 1, 1955, in Montgomery, Alabama, the arrest of a black
woman, Rosa Parks, for disregarding an order to surrender her bus seat to a
white passenger galvanized a growing movement to desegregate public
transportation, and marked a historic turning point in the African American
battle for civil rights. Yet Parks was much more than an accidental symbol.
It is sometimes overlooked that at the time of her arrest she was no ordinary
bus rider, but an experienced activist with strong beliefs.

Parks was the granddaughter of former slaves and the daughter of James
McCauley, a carpenter, and Leona McCauley, a rural schoolteacher. The
future civil rights leader grew up in Montgomery, Alabama, where she
attended the all-black Alabama State College. In 1932 Parks married Raymond Parks, a barber, with whom she became active in Montgomery's
chapter of the National Association for the Advancement of Colored
People (NAACP).

Raymond Parks's volunteer efforts went toward helping to free the
defendants in the famous Scottsboro case, and Rosa Parks worked as the
chapter's youth advisor. In 1943, when Rosa Parks actually joined the
NAACP, her involvement with the organization became even greater as she
worked with the organization's state president E. D. Nixon to mobilize a
voter registration drive in Montgomery. That same year Parks also was
elected secretary of the Montgomery branch.

In the early 1950s Parks found work as a tailor's assistant at the Montgomery Fair department store. She had a part-time job working as a seamstress for Virginia and Clifford Durr, a white liberal couple who encouraged
Parks in her civil rights work. Six months before her famous protest, Parks
received a scholarship to attend a workshop on school integration for community leaders at the Highlander Folk School in Monteagle, Tennessee, and
spent several weeks there.

The segregated seating policies on public buses had long been a source
of resentment within the black community in Montgomery and in other
cities throughout the Deep South. African Americans were required to pay
their fares at the front of the bus and then re-board through the back door.
The white bus drivers, who were invested with police powers, frequently
harassed blacks, sometimes driving away before African American passengers were able to get back on the bus. At peak hours the drivers pushed
back boundary markers segregating the bus, crowding those in the "colored
section" so that whites could be provided with seats.

On December 1, 1955, Parks took her seat in the front of the "colored
section" of a Montgomery bus. When the driver asked Parks and three other
black riders to relinquish their seats to whites, Parks refused (the others

complied). The driver called the police, and Parks was arrested. Later that night she was released, after Nixon and the Durrs posted a $100 bond.

Although three black women had been arrested earlier that year for similar acts of defiance, and Parks herself had been thrown off a bus by the same driver 12 years before, this time the opponents of segregation were prepared to mount a counterattack. The Montgomery chapter of the NAACP had been looking for a test case to challenge the legality of segregated bus seating, and to woo public opinion with a series of protests. The morning after her arrest Parks agreed to let the NAACP take on her case. Another organization, the Women's Political Council (WPC), led by JoAnn Robinson, initiated the idea of a one-day bus boycott. Within 24 hours of Parks's defiance, the WPC had distributed more than 52,000 fliers announcing the bus boycott that was to take place the day of Parks's trial. On December 5, as buses went through their routes virtually empty, Parks was convicted by the local court. She refused to pay the fine of $14, and with the help of her lawyer, Ed D. Gray, appealed to the circuit court.

On the evening of December 5, several thousand protesters crowded into the Holt Street Baptist Church to create the Montgomery Improvement Association (MIA) and to rally behind its new president, Rev. Martin Luther King Jr., who had just moved to Montgomery as the new pastor at the Dexter Avenue Baptist Church. What was planned as a day-long bus boycott swelled to 381 days, during which time 42,000 protesters walked, carpooled, or took taxis, rather than ride the segregated city buses of Montgomery. In a move designed to reverse the segregation laws on public transportation, King and the MIA filed a separate case in United States District Court. The district court ruled for the plaintiffs, declaring segregated seating on buses unconstitutional, a decision later upheld by the U.S. Supreme Court.

Parks was widely known as "the Mother of the Civil Rights Movement," but her iconic stature afforded her little financial security. She lost her job as a seamstress at Montgomery Fair and was unable to find other work in Montgomery. Parks and her husband relocated to Detroit, Michigan, in 1957, where they struggled financially for the next eight years. Parks's fortunes improved somewhat in 1965, when Congressman John Conyers hired her as an administrative assistant, a position she held until 1987.

Parks has remained a committed activist. In the 1980s she worked in support of the South African antiapartheid movement, and in 1987 she founded the Rosa and Raymond Parks Institute for Self-Development in Detroit, a career counseling center for black youth.

A friend once described Parks as someone who, as a rule, did not defy authority, but once determined on a course of action, refused to back down: "She might ignore you, go around you, but never retreat."

North America

# Passing in the United States,

the phenomenon of African Americans, who in physical appearance approach the "white" racial type, choosing to live and identify themselves, whether temporarily or permanently, as white.

# Patterson, William

(b. August 27, 1891, San Francisco, Calif.; d. March 5, 1980, Bronx, N.Y.), African American attorney, civil rights activist, and Communist Party leader who publicly charged the United States with genocide against African Americans.

Born and raised in the San Francisco area, William L. Patterson attended local public schools and later abandoned studies in engineering at the University of California at Berkeley to pursue a J.D. at the Hastings College of Law in San Francisco. At Hastings, Patterson began a lifelong involvement in political issues, protesting racism and arguing against African American participation in the "white man's" World War I. Earning his law degree in 1919, Patterson moved to New York City and established a legal practice in Harlem with two colleagues. His years in New York coincided with the height of the Harlem Renaissance, and Patterson developed relationships with Paul Robeson, W. E. B. Du Bois, and other prominent African American activists. He began to work increasingly with left-wing causes and was active in the ultimately fruitless campaign to free Nicola Sacco and Bartolomeo Vanzetti, immigrant Italian anarchists who were convicted of murder and executed in 1927.

Convinced that African American oppression was caused by capitalism and economic exploitation, Patterson devoted himself to anti-capitalist activities, joining the Communist Party USA, in 1927 (one of the few African Americans to do so) and studying for three years at the University of the Toiling People of the Far East in Moscow. After returning from the Soviet Union in 1930 Patterson continued his leftist political activities: in 1932 he was elected to the Central Committee of the Communist Party and was the Communist candidate in the New York City mayoral election. Putting his electoral ambitions on hold after failing to win public office, from 1932 to 1946 Patterson focused on legal work as executive director of the Communist-influenced International Labor Defense, helping to plan the legal strategy for the Scottsboro Case defendants.

After moving to Chicago in 1938 Patterson became a community organizer on Chicago's South Side and a writer and editor for Communist newspapers such as the *Daily Record* and the *Daily Worker*. He also worked to safeguard the rights of African Americans and radical activists as the executive director of the Civil Rights Congress, a post he held from 1946 to 1956.

In 1951 Patterson edited *We Charge Genocide: The Crime of Government Against the Negro People*, and joined Paul Robeson in submitting a petition to the United Nations that accused the United States of genocide against African Americans. A year earlier the United States Congress's House Committee on Un-American Activities (HUAC) had demanded that Patterson testify about his Communist associations, and in 1954 he was found in contempt for his refusal to answer HUAC's questions. After three months in prison he was released upon successful appeal of the contempt citation.

Patterson published his autobiography, *The Man Who Cried Genocide*, in 1971. Though Patterson's political activities had raised the ire of the U.S. government, they earned him the praise of many Communist countries: in 1978 he was awarded the Paul Robeson Memorial Medal by East Germany's Academy of Arts.

## North America

### *Plessy v. Ferguson,*

**1896 United States Supreme Court case that reconciled the equal protection clause of the Fourteenth Amendment with a system of state-imposed racial segregation via the formula "separate but equal."**

When 30-year-old shoemaker Homer Plessy refused to leave his seat on a New Orleans train in 1892, he set in motion a battle that traveled all the way to the U.S. Supreme Court. The court's 1896 decision, *Plessy v. Ferguson*, permitted states to institute racially separate public accommodations despite the Constitution's Fourteenth Amendment, which guarantees all citizens equal protection under the law. It would take nearly 60 years for the court to reverse itself, in *Brown v. Board of Education* (1954), and overturn the judicial precedent for segregation.

The segregated public transportation system that Plessy challenged in 1892 was relatively new to New Orleans, whose French and Spanish roots, many free blacks, and community of prominent Creole citizens made it one of America's most socially and economically progressive cities. Plessy himself had been born free in 1862, the second year of the Civil War, in which Union forces took control of the city's port. Throughout the war and Reconstruction, the Northern army provided a check on the Southern Democrats who sought a restoration of white power at all costs.

Just before the war, in 1860, New Orleans's trains were first segregated. Those adorned with black stars were meant for black passengers only. The rule was difficult to enforce because of the many mixed-race people and mixed marriages in New Orleans. Plessy himself was fair-skinned enough to pass for white. In 1867 the city removed the black stars from its trains, and the system returned to its earlier, integrated state.

But with the declining support of the Republican-controlled U.S. government, Reconstruction faltered. Increasingly, Southern Democrats took back the power they had lost in Louisiana. In 1890 Governor Francis T. Nicholls—elected as part of an 1876 compromise balancing a Republican president with Democratic control of the South—signed the law re-segregating Louisiana's railways. It stated that train companies had to provide "equal but separate" cars for blacks and whites, and that individuals of different races could not ride together without risking a $25 fine or 20 days in jail. The Louisiana Senate passed the law by a vote of 23 to 6.

African Americans and Creoles in New Orleans mobilized to fight the law. Rodolphe Desdunes, columnist for the *Crusader*, a black-owned newspaper, proposed that African Americans boycott the train system, writing that blacks "can withdraw the patronage from these corporations and travel only by necessity." But his idea did not take hold. Fears of violent white reprisals limited black political activism, and noted African American leaders like Booker T. Washington preached patience and accommodation.

A Louisiana group calling itself the *Comité des Citoyens* (Citizens' Committee) planned to test the law's constitutionality—specifically, to prove that the law violated the Fourteenth Amendment to the U.S. Constitution, which guarantees all citizens "the equal protection of the laws." Made up of prominent New Orleans blacks and whites, including the *Crusader*'s publisher, Louis Martinet, and Desdunes, the committee arranged for Plessy to board a whites-only train. By pre-arrangement with contacts in the East Louisiana Railroad Company, a conductor asked Plessy, who was of mixed race, if he was a "colored man." When Plessy said he was, and refused to move, the conductor and private detective hired by the *Comité* accompanied him to the police station, where he was booked and then released on $500 bond posted by a *Comité* member.

Judge John H. Ferguson, a Massachusetts native, presided over Plessy's arraignment a month later. Ferguson had earlier ruled the Louisiana law unconstitutional when it demanded segregated train cars for travel between states. Martinet had written in the Crusader that, with this decision, "Jim Crow is dead as a doornail." But in Plessy's case Ferguson sided with the state, saying that Louisiana, in compelling racial segregation on its in-state train system, had not violated African Americans' constitutional rights.

Louisiana's state supreme court agreed with Ferguson, citing a Massachusetts case, *Roberts v. City of Boston*, in which the state's chief justice had written that "prejudice, if it exists, is not created by law and cannot be changed by law." In addition, Roberts was the source of the phrase "separate but equal." The opinion also quoted a Pennsylvania case whose ruling rested upon the "natural, legal, and customary difference between the black and white races."

Plessy's lawyer, the white activist and writer Albion Tourgée, brought the case before the U.S. Supreme Court in 1896. Tourgée's brief argued that the Louisiana law "is obnoxious to the spirit of republican institutions, because it is a legalization of caste." He also stated that the law violated both the Thirteenth and Fourteenth Amendments in limiting "the natural rights of man."

The Court ruled seven to one (one justice did not participate) that Plessy's constitutional rights had not been violated. Writing for the majority, Justice Henry B. Brown wrote that while the Fourteenth Amendment had "undoubtedly" been meant to enforce "absolute equality" between the races, it did not "abolish distinction based on color," citing many states' laws mandating separate schools and prohibiting interracial marriages—laws that were themselves ruled unconstitutional later. The opinion went on to say that "legislation is powerless to eradicate racial instincts or to abolish distinctions."

In a lone but strong dissent, Justice John Marshall Harlan, a Southerner, cited cases in which segregated juries had been found unconstitutional, and went on to say in plain language what Plessy's opponents would not admit: that the separate car law not only separated the races but did so to accommodate white racial prejudice. Legal segregation, Harlan wrote, allowed "the seeds of race hate to be planted under the sanctions of law." He went on to say that "the thin disguise of 'equal' accommodations . . . will not mislead anyone, nor atone for the wrong this day done."

Harlan's words proved prophetic. The "separate but equal" doctrine relegated African American children to inadequate, unsafe schools, while the South's Jim Crow laws forbade black citizens from exercising their rights as citizens on an equal footing with white citizens. Not until the Supreme Court reversed itself in 1954's *Brown v. Board of Education* would African Americans be able to claim the rights promised in the U.S. Constitution.

North America

# Poor People's Washington Campaign,

**a demonstration in Washington, D.C., organized in 1968 by the Southern Christian Leadership Conference (SCLC) to demand federal legislation ensuring employment, income, and housing for the poor.**

On June 19, 1968, more than 50,000 people assembled in Washington, D.C., to voice their support for the Poor People's Campaign for economic justice in America. The day was the highlight of the Southern Christian Leadership Conference (SCLC) campaign, set in motion by Martin Luther King Jr. to secure federal legislation guaranteeing employment, income, and housing for the poor. Considered only minimally successful by most historians, the Poor People's Campaign has been called the last of the 1960s mass mobilizations of nonviolent resistance.

The Poor People's Campaign marked several important shifts in the orientation of SCLC as a whole, and in the thinking of King, its leader. The SCLC had expanded its operations from a regional base in the South to a national operation by the mid-1960s. In the South rural blacks had faced debilitating poverty and segregation: a National Association for the Advancement of Colored People (NAACP) survey in Mississippi found that blacks there suffered from hunger, malnutrition, and even starvation. In Northern cities such as Chicago the SCLC found an urban crisis of poverty grounded in ingrained racist economic structures. Here, the organization found, the forces of institutionalized racism did not yield to the strategies of resistance used against segregation in the South.

King became increasingly critical of a federal government and capitalist system that left a large population of African Americans, urban and rural, in poverty. He said: "We are called upon to help the discouraged beggars in life's market place. But one day we must come to see that an edifice which produces beggars needs restructuring." King pointed directly at the "edifice" of the federal government, which he had formerly viewed as a benevolent force that needed only to understand the conditions under which blacks lived in order to join the fight for change. Poverty, King now claimed, was to blame for the urban riots that plagued the country, and capitalism was to blame for poverty: "When you begin to ask why are there 40 million poor people in America, you are raising questions about the economic system, about a broader distribution of wealth. When you ask that question, you begin to question the capitalistic economy."

King took up the suggestion of Marian Wright to have the poor demonstrate in Washington, D.C., and if necessary, disrupt the national government. He envisioned a "tent city," with protesters living out of temporary structures on the mall of Capitol Hill. Unlike King's earlier campaigns for African American equality, this movement was to be staged on behalf of a spectrum of peoples, including Native Americans, Mexican Americans, Puerto Ricans, and Appalachian whites.

King began mobilizing the SCLC for a national campaign amid fears of an increasingly violent turn in the struggle for rights. The campaign moved slowly, in part for this reason and in part because of financial and organizational difficulties. Civil rights activists, such as Bayard Rustin and NAACP Executive Secretary Roy Wilkins, questioned the wisdom of a mass march on Washington that might lead to violence, while others, namely President Lyndon B. Johnson and the Federal Bureau of Investigation, waged an outright campaign to derail the organizing process. When a march led by King in Memphis, Tennessee, to support striking sanitation workers turned violent, it seemed to be the end of the campaign to march on Washington.

King's assassination on April 4, 1968, turned the tide of support for the march, and within a month over $500,000 in donations poured in for King's movement. The new SCLC leader, the Rev. Ralph Abernathy, kept the movement going, and former opponents of the march, such as Rustin, now joined in.

On May 13 the first residents of Resurrection City set up house, populating West Potomac Park in tents made from canvas and plywood. By late May, 2,500 people were living there, including groups from Tennessee, New Mexico, Chicago, and the Mississippi Delta. Each day Resurrection City residents marched to various federal agencies to present demands. They joined more than 50,000 others on Solidarity Day, June 19, for a mass demonstration organized by Sterling Tucker and led by Abernathy and Coretta Scott King. Five days later 1,500 police arrived, arresting hundreds and destroying Resurrection City.

For some who had been active in the early successes of the SCLC, the Poor People's Campaign was a failure. Many found the protest poorly organized despite its ample funding, and some protesters were critical of SCLC leaders who slept at night in a motel. For others, who remembered King's prophecy that organizing around the basic rights of jobs and income would prove even more difficult than opposing the Vietnam War, the Poor People's Campaign was a necessary turn from protests against segregation to a larger demand for economic justice.

# QR

## Race Riots in the United States,

over the course of the past hundred years a recurring part of American life; incidents include the Wilmington, N.C., Riot of 1898; New Orleans Riot of 1900; Atlanta Riot of 1906; East St. Louis Riot of 1917; Chicago Riots of 1919; Elaine, Arkansas, Race Riot of 1919; Tulsa Riot of 1921; Harlem Riots of 1935; Detroit Riot of 1943; Harlem Riots of 1943; Harlem Riot of 1964; Los Angeles Watts Riot of 1965; Detroit Riot of 1967; Miami Riot of 1980; and Los Angeles Riot of 1992.

## Racial Stereotypes

Sticks and stones will break my bones, but names will never hurt me. Our era has moved beyond this proverb, which parents teach vulnerable children. Forget sticks—we worry now about deadly weapons. Forget names—we all have to deal with racial and ethnic stereotypes. Stereotypes are proverbial generalizations broadcast by the powerful media of the modern era. Their racial dimensions are what concern us here, but first let us look at the broad issues stereotypes provoke and the history of the term.

The term "stereotype," now used with reference to our society's old problem with nasty names, was developed when, at the outset of the modern industrial age in 1798, two European printers invented a new way to reproduce images that would fix them permanently. The image-setting process was called stereotyping, and in time the word "stereotype" came to apply to the fixing of intellectual, as opposed to printed, images. One's stereotype of a jet, for instance, wipes away the marks of specific makes in order to stand in for all jets. One's stereotype of a ballet dancer may not be male or female and may not have a realized face; thus the image can represent all ballet dancers. Stereotypes simplify real images in order to make a generalization. All peoples produce stereotyped ideas in order to create a shorthand form of communication among themselves.

All peoples also produce racial stereotypes about themselves and others. That is, people simplify the intellectual images they maintain of specific ethnic groups, including their own, often in cruel or damaging ways. Poor white Southerners ("Crackers") are said to be slow, red-necked, and fat. Immigrant Italians ("Wops") are said to be short, oily, and hot-tempered. Upper-class whites ("Wasps") are said to be greedy, emotionally cold, and haughty. Negroes ("Niggers") are said to be stupid, promiscuous, and happy. These generalizations are not accurate, but they are spread widely—not only by word of mouth but also through images in television, movies, newspapers, music, comic books, talk shows, pseudo-scientific research, and even textbooks. These media make stereotypes, whose dissemination was once confined to oral transmission from one person to another, seem more like factual knowledge than personal opinion.

Perhaps the most chilling aspect of racial stereotyping is that members of groups being characterized sometimes come to believe the generalizations' damaging simplifications. Members of target groups may even try to fulfill the stereotypes. The media regularly depict people of African descent as drug dealers and teen mothers, and so it is not surprising when young black artists also adopt the roles of thugs and "bitches 'n 'ho's." Even stereotypes that include positive human attributes can warp people. For instance, if the dominant culture emphasizes that men of African descent are excellent athletes or entertainers, the glamour associated with these professions may influence the youth of that group. They may try to fulfill a simplified stereotype of their potential rather than develop other traits. That is the force of stereotypes.

Racial stereotypes reflect and are facilitated by power relations in a society. Stereotypes of a demeaned group are frequently accepted as the truth and are not understood as problematic until the group can manifest its fully human condition. As the group's relative power grows, it can sometimes stop the public proliferation of blatant stereotypes about it. That's what happened in the 1950s when the National Association for the Advancement of Colored People (NAACP) made concerted complaints about minstrel shows. The NAACP effectively stopped the practice of white Americans blacking up to represent black people in ragged, ignorant, and grotesque stereotypes. (Isolated examples of whites mounting minstrel shows continued in backwaters of the north and south United States into the 1980s. "Darkie Days" have survived in England, as in Padstow, Cornwall, right through the late 1990s, finally causing a member of Parliament to complain in 1998. Blacks in England remain much less empowered than those in the United States.)

The many paradoxes in stereotypes are analytically useful. When one group creates stereotypes to manage its thoughts about others, dispassionate observers gain access to the compact assumptions controlling that group's thought. Created in moments and locations of stress and anxiety, stereotypes satisfy various functions for their creators. One group will create stereotypes about another group in order to control them (or to fight back against control) or to justify their power over that group (or to strike back against that power). By classifying the target group as subhuman or grotesque, stereotypes are likely to minimize their creators' misgivings about participating in uneven power relations. A stereotype always isolates one perhaps imagined aspect of the target group and substitutes it for the whole. Because it denies the complex humanity of the demeaned target, every racial stereotype says much more about the creators' needs than about the target's nature. Because they always display their creators' dread of the target group, racial stereotypes eventually subvert their makers' cruel intentions. For instance, a cultural group that classifies women of another culture exclusively as mammies displays alarm about its own nurturing capacity. A people that stereotypes others as greedy money-changers betrays its own concern for prosperity.

Studying stereotypes reveals both their present power and their historical flow. Despite their power to disturb us in the present, stereotypes turn in cycles. Their meanings can change dramatically over time. The Jim Crow figure, which rapidly became a stereotype standing for United States racism, began (and persists) as a figure of black folklore. Poor white actors and workers who identified with the suffering of black slaves in the early 1800s copied their gestures to speak out against employers. But their opponents, in turn, used the image of this Jim Crow mimicry to mock the alliance between blacks and their sympathizers. It was a full century before the NAACP could gain some control over the stereotype. The evolutionary nature of stereotypes shows that they are anything but permanent. Indeed, they may help change social attitudes over time. Many sensitive artists of every hue have known how to turn stereotypes inside out. They push them hard enough so that audiences see both the stereotypes' cruelty and their makers' weakness.

North America

# Randolph, Asa Philip

**(b. April 15, 1889, Crescent City, Fla.; d. May 16, 1979, New York, N.Y.), founder and president of the Brotherhood of Sleeping Car Porters (BSCP); editor of the Messenger; and architect of the March on Washington Movement in 1941, which led to the establishment of the Fair Employment Practices Committee (FEPC), and the 1963 March on Washington.**

Although many civil rights leaders focused on voting, education, and other governmental functions, A. Philip Randolph spent his long career as a labor leader working to bring more and better jobs to African Americans. After a long, successful battle to win representation for the nation's Pullman porters, Randolph was instrumental in the formation of the FEPC, which protected African Americans against job discrimination in the army and defense industries. In addition, Randolph co-founded and edited the *Messenger*, the socialist black magazine.

The son of a minister, Randolph grew up in Jacksonville, Florida, and graduated from the Cookman Institute in 1907. A lack of economic opportunity for blacks led Randolph, the class valedictorian, into a series of menial jobs until 1911, when he moved to New York City. Working as an elevator operator and living in Harlem, Randolph took classes at the City College of New York and New York University, acted in amateur theatricals, and eventually took a job with a Harlem employment agency.

In 1914 Randolph met Chandler Owen, whose progressive politics and interest in socialism matched his own. In 1917 the two founded the *Messenger*, whose editorials strongly opposed United States entry into World War I, saying that "no intelligent Negro is willing to lay down his life for the United States as it now exists." Though the magazine was never profitable, it was influential, offering a more radical voice than that of W. E. B. Du Bois's the *Crisis* or the even more conventional *New York Age*. The *Messenger*, with its advocacy of labor unions, was especially popular among Pullman porters—all of whom were black—who served white railroad passengers in luxurious sleeping cars. Founded just after the Civil War, the Pullman company had by the 1920s become the nation's single largest employer of African Americans. Many of the Pullman porters were college graduates who enjoyed great respect within their communities, but at work they were subjected to unfair and discriminatory practices.

In 1925 with Randolph at the helm, the BSCP began organizing the nearly 10,000 porters. For ten years Randolph kept the members unified and inspired, often in the face of intimidation and firings, while he negotiated with the president and Congress to amend the Railway Labor Act. Finally, in a hard-won victory hailed by African Americans and progressives nationwide, the company recognized their union in 1935.

Randolph continued to fight for racial and economic justice in the late 1930s as president of the National Negro Congress before resigning in protest over its increasing domination by Communists. In 1940 he returned to the issue of jobs, joining Walter White, secretary of the National Association for the Advancement of Colored People (NAACP), and T. Arnold Hill of the National Urban League in urging President Franklin D. Roosevelt to desegregate the military and defense industries before World War II. After an unsatisfactory resolution to a meeting with the president, Randolph began planning a march on Washington, D.C., by the BSCP and others to demand "the right to work and fight for our country." The date for at least 10,000 African Americans to demonstrate before the Lincoln Memorial was set for July 1, 1941. Despite the president's wish to avoid a mass demonstration, Randolph refused to call off the march unless Roosevelt banned discrimination in the burgeoning defense industries. Following another meeting with Randolph and White, the president at last issued Executive Order 8002, which not only outlawed such discrimination but also established the FEPC to investigate breaches of the order.

Though the FEPC operated only from 1941 to 1946, Randolph continued to push for his other goal: desegregation of the U.S. armed forces.

A. Philip Randolph stands before the Lincoln Memorial on August 28, 1963, the day of the March on Washington, an event that was the culmination of Randolph's long career as an advocate of racial and economic justice. *CORBIS/Bettmann*

When President Harry S. Truman instituted a peacetime draft, Randolph told him "this time Negroes will not take a Jim Crow draft lying down." In July 1948 Truman signed Executive Order 9981, finally ending the historic segregation of African American soldiers.

Throughout the 1950s Randolph worked with the NAACP and other civil rights leaders. He helped plan and spoke at Pilgrimage Day, a 1957 prayer meeting in Washington, D.C. He met with President Dwight D. Eisenhower to push for faster school integration in the wake of *Brown v. Board of Education* and planned a 1958 Youth March for Integrated Schools. He also continued his union work and became vice president of the newly consolidated AFL-CIO from 1955 to 1968.

Randolph's brainchild, the March on Washington Movement, bore new fruit in 1963 with the help of Bayard Rustin and Rev. Martin Luther King Jr., who, along with Randolph, mobilized the largest demonstration of the Civil Rights Movement. Speaking before King did, the 74-year-old Randolph exhorted the crowd of 250,000 to take part in a "revolution for jobs and freedom." The next year President Lyndon B. Johnson signed the Civil Rights Act of 1964 and awarded Randolph the Presidential Medal of Freedom. In his final years Randolph established the A. Philip Randolph Institute, a job skills and training bureau in Harlem. Upon Randolph's death in 1979, Rustin said of his late colleague, "No individual did more to help the poor, the dispossessed and the working class . . . than A. Philip Randolph."

# Rangel, Charles Bernard

(b. June 11, 1930, Harlem, N.Y.), 14-term member of the United States House of Representatives from New York.

Charles Rangel was born in Harlem. Raised by his mother and grand-mother after his parents' separation, he dropped out of high school and held several jobs until joining the army in 1948. He served until 1952 and saw action in South Korea, for which he was awarded the Bronze Star and the Purple Heart.

Rangel returned to New York and resumed his high school career, obtaining his diploma in 1953. He earned a B.S. from the New York School of Commerce in 1957 and a law degree from St. John's Law School in 1960. Rangel held various positions before entering politics. Directly after graduating from law school he served as an attorney for civil rights activists. In 1961 he was appointed assistant district attorney for the Southern District of New York. Rangel then began to work in politics, serving as legal council for the New York City Housing and Redevelopment Board, as legal assistant to then-speaker of the New York State Assembly, Judge James L. Watson. In addition, with close friend Percy Sutton, Rangel helped to found the John F. Kennedy Democratic Club in Harlem (later named the Rev. Martin Luther King Jr. Democratic Club). Rangel first entered political office locally and was elected in 1966 to the New York State Assembly as representative from central Harlem.

Rangel's congressional career began when he unseated Harlem Democratic political stalwart Adam Clayton Powell Jr. in the closely contested 1970 primary election. Rangel held the seat for 14 terms despite a challenge from Powell's son, Adam Clayton Powell IV, in 1994. During Rangel's lengthy legislative career, he distinguished himself as one of the most liberal members of the House. He consistently supported a woman's right to abortion, voted for busing to desegregate public schools, opposed the Vietnam War, and opposed the illegal drug trade. In 1974 he served on the House Judiciary Committee during its hearings on the impeachment of President Richard Nixon. In 1997 Rangel cosponsored the African Growth and Opportunities Act, which was designed to promote economic investment in Africa. In addition, Rangel helped found and chaired the Congressional Black Caucus.

# Reconstruction,

the period immediately following the Civil War during which the United States sought to rebuild the South physically, politically, socially, and economically.

Reconstruction, also called the "Second American Revolution," is an often misunderstood era of United States history. For decades historians presented

Reconstruction as a time when the South was a region besieged by a punitive North. According to this view President Abraham Lincoln initially offered reasonable terms to the rebellious Southern states to speed reunion; but Radical Republicans, the liberal wing of the Republican Party, instituted a period of "Negro rule" in which blacks, incompetent to govern, mismanaged the South. In this interpretation conscientious whites "redeemed" the South by using secret patriotic organizations such as the Ku Klux Klan to depose black rule. Only during the "Second Reconstruction," the Civil Rights Movement, did most historians begin to reevaluate previous conclusions about Reconstruction. Concurring with W. E. B. Du Bois, most scholars now agree that Reconstruction was a period of progressive politics in which newly emancipated blacks, with the help of the federal government and sympathetic whites in the South, helped build a more democratic society.

This 1880 Reconstruction-era diagram of a family tree contrasts farm life before and after the Civil War. The slave family on the left works under the watchful eye of a white master. The free family on the right enjoys leisure time together. *CORBIS*

## The Federal Government During Reconstruction

Most historians consider Reconstruction to encompass the years between 1865 and 1877. But the course Reconstruction would take and the questions associated with it were the subjects of national debate even before the end of the Civil War. Who should be punished for inciting secession and the war? How would the Southern states be readmitted to the Union? What penalties would apply? What was the federal government's responsibility to the freed slaves? Should the government extend rights to former slaves, and, if so, which rights? How would the Southern economy replace slave labor with free labor? Finally, and perhaps most important to the federal government, who was responsible for implementing Reconstruction policy—the president or Congress? Although Lincoln had been granted far-reaching powers during the war, Congress could not allow the president such latitude in peacetime.

By issuing the Emancipation Proclamation on January 1, 1863, Lincoln committed the United States to abolishing slavery. Because slavery had been part of the American social fabric from the nation's beginning, its abolition would fundamentally alter the nation. Combined with this drastic social and political change was the need to rebuild the war-torn South. Many Southern cities lay in ruins. In addition, the loss of farmland and animals, as well as human labor—not only black slaves but whites killed or disabled in the war—jeopardized its agrarian economy.

## Presidential Reconstruction

In December 1863 Lincoln introduced the first Reconstruction scheme, the Ten Percent Plan, thus beginning the period known as Presidential Reconstruction. The plan decreed that when 10 percent of a state's prewar voters had taken an oath of loyalty to the U.S. Constitution, its citizens could elect a new state government and apply for readmission to the Union. In addition, Lincoln promised to pardon all but a few high-ranking Confederates if they would take this oath and accept the fact of abolition. The plan also required that states amend their constitutions to abolish slavery. Conspicuous in this plan was the stipulation that only whites could vote or hold office. Despite the objections of Northern abolitionists, Lincoln began to implement the plan in Louisiana, which the Union army had occupied since 1862. In a private meeting at the White House a group of highly accomplished free blacks from New Orleans objected to their unequal status. Spurred by this protest, Lincoln unsuccessfully urged Louisiana's governor to allow the state's qualified free blacks to vote.

Congress, believing that Lincoln's Reconstruction plan was too permissive, took a series of steps to counteract it. Congress passed the Wade-Davis Bill in late 1864, which contained more stringent readmission policies. It required that 50 percent of a state's voters declare loyalty to the Constitution before the state could create a new government, and also that these new governments recognize freed people as equal before the law. In addition, in January 1865 Congress approved the Thirteenth Amendment, which constitutionally ended slavery. It was ratified in December of that year, and in March 1865 Congress established the Bureau of Refugees, Freedmen and Abandoned Lands, or Freedmen's Bureau, a relief agency for needy refugees. Although the agency represented both black and white refugees, it was primarily intended to aid blacks in the transition from slavery to freedom.

Lincoln indirectly vetoed Wade-Davis by leaving it unsigned until Congress adjourned in late March 1865. He considered the Ten Percent Plan experimental, however, and in his final speech indicated that at least some blacks should vote. Because of this, many historians believe he might have adapted his Ten Percent Plan had he not been assassinated. It was obvious, however, that Lincoln and Congress disagreed on the basic nature of Reconstruction policy. When the war ended and Reconstruction began in earnest, the federal government had no solid plan for its direction.

Congress had adjourned by the end of the war and did not reconvene until December. With Lincoln's assassination in early April 1865, Vice President Andrew Johnson became president, controlling Reconstruction policy at its crucial beginning. Johnson, a poor white from Tennessee, harbored disdain for both the Southern planter aristocracy and blacks. In May 1865 he began issuing proclamations that were even more lenient than Lincoln's.

Johnson pardoned all Southern whites except Confederate leaders and persons whose wealth exceeded $20,000. They would have to apply personally for Johnson's pardon. Johnson appointed provisional governors and required that to rejoin the union, the states need only abolish slavery and repudiate both secession and the Confederate war debt. After the rebellious states met these requirements they were considered "reconstructed." In addition, Johnson ordered that abandoned plantations be returned to their former owners. Though representatives from the Freedmen's Bureau initially refused to follow Johnson's directive, he ultimately sent federal troops to force the return of these lands.

Southern states, encouraged by Johnson's leniency, began to return the old elites to power. In addition, Southern state governments issued Black Codes, laws that aimed to limit black mobility and economic options, and virtually to reinstate the plantation system. Under the Black Codes interracial marriages were banned and blacks could be forced to sign yearly contracts. They could also be declared vagrants for not having a certain (typically unreasonable) amount of money on their person and be sentenced to labor on a white-owned plantation. In addition, these laws limited the types of occupations and property blacks could hold. Other laws sought

The political cartoon, *Re-Construction, or "A White Man's Government,"* presents a drowning white Southerner refusing the help of a black man, who clings to an allegorical "Tree of Liberty." President Ulysses S. Grant stands onshore, urging the desperate man to accept whatever help he is offered. *CORBIS*

forcibly to apprentice black children. As a result, freed people existed somewhere between freedom and slavery.

Congress had observed these events during adjournment and, upon returning to Washington, D.C., in December 1865, sought to alter Johnson's policies. When the newly elected Southern representatives arrived and Northern congressmen discovered that many of them were former Confederate cabinet members, congressmen, and generals who had won congressional seats in the state governments restored under Johnson, Congress refused to seat them. Many congressional Republicans, especially Radical Republicans such as Thaddeus Stevens in the House and Charles Sumner in the Senate, believed that the Johnson state governments should be dissolved and Reconstruction begun again, this time based on equality under law and universal male suffrage. Moderate members of the party, however, attempted to work with Johnson and convince him to modify his policies.

In early 1866 Congress sought to advance Reconstruction by passage of the Freedmen's Bureau Act and the Civil Rights Act. The Freedmen's Bureau Act extended the agency's life for another year. The Civil Rights Act defined people born in the United States as national citizens and stated explicitly the rights to which they were entitled regardless of race. Johnson vetoed both bills, insisting that they violated states' rights. Congress quickly overrode Johnson's vetoes. Shortly thereafter, Congress approved the Fourteenth Amendment, which was ratified in 1868. Designed to protect the rights of freed people and to restrict the political power of former Confederates, the Fourteenth Amendment defined U.S. citizenship in much the same way as the Civil Rights Bill had and prohibited states from abridging the "privileges or immunities" of citizens without due process. Rather than prohibit states from restricting suffrage, it encouraged Southern states to allow black suffrage by reducing representation in states that disfranchised any male citizens.

Hiram Rhoades Revels (1822–1901) was the son of former slaves. He became a Methodist minister, an educator, and the first African American in the United States Senate. *CORBIS*

Johnson's Reconstruction program became the decisive issue in the 1866 congressional elections. Although Johnson had toured the North to win support for candidates sympathetic to his program, his efforts were mostly unsuccessful. His rhetoric was more influential in the South: all of the former confederate states, except Tennessee, rejected the Fourteenth Amendment, which Johnson had publicly disavowed. By 1867 moderate and radical Republicans in Congress, tired of Johnson's obstruction to their more ambitious Reconstruction plan, began to take advantage of the president's waning power to forge an era of Congressional Reconstruction.

## Congressional Reconstruction

After a series of compromises Congress decided upon a Reconstruction plan that was far more broad-ranging than Johnson's. In March 1867 Congress began by passing the Reconstruction Acts, which divided the ten unreconstructed states (except Tennessee, which had already ratified the Fourteenth Amendment) into five military districts, each headed by a commander whose responsibilities included overseeing the writing of new constitutions that provided for enfranchisement of all adult males.

Only after ratifying the new state constitution and the Fourteenth Amendment would a state be considered reconstructed and readmitted to the Union. In addition, Congress passed several laws to restrict Johnson's power to undermine congressional policy. In response, Johnson removed military officers who were enforcing the Reconstruction Act and fired his secretary of war. Shortly thereafter Congress began impeachment proceedings against Johnson, ultimately coming within one vote of conviction.

In 1869 Congress passed the Fifteenth Amendment, which broadened the Fourteenth Amendment's protection of black voting rights, stating that no citizen could be denied the vote on the basis of race, color, or "previous condition of servitude." It was ratified in 1870. In addition, Congress passed the Civil Rights Act of 1875, which barred discrimination by hotels, theaters, and railroads. The act, however, was rarely enforced.

## The Supreme Court and Reconstruction

The Supreme Court, which had been largely silent during the war years, became active during this period, facilitating a retreat from Reconstruction by overturning many congressional measures. In *Bradwell v. Illinois* (1873) the Court ruled against a female attorney who claimed that in prohibiting her from practicing law because of her gender, Illinois had violated the "privileges and immunities" clause of the Fourteenth Amendment.

The following day the Court further narrowed the Fourteenth Amendment's scope in the *Slaughterhouse* cases (1873), rejecting the argument that the Fourteenth Amendment had transformed citizenship by making it the federal government's responsibility. In *United States v. Cruikshank* (1876), it ruled that the duty to protect citizens' rights rested with states. In *United States v. Reese* (1876), the Court ruled that the Fifteenth Amendment did not guarantee citizens the right to vote, but listed the grounds impermissible for denying the vote. Southern states now had a clear path toward the disfranchisement of black voters.

## Freed people During Reconstruction

The first decision facing former slaves was often whether to stay on the plantation or to move. In general, the choice depended on the disposition of the former master: if a master had been mean or violent, few of his former slaves were likely to remain; if the master had been fair, however, former slaves did often stay. Southern whites exaggerated the number of black men who refused to work after emancipation as a supporting argument for black inferiority, but these numbers were in fact low. Many freedwomen, however, refused to work in the fields any longer after emancipation, choosing instead to remain at home with their children.

To some freed people, emancipation meant the freedom to move about, either because it had been prohibited or because they wished to search for family members who had been sold away during slavery. The Reconstruction era produced many touching stories of ex-slaves who traveled thousands of miles, with very little information about their relatives' whereabouts, to reunite with family members. Others found no success in their searches.

Blacks, denied literacy during slavery, also sought education, often paying for it themselves. By 1877 more than 600,000 African Americans had enrolled in elementary schools throughout the South. The Freedmen's Bureau founded more than 4,000 schools, including Howard University, and many benevolent organizations, black and white, offered education. The American Missionary Association founded seven colleges, including Fisk and Atlanta universities.

Freed people established other black institutions, especially churches, that profoundly affected African American history. As slaves, blacks had been forced to worship in their masters' churches. After emancipation freed-people founded their own churches or moved to black denominations, which served as social and political centers in the black community. Ministers often became community leaders, a practice that continues to this day.

Freed people also knew that land meant independence and that they were entitled to some of the lands of their former owners. Early in the war, as the U.S. Navy approached South Carolina, Confederates abandoned their lands on the Sea Islands. Freed people immediately lobbied for ownership of the land, insisting that it was rightfully theirs after generations of forced servitude. Instead, the U.S. government implemented the Port Royal Experiment, in which freed people labored in the abandoned Sea Island lands as wage workers. Eventually, Gen. William T. Sherman issued Special Order No. 15, which gave the land to the freed people. President Johnson, however, rescinded the order, and the land reverted to its original owners. One of Reconstruction's great failings is that the U.S. government did not effectively redistribute land after the Civil War.

Most freed people were unable to buy land and instead rented it for farming. Freedmen's Bureau agents, many of whom wanted to change the Southern economy by introducing Northern concepts such as wage labor, needed to retain enough of the old system to ensure stability. To do this efficiently, Freedmen's Bureau agents developed work contracts, which, in the cash-poor South, would promise the slave a certain wage in exchange for crops. Although intended to mediate disputes, bureau agents often sided with the former master. The Freedmen's Bureau grew less active after 1866, leaving tenants and planters to find their own way. Thus, contracts between former slaves and masters were not enforced, and slaves often depended on the good will of their former owners.

Freed people also took advantage of the franchise, voting almost unanimously for Republican candidates in the 1866 congressional elections. Freed people also joined governments. Largely because of large black turnout and because Congress banned many former Confederates from politics, the Republican Party won control of many Southern constitutional conventions. Of the 1,000 Republican delegates to constitutional conventions throughout the South, 265 were black.

Participation in government among blacks was greatest in state and local governments, where many attained high rank. Francis Cardozo was a member of South Carolina's constitutional convention and later served as state Secretary of the Treasury and as South Carolina's secretary of state. In Louisiana P. B. S. Pinchback became the first black governor in U.S. history. He also served as lieutenant governor and he was elected to both the U.S. Senate and the U.S. House of Representatives. Blanche K. Bruce was a U.S. senator from Mississippi, as was Hiram Revels. In all, 16 blacks served in the U.S. Congress during Reconstruction.

Although whites who sought to disfranchise blacks justified their actions by claiming that they had been subjected to incompetent "Negro rule," blacks constituted the majority in only two state conventions, and only in South Carolina's lower house were black representatives a majority. In many ways the biracial coalitions of which most Republican governments were composed made progressive changes, such as creating state-funded public schools and a fairer tax system, outlawing discrimination in public transportation, and ending the death penalty.

## Opposition to Reconstruction

As Reconstruction was implemented, a struggle began in the South over the new social order. On one side were the freed people and their allies, who wanted to participate in a free society. On the other side were white elites and their followers, who wanted to restore the old order. Many whites—even those who had not owned slaves before the Civil War—found it difficult to imagine a society in which blacks had the same rights as they.

Reconstruction inspired deep

A.R. Waud's 1867 illustration, *The First Vote*, shows recently freed African American men going to the polls for the first time in a state election in the South. *CORBIS/Bettmann*

resentment among Southern whites. Former Confederates were bitter about losing the war and facing their new prospects. They believed that white Republicans were race traitors, and they objected to the high taxes that Republicans imposed to pay for Reconstruction. Many believed that Reconstruction politics and the politicians who practiced them were corrupt. Though Southerners did not have a defined course, to restore white rule meant white unity. In states with white majorities, convincing white Democrats to vote Democratic was enough to eliminate Republican rule, and by 1871 Democrats had taken back Tennessee, North Carolina, Virginia, and Georgia.

In other states, however, where Republican rule depended on interracial coalitions, white Democrats were determined to convince some people not to vote, often through the violence and intimidation of such terrorist organizations as the Ku Klux Klan, which was founded in late 1865. Often led by the most prominent whites in a community, Klan members concealed themselves in white robes and hoods and often acted at night, beating, lynching, burning, or merely threatening.

Problems existed between the elite planters, who were almost unanimously Democrats, and the Republicans, who represented three main groups: freed people, carpetbaggers (as Northern republicans were called, supposedly because they had come South with all their possessions in carpetbags), and scalawags, those white Southerners who supported Reconstruction. Wherever possible, white Southerners reasserted themselves and their control; forcing blacks to stop voting was their primary tool to regain control of the South. In addition, whites still exercised a great deal of economic control over blacks, who usually had to work for whites. During this period many blacks were told explicitly, "If you vote, don't come back to work."

Another method of increasing the dependence of blacks on whites was sharecropping, in which a farmer provided a tenant land and materials in exchange for a share of the crop. Although sharecropping began as a way to maximize land under cultivation and extend credit in a credit-poor region, it relegated many freed people and poor whites to a state of virtual peonage. Sometimes the conditions in which peonage and sharecropping put blacks were even worse materially than slavery.

## End of Reconstruction

The country had been in an economic depression since around 1873, and white Northern attention turned from the plight of black people in the South to the national economy. State by state, Southern Democrats began to take control of local governments, working to reinstate the conditions of the antebellum South. Southern white supremacists believed, correctly, that Northern whites would no longer enforce Reconstruction policy. They began to subjugate blacks again, reinstating the Black Codes. Many Southern states began to pass segregation or Jim Crow laws.

For many the Compromise of 1877 marks the end of Reconstruction. In the presidential election of 1876, Republican Rutherford B. Hayes and

Democrat Samuel J. Tilden were virtually deadlocked. Tilden won the popular vote, but Republicans had control of South Carolina, Florida, and Louisiana, thus giving them control of the electoral college. Because each party in those three states had competing electors, however, Congress needed to decide the election. Hayes, the incumbent, appointed an electoral commission, which, with one more Republican than Democrat, declared him the winner.

The Democrats and the Republicans had worked out a deal, however, in which the Democrats conceded the White House in exchange for "Home Rule" in the critical three states. In a meeting that, ironically, took place in the black-owned Wormly House Hotel, the Republicans agreed. The remaining military presence in the three states departed, and Republican rule crumbled: the Democrats had won back the South. Though it would take until the 1890s for them to finish the job, the white supremacists were well on their way to what Southerners referred to as "Redemption."

Historians have presented differing interpretations of the legacy of Reconstruction. Many historians now argue that Reconstruction fundamentally changed how the United States defined citizenship, as well as the way in which U.S. citizens perceive the power and role of the federal government. The Bill of Rights, for instance, was created to prevent the federal government from infringing on the rights of the people. The Thirteenth, Fourteenth, and Fifteenth Amendments, however, placed the federal government in the role of protector of citizens' rights. This new concept of federal power and responsibility provided a framework for the Civil Rights Movement, which, a century later, finally realized what Reconstruction had begun.

North America

# Reparations,

**government-administered funding and social programs intended to compensate African Americans for the past injustices of slavery and discrimination.**

In 1988 the United States government issued a national apology to Japanese Americans who had been placed in American internment camps during World War II and paid $20,000 to each victim. This prompted many African Americans to press for similar reparations. Cited as grounds for compensation were the unfulfilled Civil War promise that each slave would receive forty acres and a mule; the millions of dollars of German aid to Jews following the Holocaust; and the U.S. Marshall Plan, which rebuilt Europe after World War II.

Advocates of reparations have proposed packages that range from $700 billion to $4 trillion. Most favor investing the money in education and economic development for the African American community. This proposed use of reparations contrasts with that of some earlier reparation movements, which sought to found an independent black state (in Africa or in the southern United States) or secure pensions for ex-slaves and their descendants.

Some opponents of reparations believe that such payments cannot truly make up for past injustices. Jesse Jackson's aide Frank Watkins draws this conclusion through analogy: "If you have two people running in a mile race around a track and one has a ball and chain tied around his leg for three laps, you can't take the ball and chain off for the final lap and still expect him to win." Although the U.S. government has not yet awarded reparations to African Americans or made a formal apology for nearly 250 years of slavery, many African Americans continue to demand that the nation officially confront and redress its past injustices.

North America

# Revolutionary Action Movement,

**an African American nationalist organization, in operation between 1963 and 1968, that advocated violence to achieve black empowerment.**

During the 1960s some African Americans, frustrated by the government's lack of responsiveness to problems in the black community such as unemployment, overcrowded housing, and police brutality, formulated and organized radical ways of effecting political and social change. This large-scale effort became known, overall, as the Black Power Movement. The Revolutionary Action Movement (RAM), one of the earliest Black Nationalist organizations of the 1960s, asserted that violence was the only way to alter fundamentally the structure of American society.

Through grassroots organizing that included African American history classes, RAM built up a liberation army in Philadelphia and New York. The organization also published a bimonthly magazine, *Black America*, and a free weekly, *RAM Speaks*. Its several hundred members included teachers, students, and businesspeople. Robert Franklin Williams, a former leader of a North Carolina branch of the National Association for the Advancement of Colored People (NAACP), served as RAM's president while in self-imposed exile, first in Cuba, then in China.

Because of RAM's militant ideology and grassroots activism, the United States Federal Bureau of Investigation (FBI) tried to destroy it. Two 1967 FBI raids of RAM headquarters in New York City led to 24 arrests and the seizure of about 130 weapons. Nine RAM members were convicted and imprisoned for conspiring to poison the police force, blow up city hall, and/or murder local and national leaders, including leaders of the NAACP and the National Urban League. RAM leaders not imprisoned either left the country or were placed under surveillance. This resulted in the collapse of the organization in 1968. In spite of the group's short existence, many former RAM members went on to contribute to the formation of other Black Nationalist organizations, such as the Republic of New Africa.

# Robeson, Eslanda Cardozo Goode

(b. December 15, 1896, Washington, D.C.; d. December 13, 1965, New York, N.Y.), African American activist and writer who advocated African independence and managed the singing and acting career of her husband, Paul Robeson.

Eslanda Robeson's father died when she was six years old, and the family moved to New York City. In 1921 she married Paul Robeson. Eslanda ("Essie") Robeson received a B.S. in chemistry from Columbia University and, in 1945, a Ph.D. in anthropology from the Hartford Seminary Foundation. She co-founded the Council for African Affairs in 1941 and participated in many left-wing causes. Robeson was the author of two books: *Paul Robeson, Negro* (1930) and *African Journey* (1945).

# Robeson, Paul

(b. April 9, 1898, Princeton, N. J.; d. January 23, 1976, Philadelphia, Pa.), African American dramatic actor, singer of spirituals, civil rights activist, and political radical.

Paul Robeson was one of the most gifted men of this century. His resonant bass and commanding presence made him a world-renowned singer and actor and proved equally valuable when he spoke out against bigotry and injustice. By the 1930s Robeson was active in a wide range of causes, but his radicalism led to a long period of political harassment that culminated in his blacklisting during the McCarthy era. Although he resumed public performances in the late 1950s, this return to active life was brief. In the 1960s serious health problems sidelined him definitively.

### Family Background and Education

Robeson's father, William Drew Robeson, was a North Carolina slave who escaped to freedom at age 15, graduated from college, and entered the ministry. Robeson's mother was Maria Louisa Bustill, a teacher and member of one of Philadelphia's leading black families. The youngest of five children, Robeson was only six years old when his mother died. His father set high expectations for his children and sent them to high school in the neighboring town of Somerville, New Jersey, because Princeton's segregated system offered no secondary education for blacks.

In 1915 Robeson won a scholarship to Rutgers College, where he excelled academically, becoming a junior-year Phi Beta Kappa, a champion debater, and class valedictorian. He was equally triumphant on the athletic field, where his imposing 1.89 m (6 ft 2 in), 86 kg- (190 lb-) frame served him well. Twice named an All-American in football, Robeson also lettered in baseball, basketball, and track. He graduated in 1919. Two years later, while a student at Columbia University Law School, he married Eslanda Goode. Paul and Essie Robeson's relationship would be a rocky one, but her assertiveness and gift for organization proved vital to his career. Their only son, Paul Robeson Jr., was born in 1927. In 1923, after earning his law degree and joining an otherwise all-white firm, Robeson decided to leave the legal profession. He had found his true calling as a performing artist.

## Stage, Concert, and Film Career

While in law school Robeson had occasionally taken parts in amateur the-atrical productions, leading in 1922 to his first professional roles—a lead in the short-lived Broadway play *Taboo* and as a replacement cast member in Eubie Blake and Noble Sissle's pioneering all-black musical, *Shuffle Along.* Robeson's career-making opportunity came when he was asked to join the Provincetown Players, an influential Greenwich Village theater company that included the playwright Eugene O'Neill among its three associate directors. In 1924 Robeson appeared in a revival of O'Neill's *The Emperor Jones* and premiered in the playwright's *All God's Chillun Got Wings.* In reviewing the latter, the American Mercury drama critic George Jean Nathan praised Robeson as "one of the most thoroughly eloquent, impres-sive, and convincing actors that I have looked at and listened to in almost twenty years of professional theater-going." Soon Robeson was offered other roles, most notably in a 1930 London production of *Othello* opposite Peggy Ashcroft; in a 1932 Broadway revival of Oscar Hammerstein II and Jerome Kern's musical, *Show-boat*, which featured Robeson's dramatic rendition of *Ol' Man River*; and in a long-running, criti-cally acclaimed 1943 production of *Othello* on Broadway.

Singer, actor, and activist Paul Robeson played Othello in 1943 on Broadway. Here Robeson rehearses his part. *CORBIS/Hulton-Deutsch Collection*

Equally significant were Robeson's musical contributions. Robeson and his longtime pianist and arranger Lawrence Brown played a pivotal role in bringing spirituals into the classical music repertory. Robeson's 1925 recital at the Greenwich Village Theater was the first in which a black soloist sang an entire program of spirituals. The concert garnered superlative reviews, propelling Robeson into a new career as a concert singer and inspiring similar recitals by other black artists.

Robeson also signed a recording contract with the Victor Talking Machine Company, which released his first recorded spirituals later that same year. Although Robeson would sing a wide range of material—including sentimental popular tunes, work songs, political ballads, and folk music from many different lands—he made his mark as an interpreter of spirituals.

During the 1930s Robeson also emerged as a film star. His first role was in the black director Oscar Micheaux's *Body and Soul* (1925), but he was most active on the screen between 1933 and 1942, a period in which he was prominently featured in Hollywood versions of *The Emperor Jones* (1933) and *Show Boat* (1936), *Tales of Manhattan* (1942), and several British films. Robeson, however, was dissatisfied with his work in motion pictures. He came to believe that—with the exceptions of his roles in *Song of Freedom* (1936) and *The Proud Valley* (1940)—his characters reflected current racial stereotypes, or what Robeson derided as "Stepin Fetchit comics and savages with leopard skin and spear." Working in films like *Sanders of the River* (1935), which sang the praises of British imperialism, became particularly distasteful as Robeson discovered his African heritage.

### His Discovery of Africa

During the 1930s Robeson made London his primary residence, and "it was there," he recalled, "that I 'discovered' Africa." In 1933 he undertook the study of several African languages at the University of London. He also took part in activities sponsored by the West African Students Union and became acquainted with future African leaders Jomo Kenyatta of Kenya and Nnamdi Azikiwe of Nigeria. Robeson began to stress the positive aspects of African life. African culture, he argued, was more spiritual and more grounded in community than that of Europe or white America. Long before the Black Power Movement, he stressed the need to be "proud of being black . . . . For no one respects a man who does not respect himself."

Unlike many American blacks, who saw their role as one of helping to "uplift" and modernize the African people, Robeson thought it imperative that the American-born regain their own African roots. He rejected the assimilationism then prevalent among the black elite, insisting that "in every black man flows the rhythm of Africa." Indeed, he wrote, "I came to consider that I was an African." Yet Robeson clearly saw this "return to Africa" as a spiritual, rather than a literal journey. He rejected separatism no less than assimilationism and never abandoned his vision of an integrated society. Instead he fashioned a world-view that anchored cultural diversity in universal values, among which the most important was a faith in human solidarity that lay at the heart of his encounter with socialism.

### Socialism and Political Activism

During the 1930s Robeson began reading about socialism and taking part in political discussions with various activists and scholars, including C. L. R. James, the radical Caribbean theorist; William L. Patterson, a black Communist and American trade unionist; and the American anarchist Emma

Goldman. In 1934 Robeson made the first of many visits to the Soviet Union. He was impressed by the seeming lack of racial prejudice in the USSR and by the Soviet Constitution, which guaranteed citizens equality, "irrespective of their nationality or race." About the same time Robeson became active in various radical causes. In England he took part in labor and peace rallies, Save China assemblies, and meetings to protest British colonialism in Jamaica. He spoke at a London rally for India's Jawaharlal Nehru, performed at benefit concerts for the Spanish Republic, and in 1938 traveled there to sing for republican troops.

In 1939 Paul and Essie Robeson returned to the United States, where he continued to be politically active. Robeson sang the egalitarian *Ballad for Americans* over national radio late that year and recorded a best-selling version of the song for Victor. He supported the United Auto Workers and other unions of the Congress of Industrial Organizations (CIO); he served on the board of the new Negro Playwrights' Company; and he became chairman of the Council on African Affairs, an American-based organization that provided information on African struggles for freedom and lobbied African concerns. During World War II Robeson committed his prodigious energies in support of the Allied war effort and in protests against the poll tax, the segregation of America's armed forces, and the segregated venues for some of his own concerts. After the war Robeson, W. E. B. Du Bois, and Bartley Crum, a liberal white lawyer, called for a national conference to secure a federal antilynching law. Robeson also protested the anti-labor Taft-Hartley Act and campaigned for the Progressive Party in the 1948 election. Robeson highlighted the black struggle for equality in all his campaign speeches, even those he delivered—at considerable risk—in the Deep South.

## Difficulties During the Cold War Era

However, as the United States entered the cold war, Robeson found himself increasingly isolated. Although he was not in fact a member of the Communist Party, he had close ties to many in the party's leadership, and he staunchly defended the Soviet Union despite the 1939 Nazi-Soviet Pact and Nikita Khrushchev's 1956 revelations about Joseph Stalin's purges. The Federal Bureau of Investigation (FBI) placed Robeson under surveillance as early as 1941 and compiled a massive dossier on his activities. Yet it seems clear that he was targeted as much for his militancy on civil rights issues as for his alleged Communism. The real turning point for Robeson came in 1949 when the Associated Press, in reporting his criticisms of the United States at a Paris peace conference, quoted him as saying: "It is unthinkable that American Negroes would go to war on behalf of those who have oppressed us for generations against a country [the Soviet Union] which in one generation has raised our people to the full dignity of mankind."

Most Americans were outraged. The House Committee on Un-American Activities (HUAC) announced that it would hold hearings to investigate Robeson and the loyalty of black Americans. White liberals and the black establishment, offended by his growing stridency and fearful of the taint of Communism, distanced themselves from him. Even one-time friends, such as Walter White, executive director of the National Association for the Advancement of Colored People, and Max Yergan, former executive director of the Council on African Affairs, denounced his remarks.

Later that year a mob of young white men disrupted an outdoor Robeson concert near Peekskill, New York, attacking concertgoers and sending a dozen to the hospital. Robeson himself narrowly escaped injury. A rescheduled concert, guarded by members of several left-wing CIO unions, came off without incident, but at its conclusion the audience found itself facing a gauntlet of enraged, rock-throwing locals. State and local police did little to restrain the attackers; indeed many joined the mob. But a grand jury investigation wrote off the violence as having been provoked by Robeson's previous unpatriotic remarks.

Ultimately, Robeson was silenced, but doing so required the combined efforts of the black establishment—including leaders of the fledgling Civil Rights Movement—white liberals, the entertainment industry, and the government. In 1950 the State Department rescinded Robeson's passport, preventing him from performing or traveling abroad. At home he found himself blacklisted by Broadway and Hollywood, by concert halls and record companies, radio, and television. His only opportunities to perform were at small affairs organized by a dwindling core of radicals and at a few black churches like Harlem's Mother African Methodist Episcopal Zion Church, whose pastor was Robeson's brother, Rev. Benjamin C. Robeson. Denied a public voice, Robeson struggled mightily to vindicate himself and win back his freedom of travel. In his 1956 testimony before HUAC, Robeson offered a powerful indictment of America's continuing racial injustice, but he steadfastly refused to condemn the Soviet Union, to provide the names of American Communists, or to answer whether he was a party member, a question that he viewed as a violation of his Constitutional rights. In 1957, after a seven-year delay, the State Department finally granted him a hearing on the revocation of his passport. The result was a six-hour grilling, but no change in the government's policy.

### The Final Years

Robeson fought his lonely battle at great personal cost. In 1955 he began to show the first clear signs of the emotional difficulties—probably bipolar disorder, a condition once known as manic-depression—that would eventually halt his public activities. It is ironic that he should pay so dearly for his alleged Communism. In truth, what lay at the heart of Robeson's political convictions was not Marxism so much as an empathy for African culture and an identification with common people, the poor, and the oppressed.

By the end of the decade the worst years of the cold war had passed, and Robeson's troubles began to ease. In 1958 he gave his first commercial concerts in several years, appearing in Chicago, Portland, and several California cities. He published *Here I Stand*, a trenchant autobiography written with Lloyd Brown. And a Supreme Court decision once again permitted him to travel abroad. The next few years were busy ones, with American concerts and recording sessions for Vanguard; concert tours of Europe, Australia, and New Zealand; visits to the Soviet Union; and in 1959 another London production of *Othello*. But on March 27, 1961, Robeson suffered a nervous breakdown and attempted suicide. For the rest of his life he would struggle with severe depression, and his public appearances would be extremely rare. Robeson dropped out of public awareness and was largely ignored by the leadership of the Civil Rights Movement, except for the militant young leaders of the Student Nonviolent Coordinating Committee (SNCC). At a gala celebration for his 67th birthday, Robeson was deeply moved when keynote speaker John Lewis, then the chairman of SNCC, proclaimed, "We of SNCC are Paul Robeson's spiritual children. We too have rejected gradualism and moderation." Yet there was more to Robeson than this. Beneath his militancy—and intertwined with it—was a profound compassion and a deep bond with Africa best seen in a passage he wrote in 1936: "I am a singer and an actor. I am primarily an artist. Had I been born in Africa, I would have belonged, I hope, to that family which sings and chants the glories and legends of the tribe. I would have liked in my mature years to have been a wise elder, for I worship wisdom and knowledge of the ways of men."

Robeson's final public appearance was at a 1966 benefit dinner for SNCC.

North America

# Robinson, JoAnn Gibson

(b. April 17, 1912, Culloden, Ga.), African American civil rights activist; a leader in the Montgomery Bus Boycott.

JoAnn Robinson attended Fort Valley State College and earned an M.A. in English from Atlanta University in 1948, after which she taught at Alabama State College in Montgomery. It was in Montgomery that she became active in the Civil Rights Movement.

Robinson became the president of the Women's Political Council (WPC), an organization composed mainly of middle-class black women and committed to increasing African American participation in civic affairs. The WPC challenged Montgomery's policy of segregated seating on public transportation by organizing a successful bus boycott after Rosa Parks's arrest for violating segregation laws in 1955. Robinson left Alabama State College in 1960 and taught English in Los Angeles until retiring in 1976.

Robinson's 1987 memoir, *The Montgomery Bus Boycott and the Women Who Started It*, was awarded special acclaim by the Southern Association for Women's Historians. Her book emphasized the important role women played in the daily organization and the planned activities of the Civil Rights Movement.

# Robinson, Ruby Doris Smith

(b. April 25, 1942, Atlanta, Ga.; d. October 7, 1967, Atlanta, Ga.), American civil rights activist and a founder of the Student Nonviolent Coordinating Committee (SNCC).

Ruby Doris Smith Robinson was inspired as a teenager by media images of the Montgomery bus boycott that occurred in 1955–1956. After joining the Civil Rights Movement, Robinson was arrested for the first time as part of a lunch counter desegregation sit-in in 1959 while she was a sophomore at Spelman College in Atlanta. In 1960 she became one of the founding members of the Student Nonviolent Coordinating Committee (SNCC).

Robinson was one of the original Freedom Riders, and she helped create SNCC's "jail, no bail" policy, a strategy to fill Southern jails with protesters and thus keep public attention on the movement. In 1966 Robinson became SNCC's first (and only) female executive secretary. She left SNCC in early 1967, and died of leukemia that October.

# Rosewood Case,

one of the worst race riots in American history, in which hundreds of angry whites killed an undetermined number of blacks and burned down their entire Florida community.

In 1922 Rosewood, Florida, was a small, predominantly black town. During the winter of 1922 two events in the vicinity of Rosewood aggravated local race relations: the murder of a white schoolteacher in nearby Perry, which led to the murder of three blacks, and a Ku Klux Klan rally in Gainesville on New Year's Eve.

On New Year's Day of 1923, Fannie Taylor, a young white woman living in Sumner, claimed that a black man sexually assaulted her in her home. A small group of whites began searching for a recently escaped black convict named Jesse Hunter, whom they believed to be responsible. They incarcerated one suspected accomplice, Aaron Carrier, and lynched another, Sam Carter. The men then targeted Aaron's cousin Sylvester Carrier, a fur trapper and private music instructor who was rumored to be harboring Jesse Hunter.

A group of 20 to 30 white men came to Sylvester Carrier's house to confront him. They shot his dog, and when his mother, Sarah, stepped outside to talk with the men, they shot her. Carrier killed two men and wounded four in the shootout that ensued. After the men left, the women and children, who prior to this had gathered in Carrier's house for protection, fled to the swamp where the majority of Rosewood's residents had already sought refuge.

The white men returned to Carrier's house the following evening. After a brief shootout they entered the house, found the bodies of Sarah Carrier and a black man whom they believed to be Sylvester Carrier, and set the residence on fire. The men then proceeded on a rampage through Rosewood, torching other buildings and slaughtering animals. They were joined by a mob of approximately 200 whites who converged on Rosewood after finding out that a black man had killed two whites.

That night two local white train conductors, John and William Bryce, who knew all of Rosewood's residents, picked up the black women and children and took them to Gainesville. John Wright, a white general-store owner who hid a number of black women and children in his home during the riot, planned and helped carry out this evacuation effort. The African Americans who escaped by foot headed for Gainesville or for other cities in the northern United States.

By the end of the weekend all of Rosewood, except the Wright house and general store, was leveled. Although the state of Florida claimed that only eight people died in the Rosewood riot—two whites and six blacks—survivors' testimonies suggest that more African Americans perished. No one was charged with the Rosewood murders. After the riot the town was deserted, and even blacks living in surrounding communities moved out.

It is unclear what became of Jesse Hunter. Residents of nearby Cedar Key claimed that he was captured and killed after the massacre. The descendants of the Carrier family, however, contend that Jesse Hunter was not the man who had attacked Taylor. Philomena Carrier, who had been working with her grandmother Sarah Carrier at Fannie Taylor's house at the time of the alleged sexual assault, claimed that the man responsible was a white railroad engineer. She said that the man had come to see Taylor the morning of January 1 after her husband left for work. After an argument between them erupted, Philomena witnessed the man exit the back door and jog down the road toward Rosewood.

The Carriers' descendants maintain that the man was a Mason who persuaded Aaron Carrier, a member of Rosewood's black Masonic lodge, to help him escape by appealing to the society's code requiring members to help one another regardless of race. Carrier in turn persuaded another black Mason, Sam Carter, one of the few men in Rosewood with a wagon, to pick up the white man at Carrier's house and drop him off in the swamp, where he disappeared without a trace.

Though the Rosewood riot received national coverage in the *New York Times* and *Washington Post* as it unfolded, it was neglected by historians. Survivors of Rosewood did not come forward to tell their stories because of the shame they felt for having been connected with the riot and their fear of being persecuted or killed. In 1993 the Florida Department of Law Enforcement conducted an investigation into the case, which led to the drafting of a bill to compensate the survivors of the massacre.

After an extended debate and several hearings, the Rosewood Bill, which awarded $150,000 to each of the riot's nine eligible black survivors, was passed in April 1994. In spite of the state's financial compensation, the survivors remained frightened. When asked if he would go back to

Rosewood, survivor Wilson Hall said, "No, . . . They still don't want me down there."

The director John Singleton, best known for his film *Boyz 'N the Hood*, released a fictionalized account of the massacre, called *Rosewood* and based on survivors' testimony, in 1997.

North America

# Ruffin, Josephine Saint Pierre

(b. 1842, Boston, Mass.; d. March 13, 1924, Boston, Mass.), African American journalist, civic leader, civil rights activist, and suffragist.

Josephine Saint Pierre Ruffin's long career of humanitarian work began during the Civil War, when she and her husband George recruited soldiers for the Fifty-fourth and Fifty-fifth Colored Regiments of Massachusetts. She was active in integrated and African American women's clubs and charitable organizations, including the Associated Charities of Boston and the Massachusetts State Federation of Women's Clubs. In 1893 she founded and was president of the Women's Era Club (WEC) and edited its newspaper, the *Women's Era*, the first newspaper to be owned, managed, and published by African American women.

In 1895, in response to a Missouri editor's assertions that African American women were without virtue, Ruffin organized a national convention of African American women's clubs. Twenty clubs met and formed the National Federation of Afro-American Women. In 1896 they merged with the National Association of Colored Women.

Resistance to integrated clubs led to the "Ruffin Incident" in 1900 at the General Federation of Women's Clubs' biennial meeting in Milwaukee. When the executive board learned that the WEC's members were African Americans, it refused to seat Ruffin, who then refused to leave. Although Northern and Midwestern delegates backed Ruffin, the Southern contingent successfully blocked her participation.

After the WEC disbanded in 1903, Ruffin helped found the Association for the Promotion of Child Training in the South and the first branch of the National Association for the Advancement of Colored People in Boston.

North America

# Rustin, Bayard

(b. March 17, 1910, West Chester, Pa.; d. August 24, 1987, New York, N.Y.), African American civil rights leader and political organizer.

Bayard Rustin was born into a Quaker family, and the pacifism he learned from the Society of Friends remained with him his entire life. After a comfortable childhood in West Chester, Pennsylvania, he studied at West Chester State College. Before graduating, he moved to Harlem during the

1930s and began studying at City College, while singing in local clubs with African American folk artists Josh White and Huddie Ledbetter. Attracted to the Young Communist League's stance on race issues, Rustin joined the group in 1936 and worked as an organizer until 1941, when he quit the party.

However, his resistance to the American government continued throughout 1941. Rustin was asked by A. Philip Randolph to help plan a 1941 march on Washington, D.C., to protest discrimination in defense industries. The march was called off when President Roosevelt made concessions. During World War II Rustin traveled to California to help interned Japanese Americans protect their property. As a pacifist Rustin spent two and a half years in prison for refusing to serve in the military.

Rustin's involvement in the Fellowship of Reconciliation, a radical pacifist movement, connected him to the establishment of the New York branch of the Congress of Racial Equality. Throughout the 1940s and 1950s he led weekend seminars on nonviolent action for both groups. Rustin helped organize the Montgomery Bus Boycott in 1955, and he was also involved in the formation of the Southern Christian Leadership Conference. In August 1963 he served as the coordinator of the March on Washington, an event attended by 200,000 people. Rustin was arrested 23 times in his lifetime, but he continued to believe that racial equality should be pursued through nonviolent means.

# S

## Sanchez, Sonia

**(b. September 9, 1934, Birmingham, Ala.), African American writer, activist, and educator who focuses on black women's struggle with racism.**

Born Wilsonia Driver, Sonia Sanchez moved with her family to Harlem when she was a young girl. She received a B.A. in 1955 from Hunter College in New York City and spent the next year studying poetry at New York University.

An activist associated first with the Congress of Racial Equality, Sanchez was further radicalized by Malcolm X and the Nation of Islam in the early 1970s. Her first volume of poetry, *Homecoming*, appeared in 1969, after several years of publishing in journals with other Black Nationalist poets such as Larry Neal and LeRoi Jones (Amiri Baraka). Sanchez's poems from this period were experimental and irreverent in style, content, and presentation. She became famous for bravura spoken-word performances that captured the cadences of African American speech. From 1965 to 1969 she taught in San Francisco and was actively involved in the founding of a controversial black studies program at San Francisco State University.

Sanchez left the Nation of Islam in the early 1970s to protest the organization's treatment of women. Her poetry and activism since have highlighted black women's struggle with racism from the dominant culture and within the black community. Her best-known collections of poetry are *A Blues Book for Blue Black Magical Women* (1973), a spiritual autobiography, and *homegirls and handgrenades* (1984), for which she earned an American Book Award in 1985. In addition to being a poet, Sanchez is an accomplished playwright, the author of children's books, and the mother of three. More recently, Sanchez has taught creative writing and black literature at Temple University in Philadelphia.

# Scottsboro Case,

an international cause célèbre during the 1930s in which nine young black men were accused of raping two white women in Alabama.

The Scottsboro case began in 1931 when two white women falsely accused nine young African Americans of rape. Throughout the world of the 1930s the Scottsboro defendants came to symbolize the racism and injustice of the American South. In their initial trials the defendants received what critics described as a "legal lynching." But the assistance of the Communist Party of the United States of America (CPUSA) gave the young men a second chance, and the ensuing struggle became one of the great civil rights cases of the twentieth century.

After several retrials, worldwide protests, massive publicity, and two landmark rulings by the Supreme Court of the United States, only four of the men gained their freedom, after having spent six years in jail. Full vindication did not come until 1976, when Alabama governor George Wallace pardoned all nine "Scottsboro boys." At that time only one of the defendants, Clarence Norris, was still alive to hear the news.

On March 25, 1931, after several young white men complained that a "bunch of Negroes" had thrown them off a freight train, a posse in Paint Rock, Alabama, searched the train and arrested nine black males. The posse also discovered two white females wearing men's caps and overalls. Within an hour the young blacks and both women were taken to Scottsboro, the seat of Jackson County. The women were examined by two physicians, who found evidence of sexual activity, though probably not within the previous twelve hours, and no signs of rape. The young men—Norris, Olen Montgomery, Haywood Patterson, Ozie Powell, Willie Roberson, Charlie Weems, Eugene Williams, and Andrew and Leroy Wright—were jailed. At 20 years of age, Weems was the oldest; the youngest, Leroy Wright, was 13.

Although the women initially denied that any assault had taken place, under the pressure of a lynch mob that filled the streets that evening and after repeated goading by a local prosecutor, they conceded that they had been raped by the black youths. Although later investigation revealed that the women were "notorious prostitutes" with prior arrest records on a variety of charges, nothing could shake the Southern ethos that made them symbols of endangered "white Southern womanhood."

During their trials the nine men received inadequate legal counsel. They were given no witness preparation before entering the courtroom, and in none of the cases did their court-appointed attorneys make closing arguments to the jury. As was customary, each jury was composed only of white men. The trials were concluded in four days with eight guilty verdicts and eight sentences of death. In the case of Leroy Wright, the youngest defendant, the jury could not reach agreement. Jurors had no doubt as to his guilt, but 11 insisted on nothing less than death, although the state had asked only for life imprisonment. The judge reluctantly declared a mistrial.

Sentencing eight men to death on a single day for the same crime was

Protesters pass by the White House on their way to deliver a petition to the president urging the release of the Scottsboro Nine, a group of black men falsely accused of rape.
*CORBIS/Underwood & Underwood*

"without parallel in the history of the nation," the *Birmingham Age-Herald* observed in concluding its trial coverage. But the Scottsboro case was far from over. Even as the trials were under way, the judge received a telegram from the Inter-national Labor Defense (ILD), a Communist-front legal organization, demanding a change of venue. The Communist Party decided to take up the young men's defense on the basis of reports from two party representatives, one black and one white, who had been sent to observe the trials. The party's enthusiastic involvement transformed what had essentially been a local matter into a cause of national importance.

In contrast, the National Association for the Advancement of Colored People (NAACP) remained aloof. Protective of its reputation, the NAACP was unwilling to aid a group of poor black hoboes unless it was certain of their innocence. Only after the case reached international proportions did the organization offer financial assistance to the ILD. Initially, NAACP representatives had warned the defendants that the Communists were only interested in them for propaganda purposes.

Communist organizing efforts made the Scottsboro case an international cause célèbre, as well as one of the decade's top news stories. The effectiveness of the party's response significantly increased its stature among Depression-era African Americans. Communist-sponsored protests took place in many Northern cities as well as in London, Moscow, and elsewhere around the world. These protests garnered invaluable publicity for CPUSA itself, but in the main its efforts drew attention to the plight of the defendants. In so doing, the party challenged the deeper symbolism of the Scottsboro case, particularly by confronting the virtual equation of "black man" and "rapist."

At the outset public understanding of the case had been tainted by white visions of black sexual depravity and by a presumption of the defendants' guilt. The party worked to humanize the image of the nine men, especially through rallies and marches that featured their mothers. It inspired sympathetic news stories about the defendants during their lengthy incarceration. As a result of this dogged publicity work, the Scottsboro case came to be seen as a great miscarriage of justice, and its defendants were increasingly regarded as innocent victims of Southern racism. At the same time the party refused to limit itself to symbolic action; it also mounted an aggressive legal defense.

The ILD provided experienced attorneys to aid in the young men's defense, the most important of whom was the distinguished lawyer Samuel Leibowitz. Over the next five years Leibowitz defended the Scottsboro Nine a total of five times. The ILD won the defendants retrials as a result of its successful appeal to the United States Supreme Court. The Court ruled, in *Powell v. Alabama* (1932), that defendants being tried for capital crimes must receive more than a perfunctory or *pro forma* defense. Following a change of venue, the trials opened in Decatur, Alabama, before Judge James E. Horton.

In Decatur, Ruby Bates renounced her previous testimony against the nine defendants. Indeed, during 1933 and 1934 she appeared at Communist-organized Scottsboro rallies, posed in photographs with the Scottsboro mothers, and joined 3,000 protesters in a march to the White House seeking the defendants' release from prison. Nonetheless, the first jury, in the trial of Patterson, again returned a verdict of guilty. Convinced that Patterson and the other defendants were innocent, Judge Horton set the verdict aside and ordered new trials. As a result, however, Horton was defeated in the May 1934 primary election and replaced by a man far more friendly to the prosecution.

The ILD once more made a successful appeal to the Supreme Court, this time challenging the systematic exclusion of blacks from Alabama jury rolls. In *Norris v. Alabama* (1935), Chief Justice Charles Evans Hughes ruled that the exclusion of African Americans from jury service did in fact deprive black defendants of equal protection under the law, as guaranteed by the Fourteenth Amendment. In essence, the Court remanded the case back to the state for retrial. Thus the Scottsboro Nine returned to the courtroom yet again. By this point a vast amount of testimony had revealed much more than a reasonable doubt as to the young men's guilt.

In 1936, as part of the CPUSA's coalition-oriented Popular Front strategy, the ILD relinquished its primary role in the case to a broader group that included the NAACP, the Socialist Party's League for Industrial Democracy, the American Civil Liberties Union, and the Methodist Federation for Social Service. Although Leibowitz continued as the defendants' counsel, the state of Alabama used the seeming displacement of the Communists as a pretext for seeking a legal compromise.

In the final set of trials that began in 1937, the state dropped all charges against the four youngest defendants—Leroy Wright, Montgomery, Roberson, and Williams. The others were duly convicted, but rather than the death penalty they received sentences ranging from 20 years to life. Norris, Powell, Patterson, Weems, and Andrew Wright gained their freedom piecemeal between 1943 and 1950. All told, the nine men spent more than 100 years in the jails and penitentiaries of Alabama.

# Seale, Bobby

(b. October 22, 1936, Dallas, Tex.), political and social activist of the 1960s; cofounder of the militant Black Panther Party.

Bobby Seale, the son of George and Thelma Seale, moved to California with his family at age ten. He entered the United States Air Force at age 18 and served as an aircraft-sheet mechanic. Three years later he was dishonorably discharged for insubordination and absence without leave. In 1961 he was admitted to Merritt College in Oakland, California.

While at Merritt, Seale became a member of the Afro-American Association in Oakland. Through this militant organization, Seale met and befriended fellow student Huey Newton. Together, Newton and Seale formed the Soul Students Advisory Committee at Merritt. In 1966 the two created the Black Panther Party, whose political platform called for equality of opportunity for African Americans and an end to police brutality against black people.

Seale was arrested in 1968 for his participation in anti-Vietnam War demonstrations at the Democratic National Convention in Chicago, and spent two years in jail. He was arrested a second time in 1972 for the murder of suspected Black Panther informer Alex Rackley, but the charges against him were dropped. In 1973 he made an unsuccessful bid for the office of mayor of Oakland, and in 1974 he resigned as chairman of the Black Panther Party. In the 1980s Seale became involved in an organization called Youth Employment Strategies. He published two autobiographies, *Seize the Time: The Story of the Black Panther Party and Huey P. Newton* in 1970 and *A Lonely Rage* in 1978.

# Seattle, Washington,

American city whose black population long endured mixed messages of racial tolerance in public and private life.

Very few blacks lived in Seattle during the city's first 80 years. African Americans did not arrive in Seattle until 1858, and in 1900 fewer than 400 African Americans lived there. Even by World War II, the population remained below 4,000. As a result, Seattle whites often took unwarranted pride in their city's racial climate. In an era when other American cities faced massive immigration, racial tension, and ghettoization, Seattle seemed a stable and racially reconciled town.

Although African Americans in Seattle lived where they pleased, voted freely, and shared public transit with whites, they faced persistent economic discrimination. White people cornered blacks into unskilled labor and domestic servitude, often presuming that African Americans accepted such work because of inbred servility. In truth, the small size of the black community left it powerless to voice dissent, and this silence perpetuated the oppressive stereotypes of white employers.

World War II transformed Seattle. In 1942 the War Manpower Commission and the Civil Service Commission began recruiting African Americans from across the nation to work in the industries of the northwest coast. During the war the black population of Seattle grew from about 4,000 to 16,000. Seattle's shipyards, the Boeing Aircraft Company, and numerous nonmilitary government jobs readily employed newcomers.

Unlike companies that faltered after the wartime boom, Boeing's success continued throughout the century. While Boeing's demand for labor remained high, however, mass immigration exceeded the company's needs, causing poverty, overcrowding, and residential segregation. Seattle's predominantly black Central District grew, schools began to reflect the segregated composition of neighborhoods, and whites elbowed blacks out of white neighborhoods. As a result, African Americans in Seattle embraced the Civil Rights Movement in the 1960s. Though violence never erupted from protests in Seattle as it did in other cities, minor skirmishes between activists and police disrupted many businesses in 1967 and 1968.

In the 1970s and 1980s Seattle's growing financial services and budding computer industry joined Boeing as major employers of blacks. The prospering economy and growing African American population helped to support black politicians. In 1989 Norman Rice was elected the city's first black mayor with significant support from Seattle whites. In the 1990s Seattle began to reflect the kind of tolerance and equality that had falsely characterized the first half of its history.

North America

# Segregation in the United States,

systematic separation of blacks and whites that circumscribed African American life in much of the country. The most thorough going system of racial segregation and disfranchisement was that found in the South and known as Jim Crow.

North America

# Shabazz, Hajj Bahiyah Betty

(1936–1997), American educator and widow of black leader Malcolm X who became an international black cultural icon symbolizing the growing influence of Malcolm's name and nationalist message.

There is some uncertainty about Betty Shabazz's origins and early life. Reportedly the daughter of Shelman Sandlin and a woman named Sanders, she was born Betty Sanders and grew up as a foster child in the Detroit, Michigan, home of a black family named Malloy. As a youth she was active in her local African Methodist Episcopal Church. She briefly attended Tuskegee Institute in Alabama, but moved to New York City to escape Southern racism and to study at the Brooklyn States Hospital School of Nursing. During her junior year she attended the Nation of Islam's Temple No. 7 in Harlem. There she taught a women's health and hygiene class and was noticed by Malcolm X, who was a minister at the temple. He proposed by telephone from Detroit, and they eloped and were married in 1958.

Shabazz converted to Islam and became a dutiful Muslim wife. She left Malcolm temporarily on several occasions, however, presumably over disagreements caused by his extensive travel schedule as a spokesman for the Nation of Islam. They became the parents of six daughters, Attallah, Qubilah, Ilyasah, Gamilah, Malaak, and Malikah. Shabazz was pregnant with the twins Malaak and Malikah when Malcolm was assassinated in the Audubon Ballroom in New York City on February 21, 1965, an event she and her other children witnessed.

After Malcolm's death Shabazz raised her children and continued her education, which culminated in a Ph.D. in educational administration from the University of Massachusetts in 1975. She taught health sciences and then became head of public relations at Medgar Evers College in Brooklyn. She left the Nation of Islam at Malcolm's death, but took the hajj, the sacred Islamic pilgrimage to Mecca, in Saudi Arabia, and considered herself a Sunni Muslim. She believed that Malcolm had been murdered by the Nation and said so in interviews until a public reconciliation in 1995 with Louis Farrakhan, the head of the Nation of Islam and a rival of Malcolm's at the time of his assassination.

Her reconciliation with Farrakhan helped to establish his legitimacy in the black community, but Shabazz's presence aided even more in the rehabilitation of Malcolm X himself. During the Civil Rights Movement Malcolm was considered by many blacks and whites to be a nationalist, a separatist, even a racist. After his death, however, Malcolm's ideas took on increasing authority as integration failed to solve the crisis of the black urban underclass. Betty Shabazz's existence helped keep Malcolm's name and message fresh, although she personally espoused the more accommodationist self-help doctrine of Booker T. Washington, founder of Tuskegee Institute. She was also active in black social organizations such as the Links, Delta Sigma Theta, and Jack and Jill of America.

On June 1, 1997, Betty Shabazz's only grandson, 12-year-old Malcolm Shabazz, set fire to her apartment in Yonkers, New York. A troubled child, he was staying with his grandmother because his mother, Qubilah, had problems of her own, including substance abuse and involvement in a plot to kill Farrakhan. In the fire Shabazz received third-degree burns over 95 percent of her body, and she died three weeks later. Shabazz was widely honored at her death, especially by black women, in part because the once-reviled Malcolm X had now become a cultural hero, but primarily because her own life had come to exemplify extraordinary courage and perseverance in the face of great difficulties.

# Sharpton, Alfred (Al), Jr.

(b. October 3, 1954, Brooklyn, N.Y.), African American Pentecostal minister, controversial civil rights activist, and first African American candidate for New York State Senate.

Rev. Al Sharpton made a reputation as a leader who does not shy away from controversy. Some observers have criticized him as an attention-seeking self-promoter, but none can discount his long career of activism and protest on behalf of African Americans and especially of the poor. In the pulpit at age 4, Sharpton—known as "the Wonderboy"—spent his early years as a sensation on the Pentecostal preaching circuit. For years he traveled to various Pentecostal churches, including a tour with famed gospel music performer Mahalia Jackson.

In 1969 Rev. Jesse Jackson chose Sharpton as youth director of Operation Breadbasket, during which Sharpton organized protest demonstrations and boycotts to pressure businesses to hire more minority employees. At around the same time, Sharpton began his own organization, the National Youth Movement, and met longtime friend and mentor, musician James Brown. From 1973 to the early 1980s, in addition to his civil rights activism, Sharpton served as one of Brown's tour managers. Sharpton's wife, Kathy Jordan-Sharpton, is a gospel singer and former back-up vocalist for Brown. The couple have two daughters, Dominique and Ashley.

Although he had entered politics in 1978 with an unsuccessful run for the new York state senate, Rev. Sharpton did not gain wide recognition until 1985, with his public statements in the case of Bernard Goetz, a white man who shot four young black men on the New York subway, permanently disabling one of them. Sharpton continued to speak out in 1986, when he called for a special prosecutor in the aftermath of the Howard Beach racial incident, in which a crowd of whites chased a black man named Michael Griffiths onto a highway where he was struck and killed by a passing car. Two years later Sharpton served as adviser to Tawana Brawley, a black teenager who claimed that she had been abducted and raped by three white police officers. Although a grand jury ultimately concluded that her accusations were a hoax, Sharpton continues to maintain that the officers are guilty. In 1989 Rev. Sharpton played a prominent role in the protests that followed the shooting death of Yusef Hawkins, a black youth who encountered a white mob in the Bensonhurst section of New York City.

Sharpton garnered both praise and criticism for his unceasing activism. His National Youth Movement faced charges of fraud and Sharpton was stung by allegations that he was an informant for the Federal Bureau of Investigation (FBI). Still, Sharpton's mastery at organizing demonstrations and delivering newsworthy sound bites quickly made him a fixture in New York City's tumultuous local politics. During the 1990s he began attempting to refine and tone down his public image, although he remained a controversial figure. As he prepared to lead a demonstration in

1991, Sharpton was attacked and stabbed by Michael Riccardi, a white resident of Bensonhurst.

In 1990 Sharpton served a 15-day sentence for disorderly conduct, and on March 9, 1993, he was remanded to Rikers Island to begin a 45-day sentence incurred as a result of a demonstration that took place in the late 1980s. Sharpton took his difficulties in stride. "This is the first time since I was 17," he told the *New York Post*, "that James Brown will play New York without me there."

After failed bids for the United States Senate in 1992 and 1994, in 1997 Sharpton made an impressive showing in the city's Democratic Mayoral primary, winning 32 percent of the vote. While recasting his public persona, Sharpton insisted that fundamentally he had not changed. "I don't think that I've changed in terms of basics," he explained to the *New York Times*. "I think I've changed in terms of style . . . . In the 1980s I was . . . concerned about getting my issues straight in the newspapers. In the 1990s, I'm far more concerned about getting our message straight in history."

North America

# Sherrod, Charles

(b. January 2, 1937, St. Petersburg, Va.), African American civil rights activist and field secretary of the Student Nonviolent Coordinating Committee (SNCC) (1961–1966).

After putting himself through Virginia Union University, where he received a B.A. in 1958 and a B.D. in 1961, Charles Sherrod took part in the struggle against racial discrimination in the United States by joining SNCC. With the two-pronged aim of desegregation and voter registration, Sherrod settled in Georgia, where he and other SNCC members united with local leaders of the African American community to defeat racist laws and practices. Sherrod broke with SNCC in 1966, largely because of his support of white inclusion in the organization. Subsequently, he organized the Southwest Georgia Independent Voters Project, which he directed until 1987, and he worked toward creating agricultural cooperatives in the area. In 1976 he was elected city commissioner in Albany, Georgia, the site of his early work with SNCC.

North America

# Shuttlesworth, Fred L.

(b. March 18, 1922, Mugler, Ala.), African American Baptist minister and civil rights leader who was a founding member and secretary of the Southern Christian Leadership Conference (SCLC).

After receiving a B.A. from Selma University in Alabama in 1951 and a B.S. from Alabama State Teachers College in 1952, Fred Shuttlesworth became pastor first of Bethel Baptist Church, and then of the First Baptist Church in Birmingham, Alabama.

Shuttlesworth formed the Alabama Christian Movement for Human Rights (ACMHR) in 1956. As president from its inception until 1969, Shuttlesworth led Birmingham's integration movement. He became secretary of the SCLC, founded in 1958. With Martin Luther King Jr., Shuttlesworth was instrumental in uniting the two organizations in an anti-segregation campaign; the joining of forces led to the Birmingham demonstration of the spring of 1963. Shuttlesworth continued to organize demonstrations and marches, and finished his term as secretary of the SCLC in 1970. As a minister in Cincinnati, Ohio, Shuttlesworth has remained committed to issues of social justice.

North America

# Simkins, Mary Modjeska Monteith

(b. December 5, 1899, Columbia, S.C.; d. May 15, 1992, Columbia, S.C.), African American civil rights activist known for her lifetime commitment to progressive causes.

The child of prosperous parents Henry Clarence Monteith and Rachel Evelyn Hull Monteith, Mary Modjeska Monteith Simkins was instilled early on with a sense of both gentility and the duty to fight for equality. After graduating from Benedict College in 1921 with a B.A., she remained at the school until she was hired by the Booker T. Washington School in Columbia, South Carolina, a year later. When she married Andrew Whitfield Simkins in 1929, Modjeska was required to leave her job due to the city policy that married women could not teach in public schools.

In 1931 Simkins began working for the South Carolina Tuberculosis Association as director of Negro Work, establishing clinics and educating the population about the disease. In addition to organizing for several alternative political parties, she was one of the founding members of the South Carolina Conference of Branches of the National Association for the Advancement of Colored People (NAACP). In 1942, due to her civil rights activities she was fired from her job with the South Carolina Tuberculosis Association.

Elected state secretary of the NAACP the same year, Simkins led victorious fights for equalizing wages for African American public school teachers and countermanding the segregated primary elections in South Carolina. Simkins and the NAACP helped to desegregate the South Carolina public schools by filing *Briggs v. Elliot* in 1951, paving the way for *Brown v. Board of Education* in 1954, which ended legal segregation in public schools. Despite her many successful projects, she was not reelected to her post as state secretary due to her affiliation with the Communist Party. Turning her focus to issues of community development, Simkins worked for African American-owned Victory Savings Bank in Columbia until her retirement.

North America

# Sit-Ins,

**series of African American student protests in 1960 in which black students occupied "white-only" lunch counters and other segregated public institutions throughout the South to protest segregated seating.**

On February 5, 1960, four black college students sat down at a "white-only" department store lunch counter in Greensboro, North Carolina. This Woolworth's counter was but one of the many segregated public facilities in the American South where African Americans were prohibited from such activities as eating, swimming, and drinking by whites who not only opposed equal treatment of the races, but feared any possibility of bodily contact. When the restaurant refused these students service, they remained seated until the store closed for the evening. The students returned each morning for the next five days to occupy the lunch counter, joined by a group of protesters that grew to the hundreds. Faced by a mob of angry white residents and management that refused to serve them a cup of coffee, the students maintained their protest until they forced the store to close its doors.

The protest by Joseph McNeil, Franklin McCain, Ezell Blair Jr., and David Richmand marked the beginning of a grassroots sit-in movement led by African American students against the segregated public spaces of the South. Black or racially integrated groups of students would sit down in white-only spaces and refuse to move until they were served or forcibly removed. By the end of 1960 about 70,000 black students had participated in a sit-in or marched in support of the demonstrators.

Although there had been a few sit-in protests before 1960, including two in 1943, the mass mobilization of 1960 was new. Few in the economically struggling black community of the South had been willing to undertake these types of direct-action protests, since they would be in danger of losing their jobs after an arrest. Black students generally had fewer financial responsibilities than their older counterparts, and they were interested in forcing change more immediate than that promised by the legal reform advocated by the National Association for the Advancement of Colored People (NAACP).

In 1960, as African American students entered the political arena in large numbers for the first time, the character of the civil rights protesting began to change. Influenced by the successful protests led by Mohandas K. Gandhi in India's Independence Movement, black students saw the potential for using nonviolent resistance to undermine the segregationist system and ideologies that supported it. Nonviolence was not just a strategy, although it did garner sympathy from many whites and the national press; it was a moral and revolutionary philosophy. Proponents such as James Lawson Jr. felt that nonviolence was an "invincible instrument of war," imbued with "soul force" and moral integrity, which would use the mass organization of bodies to strike at the heart of the morally unsound system of segregationism.

The pivotal demonstration was the Greensboro sit-in. But students had already begun organizing elsewhere. Shortly after the Greensboro protest Lawson and the Nashville Student Movement launched a well-organized and orchestrated campaign to integrate the lunch counters of Nashville, Tennessee. In less than a month Nashville yielded to the pressure of the protests. The success of these original protests inspired other black students throughout the South, who organized sit-ins to force the desegregation of public places.

During 1960 sit-ins began to break down the segregation of the upper South, and lunch counters were integrated in cities in Texas, North Carolina, and Tennessee. The reasons for integration were economic as well as moral. Boycotters, both black and white, supported the protesters, and many merchants did not want to lose the revenue of customers.

In the Deep South, however, including Louisiana, Mississippi, Alabama, Georgia, and South Carolina, white supremacy was more entrenched in the community and local government. Cities such as Montgomery, Alabama, outlawed the demonstrations, and white store owners refused to serve blacks under the rationale that they could make the rules on their own private property.

Throughout the South protesters faced not only arrest but vigilante violence as police and the Ku Klux Klan worked hand-in-hand to suppress the protests. By the end of 1960, 36,000 students had been arrested, and thousands expelled from college.

With support from Ella J. Baker of the Southern Christian Leadership Conference, students formed a permanent organization in April 1960: the Student Nonviolent Coordinating Committee (SNCC). SNCC maintained the autonomy of the grassroots students' movement and facilitated training in nonviolent resistance. The strategy of occupying a place as a means of nonviolent protest gained currency in the Civil Rights Movement. Sit-ins at lunch counters inspired similar forms of protest at other types of segregated facilities, such as wade-ins at swimming places.

The efficacy of nonviolent resistance was one of the most important legacies of the 1960 sit-in protests. Segregation was seen to be a moral, as well as a legal issue, and the dignity of blacks in the face of white supremacist rage went far to win white and black support for the movement. In the words of SNCC's founding members, "By appealing to conscience and standing on the moral nature of human existence, non-violence nurtures the atmosphere in which reconciliation and justice become actual possibilities."

North America

# Sixteenth Street Baptist Church (Birmingham, Ala.),

center for civil rights in Birmingham, Alabama; site of the 1963 bombing that killed four African American girls.

On September 15, 1963, 4 young black girls were killed and 20 other people wounded when a bomb planted by Ku Klux Klan member Robert

Edward Chambliss exploded at the 16th Street Baptist Church in Birmingham, Alabama. The terrorist attack revealed the growing hostility of segregationists toward the Civil Rights Movement as it was making inroads in the Deep South. At the time of the bombing Birmingham was in a battle over the desegregation of schools; only weeks before, the National Guard had been called in to protect black students. For civil rights leaders the bombing, which followed less than three weeks after the euphoria of the 1963 March on Washington, was a reminder of the long struggle that remained.

The 16th Street Baptist Church was a center for the Civil Rights Movement in Birmingham. Martin Luther King Jr., Andrew Young, Fred L. Shuttlesworth, James Bevel, Dick Gregory, and Ralph Abernathy all regularly took the pulpit at mass rallies of Birmingham's black community, such as the one following King's April 1963 arrest. The church had been the headquarters for a number of desegregation protests, including the May 1963 Southern Christian Leadership Conference (SCLC) rally in which more than 2000 black youth marched from the church through Birmingham.

The Ku Klux Klan targeted the church on the annual Youth Sunday. Eleven-year-old Denise McNair was with Cynthia Wesley, Carole Robertson, and Addie Mae Collins, all age 14, in the basement of the church. They were preparing to take their special roles as ushers when the bomb exploded, killing them and burying them in rubble. Twenty others, many children, were injured by the blast. In the day of increased tension that followed, two other black youths were killed. A black 13-year-old was shot by two Eagle Scouts who were on the way home from a white supremacist rally. That evening a 16-year-old black boy was shot by one of 300 state troopers ordered into the city by Gov. George C. Wallace to preserve the peace in Birmingham.

As black and white youths battled in the streets of Birmingham the night of the bombing, many white residents wavered between fear of anti-white violence and feelings of guilt. In the words of white lawyer Charles Morgan the next day, "We all did it . . . every person in this community who has in any way contributed . . . to the popularity of hatred is at least as guilty . . . as the demented fool who threw that bomb." Many in the community, and indeed in the nation, struggled with a new awareness of the brutal underside of what had been characterized as simply the Southern way of life.

Connie Lynch articulated the white supremacist reaction. Rallying the Klan shortly after the bombing, Lynch said the victims "weren't children. Children are little people, little human beings, and that means white people . . . They're just little niggers, and if there's four less niggers tonight, then I say, 'Good for whoever planted the bomb!'"

Eight thousand people attended a joint funeral for three of the girls. Martin Luther King Jr. gave the eulogy to a community that, having witnessed seven bombings within the previous six months, was torn between exhaustion and rage.

An eyewitness reported seeing four men plant the bomb. Police arrested

Chambliss after the bombing, but let him go shortly after. In 1977 Alabama Attorney General William Baxley reopened the case, and Chambliss was tried and convicted of first-degree murder.

# Slavery in the United States

Slavery has appeared in many forms throughout its long history. Slaves have served in capacities as diverse as concubines, warriors, servants, craftsmen, tutors, and victims of ritual sacrifice. In the New World (the Americas), however, slavery emerged as a system of forced labor designed to facilitate the production of staple crops. Depending on location, these crops included sugar, coffee, tobacco, and cotton; in the southern United States, by far the most important staples were tobacco and cotton. A stark racial component distinguished this modern Western slavery from the slavery that existed in many other times and places: the vast majority of slaves consisted of Africans and their descendants, whereas the vast majority of masters consisted of Europeans and their descendants.

Slavery has played a central role in the history of the United States. It existed in all the English mainland colonies and came to dominate productive relations from Maryland south. Most of the Founding Fathers were large-scale slaveholders, as were 8 of the first 12 presidents of the United States. Debate over slavery increasingly dominated American politics, leading eventually to the nation's only civil war, which in turn finally brought slavery to an end. After emancipation, over-coming slavery's legacy remained a crucial issue in American history, from Reconstruction following the Civil War to the Civil Rights Movement a century later.

## The Introduction of Slavery

There was nothing inevitable about the use of black slaves. Although Dutch traders brought 20 Africans to Jamestown, Virginia, as early as 1619, throughout most of the seventeenth century the number of Africans in the English mainland colonies grew very slowly. During those years colonists experimented with two other sources of unfree labor: Native American slaves and European indentured servants.

Although some Native American slaves existed in every colony, the number was limited. Indian men balked at performing agricultural labor, which they regarded as women's work, and colonists complained that they were "haughty" and made poor slaves. Even more important, the settlers found it more convenient to sell Native Americans captured in war to planters in the Caribbean than to turn them into slaves on their own terrain, where escape was relatively easy and violent resistance a constant threat. Ultimately, the policy of killing Indians or driving them away from white settlements proved incompatible with their widespread employment as slaves.

Far more important as a form of labor than Indian slavery was white indentured servitude. Most indentured servants were poor Europeans who, desiring to escape harsh conditions and take advantage of fabled opportunities in America, traded four to seven years of their labor in exchange for the transatlantic passage. At first predominantly English but later increasingly Irish, Welsh, and German, servants consisted primarily (although not exclusively) of young males. Once in the colonies, they were essentially temporary slaves; most served as agricultural workers although some, especially in the North, were taught skilled trades. During the seventeenth century they performed most of the heavy labor in the Southern colonies and also provided the bulk of immigrants to those colonies.

For a variety of reasons, foremost among them improved conditions in England, the number of persons willing to sell themselves into indentured servitude declined sharply toward the end of the seventeenth century. Since the labor needs of the rapidly growing colonies were increasing, this decline in servant migration produced a labor crisis. To meet their needs, landowners turned to African slaves, who from the 1680s began to supplant indentured servants; in Virginia, for example, blacks (the great majority of whom were slaves) increased from about 7 percent of the population in 1680 to more than 40 percent by the middle of the eighteenth century. During the first two-thirds of the seventeenth century Holland and Portugal had dominated the African slave trade, and the number of Africans available to English colonists was limited. During the late seventeenth and eighteenth centuries, by contrast, naval superiority gave England a dominant position in the slave trade, and English traders (some of whom lived in English America) transported millions of Africans across the Atlantic.

The transatlantic slave trade produced one of the largest forced migrations in history. From the early sixteenth century to the mid-nineteenth century about 12 million Africans were torn from their homes, herded onto ships where they were sometimes so tightly packed that they could barely move, and deposited in a strange new land. (Since others died in transit, Africa's population loss was greater still.) By far the largest importers of slaves were Brazil and the Caribbean sugar colonies; together they received well over three-quarters of all Africans brought to the New World. About 6 percent of the total (600,000 to 650,000 persons) came to the area of the present United States.

## Slavery in the Colonial Era

Slavery spread quickly in the American colonies. At first the legal status of Africans in America was poorly defined, and some—like European indentured servants—managed to become free after several years of service. From the 1660s, however, the colonies began enacting laws that defined and regulated slave relations; central to these laws was the provision that black slaves, and the children of slave women, would serve for life. By the eve of the American Revolution slaves constituted about 40 percent of the population of the southern mainland colonies, with the highest concentration in South Carolina, where well over half the population were slaves.

Slaves performed numerous tasks, from clearing the forest to serving as craftsmen, guides, trappers, nurses, and house servants, but they were most essential as agricultural laborers and most numerous where land-owners sought to grow staple crops for market. The most important of these crops were tobacco in the upper South (Maryland, Virginia, and North Carolina) and rice in the lower South (South Carolina and Georgia); farther south still, on Caribbean islands such as Barbados, Jamaica, and Saint-Domingue (present-day Haiti), sugar was an even more valuable slave-grown commodity. Slaves also worked on large wheat-producing estates in New York and on horse-breeding farms in Rhode Island, but climate and soil restricted the development of commercial agriculture in the Northern colonies, and slavery never became as economically central there as it was in the South. Slaves in the North were typically held in small numbers, and most served as domestic servants; only in New York, with its Dutch legacy, did they form more than 10 percent of the population. In the North as a whole, less than 5 percent of the inhabitants were slaves.

By the mid-eighteenth century American slavery had acquired a number of distinctive features. Well over 90 percent of American slaves lived in the South, where demographic conditions contrasted sharply with those to both the south and the north. In Caribbean colonies such as Jamaica and Saint-Domingue, blacks outnumbered whites by more than ten to one, and slaves often lived on huge estates whose inhabitants numbered in the hundreds. In the Northern colonies blacks were few, and slaves were typically held in small groups of less than five. The South, by contrast, was neither overwhelmingly white nor overwhelmingly black: slaves formed a large minority of the population (in some areas, of course, they formed the majority), and despite regional variations, most slaves lived on small and medium-sized holdings containing between 5 and 50 slaves.

A second distinctive feature was the rapid "Americanization" of both masters and slaves. English colonists quickly came to feel "at home" on their American holdings. Few sought to make quick killings on their planting ventures and then retire to a life of leisure in England, and the kind of absentee ownership common in much of the Caribbean was relatively rare in the American South; instead, masters typically took an active role in running their farms and plantations. Equally significant was the shift from an African to an African American slave population. By the eve of the American Revolution only about 20 percent of American slaves were African-born (although the concentration of Africans remained higher in South Carolina and Georgia), and after the outlawing of new slave imports beginning in 1808, the proportion of African-born slaves became tiny. The emergence of a native-born slave population had numerous important consequences. To take one example, among African-born slaves (imported primarily for their ability to perform physical labor) there were few children, and men outnumbered women by about two to one; American-born slaves, by contrast, began their slave careers as children, and there were approximately even numbers of males and females in their ranks.

This shift from African to African American was closely related to a third distinctive characteristic of American slavery that was in many ways

A group of slaves stands outside their quarters on a plantation on Cockspur Island, Georgia, one of the barrier reef Sea Islands that stretch along the coasts of Florida, Georgia, and South Carolina. *CORBIS*

the most important of all: in contrast to most other slaves in the New World, those in the United States experienced what demographers refer to as "natural population growth." Elsewhere, in regions as diverse as Brazil, Jamaica, Saint-Domingue, and Cuba, slave mortality rates exceeded birth rates, and growth of the slave population depended on the importation of new slaves from Africa; as soon as that importation ended, the slave population began to decline. At first, deaths among slaves also exceeded births in the American colonies, but in the eighteenth century those colonies experienced a demographic transition as birth rates rose, mortality rates fell, and the slave population became self-reproducing. This transition, which occurred earlier in the upper than in the lower South, meant that even after the outlawing of slave imports, the number of slaves would continue to grow rapidly; during the next half century the slave population of the United States more than tripled, from about 1.2 million to almost 4 million in 1860. The natural growth of the slave population shaped a distinctive slavery in the American South and hastened the transition among slaves from African to African American.

## The Revolutionary Challenge

Throughout most of the colonial period opposition to slavery among white Americans was virtually nonexistent. Settlers in the seventeenth and early eighteenth centuries came from a sharply stratified society in which the upper classes savagely exploited members of the "lower orders"; lacking a later generation's belief in natural human equality, they saw little reason to question the enslavement of Africans. As they sought to mold a docile labor force, these planters resorted to harshly repressive measures that included whippings and brandings.

Gradually, as slavery became more entrenched, changes occurred in the way masters looked on their slaves (and themselves). Many second-generation masters, who unlike their parents had grown up with slaves, came to regard slaves as inferior members of their extended families, and to look upon themselves as kindly patriarchs who, like benevolent despots, ruled their "people" firmly but fairly and looked after their needs. Such slave owners continued to rely heavily on the lash (and other forms of punishment) for discipline, and few slaves saw their owners as the kindly guardians that they proclaimed themselves to be. Still, the most extreme forms of physical abuse became less common over the course of the eighteenth century, at the same time that many slave owners accepted the idea that they should treat their slaves humanely.

Some slave owners went further. The last third of the eighteenth century saw the first widespread questioning of slavery by white Americans. This questioning was boosted by the American Revolution, which sparked a sharp increase in egalitarian thinking. Many of the Founding Fathers, including George Washington and Thomas Jefferson, while slaveholders, were profoundly troubled by slavery; leery of rash actions, they initiated a series of cautious acts that they thought would lead to slavery's gradual abolition.

These acts included measures in all states north of Delaware to abolish slavery. A few states did away with slavery immediately. More typical were gradual emancipation acts such as that passed by Pennsylvania in 1780, whereby all children born to slaves in the future would be freed at age 28. Two significant measures dating from 1787 were the Northwest Ordinance, which barred slavery from the Northwest Territory (including much of what is now the upper Midwest), and a compromise reached at the Constitutional Convention that would allow Congress to outlaw the importation of slaves in 1808. Meanwhile, a number of states passed acts to ease the freeing of slaves by slave owners, hundreds of whom—especially in the upper South—set some or all of their slaves free. In addition, tens of thousands of slaves acted on their own, taking advantage of wartime disruption to escape bondage. As a result the number of free blacks, which had been tiny before the Revolution, surged during the last quarter of the eighteenth century.

Nevertheless, the Revolutionary-era challenge to slavery proved successful only in the North, where the investment in slaves was small. The antislavery movement never made much headway in Georgia and South Carolina, where labor-hungry planters rushed to import tens of thousands of Africans before the 1808 cutoff. In the upper South, Revolution-inspired egalitarianism withered in the 1790s and 1800s. And because the American slave population was self-reproducing, the end of slave imports in the United States did not undermine slavery as it did elsewhere, or as many of the Founding Fathers expected. Ultimately the first antislavery movement rendered slavery a newly sectional institution that was on the road to abolition throughout the North but largely unscathed in the South.

## Slavery in the Antebellum Era

During the antebellum (pre–Civil War) years slavery expanded aggressively along with the United States. Fueled by a surging world demand for cotton, slavery spread quickly into the new states of the Southwest; by the 1830s Alabama, Mississippi, and Louisiana formed the heart of a new "cotton kingdom," together producing more than half of the nation's supply of the crop. The great bulk of this cotton was cultivated by slaves. Between 1790 and 1860 about 1 million slaves (almost twice the number of Africans shipped to the United States during the whole period of the transatlantic slave trade) moved west, some together with their masters and others as part of a new domestic trade in which owners from the seaboard states provided "surplus" slaves to planters in the Southwest.

As slavery grew, so too did its diversity. Slavery varied according to region, crops, and size of holdings. On farms and small plantations most slaves came in frequent contact with their owners, but on very large plantations, where slave owners often employed overseers, slaves might rarely see their masters. Some owners left their holdings entirely in the care of subordinates, usually hired white overseers but sometimes slaves. A few slave owners were even black themselves: a small percentage of free blacks owned slaves, in some cases essentially as a fiction so that they could protect family members, but more often to profit, like other slaveholders, from unfree labor. Most slaves on large holdings worked in gangs, under the supervision of overseers and (slave) drivers. Some, however, especially in the coastal region of South Carolina and Georgia, labored under the "task" system: assigned a certain amount of work to complete in a day, they received less supervision than gang laborers and were free to use their time as they wished once they had completed their daily assignments. In addition to performing fieldwork, slaves served as house servants, nurses, midwives, carpenters, blacksmiths, drivers, preachers, gardeners, and handymen.

Two African slave boys in a nineteenth-century photograph. *CORBIS/Hulton-Deutsch Collection*

Despite such variations there were a number of dominant trends. First, slavery was overwhelmingly rural: in 1860 only about 5 percent of all slaves lived in towns of at least 2,500 persons. Second, although some slaves lived on giant estates and others on small farms, the norm was in between: in 1860 about one-half of all slaves lived on plantations with 10 to 49 other slaves, about one-quarter on smaller and one-quarter on larger units. (Holdings tended to be bigger in the Deep South than in the upper South.) Third, most slaves lived with resident masters; owner absenteeism was most prevalent in the South Carolina and Georgia low country, but in the South as a whole it was less common than in the Caribbean. Fourth, most able-bodied adult slaves engaged in field work. Owners relied heavily on children, the elderly, and the infirm for "nonproductive" work (such as house service); only the largest plantations could spare healthy adults for exclusive assignment to specialized occupations. The main business of Southern farms and plantations—and of the slaves who supported them—was to grow cotton, tobacco, rice, corn, wheat, hemp, and sugar.

Southern slaveholders took an active role in managing their human property. Viewing themselves as the slaves' guardians, they stressed the degree to which they cared for their "people." The character of such care varied, but in purely material terms—food, clothing, housing, medical attention—it was generally better in the antebellum than in the colonial period and (judging by measurable criteria such as slave height and life expectancy) better in the American South than in the Caribbean or Brazil. Although young children were often malnourished, most working slaves received a steady supply of pork and corn which, if lacking in nutritional balance (about which antebellum Americans knew nothing), provided sufficient calories to fuel their labor, especially when supplemented with produce that slaves raised on the garden plots that they were often allotted. Clothing and housing were crude but functional: slaves typically received four coarse "suits" per year (pants and shirts for men, dresses for women, long shirts for children) and lived in small wooden cabins, one to a family. Wealthy slave owners often sent for physicians to treat slaves who became ill; given the state of medical knowledge, however, such treatment—which could range from providing various concoctions to "bleeding" a patient— often did as much harm as good.

Masters intervened continuously in the lives of their slaves, from directing their labor to approving (and disapproving) marriages. Some masters made elaborate written "rules" and most engaged in constant meddling—directing, nagging, threatening, and punishing. Many took advantage of their position to exploit slave women sexually. What slaves hated most about slavery was not the hard work to which they were subjected (most people in the rural United States expected to engage in hard physical labor), but the lack of control over their lives—their lack of freedom. Masters may have prided themselves on the care they provided for their "people"; the slaves, however, had a different idea of that care. They resented the constant interference in their lives and struggled to achieve whatever autonomy they could.

## Slave Life and Slave Resistance

Such autonomy was not totally lacking. In the quarters—the collection of slave cabins that on large plantations resembled a miniature village—slaves developed their own way of life. The degree of social independence available to slaves was not constant: throughout the South a continuing power struggle raged in which slaves strove to increase and masters strove to limit this independence. The character and resolution of this struggle in turn depended on a host of factors, from size of holdings and organization of production to residence and disposition of masters. Masters rarely were able, however, to shape the lives of their slaves as fully as they wanted.

Away from the view of owners and overseers, slaves lived their own lives. They made friends and made love, played and prayed, sang, told stories, cooked, joked, quarreled, and engaged in the necessary chores of day-to-day living, from cleaning house, cooking, and sewing to working on their garden plots. Especially important as anchors of the slaves' lives were their families and their religion.

Throughout the South the family defined the actual living arrangements of slaves: most slaves lived together in nuclear families—mother, father, children. The security and stability of these families faced severe challenges: no state law recognized marriage among slaves, masters rather than parents had legal authority over slave children, and the possibility of forced separation through sale hung over every family. (Such separations were especially frequent in the slave-exporting states of the upper South.) Still, despite their tenuous status, families served as the slaves' most basic refuge, the center of private lives that owners could never fully control.

Religion served as a second refuge. Although African slaves usually clung to their native religions, and many slave owners in the early colonial period were leery of those who sought to convert their slaves to Christianity (in part because of fears that converted slaves would have to be freed), during the antebellum years Christianity was increasingly central to the slaves' cultural life. Many slaves were converted during the religious revivals that swept the South in the late eighteenth and early nineteenth centuries. Slaves typically belonged to the same denominations as white Southerners—Baptists and Methodists were the largest groups—and some masters encouraged their "people" to come to the white church, where they usually sat in a special "slave gallery" and received advice about being obedient to their masters. In the quarters, however, there developed a parallel ("invisible") church controlled by the slaves themselves, who listened to sermons delivered by their own preachers. Not all slaves had access to these preachers and not all accepted their message, but for many, religion served as a great comfort in a hostile world.

If their families and religion helped slaves to avoid total control by their owners, slaves also more directly challenged that control through active resistance. The limits of such resistance must be kept in mind. Unlike slaves in Saint-Domingue, who rose up against their French masters in bloody rebellion and established the black republic of Haiti in 1804, American slaves faced a balance of power that discouraged armed resistance. When it occurred, such resistance was always quickly suppressed and followed by harsh repression designed to discourage repetition. Aside from "conspiracies" aborted before any actual outbreak of violence in New York (1741), Virginia (1800), and South Carolina (1822), the most noted uprisings included the Stono Rebellion near Charleston, South Carolina (1739), an attempted attack on New Orleans (1811), and the Nat Turner insurrection that rocked Southampton County, Virginia, in 1831. The Turner insurrection, which at its peak included 60 to 80 rebels, resulted in the deaths of about 60 whites; the number of blacks killed during the uprising and executed or lynched afterward may have reached 100. But the rebellion lasted less than two days and was easily suppressed by local residents. Like other slave uprisings in the United States, it caused enormous fear among whites but did not seriously threaten the slave regime.

Lower-level resistance was both more widespread and more successful. This included "silent sabotage," or foot dragging, by slaves who pretended to be sick, feigned difficulty understanding instructions, and "accidentally" misused tools and animals. It also included small-scale resistance by individuals who fought back physically—at times successfully—against what they regarded as unjust treatment. But the most common form of resistance was flight. About 1,000 slaves per year managed to escape to the North during the late antebellum period (most from the upper South), but this represented only the tip of the iceberg, since for every slave who made it to freedom, several more tried. Other fugitives remained within the South, heading for cities or swamps, or hiding out near their plantations for days or weeks before either returning voluntarily or being tracked down and captured. On a continuing basis, slaves "voted with their feet" against slavery.

Like all people, slaves felt diverse, overlapping attachments. They identified themselves as members of families, parishioners of churches, residents of particular farms and plantations, and members of an exploited class, the fruits of whose labor were appropriated by their owners. They also identified themselves as African Americans and saw themselves as an oppressed people. Because most blacks in the antebellum South were slaves, the line separating black from white approximated that separating slave from free, and the class exploitation of slave by master often appeared indistinguishable from the racial oppression of black by white. Racial identification drew support not only from common African origins and the close ties that often existed between slaves and free blacks but also from the virulent racism of many non-slaveholding whites that made it easy for slaves to look upon whites in general as their oppressors. Early African American cultural identity was forged in the crucible of slavery.

## Sectional Tensions over Slavery

Slavery was an increasingly Southern institution. Abolition of slavery in the North, begun in the Revolutionary era and largely complete by the 1830s, divided the United States into the "slave" South and the "free" North. As this happened, slavery came—both to Northerners and Southerners—to define the essence of the South: to defend slavery was to be "pro-Southern," whereas opposition to slavery was "anti-Southern." Although most Southern whites did not own slaves (the proportion of white families that owned slaves declined from 35 percent to 26 percent between 1830 and 1860), slavery more and more set the South off from the rest of the country—and the Western world. If at one time slavery had been common in much of the New World, by the middle of the nineteenth century it remained only in Brazil, Cuba, Puerto Rico, and the southern United States. In an era that celebrated liberty and equality, the slave South came to seem backward and repressive, associated in many people's minds with that other bastion of reaction, serf-holding Russia.

In fact, the slave economy grew rapidly, enriched by the spectacular increase in cotton cultivation to meet the burgeoning demand of Northern and European textile manufacturers. But Southern economic growth was based largely on putting more acreage under cultivation; the South did not undergo the kind of industrial revolution that was beginning to transform the North, and the South remained almost entirely rural. In 1860 there were only five Southern cities with more than 50,000 inhabitants (only one of which, New Orleans, was in the Deep South); less than 10 percent of Southerners lived in towns of at least 2,500 persons, compared to more than 25 percent of Northerners. The South also increasingly lagged in other indices of modernization, from railroad construction to literacy and public education.

But the biggest gap between North and South was ideological. As Northern states abolished slavery and then saw the growth of a small but articulate abolitionist movement, Southern white spokesmen—from politicians to ministers, newspaper editors, and authors—rallied around slavery as the bedrock of Southern society. Defenders of slavery developed a wide range of arguments to buttress their cause, from those that stressed the institution's "practical" necessity to those that depicted it as a "positive good." They made heavy use of religious themes, pointing to the biblical "curse of Ham" to explain the origins of black bondage and portraying slavery as part of God's plan for civilizing a primitive, heathen people.

Racial justifications were especially prevalent in pro-slavery arguments, in part because of the widespread racism that united most white Americans and in part because such arguments were especially effective in appealing to the majority of Southern whites who did not own slaves. The extreme—"scientific"—version of these arguments purported to prove that blacks were so physiologically different from whites that they amounted to a different species (or, in the reformulation of some theoreticians, were the products of a separate creation). Such an approach violated the Christian sensibilities of too many Southern whites, however, to become a central staple of pro-slavery propaganda. Far more common were brief, unscientific, and vaguely supported assertions that blacks were by nature different, inferior, and therefore unsuited for freedom. Hardworking, loyal, and productive under loving but firm direction (i.e., slavery), blacks supposedly lacked the intellectual capacity for independent existence and in freedom would quickly degenerate, perhaps even fall into extinction.

During the 1840s and 1850s Southern spokesmen increasingly based their case for slavery on social arguments that contrasted the harmonious, orderly, religious, and conservative society that supposedly existed in the South with the tumultuous, heretical, and mercenary ways of a North torn apart by radical reform, individualism, class conflict, and—worst of all— abolitionism. Insisting that Southern slaves were treated far better than Northern wage laborers, pro-slavery ideologues developed a biting critique of free-labor capitalism ("wage-slavery") as cruel, exploitative, and selfish, and pointed to the degraded condition of supposedly free British paupers and Irish peasants. This defense in many ways represented the mirror image of the "free-labor" argument increasingly prevalent in the North: as free-labor spokesmen argued that slavery kept the South backward, poor, ineffi-cient, and degraded, pro-slavery advocates retorted that only slavery could save the South (and the world) from the evils of modernity run wild.

From the mid-1840s the struggle over slavery became more and more central to American politics. Northerners committed to the concept of "free soil" (the idea that new, western territories should be reserved exclusively for free white settlers) clashed repeatedly with Southern spokesmen who insisted that any limitation on slavery's expansion represented unconstitu-tional meddling with the Southern order and a grave affront to Southern honor. In 1860 the election of Abraham Lincoln as president on a free-soil platform set off a major political and constitutional crisis, as seven states in the Deep South seceded from the United States and formed the Confed-erate States of America; the start of hostilities between the United States and the rebel Confederates in April 1861 led to the additional secession of four states in the upper South. (Four other slave states—Maryland, Delaware, Kentucky, and Missouri—remained in the Union, as did the new state of West Virginia, which split off from Virginia.)

## Emancipation—and After

Ironically, although Southern politicians supported secession in order to pre-serve slavery, their action led instead to slavery's death. As the war dragged on, Northern war aims gradually shifted from preserving the Union to abol-ishing slavery and remaking the Union. Two especially important catalysts of this shift were the following: (1) the war-time behavior of Southern blacks, who under conditions of weakened authority at home increasingly refused to behave like slaves; and (2) the changing views of Northern whites, a growing number of whom accepted the Radical Republican posi-tion that the war provided an ideal opportunity to overthrow slavery and institute a sweeping transformation of the Southern social order.

Slavery ended for hundreds of thousands of Southern blacks well before the Confederate surrender, as Union troops occupied larger and larger areas of the South and as increasing numbers of slaves fled from their owners and sought refuge within Union lines. In Union-occupied areas of the

South, blacks experienced a rehearsal for Reconstruction, as federal officials experimented with various forms of free and semi-free labor and as
Northern missionaries established schools to help turn slaves into citizens.
The freed people's enthusiasm for education, in turn, created a powerful
impression among Northern whites and contributed to their growing determination that the war must yield what President Lincoln termed "a new
birth of freedom."

This goal received symbolic recognition with the Emancipation Proclamation that Lincoln issued on January 1, 1863. Although the proclamation
applied only to areas under rebel control and did not end slavery in the
United States, it marked a clear turning point in the struggle against the
"peculiar institution": a war for union had become a war for freedom, and
henceforth everyone recognized that a federal victory would mean the
death of slavery. During the second half of the war, as slavery crumbled in
much of the South, more than 188,000 African Americans, both Southern
and Northern, served in the Union's armed forces, fighting to hasten that
death. The Thirteenth Amendment to the Constitution, passed by Congress
in January and ratified by the states in December 1865, completed the
process, outlawing slavery everywhere in the United States.

A plaque identifies the block on a Fredericksburg, Virginia, street where slaves were sold at
auction. *CORBIS/Bettmann*

Despite the overthrow of slavery, at war's end the future status of the former slaves remained unclear, and resolving that status remained at the center of the nation's political agenda. An intense struggle ensued, as freed people strove for economic security, social autonomy, and civil rights; former slave owners sought to preserve their old prerogatives; and Northern politicians became divided over the proper course of Reconstruction. The compromise that resulted from this struggle yielded an unprecedented—although temporary—national commitment to turn former slaves into citizens, anchored by the Fourteenth and Fifteenth Amendments to the United States Constitution and the Reconstruction Acts of 1867. Together these measures provided basic civil rights to former slaves, enfranchised black males, and imposed a largely self-administered democratization process on the former Confederate states, under federal supervision.

Emancipation brought many tangible rewards. Among the most obvious was the significant increase in personal freedom that came with no longer being someone else's property: whatever hardships they faced, free blacks could not be forcibly sold away from their loved ones. But emancipation did not bring full equality, and many of the most striking gains of Reconstruction—including the substantial political power that African Americans were briefly able to exercise—were soon lost. In the decades after Reconstruction African Americans experienced continued poverty and exploitation and a rising tide of violence at the hands of whites determined to re-impose black subordination. They also experienced new forms of discrimination, spearheaded by a variety of state laws that instituted rigid racial segregation in

A soldier guards a group of slaves linked together by chains in 1896.
*Hulton-Deutsch Collection/Corbis*

virtually all areas of life and that (in violation of the Fourteenth and Fifteenth Amendments) effectively disfranchised black voters. The struggle to overcome the bitter legacy of slavery would be long and arduous.

North America

# Socialism,

the economic and social doctrine that critiques capitalist production and advocates state control over vital industries, income distribution, and private property.

## American Socialism

The roots of American socialism can be found in antebellum communitarian settlements, such as the Shakers, and other utopian experiments that sought to establish cooperative societies within the emerging nation. Although some of these settlements were officially abolitionist, few offered refuge to African Americans. With the industrial boom that followed the Civil War, however, immigrant socialists lay the groundwork for a well-defined socialist doctrine and political party that—at least in theory—represented working people of all races against the growing might of American capitalism.

German immigrants brought Marxist socialist ideals to American organizations and in 1877 helped form the Socialist Labor Party. Meanwhile, American utopian reformers such as Edward Bellamy and Laurence Gronlund sought to achieve a classless society through peaceful means. From these two strands emerged a socialist doctrine reflecting the labor conditions particular to post-Civil War industrialization in the United States.

## African Americans in American Socialism

Prior to World War I the socialist movement in the United States devoted little attention to racial inequality. Formed in 1901 from socialist parties in several states, the Socialist Party of America urged African Americans to join the party and participate in the "world movement for economic emancipation." The party did not, however, establish a policy of race issues. As a result socialist positions on race differed from member to member and reflected particular attitudes and beliefs.

Socialist leader and presidential candidate Eugene V. Debs, for example, refused to address racial inequality as an issue separate from the issue of class. Instead, he maintained that there was "no Negro question outside the labor question" and believed that the overthrow of the capitalist system would free both whites and blacks. Debs claimed that African Americans, as a group that suffered keenly from capitalism and the wage labor system, would reap great benefits from the work of the socialist party and the eventual overthrow of capitalism. As a result Debs recruited African Americans and refused to address segregated audiences.

Other members of the Socialist Party of America took a more active position on race; William English Walling and Mary White Ovington, for example, worked against racial inequality and helped found the National Association for the Advancement of Colored People in 1909. On the other hand, some members, such as Victor L. Berger and William Noyes, refused to address black audiences due to their belief that "negroes and mulattos constitute a lower race."

As a result of these divergent attitudes, state socialist parties varied greatly in the extent to which they challenged the economic, social, and political inequalities faced by blacks. Socialists in Louisiana actively recruited African Americans, but insisted on segregated chapters of the state party; Oklahoma socialists promoted black voting rights and economic equality but, like other socialist parties in the South and southwest, refused to support social equality for blacks for fear that it would promote miscegenation. In contrast, some Northern Socialist parties advocated complete equality for blacks and made concerted efforts toward those goals. The New York party, for example, nominated African American candidates such as A. Philip Randolph for municipal and state public offices. Regardless of state policies, however, the national Socialist Party of America remained conspicuously silent on the issue of race and did little to recruit black members at the national level.

Nevertheless, some African Americans did join the Socialist Party. George Washington Woodbey, a Baptist minister, was the first black to join; he later actively recruited other African Americans. Like Debs, Woodbey did not consider racial inequality to be an issue separate from class. Other African American socialists, however, criticized those in the party who marginalized the issue of race. Hubert H. Harrison, for example, chastised the Socialist Party of America for its failure to understand that blacks suffered more acutely than white workers the indignities of capitalism. Harrison argued against the party's ineffectual efforts to counter African American political disfranchisement and eventually formed his own party, the Liberty League of Negro-Americans.

Two of the most notable African American socialists were A. Philip Randolph and Chandler Owen. Randolph and Owen worked together to transgress racial boundaries in the labor force and in unions. Beginning in 1917 they published the *Messenger*, a radical magazine promoting desegregated labor unions. During the 1920s Randolph used the *Messenger* to denounce the Pullman company and its union and to issue support for the nascent Brotherhood of Sleeping Car Porters, an independent black union.

By this time, however, the Socialist Party of America had splintered into factions and lost political credibility, due in part to the party's split during World War I. Ironically, the party had just started to establish a consistent policy on race and had begun working to eradicate racial inequality. Apart from a short resurgence prior to World War II, American socialism all but disappeared after World War II and the McCarthy era, when cold-war politics prompted government intimidation and discrimination against socialists. The socialist organizations that do exist today, however, tend to be closely involved with antiracist and anti-imperialist politics.

North America

# Southern Christian Leadership Conference,

civil rights organization led by Martin Luther King Jr. and a coalition of other Southern black ministers that organized protests in the 1950s and 1960s against segregation and barriers to voting.

The civil rights activist Bayard Rustin once described the Southern Christian Leadership Conference (SCLC) as the "dynamic center" of the cluster of organizations that made up the Civil Rights Movement. It differed from such organizations as the Student Nonviolent Coordinating Committee (SNCC) and the National Association for the Advancement of Colored People (NAACP), which functioned nationwide and sought to recruit individual members. SCLC served as an umbrella group for affiliates and initially concentrated its energies on America's segregated South. With prominent black ministers on its executive board and Rev. Martin Luther King Jr. at its helm, SCLC proved to be a guiding force and inspiration to the organizations and protesters engaged in the struggle for civil rights. In the words of one activist, "Southern Christian Leadership Conference is not an organization—it's a church."

In January 1957, 60 activists responded to a call for an Atlanta conference on nonviolent integration. Among the leaders were Northern activists Rustin, Ella J. Baker, and Stanley Levison, and Southern civil rights veterans King, Fred L. Shuttlesworth, Ralph Abernathy, C. K. Steele, Joseph Lowery, and William Holmes Borders. Shortly after this meeting the group established a permanent organization, the Southern Christian Leadership Conference, and elected King as president. The goal was to "to redeem the soul of America" through nonviolent resistance based on the teachings of Mohandas Gandhi. The organization drew its strength from the black churches of the South, whose ministers were said to mirror the spirit of the community.

John Tilley and, later, Baker took the job of running the Atlanta headquarters. Despite the increasingly contentious climate in the South, where black students led sit-ins and Freedom Rides to protest segregation, SCLC's early activities were fairly mild, focusing on education programs and on bringing rural blacks to the voting booth.

A SNCC-led protest against segregation in Albany, Georgia, was already under way in late November 1961, when King and executive director Wyatt T. Walker brought the SCLC into its first major nonviolent campaign. In some ways it was unsuccessful; demonstrations and arrests provoked few changes and garnered little national attention. The federal courts, which had acted in support of earlier desegregation disputes, refused to back up the protesters. After a failed attempt to raise national support by calling attention to the imprisonment of King and Abernathy, SCLC retreated from Albany.

The SCLC's 1963 campaign in Birmingham, Alabama, succeeded in every way the Albany campaign had not. In a city where white supremacist Eugene "Bull" Connor controlled the police, SCLC launched Project C ("C" for confrontation). The movement drew criticism from white liberals like Robert Kennedy, as well as some blacks, who suggested that the protesters await the reforms promised by the recently elected mayor. But as King pointed out: "Justice too long delayed is justice denied." Without its usual supporters, the demonstration limped on, and black protesters who sat-in at white-only counters soon crowded the city jails.

A brilliant strategic move turned the tide of the faltering demonstration. On May 2, 1963, 700 black children marched from the 16th Street Baptist Church in through town. After police wagons were filled, the children were carted to jail in school buses. When 2,500 more young protesters marched the next day, the police turned fire hoses on them, and the international press turned its lenses on Birmingham's police. The world saw pictures of black children knocked down by a force of water so powerful that it tore the bark off nearby trees. Now under international pressure and the growing threat of a riot, Birmingham's officials returned to the bargaining table more willing to deal with SCLC.

As a result of the Birmingham protest, SCLC won a desegregation settlement. More important, the protest laid the groundwork for the nation's 1964 Civil Rights Act. After its Birmingham triumph, SCLC organized other desegregation campaigns in Savannah, Georgia, and St. Augustine, Florida, and played a pivotal role in the 1963 March on Washington. During Freedom Summer of 1964, it joined the Congress of Racial Equality (CORE) for a massive voter registration campaign.

In its 1965 campaign in Selma, Alabama, SCLC took aim at unjust registration tests designed to keep blacks from voting. In some Southern counties less than 5 percent of the eligible black population was registered; in other counties no blacks could vote. When 400 prospective black voters, led by King and John Lewis, staged a "stand-in" at the Dallas County Courthouse, they were harassed and arrested. As King wrote in the *New York Times*, more blacks were in Selma jails than were registered to vote.

Galvanized by a surge of police brutality in neighboring Marion County, SCLC organized a 50-mile march from Selma to Montgomery. As 600 marchers began the walk, state troopers, under orders from Governor George Wallace, attacked them with clubs and tear gas. The day was dubbed Bloody Sunday.

More protesters came to Selma to undertake the march again, but tension between the two organizers, SCLC and SNCC, delayed the protest. King led a second march just over the Pettus Bridge. SNCC members accused King of mapping this partial march after negotiating a compromise with Wallace, and the rift between the organizations widened. By the time the full march led by both organizations took place in March, the landmark Voting Rights Act banning unfair voting tests had already been passed. The march took place anyway as a symbolic gesture of the solidarity needed for the long journey ahead.

Some observers criticized the SCLC for being too dependent on white liberal support and, as compared to the rising Black Power movement, too moderate. SCLC responded to the criticism by expanding its operations north to Chicago, Illinois, where, according to one historian, "SCLC discovered . . . that discrimination was a far more insidious and tenacious enemy than segregation." The organization shifted its attention to economic inequality.

Operation Breadbasket, organized in July 1967 as a national program to put "bread, money, and income into the baskets of black and poor people," became the economic arm of SCLC, organizing black consumers to press for jobs and to encourage black-owned businesses. Seeing poverty as the root of inner-city violence, SCLC began planning the Poor People's Campaign that would push for federal legislation to guarantee employment, income, and housing for the nation's economically disadvantaged blacks.

The assassination of King on April 4, 1968, interrupted plans for the Poor People's Campaign. The SCLC resumed planning the Washington demonstration. Under its newly elected leader, Ralph Abernathy, the SCLC brought between 50,000 and 100,000 people to Washington to rally support for economic justice for African Americans.

After King's death the organization went into a tailspin, beset by a decline in contributions and internal dissension over Abernathy's leadership. Lowery revived the SCLC in the late 1970s by expanding the organization's operations beyond traditional civil rights programs, but the organization never regained its original stature.

North America
# Southern Negro Youth Congress,
**organization established in Richmond, Virginia, in February 1937; until its demise in 1949 the Southern Negro Youth Congress (SNYC) played a critical role in the struggle of black Americans for full citizenship and for social, political, and economic justice.**

In the spring of 1937 black tobacco stemmers spontaneously walked out of Richmond-area tobacco plants protesting poor wages and hazardous working conditions. With the American Federation of Labor refusing assistance, C. Columbus Alston, Francis Grandison, and James E. Jackson Jr. helped the stemmers organize a Congress of Industrial Organizations (CIO)-affiliated union, which successfully struck Richmond's Export Leaf Tobacco Company. The victory had the effect of raising wages throughout the tobacco industry, and it inaugurated the SNYC's work in the South. By 1939 the organization had established a headquarters in Birmingham, Alabama, from which it coordinated organizing efforts across the South.

The SNYC's initial membership drew from the 1930s student movement, the Communist Party, and the CIO. Early leaders included Edward Strong, William Richardson, Louis Burnham, and Jackson. These men worked to connect the ongoing black struggle for civil rights to the industrial union movement of the late 1930s. But from the inception of the SNYC women played key roles in the organization, and by the early 1940s they assumed formal leadership positions. Esther Cooper Jackson served as

SNYC's executive secretary during the 1940s. Jackson, Sallye Davis, Dorothy Burnham, and Augusta Jackson Strong agitated for gender equity within the organization. At the same time they worked to establish ties between the SNYC and pre-existing networks of protest and resistance within Southern black communities.

The SNYC's connection with the Communist Party provided important links to an international arena of struggle and to a cadre of aggressive grass-roots organizers. The SNYC was, however, firmly rooted in the institutional and intellectual life of black communities across the South. Its members and constituencies came to the organization from the black Baptist church, the National Association for the Advancement of Colored People (NAACP), women's clubs, and fraternal and benevolent associations. Members of the SNYC worked hard to build coalitions, drawing on organizations, institutions, and individuals across lines of class, gender, and generation. They also attempted to reach out to white Southerners interested in economic and political transformation.

During its 12-year existence the SNYC organized eight youth legislatures in cities like Richmond; Birmingham; Chattanooga, Tennessee; and Columbia, South Carolina. The youth legislatures were living laboratories of the SNYC's vision of life and struggle. The meetings brought together various individuals and organizations active in struggles for justice in the South and the nation. Local advisory boards were formed, and older leaders from respective host cities filled positions in them. Federal government officials, national labor leaders, and icons of the black struggle for freedom, like W. E. B. Du Bois and Paul Robeson, attended and addressed meetings of the youth legislature. Through small working groups, legislature participants developed plans of action and drew up resolutions for federal government legislation. The legislatures invigorated local struggles and helped garner support for the SNYC's agenda of political and economic transformation. They also provided important venues for connecting local struggles to broader international ones. At the 1946 Columbia, South Carolina, meeting Du Bois explained, "This is the firing line not simply for the emancipation of the American Negro but for the emancipation of the African Negro and the Negroes of the West Indies . . . and for the emancipation of the white slaves of modern capitalist monopoly."

In 1940 the House Un-American Activities Committee listed the SNYC as a Communist Party front and agent of foreign powers. The Federal Bureau of Investigation placed the organization and its leaders under surveillance over the next 12 years. Although the SNYC's affiliation with the Communist Party did little to hamper its support in black communities through the World War II years, by 1947 and the advent of the cold war, the organization encountered increased opposition along many fronts. In 1948 the Internal Revenue Service withdrew the group's tax-exempt status. Liberal organizations stopped providing financial and public support. The SNYC's final youth legislature, held in Birmingham, was disrupted by local vigilantes and the city's chief of police, Eugene "Bull" Connor. By 1949 the organization ceased operations, and its members were forced to pursue new avenues of struggle. The SNYC, however, anticipated the student movement of the 1960s and left a lasting imprint on African Americans' struggle for freedom.

North America

# Stewart, Maria Miller

(b. 1803?, Hartford, Conn.; d. December 17, 1879, Washington, D.C.), African American women's rights activist, orator, writer, educator, first United States-born woman to speak publicly on political issues before a mixed-gender audience.

Born to a free family but orphaned at age five, Maria Stewart lived with the family of a clergyman until age 15. She acquired literacy and a religious education at Sabbath schools. Stewart married James Stewart on August 10, 1826, in Boston, Massachusetts. After her husband's death in 1829 and through the 1860s, Stewart worked as a teacher in the public school systems of New York City, Baltimore, Maryland, and Washington, D.C. In Washington she established a Sunday school for children in 1871 and worked and lived at the Howard University-affiliated Freedmen's Hospital for the last nine years of her life.

Stewart's two-year speaking career began in 1832 and included four lectures, all published in William Lloyd Garrison's abolitionist newspaper, the *Liberator*. Her lecture to the New England Anti-Slavery Society on September 21, 1832, was the first public lecture by an American-born woman before an audience of men and women. Stewart's speeches and subsequent writings emphasized women's ability and activism: "Daughters of Africa, awake! arise! distinguish yourselves." Her words were imbued with religious significance and delivered with a militancy also inherent in the writings of her contemporary David Walker. Stewart criticized racism and sexism in an era in which it was deemed inappropriate for women to participate publicly in political debates. She is the author of *Religion and the Pure Principles of Morality, the Sure Foundation on Which We Must Build* (1831), *Productions of Mrs. Maria W. Stewart* (1835), and *Meditations From the Pen of Mrs. Maria W. Stewart* (1879).

North America

# Student Nonviolent Coordinating Committee (SNCC) (pronounced "snick"),

civil rights group that played a major role in the 1960s campaign to end segregation in the southern United States.

### Founding and Early Protest

On February 1, 1960, four black college students attracted widespread attention when they refused to leave a whites-only lunch counter in an F. W. Woolworth store in Greensboro, North Carolina. The sit-in continued for several weeks and inspired dozens of similar sit-ins across the South. Although not the first time students had taken part in civil rights protests, the sit-in movement was among the largest and most spontaneous. Reacting to the protests, Ella J. Baker, executive director of the Southern Christian Leadership Conference (SCLC), held a conference for student activists in April at Shaw University in Raleigh, North Carolina. Baker believed that larger, more cautious civil rights groups such as the SCLC might have failed to serve students who were impatient for racial equality. She urged the 200 attendees to establish a new student group that would harness its energy and frustration to challenge white racism as well as the larger and more conventional civil rights groups.

Other civil rights leaders, such as SCLC's Martin Luther King Jr., argued that a united movement would be stronger than a divided one and invited the students to create a wing within SCLC. Representatives of the National Association for the Advancement of Colored People (NAACP) and the National Urban League made similar invitations. The students created a Temporary Coordinating Committee to debate the issue; in May the committee embraced the mainstream's practice of nonviolence but created an independent group, the Temporary Student Nonviolent Coordinating Committee. ("Temporary" was dropped from the name in October.) Made up of both black and white members, the group elected Marion Barry, a student at Nashville's Fisk University who would later become mayor of Washington, D.C., SNCC's first chairman and set up its headquarters in Atlanta, Georgia. When Barry returned to graduate studies a few months later, he was replaced by Charles McDew, a student at South Carolina State College.

In its first months SNCC served mostly as a channel for student groups to communicate and coordinate the sit-in campaign. The images on national television of well-groomed, peaceful protesters being refused a cup of coffee and, in some instances, being hauled off to jail, generated sympathy among many whites across the country. Several SNCC and other protesters capitalized on the publicity with a "jail-no-bail" campaign. Refusing to pay fines or bail, the students served jail sentences, thereby filling Southern jails and continuing media coverage. By the end of 1960 several chain stores in the upper South and Texas responded to the movement by ending segregation at their lunch counters. Several cities also agreed to desegregate public restaurants.

## Freedom Rides

From the end of 1960 through the fall of 1961 SNCC underwent a critical internal debate that it never completely resolved. One faction wanted to continue generating white sympathy through sit-ins and demonstrations, while another faction wanted to give Southern blacks power more directly by helping them register to vote. SNCC's James Forman, a schoolteacher-turned-coordinator who was well respected among students, urged the group in late 1961 to pursue both goals. Forman reasoned that helping blacks register to vote was a form of nonviolent protest that would stir up

Southern hostility, generate white sympathy, and give blacks more power. SNCC's membership agreed.

As the debate over SNCC's direction was taking place, the Congress of Racial Equality (CORE) was undertaking the Freedom Ride of 1961. On May 4 seven blacks and six whites left Washington, D.C., on two public buses bound for the Deep South. They intended to test the Supreme Court's ruling in *Boynton v. Virginia* (1960), which declared segregation in interstate bus and rail stations unconstitutional. In the first few days the riders encountered only minor hostility, but in the second week the riders were severely beaten. Outside Anniston, Alabama, one of their buses was burned, and in Birmingham several dozen whites attacked the riders only two blocks from the sheriff's office. With the intervention of the United States Justice Department, most of CORE's Freedom Riders were evacuated from Birmingham, Alabama to New Orleans. John Lewis, a former seminary student who would later lead SNCC and become a U.S. Congressman, stayed in Birmingham, as did another rider.

SNCC leaders hurriedly decided that letting violence end the trip would send the wrong signal to the country. They reinforced the pair of remaining riders with volunteers, and under SNCC leadership the trip continued. The group traveled from Birmingham to Montgomery without incident, but on their arrival in Montgomery they were savagely attacked by a mob of more than 1,000 whites. The extreme violence and the indifference of local police prompted a national outcry of support for the riders, putting pressure on President John F. Kennedy to end the violence. The riders continued to Mississippi, where they endured further brutality and jail terms but generated more publicity and inspired dozens more Freedom Rides. By the end of the summer the protests had spread to train stations and airports across the South, and in November the Interstate Commerce Commission issued rules prohibiting segregated transportation facilities.

### Winning the Vote

Following the sit-in and Freedom Ride victories, SNCC joined with CORE, the NAACP, SCLC, and the Urban League in the Voter Education Project (VEP). Funded by large private grants, VEP sought to increase the number of Southern blacks registered to vote. SNCC had failed at a similar voter-registration effort in rural Georgia in 1961 and 1962. When VEP funds became available in 1962, SNCC shifted its focus to Mississippi and Louisiana, where it also met stern resistance and succeeded in registering only a few blacks.

In 1963, however, several highly publicized conflicts changed the course of the movement. In May police in Birmingham brutally beat black and white protesters, prompting another wave of public sympathy. The next month Kennedy introduced a strong civil rights bill to Congress, which was passed during the administration of Lyndon Johnson as the Civil Rights Act of 1964. (The act prohibited segregation in several types of public facilities.) Liberal contributors responded to the violence by pouring large donations into virtually all of the civil rights groups, whose staffs and programs grew accordingly. In late 1963, when VEP decided to abandon Mississippi for lack of progress, SNCC, now led by John Lewis, could afford to stay.

Many SNCC activists were critical of the way larger civil rights groups "invaded" towns for a protest, then left after the protest ended. SNCC's field workers in Mississippi believed they could best help blacks by living in their communities and working with them over the long term. In late 1963, with help from CORE and, nominally, other civil rights groups, SNCC revitalized the Council of Federated Organizations (COFO); COFO had been created in 1961 to help free jailed Freedom Riders. It would now oversee voter registration in Mississippi. Bob Moses, a Harvard graduate student, veteran SNCC field worker, and leading advocate of commitment to communities, was placed in charge of COFO. COFO functioned largely as an arm of SNCC.

Despite COFO's efforts whites effectively used intimidation and discriminatory tactics to keep blacks from registering to vote in Mississippi. To Northern reporters, Mississippi officials argued that the state's blacks did not vote because they were too apathetic. COFO countered the claim by holding a Freedom Vote at the same time as the November 1963 elections. In mock elections 80,000 blacks cast ballots in their own communities, where they did not have to face hostile whites.

Amid the success many of COFO's black workers were angered by the role whites were playing in the organization. White students often came to the South for a few months (typically a summer), assumed high-profile leadership positions while there, then returned to safe campuses in the North while blacks continued the hard work. Many black activists were also tired of accepting beatings and jail sentences in order to win sympathy from white federal officials, white liberal donors, and the white public. They were weary as well of having to tone down their militancy and rhetoric at the request of whites in power. SNCC's Lewis voiced many of these frustrations during a speech in the March on Washington of August 1963; that Lewis was made to tone down his remarks by mainstream civil rights groups and white officials only further angered blacks in SNCC. For these reasons many COFO activists argued it was important for blacks to succeed on their own, without the help of white volunteers. Some even wondered if it would be possible to continue working with mainstream civil rights groups.

Moses was forced to address this debate when he proposed the Freedom Summer of 1964, a registration and education project that would build on the Freedom Vote. Moses argued forcefully that if COFO excluded whites, blacks had no moral standing to demand integration. Moreover, the movement would not receive as much publicity since national news groups would pay more attention to violence against whites than blacks. Moses's words were borne out when COFO's Michael Schwerner, James Chaney, and Andrew Goodman were murdered in June (Schwerner and Goodman were white) and the press and public responded with shock and outrage.

For years murders of blacks by whites in the South had gone unnoticed in the national media. President Johnson ordered a large FBI presence in Mississippi, and many whites became aware of the obstacles blacks faced when trying to vote in the Deep South. Still, COFO's 1,000 volunteers managed to register only ,1200 blacks statewide. Within COFO many student workers were convinced after the Schwerner, Chaney, and Goodman murders that nonviolence would not win blacks the vote. By the end of the summer SNCC officially defended the right of its Mississippi field secretaries to carry weapons.

Moses was able to exploit COFO's failure to register voters by creating a new party, the Mississippi Freedom Democratic Party (MFDP). Some 60,000 blacks joined the MFDP, which served as an alternative to Mississippi's all-white Democratic Party. With the presidential election of 1964 approaching, the MFDP sent 44 delegates to the national Democratic convention in Atlantic City, New Jersey. The delegation demanded to be seated at the convention in place of the regular Mississippi delegation. They were pledged to Johnson, while the white Democratic delegates were not. Although several Northern states supported seating the MFDP, Southern states threatened to walk out of the convention if the MFDP delegates were seated. Johnson, wary of losing the conservative South in the general election that fall, offered the MFDP a compromise: two of its black delegates would be seated along with the white delegates. The MFDP rejected the offer and, in a move largely coordinated by SNCC, walked out of the convention. In the aftermath, many whites across the country saw SNCC as an extremist group unwilling to bend, while many blacks became even more convinced that they could not work with whites.

## Selma and Beyond

In early 1965 King and SCLC attempted to register voters in Selma, Alabama. Learning from past mistakes, state and local officials denied the SCLC the brutal attacks that had created sympathy for blacks elsewhere. Instead, officials simply jailed blacks who tried to register. In March King called for a march from Selma to the capitol in Montgomery to protest black exclusion from the polls; however, he abruptly called off the protest on the eve of the march, probably to avoid antagonizing Johnson. After King left Selma, SNCC field workers and other activists urged local SCLC leaders to go ahead with the march. On March 7, 500 protesters headed by the SCLC's Hosea Williams and SNCC's Lewis began the march. In a matter of minutes a large deputized posse and dozens of state troopers attacked the marchers. The gruesome reports and photographs prompted one of the nation's largest outcries in support of the Civil Rights Movement. Largely as a result, Congress passed the Voting Rights Act of 1965, which provided federal protections and guarantees for black voters.

Though many SNCC members were pleased the events in Selma had generated white sympathy, many others were again weary of taking abuse. They were also angered that a second Selma march, led by King a week later, was cut short after federal officials cautioned against it. When riots broke out in the black Watts neighborhood of Los Angeles in the summer of 1965, many SNCC members argued that the time had come for blacks to seize power rather than seek accommodation with whites. In May 1966 SNCC formalized its shift in this direction by electing Stokely Carmichael (later Kwame Turé), a recent graduate of Howard University, to the chairmanship over John Lewis. Rejecting nonviolence, Carmichael argued at first that violence should be used in self-defense; later he called for offensive violence to overthrow oppression. Carmichael also denounced Johnson's civil rights bills, which were supported by the SCLC and the NAACP.

In June 1966, in Greenwood, Mississippi, Carmichael advocated Black Power in a well-publicized speech. Although "Black Power" had been used before as a shorthand for black pride and political equality, Carmichael popularized the term through repeated speeches. Many whites were offended by Carmichael's views, which they saw as racist or separatist, and most of the mainstream civil rights groups severed their few remaining ties with SNCC. SNCC's white staff and volunteers, who had already begun to drift away from the group, soon left. Eventually Carmichael expelled the remaining white staff and denounced SNCC's white donors. By early 1967 SNCC was near bankruptcy, and both its staff and membership had dwindled.

In June 1967, when Carmichael left SNCC to help lead the Black Panther Party, he was replaced by 23-year-old H. Rap Brown. In his first months Brown removed the word "Nonviolent" from SNCC (renaming the group the Student National Coordinating Committee) and made urgent calls for violence. When Detroit rioted in the summer of 1967, Brown urged an audience in Cambridge, Massachusetts, to do the same. When a Cambridge school was set aflame hours later, Brown was charged with inciting a riot, one of several charges he would face in the following years. In May 1968 his legal problems forced him to resign SNCC's chairmanship. SNCC continued to operate into the early 1970s, but its impact on politics was minimal.

North America

# Sullivan, Leon Howard

**(b. October 16, 1922, Charleston, W.Va.), African American minister; author of the "Sullivan Principles," guidelines for American companies doing business in South Africa.**

Raised by his grandmother, who encouraged him to help the disadvantaged, Leon Sullivan pursued this goal by entering the ministry. He was pastor of Philadelphia's Zion Baptist Church from 1950 to 1988. In 1964 he founded the Opportunities Industrialization Centers of America (OIC), which provided educational and vocational training for unskilled African American workers. For this work Sullivan was awarded the National Association for the Advancement of Colored People's prestigious Spingarn Medal in 1971. By 1980 the OIC had grown into a national force and, by 1993, despite funding cuts, the OIC's programs had been instituted in several sub-Saharan African countries.

In 1977 Sullivan enumerated six principles that were guidelines for American corporations doing business in South Africa. Known as the Sullivan Principles, these guidelines were designed to use American corporate power to promote fair treatment for black workers. The principles concerned equal pay, equal working conditions, integration of blacks and whites in work facilities, training programs, supervisory positions for blacks, and improvements in living conditions outside the workplace. Sullivan declared the principles a failure in 1987 because apartheid continued. In 1991 he received two honors for his work with the American and African poor: the Presidential Medal of Freedom in the United States, and the Distinguished Service Award, the highest honor awarded in the Côte d'Ivoire.

North America
_____

## Sweatt v. Painter,

**1950 United States Supreme Court case that outlawed segregation in graduate education, providing a legal basis for Brown v. Board of Education (1954).**

After decades of challenging state-imposed segregation, the National Association for the Advancement of Colored People (NAACP) in 1946 joined in a lawsuit that paved the way for its eventual victory in *Brown v. Board of Education* (1954). The case, *Sweatt v. Painter*, originated when Heman Sweatt, an African American letter carrier, was rejected on racial grounds for admission to the University of Texas Law School. Following his protest a district court ordered Texas to provide a law school for black students. Rather than accept the state's attempts at compliance—first by appending law classes to a black vocational school, then by renting rooms in an office building and hiring three part-time law professors—Sweatt chose to pursue his case.

Sweatt was represented by Thurgood Marshall of the NAACP Legal Defense Fund. The NAACP's longstanding strategy—paradoxically based on *Plessy v. Ferguson*, an earlier case that defended segregation—was to force states into choosing between providing expensive "equal" graduate schools and admitting black students to existing schools. In *Sweatt* and a related case, *McLaurin v. Oklahoma*, Marshall went further. Using sociological and psychological testimony, he argued that a segregated education, however comparable the physical facilities, was inherently unequal in that it denied black students interaction with classmates, access to extra-curricular activities, and the status and alumni network of established white schools.

In a sign of the case's significance, several groups filed *amicus curiae* (friend of the court) briefs when it reached the Supreme Court. Eleven southern states argued in support of Texas's segregation, while nearly 200 law professors signed a brief backing the NAACP. Perhaps the most influential amicus brief was presented by the U.S. Justice Department. For the first time the U.S. government said it was time to overturn *Plessy*.

The justices, however, were not prepared to go that far. Writing for a unanimous court, Chief Justice Fred Vinson declared that Heman Sweatt was denied an equal legal education in the segregated school. But the cautious opinion declined to comment on the constitutionality of "separate but equal." Despite this shortcoming, *Sweatt* and its companion cases helped prepare the court for its most significant civil rights case of the twentieth century, *Brown v. Board of Education* (1954).

# T

## Taylor, Gardner Calvin

(b. June 8, 1918, Baton Rouge, La.), African American Baptist minister known as the "Dean of Black Preachers" who led church support for the civil rights struggle.

With a bachelor's degree from Leland College, Gardner C. Taylor began his theological training at Oberlin Theological Seminary in 1937. He was ordained a Baptist minister in 1939, and he followed his theological degree (1940) with pastorates in New Orleans and Baton Rouge.

In 1948 Taylor moved to New York City to preach at the Concord Baptist Church of Christ in the Bedford-Stuyvesant section of Brooklyn. He was a dynamic leader, establishing social service programs such as a nursing home and clothing exchange. In 1962, with 12,000 members, the church became the largest Protestant congregation in the United States. Taylor was known internationally for the brilliance of his preaching, and was called the best preacher in America.

An active proponent of educational reform, Taylor risked his position on the New York City Board of Education in 1958 to support the demand for better school conditions for African American children. He served on the Citywide Committee for Integrated Schools, and in 1961 he and his wife, Laura, founded the Concord Elementary Day School.

During the 1960s Taylor rose to prominence as a civil rights leader through his involvement in the Congress of Racial Equality (CORE). During this time he worked closely with a group of Baptist ministers that included the Reverend Martin Luther King Jr. In 1961, dissatisfied with the leadership of Joseph H. Jackson, the group split from the National Baptist Convention, USA, Inc. The newly formed Progressive National Baptist Convention (PNBC) publicly supported civil rights struggles of CORE and the Southern Christian Leadership Conference (SCLC).

Renowned for his mastery of the spoken word, Taylor continued to serve as a visiting and guest preacher after his retirement in 1990 from Concord Baptist Church of Christ.

# Terrell, Mary Eliza Church

(b. September 23, 1863, Memphis, Tenn.; d. July 24, 1954, Washington, D.C.), African American educator and a prominent advocate for African American civil rights and women's rights, and for nineteenth-century black women's club organizations.

Mary Church Terrell was born to Louisa and Robert Church, who had emerged from slavery to become prosperous business owners. Although the couple separated, Robert Church financially supported his daughter as she completed a classical education at Oberlin College. When she received her bachelor's degree in 1884, her father wanted her to assume the role of hostess, a refined position he felt appropriate for the daughter of the wealthiest black man in the South. She refused the conventional role, however, and entered the professional world of education instead.

Mary Church put her energy and training to work as a teacher at Ohio's black Wilberforce College in 1885. Two years later she moved to the M Street High School in Washington D.C., where she met her future husband, Robert Heberton Terrell. She completed a master's degree at Oberlin, followed, in 1888, by a two-year European tour. For an African American woman, this American rite of passage, usually reserved for the white elite, provided more than the opportunity to see diverse cultures: it was also a chance for her to experience a different racial environment than that of the United States. Church also used the trip to develop the language skills she would later use in Europe to promote the cause of African American equality.

When Church returned to the United States in 1890, she married Terrell, retired from teaching, and focused on managing her household. That quiet life ended in 1892, when a lifelong friend, Tom Moss, was lynched in Memphis. Mary Church Terrell, along with her friend Frederick Douglass, demanded a meeting with President Benjamin Harrison. Although they did receive a hearing, Harrison made no public statement opposing the violence. The event galvanized Terrell into activism, a vocation which lasted for more than 60 years.

Terrell became an active participant in the women's club movement, leading the Colored Women's League in 1892. When this group merged with several others to form the National Association of Colored Women (NACW) in 1896, she became the president of this first American national black organization. Under Terrell's leadership NACW organized around issues of health, housing, employment, and child care, as these matters specifically applied to the lives of African American women.

As a member of the National American Woman Suffrage Association, Terrell took the podium for the cause of women's voting rights, often speaking before all-white audiences. She was striking in her learning and political savvy: at the 1904 International Council of Women conference in Berlin, for instance, she delivered her speech in German, and then translated into French and English.

Terrell worked alongside many of the prominent African American activists of the era on issues of racial equity. She supported the work of Booker T. Washington, despite others' criticism of his vocational educational programs. In 1909 she joined W. E. B. Du Bois as a founding member of the National Association for the Advancement of Colored People (NAACP).

An active supporter of the Republican Party until 1952 and the wife of a federal judge, Terrell used her political clout in the upper echelons of American politics to fight for social justice for African Americans. Yet she often risked this position to speak what she saw to be the truth. In 1906, when three companies of black soldiers were dismissed from the United States Army without a hearing after a racial incident in Brownsville, Texas, Terrell publicly attacked President Theodore Roosevelt's decision. After her meeting with Secretary of War William Howard Taft, the soldiers were granted a hearing, although the dismissal ultimately remained in place.

During World War I and World War II, Terrell positioned herself as an advocate for the black women and girls who were entering the employment arena. Following World War II she became even more militant in her activism, as she saw the discrimination and economic hardship that continued in the nation even after black soldiers had given their lives abroad.

Despite the privileges afforded her by her social status and fair skin, Terrell encountered the same discrimination faced by other African Americans. In her autobiography, *A Colored Woman in a White World* (1940), she wrote of the difficulty of being black and female: "A White woman has only one handicap to overcome—that of sex. I have two—both sex and race."

In 1950 Terrell entered a segregated Washington, D.C., restaurant with an interracial group. After the blacks were refused service, they filed affidavits against the restaurant. Three years of protest and legal battles ended in the protesters' favor, in *District of Columbia v. John Thompson*, and at 90 years of age, Terrell saw the desegregation of eating facilities in Washington, D.C.

North America

# Thirteenth Amendment of the United States Constitution and the Emancipation Proclamation,

document that signaled the government's commitment to ending slavery, which was followed by the constitutional amendment that officially abolished slavery in the United States.

The Thirteenth Amendment is best understood against the background of the American Civil War. Although President Abraham Lincoln personally opposed slavery, ending slavery was not one of his administration's initial war aims. Instead he sought to "save the Union, and not either to save or

THE AMERICAN DECLARATION OF INDEPENDENCE ILLUSTRATED.

In 1867 Louis Prang & Co., lithographers in Boston, issued *The American Declaration of Independence Illustrated*, in which the American Eagle lifts a recently freed black man and a white to freedom. Above their heads is the line: "Break every yoke; let the oppressed go free." *CORBIS/Bettmann*

destroy slavery." As president, Lincoln had sworn to uphold the Constitution; the Supreme Court had affirmed the constitutionality of slavery in its 1857 *Dred Scott* decision. As Southern states seceded, Lincoln had serious concerns about keeping the four border states—Delaware, Maryland, Kentucky, and Missouri—in the Union and about the loyalty of Northern Democrats. Also, he had promised slaveholders who were loyal to the federal government that they would be able to keep their slaves. Lincoln had first attempted to convince slaveholders in the border states gradually to eliminate slavery in return for compensation, but the slaveholders refused.

Lincoln's commitment to winning the war led him by 1862 to see emancipation as a necessity because he realized that slaves were a vital component of the Southern economy and that freeing slaves would destabilize the South. Thus in July 1862 Congress passed two laws regarding slaves. The first was a confiscation act that freed slaves from owners who had rebelled against the United States. The second was a militia act that enabled the president to use freed slaves in the army. In this context Lincoln was prepared to use presidential war powers to emancipate slaves in the rebel states.

Lincoln issued the Emancipation Proclamation on January 1, 1863, declaring that slaves in all states still at war with the federal government were free and would remain so. While taking care to exempt border slave states and the three Confederate states that the Union controlled, Lincoln nevertheless endorsed the idea of recruiting freed slaves and free blacks for service in the armed forces. The Emancipation Proclamation, however, technically freed no one, because Lincoln's authority was not recognized in the Confederacy.

Many Republican Party members recognized that the proclamation was only a war measure that might have no lasting impact on the institution of slavery. Still, its effect was to signal the federal government's opposition to slavery and to bolster the abolitionist cause. The war ceased to be one aimed only at saving the Union and became a war to end slavery as well. An initial stream of escaping slaves slowly expanded to become a flood of runaways. In response to the proclamation's endorsement of black military enlistment, more than 180,000 blacks enrolled in the army and 10,000 in the navy by the end of the war.

A variety of forces began to press for a constitutional amendment to abolish slavery permanently. Women's groups were in the forefront in this battle, particularly the National Women's Loyal League, a predominantly white organization led by suffragists Susan B. Anthony and Elizabeth Cady Stanton. They believed that chattel slavery as practiced in the United States was closely linked to women's inferior place in society, and that progress in one area could result in progress in another. The Republican Party outlined support for such an amendment in its 1864 platform. Lincoln, after winning the 1864 presidential election, began pushing Congress to pass an amendment, using both his electoral mandate and his political skills to overcome Democratic opposition.

Early in 1865, shortly before the end of the Civil War and Lincoln's assassination, Congress approved the amendment. Its simplicity and brevity belies the fundamental changes it made to American society. Section 1 states that, "Neither slavery nor involuntary servitude, except as a punishment for crime whereof the party shall have been duly convicted, shall exist within the United States, or any place subject to their jurisdiction." Section 2 gives Congress the "power to enforce this article by appropriate legislation."

Although it was approved by Congress, the amendment had to be ratified by three-fourths of the states before becoming part of the Constitution. Most Northern states had ratified it, but it was up to President Andrew Johnson, who assumed the presidency after Lincoln's assassination in April 1865, to secure the necessary approval from Southern states. Johnson set very lenient terms for Southern reentry into American political society, but he required that Southern states ratify the amendment as a condition of readmission. Many state constitutional conventions, including those of Delaware and Kentucky, which had never outlawed slavery, opposed this requirement. Southern states especially disliked the second section, which provided for federal intervention if slavery were practiced. Johnson's tactics gained cooperation of enough states and the amendment was ratified on December 18, 1865, finally abolishing legalized slavery throughout the United States.

North America

# Thomas, Clarence

(b. June 23, 1948, Pin Point, Ga.), African American associate justice of the United States Supreme Court known for his conservative views and judicial record.

Clarence Thomas was raised by his grandparents in Savannah, Georgia. He attended Roman Catholic schools, and in 1967 enrolled in Immaculate Conception Seminary in Conception, Missouri, to study to become a priest.

Subjected to overt racism at the school, however, he transferred to Holy Cross College in Worcester, Massachusetts, where he became active in the Black Power Movement.

After graduating cum laude with an A.B. in English literature in 1971, Thomas entered Yale University Law School later that year. At Yale Thomas developed the view that the Democratic Party had failed and was failing African Americans. By the time of his graduation in 1974, Thomas had become staunchly conservative and decided to work for John Danforth, Missouri's Republican attorney general, whom he followed to Washington, D.C., when Danforth became a U.S. Senator.

Known within the Republican Party as a consistently conservative critic of governmental civil rights activity and of affirmative action, Thomas was appointed assistant secretary for civil rights in the Department of Education. In 1982 President Ronald Reagan named Thomas chair of the Equal Employment Opportunity Commission (EEOC), a post to which he was reappointed in 1986, passing both confirmation processes with little difficulty despite opposition from civil rights groups.

In 1989 President George Bush nominated Thomas for the U.S. Circuit Court of Appeals, and he was confirmed by the Senate Judiciary Committee on March 6, 1990 by a vote of 13 to 1. When Thurgood Marshall announced his retirement from the Supreme Court in July 1991, Bush nominated Thomas for the opening, despite his brief judicial record. The committee reached an impasse regarding Thomas's nomination and, for the first time in U.S. history, a Supreme Court nominee was sent to the Senate floor without recommendation. Soon after, Anita Hill, a University of Oklahoma law professor, went public with allegations that Thomas had sexually harassed her during the time she worked with him as an EEOC staff attorney. Hearings held in October to examine Hill's claims were given extraordinary popular media coverage. Despite heated sentiment against Thomas from many groups, the Senate voted 52 to 48 to confirm Thomas by the second closest margin ever for a Supreme Court nominee. Thomas was sworn in on October 19, 1991, and has not only amassed one of the Court's most conservative records, but has also attracted public criticism from many prominent African Americans.

North America

# Till, Emmett Louis

(b. July 25, 1941, Chicago, Ill.; d. August 28, 1955, LeFlore County, Miss.),
African American teenager who was an early victim of civil rights-era violence.

Emmett Till was born and raised in Chicago, Illinois. When he was 14 years of age, he was sent to Mississippi to spend the summer with his uncle. Because of his Northern upbringing, Till was not accustomed to the racial taboos of the segregated South; he bragged to his Southern black friends that in Chicago he even had a white girlfriend. These unbelieving friends dared him to enter a store and ask a white woman for a date. Inside, Till hugged Carol Bryant's waist and squeezed her hand, then whistled at her as his friends rushed him away.

On August 28, 1955, Carol Bryant's husband, Roy, and his half-brother, J.W. Milam, abducted Till from his uncle's home. Three days later his naked, beaten, decomposed body was found in the Tallahatchie River; he had been shot in the head. The two white men were tried one month later by an all-white jury, and despite the fact that they admitted abducting Till, they were acquitted because the body was too mangled to be positively identified.

Till's murder became a rallying point for the Civil Rights Movement. Photographs of his open casket were reprinted across the country, and protests were organized by the National Association for the Advancement of Colored People (NAACP), the Brotherhood of Sleeping Car Porters, and such leaders as W. E. B. Du Bois. The public outrage over the injustice of the trial helped ensure that Congress included a provision for federal investigations of civil rights violations in the Civil Rights Act of 1957.

North America

## Tulsa Riot of 1921,

white riot that devastated some 40 city blocks in the mostly black Greenwood district of Tulsa, Oklahoma.

The growth of the oil industry made Tulsa, Oklahoma, a rich town by 1921. Its predominantly black section, Greenwood, achieved a level of wealth that earned it a reputation as the "Negro Wall Street of America." African Americans constituted about 12 percent of the overall population. Whites reacted violently to the success of African Americans—forming "whipping parties" that randomly assaulted blacks on a daily basis. There had also been several lynchings in the vicinity of Tulsa, a major Ku Klux Klan center, and blacks armed themselves for protection. The riot of 1921 was the culmination of these racial tensions.

In 1921 a 19-year-old black man named Dick Rowland took a break from his downtown job as a shoe shiner to use the restroom at the top of a nearby building. Sarah Page, a 17-year-old white girl who was operating the elevator there, claimed that Rowland assaulted her. Rowland was arrested the following day and incarcerated at the local courthouse.

Before the incident had been investigated, the May 31 *Tulsa Tribune* reported that Rowland, who was identified only by his color, "attacked [Page], scratching her hands and face, and tearing her clothes off." That evening a crowd of whites began to gather outside the courthouse in response to the paper's assertion that Rowland was going to be lynched.

The sheriff tried unsuccessfully to disperse the crowd, which by 10:30 p.m. had grown to nearly 2,000. A group of 50 to 75 armed black men, who previously had been turned away, returned to the courthouse to help the sheriff defend Rowland. One of the white men tried to disarm one of the blacks, a shot was fired, and the two groups opened fire. Vastly outnumbered, the blacks retreated to Greenwood. Whites who did not have arms stole them from hardware stores and pawnshops and headed for the Frisco Railroad tracks, the boundary line that separated the black and white communities. Around 1:00 a.m. on June 1st, warfare resumed.

After several drive-by shootings, whites invaded the Greenwood district in force around 6:00 a.m. and began to burn houses and businesses. They shot at the fleeing blacks, whom they sometimes threw back into the flames. Blacks were largely outnumbered and, during the rioting, police worked continuously to disarm them. When the National Guard arrived at 9:15 a.m. the gunfire had diminished, and the Guard began to help the police round up and place African Americans in holding areas, which were manned by armed guards. Approximately 6,000 blacks—half of Tulsa's African American population—were reported to have been incarcerated during the riot.

By 11:30 a.m. violence had ceased, and the Red Cross had arrived to provide medical treatment to the injured blacks. In the following week the Red Cross treated 531 persons and operated on an additional 163. They also erected 350 tents for African Americans whose homes had been destroyed, and they continued to administer aid through the late fall of 1921. Records kept by the Red Cross estimate that 1,115 houses and businesses belonging to black people had been burned down, and that another 314 had been looted; that 715 families left Tulsa, some of whom returned after the riot; and that 300 people died, of whom only a small percentage were white. Historical sources disagree about these statistics.

In the midst of Red Cross relief efforts Tulsa's white authorities announced to the nation that they would assume the responsibility of rebuilding Greenwood, and that additional external assistance would not be accepted. The white community, however, abandoned the reconstruction project and tried unsuccessfully to prevent African Americans from rebuilding on their own land. Because the city's white officials delayed their reconstruction efforts, 1,000 black Tulsans spent the winter of 1921–1922 in tents.

In the end blacks were blamed for inciting the riot by showing up at the courthouse with firearms. No white Tulsans were arrested or jailed. Page refused to prosecute Rowland: follow-up investigation found that Rowland had stumbled into the girl as he was getting off the elevator, and all charges were dropped. Little discussion of the riot occurred before its 75th anniversary on June 1, 1996, when, at a ceremony in Tulsa, African American survivors of the riot addressed the public. Both whites and blacks in Tulsa had avoided serious discussion of the riot until that event.

# United States Judiciary, Blacks in the

The nominee for the newly created position on the United States Court of Appeals for the Third Circuit approached confirmation hearings with impressive credentials. He was a graduate of Amherst College (Phi Beta Kappa and magna cum laude) and Harvard Law School (J.D., S.J.D.; law review editor) as well as a member of the faculty, and later dean, of Howard University School of Law. He served as assistant solicitor in the U.S. Department of the Interior, civilian aide to the secretary of war in World War II, and was a personal adviser to President Truman. He was a former governor and U.S. District Court judge. The nominee in question was William Henry Hastie, the first African American appointed to the federal bench. His nomination was roundly endorsed by the attorney general and the American Bar Association. Moreover, the sitting judges on the third circuit—his colleagues by virtue of his recess appointment to the new judgeship—actively lobbied their U.S. senators on his behalf. Yet his unprecedented appointment was engulfed in often vicious political controversy—this at one point even degenerated to Hastie's being branded by some as a Communist, which, in the climate of the times, was a deadly accusation. Between his nomination and eventual confirmation fully ten months later, hearings were postponed, a special subcommittee was impaneled to consider his nomination, and the political nerves of those both on and off the bench were rubbed raw.

Federal judges are important not only because they decide conflicts (cases) between individuals and groups in society, but also because they interpret the Constitution. In the process they determine how broad statements like "equal protection under the laws" in the Fourteenth Amendment apply to specific situations such as the legality of segregation or affirmative action. Federal judges are nominated by the president and must be confirmed by the U.S. Senate. They "hold their Offices during good Behavior," which means they serve for life unless removed from office (a truly extraordinary event). Consequently, the mark that presidents make on the courts with their appointments is evident for years or even decades after they leave office. For example, 23 years after Lyndon Johnson left the White House, Thurgood Marshall was still on the Supreme Court.

At the dawn of the twenty-first century some are proclaiming the start of an almost revolutionary diversification of the federal courts. This process was spearheaded by the efforts of President Bill Clinton, who promised to use his appointment power to create a bench that "looks like America." Even though almost 20 percent of President Clinton's appointments went to African Americans, the overall percentage of African Americans on the bench at the end of 1996 stood at only 9.2 percent, fully 25 percent lower than the percentage of African Americans in the general population (12.7 percent). Additionally, the preponderance of Clinton's appointments were to certain states or regions. Indeed, almost half (23) of the states in this country never have had an African American federal judge. The general trend toward diversification is diluted further because most appointments have been to the district courts, rather than to the more prestigious and powerful appeals courts, where the number of sitting African American judges amounts to only 5.8 percent.

Research on federal judicial selection tells us that minority appointments are likely to come from areas where there are higher concentrations of African American voters and economic power, often in the form of business ownership. The African American community in those areas is a force to be recognized and reckoned with, which leads to representation on the bench. Given the structure of the judicial selection process, however, the role of the president is central, and the degree to which diversification is achieved is, in large measure, a product of how important that goal is to a president.

## The First Inroads: 1937–1976

The federal judiciary—by nature of a shared institutional appointment process—is inextricably bound to the president and Congress, which in turn interact with the larger society. Genuine progress is rarely made until all the elements in this complex mix are prepared to support change. This principle is demonstrated in the chain of events that started with the Supreme Court's decision in *Brown v. Board of Education* in 1954, which, among other things, set the stage for congressional approval of the Civil Rights Act of 1964 and the Voting Rights Act of 1965. These two acts were in turn enforced vigorously by President Johnson's attorney general, Ramsey Clark.

No African American was appointed to the federal judiciary until 1937. Even after that, the first two—William Hastie and his successor, Herman Moore—were named as district judges to the Virgin Islands. Unlike judicial appointments from states, territorial appointments are set for a fixed term rather than for life. Additionally, even though territorial appointees must be confirmed by the Senate, they do not serve an area that is represented by a senator. Accordingly, they elide the "not in my backyard" mentality of elected politicians serving in a pervasively racist political climate. Hastie's appointment, in other words, was part of no grand effort to diversify the judiciary. Prior to his nomination he served with distinction as the Interior Department's assistant solicitor in charge of the Virgin Islands; he was subsequently the governor of this territory. Interior Secretary Harold Ickes recommended him to President Roosevelt when a vacancy occurred on the Virgin Islands court.

For his time Roosevelt's successor, Harry Truman, was progressive with regard to issues of race; he ordered the desegregation of the armed forces and an end to discrimination in the civil service. Although he commissioned only three African American judges, two of the three are of special significance. Irvin Mollison was the first African American lifetime appointee, albeit one to the Customs Court, which has a specialized rather than a general jurisdiction. Hastie reemerged as another first—this time as the first African American appointed to the prestigious Circuit Court of Appeals, where he served with distinction until his retirement in 1971.

The election of Dwight Eisenhower in 1952 stalled the process of bench diversification. Eisenhower's opposition to racial justice in general and to the decision in *Brown v. Board of Education* in particular are well documented. Both are illustrated in his judicial appointees: in his eight years as president Eisenhower allowed only 1 of his 173 appointments to go to an African American candidate—Walter Gordon, who was posted to the Virgin Islands.

To some John F. Kennedy symbolized a commitment to racial justice, and his election in 1960 heralded to many a new dawn in securing minority appointments to the federal courts. The fact remains, however, that throughout his abbreviated presidency Kennedy was very careful not to antagonize powerful Southerners in the Congress. While it is impossible to know what might have transpired had he served two full terms, Kennedy's timidity in this regard is reflected in his judicial appointments: only 3 percent (4 of 128) went to African Americans. Judge Spottswood Robinson's appointment to the District of Columbia notwithstanding, all of Kennedy's African American appointments were to federal courts in Northern states.

Judicial diversity was fundamentally advanced under Lyndon Johnson. Johnson, for one thing, appointed more than twice as many African Americans (9) as did his predecessor. Further, in 1966 he nominated Constance Baker Motley, the first female African American jurist, to the Southern District of New York. He followed that appointment in 1967 with the stunning announcement that Thurgood Marshall was his choice for a seat on the Supreme Court.

Judge Motley was born in New Haven, Connecticut, in 1921 and graduated from New York University and Columbia Law School. Prior to her appointment to the bench she was an attorney for the National Association for the Advancement of Colored People (NAACP) Legal Defense Fund, a New York state senator, and borough president of Manhattan. She retired from the court in 1986. Justice Marshall was born in Baltimore, Maryland, in 1908 and graduated from Lincoln University and Howard University Law School. He was solicitor general of the United States (the government's chief lawyer) and prior to his elevation to the Supreme Court he served on the Second Circuit Court of Appeals. He received national prominence when, as director of the NAACP Legal Defense Fund, he argued *Brown v. Board of Education* before the Supreme Court. He retired from the bench in 1991.

Richard Nixon, in his 1968 presidential campaign, complained often and vehemently about the liberal decisions made by the Supreme Court in the 1950s and 1960s and pledged that he would appoint only "strict constructionists" to the federal bench. Then and again in his reelection effort in 1972 he pursued a "Southern strategy" designed to attract voters from the nation's Southland who otherwise might be inclined to vote for segregationist George Wallace. Once Nixon was elected, the consequences for the federal bench were predictable. Nixon and his caretaker successor, Gerald Ford, appointed only ten African Americans to the federal bench, and six of those were Republicans; none was appointed to either the more prestigious circuit courts or the Supreme Court. In one case Whitney Young, executive director of the National Urban League, lobbied the president to replace the retired Hastie with Clarence Ferguson. The latter was a lifelong Republican, former dean of Howard University Law School, and professor at Rutgers Law School. Despite Young's contention that Hastie's replacement was a matter of grave concern to the black community, Ferguson was rejected as being too liberal, and Hastie's seat went to a white male.

## Jimmy Carter: 1977–1980

Carter was the first president elected from the Deep South in more than a century, and he brought to the Oval Office a personal commitment to racial progress. African Americans were a crucial element of his electoral coalition, especially in the Southern states that ended up leading his margin of victory. During the 1976 campaign he pledged to appoint judges on the basis of merit rather than traditional political considerations, and once in office he worked with Congress to establish merit selection commissions in the states and circuits. Throughout its term the Carter administration promoted racial and gender diversification. Compared to those of his predecessors, Carter's results were stunning. Thirty-eight (14 percent) of his appointments went to African Americans. In contrast to that of other presidents, Carter's appointment rate for African Americans was higher in the circuit courts than in the district courts (he made no appointments to the Supreme Court). Carter made the first African American judicial appointment to a Deep South state—Robert Collins to the Eastern District of Louisiana. Moreover, by the time he left office he had made the first African American appointments to 14 states, including 11 Southern and border states, as well as the first such appointment on 3 circuits. So, in just four years Carter made considerable strides in diversifying the bench in two respects—numerically and geographically.

## The Republican Reversal: 1981–1992

Ronald Reagan entered office armed with a conservative political agenda and an avowed hostility to affirmative action. The consequences for racial diversification of the federal bench followed suit: only 7 of Reagan's 369 appointees (1.9 percent) were African American. Only one African American was placed on the circuit courts, and none went to the Supreme Court. Perhaps the only saving grace of Reagan's appointments was that they completed the task—spearheaded by Carter—of integrating the Deep South bench by assigning African American district judges to Virginia and Mississippi.

As Reagan's administration wore on, the level of criticism by the Democrat-controlled Senate rose over the president's apparent inattention to racial and gender diversity on the federal courts. George Bush experienced pressure from the same criticism when he entered office. Additionally, post-election analyses revealed that Bush faced a "gender gap" with female voters (a considerably lower percentage of his supporters were women), and minority voters held the balance of power in several states that would be critical to his reelection efforts. Accordingly, Bush was more attentive to appointing women and Latinos than African Americans, yet he nonetheless improved on Reagan's record by awarding 13 of his 187 appointments to African Americans. Bush also appreciated that minority candidates could be nominated without conceding political or legal agendas contrary to his own: only 2 of Bush's 13 appointees were Democrats. Judge Clarence Thomas was appointed to the Supreme Court in 1991, and he is now one of the staunchest conservatives on the high court.

Justice Thomas was born in Savannah, Georgia, and was educated at Holy Cross College and Yale Law School. He was assistant attorney general for the State of Missouri, legislative assistant to Senator John Danforth (MO), assistant secretary for civil rights in the U.S. Department of Education, and chair of the Equal Employment Opportunity Commission. Prior to his elevation to the Supreme Court he was appointed to the U.S. Court of Appeals for the District of Columbia Circuit by President Bush in 1990.

## A Bench That Looks Like America: 1993–

Clinton entered office without wanting to recast the ideological profile of the federal judiciary; he did not base his selection of appointees on litmus tests on issues such as abortion, as had the Reagan administration. While Clinton did have perhaps the most ambitious domestic policy agenda in a generation, he sought to implement it in ways other than a judicial selection strategy. Reluctant to have heated confirmation battles jeopardize his policy aspirations in other areas, he consistently nominated moderate candidates with sound credentials. Nevertheless, during his campaign and once in office

Clinton was unambiguous in his intention to broaden representation both in the executive branch and on the federal courts. He made good on his promise by appointing the largest percentage of African Americans in history (19.6); these were by and large moderates, to be sure.

The pace of diversification slowed somewhat once the Republicans wrested control of the Congress from the Democrats in 1994, so Clinton's place in the history of bench diversification remains to be seen. African Americans currently are represented on only 5 of the 12 circuit courts and on the district courts of 25 states. Even so, Carter or Clinton alone had a hand in all but one of the circuit appointments, and in 17 of those to the states.

# Voting Rights Act of 1965,

legislation that charged the federal government of the United States with helping disfranchised African Americans regain the right to vote in the South.

In the century following Reconstruction, African Americans in the South faced overwhelming obstacles to voting. Despite the Fifteenth and Nineteenth Amendments to the United States Constitution, which had enfranchised black men and all women respectively, Southern voter registration boards used poll taxes, literacy tests, and other bureaucratic impediments to deny African Americans their legal rights. Southern blacks also risked harassment, intimidation, economic reprisals, and physical violence when they tried to register or vote. As a result African Americans had little if any political power, either locally or nationally. In Mississippi, for instance, only 5 percent of eligible blacks were registered to vote in 1960.

The Voting Rights Act of 1965, meant to reverse this disfranchisement, grew out of both public protest and private political negotiation. Starting in 1961, the Southern Christian Leadership Conference (SCLC), led by Rev. Martin Luther King Jr., staged nonviolent demonstrations in Albany, Georgia, and Birmingham, Alabama. King and the SCLC hoped to attract national media attention and pressure the U.S. government to protect African Americans' constitutional rights. The strategy worked. Newspaper photos and television broadcasts of Birmingham's notoriously racist police commissioner, Eugene "Bull" Connor, and his men violently attacking the SCLC's peaceful protesters with water hoses, police dogs, and nightsticks awakened the consciences of white Americans.

Selma, Alabama, was the site of the next campaign. In the first three months of 1965 the SCLC led local residents and visiting volunteers in a series of marches demanding an equal right to vote. As they did in Birmingham, protesters met with violence and imprisonment in Selma. King himself wrote a letter from the Selma jail, published in the *New York*

A federal vote registrar fills out forms for prospective black voters in Canton, Mississippi, under the Voting Rights Act of 1965. *CORBIS*

*Times*, in which he said, "There are more Negroes in jail with me than there are on the voting rolls" in Selma. In the worst attack yet, on Sunday, March 7, a group of Alabama state troopers, local sheriff's officers, and unofficial possemen used tear gas and clubs against 600 peaceful marchers. By now, as King had predicted, the nation was watching.

President Lyndon B. Johnson, who succeeded to the presidency after the 1963 assassination of John F. Kennedy, made civil rights one of his administration's top priorities, using his formidable political skills to pass the Twenty Fourth Amendment, which outlawed poll taxes, in 1964. Now, a week after "Bloody Sunday" in Selma, Johnson gave a televised speech before Congress in which he not only denounced the assault but called it "wrong—deadly wrong" that African Americans were being denied their constitutional rights. Johnson went on to dramatically quote the movement's motto, "we shall overcome."

Two days later the president sent the voting rights bill to Congress. The resolution, signed into law on August 6, 1965, empowered the federal government to oversee voter registration and elections in counties that had used tests to determine voter eligibility or where registration or turnout had been less than 50 percent in the 1964 presidential election. It also banned discriminatory literacy tests and expanded voting rights for non-English-speaking Americans.

The law's effects were wide and powerful. By 1968 nearly 60 percent of eligible African Americans were registered to vote in Mississippi, and other Southern states showed similar improvement. Between 1965 and 1990 the number of black state legislators and members of Congress rose from 2 to 160. Despite finally reclaiming their constitutional voting rights, however, many African Americans in the South and elsewhere saw little progress on other fronts. They still faced illegal job discrimination, substandard schools, and unequal health care. Following its major victories—the Civil Rights Act of 1964 and the Voting Rights Act of 1965—the liberal, integrationist Civil Rights Movement began to be eclipsed by the more radical Black Power Movement.

The Voting Rights Act was extended in 1970, 1975, and 1982—the last time despite vigorous resistance from the Reagan administration. Fearing a largely Democratic black vote, the Republican Party adopted various means to minimize it, including at-large elections and redistricting to dilute black representation. The party also attacked as racial gerrymandering the new "majority-minority" congressional districts drawn by the U.S. Justice Department. In 1996 the Supreme Court agreed, outlawing the use of racial factors in deciding district lines. Some prominent African Americans, like Harvard University law professor Lani Guinier, argued that minority votes would be more effective in a system of proportional representation.

Despite these setbacks and debates, the Voting Rights Act had an enormous impact. It re-enfranchised black Southerners and helped elect African Americans at the local, state, and national levels. By 1989 there were an estimated 7,200 black officeholders, of whom 67 percent were in the South.

# Walker, David

**(b. 1785?, Wilmington, N.C.; d. June 28, 1830, Boston, Mass.), African American abolitionist, civil rights activist, and advocate of African independence best known for his fiery pamphlet *Walker's Appeal . . . to the Colored Citizens of the World* (1829).**

During the antebellum years David Walker was prominent among a generation of politically outspoken free blacks that included Frederick Douglass, Martin Robison Delany, and the Reverend Henry Highland Garnet. Walker, according to historian Sterling Stuckey, deserves recognition as "the father of black nationalist theory in America." His most lasting achievement was his essay, *Walker's Appeal . . . to the Colored Citizens of the World*, which in part called on African American slaves to revolt against their masters to gain their freedom.

The son of a white mother and a slave father, Walker was born free, taking the status of his mother as stipulated by North Carolina law. Little is known of his life before he moved to Boston in the late 1820s. In particular, it is not known how he learned to read and write. The antebellum South made scant provision for educating African Americans, whether slave or free. Yet before moving to the North, Walker had acquired an education that included a familiarity with Thomas Jefferson's *Notes on the State of Virginia* (1785). He also had ample opportunity to observe the evils of slavery firsthand.

In Boston Walker commenced a used clothes business and quickly gained recognition in the local black community. Walker was evidently a natural leader. He was physically impressive: his wife Eliza described him as "prepossessing, being six feet in height, slender and well-proportioned. His hair was loose, and his complexion was dark." Walker played an active role in the Massachusetts General Colored Association, established in 1826, and was an agent for the first African American newspaper, *Freedom's Journal* (1827–1829).

In an 1828 address to the Massachusetts General Colored Association, Walker exhorted free blacks to improve their lot through mutual aid and self-help organizations. He roundly condemned the passivity of those who acquiesced in racial injustice. In September of the following year Walker published his *Appeal*, which further extended his argument for black activism and solidarity. Rejecting Jefferson's contention in *Notes on the State of Virginia* that blacks were inherently inferior, Walker called on African Americans to acquire copies of the book, in order to study and refute it. "[L]et no one of us suppose," he wrote, "that the refutations which have been written by our white friends are enough—they are whites—we are blacks."

Besides advocating the violent overthrow of slavery and the formation of black civil rights and self-help organizations, the Appeal called for racial equality in the United States and independence for the peoples of Africa. As Stuckey observed, Walker was "the precursor of a long line of advocates of African freedom, extending all the way to Paul Robeson and Malcolm X in our time."

To distribute his pamphlet, Walker relied on the mails and on seamen traveling to Southern ports. Alarmed Southern leaders responded by passing stricter laws against such "seditious" literature and against teaching free blacks to read or write. The Georgia state legislature went so far as to place a price on Walker's head: $10,000, if he were delivered alive, or $1,000, if dead. Walker encountered sharp criticism in the North as well, even from such white abolitionists as William Lloyd Garrison and Benjamin Lundy. In 1830, nine months after publishing his *Appeal*, Walker died under mysterious circumstances. Rumor held that he had been poisoned, but the charge was never verified.

North America

# Walker, Wyatt Tee

**(b. August 16, 1929, Brockton, Mass.), African American minister, chief strategist for the Southern Christian Leadership Conference during the Civil Rights Movement.**

Wyatt Tee Walker left a ministerial post in Petersburg, Virginia, in 1960 to become executive director of the Southern Christian Leadership Conference (SCLC). He proved an excellent tactician, authoring protest strategies that included the Birmingham campaign of April 1963.

Walker left the SCLC in 1964, settled in New York City, and continued to work for social justice. An expert on gospel music, he wrote *Somebody's Calling My Name: Black Sacred Music and Social Change* (1979). He has been the pastor of Canaan Baptist Church of Christ in Harlem since 1967.

North America

# Waller, Odell,

**(b. March 6, 1917?, Pittsylvania, Va.; d. July 2, 1942, Richmond, Va.), African American sharecropper whose conviction on murder charges highlighted the need to integrate Southern juries.**

In July 1940 Odell Waller, a sharecropper, shot and killed his white land-lord in a dispute over the shares owed to him. Waller claimed self-defense, but the all-white jury found him guilty of first-degree murder and sen-tenced him to death. Waller's defense attorneys argued that Waller did not receive a fair trial because sharecroppers did not pay the poll tax and were thus excluded from jury service. Though several civil rights organizations appealed Waller's conviction for more than two years, he was executed on July 2, 1942.

North America

# Wall of Respect, The,

a street mural on the South Side of Chicago, Illinois, depicting numerous black heroes; considered the founding work of the black mural movement.

In 1967, at the beginning of the Black Power Movement, painter William Walker assembled a group of some 20 African American artists to execute a mural celebrating prominent figures in black history. Most of these artists were members of a Chicago-based organization called the Visual Arts Workshop of OBAC (Organization of Black American Culture). Together these artists planned the mural's design and raised the money needed to finance the project. They decided to paint the mural on the side of a two-story, boarded-up tenement building at the intersection of 43rd Street and Langley Avenue. Once a thriving part of the city, this predominantly black area of Chicago had deteriorated into a slum. The mural is a patchwork of famous African Americans, including Charlie "Bird" Parker, Muhammad Ali, and Gwendolyn Brooks.

The artists' objective in painting the Wall of Respect was to lift the local black community's morale through highly visible, dignified images of famous black Americans. The response was overwhelmingly positive. People arrived from miles around to view the mural, and the publicity it generated led to the construction of a human resources center in the impoverished neighborhood. Furthermore, the Wall of Respect sparked a national black mural movement in which inner-city African American artists began to embellish their neighborhoods with positive black imagery. This movement was ideologically linked to the contemporary Black Power Movement in that it sought to challenge the white-supremacist social order, and aestheti-cally linked to the mural traditions of post-revolutionary Mexico and Depression-era America in that its artists portrayed historical figures in a social realist vein.

Shortly after the Wall of Respect was finished, the Visual Arts Work-shop of OBAC broke up. Many of the artists went on to found AfriCOBRA (African Commune of Bad Relevant Artists) in 1968. Although a fire destroyed the Wall of Respect in 1971, AfriCOBRA has continued to produce public works of art meant to liberate and uplift the African American community.

# Walters, Alexander

(b. August 1, 1858, Bardstown, Ky.; d. February 2, 1917, Brooklyn, N.Y.), African Methodist Episcopal Zion Church leader and early twentieth-century civil rights advocate.

Alexander Walters was born into a slave family, the sixth of eight children. Displaying academic promise, he was awarded a scholarship by the African Methodist Episcopal Zion Church (AMEZ) to attend private school in 1868. Receiving his license to preach in 1877, he began his pastoral duties in Indianapolis, Indiana. He went on to serve as pastor in Louisville; San Francisco; Portland, Oregon; and Chattanooga and Knoxville, Tennessee. After taking a church in New York City, he continued as a minister until he was consecrated in 1892 as bishop at the seventh district of the AMEZ Church.

Walters's contribution to civil rights activism began in 1898, when he and T. Thomas Fortune, the editor of the *New York Age*, founded the National Afro-American Council. As president of this council, Walters focused on several issues at the heart of current politics: battling the *Plessy v. Ferguson* "separate but equal" Supreme Court ruling of 1896, opposing Bishop Henry McNeal Turner's call for blacks to return to Africa, and challenging Booker T. Washington's ideas of accommodation to segregation and discrimination. A conflict in 1902 with Fortune over Washington's views resulted in Walters's removal as president of the council.

In 1908 Walters joined activist W. E. B. Du Bois's Niagara Movement, and he helped organize the founding conference of the National Association for the Advancement of Colored People (NAACP). He became vice president of this organization in 1911. After leading AMEZ churches and education programs in West Africa, Walters felt compelled to encourage the American government to increase economic support in Africa. In 1915 President Woodrow Wilson offered Walters a post as minister to Liberia, which he declined in order to continue organizing AMEZ Church education programs in the United States and internationally. Walters maintained this involvement in AMEZ Church affairs until his death in 1917.

# Washington, Booker Taliaferro

(b. April 5, 1856, Franklin County, Va.; d. November 14, 1915, Tuskegee, Ala.), African American founder of the Tuskegee Institute, who urged blacks to accommodate themselves to the white South and concentrate on economic self-advancement; supported by influential whites, he became the most prominent black American of the late nineteenth and early twentieth century.

### Discipline and Efficiency

Booker T. Washington was born Booker Taliaferro, a slave, in rural Virginia. His mother, Jane, was the plantation's cook; his father was a white man whose identity he never knew. Washington worked as a servant in the plantation house until he was liberated by Union troops near the end of the Civil War. After the war his family moved to Malden, West Virginia, where they joined Washington Ferguson, also a former slave, whom Jane had married during the war.

To help support the family Washington worked first in a salt furnace, then in a coal mine, and later as a house-boy in the home of Gen. Lewis Ruffner, who owned the mines. Here he came under the influence of Viola Ruffner, the general's wife, who taught him a respect for cleanliness, efficiency, and order. During this time, and despite opposition from his stepfather, Booker attended a school for blacks while continuing to work. At school he gave himself the last name Washington for reasons still debated by historians.

In 1872 Washington left Malden, traveling on foot to Virginia's Hampton Institute, which had opened only a few years earlier as a school for blacks. Its white principal, Gen. Samuel Chapman Armstrong, was the son of missionaries to Hawaii and a commander of black Union troops during the war. The South's freed blacks, Armstrong believed, needed a practical, work-based education that would also teach character and morality. Hampton offered not only agricultural and mechanical classes but training in cleanliness, efficiency, discipline, and the dignity of manual labor as well.

Washington arrived at the school dirty and penniless. He was given work as a janitor, which paid for his room and board, and Armstrong secured a white benefactor to pay his tuition. Washington was a diligent student, adopting Armstrong's credo so thoroughly that many historians have concluded that the rest of Washington's public life was a manifestation of Armstrong's philosophy.

Graduating with honors in 1875, Washington returned to West Virginia to teach. In 1878 he attended Wayland Seminary in Washington, D.C., a school offering a decidedly conventional training in the liberal arts. Washington's experience at Wayland—where the black students knew little of manual labor, and, moreover, seemed uninterested in returning South to help rural blacks—further convinced him of the rightness of Armstrong's methods. After a year at Wayland, Washington returned to Hampton, this time as a member of the faculty. He grew closer to Armstrong, and in 1881, when Armstrong was asked by the state of Alabama to name a white principal to head a new school for blacks, he instead suggested Washington.

## Tuskegee

The Tuskegee Institute in Macon County, Alabama, had been apportioned $2,000 by the state legislature for salaries, but nothing for land or buildings. Washington began classes with a handful of students in a shanty owned by a black church. Intending Tuskegee to be a replica of Hampton, he established a vocational curriculum for both boys and girls that included such courses as carpentry, printing, tinsmithing, and shoemaking. Girls also took classes in cooking and sewing, and boys learned farming and dairying.

Manners, hygiene, and character also received heavy emphasis, and each day was framed by a rigid schedule that included daily chapel. The earliest students were set to work building a kiln, then making bricks, then erecting buildings. The school sold additional bricks to pay part of its expenses, and Washington secured the rest of the funds from philanthropists, mostly white and mostly Northern, to whom Armstrong had introduced him.

A good deal of Washington's work took place beyond the school's walls. He placated the hostile whites of Tuskegee with assurances that he was counseling his students to set aside political activism in favor of economic gains. He also assured skeptical legislators that his students would not flee the South after their education but instead would be productive contributors to the rural economy. These messages resonated with whites not just in the South but also in the North among Tuskegee's benefactors.

Steel magnate Andrew Carnegie, who became the most generous donor to Tuskegee during Washington's lifetime, said Washington was "one of the most wonderful men . . . who has ever lived." Blacks also praised the man who built a school from the dirt of the Deep South that had succeeded, by 1890, in training 500 African Americans a year on 500 acres of land.

These triumphs, however, were underscored by pockets of tragedy in Washington's personal life. His first wife, Fanny Smith Washington, a graduate of Hampton and Washington's girlfriend since Malden, died from a fall in 1884, just two years after their marriage. His second wife, Olivia Davidson Washington, also a graduate of Hampton and in chronically poor health, died in 1889. Washington's third wife, Margaret Murray Washington, was a graduate of Fisk University and, like Olivia Washington, held the title of lady principal of Tuskegee. Margaret Washington helped her husband for the rest of his life and also led regional and national federations of black women.

## National Prominence

Although Tuskegee earned him a measure of popularity, Washington did not become a national leader until he spoke, in September 1895, at the Cotton States and International Exposition in Atlanta, Georgia. Over the previous several years relations between the races had steadily deteriorated. The South had codified its discriminatory Jim Crow laws, and violence, especially lynching, was common. Earlier in the year Frederick Douglass, the acknowledged leader of blacks North and South, died, and no clear successor had yet emerged. Washington was the only black speaker chosen to address the mixed-race crowd in Atlanta.

He urged Southern blacks to "cast down your bucket where you are"—that is, to remain in the South—and to accept discrimination as unchangeable for the time being. "In all things that are purely social," he said, "we can be as separate as the fingers, yet one as the hand in all things essential to mutual progress." Blacks should first commit themselves to economic improvement, Washington stated; once they had achieved that, he assured his listeners, improvement in civil rights would follow.

The speech, which critics called the Atlanta Compromise, won nearly unanimous acclaim from both blacks and whites. Even the black intellectual W. E. B. Du Bois, who later broke sharply with Washington's accommodating position, praised Washington's message at the time. Donations from white Americans flowed in larger amounts to Tuskegee, and soon white journalists, politicians, and philanthropists sought Washington's word on all things racial.

In 1898 President William McKinley visited Tuskegee, offering praise that further elevated Washington's stature. Although in public Washington disdained politics, in private he assiduously cultivated his own power. He secretly owned stock in several black newspapers, which he influenced to provide favorable reports about him and Tuskegee. Other black newspapers he quietly cajoled, persuaded, and occasionally coerced into giving him positive coverage. At his heavily attended lectures around the country, he endeared himself to whites by telling stories about "darkies"—blacks who fit racist stereotypes—portraying them as lovable, gullible, and shiftless. These stories alienated black intellectuals.

In 1901 Washington published his ghostwritten autobiography, *Up From Slavery*. Told simply but movingly, it is a classic American tale of success through hard work. Almost instantly it became a bestseller and was translated into several languages. Theodore Roosevelt, who had become president the same year, invited Washington to the White House for lunch, prompting a flurry of angry editorials in the white South but further increasing Washington's power and appeal elsewhere. Roosevelt (as did President William Howard Taft after him) sought Washington's advice on racial and Southern issues.

In a short time Washington became a dispenser of Republican Party patronage throughout the South and parts of the North. Blacks soon learned that Washington's endorsement was essential for any political appointment or, for that matter, for funding by white philanthropic groups, who readily deferred to Washington's opinions. He, in turn, used his wealth and power secretly to finance some court cases and other activities challenging Jim Crow laws. He also provided the main impetus for founding the National Negro Business League, which served to advocate his Tuskegee philosophy throughout the country. Some observers referred to the powerful Washington as the Wizard of Tuskegee, and to his operation as the Tuskegee Machine.

## "Of Mr. Booker T. Washington and Others"

In 1903 W. E. B. Du Bois published *The Souls of Black Folk*. In one of its essays, "Of Mr. Booker T. Washington and Others," he criticized Washington for failing to realize that economic power could not be had without political power, because political power was needed to protect economic gains. Moreover, Du Bois believed that Washington's disparagement of liberal arts education would rob the race of well-trained leaders.

Du Bois insisted that in a time of increasing segregation and discrimination, blacks must struggle for their civil rights rather than accommodate inequality. Washington, then at the peak of his power, was stung by Du

Bois's criticisms, and "Of Mr. Booker T. Washington and Others" allowed critics to be more open over the next several years.

The greatest threat to Washington's conservatism and power came in 1909 with the founding of the National Association for the Advancement of Colored People (NAACP). The NAACP, which sought to address the neglected civil rights of blacks, was a direct challenge to Washington, as was its predecessor, Du Bois's Niagara Movement. Washington tried at first to stifle the group; failing that, he sought a rapprochement. As that, too, failed, increasing numbers of blacks gravitated to the NAACP, and Washington's base of power began to weaken.

The election in 1913 of Democrat Woodrow Wilson to the presidency dealt Washington another blow, as his duties as dispenser of Republican patronage came to an end. Washington nonetheless remained personally prominent until his death in 1915. At that time the Tuskegee Institute had a faculty of 200, an enrollment of 2,000, and an endowment of $2 million.

North America

# Washington, D.C.,

**capital city of the United States and the only major city whose citizens—the majority of whom are black—lack the authority to govern fully their own affairs.**

Established under the direction of President George Washington and named in his honor, Washington, D.C., was created to meet the constitutional mandate for the establishment of a federal district. (Washington originally intended the city's name to be the "District of Columbia" in honor of Christopher Columbus.) Established as a unique entity, separate from the states, Washington, D.C., has been hampered by its ambiguous position, both in terms of racial issues and voting rights. Located between a free and a slave state—Maryland and Virginia, respectively—Washington, D.C., has struggled throughout much of its existence to be both a city for the nation and for its residents.

At the time of its founding in 1800, Washington's population of 14,103 persons comprised 10,066 whites, 793 free blacks, and 3244 slaves. Designed principally by the French architect Pierre L'Enfant, the survey for the city was completed in part by the self-taught African American scientist and mathematician Benjamin Banneker. Arranged in a grid format with four quadrants, Washington, D.C., is some 175.5 sq km (63 sq mi) in size and includes both the Potomac and Anacostia rivers.

During its first 50 years Washington, D.C., became a center for both abolitionist activity as well as the establishment of businesses and institutions led by free blacks, including the several schools organized by and for African American women (the most notable being the Miner Normal School, which later evolved into the University of the District of Columbia). Due in part to the federal government's growing uneasiness with the slave trade, this activity increased the city's attractiveness to free blacks, who began to migrate there in significant numbers after 1820.

However, the increase in the number of free blacks coming to the nation's capital led to unease among the leaders of the city itself. The District's city council and other local city councils responded by passing laws that attempted to restrict blacks' movement and activities—including preaching and business ownership. Tensions erupted in the Washington Navy Yard and Georgetown during 1835 and 1836 when whites rioted against abolitionists and free blacks.

With the Civil War under way, Congress moved to redress these problems by abolishing slavery in the capital in 1862, several months before the Emancipation Proclamation. More than 3,000 black residents of the district volunteered in the Union army, and the city itself became an important stop for runaway slaves. The war also encouraged the formation of several black charitable organizations, including the Contraband Relief Organization and Freedman's Hospital. With Reconstruction, many notable African Americans settled in Washington, D.C., including Frederick Douglass, Alexander Crummell, and Senator Blanche K. Bruce of Mississippi. By 1880 more than 175,000 people lived in Washington, of whom one-third were African Americans.

Although home rule had been a part of the city's political charter since its beginning, suffrage for black voters was repeatedly denied by popular election in the city from 1856 until 1864. It was only after the Civil War that voting rights were conferred on black males by virtue of an act of Congress (the Sumner Civil Rights Amendment). Shortly thereafter, in 1868, the first black mayor of Washington—Sayles Jenks Bowen—was elected. Defeated two years later in his re-election bid by anti-suffrage forces, Bowen and other members of Washington's new black political establishment suffered a grievous defeat in 1871 when Congress reversed itself and established a governing body for the city that was appointed by the president and Congress. For the next 100 years African American efforts to assume control of the city would be for naught as the city's political activities were dictated by Congress through a three-member commission whose members would remain exclusively white until 1961.

From Reconstruction until World War I black life in Washington, D.C., advanced most importantly with the establishment of learning organizations such as the American Negro Academy (established by Crummell) and the Association for the Study of Negro Life and History (founded by Carter G. Woodson), and fraternities and sororities such as Omega Psi Phi and Alpha Kappa Alpha, and the founding of Howard University in 1867. Newspapers such as the *Washington Bee* and *Washington Afro-American* also contributed to the city's black life. In addition, Washington continued to attract a large number of black migrants from the South; by 1910 nearly 100,000 African Americans lived in the city, with poor blacks often living in hastily constructed alleys and elite members of the African American community living in neighborhoods such as Le Detroit Park.

Despite the distinct class differences that appeared within the black community in Washington, D.C., the continued growth of the black population in Washington remained a tense issue with its white leaders and their followers. Two days of riots in 1919 confirmed the impression that racial tensions were an indelible part of the city's character. Fueled by newspaper accounts of alleged crimes against white women by black men, the city endured one of its worst race riots. In a city populated with soldiers returning from World War I, whites attacked black citizens in many down-town locations, and black citizens retaliated with attacks in white neighbor-hoods. Four people died as a result of the riot, including two African Americans, and federal troops were called in to restore calm.

With the establishment of the New Deal in 1932 and the rise of Howard University as a center for some of the leading black activists and writers of the day—including Charles Hamilton Houston, Ralph Bunche, and E. Franklin Frazier—organized protests within the district's black community became more common. For instance, the New Negro Alliance, whose members included Houston, Robert C. Weaver, and Mary McLeod Bethune, successfully led protests against employment discrimination. Organized black protest in Washington, D.C., achieved national recognition when the accomplished opera singer and contralto Marian Anderson was denied use of Constitution Hall by the Daughters of the American Revolution in 1939, and instead sang at the Lincoln Memorial before an audience of 75,000 people. (Ironically, the dedication of the Lincoln Memorial itself in 1922 occurred under segregated conditions.) Despite these successes, primary control of Washington remained firmly in the hands of the three-member commission appointed by Congress, and inevitably in the hands of individual Congress members, some of whom—such as Mississippi Democrats Senator Theodore Bilbo and Congressman Ross Collins—were avowed racists.

While congressional oversight of district matters continued, organized efforts to remove Jim Crow laws, coupled with strong migration to the city, meant that the district's black population grew significantly after World War II. By 1960 the black population of Washington, D.C., exceeded 411,000 and represented more than half of the city's citizens. In 1961 ratification of the Twenty-third Amendment to the Constitution occurred, giving residents of Washington, D.C., the right to vote in presidential elections for the first time. The growth of the Civil Rights Movement, and the use of Washington, D.C., as a site for protests by other activist movements brought additional political reforms to the district, including the appointment of African Americans to the newly established office of mayor and the three-member commission. Political reform was hastened by the riots of 1968, which occurred shortly after the assassination of Martin Luther King Jr. Reaction to King's assassination began peacefully when Black Power advocate Stokely Carmichael (Kwame Turé) asked downtown businesses to close their doors out of respect to the slain civil rights leader. The reaction grew violent as large crowds gathered and reacted to the news of King's death. For three days rioting and looting occurred at a cost of 12 lives, 7,600 arrests, and $27 million in property damage, before federal troops were able to restore order.

The 1968 riots, despite the economic devastation they caused, sped the reestablishment of home rule in the city. In 1974, for the first time in nearly 100 years, all citizens of Washington, D.C., were permitted to elect a city council and a mayor. The previously appointed mayor, Walter Washington, was elected mayor in 1974. Marion Barry—a former leader of the Student Nonviolent Coordinating Committee (SNCC), who moved to Washington, D.C., after working in Mississippi—was elected to the post in 1978 to serve the first of three consecutive terms as mayor. A populist leader whose first-term coalition of poor blacks and white downtown real estate developers would undergo substantial changes in subsequent years, Barry was initially an effective leader who revitalized the downtown and energized long-neglected citizens with his pledges

Marion S. Barry celebrates after winning the Democratic mayoral primary in Washington D.C., in 1994. Barry went on to win his fourth term as mayor. *CORBIS*

of inclusion. However, Barry's own struggles with drug use, coupled with his desire to expand the city bureaucracy significantly, severely limited his effectiveness as a mayor. In the 1991 election the voters chose to replace Barry with a newcomer, Sharon Pratt Kelly.

The first black woman elected mayor of a major city, Kelly directed reform efforts that failed largely as a result of her inexperience, leaving the city with mounting financial deficits and increasingly frustrated citizens. When Barry was returned to the office of mayor in 1994, the Congress and President Bill Clinton responded to his election and the continued fiscal crisis by establishing the D.C. Control Board, another congressionally appointed body with the power to manage most of the fiscal and administrative affairs of the district until such time as its fiscal condition is stabilized. Despite some successes, the control board has struggled to convince the city's residents that meaningful reform is possible without a self-representative governing body. Its efforts, coupled with Barry's decision in 1998 not to seek reelection, mean that Anthony A. Williams, who was elected mayor in November 1998, faces a daunting but familiar set of problems.

North America

# Washington, Harold

(b. April 15, 1922, Chicago, Ill.; d. November 25, 1987, Chicago, Ill.), African American politician, the first African American mayor of Chicago, Illinois (1983–1987).

Harold Washington was born to Bertha and Roy Lee Washington, who separated when their son was young, and Washington was raised by his father. After dropping out of high school during his junior year, Washington earned a high school equivalency certificate in the army, after he was drafted during World War II. He graduated from Roosevelt University in 1949 with a degree in political science and earned a degree in law from Northwestern University in 1952.

Washington began his political career when he succeeded his deceased father in 1953 as a Democratic Party precinct captain. After holding positions as a city attorney (1954–1958) and a state labor arbitrator (1960–1964), he served in the Illinois House of Representatives (1965–1976). He then advanced to seats in the Illinois State Senate (1976–1980) and the United States House of Representatives (1980–1983). He was active in the 1982 effort to extend the 1965 Voting Rights Act.

In 1977 Washington made an unsuccessful bid to become the mayor of Chicago. In 1983 he again entered the mayoral race and defeated Jane Byrne and Richard M. Daley in the primaries. He edged out Republican Bernard Epton in the general election on April 12, 1983, to become the city's first African American mayor.

Washington increased racial diversity in city administration, assuring equal opportunities for women and minorities seeking employment, and ended city patronage. He had difficulty implementing his initiatives since the majority of the 50 city council seats were held by his political opponents. In 1986, after a federal court called for new elections in certain wards that were deemed racially biased, however, Washington achieved more legislative success. He unexpectedly died of a heart attack shortly after his reelection in 1987, ending hope for a popular, progressive, multiracial city government.

North America

# Washington, Margaret Murray

(b. 1861, Macon, Miss.; d. June 4, 1925, Tuskegee, Ala.), African American educator and president of the National Association of Colored Women's Clubs.

After graduating in 1889 from Fisk University's preparatory school in Nashville, Tennessee, Margaret Murray Washington joined the faculty at Tuskegee Institute (later Tuskegee University), becoming dean of the women's department in 1890. In 1891 she married Tuskegee's president and founder, Booker T. Washington.

In addition to teaching and helping her husband administer Tuskegee, Washington participated in women's clubs, becoming the president of the National Association of Colored Women's Clubs in 1914. She was also involved in the temperance movement and coordinated self-improvement programs for women in the Tuskegee area. After Booker T. Washington's death in 1915, she continued to work at Tuskegee.

North America

# Waters, Maxine Moore

(b. August 15, 1938, St. Louis, Mo.), African American state assemblywoman and United States Democratic Congresswoman from California known for her commitment to urban renewal.

Maxine Moore Waters gained national recognition during the 1992 Los Angeles riots, when she emerged as one of the black community's principal voices in Congress. She assailed the long-term neglect of America's inner cities, an issue that had propelled her political career from its beginning.

The 5th of 13 children born to Remus and Velma Lee Carr Moore, Waters grew up in a housing project in St. Louis, Missouri. Inspired by a fifth-grade math teacher who took a special interest in her, Waters set high expectations for herself and assumed leadership roles in school. In the late 1960s she became a spokesperson for the Los Angeles-based Head Start program, in which she taught after working as a factory worker and telephone operator. Meanwhile, Waters attended California State University, majoring in sociology, and brought up her two children with her husband, Edward Waters.

In 1973 Waters was appointed chief deputy to city council member David Cunningham; she later campaigned for U.S. senator Alan Cranston and Los Angeles mayor Tom Bradley. She launched her own political career in 1976, when she was elected to the California State Assembly. During her 14-year tenure as an assemblyperson, her legislative successes were numerous and diverse, ranging from a law that curbed California's business investment in South Africa to a training program for child abuse prevention. She prioritized women's rights and helped to found the National Political Congress of Black Women in 1984. In 1990 Waters was elected to the U.S. Congress, where she advocated for minorities and urban renewal. In 1993 she introduced and won passage of a bill that provided $50 million for an innovative training program for disadvantaged youth nationwide. In 1997 she became the third woman to chair the Congressional Black Caucus.

North America

# Wattleton, Faye

**(b. July 8, 1943, St. Louis, Mo.), former president of the Planned Parenthood Federation of America (PPFA) and the person most responsible for the group's advocacy of abortion rights.**

Alyce Faye Wattleton was born the only child of Ozie Walton, a seamstress and minister, and George Wattleton, a factory worker, in St. Louis, Missouri. She graduated from high school at age 16 and attended Ohio State University, from which she received a degree in nursing in 1964. She later entered Columbia University to pursue a master's degree in maternal and infant care. At Columbia—during a time when almost all abortions were illegal—her patients included many girls and women who had attempted abortions with dreadful results. Wattleton soon became active in Planned Parenthood. In the late 1960s she headed a local chapter in Dayton, Ohio, dramatically expanding its services to women and children as well as its donor base. In 1978 she was named president of the PPFA.

At the time Planned Parenthood was known mainly for its several hundred United States clinics offering services such as birth control, prenatal care, and abortions. Although most types of abortions became legal after the

Supreme Court confirmed their constitutionality in the 1973 case *Roe v. Wade*, abortion opponents were fighting back: the 1977 congressional Hyde Amendment restricted federal funding for abortions, and in 1980 Ronald Reagan became president promising to support the "pro-life" cause.

Eloquent and poised, Wattleton used her position in Planned Parenthood to advocate reproductive rights. Along with other abortion-rights groups, she fought to secure federal funding for birth control and prenatal programs; to forbid states from restricting abortions; and to legalize the sale in the United States of RU-486, the French-made pill that induces abortions. The efforts of Wattleton and others encountered a number of setbacks, including the Supreme Court's 1989 decision in *Webster v. Reproductive Health Services* to allow states to restrict abortions. Wattleton used such defeats to mobilize activists and donors further. In 1992 she resigned from Planned Parenthood to host a talk show based in Chicago. She has one daughter, Felicia, from a marriage in the 1970s.

North America

# Watt, Melvin

(b. August 26, 1945, Steele Creek, N.C.), Democratic member of the United States House of Representatives from North Carolina (1993– ).

Melvin Watt was born in Steele Creek, North Carolina. He received a bachelor's degree from the University of North Carolina at Chapel Hill in 1967 and a law degree from Yale University in 1970. He pursued a career as a civil rights attorney in Charlotte, North Carolina, between 1971 and 1992. Watt served one term in the North Carolina Senate from 1985 to 1987. In 1992 Watt ran successfully for a seat in the U.S. House representing North Carolina's 12th Congressional District. He was easily reelected in 1994 and 1996.

The 12th Congressional District's boundary connects predominately black areas from ten counties in a narrow strip. The district was created in 1992 as one of two North Carolina minority districts mandated by the U.S. Justice Department. However, in June 1996 the U.S. Supreme Court declared the district illegally drawn. In March 1997 the North Carolina Legislature reshaped the district and reduced its number of minority voters. The district's economy relies on tobacco production, furniture manufacture, and textile production. Duke University in Durham is a major employer.

In the 105th Congress (1997–1999), Watt served on the Judiciary Committee and the Banking and Financial Services Committee. He was ranking member of the Immigration and Claims Subcommittee of the Judiciary Committee. He was also a member of the Congressional Black Caucus.

North America

# Weaver, Robert Clifton

(b. December 29, 1907, Washington, D.C.; d. July 17, 1997, New York, N.Y.), first African American United States cabinet member; secretary of housing and urban development (1966–1968).

The son of Mortimer and Florence Weaver, Robert Clifton Weaver grew up attending segregated schools in Washington, D.C. After graduating from high school, he attended Harvard, where his older brother, Mortimer, was pursuing graduate studies in English. Weaver was refused dormitory accommodations because he was black, so he moved off campus to become his brother's roommate. He graduated cum laude with a degree in economics in 1929, the same year Mortimer died unexpectedly. Weaver remained at Harvard, taking an M.A. in 1931 and a Ph.D. in economics in 1934.

President Lyndon Johnson congratulates Robert C. Weaver at his swearing in as secretary of the Department of Housing and Urban Development in 1966. *CORBIS*

Weaver began his government career in 1933 when Secretary of the Interior Harold Ickes hired him as a race relations advisor in the housing division. By 1937 Weaver had become special assistant to the administrator of the U.S. Housing Authority, a post he held until 1940. As a high-ranking African American in President Franklin D. Roosevelt's administration, Weaver was a member of the "Black Cabinet," an informal network of African Americans who worked to end racial discrimination in the federal government and the programs it administered.

In 1944, after serving on the National Defense Advisory Committee, the Manpower Commission, and the War Production Board, Weaver was appointed the director of the Mayor's Committee on Race Relations in Chicago, Illinois, and then of the American Council on Race Relations. During this time he published two critical studies of discrimination in the United States, *Negro Labor: A National Problem* (1946) and *The Negro Ghetto* (1948).

In 1955 New York governor Averell Harriman made Weaver the first African American to hold a state cabinet-level position by naming him state rent commissioner. Weaver held this post until 1960, when President John F. Kennedy named him director of the U.S. Housing and Home Finance Agency, making him the highest-ranking African American in government.

Kennedy intended to establish a cabinet-level agency to address urban affairs with Weaver as its head. However, Southern members of Congress who opposed an African American cabinet member in general and Weaver's strong support of integrated housing in particular blocked Kennedy's plan. The agency, the Department of Housing and Urban Development (HUD), was not established until President Lyndon B. Johnson was elected in 1965. In 1966, with Johnson better able to exercise power in the Congress, Weaver became the first HUD secretary and the first African American cabinet member.

Weaver effectively administered HUD, but his more ambitious and imaginative plans, such as Demonstration Cities and the Metropolitan Development Act, were unsupported because of the precedence given by the federal government to the Vietnam War and because of conservative reaction to ghetto rioting from 1965 to 1968. In 1969 Weaver ended his career in government, becoming president of City College of New York's (CCNY's) Baruch College. In 1971 he became distinguished professor of urban affairs at CCNY's Hunter College, and he became professor emeritus in 1978.

Weaver's public service extended beyond his careers in government and education. He chaired the board of directors of the National Association for the Advancement of Colored People (NAACP) in 1960, and was president of the National Committee against Discrimination in Housing from 1973 to 1987. In addition, Weaver received the Spingarn Medal in 1962, the New York City Urban League's Frederick Douglass Award in 1977, the Schomburg Collection Award in 1978, and the Equal Opportunity Day Award from the National Urban League in 1987.

# W. E. B. Du Bois: An Interpretation

### Cornel West

W. E. B. Du Bois is the towering black scholar of the twentieth century. The scope of his interests, the depth of his insights, and the sheer majesty of his prolific writings bespeak a level of genius unequaled among modern black intellectuals. Yet, like all of us, Du Bois was a child of his age. He was shaped by the prevailing presuppositions and prejudices of modern Euro-American civilization. And despite his lifelong struggle—marked by great courage and sacrifice—against white supremacy and for the advancement of Africans around the world, he was, in style and substance, a proud black man of letters primarily influenced by nineteenth-century, Euro-American traditions.

For those of us interested in the relation of white supremacy to modernity (African slavery in the New World and European imperial domination of most of the rest of the world) or the consequences of the construct of "race" during the Age of Europe (1492–1945), the scholarly and literary works of Du Bois are indispensable. For those of us obsessed with alleviating black social misery, the political texts of Du Bois are insightful and inspiring. In this sense, Du Bois is the brook of fire through which we all must pass in order to gain access to the intellectual and political weaponry needed to sustain the radical democratic tradition in our time.

Yet even this great titan of black emancipation falls short of the mark. This is not to deny the remarkable subtlety of his mind or the undeniable sincerity of his heart. The grand example of Du Bois remains problematic principally owing to his inadequate interpretation of the human condition and his inability to immerse himself fully in the rich cultural currents of black everyday life. His famous notion of the Talented Tenth reveals this philosophic inadequacy and personal inability.

What does it mean to claim that Du Bois put forward an inadequate interpretation of the human condition or that he failed to immerse himself fully in the cultural depths of black everyday life? Are these simply rhetorical claims devoid of content—too abstract to yield conclusions and too general to evaluate? Are some interpretations of the human condition and cultural ways of life really better than others? If so, why? These crucial questions sit at the center of my critique of Du Bois because they take us to the heart of black life in the profoundly decadent American civilization at the end of the twentieth century—a ghastly century whose levels of barbarity, bestiality, and brutality are unparalleled in human history.

My assessment of Du Bois primarily concerns his response to the problem of evil—to undeserved harm, unjustified suffering, and unmerited pain. Do his evolving world-view, social analysis, and moral vision enable us to understand and endure this "first century of world wars" (Muriel Rukeyser's apt phrase) in which nearly 200 million fellow human beings have been murdered in the name of some pernicious ideology? Does his work contain the necessary intellectual and existential resources to enable us to confront the indescribable agony and unnameable anguish likely to be unleashed in the twenty-first century—the first century involving a systemic gangsterization of everyday life, shot through with revitalized tribalisms—under the aegis of an uncontested, fast-paced global capitalism? As with any great figure, to grapple with Du Bois is to wrestle with who we are, why we are what we are, and what we are to do about it.

Du Bois was first and foremost a black New England Victorian seduced by the Enlightenment ethos and enchanted with the American Dream. His interpretation of the human condition—that is, in part, his idea of who he was and could be—was based on his experiences and, most important, on his understanding of those experiences through the medium of an Enlightenment world-view that promoted Victorian strategies in order to realize an American optimism; throughout this essay, I shall probe these three basic foundations of his perspective. Like many of the brilliant and ambitious young men of his time, he breathed the intoxicating fumes of "advanced" intellectual and political culture. Yet in the face of entrenched evil and demonic power, Du Bois often found himself either shipwrecked in the depths of his soul or barely afloat with less and less wind in his existential sails.

My fundamental problem with Du Bois is his inadequate grasp of the tragicomic sense of life—a refusal candidly to confront the sheer absurdity of the human condition. This tragicomic sense—tragicomic rather than simply "tragic," because even ultimate purpose and objective order are called into question—propels us toward suicide or madness unless we are buffered by ritual, cushioned by community, or sustained by art. Du Bois's inability to immerse himself in black everyday life precluded his access to the distinctive black tragicomic sense and black encounter with the absurd. He certainly saw, analyzed, and empathized with black sadness, sorrow, and suf-

fering. But he didn't feel it in his bones deeply enough, nor was he intellec-
tually open enough to position himself alongside the sorrowful, suffering,
yet striving ordinary black folk. Instead, his own personal and intellectual
distance lifted him above them even as he addressed their plight in his progressive writings. Du Bois was never alienated by black people: he lived in
black communities where he received great respect and admiration. But
there seemed to be something in him that alienated ordinary black people.
In short, he was reluctant to learn fundamental lessons about life—and
about himself—from them. Such lessons would have required that he, at
least momentarily, believe that they were or might be as wise, insightful,
and "advanced" as he; and this he could not do.

Du Bois's Enlightenment world-view—his first foundation—prohibited
this kind of understanding. Instead, he adopted a mild elitism that underes-
timated the capacity of everyday people to "know" about life. In "The Talented Tenth," he claims, "knowledge of life and its wider meaning, has been
the point of the Negro's deepest ignorance." In his classic book *The Souls of
Black Folk* (1903), there are 18 references to "black, backward, and
ungraceful" folk, including a statement of his intent "to scatter civilization
among a people whose ignorance was not simply of letters, but of life itself."

My aim is not to romanticize those whom Sly Stone calls "everyday
people" or to cast them as the sole source of wisdom. The myths of the
noble savage and the wise commoner are simply the flip sides of the Enlightenment attempts to degrade and devalue everyday people. Yet Du Bois,
owing to his Puritan New England origins and Enlightenment values, found
it difficult not to view common black folk as some degraded "other" or
"alien" no matter how hard he resisted. His honest response to a church service in the backwoods of Tennessee at a "Southern Negro Revival" bears this
out. "A sort of suppressed terror hung in the air and seemed to seize us,—a
pythian madness, a demoniac possession, that lent terrible reality to song and
word. The black and massive form of the preacher swayed and quivered as
the words crowded to his lips and flew at us in singular eloquence. The
people moaned and fluttered, and then the gaunt-cheeked brown woman
beside me suddenly leaped straight into the air and shrieked like a lost soul,
while round about came wail and groan and outcry, and a scene of human
passion such as I had never conceived before. Those who have not thus witnessed the frenzy of a Negro revival in the untouched backwoods of the
South can but dimly realize the religious feeling of the slave; as described,
such scenes appear grotesque and funny, but as seen they are awful."

Du Bois's intriguing description reminds one of an anthropologist visiting some strange and exotic people whose rituals suggest not only the
sublime but also the satanic. The "awfulness" of this black church service,
similar to that of my own black Baptist tradition, signifies for him both
dread and fear, anxiety and disgust. In short, a black ritualistic explosion of
energy frightened this black rationalist. It did so not simply because the
folk seem so coarse and uncouth, but also because they are out of control,
overpowered by something bigger than themselves. This clearly posed a
threat to him.

Like a good Enlightenment philosophe, Du Bois pits autonomy against authority, self-mastery against tradition. Autonomy and self-mastery connote self-consciousness and self-criticism; authority and tradition suggest blind deference and subordination. Self-consciousness and self-criticism yield cosmopolitanism and highbrow culture. Authority and tradition reinforce provincialism and lowbrow culture. The educated and chattering class—the Talented Tenth—are the agents of sophistication and mastery, while the uneducated and moaning class—the backward masses—remain locked in tradition; the basic role of the Talented Tenth is to civilize and refine, uplift and elevate the benighted masses.

For Du Bois education was the key. Ignorance was the major obstacle—black ignorance and white ignorance. If the black masses were educated—in order to acquire skills and culture—black America would thrive. If white elites and masses were enlightened, they would not hate and fear black folk. Hence America—black and white—could be true to its democratic ideals. "The Negro Problem was in my mind a matter of systematic investigation and intelligent understanding. The world was thinking wrong about race, because it did not know. The ultimate evil was stupidity. The cure for it was knowledge based on scientific investigation."

This Enlightenment naiveté—not only in regard to white supremacy but with respect to any form of personal and institutional evil—was momentarily shaken by a particular case involving that most peculiar American institution—lynching.

"At the very time when my studies were most successful, there cut across this plan which I had as a scientist, a red ray which could not be ignored. I remember when it first, as it were, startled me to my feet: a poor Negro in central Georgia, Sam Hose, had killed his landlord's wife. I wrote out a careful and reasoned statement concerning the evident facts and started down to the Atlanta Constitution office . . . . I did not get there. On the way news met me: Sam Hose had been lynched, and they said that his knuckles were on exhibition at a grocery store farther down on Mitchell Street, along which I was walking. I turned back to the university. I began to turn aside from my work . . . . "

"Two considerations thereafter broke in upon my work and eventually disrupted it: first, one could not be a calm, cool, and detached scientist while Negroes were lynched, murdered and starved; and secondly, there was no such definite demand for scientific work of the sort that I was doing . . . . "

Then, in the very next month, Du Bois lost his 18-month-old son, Burghardt, to diphtheria. If ever Du Bois was forced to confront the tragedy of life and the absurdity of existence, it was in the aftermath of this loss, which he describes in his most moving piece of writing, "Of the Passing of the First-Born," in *The Souls of Black Folk*. In this powerful elegiac essay Du Bois not only mourns his son but speaks directly to death itself—as Prometheus to Zeus or Jesus to his Heavenly Father. "But hearken, O Death! Is not this my life hard enough, is not that dull land that stretches its sneering web about me cold enough,—is not all the world beyond these four little walls pitiless enough, but that thou must needs enter here,—thou, O Death? About my head the thundering storm beat like a heartless voice, and the crazy forest pulsed with the curses of the weak; but what cared I, within my home beside my wife and baby boy? Wast thou so jealous of one little coign of happiness that thou must needs enter there,—thou, O Death?"

This existential gall to go face-to-face and toe-to-toe with death in order to muster some hope against hope is echoed in his most tragic characterization of the black sojourn in white supremacist America. "Within the Veil was he born, said I; and there within shall he live,—a Negro and a Negro's son. Holding in that little head—ah, bitterly!—the unbowed pride of a hunted race, clinging with that tiny dimpled hand—ah, wearily!—to a hope not hopeless but unhopeful, and seeing with those bright wondering eyes that peer into my soul a land whose freedom is to us a mockery and whose liberty a lie."

What is most revealing in this most poignant of moments is Du Bois's refusal to linger with the sheer tragedy of his son's death (a natural, not a social, evil)—without casting his son as an emblem of the race or a symbol of a black deliverance to come. Despite the deep sadness in this beautiful piece of writing, Du Bois sidesteps Dostoyevsky's challenge to wrestle in a sustained way with the irrevocable fact of an innocent child's death. Du Bois's rationalism prevents him from wading in such frightening existential waters. Instead, Du Bois rushes to glib theodicy, weak allegory, and superficial symbolism. In other words his Enlightenment world-view falters in the face of death—the deaths of Sam Hose and Burghardt. The deep despair that lurks around the corner is held at arm's length by rational attempts to boost his flagging spirit.

Du Bois's principal intellectual response to the limits of his Enlightenment world-view was to incorporate certain insights of Marx and Freud. Yet Marx's powerful critique of the unequal relations of power between capitalists and the proletariat in the workplace and Freud's penetrating attempt to exercise rational control over the irrational forces at work in self and society only deepened Du Bois's commitment to the Enlightenment ethos. And though particular features of this ethos are essential to any kind of intellectual integrity and democratic vision—features such as self-criticism and self-development, suspicion of illegitimate authority and suffocating tradition—the Enlightenment world-view held by Du Bois is ultimately inadequate, and, in many ways, antiquated, for our time. The tragic plight and absurd predicament of Africans here and abroad requires a more profound interpretation of the human condition—one that goes far beyond the false dichotomies of expert knowledge versus mass ignorance, individual autonomy versus dogmatic authority, and self-mastery versus intolerant tradition. Our tragicomic times require more democratic concepts of knowledge and leadership which highlight human fallibility and mutual accountability; notions of individuality and contested authority which stress dynamic traditions; and ideals of self-realization within participatory communities.

The second fundamental pillar of Du Bois's intellectual project is his Victorian strategies—namely, the ways in which his Enlightenment world-view can be translated into action. They rest upon three basic assumptions. First, that the self-appointed agents of Enlightenment constitute a sacrificial cultural elite engaged in service on behalf of the impulsive and irrational masses. Second, that this service consists of shaping and molding the values and viewpoints of the masses by managing educational and political bureaucracies (e.g., schools and political parties). Third, that the effective management of these bureaucracies by the educated few for the benefit of the pathetic many promotes material and spiritual progress. These assumptions form the terrain upon which the Talented Tenth are to operate.

In fact, Du Bois's notion of the Talented Tenth is a descendant of those cultural and political elites conceived by the major Victorian critics during the heyday of the British Empire in its industrial phase. S. T. Coleridge's secular clerisy, Thomas Carlyle's strong heroes, and Matthew Arnold's disinterested aliens all shun the superficial vulgarity of materialism and the cheap thrills of hedonism in order to preserve and promote highbrow culture and to civilize and contain the lowbrow masses. The resounding first and last sentences of Du Bois's essay "The Talented Tenth" not only echo the "truths" of Victorian social criticism, they also bestow upon the educated few a salvific role. "The Negro race, like all races, is going to be saved by its exceptional men." This bold statement is descriptive, prescriptive, and predictive. It assumes that the exceptional men of other races have saved their "race" (Gladstone in Britain, Menilek in Ethiopia, Bismarck in Germany, Napoleon in France, Peter in Russia). Here Du Bois claims that exceptional black men ought to save their "race" and asserts that if any "race"—especially black people—is to be saved, exceptional men will do it. The patriarchal sensibilities speak for themselves.

Like a good Victorian critic, Du Bois argues on rational grounds for the legitimacy of his cultural elite. They are worthy of leadership because they are educated and trained, refined and civilized, disciplined and determined. Most important, they have "honesty of heart" and "Purity of motive." Contrast Matthew Arnold's disinterested aliens, "who are mainly led, not by their class spirit, but by a general humane spirit, by the love of human perfection," in *Culture and Anarchy* (1869) with Du Bois's Talented Tenth.

"The men of culture are the true apostles of equality. The great men of culture are those who have had a passion for diffusing, for making prevail, for carrying from one end of society to the other, the best knowledge, the best ideas of their time, who have laboured to divest knowledge of all that was harsh, uncouth, difficult, abstract, professional, exclusive; to humanize it, to make it efficient outside the clique of the cultivated and learned, yet still remaining the best knowledge and thought of the time, and a true source, therefore, of sweetness and light. Who are today guiding the work of the Negro people? The "exceptions" of course . . . . A saving remnant continually survives and persists, continually aspires, continually shows itself in thrift and ability and character . . . . Can the masses of the Negro people be in any possible way more quickly raised than by the effort and example of this aristocracy of talent and character? Was there ever a nation on God's fair earth civilized from the bottom upward? Never; it is, ever was and ever will be from the top downward that culture filters. The Talented Tenth rises and pulls all that are worth the saving up to their vantage ground. This is the history of human progress; and the two historic mistakes which have hindered that progress were the thinking first that no more could ever rise save the few already risen; or second, that it would better the unrisen to pull the risen down."

Just as Arnold seeks to carve out discursive space and a political mission for the educated elite in the British Empire somewhere between the arrogance and complacency of the aristocracy and the vulgarity and anarchy of the working classes, Du Bois wants to create a new vocabulary and social vocation for the black educated elite in America somewhere between the hatred and scorn of the white supremacist majority and the crudity and illiteracy of the black agrarian masses. Yet his gallant efforts suffer from intellectual defects and historical misconceptions.

Let us begin with the latter. Is it true that in 1903 the educated elite were guiding the work of the Negro people? Yes and no. Certainly the most visible national black leaders tended to be educated black men, such as the ubiquitous Booker T. Washington and, of course, Du Bois himself. Yet the two most effective political forms of organizing and mobilizing among black people were the black women's club movement led by Ida B. Wells and the migration movement guided by Benjamin "Pap" Singleton, A. A. Bradley, and Richard H. Cain. Both movements were based in black civil society—that is, black civic associations like churches, lodges, fraternal orders, and sororities. Their fundamental goals were neither civil rights nor social equality but rather respect and dignity, land and self-determination. How astonishing—and limiting—that Du Bois fails to mention and analyze these movements that will result in the great Mary McLeod Bethune's educational crusade and the inimitable Marcus Garvey's Back-to-Africa Movement in a decade or so!

Regarding the intellectual defects of Du Bois's noble endeavor: first, he assumes that highbrow culture is inherently humanizing, and that exposure to and immersion in great works produce good people. Yet we have little reason to believe that people who delight in the works of geniuses like Mozart and Beethoven or Goethe and Wordsworth are any more or less humane than those who dance in the barnyards to the banjo plucking of nameless rural folk in Tennessee. Certainly those fervent white supremacists who worship the Greek and Roman classics and revel in the plays of the incomparable Shakespeare weaken his case. Second, Du Bois holds that the educated elite can more easily transcend their individual and class interests and more readily act on behalf of the common good than the uneducated masses. But is this so? Are they not just as prone to corruption and graft, envy and jealousy, self-destructive passion and ruthless ambition as everyone else? Were not Carlyle's great heroes, Cromwell and Napoleon, tyrants? Was it not Arnold's disinterested aliens who promoted and implemented the inhumane policies of the imperial British bureaucracies in India and Africa? Was not Du Bois himself both villain and victim in petty political games as well as in the all-too-familiar social exclusions of the educated elite?

Du Bois wisely acknowledges this problem in his 1948 revision of "The Talented Tenth": "When I came out of college into the world of work, I realized that it was quite possible that my plan of training a talented tenth might put in control and power, a group of selfish, self-indulgent, well-to-do men, whose basic interest in solving the Negro Problem was personal; personal freedom and unhampered enjoyment and use of the world, without any real care, or certainly no arousing care, as to what became of the mass of American Negroes, or of the mass of any people. My Talented Tenth, I could see, might result in a sort of interracial free-for-all, with the devil taking the hindmost and the foremost taking anything they could lay hands on."

He then notes the influence of Marx on his thinking and adds that the Talented Tenth must not only be talented but have "expert knowledge" of modern economics, be willing to sacrifice and plan effectively to institute socialist measures. Yet there is still no emphatic call for accountability from below, nor any grappling with the evil that lurks in the hearts of all of us. He recognizes human selfishness as a problem without putting forward adequate philosophical responses to it or institutional mechanisms to alleviate it. In the end he throws up his hands and gives us a grand either/or option. "But we must have honest men or we die. We must have unselfish, far-seeing leadership or we fail."

Victorian social criticism contains elements indispensable to future critical thought about freedom and democracy in the twenty-first century. Most important, it elevates the role of public intellectuals who put forward overarching visions and broad analyses based on a keen sense of history and a subtle grasp of the way the world is going in the present. The rich tradition of Victorian critics—Thomas Carlyle, John Ruskin, Matthew Arnold, John Morley, William Morris, and, in our own century, L. T. Hobhouse, J.A. Hobson, C. E. G. Masterman, R. H. Tawney, Raymond Williams, E. P. Thompson, and others—stands shoulders above the parochial professionalism of much of the academy today. In our era scholarship is often divorced from public engagement, and shoddy journalism often settles for the sensational and superficial aspects of prevailing crises. As the distinguished European man of letters George Steiner notes in regard to the academy, "Specialization has reached moronic vehemence. Learned lives are expended on reiterative minutiae. Academic rewards go to the narrow scholiast, to the blinkered. Men and women in the learned professions proclaim themselves experts on one author, in one brief historical period, in one aesthetic medium. They look with contempt (and dank worry) on the 'Generalist.' . . . It may be that cows have fields. The geography of consciousness should be that of unfenced errance, Montaigne's comely word."

Yet the Victorian strategies of Du Bois require not piecemeal revision but wholesale reconstruction. A fuller understanding of the human condition should lead us far beyond any notions of free-floating elites, suspicious of the tainted masses—elites who worship at the altar of highbrow culture while ignoring the barbarity and bestiality in their own ranks. The fundamental role of the public intellectual—distinct from, yet building on, the indispensable work of academics, experts, analysts, and pundits—is to create and sustain high-quality public discourse addressing urgent public problems which enlightens and energizes fellow citizens, prompting them to take public action. This role requires a deep commitment to the life of the mind—a perennial attempt to clear our minds of cant (to use Samuel Johnson's famous formulation)—which serves to shape the public destiny of a people. Intellectual and political leadership is neither elitist nor populist; rather it is democratic, in that each of us stands in public space, without humiliation, to put forward our best visions and views for the sake of the public interest. And these arguments are presented in an atmosphere of mutual respect and civic trust.

The last pillar of Du Bois's project is his American optimism. Like most intellectuals of the New World, he was preoccupied with progress. And given his genuine commitment to black advancement, this preoccupation is understandable. Yet, writing as he was in the early stages of the consolidation of the American Empire (some 8 million people of color had been incorporated after the Spanish-American War), when the United States itself was undergoing geographical and economic expansion and millions of "new" Americans were being admitted from eastern Europe, Du Bois tended to assume that United States expansionism was a sign of probable American progress. In this sense, in his early and middle years he was not only a progressivist but also a kind of American exceptionalist. It must be said, to be sure, that unlike most American exceptionalists of his day, he considered the color line the major litmus test for the country. Yet he remained optimistic about a multiracial democratic America.

Du Bois never fully grasped the deeply pessimistic view of American democracy behind the Garvey movement. In fact, he never fully understood or appreciated the strong—though not central—black nationalist strain in the Black Freedom Movement. As much as he hated white supremacy in America, he could never bring himself to identify intimately with the harsh words of the great performing artist Josephine Baker, who noted in response to the East St. Louis Riot of July 1917 that left more than 200 black people dead and more than 6,000 homeless, "The very idea of America makes me shake and tremble and gives me nightmares." Baker lived most of her life in exile in France. Even when Du Bois left for Africa in 1961—as a member of a moribund Communist Party—his attitude toward America was not that of an Elijah Muhammad or a Malcolm X. He was still, in a significant sense, disappointed with America, and there is no disappointment without some dream deferred. Elijah Muhammad and Malcolm X were not disappointed with America. As bona fide black nationalists, they had no expectations of a white supremacist civilization; they adhered neither to American optimism nor to exceptionalism.

Black Nationalism is a complex tradition of thought and action, a tradition best expressed in the numerous insightful texts of black public intellectuals like Maulana Karenga, Imamu Amiri Baraka, Haki R. Madhubuti, Marimba Ani, and Molefi Asante. Black nationalists usually call upon black people to close ranks, to distrust most whites (since the reliable whites are few and relatively powerless in the face of white supremacy), and to promote forms of black self-love, self-defense, and self-determination. Black Nationalism views white supremacy as the definitive systemic constraint on black cultural, political, and economic development. More pointedly, black nationalists claim that American democracy is a modern form of tyranny on the part of the white majority over the black minority. For them, black sanity and freedom require that America not serve as the major framework in which to understand the future of black people. Instead, American civilization—like all civilizations—rises and falls, ebbs and flows. And owing to its deep-seated racism, this society does not warrant black allegiance or loyalty. White supremacy dictates the limits of the operation of American democracy—with black folk the indispensable sacrificial lamb vital to its sustenance. Hence black subordination constitutes the necessary condition for the flourishing of American democracy, the tragic prerequisite for America itself. This is, in part, what Richard Wright meant when he noted, "The Negro is America's metaphor."

The most courageous and consistent of twentieth-century black nationalists—Marcus Garvey and Elijah Muhammad—adamantly rejected any form of American optimism or exceptionalism. Du Bois feared that if they were right, he would be left in a state of paralyzing despair. A kind of despair that results not only when all credible options for black freedom in America are closed, but also when the very frame-work needed to understand and cope with that despair is shattered. The black nationalist challenge to Du Bois cuts much deeper than the rational and political possibilities for change; it resides at the visceral and existential levels of what to do about "what is" or when "what ought to be done" seems undoable. This frightening sense of foreboding pervades much of black America today—a sense that fans and fuels Black Nationalism.

Du Bois's American optimism screened him from this dark night of the soul. His American exceptionalism guarded him from that gray twilight between "nothing to be done" and "I can't go on like this"—a Beckett-like dilemma in which the wait and search for Godot, or for freedom, seem endless. This militant despair about the black condition is expressed in that most arresting of black nationalist speeches by Rev. Henry Highland Garnet in 1843: "If we must bleed, let it come all at once—rather die freemen than live to be slaves. It is impossible like the children of Israel, to make a grand Exodus from the land of bondage. The pharaoh's on both sides of the blood-red waters!"

Du Bois's response to such despair is to say, "we surely must do something"—for such rebellion is suicidal and the notion of a separate black nation quixotic. So, he seems to say, let us continue to wait and search for Godot in America—even if it seems, with our luck, that all we get is "Pozzo" (new forms of disrespect, disregard, degradation, and defamation). American optimism couched within the ideals of the American experiment contains crucial components for any desirable form of black self-determination or modern nationhood: precious standards of constitutional democracy, the rule of law, individual liberties, and the dignity of common folk. Yet

American optimism—in the ugly face of American white supremacist practices—warrants, if not outright rejection, at least vast attenuation. The
twenty-first century will almost certainly not be a time in which American
exceptionalism will flower in the world or American optimism will flourish
among people of African descent.

If there are any historical parallels between black Americans at the end
of the twentieth century and other peoples in earlier times, two candidates
loom large: Tolstoy's Russia and Kafka's Prague—soul-starved Russians a
generation after the emancipation of the serfs in 1861 and anxiety-ridden
Central European Jews a generation before the European Holocaust in the
1940s. Indeed, my major intellectual disappointment with the great Du
Bois lies in the fact that there are hardly any traces in his work of any
serious grappling with the profound thinkers and spiritual wrestlers in the
modern West from these two groups—major figures obsessed with the
problem of evil in their time.

We see in Du Bois no engagement with Leo Tolstoy, Fyodor Dostoyevsky, Ivan Turgenev, Alexander Herzen, Lev Shestov, Anton Chekhov,
or Franz Kafka, Max Brod, Kurt Tucholsky, Hermann Broch, Hugo
Bergmann, or Karl Kraus. These omissions are glaring because the towering
figures in both groups were struggling with political and existential issues
similar to those facing black people in America. For example, the Russian
situation involved the humanity of degraded, impoverished peasants, the
fragile stability of an identity-seeking empire, and the alienation of super-
fluous intellectuals; the Central European Jewish circumstance, the
humanity of devalued middle-class Jews, the imminent collapse of a decadent empire, and the militant despair of self-hating intellectuals. The intellectual response on the part of the Russian authors was what Hegel would
call "world-historical": they wrote many of the world's greatest novels, short
stories, essays, and plays. The writers I cite put forward profound interpretations of the human condition that rejected any Enlightenment world-view,
Victorian strategy, or worldly optimism. And although the Central European Jewish authors are often overlooked by contemporary intellectuals—
owing to a tendency to focus on Western Europe—their intellectual
response was monumental. They composed many of this century's most
probing and penetrating novels, short stories, autobiographies, and letters.

Both Russian and Central European Jewish writers share deep elective
affinities that underlie their distinctive voices: the "wind of the wing of
madness" (to use Baudelaire's phrase) beats incessantly on their souls. The
fear of impending social doom and dread of inevitable death haunt them,
and they search for a precious individuality in the face of a terror-ridden
society and a seductive (yet doubtful) nationalist option. In short, fruitful
comparisons may be made between the Russian sense of the tragic and the
Central European Jewish sense of the absurd and the black intellectual
response to the African American predicament. Tolstoy's *War and Peace*
(1869), *The Death of Ivan Ilych* (1886), and "How Much Land Does a Man
Need?" (1886), Chekhov's *The Three Sisters* (1901)—the greatest novel,
short story, brief tale, and play in modern Europe—and Kafka's "The Judg-

ment" (1913), "The Metamorphosis" (1915), "In the Penal Colony" (1919), and "The Burrow"(1923)—some of the grandest fictive portraits of twentieth-century Europe—constitute the highest moments and most ominous murmurings in Europe before it entered the ugly and fiery inferno of totalitarianism. Similarly, the intellectual response of highbrow black artists—most of whom are musicians and often of plebeian origins—probes the depths of a black sense of the tragic and absurd that yields a subversive joy and sublime melancholia unknown to most in the New World. The form and content of Louis Armstrong's *West End Blues*, Duke Ellington's *Mood Indigo*, John Coltrane's *Alabama*, and Sarah Vaughan's *Send in the Clowns* are a few of the peaks of the black cultural iceberg—towering examples of soul-making and spiritual wrestling that crystallize the most powerful interpretations of the human condition in black life. This is why the best of the black musical tradition in the twentieth century is the most profound and poignant body of artistic works in our time.

Like their Russian and Central European Jewish counterparts, the black artists grapple with madness and melancholia, doom and death, terror and horror, individuality and identity. Unlike them, the black artists do so against the background of an African heritage that puts a premium on voice and body, sound and silence, and the foreground is occupied by an American tradition that highlights mobility and novelty, individuality and democracy. The explosive products of this multilayered cultural hybridity—with its new diasporic notions of time and space, place and face—take us far beyond Du Bois's enlightened optimism. Instead, the profound black cultural efforts to express the truth of modern tragic existence and build on the ruins of modern absurd experiences at the core of American culture take us to the end of this dreadful century. These black artistic endeavors prefigure and pose the most fundamental and formidable challenges to a twilight civilization—an American Empire adrift on turbulent seas in a dark fog. William Faulkner, Mark Twain, Thomas Pynchon, and, above all, the incomparable Herman Melville—the only great Euro-American novelists to be spoken of in the same breath as Tolstoy and Kafka, Armstrong and Coltrane—grasp crucial aspects of this black condition. Just as Richard Wright, Ralph Ellison, James Baldwin, and, preeminently, Toni Morrison guide us through the tragedies and absurdities within the Veil (or behind the color curtain) to disclose on the page what is best revealed in black song, speech, sermon, bodily performance, and the eloquence of black silence. Yet despite his shortcomings, the great Du Bois remains the springboard for any examination of black strivings in American civilization.

## On Black Strivings

Black strivings are the creative and complex products of the terrifying African encounter with the absurd in America—and the absurd as America. Like any other group of human beings, black people forged ways of life and ways of struggle under circumstances not of their own choosing. They constructed structures of meaning and structures of feeling in the face of the fundamental facts of human existence—death, dread, despair, disease, and disappointment. Yet the specificity of black culture—namely, those features that distinguish black culture from other cultures—lies in both the African and American character of black people's attempts to sustain their mental sanity and spiritual health, social life and political struggle in the midst of a slaveholding, white supremacist civilization that viewed itself as the most enlightened, free, tolerant, and democratic experiment in human history.

Any serious examination of black culture should begin with what Du Bois dubbed, in Faustian terms, the "spiritual strivings" of black people—the dogged determination to survive and subsist, the tenacious will to persevere, persist, and maybe even prevail. These "strivings" occur within the whirl-wind of white supremacy—that is, as responses to the vicious attacks on black beauty, black intelligence, black moral character, black capability, and black possibility. To put it bluntly, every major institution in American society—churches, universities, courts, academies of science, governments, economies, newspapers, magazines, television, film, and others—attempted to exclude black people from the human family in the name of white supremacist ideology. This unrelenting assault on black humanity produced the fundamental condition of black culture—that of black invisibility and namelessness.

This basic predicament exists on at least four levels: existential, social, political, and economic. The existential level is the most relevant here because it has to do with what it means to be a person and live a life under the horrifying realities of racist assault. To be a black human being under circumstances in which one's humanity is questioned is not only to face a difficult challenge but also to exercise a demanding discipline.

The sheer absurdity of being a black human being whose black body is viewed as an abomination, whose black thoughts and ideas are perceived as debased, and whose black pain and grief are rendered invisible on the human and moral scale is the New World context in which black culture emerged. Black people are first and foremost an African people, in that the cultural baggage they brought with them to the New World was grounded in their earlier responses to African conditions. Yet the rich African tradi-tions—including the kinetic orality, passionate physicality, improvisational intellectuality, and combative spirituality—would undergo creative transfor-mation when brought into contact with European languages and rituals in the context of the New World. For example, there would be no jazz without New World Africans with European languages and instruments.

On the crucial existential level relating to black invisibility and name-lessness, the first difficult challenge and demanding discipline are to ward off madness and discredit suicide as a desirable option. A central preoccupa-tion of black culture is that of confronting candidly the ontological wounds, psychic scars, and existential bruises of black people while fending off insanity and self-annihilation. Black culture consists of black modes of being-in-the-world obsessed with black sadness and sorrow, black agony and anguish, black heartache and heartbreak without fully succumbing to the numbing effects of such misery—to never allow such misery to have the last word. This is why the "urtext" of black culture is neither a word nor a book, not an architectural monument or a legal brief. Instead, it is a guttural cry and a wrenching moan—a cry not so much for help as for home, a moan less out of complaint than for recognition. The most profound black cultural products—John Coltrane's saxophone solos, James Cleveland's gut gospels, Billie Holiday's vocal leaps, Rev. Gardner Taylor's rhapsodic sermons, James Baldwin's poignant essays, Alvin Ailey's graceful dances, Toni Morrison's dissonant novels—transform and transfigure in artistic form this cry and moan. The deep black meaning of this cry and moan goes back to the indescribable cries of Africans on the slave ships during the cruel transatlantic voyages to America and the indecipherable moans of enslaved Afro-Americans on Wednesday nights or Sunday mornings near godforsaken creeks or on wooden benches at prayer meetings in makeshift black churches. This fragile existential arsenal—rooted in silent tears and weary lament—supports black endurance against madness and suicide. The primal black cries and moans lay bare the profoundly tragicomic character of black life. Ironically, they also embody the life-preserving content of black styles—creative ways of fashioning power and strength through the body and language that yield black joy and ecstasy.

Du Bois captures one such primal scene of black culture at the beginning of *The Souls of Black Folk*, in chapter 1, "Of Our Spiritual Strivings." He starts with 13 lines from the poem "The Crying of Water" by Arthur Symons, the English symbolist critic and decadent poet who went mad a few years after writing the poem. The hearts of human beings in a heartless slave trade cry out like the sea: "All life long crying without avail, / As the water all night long is crying to me."

This metaphorical association of black hearts, black people, and black culture with water (the sea or a river) runs deep in black artistic expression—as in Langston Hughes's recurring refrain "My soul has grown deep like the rivers" in "The Negro Speaks of Rivers." Black striving resides primarily in movement and motion, resilience and resistance against the paralysis of madness and the stillness of death. As it is for Jim in Mark Twain's *The Adventures of Huckleberry Finn* (1885), the river—a road that moves—is the means by which black people can flee from a menacing racist society. Du Bois continues with the musical bars of the Negro spiritual *Nobody Knows the Trouble I've Seen*. This spiritual is known not simply for its plaintive melody but also for its inexplicable lyrical reversal.

> *Nobody knows the trouble I've seen*
> *Nobody knows but Jesus*
> *Nobody knows the trouble I've seen*
> *Glory hallelujah!*

This exemplary shift from a mournful brooding to a joyful praising is the product of courageous efforts to look life's abyss in the face and keep "keepin' on." This struggle is sustained primarily by the integrity of style, song, and spirituality in a beloved community (e.g., Jesus' proclamation of the Kingdom). It is rather like Ishmael's tragicomic "free and easy sort of genial, desperado philosophy" in Moby Dick, but it is intensified by the fiery art of Aretha Franklin's majestic shouts for joy.

The first of Du Bois's own words in the text completes the primal scene of black culture: "Between me and the other world there is ever an unasked question: unasked by some through feelings of delicacy; by others through the difficulty of rightly framing it. All, nevertheless, flutter round it. They approach me in a half-hesitant sort of way, eye me curiously or compassionately, and then, instead of saying directly, How does it feel to be a problem? they say, I know an excellent colored man in my town; or, I fought at Mechanicsville; or, Do not these Southern outrages make our blood boil? At these I smile, or am interested, or reduce the boiling to a simmer, as the occasion may require. To the real question, How does it feel to be a problem? I answer seldom a word. And yet, being a problem is a strange experience,—peculiar even for one who has never been anything else, save perhaps in babyhood . . . . "

This seminal passage spells out the basic components of black invisibility and namelessness: black people as a problem-people rather than people with problems; black people as abstractions and objects rather than as individuals and persons; black and white worlds divided by a thick wall (or a Veil) that requires role-playing and mask-wearing rather than genuine humane interaction; black rage, anger, and fury concealed in order to assuage white fear and anxiety; and black people rootless and homeless on a perennial journey to discover who they are in a society content to see blacks remain the permanent underdog.

To view black people as a problem-people is to view them as an undifferentiated blob, a homogeneous bloc, or a monolithic conglomerate. Each black person is interchangeable, indistinguishable, or substitutable since all black people are believed to have the same views and values, sentiments and sensibilities. Hence one set of negative stereotypes holds for all of them, no matter how high certain blacks may ascend in the white world (e.g., "savages in a suit or suite"). And the mere presence of black bodies in a white context generates white unease and discomfort, even among whites of goodwill.

This problematizing of black humanity deprives black people of individuality, diversity, and heterogeneity. It reduces black folk to abstractions and objects born of white fantasies and insecurities—as exotic or transgressive entities, as hypersexual or criminal animals. The celebrated opening passage of Ralph Ellison's classic novel, *Invisible Man* (1952), highlights this reduction. "I am an invisible man. No, I am not a spook like those who haunted Edgar Allan Poe; nor am I one of your Hollywood-movie ectoplasms. I am a man of substance, of flesh and bone, fiber and liquids—and I might even be said to possess a mind. I am invisible, understand, simply because people refuse to see me. Like the bodiless heads you see sometimes in circus sideshows, it is as though I have been surrounded by mirrors of hard, distorting glass. When they approach me they see only my surroundings, themselves, or figments of their imagination—indeed, everything and anything except me."

This distorted perception—the failure to see the humanity and individuality of black people—has its source in the historic "Veil" (slavery, Jim Crow, and segregation) that separates the black and white worlds. Ironically, this refusal to see a people whose epidermis is most visible exists alongside a need to keep tight surveillance over these people. This Veil not only precludes honest communication between blacks and whites, it also forces blacks to live in two worlds in order to survive. Whites need not understand or live in the black world in order to thrive. But blacks must grapple with the painful "doubleconsciousness" that may result in "an almost morbid sense of personality and a moral hesitancy which is fatal to self-confidence." Du Bois notes, "The worlds within and without the Veil of Color are changing, and changing rapidly, but not at the same rate, not in the same way; and this must produce a peculiar wrenching of the soul, a peculiar sense of doubt and bewilderment. Such a double life, with double thoughts, double duties, and double social classes, must give rise to double words and double ideals, and tempt the mind to pretence or to revolt, to hypocrisy or to radicalism."

Echoing Paul Laurence Dunbar's famous poem "We Wear the Mask," Du Bois proclaims that "the price of culture is a Lie." Why? Because black people will not succeed in American society if they are fully and freely themselves. Instead, they must "endure petty insults with a smile, shut [their] eyes to wrong." They must not be too frank and outspoken and must never fail to flatter and be pleasant in order to lessen white unease and discomfort. Needless to say, this is not the raw stuff for healthy relations between black people and white people.

Yet this suppression of black rage—the reducing "the boiling to a simmer"—backfires in the end. It reinforces a black obsession with the psychic scars, ontological wounds, and existential bruises that tend to reduce the tragic to the pathetic. Instead of exercising agency or engaging in action against the odds, one may wallow in self-pity, acknowledging the sheer absurdity of it all. After playing the role and wearing the mask in the white world, one may accept the white world's view of one's self. As Du Bois writes, "It is a peculiar sensation, this double-consciousness, this sense of always looking at one's self through the eyes of others, of measuring one's soul by the tape of a world that looks on in amused contempt and pity."

Toni Morrison explores this dilemma of black culture through her moving portrayal of the character of Sweet Home in her profound novel *Beloved* (1987), similar to Jean Toomer's Karintha and Fern in his marvelous and magical text *Cane* (1923). "For the sadness was at her center, the desolated center where the self that was no self made its home."

This theme of black rootlessness and homelessness is inseparable from black namelessness. When James Baldwin writes about these issues in *Nobody Knows My Name* (1961) and *No Name in the Street* (1972), he is trying to explore effective ways to resist the white supremacist imposition of subordinate roles, stations, and identities on blacks. He is attempting to devise some set of existential strategies against the overwhelming onslaught of white dehumanization, devaluation, and degradation. The search for black space (home), black place (roots), and black face (name) is a flight from the visceral effects of white supremacy. Toni Morrison characterizes these efforts as products of a process of "dirtying you." "That anybody white could take your whole self for anything that came to mind. Not just work, kill, or maim you, but dirty you. Dirty you so bad you couldn't like yourself anymore. Dirty you so bad you forgot who you were and couldn't think it Up."

Toni Morrison's monumental novel holds a privileged place in black culture and modernity precisely because she takes this dilemma to its logical conclusion – that black flight from white supremacy (a chamber of horrors for black people) may lead to the murder of those loved ones who are candidates for the "dirtying" process. The black mother, Sethe, kills her daughter, Beloved, because she loved her so, "to out-hurt the hurter," as an act of resistance against the "dirtying" process. "And though she and others lived through and got over it, she could never let it happen to her own. The best thing she was, was her children. Whites might dirty her all right, but not her best thing, her beautiful, magical best thing—the part of her that was clean. No undreamable dreams about whether the headless, feetless torso hanging in the tree with a sign on it was her husband or Paul A; whether the bubbling-hot girls in the colored-school fire set by patriots included her daughter; whether a gang of whites invaded her daughter's private parts, soiled her daughter's thighs and threw her daughter out of the wagon. She might have to work the slaughterhouse yard, but not her daughter. And no one, nobody on this earth, would list her daughter's characteristics on the animal side of the paper. No. Oh no . . . . Sethe had refused—and refused still . . . . [W]hat she had done was right because it came from true love."

Is death the only black space (home), place (roots), and face (name) safe from a pervasive white supremacy? Toni Morrison's Sethe echoes Du Bois's own voice upon the painful passing of his first-born. For Sethe, as for Tolstoy's Ivan, Chekhov's Bishop Pyotr, Kafka's Josephine, Hawthorne's Goodman Brown, Hardy's Jude, Bilchner's Woyzeck, Drelser's Hurstwood, and Shakespeare's Lear, death is the great liberator from suffering and evil.

"But Love sat beside his cradle, and in his ear Wisdom waited to speak. Perhaps now he knows the All-love, and needs not to be wise. Sleep, then, child,—sleep till I sleep and waken to a baby voice and the ceaseless patter of little feet—above the Veil." The most effective and enduring black responses to invisibility and namelessness are those forms of individual and collective black resistance predicated on a deep and abiding black love. These responses take the shape of prophetic thought and action: bold, fearless, courageous attempts to tell the truth about and bear witness to black suffering and to keep faith with a vision of black redemption. Like the "urtexts" of the guttural cry and wrenching moan—enacted in Charlie Parker's bebop sound, Dinah Washington's cool voice, Richard Pryor's comic performances, and James Brown's inimitable funk—the prophetic utterance that focuses on black suffering and sustains a hope-against-hope for black freedom constitutes the heights of black culture. The spiritual depths (the how and what) of Martin Luther King's visionary orations, Nat King Cole's silky soul, August Wilson's probing plays, Martin Puryear's unique sculpture, Harold and Fayard Nicholas's existential acrobatics, Jacob Lawrence's powerful paintings, Marvin Gaye's risky falsettos, Fannie Lou Hamer's fighting songs, and, above all, John Coltrane's *A Love Supreme* exemplify such heights. Two of the greatest moments in black literature also enact such high-quality performances. First, James Baldwin's great self-descriptive visionary passage in *Go Tell It on the Mountain* (1953): "Yes, their parts were all cut off, they were dishonored, their very names were nothing more than dust blown disdainfully across the field of time—to fall where, to blossom where, bringing forth what fruit hereafter, where? – their very names were not their own. Behind them was the darkness, nothing but the darkness, and all around them destruction, and before them nothing but the fire—a bastard people, far from God, singing and crying in the wilderness! Yet, most strangely, and from deeps not before discovered, his faith looked up; before the wickedness that he saw, the wickedness from which he fled, he yet beheld, like a flaming standard in the middle of the air, that power of redemption to which he must, till death, bear witness; which, though it crush him utterly, he could not deny; though none among the living might ever behold it, he had beheld it, and must keep the faith."

For Baldwin the seemingly impossible flight from white supremacy takes the form of a Chekhovian effort to endure lovingly and compassionately, guided by a vision of freedom and empowered by a tradition of black love and faith. To be a bastard people—wrenched from Africa and in, but never fully of, America—is to be a people of highly limited options, if any at all. To bear witness is to make and remake, invent and reinvent oneself as a person and people by keeping faith with the best of such earlier efforts, yet also to acknowledge that the very new selves and peoples to emerge will never fully find a space, place, or face in American society—or Africa. This perennial process of self-making and self-inventing is propelled by a self-loving and self-trusting made possible by overcoming a colonized mind, body, and soul.

This is precisely what Morrison describes in the great litany of black love in Baby Suggs's prayer and sermon of laughter, dance, tears, and silence in "a wide-open place cut deep in the woods nobody knew for what at the end of a path known only to deer and whoever cleared the land in the first place." On those hot Saturday afternoons, Baby Suggs "offered up to them her great big heart." "She told them that the only grace they could have was the grace they could imagine. That if they could not see it, they would not have it. 'Here,' she said, 'in this here place, we flesh; flesh that weeps, laughs; flesh that dances on bare feet in grass. Love it. Love it hard. Yonder they do not love your flesh. They despise it. They don't love your eyes; they'd just as soon pick em out. No more do they love the skin on your back. Yonder they flay it. And O my people they do not love your hands. Those they only use, tie, bind, chopoff and leave empty. Love your hands! Love them. Raise them up and kiss them. Touch others with them, pat them together, stroke them on your face 'cause they don't love that either.

You got to love it, you! And no, they ain't in love with your mouth. Yonder, out there, they will see it broken and break it again. What you say out of it they will not heed. What you scream from it they do not hear. What you put into it to nourish your body they will snatch away and give you leavins instead. No, they don't love your mouth. You got to love it. This is flesh I'm talking about here. Flesh that needs to be loved. Feet that need to rest and to dance; backs that need support; shoulders that need arms, strong arms I'm telling you. And O my people, out yonder, hear me, they do not love your neck unnoosed and straight. So love your neck; put a hand on it, grace it, stroke it and hold it up. And all your inside parts that they'd just as soon slop for hogs, you got to love them. The dark, dark liver—love it, love it, and the beat and beating heart, love that too. More than eyes or feet. More than lungs that have yet to draw free air. More than your life-holding womb and your life-giving private parts, hear me now, love your heart. For this is the prize.' Saying no more, she stood up then and danced with her twisted hip the rest of what her heart had to say while the others opened their mouths and gave her the music. Long notes held until the four-part harmony was perfect enough for their deeply loved flesh."

In this powerful passage Toni Morrison depicts in a concrete and graphic way the enactment and expression of black love, black joy, black community, and black faith that bears witness to black suffering and keeps alive a vision of black hope. Black bonds of affection, black networks of support, black ties of empathy, and black harmonies of spiritual camaraderie provide the grounds for the fragile existential weaponry with which to combat black invisibility and namelessness.

Yet these forceful strategies in black culture still have not successfully come to terms with the problem. The black collective quest for a name that designates black people in the United States continues—from colored, Negro, black, Afro-American, Abyssinian, Ethiopian, Nubian, Bilalian, American African, American, African to African American. The black individual quest for names goes on, with unique new ones for children—e.g., Tarsell, Signithia, Jewayne—designed to set them apart from all others for the purpose of accenting their individuality and offsetting their invisibility. And most important, black rage proliferates—sometimes unabated.

Of all the hidden injuries of blackness in American civilization, black rage is the most deadly, the most lethal. Although black culture is in no way reducible to or identical with black rage, it is inseparable from black rage. Du Bois's renowned eulogy for Alexander Crummell, the greatest nineteenth-century black intellectual, is one of the most penetrating analyses of black rage. Du Bois begins his treatment with a virtually generic description of black childhoods—a description that would hold for Arthur Ashe or Ice Cube, Kathleen Battle or Queen Latifah. "This is the history of a human heart,—the tale of a black boy who many long years ago began to struggle with life that he might know the world and know himself. Three temptations he met on those dark dunes that lay gray and dismal before the wonder-eyes of the child: the Temptation of Hate, that stood out against the red dawn; the Temptation of Despair, that darkened noonday; and the

Temptation of Doubt, that ever steals along with twilight. Above all, you must hear of the vales he crossed,—the Valley of Humiliation and the Valley of the Shadow of Death."

Black self-hatred and hatred of others parallels that of all human beings, who must gain some sense of themselves and the world. But the tremendous weight of white supremacy makes this human struggle for mature black selfhood even more difficult. As black children come to view themselves more and more as the degraded other, the temptation of hate grows, "gliding stealthily into [their] laughter, fading into [their] play, and seizing [their] dreams by day and night with rough, rude turbulence. So [they ask] of sky and sun and flower the never-answered Why? and love, as [they grow], neither the world nor the world's rough ways."

The two major choices in black culture (or any culture) facing those who succumb to the temptation of hate are a self-hatred that leads to self-destruction or a hatred of others—degraded others—that leads to vengeance of some sort. These options often represent two sides of the same coin. The case of Bigger Thomas, portrayed by Richard Wright in his great novel *Native Son* (1940), is exemplary in this regard. "Bigger's face was metallically black in the strong sunlight. There was in his eyes a pensive, brooding amusement, as of a man who had been long confronted and tantalized by a riddle whose answer seemed always just on the verge of escaping him, but prodding him irresistibly on to seek its solution. The silence irked Bigger; he was anxious to do something to evade looking so squarely at this problem."

The riddle to which Bigger seeks an answer is the riddle of his black existence in America—and he evades it in part because the pain, fear, silence, and hatred cut so deep. Like the "huge black rat" that appears at the beginning of the novel, Bigger reacts to his circumstances instinctually. Yet his instinct to survive is intertwined with his cognitive perception that white supremacy is out to get him. To make himself and invent himself as a black person in America is to strike out against white supremacy—out of pain, fear, silence, and hatred. The result is psychic terror and physical violence—committed against black Bessie and white Mary. "Bigger rose and went to the window. His hands caught the cold steel bars in a hard grip. He knew as he stood there that he could never tell why he had killed. It was not that he did not really want to tell, but the telling of it would have involved an explanation of his entire life. The actual killing of Mary and Bessie was not what concerned him most; it was knowing and feeling that he could never make anybody know what had driven him to it. His crimes were known, but what he had felt before he committed them would never be known. He would have gladly admitted his guilt if he had thought that in doing so he could have also given in the same breath a sense of the deep, choking hate that had been his life, a hate that he had not wanted to have, but could not help having. How could he do that? The impulsion to try to tell was as deep as had been the urge to kill."

The temptation to hate is a double-edged sword. Bigger's own self-hatred not only leads him to hate other blacks but also to deny the humanity of whites. Yet he can overcome this self-hatred only when he views himself as a self-determining agent who is willing to take responsibility for his actions and acknowledge his connection with others. Although Wright has often been criticized for casting Bigger as a pitiful victim, subhuman monster, and isolated individualist—as in James Baldwin's "Everybody's Protest Novel" and "Many Thousands Gone" in *Notes of a Native Son* (1955)—Wright presents brief moments in which Bigger sees the need to transcend his victim status and rapacious individualism. When his family visits him in jail, Bigger responds to their tears and anger. "Bigger wanted to comfort them in the presence of the white folks, but did not know how. Desperately, he cast about for something to say. Hate and shame boiled in him against the people behind his back; he tried to think of words that would defy them, words that would let them know that he had a world and life of his own in spite of them."

Wright does not disclose the internal dynamics of this black world of Bigger's own, but Bigger does acknowledge that he is part of this world. For example, his actions had dire consequences for his sister, Vera. "'Bigger,' his mother sobbed, trying to talk through her tears. 'Bigger, honey, she won't go to school no more. She says the other girls look at her and make her 'shamed . . . . ' He had lived and acted on the assumption that he was alone, and now he saw that he had not been. What he had done made others suffer. No matter how much he would long for them to forget him, they would not be able to. His family was a part of him, not only in blood, but in spirit. He sat on the cot and his mother knelt at his feet. Her face was lifted to his; her eyes were empty, eyes that looked upward when the last hope of earth had failed."

Yet even this family connection fails to undercut the layers of hate Bigger feels for himself and them. It is only when Bigger receives unconditional support and affirmation across racial lines that his self-hatred and hatred of others subsides—for a moment, from white Jan, the boyfriend of the slain Mary. "He looked at Jan and saw a white face, but an honest face. This white man believed in him, and the moment he felt that belief he felt guilty again; but in a different sense now. Suddenly, this white man had come up to him, flung aside the curtain and walked into the room of his life. Jan had spoken a declaration of friendship that would make other white men hate him: a particle of white rock had detached itself from that looming mountain of white hate and had rolled down the slope, stopping still at his feet. The word had become flesh. For the first time in his life a white man became a human being to him; and the reality of Jan's humanity came in a stab of remorse: he had killed what this man loved and had hurt him. He saw Jan as though someone had performed an operation upon his eyes, or as though someone had snatched a deforming mask from Jan's face."

In both instances Bigger lurches slightly beyond the temptation of hate when he perceives himself as an agent and subject accountable for the consequences of his actions—such as the victimization of his own black sister and a white person. Yet the depths of his self-hatred—his deep-seated colonized mind—permit only a glimpse of self-transformation when the friendship of a white fellow victim is offered to him.

Similar to Bigger Thomas, Alexander Crummell was inspired by a white significant other—Beriah Green. This sort of sympathetic connection makes the temptation of hate grow "fainter and less sinister. It did not wholly fade away, but diffused itself and lingered thick at the edges." Through both Bigger Thomas and Alexander Crummell we see the tremendous pull of the white world and the tragic need for white recognition and affirmation among so many black people.

The temptation of despair is the second element of black rage in Du Bois's analysis. This temptation looms large when black folk conclude that "the way of the world is closed to me." This conclusion yields two options— nihilism and hedonism. Again, two sides of the same coin. This sense of feeling imprisoned, bound, constrained, and circumscribed is a dominant motif in black cultural expressions. Again, Wright captures this predicament well with Bigger Thomas. "'Goddammit!' 'What's the matter?' 'They don't let us do nothing.' 'Who?' 'The white folks.' 'You talk like you just now finding that out,' Gus said. 'Naw. But I just can't get used to it,' Bigger said. 'I swear to God I can't. I know I oughtn't think about it, but I can't help it. Every time I think about it I feel like somebody's poking a red-hot iron down my throat. Goddammit, look! We live here and they live there. We black and they white. They got things and we ain't. They do things and we can't. It's just like living in jail. Half the time I feel like I'm on the outside of the world peeping in through a knot-hole in the fence.'"

The temptation of despair is predicated on a world with no room for black space, place, or face. It feeds on a black futurelessness and black hopelessness—a situation in which visions and dreams of possibility have dried up like raisins in the sun. This nihilism leads to lives of drift, lives in which any pleasure, especially instant gratification, is the primary means of feeling alive. Anger and aggression usually surface in such lives. Bigger says, "I hurt folks 'cause I felt I had to; that's all. They was crowding me too close; they wouldn't give me no room . . . . I thought they was hard and I acted hard . . . . I'll be feeling and thinking that they didn't see me and I didn't see them."

The major black cultural response to the temptation of despair has been the black Christian tradition, dominated by music in song, prayer, and sermon. The unique role of this tradition is often noted. Du Bois writes "that the Negro church antedates the Negro home, leads to an explanation of much that is paradoxical in this communistic institution and in the morals of its members. But especially it leads us to regard this institution as peculiarly the expression of the inner ethical life of a people in a sense seldom true elsewhere."

Even Bigger Thomas—the most cynical and secular of rebels in the black literary tradition—is captivated by the power of black church music, the major caressing artistic flow in the black *Sittlichkeit* (ethical life). "The singing from the church vibrated through him, suffusing him with a mood of sensitive sorrow. He tried not to listen, but it seeped into his feelings, whispering of another way of life and death . . . . The singing filled his ears; it was complete, self-contained, and it mocked his fear and loneliness, his deep yearning for a sense of wholeness. Its fullness contrasted so sharply with his hunger, its richness with his emptiness, that he recoiled from it while answering it."

The black church tradition, along with the rich musical tradition it spawned, generates a sense of movement, motion, and momentum that keeps despair at bay. As with any collective project or performance that puts a premium on change, transformation, conversion, and future possibility, the temptation of despair is not eliminated but attenuated. In this sense, the black church tradition has made ritual art and communal bonds out of black invisibility and namelessness. Ralph Ellison updates and secularizes this endeavor when he writes, "Perhaps I like Louis Armstrong because he's made poetry out of being invisible. I think it must be because he's unaware that he is invisible. And my own grasp of invisibility aids me to understand his music . . . . Invisibility, let me explain, gives one a slightly different sense of time, you're never quite on the beat. Sometimes you're ahead and sometimes behind. Instead of the swift and imperceptible flowing of time, you are aware of its nodes, those points where time stands still or from which it leaps ahead. And you slip into the breaks and look around. That's what you hear vaguely in Louis' music."

The temptation of doubt is the most persistent of the three temptations. White supremacy drums deeply into the hearts, minds, and souls of black people, causing them to expect little of one another and themselves. This black insecurity and self-doubt produces a debilitating black jealousy in the face of black "success"—a black jealousy that often takes the form of what Eldridge Cleaver called "nigger rituals"—namely, a vicious trashing of black "success" or a black "battle royal" for white spectators. Understandably, under conditions of invisibility and namelessness, most of those blacks with "visibility" and a "name" in the white world are often the object of black scorn and contempt. Such sad, self-fulfilling prophecies of black cowardice make the temptation of doubt especially seductive—one that fans and fuels the flames of black rage. Du Bois states, "Of all the three temptations, this one struck the deepest. Hate? He had outgrown so childish a thing. Despair? He had steeled his right arm against it, and fought it with the vigor of determination. But to doubt the worth of his life-work,—to doubt the destiny and capability of the race his soul loved because it was his; to find listless squalor instead of eager endeavor; to hear his own lips whispering, 'They do not care; they cannot know; they are dumb driven cattle,—why cast your pearls before swine?'—this, this seemed more than man could bear; and he closed the door, and sank upon the steps of the chancel, and cast his robe upon the floor and writhed."

The two principal options for action after one yields to the temptation of doubt in black culture are authoritarian subordination of the "ignorant" masses or individual escape from these masses into the white mainstream. These two options are not two sides of the same coin, though they often flow from a common source: an elitist vision that shuns democratic accountability. And although this elitist vision—that of the Exceptional Negro or Talented Tenth who is "better than those other blacks"—is found more readily among the black educated and middle class, some of the black working poor and very poor subscribe to it too. Even Bigger Thomas. "As he rode, looking at the black people on the sidewalks, he felt that one way to end fear and shame was to make all those black people act together, rule them, tell them what to do, and make them do it . . . . But he felt that such would never happen to him and his black people, and he hated them and wanted to wave his hand and blot them out. Yet, he still hoped, vaguely. Of late he had liked to hear tell of men who could rule others, for in actions such as these he felt that there was a way to escape from this tight morass of fear and shame that sapped at the base of his life. He liked to hear of how Japan was conquering China; of how Hitler was running Jews to the ground; of how Mussolini was invading Spain. He was not concerned with whether these acts were right or wrong; they simply appealed to him as possible avenues of escape. He felt that some day there would be a black man who would whip the black people into a tight band and together they would act and end fear and shame. He never thought of this in precise mental images; he felt it; he would feel it for a while and then forget. But hope was always waiting somewhere deep down in him."

This hope for black unity and action was based on a profound doubt concerning the ability of black people to think for themselves and act on principles they had examined, scrutinized, and deliberately chosen. Ironically, this same elitist logic is at work among those who uncritically enter the white mainstream and accuse black people of lacking discipline and determination. Alexander Crummell overcame the difficult challenge of self-doubt and the doubt of other black folk by moving to Africa and later returning to America to fight for and "among his own, the low, the grasping, and the wicked, and with that unbending righteousness which is the sword of the just."

In the end, for Du Bois, Alexander Crummell triumphed over hate, despair, and doubt owing to "that full power within, that mighty inspiration" within the Veil. He was able to direct his black rage through moral channels sustained primarily by black bonds of affection, black networks of support, and black ties of empathy. Yet few today know his name and work, principally due to the thick Veil of color then and now: "His name today, in this broad land, means little, and comes to fifty million ears laden with no incense of memory or emulation. And herein lies the tragedy of the age: not that men are poor,—all men know something of poverty; not that men are wicked,—who is good? not that men are ignorant,—what is Truth? Nay, but that men know so little of men."

For Du Bois "the problem of the twentieth century is the problem of the color-line" largely because of the relative lack of communication across the Veil of color. For Du Bois the vicious legacy of white supremacy contributes to the arrested development of democracy. And since communication is the lifeblood of a democracy—the very measure of the vitality of its public life—we either come to terms with race and hang together, or ignore it and hang separately. This is why every examination of black strivings is an important part of understanding the prevailing crisis in American society.

## A Twilight Civilization in Our Time

In our time—at the end of the twentieth century—the crisis of race in America is still raging. The problem of black invisibility and namelessness, however, remains marginal to the dominant accounts of our past and present and is relatively absent from our pictures of the future. In this age of globalization, with its impressive scientific and technological innovations in information, communication, and applied biology, a focus on the lingering effects of racism seems outdated and antiquated. The global cultural bazaar of entertainment and enjoyment, the global shopping mall of advertising and marketing, the global workplace of blue-collar and white-collar employment, and the global financial network of computerized transactions and megacorporate mergers appear to render any talk about race irrelevant.

Yet with the collapse of the Soviet Empire, the end of the cold war, and the rise of Japan, corrupt and top-heavy nation-states are being eclipsed by imperial corporations as public life deteriorates owing to class polarization, racial balkanization, and especially a predatory market culture. With the vast erosion of civic networks that nurture and care for citizens—such as families, neighborhoods, and schools—and with what might be called the gangsterization of everyday life, characterized by the escalating fear of violent attack, vicious assault, or cruel insult, we are witnessing a pervasive cultural decay in American civilization. Even public discourse has degenerated into petty name calling and finger pointing, with little room for mutual respect and empathetic exchange. Increasing suicides and homicides, alcoholism and drug addiction, distrust and disloyalty, cold-heartedness and mean-spiritedness, isolation and loneliness, cheap sexual thrills and cowardly patriarchal violence are still other symptoms of this decay. Yet race—in the coded language of welfare reform, immigration policy, criminal punishment, affirmative action, and suburban privatization—remains a central signifier in the political debate.

As in late nineteenth-century Russia and early twentieth-century Central Europe, the ruling political right hides and conceals the privilege and wealth of the few (the 1 percent who own 48 percent of the net financial wealth, the top 10 percent who own 86 percent, the top 20 percent who have 94 percent!) and pits the downwardly mobile middlers against the downtrodden poor. This age-old strategy of scapegoating the most vulnerable, frightening the most insecure, and supporting the most comfortable constitutes a kind of iron law signaling the decline of modern civilizations, as in Tolstoy's Russia and Kafka's Central Europe: chaotic and inchoate rebellion from below, withdrawal and retreat from public life from above, and a desperate search for authoritarian law and order, at any cost, from the middle. In America this suggests not so much a European style of fascism but rather a homespun brand of authoritarian democracy—the systemic stigmatizing, regulating, and policing of the degraded others—women, gays, lesbians, Latinos, Jews, Asians, Indians, and especially black people. As Sinclair Lewis warned over a half century ago, fascism, American-style, can happen here.

Welfare reform means, on the ground, poor people (disproportionately black) with no means of support. Criminal punishment means hundreds of thousands of black men in crowded prisons—many in there forever. And suburban privatization means black urban poor citizens locked into decrepit public schools, dilapidated housing, inadequate health care, and unavailable child care. Furthermore, the lowest priorities on the global corporate agenda of the political right—the low quantity of jobs with a living wage and the low quality of life for children—have the greatest consequences for the survival of any civilization. Instead, we have generational layers of unemployed and underemployed people (often uncounted in our national statistics) and increasing numbers of hedonistic and nihilistic young people (of all classes, races, genders, and regions) with little interest in public life and with little sense of moral purpose.

This is the classic portrait of a twilight civilization whose dangerous rumblings—now intermittent in much of America but rampant in most of black urban America—will more than likely explode in the twenty-first century if we stay on the present conservative course. In such a bleak scenario, given the dominant tendencies of our day, Du Bois's heralded Talented Tenth will by and large procure a stronger foothold in the well-paid professional managerial sectors of the global economy, and more and more will become intoxicated with the felicities of a parvenu bourgeois existence. The heroic few will attempt to tell unpleasant truths about our plight and bear prophetic witness to our predicament as well as try to organize and mobilize (and be organized and mobilized by) the economically devastated, culturally degraded, and politically marginalized black working poor and very poor. Since a multiracial alliance of progressive meddlers, liberal slices of the corporate elite, and subversive energy from below is the only vehicle by which some form of radical democratic accountability can redistribute resources and wealth and restructure the economy and government so that all benefit, the significant secondary efforts of the black Talented Tenth alone in the twenty-first century will be woefully inadequate and thoroughly frustrating. Yet even progressive social change, though desirable and necessary, may not turn back the deeper and deadly processes of cultural decay in late twentieth-century America.

As this Talented Tenth comes to be viewed more and more with disdain and disgust by the black working poor and very poor, not only class envy but class hatred in black America will escalate in the midst of a more isolated and insulated black America. This will deepen the identity crisis of the black Talented Tenth—a crisis of survivor's guilt and cultural rootlessness. As the glass ceilings (limited promotions) and golden cuffs (big position and good pay with little or no power) remain in place for most, though not all, blacks in corporate America, we will see anguish and hedonism intensify among much of the Talented Tenth. The conservative wing of black elites will climb on the bandwagon of the political right—some for sincere reasons, most for opportunistic ones—as the black working poor and very poor try to cope with the realities of death, disease, and destruction. The progressive wing of the black elite will split into a vociferous (primarily male-led) black nationalist camp that opts for self-help at the lower and middle levels of the entrepreneurial sectors of the global economy and a visionary (disproportionately woman-led) radical democratic camp that works assiduously to keep alive a hope—maybe the last hope—for a twilight civilization that once saw itself as the "last best hope of earth."

After 95 years of the most courageous and unflagging devotion to black freedom witnessed in the twentieth century, W E. B. Du Bois not only left America for Africa but concluded, "I just cannot take any more of this country's treatment. We leave for Ghana October 5th and I set no date for return . . . . Chin up, and fight on, but realize that American Negroes can't win."

In the end Du Bois's Enlightenment world-view, Victorian strategies, and American optimism failed him. He left America in militant despair—the very despair he had avoided earlier—and mistakenly hoped for the rise of a strong postcolonial and united Africa. Echoing Tolstoy's claim that "it's intolerable to live in Russia . . . . I've decided to emigrate to England forever" (though he never followed through) and Kafka's dream to leave Prague and live in Palestine (though he died before he could do so), Du Bois concluded that black strivings in a twilight civilization were unbearable for him yet still imperative for others—even if he could not envision black freedom in America as realizable.

For those of us who stand on his broad shoulders, let us begin where he ended—with his militant despair; let us look candidly at the tragicomic and absurd character of black life in America in the spirit of John Coltrane and Toni Morrison; let us continue to strive with genuine compassion, personal integrity, and human decency to fight for radical democracy in the face of the frightening abyss—or terrifying inferno—of the twenty-first century, clinging to "a hope not hopeless but unhopeful."

North America

# Wells-Barnett, Ida Bell

**(b. July 16, 1862, Holly Springs, Miss.; d. March 25, 1931, Chicago, Ill.), African American journalist, advocate of civil rights, women's rights, and economic rights, and antilynching crusader.**

Ida B. Wells-Barnett, the first of Jim and Elizabeth Wells's eight children, was born six months before the Emancipation Proclamation went into effect. She attended Shaw University (now Rust College) in her hometown of Holly Springs, Mississippi, until she was forced to drop out when her parents died of yellow fever in 1878. Following their deaths, Wells-Barnett supported herself and her siblings by working as a schoolteacher in rural Mississippi and Tennessee. She took summer courses at Fisk University and continued to teach through 1891, when she was fired for writing an editorial that accused the Memphis school board of providing inadequate resources to black schools.

In May 1884 Wells-Barnett filed suit against a railroad company after she was forced off a train for refusing to sit in the Jim Crow car designated for blacks. She was awarded $500 by a circuit court, but the decision was overruled by the Tennessee Supreme Court in 1887, a rejection that only strengthened her resolve to devote her life to upholding justice.

Wells-Barnett embarked on a career in journalism when she was elected editor of the *Evening Star* and then the *Living Way*, weekly church newspapers in Memphis. She became the editor of *Free Speech*, also in Memphis, in 1889. Her articles, written under the alias "Iola," were direct and confrontational, and two editorials she wrote in 1892 in response to the persecution and eventual lynching of three black businessmen were particularly controversial. The first, published on March 9, encouraged blacks to leave Memphis for Oklahoma and to boycott segregated transportation. The second, which appeared on May 21, suggested that white women were often the willing initiators in interracial relationships. Whites who were angered by her work responded by wrecking the offices and press of *Free Speech*.

Wells-Barnett took refuge in the North, reporting in the black newspapers the *New York Age* and the *Chicago Conservator* on the violence and injustices being perpetrated against African Americans. Through a lecture tour of England, Scotland, and Wales in 1893 and 1894, Wells-Barnett inspired international organizations to apply pressure on America to end segregation and lynching. In 1895 she published an analysis of lynching titled *A Red Record: Tabulated Statistics and Alleged Causes of Lynching in the United States*, which argued that the impetus behind lynching was economic.

Marrying Ferdinand Barnett, a Chicago lawyer and editor, in 1895, Wells-Barnett put her writing on hold to focus on her family (the couple had four children), but she remained politically active. She helped to found the National Association of Colored Women in 1896, the Negro Fellowship League and the National Association for the Advancement of Colored People in 1910, and the Alpha Suffrage Club in 1913. In 1916 she became involved with Marcus Garvey's Universal Negro Improvement Association.

During the last 15 years of her life Wells-Barnett wrote extensively on the race riots in East St. Louis (1917), Chicago (1919), and Arkansas (1922), and continued to promote civil rights and justice for African Americans. A low-income housing project in Chicago was named in her honor in 1941, and in 1990 the United States Postal Service issued an Ida B. Wells-Barnett stamp.

North America

# White, Walter Francis

(b. July 1, 1893, Atlanta, Ga.; d. March 21, 1955, New York, N.Y.), African American civil rights leader who built the foundations of the Civil Rights Movement as an official of the National Association for the Advancement of Colored People (NAACP), and influential author of the Harlem Renaissance.

Walter White grew up in a racially mixed neighborhood and, as a light-skinned, blue-eyed man, was able to pass for white. He credited a 1906 race riot in Atlanta, during which he defended his family's home from fire, as the incident that ignited his race consciousness as a black man. From that point on, he chose to live as an African American fighting for political and social justice.

After graduating from Atlanta University in 1916, White's activism with the Atlanta branch of the National Association for the Advancement of Colored People (NAACP) became his career. In 1918 he moved to New York to serve as assistant to NAACP executive secretary James Weldon Johnson. He was an invaluable researcher for the NAACP's antilynching efforts; passing for white, he investigated lynchings and other racially motivated crimes without hindrance. White's reports for the NAACP were fodder for his fiction; his two novels, *The Fire in the Flint* (1924) and *Flight* (1926), both concern the responses of educated blacks, or "New Negroes," to racial injustice. Although the novels sometimes sacrifice plot and characterization to political message, they earned White a Guggenheim Fellowship in 1926. White used money from the fellowship for support while writing a seminal investigation of lynching, *Rope and Faggot: A Biography of Judge Lynch* (1929).

As executive secretary of the NAACP from 1931 to 1955, White worked with A. Philip Randolph to secure the establishment of the Fair Employment Practices Committee in 1941; his efforts also helped produce the executive orders banning discrimination in war-related industries that same year and in the entire United States military in 1948. A delegate with W. E. B. Du Bois and Mary McLeod Bethune to the founding of the United Nations in 1945, White also became involved with seeking justice for the African diaspora. One of White's most lasting achievements as NAACP executive secretary was the recruitment of Charles Hamilton Houston to serve as the NAACP's first full-time chief counsel. Under Houston's leadership and fueled by White's tireless fundraising efforts, the NAACP undertook a series of legal challenges to segregation, culminating in the 1954 United States Supreme Court's historic *Brown v. Board of Education* decision, which finally toppled segregated education in the United States.

North America

# Wilkins, Roy Ottoway

**(b. August 30, 1901, St. Louis, Mo.; d. September 8, 1981, New York, N.Y.), African American journalist, civil rights leader, and director of the National Association for the Advancement of Colored People (NAACP).**

Before Roy Wilkins was born, his father had been forced to flee St. Louis to avoid being lynched for refusing to follow a white man's order to get out of the road. Wilkins grew up in St. Paul, Minnesota, where he attended racially integrated schools. He became urgently aware of racial matters at age 18, when three Minnesotan black men were lynched by a mob of 5,000 whites. Upon enrolling in the University of Minnesota, Wilkins became active in the National Association for the Advancement of Colored People

(NAACP), as well as on the campus newspaper. He would pursue both interests in Kansas City following graduation. Wilkins worked for the *Kansas City Call*, an African American newspaper, until 1931. He then became assistant executive secretary for the NAACP, a position he held while editing the organization's newspaper, the *Crisis*, until 1949.

In 1955 Wilkins was appointed to serve as the NAACP's executive director, the organization's highest administrative post. He steered the NAACP through the Civil Rights Movement's most turbulent era, and with Martin Luther King Jr. helped to organize the March on Washington in 1963. Throughout his career Wilkins upheld the principle of nonviolent, legal forms of redress, which tended to alienate him from more radical black groups. Wilkins's struggles for equality and civil rights brought him many awards and earned him the nickname "Mr. Civil Rights."

North America

# Williams, Robert Franklin

(b. February 26, 1925, Monroe, N.C.; d. October 15, 1996, Grand Rapids, Mich.), civil rights activist and prominent advocate of black self-defense and revolutionary nationalism.

Robert Franklin Williams grew up in a tradition of resistance to white supremacy. His grandfather, born a slave, had been a Republican Party activist during Reconstruction after the Civil War, when former slaves sought to establish themselves as equal citizens but found their efforts dashed by white terrorists. His grandfather edited a newspaper called the *People's Voice*. His grandmother, who lived through these struggles, was a daily presence in his life as he grew to manhood. She told young Williams stories of the crusading editor's political exploits and before she died gave him his grandfather's gun.

World War II transformed Williams's life; he moved to Detroit to work in the defense industries, fought white mobs in the Detroit Riot of 1943, and marched for freedom in a segregated United States Army. Military training "instilled in us what a virtue it was to fight for democracy," he said, "but most of all they taught us to use arms."

When he returned to his birthplace, Monroe, North Carolina, in 1955 Williams served as president of the Monroe chapter of the National Association for the Advancement of Colored People (NAACP). Confronted by Ku Klux Klan terrorism, Williams organized the local chapter into a black militia that repelled armed Klan attacks. In 1959, after an all-white jury acquitted a white man charged with the attempted rape of a pregnant black woman, Williams called for blacks "to meet violence with violence," invoking "the right of armed self-defense against attack." The NAACP suspended Williams for his remarks in a struggle over the meaning of nonviolence for the African American freedom struggle. The following year Williams debated prominent pacifists, including Martin Luther King Jr., the leading spokesperson of the black freedom struggle.

In 1961 followers of King came to Monroe, many of them intent on proving that nonviolence could work. Armed racial conflict broke out, forcing Williams to flee to Cuba under federal indictment on trumped-up kidnapping charges. From Havana, Williams broadcast "Radio Free Dixie," which spread his gospel of "armed self-reliance." He also published his newsletter the *Crusader*, whose readership was about 40,000. His 1962 book *Negroes with Guns* was a decisive influence on the Black Panther Party for Self-Defense, founded in Oakland, California, in 1966, and on a generation of increasingly defiant black activists.

Moving to North Vietnam and then China in 1966, Williams wrote antiwar propaganda aimed at African American soldiers fighting in Vietnam and called for revolution in the United States. In China Williams moved in the upper circles of the Chinese government. The Revolutionary Action Movement and the Republic of New Africa, two important revolutionary black nationalist groups in the United States, both chose him as their president-in-exile. In 1969, as the U.S. government moved to open diplomatic relations with China, Williams traded his knowledge of China for safe passage home and a post at the University of Michigan's Center for Chinese Studies. Just before he died in 1996, Williams completed his autobiography, *While God Lay Sleeping*. Above the desk where he wrote hung the ancient rifle his grandmother had given him.

Williams was typical of the generation of black Southerners who launched the African American freedom movement. His evolution from local NAACP leader to international revolutionary underlines both the growing radicalism of the movement and its origins in traditions of militant African American self-assertion.

North America

# Wilmington, N.C., Riot of 1898,

white supremacist campaign of violence and murder directed at black political officials in Wilmington, North Carolina.

In 1898 Wilmington, with a population of approximately 20,000, was the major city in the eastern region of North Carolina. It was one of the most integrated cities of the South, with blacks and whites living in each of the five wards. African Americans constituted a majority of the city's residents and successfully competed with whites for jobs. A significant number of blacks were successful businessmen and professionals, and many also held important municipal positions such as police chief, deputy sheriff, and federal collector of customs. Wilmington was part of the Second Congressional District, often called the "Black Second" on account of its large number of black political officials.

Part of what had allowed black Republicans to assume important political posts was their alliance with Populists. These two parties controlled the local government until 1898 and, to ensure black representation, had passed a resolution in 1897 to appoint African Americans to five of the ten alderman positions. Blacks were approaching a level of political and social equality that many whites found unacceptable. As a result white Democrats, determined to oust the black officials from office, began campaigning well before the 1898 election. They claimed that the presence of blacks in the local government "emboldens bad Negroes to display their evil, impudent, and mean natures." White Democrats misrepresented black speakers by exaggerating their arguments and threatened to kill them if they did not withdraw from the election. Wilmington's white leaders issued a "Declaration of White Independence" calling for the expulsion of black politicians and businessmen, and organized a "secret nine" committee to facilitate this task.

As part of their attack on black Republicans, white Democrats printed and distributed 300,000 copies of an article that had been written in August 1898 by Alex Manly, editor of the *Wilmington Record* who was of mixed African descent. It read, "Our experience among poor white people in the country teaches us that the women of that race are not any more particular in the matter of clandestine meetings with colored men, than are the white men with the colored women." This assertion against white womanhood fueled anger within the white community and emboldened them to vote black officials out of office. As a result the white Democrats swept the 1898 elections.

On the morning of November 10, the day after the election, a group of approximately 500 men who had been summoned by the white Democrats took up firearms, formed a mob, and marched into Brooklyn, a predominantly black section of town. They burned down the office of Manly, who had reportedly left town 11 days earlier, and local Africans Americans began to fear that the mob would turn on them next. Upon receiving news of what had happened, African American officials resigned and many black employees at the local cotton compress left work to find and defend their families. The mob disbanded and headed home in small groups.

One of these groups of white men encountered a group of armed black men at the intersection of Fourth and Harnett streets and advised them to return to their homes. The blacks crossed the street and refused to move any farther. A shot was fired and one of the white mob, William Mayo, was injured. The two groups opened fire at each other and a shootout ensued. Whites quickly received notice of the incident and flooded the city's black neighborhoods, where they indiscriminately shot at blacks. Whites not participating in the riot sought refuge in churches and schools while blacks fled to the forest to save their lives.

The governor sent in the state militia to aid whites in disarming the blacks, who were regarded as the antagonists. Up-to-the-minute telegraph coverage was wired across the country. By 3:00 p.m., gunfire ceased. It is estimated that 7 to 30 blacks were killed. The few remaining blacks that ventured into the open to return home were stopped and searched by white soldiers and pedestrians. In the days following the riot, a large number of blacks and some whites left Wilmington. The white Democrats quickly disfranchised the remaining black community by instituting literacy tests at the polls. By the turn of the century the town had a white majority.

# Wright, Louis Tompkins

(b. July 23, 1891, La Grange, Ga.; d. October 8, 1952, New York, N.Y.), African American surgeon, hospital administrator, and chairman of the board of the National Association for the Advancement of Colored People (NAACP).

In a career combining medical and political achievements, Louis T. Wright was one of the most respected black professionals of his time. A doctor's son (and later a doctor's stepson), Wright graduated from Clark University in Atlanta, Georgia, in 1911 and went on to medical school at Harvard University. While at Harvard, Wright voiced strong objection to being treated differently when a professor tried to prevent him from delivering babies at a white teaching hospital. This became an early example of his lifelong insistence upon equal rights.

Unable to win an internship at any of Boston's many hospitals despite graduating fourth in his class at Harvard, Wright did his postgraduate internship at Freedmen's Hospital, an affiliate of Howard University in Washington, D.C. In 1916 he returned to Atlanta, went into practice with his stepfather, and joined the NAACP. When the United States entered World War I the next year, Wright served as a lieutenant in the Army Medical Corps, ran a field hospital in France, and was awarded the Purple Heart.

After the war Wright started a small, general practice in Harlem in 1919 and became affiliated with Harlem Hospital. Meanwhile he continued his NAACP work toward racial equality. As he became more prominent, Wright occasionally encountered opposition to his advocacy of more stringent educational standards; especially upset were those members of the black medical establishment who had grown used to separate and at times unequal, less rigorous schools. The New York Police Department appointed Wright police surgeon in 1929; in 1935 the NAACP made him the chairman of its board; eight years later Harlem Hospital made him its chief of surgery. None of these positions had been held before by an African American.

Wright never completely recovered from the lung damage he had suffered in the war; from 1939 to 1942 he was hospitalized for tuberculosis. In 1952 he died following a heart attack. Despite its brevity and interruptions, his medical career was impressive. Wright published 89 scientific papers, including several influential works on the treatment of bone fractures. He helped develop new antibiotics and did pioneering cancer research. In 1940 he was awarded the NAACP's Spingarn Medal. Harlem Hospital renamed its library after Louis Tompkins Wright shortly before his death.

# XYZ

## Young, Andrew

(b. October 23, 1932, New Orleans, La.), African American civil rights activist and politician who was the first black United States ambassador to the United Nations.

Raised in an affluent African American family in New Orleans, Andrew Young as a child had opportunities available to few blacks in the American South. Among these was an exceptional education: he attended Howard University and Hartford Theological Seminary. He was ordained a Congregational minister in 1955 and soon after accepted a position in a diocese in rural Georgia and Alabama. This experience made him keenly aware of the poverty African Americans suffered in the rural South and inspired his work as a civil rights activist.

In 1959 Young moved to New York City to be the assistant director of the National Council of Churches and to raise financial support for civil rights activities in the South. He returned to Georgia two years later and joined the Southern Christian Leadership Conference (SCLC). His energetic work as funding coordinator and administrator of the SCLC's Citizenship Education Programs soon won him the admiration of Martin Luther King Jr. The two men became close associates, and Young helped King organize SCLC marches in the South.

Young became executive director of the SCLC in 1964 and executive vice president in 1967. After King's death Young helped to guide the SCLC toward activities promoting social and economic improvements for African Americans. He retired from these positions in 1970, but remained on the board of directors until 1972.

In 1972 Young became the first African American to be elected to the U.S. House of Representatives from Georgia since Reconstruction. While a representative, Young played an instrumental role in winning for the presidential candidate Jimmy Carter the vital backing of those members of the

African American community who questioned Carter's commitment to civil rights.

Young resigned from the House of Representatives in 1977 when Carter appointed him U.S. ambassador to the United Nations. As ambassador Young improved communications between the United States and African nations. He was instrumental in focusing American foreign policy on sub-Saharan Africa and bringing American attention to the conditions of apartheid in South Africa. Young resigned from the position in 1979 after he was criticized for his contacts with the Palestine Liberation Organization (PLO).

In 1982 Young was elected mayor of Atlanta, an office which he held until 1989. In 1990 he made an unsuccessful bid in the Georgia gubernatorial race and retired from politics. In 1994 he published his memoir, *A Way Out of No Way*, and returned to public life to co-chair the Atlanta Committee for the 1996 Summer Olympic Games.

North America

# Young, Whitney Moore, Jr.

(b. July 31, 1921, Lincoln Ridge, Ky.; d. March 11, 1971, Lagos, Nigeria), former executive director of the National Urban League (NUL) who shaped the organization's policy and lobbied industry to provide employment opportunities for African Americans.

When he was named executive director of the National Urban League (NUL) in October 1961, many observers believed that Whitney Young Jr. was not qualified to hold the position. He had served as industrial relations secretary for the St. Paul, Minnesota, branch of the NUL from 1947 to 1949; as executive secretary of the Omaha, Nebraska, branch from 1949 to 1954; and as dean of the Atlanta University School of Social Work from 1954 to 1961. Still, by traditional NUL standards he was young and inexperienced. As executive director during the 1960s, however, Young guided the organization through one of the most socially and politically tumultuous decades in United States history.

The NUL was much less militant than many other organizations involved in the Civil Rights Movement. Since its inception in 1910 it had sought to promote African American participation in the U.S. political system, rather than to change the system itself. In the 1960s though the NUL did not embrace the direct action of other civil rights organizations— it did not sponsor sit-ins, protest marches, bus boycotts, or voter registration drives—under Young's leadership it took a more active stance that better aligned it with black political and social thought of the day. The NUL provided support for civil rights activists, including co-sponsorship of the March on Washington for Jobs and Freedom in 1963.

Young, who had grown up on the campus of the Lincoln Institute, a vocational high school for blacks at which his father was the principal and the faculty was integrated, was accustomed to interracial cooperation. He used his considerable social and political skills to become an unofficial advisor to presidents John F. Kennedy, Lyndon B. Johnson, and Richard Nixon. Johnson drew on some of Young's ideas for his War on Poverty. Young's relationships with white business leaders brought increased employment to blacks and increased funding to the NUL.

Young, who held a master's degree in social work from the University of Minnesota, also called for a "Domestic Marshall Plan" for blacks. In 1968 he introduced the NUL's New Thrust, a program designed to help eliminate ghettos and to increase affordable housing, health care, and educational opportunities for the poor. In addition, Young wrote a weekly column, "To Be Equal," for the *New York Amsterdam News*. In 1964 a collection of those columns was published as *To Be Equal*. Young died in 1971 while swimming during a visit to Nigeria.

# Select Bibliography

ABAJIAN, JAMES DE T. *Blacks and their Contributions to the American West* (1974).

ABBOTT, D. "Revolution by Other Means," interview with Angela Davis, *New Statesman* 114 (14 August 1987): 16–17.

ABBOTT, ELIZABETH. *Haiti: The Duvaliers and their Legacy* (1988).

ABDUL-JABBAR, KAREEM, WITH MIGNON MCCARTHY. *Kareem* (1990).

ABENON, LUCIEN. *Petite histoire de la Guadeloupe* (1992).

ABERNATHY, RALPH DAVID. *And the Walls Came Tumbling Down: An Autobiography* (1989).

ABRAHAMS, R. G. *The Nyamwezi Today: A Tanzanian People in the 1970s* (1981).

ABRAHAMS, ROGER D. *Deep Down in the Jungle: Negro Narrative Folklore from the Streets of Philadelphia* (1964).

——. *Singing the Master: The Emergence of African American Culture in the Plantation South* (1992).

——. *Talking Black* (1976).

ABRAHAMS, ROGER, AND JOHN SZWED. *After Africa: Extracts from British Travel Accounts and Journals of the Seventeenth, Eighteenth and Nineteenth Centuries Concerning the Slaves, their Manners, and Customs in the British West Indies* (1983).

ABREU, MAURICIO DE. *Evolução urbana do Rio de Janeiro* (1987).*****

ABU-LUGHOD, JANET L. *Rabat: Urban Apartheid in Morocco* (1980).

ABU-JAMAL, MUMIA. *Live from Death Row* (1996).

ACHEBE, CHINUA. *Hopes and Impediments: Selected Essays* (1988).

ADAIR, GENE. *George Washington Carver* (1989).

ADAMS, BARBARA ELEANOR. *John Henrik Clarke: The Early Years* (1992).

ADAMS, W. M., A. S. GOUDIE, AND A. R. ORME. *The Physical Geography of Africa* (1996).

ADÉLAÏDE-MERLANDE, JACQUES. *Delgrés, ou, la Guadeloupe en 1802* (1986).

ADENAIKE, CAROLYN KEYES, AND JAN VANSINA, EDS. *In Pursuit of History: Fieldwork in Africa* (1996).

ADJAYE, JOSEPH K., AND ADRIANNE R. ANDREWS, EDS. *Language, Rhythm, and Sound: Black Popular Cultures into the Twenty-First Century* (1997).

"African-American Quilts: Tracing the Aesthetic Principles." *Clarion* 14, no. 2 (Spring 1989): 44–54.

"African Symbolism in Afro-American Quilts." *African Arts* 20, no 1 (1986).

"Afro-Brazilian Religion." Special issue of *Callaloo* 18, no. 4 (1995).

AGRONSKY, JONATHAN. *Marion Barry: The Politics of Race* (1991).

AGORSAH, E. KOFI, ED. *Maroon Heritage: Archaeological, Ethnographic, and Historical Perspectives* (1994).

AGUIRRE BELTRÁN, GONZALO. *El negro esclavo en Nuevo España: La formación colonial, la medicina popular y otros ensayos* (1994).

ALAGOA, E. J., F. N. ANOZIE, AND NWANNA NZEWUNWA, EDS. *The Early History of the Niger Delta* (1988).

ALBERTSON, CHRIS. *Bessie* (1972).

ALGOO-BAKSH, STELLA. *Austin C. Clarke: A Biography* (1994).

ALIE, JOE A. D. *A New History of Sierra Leone* (1990).

ALLAN D. AUSTIN, ED. *African Muslims in Antebellum America: A Source Book* (1984).

ALLEN, PHILIP M. *Madagascar: Conflicts of Authority in the Great Island* (1995).

ALPERT, HOLLIS. *The Life and Times of Porgy and Bess* (1990).

ALVAREZ NAZARIO, MANUEL. *El elemento afronegroide en el español de Puerto Rico: Contribución al estudio del negro en América* (1974).

AL-AMIN, JAMIL. *See* Brown, H. Rap.

*The Amistad Case: The Most Celebrated Slave Mutiny of the Nineteenth Century*, 2 vols. (1968).

AMMONS, KEVIN. *Good Girl, Bad Girl: An Insider's Biography of Whitney Houston* (1996).

ANDERSON, JEAN BRADLEY. *Durham County: A History of Durham County, North Carolina* (1990).

ANDERSON, JERVIS. A. *Philip Randolph: A Biographical Portrait* (1973).

———. Bayard Rustin: *Troubles I've Seen: A Biography* (1997).

ANDERSON, MARIAN. *My Lord, What a Morning: An Autobiography* (1956).

ANDREWS, BENNY. *Between the Lines: 70 Drawings and 7 Essays* (1978).

ANDREWS, GEORGE REID. *Blacks and Whites in São Paulo, Brazil, 1888–1988* (1991). ****

ANDREWS, WILLIAM L. *The Literary Career of Charles W. Chesnutt* (1980).

———. *Sisters of the Spirit: Three Black Women's Autobiographies of the Nineteenth Century* (1986).

———. *To Tell a Free Story: The First Century of Afro-American Autobiography, 1760–1865* (1986).

ANDREWS, WILLIAM L., AND HENRY LOUIS GATES, JR., EDS. *The Civitas Anthology of African American Slave Narratives* (1999).

ANGELL, ROGER. *The Summer Game* (1972).

ANJOS, JOANA DOS. *Ouvindo historias na senzala* (1987).

ANTOINE, JACQUES CARMELEAU. *Jean Price-Mars and Haiti* (1981).

ANTOINE, RÉGIS. *La littérature franco-antillaise* (1992).

APARICIO, RAÚL. *Sondeos* (1983).

APPIAH, KWAME ANTHONY. *In My Father's House: Africa in the Philosophy of Culture* (1992).

APTHEKER, HERBERT. *American Negro Slave Revolts*. 6th ed. (1993).

——. *Nat Turner's Slave Rebellion* (1966).

——. *"One Continual Cry": David Walker's Appeal to the Colored Citizens of the World 1829–30: Its Setting and its Meaning, Together with the Full Text of the Third, and Last, Edition of the Appeal* (1965).

ARAUJO, EMANOEL, ED. *The Afro-Brazilian Touch: The Meaning of its Artistic and Historic Contribution.* Translated by Eric Drysdale (1988).

ARMAS, JOSÉ R. DE, AND CHARLES W. STEELE. *Cuban Consciousness in Literature: 1923–1974* (1978).

ARNOLD, A. JAMES. *Modernism and Negritude: The Poetry and Poetics of Aimé Césaire* (1981).

ASANTE, MOLEFI KETE. *The Afrocentric Idea* (1987).

——. *Afrocentricity* (1988).

——. *Kemet, Afrocentricity, and Knowledge* (1990).

ASCHENBRENNER, JOYCE. *Katherine Dunham: Reflections on the Social and Political Aspects of Afro-American Dance* (1981).

ASCHERSON, NEAL. *The King Incorporated: Leopold II in the Age of Trusts* (1963).

ASHBAUGH, CAROLYN. *Lucy Parsons: American Revolutionary* (1976).

ASHE, ARTHUR. *Days of Grace: A Memoir* (1993).

——. *A Hard Road to Glory: A History of the African-American Athlete* (1988).

AUSTERLITZ, PAUL. *Merengue: Dominican Music and Dominican Identity* (1997).

AUSTIN-BROOS, DIANE. *Jamaica Genesis: Religion and the Politics of Moral Orders* (1997).

AVERILL, GAGE. *A Day for the Hunter, A Day for the Prey* (1997).

AXELSON, ERIC. *Portuguese in South-East Africa, 1488–1600* (1973).

AYISI, RUTH A. "The Urban Influx." *Africa Report* (November-December 1989).

AYOT, H. OKELLO. *Historical Texts of the Lake Region of East Africa* (1977).

AZEVEDO, CELIA MARIA MARINHO DE. *Onda negra, medo branco: O negro no imaginario das elites, seculo XIX* (1987).

AZEVEDO, MARIO. *Historical Dictionary of Mozambique* (1991).

AZEVEDO, THALES. *Les élites de couleur dans une ville brésilienne* (1953).

BABB, VALERIE MELISSA. *Ernest Gaines* (1991).

BACELAR, JEFERSON AFONSO. *Etnicidade: Ser negro em Salvador* (1989).

BAER, HANS A., AND MERRIL SINGER. *African-American Religion in the Twentieth Century: Varieties of Protest and Accommodation* (1992).

BAILEY, PEARL. *Between You and Me: A Heartfelt Memoir of Learning, Loving, and Living* (1989).

——. *The Raw Pearl* (1968).

BAKER, DAVID. *The Jazz Style of Cannonball Adderley* (1980).

BAKER, HOUSTON A., JR. *Blues, Ideology, and Afro-American Literature: A Vernacular Theory* (1980).

BALANDIER, GEORGES. *Daily Life in the Kingdom of the Kongo: From the Sixteenth to the Eighteenth Century* (1968).

BALL, WENDY, AND TONY MARTIN. *Rare Afro-Americana: A Reconstruction of the Adger Library* (1981).

BALUTANSKY, KATHLEEN M., AND MARIE-AGNËS SOURIEAU, EDS. *Caribbean Creolization: Reflections on the Cultural Dynamics of Language, Literature, and Identity* (1998).

BANDEIRA, MARIA DE LOURDES. *Territorio negro em espaço branco: Estudo antropologico de Vila Bela* (1988).

BAQUERO, GASTON. *Indios, blancos y negros en el caldero de America* (1991).

BARAKA, AMIRI. *The Autobiography of LeRoi Jones* (1984).

BARBOSA DEL ROSARIO, PILAR. *La obra de José Celso Barbosa.* 4 vols. (1937).

BARBOUR, DOUGLAS. *Worlds Out of Words: The SF Novels of Samuel R . Delaney* (1979).

BARFIELD, THOMAS J. *The Nomadic Alternative* (1993).

BARKER, DANNY. *A Life in Jazz* (1986).

BARNES, STEVE. "The Crusade of Dr. Elders." *New York Times Magazine* (October 15, 1989): 38–41.

BARNETT, ALAN W. *Community Murals: The People's Art* (1984).

BARNWELL, P. J., AND AUGUSTE TOUSSAINT. *A Short History of Mauritius* (1949).

BARRADAS, EFRAÍN. PARA LEER EN PUERTORRIQUENO: *Acercamiento a la obra de Luis Rafael S·nchez* (1981).

BARREDA-TOM·S, PEDRO M. *The Black Protagonist in the Cuban Novel* (1979).

BARROW, STEVE, AND PETER DALTON. *Reggae: The Rough Guide* (1997).

BASH, BARBARA. *Tree of Life: The World of the African Baobab* (1994).

BASIE, WILLIAM JAMES ("COUNT"), AS TOLD TO ALBERT MURRAY. *Good Morning Blues: The Autobiography of Count Basie* (1985).

"A Basis for Interracial Cooperation and Development in the South: A Statement by Southern Negroes." *In Southern Conference on Race Relations* (1942).

BASS, CHARLOTTA SPEARS. Forty Years: Memoirs from the Pages of a Newspaper (1960).

BASTIDE, ROGER, AND FLORESTAN FERNANDES. *Relacoes raciais entre negros e brancos em Sao Paulo (1955).*

BAUM, ROBERT M. *Shrines of the Slave Trade: Diola Religion and Society in Precolonial Senegambia* (1999).

BEACH, DAVID. *The Shona and their Neighbours* (1994).

BEARDEN, JIM, AND LINDA BUTLER. *Shadd: The Life and Times of Mary Shadd Cary* (1977).

BEARDEN, ROMARE, AND HARRY HENDERSON. *A History of African-American Artists from 1792 to the Present* (1993).

BEAUFORD DELANEY: *A Retrospective* (1978).

BECHKEY, ALLEN. *Adventuring in East Africa* (1990).

BECKFORD, RUTH. *Katherine Dunham: A Biography* (1979).

BECKLES, HILARY. *Afro-Caribbean Women and Resistance to Slavery in Barbados* (1988).

——. *Black Masculinity in Caribbean Slavery* (1996).

——. *Black Rebellion in Barbados: The Struggle against Slavery, 1627–1838* (1984).

——. *A History of Barbados: Amerindian Settlement to Nation-State* (1990).

——. *Natural Rebels: A Social History of Enslaved Black Women in Barbados* (1989).

——. *White Servitude and Black Slavery in Barbados, 1627–1715* (1989).

——, ED. *Inside Slavery: Process and Legacy in the Caribbean Experience* (1996).

BECKWOURTH, JAMES P. *The Life and Adventures of James P. Beckwourth, Mountaineer, Scout and Pioneer and Chief of the Crow Nation of Indians.* Edited by T. D. Bonner (1965).

BEDINI, SILVIO. *The Life of Benjamin Banneker* (1971–1972).

BEETH, HOWARD, AND CARY WINTZ. *Black Dixie: Afro-Texan History and Culture in Houston* (1992).

BEGO, MARK. *Aretha Franklin* (1989).

BEHAGUE, GERARD H., ED. *Music and Black Ethnicity: The Caribbean and South America* (1994).

BELL, BERNARD. *The Afro-American Novel and its Tradition* (1987).

BELLEGARDE-SMITH, PATRICK. *In the Shadow of Powers: Dantès Bellegarde in Haitian Social Thought* (1985).

——. Race, Class and Ideology: Haitian Ideologies for Underdevelopment 1806–1934 (1985).

BELL, HOWARD H. *Search for a Place: Black Separatism and Africa, 1860* (1969).

BELL, MALCOM. *The Turkey Shoot: Tracking the Attica Cover-Up* (1985).

BENBERRY, CUESTA. *Always There: The African-American Presence in American Quilts* (1992).

BENNETT, LERONE, JR. *Before the Mayflower* (1962; revised ed., 1987).

BENNETT, NORMAN. *Arab versus European: Diplomacy and War in Nineteenth-Century East Central Africa* (1986).

BENNETT, ROBERT. "Black Episcopalians: A History from the Colonial Period to the Present." *Historical Magazine of the Protestant Episcopal Church 43*, no. 3 (September 1974): 231–45.

BENOIT, EDOUARD. "Biguine: Popular Music of Guadeloupe, 1940–1960." *In Zouk: World Music in the West Indies,* ed. Jocelyne Guilbault (1993).

BENSTON, KIMBERLY, ED. *Speaking for You: The Vision of Ralph Ellison* (1995).

BENTLY, GEORGE R. *A History of the Freedmen's Bureau* (1955).

BERENDT, JOACHIM. *The Jazz Book: From Rag-time to Fusion and Beyond.* 6th ed. (1992).

BERGER, PHIL. *Blood Season: Tyson and the World of Boxing* (1989).

BERLIN, IRA. *Slaves without Masters: The Free Negro in the Antebellum South* (1974).

BERNABÈ, JEAN, PATRICK CHAMOISEAU, AND RAPHAÎL CONFIANT. *Eloge de la creolite / In Praise of Creoleness.* Translated by M. B. Taleb-Khyar (1993).

BERND, ZILA. *Introducao a literatura negra* (1988).

BERNSEN, CHARLES. "The Fords of Memphis: A Family Saga." *Memphis Commercial Appeal* (July 1–4, 1990).

BERNSTEIN, IVER. *The New York City Draft Riots: Their Significance for American Society and Politics in the Age of the Civil War* (1990).

BERROU, RAPHAEL. *Histoire de la littérature haïtienne illustrée par les textes*. 3 vols. (1975–1977).

BERRY, CHUCK. *Chuck Berry: The Autobiography* (1987).

BERRY, JAMES. *Chain of Days* (1985).

BERRY, JASON. *Amazing Grace: With Charles Evers in Mississippi* (1973).

BERTLEY, LEO W. *Canada and its People of African Descent* (1977).

BEYAN, AMOS J. *The American Colonization Society and the Creation of the Liberian State: A Historical Perspective, 1822–1900* (1991).

BIANCO, DAVID. *Heat Wave: The Motown Fact Book* (1988).

BIBB, HENRY WALTON. *Narrative of the Life and Adventures of Henry Bibb, an American Slave* (1849).

BICKERTON, DEREK. "The Language Bioprogram Hypothesis." *Behavioral and Brain Sciences* 7 (1984): 173–221.

BIEBUYCK, DANIEL P., SUSAN KELLIHER, AND LINDA McRAE. *African Ethnonyms: Index to Art-Producing Peoples of Africa* (1996).

BIRMINGHAM, DAVID, AND RICHARD GRAY. *Pre-Colonial African trade: Essays on Trade in Central and Eastern Africa before 1900* (1966).

BISHOP, JACK. *Ralph Ellison* (1988).

"Black Clout in Clinton Administration." *Ebony* 48, no. 7 (May 1993): 60.

BLACK, PATTI CARR, ED. *Something to Keep You Warm* (1981).

"Blacks in U.S. Foreign Policy: A Retrospective." *TransAfrica Forum* (1987).

"Black Women: Sisters Without Leaders." *Economist* (November 1, 1997): 31.

BLAKELY, ALLISON. *Blacks in the Dutch World: The Evolution of Racial Imagery in a Modern Society* (1993).

——. *Russia and the Negro: Blacks in Russian History and Thought* (1986).

BLANCHARD, PETER. *Slavery and Abolition in Early Republican Peru* (1992).

BLAND, RANDALL W. *Private Pressure on Public Law: The Legal Career of Justice Thurgood Marshall* (1973).

BLANCQ, C. C. *Sonny Rollins: The Journey of a Jazzman* (1983).

BLASSINGAME, JOHN W., ED. *The Frederick Douglass Papers*. 4 vols. (1979–1991).

——. *The Slave Community: Plantation Life in the Antebellum South*. Rev. ed. (1979).

BLASSINGAME, JOHN W., AND MAE G. HENDERSON, EDS. *Antislavery Newspapers and Periodicals*. 5 vols. (1980).

BLESH, RUDI, AND HARRIET JANIS. *They All Played Ragtime*. 4th ed. (1971).

BLIER, SUZANNE PRESTON. *African Vodun: Art, Psychology, and Power* (1995).

——. *The Royal Arts of Africa: The Majesty of Form* (1998).

BLIGHT, DAVID W. *Frederick Douglass' Civil War: Keeping Faith in Jubilee* (1989).

BLOCH, HERMAN D. *The Circle of Discrimination: An Economic and Social Study of the Black Man in New York* (1969).

BLOCH, M. *Placing the Dead: Tombs, Ancestral Villages, and Kinship Organization in Madagascar* (1971).

BLY, NELLIE. *Oprah! Up Close and Down Home* (1993).

BOFF, C., AND L. BOFF. *Introducing Liberation Theology* (1987).

BOGGS, VICTOR. *Salsiology: Afro-Cuban Music and the Evolution of Salsa in New York City* (1992).

BOGLE, DONALD. *Blacks in American Films and Television: An Illustrated Encyclopedia* (1988).

——. *Dorothy Dandridge: A Biography* (1997).

——. *Toms, Coons, Mulattoes, Mammies, and Bucks : An Interpretive History of Blacks in American Films.* 3d ed. (1994).

BOLCOM, WILLIAM, AND ROBERT KIMBALL. *Reminiscing with Sissle and Blake* (1973).

BOLLAND, O. NIGEL. *A History of Belize: Nation in the Making* (1997).

BOLOUVI, LEBENE PHILIPPE. *Nouveau dictionnaire étymologique afro-brésilien: Afro-brasilérismes d'origine Ewe-Fon et Yoruba* (1994).

BONGIE, CHRIS. "The (Un)Exploded Volcano: Creolization and Intertextuality in the Novels of Daniel Maximin." *Callaloo* 17, no. 2 (Summer 1994): 627–42.

BONILLA, ADRIAN. "Conversación con Adalberto Ortiz." *Cultura: Revista del Banco Central del Ecuador* 6, no. 16 (1983): 189–96.

BOODOO, KEN I., ED. *Eric Williams: The Man and the Leader* (1986).

BOONE, GRAEME M., AND JAMES CLYDE SELLMAN, "The Jook Joint: An Historical Note." Liner essay to *Quincy Jones, Q's Jook Joint* (1995).

BORDERS, WILLIAM H. *Seven Minutes at the Mike in the Deep South* (1943).

BOSKIN, JOSEPH. *Sambo: The Rise and Demise of an American Jester* (1986).

BOURDILLON, M. F. C. *The Shona Peoples: An Ethnography of the Contemporary Shona, with Special Reference to their Religion* (1987).

BOURNE, M. "Bob, Baroque, the Blues: Modern Jazz Quartet." *Down Beat* 59, no.1 (January 1992): 24.

BOVILL, E. W. *The Niger Explored* (1968).

BOWMAN, J. WILSON. *America's Black Colleges: The Comprehensive Guide to Historically and Predominantly Black 4-Year Colleges and Universities* (1992).

BOWMAN, LARRY W. *Mauritius: Democracy and Development in the Indian Ocean* (1991).

BOWSER, FREDERICK P. *The African Slave in Colonial Peru 1524–1650* (1974).

BOXER, C.R. *The Dutch in Brazil, 1624–1654* (1957).

——. *The Portuguese Seaborne Empire, 1415–1825* (1969).

BOYER, JAY. *Ishmael Reed* (1993).

BOYKIN, KEITH. *One More River to Cross: Black & Gay in America* (1996).

BOZONGWANA, WALLACE. *Ndebele Religion and Customs* (1983).

BRACEY, JOHN H., JR., ET AL, EDS. *Black Nationalism in America* (1970).

BRAGG, GEORGE FREEMAN. *The History of the Afro-American Group of the Episcopal Church* (1968).

——. *The Story of the First Blacks: Absalom Jones* (1929).

BRANCH, TAYLOR. *Parting the Waters: America in the King Years: 1954–63* (1988).

BRANDSTRÖM, PER. "Who is Sukuma and Who is a Nyamwezi?: Ethnic Identity in West-Central Tanzania." In *Working Papers in African Studies* no. 27 (1986).

BRAND-WILLIAMS, ORALANDAR. "Million Woman March: Black Women Vow to 'Act on Power,'" *Detroit News* (October 26, 1997).

BRATHWAITE, EDWARD KAMAU. *Roots* (1993).

BRAUSCH, GEORGES. *Belgian Administration in the Congo* (1961).

BRIGHAM, DAVID R. "Bridging Identities (The Works of Dox Thrash, Afro-American Artist)." *Smithsonian Studies in American Art* (Spring 1990).

BRISBANE, ROBERT. *Black Activism: Racial Revolution in the U.S., 1954–70* (1974).

BRISTOW, PEGGY, ET AL. *We're Rooted Here and They Can't Pull Us Up: Essays in African Canadian Women's History* (1994)

BRITT, STAN. *Dexter Gordon: A Musical Biography* (1989).

BRODE, DOUGLAS. *Denzel Washington: His Films and Career* (1996).

BRODERICK, FRANCIS L., AUGUST MEIER, AND ELLIOTT M. RUDWICK. *Black Protest Thought in the Twentieth Century.* 2d ed. (1971).

BROOKSHAW, DAVID. *Race and Color in Brazilian Literature* (1986).

BROUGHTON, SIMON, MARK ELLINGHAM, DAVID MUDDYMAN, AND RICHARD TRILLO. *World Music: The Rough Guide* (1994).

BROUSSARD, ALBERT S. *Black San Francisco: The Struggle for Racial Equality in the West, 1900–1954* (1993).

BROWN, A. THEODORE, AND LYLE W. DORSETT. *K.C.: A History of Kansas City, Missouri* (1978).

BROWN, CLAUDE. *Manchild in the Promised Land* (1965).

BROWN, DIANA DEGROAT. *Umbanda: Religion and Politics in Urban Brazil* (1994).

BROWN, GEOFF, AND CHRIS CHARLESWORTH. *A Complete Guide to the Music of Prince* (1995).

BROWN-GUILLORY, ELIZABETH. "Alice Childress: A Pioneering Spirit," *Sage: A Scholarly Journal on Black Women* (Spring 1987): 104–9.

BROWN, HENRY. *Narrative of Henry Box Brown Who Escaped from Slavery Enclosed in a Box Three Feet Long and Two Wide, with Remarks upon the Remedy for Slavery* (1849).

BROWN, H. RAP. *Die, Nigger, Die!* (1969).

BROWNING, BARBARA. *Samba: Resistance in Motion* (1995).

BROWN, MERVYN. *A History of Madagascar* (1995).

———. Madagascar Rediscovered: A History from Early Times to Independence (1978).

BROWN, RUTH, WITH ANDREW YULE. *Miss Rhythm: The Autobiography of Ruth Brown, Rhythm & Blues Legend* (1996).

BROWN, SCOTT E. *James P. Johnson: A Case of Mistaken Identity* (1986).

BROWN, STERLING A. "A Century of Negro Portraiture in American Literature." In *Black Insights: Significant Literature by Black Americans-1760 to the Present*, ed. Nick Aaron Ford (1971): 66–78.

BROWN, TONY. *Black Lies, White Lies: The Truth According to Tony Brown* (1995).

BRUCE, DICKSON D., JR. *Black American Writing from the Nadir: The Evolution of a Literary Tradition, 1877–1915* (1989).

BRUNDAGE, W. FITZHUGH, ED. *Under Sentence of Death: Lynching in the South* (1997).

BRYAN, T. J. "The Published Poems of Helene Johnson," *Langston Hughes Review* 6 (Fall 1987): 11–21.

BRYANT-JACKSON, PAUL, AND LOIS MORE OVERBECK, EDS. *Intersecting Boundaries: The Theater of Adrienne Kennedy* (1992).

BUCKLER, HELEN. *Daniel Hale Williams: Negro Surgeon* (1968)

BUCKLEY, GAIL LUMET. *The Hornes: An American Family* (1986).

BUENO, EVA PAULINO. *Resisting Boundaries: The Subject of Naturalism in Brazil* (1995).

BUGNER, LADISLAS, ED. *The Image of the Black in Western Art* (1976– ).

BUHLE, PAUL. *C. L. R. James: The Artist as Revolutionary* (1988).

BULHAN, HUSSEIN ABDILAHI. *Frantz Fanon and the Psychology of Oppression* (1985).

BULLOCK, PENELOPE L. *The Afro-American Periodical Press, 1838–1909* (1981).

BUNI, ANDREW. *The Negro in Virginia Politics, 1902–1965* (1967).

BUNWAREE, SHEILA S. *Mauritian Education in a Global Economy* (1994).

BURCKHARDT, TITUS. *Fez, City of Islam* (1992).

BURDICK, JOHN. *Blessed Anastacia: Women, Race and Popular Christianity in Brazil* (1998).

——. "The Spirit of Rebel and Docile Slaves: The Black Verson of Brazilian Umbanda." *Journal of Latin American Love* 18 (1992): 163–87.

BURNS, KHEPHRA. "A Love Supreme: Ruby Dee & Ossie Davis." *Essence* (December 1994).

BUSBY, MARK. *Ralph Ellison* (1991).

BUSH, MARTIN. *The Photographs of Gordon Parks* (1983).

BUSTIN, EDOUARD. *Lunda under Belgian Rule: The Politics of Ethnicity* (1975).

BUTLER, ADDIE LOUISE JOYNER. *The Distinctive Black College: Talladega, Tuskegee and Morehouse* (1977).

CAAMAÑO DE FERNÀNDEZ, VICENTA. *El negro en la poesía dominicana* (1989).

CABRERA GOMEZ, JORGE. *El Baobab* (1996).

CABRERA, LYDIA. *Anaforuana: Ritual y simbolos de la iniciacion en la sociedad secreta* (1975).

——. Anago: *Vocabulario lucumi (el yoruba que se habla in Cuba)* (1957).

——. *Los animales en el folklore y la magia de Cuba* (1988).

——. *Cuentos negros de Cuba* (1972).

——. *Francisco y Francisca: Chascarrillos de negros viejos* (1976).

——. *La lengua sagrada de los nanigos* (1988).

——. *El monte, Igbo, Finda, Ewe orisha, vitti nfinda: (Notas sobre las religiones, la magia, las supersticiones y el folklore de los negros criollos y del pueblo de Cuba)* (1968).

——. *La Regla Kimbisa del Santo Cristo del Buen Viaje* (1977).

——. *Reglas de Congo: Palo Monte Mayombe* (1979).

——. *La sociedad secreta Abakua, narrada por viejos adeptos* (1959).

——. *Yemaya y Ochun* (1974).

CAGIN, SETH, AND PHILIP DRAY. *We Are Not Afraid: The Story of Goodman, Schwerner, and Chaney and the Civil Rights Campaign for Mississippi* (1988).

CALCAGNO, FRANCISCO. *Poetas de color* (1878).

CALLAGHAN, BARRY, ED. *The Austin Clarke Reader* (1996).

CALVO OSPINA, HERNANDO. *Salsa! Havana Heat, Bronx Beat.* (1992).

CAMARGO, OSWALDO. *A raz„o da chama: Antologia de poetas negros brasileiros* (1986).

CAMINHA, ADOLFO. *The Black Man and the Cabin Boy.* Translated by E. Lacey (1982).

CAMPBELL, ELAINE, AND PIERRETTE FRICKEY, EDS. *The Whistling Bird: Women Writers of the Caribbean* (1998).

CAMPBELL, JAMES T. *Songs of Zion: The African Methodist Episcopal Church in the United States and South Africa* (1995).

CAMPBELL, STANLEY W. *The Slave Catchers: Enforcement of the Fugitive Slave Law, 1850–1860* (1968).

CANNON, STEVE, TOM FINKELPEARL, AND KELLIE JONES. *David Hammons: Rousing the Rubble* (1991).

CANTAROW, ELLEN, AND SUSAN GUSHEE O'MALLEY. "Ella Baker: Organizing for Civil Rights." In *Moving the Mountain: Women Working for Social Change* (1980).

CAPECI, DOMINIC J., JR. *The Harlem Riot of 1943* (1977).

CARBY, HAZEL V. *Reconstructing Womanhood: The Emergence of the Afro-American Woman Novelist* (1987).

CAREW, JAN. *Fulcrums of Change: Origins of Racism in the Americas* (1988).

CARMICHAEL, STOKELY, AND CHARLES V. HAMILTON. *Black Power: The Politics of Liberation in America* (1992).

CARMICHAEL, TREVOR, ED. BARBADOS: *30 Years of Independence* (1996).

CARNER, GARY, ED. *The Miles Davis Companion: Four Decades of Commentary* (1996).

CARO, TIMOTHY M. *Cheetahs of the Serengeti Plains: Group Living in an Asocial Species* (1994).

CARPENTER, BILL. "Big Mama Thornton: 200 Pounds of Bugaloo." *Living Bluesletter* no. 106 (November 1992).

CARPENTIER, ALEJO. *La m'sica en Cuba* (1946).

——. *Obras Completas* (1983– ).

CARR, IAN. *Miles Davis: A Biography* (1982).

CARROLL, PATRICK JAMES. *Blacks in Colonial Veracruz: Race, Ethnicity, and Regional Development* (1991).

CARSON, CLAYBORNE. *In Struggle: SNCC and the Black Awakening of the 1960s* (1981).

CARVALHO, JOSÉ JORGE DE, AND RITA LAURA SEGATO. *Shango Cult in Recife, Brazil* (1992).

CASH, EARL A. *John A. Williams: The Evolution of a Black Writer* (1975).

CASSIDY, FREDERIC G. *Jamaica Talk: Three Hundred Years of the English Language in Jamaica* (1961).

CASTELLANOS, JORGE, AND ISABEL CASTELLANOS. *Cultura afrocubana: Las religiones y las lenguas. 3 vols.* (1992).

CASTLEMAN, CRAIG. *Getting Up: Subway Graffiti in New York* (1984).

CASTOR, ELIE, AND RAYMOND TARCY. *Fèlix Ebouè: Gouverneur et philosophe* (1984).

CASTRO, RUY. *Chega de saudade : A história e as histórias da bossa nova* (1990).

CAYETANO, SEBASTIAN. *Garifuna History: Language and Culture of Belize, Central America and the Caribbean.* Rev. ed. (1997).

CENTRO DE ARTICULÇÁO DE POPULAÇÕES MARGINALIZADAS. *The Killing of Children and Adolescents in Brazil.* Translated by Joscelyne Vera Mello (1991).

CHAFETS, ZE'EV. *Devil's Night and Other True Tales of Detroit* (1990).

CHALLENOR, HERCHELLE SULLIVAN. "The Influence of Black Americans on U.S. Foreign Policy Toward Africa." *Ethnicity and U. S. Foreign Policy* (1981).

CHAMBERLAIN, HOPE. "Against the System: Shirley Chisholm." *In A Minority of Mem-bers: Women in the U. S. Congress* (1973).

CHAMBERLAIN, WILT. *The View From Above* (1991).

CHAMBERS, JACK. *Milestones.* 2 vols. (1983–1985).

CHAMBERS, VERONICA. "The Essence of Essence." *New York Times Magazine* (June 18, 1995).

CHANAN, MICHAEL. *The Cuban Image: Cinema and the Cultural Politics in Cuba* (1985).

CHANOCK, MARTIN. *Law, Custom and Social Order: The Colonial Experience in Malawi and Zambia* (1985).

CHAPELLE, TONY. "Vanessa's Comeback." *The Black Collegian* (February 1995).

CHAPPELL, KEVIN. "The 3 Mayors Who Made it Happen." *Ebony* (July 1996): 66.

*Charte de la révolution socialiste Malagasy Tous Azimuts* (1975).

CHARTERS, SAMUEL B. *The Bluesmen.* 2 vols. (1967–1977).

CHENEY, ANNE. *Lorraine Hansberry* (1984).

CHIGWEDERE, AENEAS S. *Birth of Bantu Africa* (1982).

CHILTON, JOHN. *The Song of the Hawk: The Life and Recordings of Coleman Hawkins* (1990).

CHISHOLM, SHIRLEY. *Unbought and Unbossed* (1970).

CHRISMAN, ROBERT, AND ROBERT L. ALLEN, EDS. *Court of Appeal: The Black Community Speaks Out on the Racial and Sexual Politics of Clarence Thomas vs. Anita Hill* (1992).

CHRISTIAN, BARBARA. *Black Feminist Criticism: Perspectives on Black Women Writers* (1985).

——. *Black Women Novelists: The Devel-opment of a Tradition, 1892–1976* (1980).

CHRISTIE, IAIN. *Samora Machel: A Biography* (1989).

CHRISTOPHER, A. J. *The Atlas of Apartheid* (1994).

CHUCHO GARCIA, JESUS. *La diaspora de los Kongos en las Americas y los Caribes* (1995).

CHURCH, ANNETTE, AND ROBERTA CHURCH. *The Robert Churches of Memphis* (1975).

CLANCY-SMITH, JULIA A. *Rebel and Saint: Muslim Notables, Populist Protest, Colonial Encounters: Algeria and Tunisia, 1800–1904* (1994).

CLAIRMONT, DONALD, AND DENNIS MAGILL. *Africville: The Life and Death of a Canadian Black Community.* Rev. ed. (1987).

CLARKE, A.M. *Sir Constantine and Sir Hugh Wooding* (1982).

CLARKE, DUNCAN. *The Art of African Textiles* (1997).

CLARKE, GEORGE ELLIOTT, ED. *Fire on the Water: An Anthology of Black Nova Scotian Writing.* 2 vols. (1991–1992).

CLARK, SEBASTIAN. *Jah Music* (1980).

CLARK, SEPTIMA. *Echo in My Soul* (1962).

CLARK, SEPTIMA, WITH CYNTHIA STOKES BROWN. *Ready from Within: Septima Clark and the Civil Rights Movement* (1986).

CLASH, M.G. *Benjamin Banneker, Astronomer and Scientist* (1971).

"Claude Albert Barnett." *New York Times* (August 3, 1967).

CLAYTON, ANTHONY. *The Zanzibar Revolution and its Aftermath* (1981).

CLAY, WILLIAM L. *Just Permanent Interests: Black Americans in Congress, 1870–1991* (1992).

COBB, W. MONTAGUE. *The First Negro Medical Society: A History of the Medico-Chirurgical Society of the District of Columbia* (1939).

COHEN, DAVID W., AND JACK P. GREENE. *Neither Slave nor Free: The Freedman of African Descent in the Slaves Societies of the New World Baltimore* (1972).

COHEN, RONALD, GORAN HYDEN, AND WINSTON P. NAGAN, EDS. *Human Rights and Governance in Africa* (1993).

COLE, HERBERT. *Christophe: King of Haiti* (1967).

COLEMAN, JAMES W. *Blackness and Modernism: The Literary Career of John Edgar Wideman* (1989).

COLEMAN, LUCRETIA NEWMAN. *Poor Ben: A Story of Real Life* (1890).

COLI, SUZANNE M. *George Washington Carver* (1990).

COLLIER, ALDORE. "Maxine Waters: Telling It Like It Is in L.A." *Ebony* (October 1992).

———. "Pointer Sisters Shed Old Look, Old Clothes to Reach New Heights." *Jet* (April 15, 1985): 58.

———. "Whatever Happened to the Nicholas Brothers?" *Ebony* (May 1985).

COLLIER, JAMES LINCOLN. *The Making of Jazz: A Comprehensive History* (1978).

COLLINS, L. M. *One Hundred Years of Fisk University Presidents* (1989).

COLLINS, R. *New Orleans Jazz: A Revised History: The Development of American Jazz from the Origin to the Big Bands* (1996).

COLLINS, ROBERT O. *The Waters of the Nile: Hydropolitics and the Jonglei Canal, 1900–1988* (1990).

CONDÉ, MARYSE, AND MADELAINE COTTENET-HAGE, EDS. *Penser la Créolité* (1995).

CONE, JAMES H. *Martin and Malcolm and America: A Dream or a Nightmare* (1991).

CONGRESS, RICK. *The Afro-Nicaraguans: The Revolution and Autonomy* (1987).

CONNIFF, MICHAEL L. *Black Labor on a White Canal: Panama 1904–1981* (1985).

CONNIFF, MICHAEL L., AND THOMAS J. DAVIS. *Africans in the Americas: The History of the Black Diaspora* (1994).

CONNOLLY, HAROLD X. *A Ghetto Grows in Brooklyn* (1977).

CONRAD, ROBERT EDGAR, ED. *Children of God's Fire: A Documentary of Black Slavery.* (1983).

————. *The Destruction of Brazilian Slavery*, 1850–1888 (1993).

CONSENTINO, DONALD J., ED. *Sacred Arts of Haitian Vodou* (1995).

COOK, DAVID, AND MICHAEL Okenimpke. *Ngugi wa Thiong'o: An Exploration of His Writing*, 2d ed. (1997).

COOLIDGE, CHRISTOPHER R. "Reply: Tolerance of Racial, Ethnic Jokes." In *ADS-L Digest 22* (February 22, 1997).

COOPER, GARY. "Stage Coach Mary: Gun Toting Montanan Delivered U.S. Mail," as told to Marc Crawford in *Ebony* 14 (October 1959): 97–100.

COOPER, RALPH, WITH STEVE DOUGHERTY. *Amateur Night at the Apollo: Ralph Cooper Presents Five Decades of Great Entertainment* (1990).

COOPER, WAYNE F. *Claude McKay: A Rebel Sojourner in the Harlem Renaissance: A Biography* (1987).

COPPIN, FANNY JACKSON. *Reminiscences of School Life, and Hints on Teaching* (1913).

CORDOBA, AMIR SMITH, ED. *Vision sociocultural del negro en Colombia* (1986).

CORNELIUS, WAYNE A. "Spain: The Uneasy Transition from Labor Exporter to Labor Importer." In *Controlling Immigration: A Global Perspective*, ed. Wayne A. Cornelius, Philip L. Martin, and James F. Hollifield (1994).

CORNISH, DUDLEY T. *The Sable Arm: Negro Troops in the Union Army*, 1861–1865 (1956).

CORTÉS LÓPEZ, JOSÉ LUIS. *La esclavitud negra en la España peninsular del siglo XVI* (1989).

Cortner, Richard C. *A Mob Intent on Death: The NAACP and the Arkansas Riot Cases* (1988).

CORY, HANS H. *Sukuma Law and Custom* (1953).

COUFFON, CLAUDE. *René Depestre* (1986).

COUNTER, S. ALLEN. *North Pole Legacy: Black, White and Eskimo* (1991).

COURTNEY-CLARKE, MARGARET. *Ndebele: The Art of an African Tribe* (1986).

COVELL, MAUREEN. *Historical Dictionary of Madagascar* (1995).

————. *Madagascar: Politics, Economics, and Society* (1987).

COX, HARVEY. *Fire From Heaven: The Rise of Pentecostal Spirituality and the Reshaping of Religion in the Twenty-First Century* (1995).

CRAFT, WILLIAM, AND ELLEN CRAFT. *Running a Thousand Miles for Freedom; or, The Escape of William and Ellen Craft from Slavery* (1860; reprint ed., 1991.).

CREEL, MARGARET WASHINGTON. *A Peculiar People: Slave Religion and Community-Culture Among the Gullahs* (1988).

CRESPO R., ALBERTO. *Esclavos negros en Bolivia* (1977).

CRIPPS, THOMAS. *Making Movies Black: The Hollywood Message Movie from World War II to the Civil Rights Era* (1993).

————. *Slow Fade to Black: The Negro in American Film 1900–1942* (1977).

CROUCHETT, LORRAINE J. *Delilah Leontium Beasley: Oakland's Crusading Journalist* (1990).

CRUISE O'BRIEN, DONALD. *The Mourides of Senegal: The Political and Economic Organization of an Islamic Brotherhood* (1971).

CUDJOE, SELWYN, ED. *Caribbean Women Writers: Essays from the First International Conference.* (1990).

——. *Resistance and Caribbean Literature* (1980).

CULLEN, COUNTEE. *My Soul's High Song: The Collected Writings of Countee Cullen, Voice of the Harlem Renaissance.* Edited by Gerald Early (1991).

CULLMAN, BRIAN. "Cheb Khaled and the Politics of Pleasure." *Antaeus* (Fall 1993).

CUNEY-HARE, MAUD. *Norris Wright Cuney: A Tribune of the Black People* (1995).

CUNNINGHAM, CAROL, AND JOEL BERGER. *Horn of Darkness: Rhinos on the Edge* (1997).

CURRY, LEONARD P. *The Free Black in Urban America, 1800–1850: The Shadow of the Dream* (1981).

CURTIN, PHILIP D. *The Atlantic Slave Trade: A Census* (1969).

CUTLER, JOHN HENRY. *Ed Brooke: Biography of a Senator* (1972).

DABNEY, VIRGINIUS. *Richmond: The Story of a City* (1976).

DABNEY, WENDELL P. *Cincinnati's Colored Citizens: Historical, Sociological, and Biographical* (1926).

DABYDEEN, DAVID. "On Not Being Milton: Nigger Talk in England Today." In *The Routledge Reader in Caribbean Literature*, ed. Alison Donnell and Sarah Lawson Welsh (1996).

DAHL, OTTO C. *Malgache et Maanjan: Une comparaison linguistigue* (1951).

DALFIUME, RICHARD M. *Desegregation of the U. S. Armed Forces: Fighting on Two Fronts, 1939–1953* (1969).

DALTON, NARINE. "The Maestros: Black Symphony Conductors are Making a Name for Themselves." *Ebony* (February 1989): 54–57.

DALY, VERE T. *A Short History of the Guyanese People* (1975).

DANCE, DARYL C. *Shuckin' and Jivin': Folklore from Contemporary Black Americans* (1978).

DANIELS, DOUGLAS HENRY. "Lester Young: Master of Jive." *American Music* 3 (Fall 1985): 313–28.

——. *Pioneer Urbanites: A Social and Cul-tural History of Black San Francisco* (1980).

DANIEL, WALTER C. *Afro-American Journals, 1827–1980: A Reference Book* (1982).

DASH, J. MICHAEL. *Edouard Glissant* (1995).

DASH, JULIE. *Daughters of the Dust: The Making of an African American Woman's Film* (1992).

DATES, JANNETTE L., AND WILLIAM BARLOW, EDS. *Split Image: African Americans in the Mass Media* (1990).

DATT, NORMAN. *CHEDDI B. JAGAN: The Legend* (1997).

DAVENPORT, M. MARGUERITE. *Azalia: The Life of Madame E. Azalia Hackley* (1947).

DAVIES, CAROL BOYCE, AND ELAINE SAVORY FIDO, EDS. *Out of the Kumbla: Caribbean Women and Literature* (1990).

DAVIS, ARTHUR P. *From the Dark Tower: Afro-American Writers, 1900–1960* (1974).

DAVIS, BENJAMIN O., JR. *Benjamin O. Davis, Jr., American: An Autobiography* (1991).

DAVIS, CHARLES T., AND HENRY LOUIS GATES, JR., EDS. *The Slave's Narrative* (1985).

DAVIS, CYPRIAN. *The History of Black Catholics in the United States* (1990).

DAVIS, DARIÉN J., ED. *Slavery and Beyond: The African Impact on Latin America and the Caribbean*.

DAVIS, DAVID BRION. *The Problem of Slavery in the Age of Revolution, 1770–1823*. 2d ed. (1998).

———. *The Problem of Slavery in Western Culture* (1966).

———. *Slavery and Human Progress* (1984).

DAVIS, H. P. *Black Democracy: The Story of Haiti* (1967).

DAVIS, JAMES J. "Entrevista con el dominicano Norberto James Rawlings." *Afro-Hispanic Review* (May 1987):16–18.

DAVIS, MICHAEL D. *Black American Women in Olympic Track and Field: A Complete Illustrated Reference* (1992).

DAVIS, RUSSELL. *Black Americans in Cleveland from George Peake to Carl B. Stokes, 1796–1969* (1972).

DAVIS, STEPHEN, AND PETER SIMON. *Reggae International* (1983).

DAVIS, THOMAS J. *A Rumor of Revolt: The "Great Negro Plot" in Colonial New York* (1985).

DAWKINS, WAYNE. *Black Journalists: The NABJ Story* (1993).

DAYAN, JOAN. "France Reads Haiti: An Interview with René Depestre." *Yale French Studies* 83: 136–153.

DEERR, NOEL. *The History of Sugar*. 2 vols. (1949–1950).

DELERIS, FERDINAND. *Ratsiraka: Socialisme et misère à Madagascar* (1986).

DELIUS, PETER. *A Lion Amongst the Cattle: Reconstruction and Resistance in the Northern Transvaal* (1996).

DEREN, MAYA. DIVINE HORSEMEN: *The Living Gods of Haiti* (1953).

DERRICOTTE, TOI. *The Black Notebooks: An Interior Journey* (1997).

DESMANGLES, LESLIE G. *The Faces of the Gods: Vodou and Roman Catholicism in Haiti* (1992).

DE WILDE, LAURENT. *Monk* (1997).

DIAWARA, MANTHIA: *Politics and Culture* (1992).

———, ED. *Black American Cinema* (1993).

DÍAZ AYALA, CRISTOBAL. *Música cubana del areyto a la nueva trova* (1981).

DIEDHIOUS, DJIB. "Paulin S. Vieyra a rencontré le cinèma africain." *Le Soleil* (December 27, 1982).

DILLON, MERTON L. *Benjamin Lundy and the Struggle for Negro Freedom* (1966).

DIOP, CHEIKH ANTA. *Nations nègres et culture: De l'antiquité Nègre-Egyptienne aux problèmes culturels de l'Afrique noire d'a. ujourd'hui*. 2d ed. (1965).

DITTMER, JOHN. *Black Georgia in the Progressive Era, 1900–1920* (1977).

———. *Local People: The Struggle for Civil Rights in Mississippi* (1995).

DIXON, WILLIE. *I Am the Blues: The Willie Dixon Story* (1989).

DOMÍNGUEZ ORTIZ, ANTONIO. "La esclavitud en Castilla durante la Edad Moderna." In *Estudios de historia social de España*, ed. Carmelo Vióas y Mey. 2 vols. (1952). Vol. II, pp. 369–427.

DONOVAN, NANCY, AND LAST, JILL. *Ethiopian Costumes* (1980).

DORSEY, CAROLYN. "Despite Poor Health: Olivia Davidson Washington's Story." *Sage: A Scholarly Journal on Black Women* (Fall 1985).

DORSEY, DAVID. "The Art of Mari Evans." In *Black Women Writers* (1984): 170–89.

DORSEY, THOMAS ANDREW. *Say Amen, Somebody* (1983).

DORSINVILLE, ROGER. *Jacques Roumain* (1981).

D'ORSO, MICHAEL. *Like Judgement Day: The Ruin and Redemption of a Town Called Rosewood* (1996).

DOUGLASS, WILLIAM. *Annals of the First African Church in the United States of America, Now Styled the African Episcopal Church of St. Thomas, Philadelphia* (1862).

DRAGO, EDMUND L. *Initiative, Paternalism, and Race Relations: Charleston's Avery Normal Institute* (1990).

DRAKE, SANDRA E. *Wilson Harris and the Modern Tradition: A New Architecture of the World* (1986).

DRAKE, ST. CLAIR. *Black Folk Here and There: An Essay in History and Anthropology.* 2 vols. (1987–1990).

DRAKE, ST. CLAIR, AND HORACE R. CAYTON. *Black Metropolis: A Study of Negro Life in a Northern City* (1945).

DRESCHER, SEYMOUR, AND STANLEY L. ENGERMAN, EDS. *A Historical Guide to World Slavery* (1998).

DRISKELL, DAVID. *Hidden Heritage: Afro-American Art, 1800–1950* (1985).

"Dr. Lillie M. Jackson: Lifelong Freedom Fighter." *Crisis* 82 (1975).

DROT, JEAN-MARIE. *Peintures et dessins, vaudou d'Haïti* (1986).

DUANY, JORGE, AND PETER MANUEL. "Popular Music in Puerto Rico: Toward an Anthropology of Salsa." *Latin American Music Review* 5 (1984): 186–216.

DUBOFSKY, MELVYN, AND STEPHEN BURWOOD, EDS. *Women and Minorities During the Great Depression* (1990).

DU BOIS, SHIRLEY GRAHAM. *His Day is Marching On: A Memoir of W. E. B. Du Bois.* (1971).

DU BOIS, W. E. B. *Black Reconstruction in America* (1935).

——. *The Souls of Black Folk: Essays and Sketches* (1903).

DUFFY, SUSAN. "Shirley Chisholm." *American Orators of the Twentieth Century*, ed. Barnard K. Duffy and Halford R. Ryan (1987).

DUGGAN, WILLIAM, AND JOHN CIVILLE. *Tanzania and Nyerere: A Study of Ujamaa and Nationhood* (1976).

DUGGY, JOHN. *PRINCE: An Illustrated Biography* (1995).

DUMMETT, CLIFTON O., AND LOIS DOYLE DUMMETT. *Afro-Americans in Dentistry: Sequence and Consequence of Events* (1978).

DUNBAR-NELSON, ALICE. *Give Us This Day: The Diary of Alice Dunbar-Nelson*, ed. Gloria T. Hull (1984).

DUNCAN, JOHN. "Negro Composers of Opera." *Negro History Bulletin* (January 1966): 79–80, 93.

DUNCAN, QUINCE. *Cultura negra y teologia* (1986).

——. *Dos estudios sobre diaspora negra y racismo* (1987).

DUNDES, ALAN, ED. *Mother Wit From the Laughing Barrel: Readings in the Interpretation of Afro-American Folklore* (1990).

DUNN, RICHARD S. *Sugar and Slaves: The Rise of the Planter Class in the English West Indies, 1624–1713* (1972).

DUNNING, JAMES MORSE. *The Harvard School of Dental Medicine: Phase Two in the Development of a University Dental School* (1981).

DURHAM, PHILIP, AND EVERETT L. JONES. *The Negro Cowboys* (1965).

DURIX, JEAN-PIERRE. *Dictionary of Literary Biography* (1992).

DUSTER, ALFREDA, ED. *Crusade for Justice: The Autobiography of Ida B. Wells* (1970).

DUSTER, TROY. *Backdoor to Eugenics* (1990).

DYNES, WAYNE R., ED. *Encyclopedia of Homosexuality* (1990).

EDELMAN, MARIAN WRIGHT. *The Measure of Our Success: A Letter to My Children and Yours* (1992).

EDRERIA DE CABALLERO, ANGELINA. *Antonio Medina, el don Pepe de la raza de color* (1938).

EGERTON, DOUGLAS R. *Gabriel's Rebellion: The Virginia Slave Conspiracies of 1800 and 1802* (1993).

EHRET, CHRISTOPHER, AND M. POSNANSKY. *The Archaeological and Linguistic Reconstruction of African History* (1982).

EHRLICH, WALTER. *They Have No Rights: Dred Scott's Struggle for Freedom* (1979).

ELDERS, JOYCELYN. *Joycelyn Elders, M.D.: From Sharecropper's Daughter to Surgeon General of the United States of America* (1997).

ELIAS, JOÃO. *A impotencia da raca negra não tira da fraqueza dos brancos.* 2d ed. (1994).

ELLISON, RALPH. *Romare Bearden: Paintings and Projections* (1968).

——. *Shadow and Act* (1964).

ELLSWORTH, SCOTT. *Death in A Promised Land: The Tulsa Race Riot of 1921* (1982).

ELY, MELVIN PATRICK. *The Adventures of Amos 'n' Andy: A Social History of an American Phenomenon* (1991).

EMECHETA, BUCHI. *Head Above Water* (1986).

EMERY, LYNNE FAULEY. *Black Dance in the United States from 1619 to 1970* (1980).

ENCICLOPÉDIA DA MÚSICA BRASILEIRA: Erudita, folclórica, popular (1977).

EQUIANO, OLAUDAH. *Equiano's Travels: His Autobiography: The Interesting Narrative of the Life of Olaudah Equiano or Gustavus Vassa, the African.* Edited by Paul Edwards (1967).

ERLEWINE, MICHAEL, ET AL, EDS. *All Music Guide to Jazz: The Experts' Guide to the Best Jazz Recordings* (1996).

ERLMANN, VEIT, AND DEBORAH PACINI HERNANDEZ, EDS. "The Politics and Aesthetics of Transnational Musics." Special issue of *World of Music* 35, no. 2 (1993).

ERSTEIN, HAP. "Richards, Wilson Team Up on Prize Dramas." *Washington Times* (November 8, 1991): E1.

ESTES, J. WORTH. *The Medical Skills of Ancient Egypt* (1993).

ESTUPIÑAN TELLO, JULIO. *Historia de Esmeraldas* (1977).

EVANS, MARI. *Black Women Writers (1950–1980): A Critical Evaluation* (1984).

EVERS, CHARLES, AND GRACE HASKELL, EDS. *Evers* (1971).

EWERS, TRAUTE. *The Origin of American Black English: Be-Forms in the HOODOO Texts* (1996).

FABRE, MICHEL. "The Last Quest of Horace Cayton." *Black World* 19 (May 1970): 41–45.

——. *The Unfinished Quest of Richard Wright*. Translated by Isabel Barzun (1973).

FAIRCLOUGH, ADAM. *To Redeem the Soul of America: The Southern Christian Leadership Conference and Martin Luther King, Jr* (1987).

FAIR, LAURA. "Dressing Up: Clothing, Class and Gender in Post-Abolition Zanzibar." *Journal of African History* 39 (1998): 63–94.

FANON, FRANTZ. *Black Skin, White Masks*. Translation of *Peau noire, masques blancs* by Charles Lam Markmann (1967).

FARMER, JAMES. *Lay Bare the Heart: An Autobiography of the Civil Rights Movement* (1985).

FARNSWORTH, ROBERT M. *Melvin B. Tolson, 1898–1966: Plain Talk and Poetic Prophecy* (1984).

FARRISON, WILLIAM EDWARD. *William Wells Brown: Author and Reformer* (1969).

FEHRENBACHER, DON E. *The Dred Scott Case: Its Significance in American Law and Politics* (1978).

FELDMAN, LINDA. "Norton Biography." *Christian Science Monitor* (March 31, 1992): 14:1

FERGUSON, JAMES. *Papa Doc, Baby Doc: Haiti and the Duvaliers* (1987).

FERGUSON, MOIRA. *Jamaica Kincaid: Where the Land Meets the Body* (1994).

FERGUSON, SHEILA. *Soul Food: Classic Cuisine from the Deep South* (1989).

FERRIS, WILLIAM, ED. *Afro-American Folk Arts and Crafts* (1983).

FERRIS, WILLIAM, AND BRENDA MCCALLUM, EDS. *Local Color: A Sense of Place in Folk Art* (1982).

FIELDS, BARBARA JEANNE. *Slavery and Freedom on the Middle Ground: Maryland During the Nineteenth Century* (1985).

FILHO, LUÍS VIANA. *O Negro na Bahia* (1988).

FITZGERALD, MARY ANN, HENRY J. DREWAL, AND MAYO OKEDIJI. "Transformation through Cloth: An Egungun Costume of the Yoruba." *African Arts* 28 (1995).

FLASCH, JOY. *Melvin B. Tolson* (1972).

FLEISCHER, NAT. *Black Dynamite: The Story of the Negro in the Prize Ring from 1782 to 1838* (1938).

FLETCHER, MARVIN E. *America's First Black General: Benjamin O. Davis, Sr.* (1989).

——. *The Black Soldier and Officer in the United States Army, 1891–1917* (1974).

FLETCHER, TOM. *One-Hundred Years of the Negro in Show Business* (1984).

FLINT, J. E. "Zanzibar 1890–1950." *In History of East Africa*, ed. Vincent Harlow and E. M. Chilver (1965).

FLOMENHAFT, ELEANOR, ED. FAITH RINGGOLD: *A 25–Year Survey* (1990).

FLOYD, SAMUEL, ED. *Black Music in the Harlem Renaissance* (1990).

FLYNN, JOYCE, AND JOYCE OCCOMY STRICKLIN, EDS. *Frye Street and Environs: The Collected Works of Marita Bonner Occomy* (1987).

FOGEL, ROBERT W. *Without Consent or Contract: The Rise and Fall of American Slavery* (1989).

FOLEY, ALBERT S. *Bishop Healy: Beloved Outcaste* (1954).

FONER, ERIC. *Reconstruction: America's Unfinished Revolution, 1863–1877* (1988).

FONER, PHILIP. *Antonio Maceo* (1977).

——. *Black Panthers Speak* (1995).

——. *Blacks in the American Revolution* (1976).

——. *Organized Labor & the Black Worker 1619–1973* (1974).

——. *The Spanish-Cuban-American War and the Birth of U.S. Imperialism. Vol. I* (1962).

FONER, PHILIP, ED. *Black Socialist Preacher: The Teachings of Reverend George Washington Woodbey and his Disciple Reverend George W. Slater, Jr.* (1983).

FONER, PHILIP, AND RONALD LEWIS. *Black Workers: A Documentary History from Colonial Times to the Present* (1989).

FOOTE, JULIA. *A Brand Plucked From the Fire. In Spiritual Narratives*, ed. Henry Louis Gates Jr. (1988).

FORBES, JACK D. *Africans and Native Americans: The Language of Race and the Evolution of Red-Black Peoples* (1988).

FORBES, STEVEN. *The Baymen of Belize and How They Wrested British Honduras from the Spaniards* (1997).

FORMAN, JAMES. *The Making of Black Revolutionaries* (1985).

FOSTER, FRANCES SMITH. "Adding Color and Contour to Early American Self-Portraitures: Autobiographical Writings of Afro-Amer-ican Women." In *Conjuring: Black Women, Fiction and Literary Tradition*, ed. Marjorie Pryse and Hortense J. Spillers (1985).

——. *Written By Herself: Literary Production by African American Women, 1746–1892* (1993).

FOUCHET, MAX POL. *Wifredo Lam.* (1976).

FOWLER, VIRGINIA. *Nikki Giovanni* (1992).

FRADY, MARSHALL. *Jesse: The Life and Pilgrimage of Jesse Jackson* (1996).

FRANCO, JOSÉ LUCIANO. *Apuntes para una historia de su vida.* 3 vols. (1951–1957).

Franco Silva, Alfonso. *La esclavitud en Sevilla y su tierra a fines de la edad media* (1979).

FRANKLIN, CHARLES LIONEL. *The Negro Labor Unionist of New York: Problems and Conditions among Negroes in the Labor Unions in Manhattan with Special Reference to the N.R.A. and Post-N.R.A. Situations* (1936).

FRANKLIN, JOHN HOPE. *The Free Negro in North Carolina, 1790–1863* (1943).

——. *From Slavery to Freedom: A History of Negro Americans* (1988).

——. *Race and History: Selected Essays, 1938–1988* (1989).

FRANKLIN, JOHN HOPE, AND AUGUST MEIER, EDS. *Black Leaders of the Twentieth Century* (1982).

FRANKLIN, VINCENT P. *The Education of Black Philadelphia: The Social and Educational History of a Minority Community, 1900–1950* (1979).

FRANK, RUSTY E. *Tap! The Greatest Tap Dance Stars and Their Stories, 1900–1955* (1990).

FRAZIER, E. FRANKLIN. "Durham: Capital of the Black Middle Class." In Alain Locke, ed. *The New Negro* (1925).

——. *On Race Relations: Selected Writings*, ed. Gilbert Edwards (1968).

FRAZIER, JOE, AND PHIL BERGER. *Smokin' Joe: The Autobiography of a Heavyweight Champion of the World, Smokin' Joe Frazier* (1996).

FREEDBERG, SYDNEY P. *Brother Love: Money, Murder, and a Messiah* (1994).

FRENCH, WILLIAM P. "Black Studies: Getting Started in a Specialty." *AB: Bookmans Weekly* (February 22, 1988): 737–41.

FREYRE, GILBERTO. *O Brasil em face das Africas negras e mesticas* (1963).

——. *The Masters and the Slaves: A Study in the Development of Brazilian Civilization*. Translation of *Casa grande e senzala* by Samuel Putnam (1986).

FREY, SYLVIA. *Water From the Rock: Black Resistance in a Revolutionary Age* (1991).

FRIEDEMANN, NINA S. DE. *Lengua y sociedad en el palenque de San Basilio* (1983).

——. *Ma ngombe: Guerreros y ganaderos en Palenque*. 2d ed. (1987).

——. *La saga del Negro: Presencia africana en Colombia* (1993).

FRIEDEMANN, NINA S. DE., AND ALFREDO VANIN, COMP. *Entre la tierra y el cielo: Magia y leyendas del Chocó* (1995).

FRIEDMAN, LAWRENCE J. *Gregarious Saints: Self and Community in American Abolitionism, 1830–1870* (1982).

FINLAYSON, IAIN. *Tangier: City of the Dream* (1992).

FOX, STEPHEN R. *The Guardian of Boston: William Monroe Trotter* (1970).

FOX, TED. *Showtime at the Apollo* (1983).

FRY, GLADYS-MARIE. *Stitched from the Soul: Slave Quilts from the Ante-Bellum South* (1990).

FREDERICKS, MARCEL, JOHN LENNON ET AL. *Society and Health in Guyana* (1986).

FUNARI, PEDRO PAUL A., MARTIN HALL, AND SIAN JONES, EDS. *Historical Archaeology: Back from the Edge* (1999).

FUNDACÓ CASA DE RUI BARBOSA. *O Abolicionista Rui Barbosa* (1988).

FUNKE, LEWIS. *The Curtain Rises: The Story of Ossie Davis* (1971).

FYFE, CHRISTOPHER. *Sierra Leone Inheritance* (1964).

GABBARD, KRIN, ED. *Representing Jazz* (1995).

GABRIEL, TESHOME. *Third Cinema in the Third World: The Aestheties of Liberation* (1982).

GADELII, KARL ERLAND. *Lesser Antillean French Creole and Universal Grammar* (1997).

GAINES, ERNEST. *Porch Talk with Ernest Gaines: Conversations on the Writer's Craft*, ed. Marcia Gaudet and Carl Wooton (1990).

GALEANO, EDUARDO. *Football in Sun and Shadow* (1998).

GAMBINO, FERRUCCIO. "The Transgression of a Laborer: Malcolm X in the Wilderness of America." *Radical History Review* 55 (Winter 1993): 7–31.

GAMBLE, DAVID. *The Wolof of Senegambia, Together with Notes on the Lebu and the Serer* (1967).

GANDY, SAMUEL LUCIUS. *Human Possibilities: A Vernon Johns Reader* (1977).

GANGITANO, LIA AND STEVEN NELSON, EDS. *New Histories* (1996).

GARCÍA, HORACIO, ED. *Pensamiento revolucionario cubano*. Vol. I (1971).

GARCÍA, JUAN. *Cuentos y décimas afro-esmeraldeñas* (1988).

GARCÍA, JUAN MANUEL. *La Masacre de Palma Sola (Partidos, lucha política y el asesino del general): 1961–1963* (1986).

GARFINKEL, HERBERT. *When Negroes March: The March on Washington Movement in the Organizational Politics for FEPC* (1959).

GARROW, DAVID J. *Bearing the Cross: Martin Luther King, Jr., and the Southern Christian Leadership Conference* (1986).

——. *Protest at Selma: Martin Luther King, Jr., and the Voting Rights Act of 1965* (1978).

GASPAR, DAVID BARRY. *Bondmen and Rebels: A Study of Master-Slave Relations in Antigua* (1985).

GATES, HENRY LOUIS, JR. *Black Literature and Literary Theory* (1984).

——. *Colored People: A Memoir* (1994).

——. *Figures in Black: Words, Signs, and the Racial Self* (1992).

——. *Loose Canons: Notes on the Culture Wars* (1992).

——. *The Signifying Monkey: Towards A Theory of Afro-American Literary Criticism* (1988).

——. *Thirteen Ways of Looking at a Black Man* (1997): 155–79.

GATES, HENRY LOUIS, JR., ED. *Bearing Witness: Selections from African-American Autobiography in the Twentieth Century* (1991).

——, ed. *The Classic Slave Narratives* (1987).

——, ed. *Collected Black Women's Narratives: The Schomburg Library of Nineteenth-Century Black Women Writers* (1988).

GATES, HENRY LOUIS, JR., AND KWAME ANTHONY APPIAH, EDS. *Richard Wright: Critical Perspectives Past and Present* (1993).

——.Gloria Naylor: *Critical Perspectives Past and Present* (1993).

GATES, HENRY LOUIS, JR., AND NELLIE Y. MCKAY. *The Norton Anthology of African American Literature* (1997).

GATES, HENRY LOUIS, JR., AND CORNEL WEST. *The Future of the Race* (1996).

GATEWOOD, WILLARD B. *Aristocrats of Color: The Black Elite, 1880–1920* (1990).

GAVINS, RAYMOND. *The Perils and Prospects of Southern Black Leadership: Gordon Blaine Hancock, 1884–1970* (1977).

GAYLE, ADDISON, JR., ED. *The Black Aesthetic* (1971).

GAY, ROBERT. *Popular Organization and Democracy in Rio de Janeiro: A Tale of Two Favelas* (1994).

GEARY, LYNETTE G. "Jules Bledsoe: The Original 'Ol' Man River'." *Black Perspective in Music* 17, nos. 1, 2 (1989): 27–54.

GEIS, IMMANUEL. *The Pan-African Movement: A History of Pan-Africanism in America, Europe and Africa* (1974).

GELPÍ, JUAN. *Literatura y paternalismo en Puerto Rico* (1993).

GENOVESE, EUGENE D. *Roll, Jordan, Roll: The World the Slaves Made* (1974).

GEORGE, CAROL V. R. *Segregated Sabbaths: Richard Allen and the Emergence of Independent Black Churches 1760–1840* (1972).

GEORGE, NELSON. *Elevating the Game: Black Men and Basketball* (1992).

——. *Where Did Our Love Go?: The Rise and Fall of the Motown Sound* (1985).

GEORGE, NELSON, ET AL., EDS. *Fresh: Hip Hop Don't Stop* (1985).

GERBER, JANE S. *Jewish Society in Fez, 1450–1700: Studies in Communal and Economic Life* (1980).

GIBB, H.A.R. IBN BATTUTA: *Travels in Asia and Africa 1325–1354* (1929).

GIBSON, BOB. *From Ghetto to Glory: The Story of Bob Gibson* (1968).

GIDE, ANDRÈ. *Travels in the Congo* (1962).

GILARD, JACQUES. "Crescencio ou don Toba? Fausses questions et vraies rèponses sur le 'vallenato'." *Cahiers du monde hispanique et luso-brésilien, Caravelle* 48 (1987): 69–80.

GILL, GERALD R. "Win or Lose -We Win." *In The Afro-American Woman: Struggles and Images* (1978).

GILLESPIE, JOHN BIRKS ("DIZZY"), WITH AL FRASER. *Dizzy To BE, or Not . . . to BOP: The Autobiography of Dizzy Gillespie* (1979).

GILROY, PAUL. *There Ain't No Black in the Union Jack: The Cultural Politics of Race and Nation* (1991).

GIRAL, SERGIO. "Cuban Cinema and the Afro-Cuban Heritage." Interview by Julianne Burton and Gary Crowdus. *In Film and Politics in the Third World*, ed. John D. H. Downing (1987).

——. "Sergio Giral on Filmmaking in Cuba." Interview by Ana M. López and Nicholas Peter Humy. *In Cinemas of the Black Diaspora: Diversity, Dependence, and Oppositionality*, ed. Michael T. Martin (1995).

GIRVAN, NORMAN. *Poverty, Empowerment and Social Development in the Caribbean* (1997).

GLAZIER, STEPHEN D. MARCHIN' the Pilgrims Home (1983).

——,ED. *Perspectives on Pentecostalism: Case Studies from the Caribbean and Latin America* (1980).

GLEN, JOHN M. *Highlander: No Ordinary School, 1932–1962* (1988).

GLISSANT, EDOUARD. *Caribbean Discourse: Selected Essays*. Translated by J. Michael Dash (1989).

GOGGIN, JACQUELINE ANNE. *Carter G. Woodson: A Life in Black History* (1993).

GOINGS, KENNETH W. *Mammy and Uncle Mose: Black Collectibles and American Stereotyping* (1994).

GOLDBERG, JANE. "A Hoofer's Homage: John Bubbles." *Village Voice* (December 4, 1978).

GONZ·LEZ BUENO, GLADYS. "An Initia-tion Ceremony in Regla de Palo." *In AfroCuba: An Anthology of Cuban Writing on Race, Politics and Culture*, ed. Pedro Pèrez Sarduy and Jean Stubbs (1993).

GONZLEZ DÍAZ, ANTONIO MANUEL. *La esclavitud en Ayamonte durante el Antiguo Régimen (siglos XVI, XVII y XVIII)* (1997).

GONZ·LEZ ECHEVARRIA, ROBERTO. *Myth and Archive: A Theory of Latin American Narrative* (1998).

——. *The Pride of Havana: The History of Cuban Baseball* (1999).

GONZALEZ-PEREZ, ARMANDO. *Acercamiento a la literatura afrocubana: Ensayos de interpretación* (1994).

GONZALEZ-WHIPPLER, MIGENE. *The Santeria Experience: A Journey into the Miraculous*. Rev. and exp. ed. (1992).

GOODHEART, LAWRENCE B., ET AL., EDS. *Slavery in American Society*. 3d ed. (1993).

GOODWIN, ANDREW, AND JOE GORE. "World Beat and the Cultural Imperialism Debate." *Socialist Review* 20, no. 3 (1990): 63–80.

GORDON, ALLAN M. *Echoes of Our Past: The Narrative Artistry of Palmer C. Hayden* (1988).

GORDON, P. "The New Right, Race, and Education." *Race and Class* 29, no. 3 (Winter 1987).

GOSNELL, HAROLD F. *Negro Politicians: The Rise of Negro Politics in Chicago* (1967).

GOURAIGE, GHISLAIN. *Histoire de la littérature haïtienne (de l'indépendance à nos jours)* (1982).

GOUREVITCH, PHILIP. *We Wish to Inform You that Tomorrow We Will Be Killed with Our Families: Stories from Rwanda* (1998).

GOURSE, LESLIE. *Unforgettable: The Life and Mystique of Nat King Cole* (1991).

GRANDA GUTIERREZ, GERMAN DE. *Estudios sobre un area dialectal hispanoamericana de poblacion negra: Las tierras bajas occidentales de Colombia* (1977)

GRANT, JOANNE. *Fundi: The Story of Ella Baker* (1981).

GRATIANT, GILBERT. *Fables créoles et autres récits* (1995).

GRAY, JOHN MILNER. *History of Zanzibar from the Middle Ages to 1856* (1962).

GRAY, RICHARD. *Black Christians and White Missionaries* (1990).

GREENBAUM, SUSAN. "A Comparison Between African-American and Euro-American Mutual Aid Societies in 19th-Century America." *Journal of Ethnic Studies* 19 (Fall 1991): 95–119.

GREENBERG, CHERYL LYNN. *"Or Does It Explode?: Black Harlem in the Great Depression* (1991).

GREENBERG, JACK. *Crusaders in the Courts: How a Dedicated Band of Lawyers Fought for the Civil Rights Revolution* (1994).

GREENE, LORENZO JOHNSTON. *Selling Black History for Carter G. Woodson* (1996).

GREENE, LORENZO JOHNSTON, GARY R. KREMER, AND ANTONIO F. HOLLAND. *Missouri's Black Heritage* (1993).

GREEN, TIM. *The Dark Side of the Game: The Unauthorized NFL Playbook* (1996).

GREGORY, DICK, WITH MARK LANE. *Up From Nigger* (1976).

GREGORY, DICK, WITH MARTIN LIPSYTE. *Nigger: An Autobiography* (1964).

GREGORY, PAYNE J., AND SCOTT C. RATZAN. *Tom Bradley: The Impossible Dream: A Biography* (1986).

GRENARD, STEVE. *Handbook of Alligators and Crocodiles* (1991).

GRIAULE, MARCEL. *Conversations with Ogotemmeli: An Introduction to Dogon Religious Ideas* (1965).

GROIA, PHILIP. *They All Sang on the Corner: A Second Look at New York City's Rhythm and Blues Vocal Groups* (1983).

GROSSMAN, JAMES R. *Land of Hope: Chicago, Black Southerners and the Great Migration* (1989).

GRUDIN, EVA UNGAR. *Stitching Memories: African-American Story Quilts* (1990).

GUERRERO, EDWARD. *Framing Blackness: The African American Image in Film* (1993).

GUILBAULT, JOCELYNE, WITH GAGE AVERILL, EDOUARD BENOîT, AND GREGORY RABESS. *Zouk: World Music in the West Indies* (1993).

GUILLÉN, NICOLAS. *Martín Morúa Delgado: ¿Quién fue?* (1984).

GURALNICK, PETER. *Searching for Robert Johnson* (1989).

———. *Sweet Soul Music: Rhythm and Blues and the Southern Dream of Freedom* (1986).

GUTMAN, BILL. *The Harlem Globetrotters* (1977).

GUTMAN, HERBERT G. *The Black Family in Slavery and Freedom, 1750–1925* (1976).

GUY-SHEFTALL, BEVERLY, AND JO MOORE STEWART. *Spelman: A Centennial Celebration* (1981).

GUZMAN, JESSIE P. *Crusade for Civic Democracy: The Story of the Tuskegee Civic Association, 1941–1970* (1985).

HABEKOST, CHRISTIAN. *Verbal Riddim: The Politics and Aesthetics of African-Caribbean Dub Poetry* (1993).

HACKETT, ROSALIND. *Art and Religion in Africa* (1996).

HAIR, WILLIAM IVY. *Carnival of Fury: Robert Charles and the New Orleans Race Riot of 1900* (1976).

HALE, LINDSAY, "Preto Velho: Resistance, Redemption and Engendered Representations of Slavery in a Brazilian Possession-Trance Religion." *American Ethnologist* 24, no. 2 (1997): 392–414.

HALL, JACQUELYN DOWD. *Revolt Against Chivalry: Jessie Daniel Ames and the Women's Campaign Against Lynching* (1979).

HALL, MARGARET, AND TOM YOUNG. *Confronting Leviathan: Mozambique Since Independence* (1997).

HALL, RICHARD. *Stanley: An Adventurer Explored* (1974).

HALL, STUART. "Racism and Reaction." *In Five Views on Multi-Racial Britain* (1978).

HALL, STUART, AND BRAM GIEBEN, EDS. *Formations of Modernity* (1992).

HALL, STUART, AND MARTIN JACQUES, EDS. *New Times: The Changing Face of Politics in the 1990s* (1990).

HAMER, MARY. *Signs of Cleopatra: History, Politics, Representation* (1993).

HAMILTON, CHARLES V. *Adam Clayton Powell, Jr.: The Political Biography of an American Dilemma* (1991).

HAMILTON, HOLMAN. *Prologue to Conflict: The Crisis and Compromise of 1850* (1964).

HAMILTON, KENNETH MARVIN. *Black Towns and Profit: Promotion and Development in the Trans-Applachian West, 1877–1915* (1991).

HAMNER, ROBERT D, ED. *Critical Perspectives on Derek Walcott* (1993).

HANCHARD, MICHAEL GEORGE. *Orpheus and Power: The Movimento Negro of Rio de Janeiro and São Paulo, Brazil, 1945–1988* (1994).

HANDY, D. ANTOINETTE. "Conversations with Mary Lou Williams: First Lady of the Jazz Keyboard." *Black Perspectives on Music* 8 (Fall 1980): 195–214.

HANDY, WILLIAM C. *Father of the Blues: An Autobiography.* Edited by Arna Bontemps (1941).

HANSEN, EMMANUEL. *Frantz Fanon: Social and Political Thought* (1977).

HARDESTY, VON, AND DOMINICK PISANO. *Black Wings: The American Black in Aviation* (1983).

HARDY, CHARLES, AND GAIL F. STERN, EDS. *Ethnic Images in the Comics* (1986).

HARDY, GAYLE J. *American Women Civil Rights Activists: Biobibliographies of 68 Leaders, 1825–1992* (1993).

HARLAN, LOUIS R. *Booker T. Washington: The Making of a Black Leader, 1856–1901* (1972).

HARPER, MICHAEL S., ET. AL., EDS. *Chant of Saints: A Gathering of Afro-American Literature, Art, and Scholarship* (1979).

HARRINGTON, OLIVER. *Why I Left America and Other Essays* (1993).

HARRIS, FRED R., AND ROGER WILKINS, EDS. *Quiet Riots: Race and Poverty in the United States* (1988).

HARRIS, JESSICA B. *Iron Pots and Wooden Spoons: Africa's Gifts to New World Cooking* (1989).

HARRIS, MICHAEL. *The Rise of the Gospel Blues: The Music of Thomas Andrew Dorsey in the Urban Church* (1992).

HARRISON, ALFERDTEEN, ED. *Black Exodus: The Great Migration from the American South* (1991).

HARRISON, EARL. *The Dream and the Dreamer* (1956).

HARRIS, ROBERT. "Early Black Benevolent Societies, 1780–1830." *Massachusetts Review* 20 (Autumn 1979): 603–28.

HARRIS, WILLIAM HAMILTON. *Keeping the Faith: A. Philip Randolph, Milton P. Webster, and the Brotherhood of Sleeping Car Porters, 1925–37* (1977).

HARRIS, WILLIAM J. *The Poetry and Poetics of Amiri Baraka: The Jazz Aesthetic* (1985).

HARRIS, WILSON. *History, Fable, and Myth in the Caribbean and the Guianas* (1970).

HART, DAVID. *The Volta River Project: A Case Study in Politics and Technology* (1980).

HASKINS, JAMES. *Black Dance in America: A History through its People* (1990).

——. *Bricktop* (1983).

——. *Mabel Mercer: A Life* (1987).

——. *Pinckney Benton Stewart Pinchback* (1973).

HASKINS, JAMES, AND N. R. MITGANG. *Mr. Bojangles: The Biography of Bill Robinson* (1988).

HAYDEN, DOLORES. "Biddy Mason's Los Angeles, 1856–1891." *California History* 68 (Fall 1989): 86–99.

HAYDEN, TOM. *Rebellion in Newark: Official Violence and Ghetto Response* (1967).

HAYES, DIANA L. *And Still We Rise: An Introduction to Black Liberation Theology* (1996).

HAYGOOD, WIL. *King of the Cats: The Life and Times of Adam Clayton Powell, Jr.* (1993).

HAYNES, KARIMA A. "Mae Jemison: Coming in from Outer Space." *Ebony* 48, no. 2 (Dec. 1992):118.

HAYWOOD, HARRY. *Black Bolshevik: Autobiography of an Afro-American Communist* (1978).

HAZAEL-MASSIEUX, MARIE-CHRISTINE. "Le Criole aux Antilles: Evolutions et Perspectives." In Yacou Alain, ed., *Creoles de la Caraïbe: Actes du Colloque universitaire en hommage á Guy Hazael-Massieux, Pointe-á-Pitre, le 27 mars 1995* (1996): 179–200.

HEDGEMAN, ANNA ARNOLD. *The Trumpet Sounds: A Memoir of Negro leadership* (1964).

HEDRICK, JOAN. *Harriet Beecher Stowe: A Life* (1994).

HEILBUT, ANTHONY. *The Gospel Sound: Good News and Bad Times* (1971).

HELDMAN, MARILYN E., STUART MUNRO-HAY, AND RODERICK GRIERSON. *African Zion: The Sacred Art of Ethiopia* (1993).

HELG, ALINE. *Our Rightful Share: The Afro-Cuban Struggle for Equality, 1886–1912* (1995).

HELLER, PETER. *Bad Intentions: The Mike Tyson Story* (1989).

HELM, MCKINLEY. *Angel Mo' and Her Son, Roland Hayes* (1942).

HEMENWAY, ROBERT. *Zora Neale Hurston: A Literary Biography* (1980).

HEMPHILL, ESSEX, ED. *Brother to Brother: New Writings by Black Gay Men* (1991).

HENDERSON, ALEXA BENSON. *Atlanta Life Insurance Company: Guardian of Black Economic Dignity* (1990).

HENDERSON, HARRY, AND GYLBERT GARVIN COKER. *Charles Alston: Artist and Teacher* (1990).

HENSON, MATTHEW A. *A Black Explorer at the North Pole 1866–1955* (1989).

HENZE, PAUL B. *The Defeat of the Derg and the Establishment of New Governments in Ethiopia and Eritrea* (1992).

HEUMAN, GAD, ED. *Out of the House of Bondage: Runaways, Resistance, and Marronage in Africa and the New World* (1986).

HEYMOUNT, GEORGE. "Blacks in Opera." *Ebony* (November 1981): 32–36.

HIDALGO ALZAMORA, LAURA. "Del ritmo al concepto en la poesía de Preciado." *Cultura, Revista del Banco Central del Ecuador 3*, no.7 (May-August 1980): 102–19.

HIGGINBOTHAM, A. LEON. *In the Matter of Color: The Colonial Period* (1978).

——. *Shades of Freedom: Racial Politics and Presumptions of the American Legal Process* (1996).

HIGGINBOTHAM, EVELYN BROOKS. *Righteous Discontent: The Women's Movement in the Black Baptist Church, 1880–1920* (1993).

HILL, DANIEL G. *The Freedom Seekers: Blacks in Early Canada* (1981).

HILL, DONALD. *Calypso Calaloo: Early Carnival Music in Trinidad* (1993).

HILL, ROBERT A., ED. *The Crusader*. 3 vols. (1987).

——. *The Marcus Garvey and Universal Negro Improvement Association Papers* (1983–1991).

HINE, DARLENE CLARK, ED. *Black Women in America: An Historical Encylopedia*. 2 vols. (1993).

HIRO, DILIP. *Desert Shield to Desert Storm: The Second Gulf War* (1992).

HIRSH, ARNOLD R., AND JOSEPH LOGSDON. *Creole New Orleans: Race and Americanization* (1992).

HIRSCHORN, H. H. "Botanical remedies of South and Central America and the Caribbean: An Archival Analysis." *Journal of Ethnopharmacology* 4, no. 2 (1981).

HOCHSCHILD, ADAM. *King Leopold's Ghost: A Story of Greed, Terror, and Heroism in Colonial Africa* (1998).

HODGES, LEROY. *Portrait of an Expatriate: William Gardner Smith, Writer* (1985).

HOFFMAN, FREDERICK J., CHARLES ALLEN, AND CAROLYN R. ULRICH. *The Little Magazine: A History and a Bibliography* (1946).

HOFFMAN, LARRY G. *Haitian Art: The Legend and Legacy of the Naïve Tradition* (1985).

HOFFMANN, LÉON-FRANÇOIS. *Littérature d'Haïti* (1995).

HOFLER, ROBERT. "Minority View: Seeing White, Being Black: Interview with Lou Gossett Jr." *Life* (March 1989).

HOLANDA, AURÉLIO BUARQUE DE. "Teixeira e Souza." In *O Romance Brasileiro*, ed. Olivio Montenegro (1952).

HOLDREDGE, HELEN. *Mammy Pleasant* (1953).

HOLLOWAY, JOSEPH E., ED. *Africanisms in American Culture* (1990).

HOLM, JOHN. *Pidgins and Creoles*. 2 vols. (1988–1989).

HOLT, RACKMAN. *Mary McLeod Bethune: A Biography* (1964).

HOLWAY, JOHN B. *Josh and Satch: The Life and Times of Josh Gibson and Satchel Paige* (1991).

HOLYFIELD, EVANDER, AND BERNARD HOLYFIELD. *Holyfield: The Humble Warrior* (1996).

HOOKS, BELL, "Black is a Woman's Color." In *Bearing Witness: Selections from African-American Autobiography in the Twentieth Century*, ed. Henry Louis Gates Jr. (1991).

HOOKS, BELL, AND CORNEL WEST. *Breaking Bread: Insurgent Black Intellectual Life* (1991).

HOPE KING, RUBY. *Education in the Caribbean: Historical Perspectives* (1987).

HORACE, LILLIAN B. *"Crowned with Glory and Honor": The Life of Rev. Lacey Kirk Williams* (1978).

HORNE, GERALD. *Communist Front? The Civil Rights Congress 1946–56* (1988).

HORTON, AIMEE ISGRIG. *The Highlander Folk School: A History of its Major Programs, 1932–1961* (1989).

HOSHER, JOHN. *God in a Rolls Royce: The Rise of Father Divine: Madman, Menace, or Messiah* (1936).

HOSIASSON, JOSE. "Kid Ory." *New Grove Dictionary of Jazz* (1988).

HOUSE, ERNEST R. *Jesse Jackson and the Politics of Charisma: The Rise and Fall of the PUSH/Excel Program* (1988).

HOWAT, GERALD. *Learie Constantine* (1975).

HOWES, R. "The Literature of Outsiders: The Literature of the Gay Community in Latin America." In *Latin American Masses and Minorities: Their Images and Realities* (1987).

HOWE, STEPHEN. *Afrocentrism: Mythical Pasts and Imagined Homes* (1998).

HOYOS, F. A. *A History from the Amerindians to Independence* (1978).

HUCKABY, ELIZABETH. *Crisis at Central High School: Little Rock, 1957–58* (1980).

HUGGINS, NATHAN IRVIN. *Harlem Renaissance* (1971).

HUGHES, C. ALVIN. "We Demand Our Rights: The Southern Negro Youth Congress, 1937–1949." *Phylon* 48, no. 1 (Spring 1987): 38–50.

HULL, GLORIA T. *Color, Sex, and Poetry: Three Women Writers of the Harlem Renaissance* (1987).

HUNTER-GAULT, CHARLAYNE. *In My Place* (1992).

HUNTINGTON, RICHARD. *Gender and Social Structure in Madagascar* (1988).

HURD, MICHAEL. *Black College Football, 1892–1992: One Hundred Years of History, Education, and Pride* (1993).

HURLEY, DANIEL. *Cincinnati, The Queen City* (1982).

HURSTON, ZORA NEALE. "Hoodoo in America." *Journal of American Folklore* 44 (1931): 414.

———. *I Love Myself When I am Laughing . . . and Then Again When I am Looking ·Mean and Impressive: A Zora Neale Hurston Reader*, ed. Alice Walker (1979).

———. *Mules and Men* (1935).

HUTCHINSON, EARL OFARI. *Betrayed: A History of Presidential Failure to Protect Black Lives* (1996).

———. *Blacks and Reds: Race and Class in Conflict, 1919–1990* (1995).

IANNI, OCTÁVIO. *Escravidão e racismo*. 2d ed. (1988).

IHONVBERE, JULIUS O. *Economic Crisis, Civil Society, and Democratization: The Case of Zambia* (1996).

ILLINOIS STATE MUSEUM. *Healing Walls: Murals and Community, A Chicago History* (1996).

"Interview: Queen Mother Moore." *Black Scholar* 4 (March-April 1973): 47–55.

IOAKIMIDIS, DEMETRE. "Chu Berry." *Jazz Monthly* (March 1964).

IRVINE, CECILIA. "The Birth of the Kimbanguist Movement in Bas-Zaire, 1921." *Journal of Religion in Africa* 6, no. 1 (1974): 23–76.

ISICHEI, ELIZABETH. *A History of African Societies to 1870* (1997).

JACKSON, CARLTON. *Hattie: The Life of Hattie McDaniel* (1990).

JACKSON, KENNETH T., AND BARBARA B. JACKSON. "The Black Experience in Newark: The Growth of the Ghetto, 1870–1970." *In New Jersey Since 1860: New Findings and Interpretations*, ed. William C. Wright (1972).

JACKSON, LUTHER P. *Free Negro Labor and Property Holding in Virginia, 1830–1860* (1942).

JACKSON, REGINALD, WITH MIKE LUPICA. *Reggie* (1984).

JACKSON, RICHARD L. *Black Writers in Latin America* (1979).

JACOBS, DONALD M. *Antebellum Black Newspapers* (1976).

———. "David Walker: Boston Race Leader, 1825–1830." *Essex Institute Historical Collections* 107 (Jan. 1971): 94–107.

JACOBS, HARRIET. *Incidents in the Life of a Slave Girl, Written by Herself*, ed. Jean Fagan Yellin (1987).

JACOBSON, MARK. "When He Was King: Former Heavyweight Boxing Champ Larry Holmes." *New York* 30, no. 28 (July 28, 1997): 32–35.

JACQUES-GARVEY, AMY, ED. *Philosophy and Opinions of Marcus Garvey* (1923–1925).

JADIN, LOUIS. *Le Congo et la secte des Antoniens* (1961).

JAGAN, CHEDDI. *The West on Trial: My Fight for Guyana's Freedom* (1967).

JAMES, ADEOLA. *In Their Own Voices: African Women Writers Talk* (1990).

JAMES, C.L.R. *The Black Jacobins: Toussaint L' Ouverture and the San Domingo Revolution* (1963).

———. *A History of Pan-African Revolt* (1969).

JAMES, M. *Ten Modern Jazzmen: An Appraisal of the Recorded Work of Ten Modern Jazzmen* (1960).

"J. A. Rogers: Portrait of an Afro-American Historian." *Black Scholar* 6, no. 5 (January-February 1975): 32–39.

JASEN, DAVID A., AND TREBOR TICHENOR. *Rags and Ragtime: A Musical History* (1989).

JEFFREY, HENRY B., AND COLIN BABER. *Guyana: Politics, Economics, and Society: Beyond the Burnham Era* (1986).

JENKINS, MARK. *To Timbuktu* (1997).

JIMÉNEZ-ROMAN, MIRIAM. "Un hombre (negro) del pueblo: José Celso Barbosa and the Puerto Rican 'Race' towards Whiteness." *Centro de Estudios Puertorriqueños* (Spring 1996).

JIMENO, MYRIAM, AND MARÍA LUCIA SOTOMAYOR, LUZ MARÍA VALDERRAMA. *Chocó: Diversidad cultural y medio ambiente* (1995).

JOHNS, CHRIS. *Valley of Life: Africa's Great Rift* (1991).

JOHNSON, ABBY ARTHUR, AND RONALD MABERRY JOHNSON. "Charting a New Course: African American Literary Politics since 1976." In *The Black Columbiad: Defining Moments in African American Literature and Culture*, ed. Werner Sollors and Maria Diedrich (1994), pp. 369–81.

———. *Propaganda and Aesthetics: The Literary Politics of African-American Magazines in the Twentieth Century* (1991).

JOHNSON, CECIL, *Guts: Legendary Black Rodeo Cowboy Bill Pickett* (1994).

JOHNSON, DIANE. *Telling Tales: The Pedagogy and Promise of African American Literature for Youth* (1990).

JOHNSON, JOHN H., AND LERONE BENNETT, JR. *Succeeding Against the Odds* (1989).

JOHNSON, JAMES WELDON. *Black Manhattan* (1930).

———. Preface to *The Book of American Negro Poetry* (1922).

JOHNSON, RANDAL. *Cinema Novo x 5: Masters of Contemporary Brazilian Film* (1984).

JOHNSTON, J. H. "Luther Porter Jackson." *Journal of Negro History* (October 1950): 352–55.

JONAS, JOYCE. *Anancy in the Great House: Ways of Reading West Indian Fiction* (1991).

JONES, HOWARD. *Mutiny on the Amistad: The Saga of a Slave Revolt and its Impact on American Abolition, Law and Diplomacy* (1987).

———. "The Peculiar Institution and National Honor: The Case of the Creole Slave Revolt." *Civil War History* 21 (1975): 28–50.

JONES, JAMES H. *Bad Blood: The Tuskegee Syphilis Experiment* (1993).

JONES, JOYCE. "The Best Commerce Secretary Ever." *Black Enterprise* 26, no. 11 (1990).

JONES, RALPH H. *Charles Albert Tindley: Prince of Preachers* (1982).

JONES, TAD. "Professor Longhair." *Living Blues* 26 (March-April 1976): 16–29.

JORDAN, BARBARA, AND SHELBY HEARON. *Barbara Jordan: A Self-Portrait* (1979).

JOSEPH, CLIFTON. "Jump Up and Beg." *Toronto Life* (August 1996).

JOYCE, DONALD FRANKLIN. *Black Book Publishers in the United States: A Historical Dictionary of the Presses, 1817–1990* (1991).

——. *Gatekeepers of Black Culture: Black-Owned Book Publishing in the United States, 1817–1981* (1983).

JOYCE, PETER. *Anatomy of a Rebel: Smith of Rhodesia: A Biography* (1974).

JOYNER, CHARLES. *Down by the Riverside: A South Carolina Slave Community* (1989).

JULIEN, ISAAC. *Looking for Langston: A Meditation on Langston Hughes (1902–1967) and the Harlem Renaissance, with the Poetry of Essex Hemphill and Bruce Nugent (1906–1987)* (1992).

KAHAN, MITCHELL D. *Heavenly Visions: The Art of Minnie Evans* (1986).

KAPLAN, SIDNEY. "The Miscegenation Issue in the Election of 1864." In *American Studies in Black and White: Selected Essays, 1949–1989*, ed. Allan D. Austin (1991): 47–100.

KAPLAN, SIDNEY, AND EMMA NOGRADY KAPLAN. *The Black Presence in the Era of the American Revolution*. 2d ed. (1989).

KAPLAN, STEVEN. *The Beta Israel (Falasha) in Ethiopia: From Earliest Times to the Twentieth Century* (1992).

KARENGA, MAULANA. *The African American Holiday of Kwanzaa: A Celebration of Family, Community, and Culture* (1988).

——. *Introduction to Black Studies*. 2d ed. (1993).

KATZ, JONATHAN. *Resistance at Christiana: The Fugitive Slave Rebellion, Christiana, Pennsylvania, September 11, 1851: A Documentary Account* (1974).

KATZMAN, DAVID. *Before the Ghetto: Black Detroit in the Nineteenth Century* (1973).

KATZ, WILLIAM L. *Black People Who Made the Old West* (1992).

——. *The Black West* (1987).

KECKLEY, ELIZABETH. *Behind the Scenes; or, Thirty Years a Slave and Four Years in the White House* (1868).

KELLEY, ROBIN D. G. *Hammer and Hoe: Alabama Communists During the Great Depression* (1990).

KENNEDY, ADRIENNE. *People Who Led to My Plays* (1987).

KENNEDY, RANDALL. *Dred Scott and African American Citizenship* (1996).

——. *Race, Crime, and the Law* (1997).

KENNEY, WILLIAM HOWLAND. *Chicago Jazz: A Cultural History, 1904–1930* (1993).

——. "Jimmie Noone, Chicago's Classical Jazz Clarinetist." *American Music* 4 (1986): 145–58.

KENYATTA, JOMO. *Facing Mount Kenya: The Tribal Life of the Gikuyu* (1938).

KEPPEL, BEN. *The Work of Democracy: Ralph Bunche, Kenneth B. Clark, Lorraine Hansberry, and the Cultural Politics of Race* (1995).

KESSELMAN, LOUIS. *The Social Politics of FEPC: A Study in Reform Pressure Movements* (1948).

KESSLER, JAMES H. *Distinguished African American Scientists of the Twentieth Century* (1996).

KESTELOOT, LILYAN. *Black Writers in French: A Literary History of Negritude.* Translated by Ellen Conroy Kennedy (1991).

KEVLES, DANIEL. *In the Name of Eugenics: Genetics and the Uses of Human Heredity* (1985).

KHAZANOV, A. *Agostinho Neto* (1986).

KIM, AEHYUNG, AND BRUCE BENTON. *Cost-benefit Analysis of the Onchocerca Control Program (OCP)* (1995).

KINCAID, JAMAICA. *A Small Place* (1988).

KING, B. B., WITH DAVID RITZ. *Blues All Around Me: The Autobiography of B. B. King* (1996).

KING, BRUCE, ED. *West Indian Literature* (1979).

KING, CORETTA SCOTT. *My Life with Martin Luther King, Jr.* (1969).

KINGDON, ZACHARY, "Chanuo Maundu: Master of Makonde Blackwood Art." *African Arts* (Autumn 1996).

KIPLE, KENNETH F. *The Caribbean Slave: A Biological History* (1984).

KIRSH, ANDREA, AND SUSAN FISHER STERLING. *Carrie Mae Weems* (1992).

KIRWAN, ALBERT DENNIS. *John J. Crittenden: The Struggle for the Union* (1962).

KISKA, TIM. "CBS' Ed Bradley Recalls Childhood Days in Detroit." *Detroit News* (March 21, 1997) A, 2:2.

KITT, EARTHA. *Alone with Me* (1976).

——. *Thursday's Child* (1956).

KITWANA, BAKARI. *The Rap on Gangsta Rap: Who Run It? Gangsta Rap and Visions of Black Violence* (1994).

KLAPISCH, BOB. *High and Tight: The Rise and Fall of Dwight Gooden and Darryl Strawberry* (1996).

KLEHR, HARVEY. *The Heyday of American Communism: The Depression Decade* (1984).

KLEIN, HERBERT S. *African Slavery in Latin America and the Caribbean* (1986).

——. *The Middle Passage: Comparative Studies in the Atlantic Slave Trade* (1978).

——. *Slavery in the Americas: A Comparative Study of Virginia and Cuba* (1967).

KLEMENT, FRANK L. *The Copperheads of the Middle West* (1972).

KLEPPNER, PAUL. Chicago *Divided: The Making of a Black Mayor* (1985).

KLOTMAN, PHYLLIS RAUCH, ED. *Screenplays of the African American Experience* (1991).

KLOTS, STEVE. *Richard Allen* (1991).

KLUGER, RICHARD. *Simple Justice: The History of Brown v. Board of Education and Black America's Struggle for Equality* (1975).

KNAACK, TWILA. *Ethel Waters: I Touched a Sparrow* (1978).

KNIGHT, FRANKLIN. *The African Dimension in Latin American Societies* (1974).

——. *Slavery and the Transformation of Society in Cuba, 1511–1760: From Settler Society to Slave Society* (1988).

KNIGHT, GLADYS. *Between Each Line of Pain and Glory: My Life Story* (1997).

KOLCHIN, PETER. *American Slavery, 1619–1877* (1993).

KONCZACKI, Z. A. *The Economics of Pastoralism: A Case Study of Sub-Saharan Africa* (1978).

KOOK, HETTY, AND GORETTI NARAIN. "Papiamento." In *Community Languages in the Netherlands*, ed. Guus Extra and Ludo Verhoeven (1993): 69–91.

KORNWEIBEL, THEODORE, JR. *No Crystal Stair: Black Life and the Messenger, 1917–1928* (1975).

KOSTARAS, JAMES GEORGE. *Fez: Transformation of the Traditional Urban Environment* (1986).

KOSTARELOS, FRANCES. *Feeling the Spirit: Faith and Hope in an Evangelical Black Storefront Church* (1995).

KOTLOWITZ, ALEX. "A Bridge Too Far? Benjamin Chavis." *New York Times Magazine* (June 12, 1994).

KOTTAK, CONRAD P. *The Past and the Present: History, Ecology, and Cultural Variation in Highland Madagascar* (1980).

KOUSSER, J. MORGAN. *The Shaping of Southern Politics: Suffrage Restriction and the Establishment of the One-Party South, 1880–1910* (1974).

KRADITOR, AILEEN S. *Means and Ends in American Abolitionism: Garrison and his Critics on Strategy and Tactics, 1834–1850* (1989).

KREAMER, CHRISTINE M. *A Life Well Lived: Fantasy Coffins of Kane Quaye* (1994).

KREMER, GARY R., ED. *George Washington Carver in His Own Words* (1987).

KUREISHI, H. "Dirty Washing." *Time Out* (London) ( November 14–20, 1985).

KUSMER, KENNETH. *A Ghetto Takes Shape: Black Cleveland, 1870–1930* (1976).

KUTZINKSI, VERA. *Sugar's Secrets: Race and the Erotics of Cuban Nationalism* (1993).

KWAMENAH-POH, M., J.TOSH, R. WALLER, AND M. TIDY, *African History in Maps* (1982).

LABELLE, MICHELINE. *Idéologie de couleur et classes sociales en Haïti*. 2d ed. (1987).

LABOV, WILLIAM. *Language in the Inner City: Studies in the Black English Vernacular* (1972).

LA GUERRE, JOHN GAFFAR. *Enemies of Empire* (1984).

LAMBERT, BRUCE. "Doxey Wilkerson is Dead at 88: Educator and Advocate for Rights." *New York Times* (June 18, 1993): D 16.

LANE, ANN J. *The Brownsville Affair: National Crisis and Black Reaction* (1971).

LANE, ROGER. *Roots of Violence in Black Philadelphia, 1860–1900* (1986).

LANNING, MICHAEL LEE, LT. COL. (RET.). *The African-American Soldier: From Crispus Attucks to Colin Powell* (1997).

LAPP, RUDOLPH M. *Blacks in Gold Rush California* (1977).

LAURINO, MARIA. "Sensitivity Comes From 'The Soles of the Feet.'" Interview with Anna Deveare Smith, *New York Newsday* (Feb. 23, 1994).

LAWLAH, JOHN W. "The President-Elect." *Journal of the National Medical Association* 55 (November 1963): 551–554.

LAWRENCE, ELIZABETH A. *Rodeo: An Anthropologist Looks at the Wild and the Tame* (1982).

LEAMAN, OLIVER. *Averroes and His Philosophy* (1988).

LEAVY, WALTER. "Howard University: A Unique Center of Excellence." *Ebony* (September 1985): 140–142.

——. "Is Tony Gwynn the Greatest Hitter in Baseball History?" *Ebony* (August 1997): 132.

LECKIE, WILLIAM. *The Buffalo Soldiers: A Narrative of the Negro Cavalry in the West* (1967).

LEEDS, ANTHONY, AND ELIZABETH LEEDS. *A Sociologia do Brasil Urbano (The Sociology of Urban Brazil)*. Translated by Maria Laura Viveiros de Castro (1977).

LEE, JARENA. *The Life and Religious Experience of Jarena Lee* (1849). Reprinted in *Sisters of the Spirit: Three Black Women's Autobiographies of the Nineteenth Century*. Edited by William L. Andrews (1986).

LEEMING, DAVID. *James Baldwin: A Biography* (1994).

LEES, GENE. *Oscar Peterson: The Will to Swing* (1988).

LEFEVER, ERNEST W. *Crisis in the Congo: A United Nations Force in Action* (1965).

LEGUM, COLIN, AND GEOFFREY MMARI. *Mwalimu: The Influence of Nyerere* (1995).

LEMANN, NICHOLAS. *The Promised Land: The Great Black Migration and How It Changed America* (1991).

LEMARCHAND, RENÈ. *Political Awakening in the Belgian Congo* (1964).

LEÓN, ARGELIERS. *Del canto y el tiempo* (1984).

LEON, ELI. *Who'd a Thought It: Improvisation in African-American Quiltmaking* (1987).

LEONS, WILLIAM, AND ALLYN MACLEON STEARMAN. *Anthropological Investigations in Bolivia* (1984).

LEREBOURS, MICHEL PHILIPPE. *Haïti et ses peintres*. 2 vols. (1989).

LERNER, GERDA, ED. *Black Women in White America: A Documentary History* (1972).

LERNER, MICHAEL, AND CORNEL WEST. *Jews and Blacks: Let the Healing Begin* (1995).

LESLAU, WOLF, TRANS. *Falasha Anthology* (1954).

LESLIE, WINESOME J. *Zaire: Continuity and Political Change in an Oppressive State* (1993).

LEVINE, DONALD N. *Greater Ethiopia: The Evolution of a Multi-Ethnic Society* (1974).

LEVINE, LAWRENCE W. *Black Culture and Black Consciousness* (1977).

LEVINE, ROBERT M., AND JOSÈ CARLOS SEBE BOM MEIHY. *The Life and Death of Carolina Maria de Jesus* (1995).

LEWIS, DAVID LEVERING. *W. E. B. Du Bois: Biography of a Race* (1993).

——. *When Harlem Was in Vogue* (1981).

LEWIS, GORDON K. *Main Currents in Caribbean Thought: The Historical Experience of Caribbean Society and its Ideological Aspects, 1492–1900* (1983).

LEWIS, LANCELOT S. *The West Indian in Panama: Black Labor in Panama, 1850–1914* (1980).

LEWIS, MARVÍN A. *Ethnicity and Identity in Contemporary Afro-Venezuelan Literature: A Culturalist Approach* (1992).

LEWIS, MARY L. "The White Rose Industrial Association: The Friend of the Strange Girl in New York." *Messenger* 7 (April 1925): 158.

LEWIS, SAMELLA. *African American Art and Artists* (1990).

——. *The Art of Elizabeth Catlett* (1984).

LEWIS, SAMELLA, AND RICHARD POWELL. *Elizabeth Catlett: Works on Paper,* *1944–1992* (1993).

LHAYA, PEDRO. *Juan Pablo Sojo, pasión y acento de su tierra* (1968).

LIBBY, BILL. *Goliath: The Wilt Chamberlain Story* (1977).

LICHTENSTEIN, GRACE, AND LAURA DANKNER. *Musical Gumbo: The Music of New* *Orleans* (1993).

LIEBENOW, J. GUS. *Colonial Rule and Political Development in Tanzania: The Case of* *the Makonde* (1971).

LIEB, SANDRA. *Mother of the Blues: A Study of Ma Rainey* (1981).

LIGHT, ALAN. "Curtis Mayfield: An Interview." *Rolling Stone* (October 28, 1993).

LINARES, OLGA. *Power, Prayer, and Production: The Jola of Casamance, Senegal* (1992).

LINCOLN, C. ERIC, AND LAWRENCE MAMIYA. *The Black Church in the African* *American Experience* (1990).

LINSLEY, ROBERT. "Wifredo Lam: Painter of Negritude." *Art History* 2, no. 4 (1988): 527–544.

LIPSKI, JOHN M. *The Speech of the Negros Congos of Panama* (1989).

LIPZITZ, GEORGE. *A Life in the Struggle: Ivory Perry and the Culture of Opposition* (1988).

LITVIN, MARTIN. *Hiram Revels in Illinois: A Biographical Novel about a Lost Chapter* *in the Life of America's First Black U.S. Senator* (1974).

LITWACK, LEON F. *Been in the Storm So Long: The Aftermath of Slavery* (1979).

———. *Trouble in Mind: Black Southerners in the Age of Jim Crow* (1998).

LITWACK, LEON F., AND AUGUST MEIER, EDS. *Black Leaders of the Nineteenth Century* (1988).

LIVINGSTON, JANE, JOHN BEARDSLEY, AND REGINIA PERRY. *Black Folk Art in America,* *1930–1980* (1982).

LLERENA VILLALOBOS, RITO. *Memoria cultural en el vallenato* (1985).

LLEWELYN-DAVIES, MELISSA. *Some Women of Marrakech.* Videotape, Granada Television (1981).

LOCKE, ALAIN. *The New Negro* (1925).

LOCKE, MARY. *Anti-Slavery in America from the Introduction of African slaves to the* *Prohibition of the Slave Trade (1619–1808)* (1901).

LOCKE, THERESA A. "Willa Brown-Chappell, Mother of Black Aviation." *Negro* *History Bulletin* 50 (January-June 1987): 5–6.

LOCKHART, JAMES. *Spanish Peru, 1532–1560: A Social History* (1994).

LODER, KURT. "Bo Diddley Interview." *Rolling Stone* (February 12, 1987).

LOFTON, JOHN. *Denmark Vesey's Revolt: The Slave Plot that Lit a Fuse to Fort Sumter* (1983).

LOGAN, RAYFORD. *Howard University: The First Hundred Years, 1867–1967* (1969).

LOGAN, RAYFORD, AND MICHAEL R. WINSTON. *Dictionary of American Negro* *Biography* (1982).

LOMAX, ALAN. *Mister Jelly Roll: The Fortunes of Jelly Roll Morton, New Orleans* *Creole and Inventor of Jazz* (1973).

———. *The Land Where the Blues Began* (1993).

LONG, RICHARD. *The Black Tradition in American Dance* (1989).

LOOS, DOROTHY SCOTT. *The Naturalistic Novel of Brazil* (1963).

LOPES, HELENA T. *Negro e cultura no Brasil* (1987).

LOPES, JOSÈ SERGIO LEITE. "Successes and Contradictions in 'Multiracial' Brazilian Football." In *Entering the Field: New Perspectives on World Football*, ed. Gary Armstrong and Richard Giulianotti (1997).

LOTZ, RAINER, AND IAN PEGG, EDS. *Under the Imperial Carpet: Essays in Black History, 1780–1950* (1990).

LOVE, NAT. *The Life and Adventures of Nat Love, Better Known in the Cattle Country as "Deadwood Dick"* (1907; reprint ed., 1995).

LOVE, SPENCIE. *One Blood: The Death and Resurrection of Charles Drew* (1996).

LOVETT, CHARLES C. *Olympic Marathon: A Centennial History of the Games' Most Storied Race* (1997).

LOZANO, WILFREDO, ED. *La cuestión haitiana en Santo Domingo* (1992).

LUIS, WILLIAM. *Literary Bondage : Slavery in Cuban Narrative* (1990).

——, ed. *Voices from Under: Black Narrative in Latin America and the Caribbean* (1984).

LUMDSEN, I. *Society and the State in Mexico* (1991).

LUNDY, ANNE. "Conversations with Three Symphonic Conductors: Dennis De Couteau, Tania Leon, Jon Robinson." *Black Perspective in Music*, no. 2 (Fall 1988): 213–25.

LYNCH, HOLLIS R. *Black American Radicals and the Liberation of Africa: The Council on African Affairs, 1937–1955* (1978).

LYNCH, JOHN ROY. *Reminiscences of an Active Life: The Autobiography of John Roy Lynch*. Edited by John Hope Franklin (1970).

LYONS, LEONARD. *The Great Jazz Pianists: Speaking of Their Lives and Music* (1983).

MACDONALD, J. FRED. *Blacks and White TV: African Americans in Television Since 1948*. Rev. ed. (1992).

MACEO, ANTONIO. *El pensamiento vivo de Maceo: Cartas, proclamas, articulos y documentas*. Edited by José Antonio Portuondo (1960).

MACGAFFEY, WYATT. *Religion and Society in Central Africa: The BaKongo of Lower Zaire* (1986).

MACHARIA, KINUTHIA. *Social and Political Dynamics of the Informal Economy in African Cities: Nairobi and Harare* (1997).

MACKEY, NATHANIEL, ED. "Wilson Harris Special Issue." *Callaloo* (1995).

MACROBERT, IAIN. *The Black Roots and White Racism of Early Pentecostalism in the U.S.A.* (1988).

MAES-JELINEK, HENA, ED. *Commonwealth Literature and the Modern World* (1975).

MAGALHÃES, R., JR. *A Vida Turbulenta de Josè do Patrocínio* (1972).

MAGUBANE, VUKANI. "Graca Machel." *Ebony* (May 1997).

MAIN, MICHAEL. *Kalahari: Life's Variety in Dune and Delta* (1987).

MAIO, MARCOS CHOR. *A História do Projeto UNESCO: Estudos raciais e ciíncias sociais no Brasil* (1997).

MAIR, GEORGE. *Oprah Winfrey: The Real Story* (1994).

MAKEBA, MIRIAM, WITH JAMES HALL. *Makeba: My Story* (1988).

MALCOLM X, WITH ALEX HALEY. *The Autobiography of Malcolm X* (1964).

MALONE, JACQUI. *Steppin' on the Blues: The Visible Rhythms of African-American Dance* (1996).

MALTBY, MARC S. *The Origins and Early Development of Professional Football* (1997).

MANDELA, NELSON. *Long Walk to Freedom: The Autobiography of Nelson Mandela* (1994).

——. *The Struggle Is My Life: His Speeches and Writings Brought Together to Mark His 60th Birthday* (1978).

MANESS, LONNIE E. "The Fort Pillow Massacre: Fact or Fiction." *Tennessee Historical Quarterly* 48 (Winter 1986): 287–315.

MANGIONE, JERRE. *The Dream and the Deal: The Federal Writers' Project, 1935–1945* (1972).

MANLEY, ALBERT E. *A Legacy Continues: The Manley Years at Spelman College, 1953–1976* (1995).

MANNICK, A. R. *Mauritius: The Politics of Change* (1989).

MANUEL, PETER, ED. *Essays on Cuban Music: North American and Cuban Perspectives* (1991).

MANUEL, PETER, WITH KENNETH BILBY AND MICHAEL LARGEY. *Caribbean Currents: Caribbean Music from Rumba to Reggae* (1995).

MANUH, TAKYIWAA. "Diasporas, Unities, and the Marketplace: Tracing Changes in Ghanaian Fashion." *Journal of African Studies* 16, no.1 (Winter 1998).

MAPP, EDWARD. *Directory of Blacks in the Performing Arts* (1990).

MARCUS, HAROLD G. *A History of Ethiopia* (1994).

MARKMANN, CHARLES LAM. *The Noblest Cry: A History of the American Civil Liberties Union* (1965).

MARKOWITZ, GERALD E., AND DAVID ROSNER. *Children, Race, and Power: Kenneth and Mamie Clark's Northside Center* (1996).

MARQUIS, DONALD M. *In Search of Buddy Bolden: First Man of Jazz* (1978).

MARSHALL, RICHARD, ET. AL. *Jean-Michel Basquiat* (1992).

MARSH, J. B. T. *The Story of the Jubilee Singers with Their Songs* (1880; reprint ed., 1971).

MARTEENA, CONSTANCE HILL. *The Lengthening Shadow of a Woman: A Biography of Charlotte Hawkins Brown* (1977).

MARTÍ, JOSÉ. CUBA, *Nuestra América, los Estados Unidos* (1973).

——. *En los Estados Unidos* (1968).

MARTIN, ESMOND BRADLEY. *Zanzibar: Tradition and Revolution* (1978).

MARTIN, JAY, ED. *A Singer in the Dawn: Reinterpretations of Paul Laurence Dunbar* (1975).

MARTIN, MARIE-LOUISE. *Kimbangu: An African Prophet and His Church* (1975).

MARTIN, MICHAEL T., ED. *Cinemas of the Black Diaspora: Diversity, Dependence, and Oppositionality* (1995).

MARTIN, REGINALD. *Ishmael Reed and the New Black Aesthetic Critics* (1988).

——. "Total Life Is What We Want: The Progressive Stages of the New Black Aesthetic in Literature." *South Atlantic Review* (November 1986): 46–47.

MARTINS, LEDA MARIA. *A cena em sombras* (1995).

MARTIN, TONY. *Race First: The Ideological and Organizational Struggles of Marcus Garvey and the Universal Negro Improvement Association* (1986).

MASON, TONY. *Passion of the People? Football in South America* (1995).

MATORY, J. LORAND. *Sex and the Empire That Is No More: Gender and the Politics of Metaphor in Oyo Yoruba Religion* (1994).

MATTA, ROBERTO DA. CARNIVALS, *Rogues, and Heroes: An Interpretation of the Brazilian Dilemma*. Translated by John Drury (1991).

MATTHEWS, MARCIA M. *Henry Ossawa Tanner, American Artist* (1969).

MATTOSO, KATIA M. DE QUEIRÓS. *To Be a Slave in Brazil, 1550–1888*. Translated by Arthur Goldhammer (1994).

MAYNARD, OLGA. *Judith Jamison: Aspects of a Dancer* (1982).

MAZRUI, ALI A. *The Africans: A Triple Heritage* (1986).

MCADAM, DOUG. *Freedom Summer* (1988).

MCBROOME, DELORES NASON. *Parallel Communities: African Americans in California's East Bay, 1850–1963* (1993).

MCCABE, BRUCE. "Bringing the Streets to the Stage." *Boston Globe* (April 18, 1997): F 3.

MCCORMICK, RICHARD P. "William Whipper: Moral Reformer." *Pennsylvania History* 43 (January 1976): 22–46.

MCDONNELL, PATRICK, KAREN O'CONNELL, AND GEORGIA RILEY DE HAVENON. *Krazy Kat: The Comic Art of George Herriman* (1986).

MCDOWELL, ROBERT. "The Assembling Vision of Rita Dove." *Callaloo* 9 (Winter 1986): 61–70.

MCELVAINE, ROBERT S. *The Great Depression: America, 1929–1941* (1984).

MCFEELY, WILLIAM S. *Frederick Douglass* (1991).

MCGOWAN, CHRIS, AND RICARDO PESSANHA. *The Brazilian Sound: Samba, Bossa Nova, and the Popular Music of Brazil* (1991).

MCKIBLE, ADAM. "'These Are the Facts of the Darky's History': Thinking History and Reading Names in Four African American Tests." *African American Review* 28 (1994): 223–35.

MCKIVIGAN, JOHN R. *The War against Proslavery Religion: Abolitionism and the Northern Churches, 1830–1865* (1984).

MCLARIN, KIMBERLY J. *Native Daughter* (1994).

MCLENDON, JACQUELYN Y. *The Politics of Color in the Fiction of Jessie Fauset and Nella Larsen* (1995).

MCMILLAN, DELLA E. *Sahel Visions: Planned Settlement and River Blindness Control in Burkina Faso* (1995).

MCMURRY, LINDA O. *Recorder of the Black Experience: A Biography of Monroe Nathan Work* (1985).

MCNEIL, GENNA RAE. *Groundwork: Charles Hamilton Houston and the Struggle for Civil Rights* (1983).

MCPHERSON, JAMES M. *The Negro's Civil War: How American Negroes Felt and Acted During the War for the Union* (1965).

MEIER, AUGUST. "Introduction: Benjamin Quarles and the Historiography of Black America." In *Benjamin Quarles, Black Mosaic: Essays in Afro-American History and Historiography* (1989): 3–21.

———. *Negro Thought in America,1880–1915: Racial Ideologies in the Age of Booker T. Washington* (1963).

MEIER, AUGUST, AND JOHN H. BRACEY, JR. "The NAACP as a Reform Movement: 1909–1965." *Journal of Southern History* 49, no. 1 (February 1993).

MEIER, AUGUST, AND ELLIOTT RUDWICK. *Black History and the Historical Profession* (1986).

———. *CORE: A Study in the Civil Rights Movement, 1942–1968* (1973).

MELHEM, D.H. "Dudley Randall: A Humanist View." *Black American Literature Forum* 17 (1983).

MELLAFE R., ROLANDO. *La introducción de la esclavitud negra en Chile: Tráfico y rutas* (1984).

MENTON, SEYMOUR. *Prose Fiction of the Cuban Revolution* (1975).

MERCER, K. "Imagining the Black Man's Sex." In *Photography/Politics: Two*, ed. P. Holland et. al. (1987).

MÉRIAN, JEAN-YVES. *Aluísio Azevedo, Vida e Obra (1857–1913): O Verdadeiro Brasil do Século XIX* (1988).

METCALF, GEORGE R. *Black Profiles* (1968).

MÉTRAUX, ALFRED. "UNESCO and the Racial Problem." *International Social Science Bulletin* 2, no. 3 (1950): 384–90.

———. *Voodoo in Haiti* (1959).

MIDDLETON, JOHN, ED. *Encyclopedia of Africa South of the Sahara.* 4 vols. (1997).

MILES, ALEXANDER. *Devil's Island: Colony of the Damned* (1988).

MILLER, ERROL. *Education for all: Caribbean Perspectives and Imperatives* (1992).

MILLER, FLOYD J. *The Search for a Black Nationality: Black Colonization and Emigration, 1787–1863* (1975).

MILLER, RANDALL M., AND JOHN DAVID SMITH, EDS. *Dictionary of Afro-American Slavery.* 2d ed. (1997).

MILLS, KAY. "Maxine Waters: 'I Don't Pretend to Be Nice No Matter What . . . '." *The Progressive* (December 1993).

MINER, HORACE. *The Primitive City of Timbuctoo* (1954).

MINNICK-TAYLOR, KATHLEEN, AND CHARLES TAYLOR II. *Kwanzaa: How to Celebrate It in Your Own Home* (1994).

MINORITY RIGHTS GROUP, ED. *No Longer Invisible: Afro-Latin Americans Today* (1995).

MINTER, WILLIAM. *Apartheid's Contras: An Inquiry into the Roots of War in Angola and Mozambique* (1994).

MINTZ, SIDNEY. *Sweetness and Power* (1985).

MINTZ, SIDNEY, AND SALLY PRICE, EDS. *Caribbean Contours* (1985).

MImanyara, ALFRED M. *The Restatement of Bantu Origin and Meru History* (1992).

MOBERG, MARK. *Myths of Ethnicity and Nation: Immigration, Work, and Identity in the Belize Banana Industry* (1997).

*Models in the Mind: African Prototypes in American Patchwork* (1992).

MOISE, CLAUDE. *Constitutions et luttes de pouvoir en Haiti (1804–1987)* (1988–1990).

MOISÉS, MASSAUD. *História da literatura Brasileira. Vol. II* (1989).

MOON, ELAINE LATZMAN, ED. *Untold Tales, Unsung Heroes: An Oral History of Detroit's African American Community, 1918–1967* (1994).

MOOREHEAD, ALAN. *The White Nile* (1971).

MOORE, JESSE THOMAS. *A Search for Equality: The National Urban League, 1910–1961* (1981).

MOORE, JOSEPH THOMAS. *Pride Against Prejudice: The Biography of Larry Doby* (1988).

MOORE, ROBIN. *Nationalizing Blackness: Afrocubanismo and Artistic Revolution in Havana, 1920–40* (1997).

MOORE, ZELBERT L. "Solano Trindade Remembered, 1908–1974." *Luso-Brazilian Review* 16 (1979): 233–38.

MORALES, FLORENTINO. "El poeta esclavo." *Conceptos* 2, no. 27 (December 1989): 2–3.

MORAN, CHARLES. *Black Triumvirate: A Study of L'Ouverture, Dessalines, Christophe: The Men Who Made Haiti* (1957).

MORDECAI, PAMELA, AND BETTY WILSON, EDS. *Her True-True Name* (1989).

MORELL, VIRGINIA. *Ancestral Passions: The Leakey Family and the Quest for Humankind's Beginnings* (1995).

MORENO NAVARRO, ISIDORO. *Los cuadros del mestizaje americano: Estudio antropológico del mestizaje* (1973).

MORGAN, PHILIP D. *Slave Counterpoint: Black Culture in the Eighteenth-Century Chesapeake and Lowcountry* (1998).

MORGAN, THOMAS L., AND WILLIAM BARLOW. *From Cakewalks to Concert Halls: An Illustrated History of African American Popular Music from 1895–1930* (1992).

MORNA, COLLEEN. "Graca Machel: Interview." *Africa Report* (July-August 1988).

MORRIS, MERVYN. "Louise Bennett." In *Encyclopedia of Post-Colonial Literatures in English*. Vol. I, ed. Eugene Benson and L. W. Conolly (1994).

MORRIS, THOMAS D. *Free Men All: The Personal Liberty Laws of the North, 1780–1861* (1974).

MORRISON, TONI. *Playing in the Dark: Whiteness and the Literary Imagination* (1992).

———, ed. *Race-ing Justice, En-gendering Power: Essays on Anita Hill, Clarence Thomas, and the Construction of Social Reality* (1992).

MORROW, CURTIS. *What's A Commie Ever Done to Black People?: A Korean War Memoir of Fighting in the U.S. Army's Last All Negro Unit* (1997).

MORSE, STEPHEN S. *Emerging Viruses* (1993).

MORSHA, A. C. "Urban Planning in Tanzania at the Crossroads." *Review of Rural and Urban Planning in Southern and Eastern Africa* (1989): 79–91.

MOSBY, DEWEY F., DARRELL SEWELL, AND RAE ALEXANDER-MINTER. *Henry Ossawa Tanner* (1991).

MOSELEY, THOMAS ROBERT. "A History of the New York Manumission Society." Ph.D. Diss. University of Michigan, 1963.

MOSES, WILSON JEREMIAH. *Black Messiahs and Uncle Toms: Social and Literary Manipulation of a Religious Myth* (1982).

———. *The Golden Age of Black Nationalism: 1850–1925* (1978).

MOSQUERA, GERARDO. "Modernism from Afro-America: Wifredo Lam." *In Beyond the Fantastic: Contemporary Art Criticism from Latin America*, ed. Gerardo Mosquera (1996).

MOSS, ALFRED A., JR. *The American Negro Academy: Voice of the Talented Tenth* (1981).

MOTA, ANA MARITZA DE LA. "Palma Sola: 1962," *Boletín: Museo de hombre dominicano* 14 (1980): 197–223.

MOTT, LUIZ. ESCRAVID„O, *Homossexualidade e Demonologia* (1988).

MOUNTOUSSAMY-ASHE, JEANNE. *View-finders: Black Women Photographers* (1986).

MUDIMBE-BOYI, ELISABETH. *L'oeuvre romanesque de Jacques-Stèphen Alexis : Une ècriture poètique, un engagement politique* (1992).

MUDIMBE, VALENTIN. *The Invention of Africa: Gnosis, Philosophy, and the Order of Knowledge* (1988).

MUNFORD, CLARENCE. *Race and Reparations: A Black Perspective for the Twenty-First Century* (1996).

MUNRO-HAY, STUART. *Aksum: An African Civilization of Late Antiquity* (1991).

MUNRO-HAY, STUART, AND RICHARD PANKHURST. *Ethiopia* (1995).

MUNSLOW, BARRY, ED. *Samora Machel, An African Revolutionary: Selected Speeches and Writings* (1985).

MURPHY, JOSEPH M. *Working the Spirit: Ceremonies of the African Diaspora* (1994).

MURRAY, PAULI. *Dark Testament and Other Poems* (1970).

———. *Proud Shoes: The Story of an American Family* (1956).

———. *Song in a Weary Throat: An American Pilgrimage* (1987).

MUSICK, PHIL. *Reflections on Roberto* (1994).

MYRDAL, GUNNAR. *An American Dilemma: The Negro Problem and Modern Democracy* (1944).

NADEL, ALAN, ED. *May All of Your Fences Have Gates: Essays on the Drama of August Wilson* (1994).

NAISON, MARK. *Communists in Harlem During the Depression* (1983).

NALTY, BERNARD C. *Strength for the Fight: A History of Black Americans in the Military* (1986).

NASCIMENTO, ABDIAS DO. *Africans in Brazil: A Pan-African Perspective* (1992).

———. *Dramas para negros e prologo para brancos: Antologia de teatro negro-brasileiro.* (1961).

———. *Orixas: Os deuses vivos da Africa* (1995).

———. *O quilombismo: Documentos de uma militancia pan-africanista* (1980).

———. *Racial Democracy in Brazil, Myth or Reality?: A Dossier of Brazilian Racism.* Translated by Elisa Larkin do Nascimento; foreword by Wole Soyinka (1977).

———, ed. *O Negro revoltado* (1968).

NASH, GARY B. *Forging Freedom: The Formation of Philadelphia's Black Community, 1720–1840* (1988).

———. *Race and Revolution* (1990).

NAVARRETE, MARÍA CRISTINA. *Historia social del negro en la colonia: Cartagena, siglo XVII* (1995).

NAVARRO, DESIDERIO. *Ejercicios del criterio* (1988).

NEFT, DAVID S. *The Football Encyclopedia: The Complete History of Professional NFL Football, from 1892 to the Present* (1991).

NEWBY, I. A. *Black Carolinians: A History of Blacks in South Carolina from 1895 to 1968* (1973).

NEWFIELD, JACK. *Only in America: The Life and Crimes of Don King* (1995).

NEWMAN, RICHARD. *Words Like Freedom: Essays on African-American Culture and History* (1996).

———. Lemuel Haynes: *A Bio-bibliography* (1984).

———, comp. *Black Access: A Bibliography of Afro-American Bibliographies* (1984).

NEWTON, HUEY P. *To Die for the People: The Writings of Huey Newton* (1972).

———. *War Against the Panthers: A Study of Repression in America* (1997).

"New Voice of the NAACP." Interview in *Newsweek* 46 (November 22, 1976).

NGUGI WA THIONG'O. *Decolonising the Mind: The Politics of Language in African Literature* (1986).

———. *Moving the Centre: The Struggle for Cultural Freedoms* (1993).

NICOLAS, ARMAND. *Histoire de la Martinique*. 2 vols. (1996).

———. *La rèvolution antiesclavagiste de mai 1848 à la Martinique* (1967).

NINA RODRIGUES, RAIMUNDO. *Os Africanos no Brasil* (1977).

NKOMO, JOSHUA. *Nkomo: The Story of My Life* (1984).

———. *Zimbabwe Must and Shall be Totally Free* (1977).

NOBLE, PETER. *The Negro in Films* (1948).

NOBRE, CARLOS. *Mães de Acari: Uma história de luta contra a impunidade* (1994).

NOONAN, JOHN T. *The Antelope: The Ordeal of the Recaptured Africans in the Administrations of James Monroe and John Quincy Adams* (1977).

NORMENT, LYNN. "Vanessa L. Williams: On her Painful Divorce, the Pressures of Superstardom and her New Life as a Single Mom." *Ebony* (October 1997).

NORRIS, H. T. *The Berbers in Arabic Literature* (1982).

NORRIS, JERRIE. *Presenting Rosa Guy* (1988).

NORTHRUP, SOLOMON. *Twelve Years a Slave: Narrative of Solomon Northrup, a Citizen of New York, Kidnapped in Washington City in 1841, and Rescued in 1853, from a Cotton Plantation near the Red River, in Louisiana* (1853).

NOTCUTT, LESLIE A., AND GEORGE C. LANTHAM. *The African and the Cinema: An Account of the Bantu Educational Cinema Experiment During the Period March 1935 to May 1937* (1937).

NOTTEN, ELEONORE VAN. *Wallace Thurman's Harlem Renaissance* (1994).

NUGENT, JOHN PEER. *Black Eagle* (1971).

NUNN, JOHN F. *Ancient Egyptian Medicine* (1996).

NYERERE, JULIUS K. *The Arusha Declaration: Ten Years After* (1977).

———. *Freedom and Socialism: Uhuru na Ujamaa: A Selection from Writings and Speeches, 1965–1967* (1968).

———. *Ujamaa: Essays on Socialism* (1971).

OATES, STEPHEN B. *The Fires of Jubilee: Nat Turner's Fierce Rebellion* (1975).

———. *To Purge This Land with Blood: A Biography of John Brown*. 2d ed. (1984).

OBADELE, IMARI. *America the Nation State: The Politics of the United States from a State-Building Perspective* (1988).

OCHS, STEPHEN J. *Desegregating the Altar: The Josephites and the Struggle for Black Priests, 1871–1960* (1970).

OFCANSKY, THOMAS, AND RODGER YEAGER. *Historical Dictionary of Tanzania* (1997).

OGOT, BETHWELL A. *Africa and the Caribbean* (1997).

OÍLIAM, JOSÉ. *O Negro na Economia Mineira* (1993).

OLANIYAN, TEJUMOLA. *Scars of Conquest/Masks of Resistance: The Invention of Cultural Identities in African, African-American, and Caribbean Drama* (1995).

OLIVER, PAUL. *Songsters and Saints: Vocal Traditions on Race Records* (1984).

——, ed. *Black Music in Britain: Essays on the Afro-Asian Contribution to Popular Music* (1990).

OLSON, JAMES STUART. *The Peoples of Africa: An Ethnohistorical Dictionary* (1996).

OLSON, SHERRY. *Baltimore: The Building of an American City*. Rev. and exp. ed. (1997).

OLWIG, KAREN FOG. *Cultural Adaptation and Resistance on St. John: Three Centuries of Afro-Caribbean Life.*

O'MEALLY, ROBERT G. *The Craft of Ralph Ellison* (1980).

OODIAH, MALENN. *Mouvement militant mauritien: 20 ans d'histoire (1969–1989)* (1989).

O'REILLY, KENNETH. *Nixon's Piano: Presidents and Racial Politics from Washington to Clinton* (1995).

ORIARD, MICHAEL. *Reading Football: How the Popular Press Created an American Spectacle* (1993).

ORMOND, ROGER. *The Apartheid Handbook: A Guide to South Africa's Everyday Racial Policies* (1985).

OROVIO, HELIO. *Diccionario de la música cubana: Biográfico y técnico* (1992).

ORTIZ, FERNANDO. *Los bailes y le teatro de los negros en el folklore de cuba* (1951).

——. *Los instrumentos de la musica afrocubana*. 5 vols. (1952–1955).

——. *La música afrocubana* (1974).

——. *Los negros brujos* (1995).

——. *Wifredo Lam y su obra vista a traves de significados criticos* (1950).

ORTIZ, RENATO, "OGUM AND THE UMBANDISTA RELIGION." *In Africa's Ogun: Old World and New*, ed. Santra Barnes (1989): 90–102.

OSOFSKY, GILBERT. *Harlem: The Making of a Ghetto: Negro New York, 1890–1930* (1971; revised ed., 1996).

OSPINA, HERNANDO CALVO. *Salsa: Havana Beat, Bronx Beat* (1985).

OSSMAN, SUSAN. *Picturing Casablanca: Portraits of Power in a Modern City* (1994).

OTHAM, HAROUB. *Zanzibar's Political History: The Past Haunting the Present?* (1993).

OTIS, JOHNNY. *Upside Your Head!: Rhythm and Blues on Central Avenue* (1993).

OTTLEY, ROI. *The Lonely Warrior: The Life and Time of Robert S. Abbott* (1955).

OTTLEY, ROI AND WILLIAM WEATHERBY, EDS. *The Negro in New York: An Informal Social History* (1967).

OWENS, THOMAS. *Bebop: The Music and its Players* (1995).

PACINI HERN·NDEZ, DEBORAH. "The Picó Phenomenon in Cartagena, Colombia." *Amèrica Negra* 6 (December 1993): 69–115.

PAINTER, NELL IRVIN. *Exodusters: Black Migration to Kansas after Reconstruction* (1986).

——. "Martin R. Delany: Elitism and Black Nationalism." In *Black Leaders of the Nineteenth Century*, ed. Leon Litwack and August Meier (1988): 148–171.

——. *Sojourner Truth: A Life, A Symbol* (1996).

PAIVA, EDUARDO FRANCA. *Escravos e libertos nas Minas Gerais do século XVIII: Estratégias de resistência através dos testamentos* (1995).

PALMER, COLIN. *Slaves of the White God: Blacks in Mexico, 1570–1650* (1976).

PALMER, RICHARD. *Oscar Peterson* (1984).

PALMER, ROBERT. *Deep Blues* (1981).

PAQUET, SANDRA POUCHET. *The Novels of George Lamming* (1982).

PARIS, PETER. *Black Religious Leaders: Conflict in Unity* (1991).

PARK, THOMAS K. *Historical Dictionary of Morocco* (1996).

PATTERSON, JAMES T. *America's Struggle Against Poverty, 1900–1994* (1994).

PATTERSON, ORLANDO. *Freedom in the Making of Western Culture* (1991).

——. *The Ordeal of Integration: Progress and Resentment in America's "Racial" Crisis* (1997).

——. *Rituals of Blood: Consequences of Slavery in Two American Centuries* (1998).

PATTERSON, WILLIAM. *The Man Who Cried Genocide: An Autobiography* (1971).

PAUL, JOAN, RICHARD V. MCGHEE, AND HELEN FANT. "The Arrival and Ascendance of Black Athletes in the Southeastern Conference, 1966–1980." *Phylon* 45, no. 4 (1984): 284–97.

PAYNE, DANIEL A. *History of the African Methodist Episcopal Church*. Vol. I (1891; reprint ed., 1968).

PEASE, JANE H., AND WILLIAM H. PEASE. *They Who Would Be Free: Blacks' Search for Freedom, 1830–1861* (1974).

PENKOWER, MONTY NOAM. *The Federal Writers' Project: A Study in Government Patronage of the Arts* (1983).

PENVENNE, JEANNE. *African Workers and Colonial Racism: Mozambican Struggles in LourenÁo Marques, 1877–1962* (1997).

PÉREZ SANJURJO, Elena. *Historia de la m'sica cubana* (1986).

PERKINS, KENNETH J. *Historical Dictionary of Tunisia* (1997).

PERKINS, LINDA M. *Fanny Jackson Coppin and the Institute for Colored Youth: A Model of Nineteenth-Century Black Female Educational and Community Leadership, 1865–1902* (1978).

PERLMAN, JANICE. *The Myth of Marginality: Urban Poverty and Politics in Rio de Janeiro* (1973).

PERN, STEPHEN. *Another Land, Another Sea: Walking Round Lake Rudolph* (1979).

PERRY, BRUCE. *Malcolm: The Life of a Man Who Changed Black America* (1991).

PERRY, REGINA A. *Free Within Ourselves: African-American Artists in the Collection of the National Museum of American Art* (1992).

PETERSON, CARLA. *Doers of the Word: African-American Women Speakers and Writers in the North (1830–1880)* (1995).

PETERSON, KIRSTEN HOLST, AND ANNA RUTHERFORD. *Chinua Achebe: A Celebration* (1991).

PETERSON, ROBERT. *Only the Ball Was White: A History of Legendary Black Players and All-black Professional Teams* (1992).

PETERS, WALLACE, AND HERBERT M. GILLES. *Color Atlas of Tropical Medicine and Parasitology* (1995).

PFAFF, FRANÇOISE. *Conversations with Maryse Condè* (1996).

PHELPS, J. ALFRED. *Chappie: America's First Black Four-Star General: The Life and Times of Daniel James, Jr.* (1991).

PHELPS, TIMOTHY M., AND HELEN WINTERNITZ. *Capitol Games: The Inside Story of Clarence Thomas and Anita Hill, and a Supreme Court Nomination* (1993).

PHILLIPS, CHRISTOPHER. *Freedom's Port: The African American Community of Baltimore, 1790–1860* (1997).

PICTON, JOHN, AND JOHN MACK. *African Textiles* (1989).

PIMPÃO, ÁLVARO JÚLIO DA COSTA. "José Basilio da Gama. Edição Comemorativa do Segundo Centenário." *Brasília* 2 (1942): 777–80.

PINO, JULIO CESAR. *Family and Favela: The Reproduction of Poverty in Rio de Janeiro* (1997).

PINTO, LUIZ DE AGUIAR COSTA. *O Negro no Rio de Janeiro: Relações de raças numa sociedade em mudança* (1953).

PIVEN, FRANCES FOX, AND RICHARD A. CLOWARD. *Poor People's Movements: Why They Succeed, How They Fail* (1977).

PLACKSIN, SALLY. *American Women in Jazz: 1900 to the Present: Their Words, Lives, and Music* (1982).

PLACOLY, VINCENT. *Dessalines, ou, la passion de l'indépendance* (1983).

PLASTOW, JANE. *Ethiopia: The Creation of a Theater Culture* (1989).

PLATO, ANN. *Essays: Including Biographies and Miscellaneous Pieces, in Prose and Poetry* (1841).

PLATT, ANTHONY M. *E. Franklin Frazier Reconsidered* (1991).

PLOWDEN, MARTHA WARD. *Olympic Black Women* (1996).

PLUCHON, PIERRE, AND LOUIS ABENON, EDS. *Histoire des Antilles et de la Guyane* (1982).

POITIER, SIDNEY. *This Life* (1980).

POLAKOFF, CLAIRE. INTO *Indigo: African Textiles and Dyeing Techniques* (1980).

POLLAK-ELTZ, ANGELINA. *Black Culture and Society in Venezuela (La Negritud en Venezuela)* (1994).

——. *La medicina popular en Venezuela* (1987).

——. *La religiosidad popular en Venezuela* (1994).

PORTER, DAVID L., ED. *Biographical Dictionary of American Sports: Basketball and Other Indoor Sports* (1989).

PORTER, DOROTHY B. "Maria Baldwin." *Journal of Negro History* (Winter 1952): 94–96.

PORTER, JAMES AMOS. *Modern Negro Art* (1943).

POSADA, CONSUELO. *Canción vallenata y tradición oral* (1986).

POTASH, CHRIS, ED. *Reggae, Rasta, Revolution: Jamaican Music from Ska to Dub* (1997).

POTTER, DAVID M. *The Impending Crisis, 1848–1861* (1976).

POUPEYE, VEERLE. *Modern Jamaican Art* (1998).

POVOAS, RUY DO CARMO. *A linguagem do candomble: Niveis sociolinguisticos de integração afro-portuguesa* (1989).

POWELL, COLIN L. *My American Journey* (1995).

POWELL, IVOR. *Ndebele: A People and Their Art* (1995).

POWELL, RICHARD J. *Black Art and Culture in the Twentieth Century* (1997).

——. *Homecoming: The Art and Life of William H. Johnson* (1991).

POWLEDGE, FRED. *Free at Last? The Civil Rights Movement and the People Who Made It* (1991).

PRANDI, J. REGINALDO. *Herdeiras do axé: Sociologia das religiões afro-brasileiras* (1996).

PRATHER, H. LEON. *We Have Taken A City: Wilmington Racial Massacre and Coup of 1898* (1984).

PRESCOTT, LAURENCE E. *Candelario Obeso y la iniciación de la poesía negra en Colombia* (1985).

PRICE, JOE X. *Redd Foxx, B.S. (Before Sanford)* (1979).

PRICE-MARS, JEAN. *La Rep'blica de Haiti y la Rep'blica Dominicana* (1958).

PRICE, RICHARD, ED. *Maroon Societies: Rebel Slave Communities in the Americas.* 3d ed. (1996).

PRICE, SALLY, AND RICHARD PRICE. *Maroon Arts: Cultural Vitality in the African Diaspora* (1999).

PRIDE, CHARLEY. *Pride: The Charley Pride Story* (1994).

PRIMM, JAMES NEAL. *Lion of the Valley, St. Louis, Missouri* (1981).

PRUTER, ROBERT. *Doowop: The Chicago Scene* (1996).

PRYSE, MARJORIE. "'Patterns Against the Sky': Deism and the Motherhood in Ann Petry's The Street." In *Conjuring: Black Women, Fiction and Literary Traditions,* ed. Marjorie Pryse and Hortense Spillers (1985).

QUARLES, BENJAMIN. *Black Abolitionists* (1969).

——. *The Negro in the American Revolution* (1961).

——. *The Negro in the Civil War* (1953).

QUERINO, MANUEL. *The African Contribution to Brazilian Civilization.* Translated by E. Bradford Burns (1978).

——. *A Bahia de Outoura* (1955).

——. *Costumes africanos no Brasil* (1938).

——. *A raça africana e os seus costumes* (1955).

QUILLEN, FRANK U. *The Color Line in Ohio* (1913).

QUILOMBHOJE. *Criação crioula, nu elefante branco* (1987).

QUINN, CHARLOTTE. *Mandingo Kingdoms of the Senegambia: Traditionalism, Islam, and European Expansion* (1972).

QUIROZ OTERO, CIRO. *Vallenato: Hombre y canto* (1982).

RABINOWITZ, HOWARD N. *Race Relations in the Urban South, 1865–1890* (1996).

RAGAN, SANDRA L. ET AL, ED. *The Lynching of Language: Gender, Politics, and Power in the Hill-Thomas Hearings* (1996).

RAHIER, JEAN. *La décima: Poesía oral negra del Ecuador* (1987).

RAINWATER, LEE. *Behind Ghetto Walls: Black Families in a Federal Slum* (1970).

RAJOELINA, PATRICK. *Quarante années de la vie politique de Madagascar, 1947–1987* (1988).

RAKE, ALAN. *Who's Who in Africa: Leaders for the 1990s* (1992).

RAKODI, CAROLE. *Harare: Inheriting a Settler-Colonial City: Change or Continuity* (1995).

RAMOS, ARTHUR. *The Negro in Brazil* (1951).

RAMOS GUEDEZ, JOSÉ MARCIAL. *El negro en Venezuela: Aporte bibliografico* (1985).

RAMPERSAD, ARNOLD. *The Art and Imagination of W. E. B. Du Bois* (1990).

——. *Jackie Robinson: A Biography* (1997).

——. *The Life of Langston Hughes.* 2 vols. (1986–1988).

RANVAUD, DON. "Interview with Med Hondo." *Framework* (Spring 1978): 28–30.

*Rap on Rap: Straight Up Talk on Hip Hop Culture.* Compiled by Adam Sexton (1995).

RASKY, FRANK. "Harlem's Religious Zealots." *Tomorrow* (Nov. 1949): 11–17.

RAPER, ARTHUR F. *The Tragedy of Lynching* (1933).

RAWLEY, JAMES A. *The Transatlantic Slave Trade: A History* (1981).

RAY, BENJAMIN. *African Religions: Symbol, Ritual, and Community* (1976).

READER, JOHN. *Africa: A Biography of the Continent* (1998).

READ, FLORENCE. *The Story of Spelman College* (1961).

REDD, LAWRENCE N. *Rock Is Rhythm and Blues: The Impact of Mass Media* (1974).

REDKEY, EDWIN S. *Black Exodus: Black Nationalist and Back-to-Africa Movements, 1890–1910* (1969).

REDMON, COATES. *Come As You Are: The Peace Corps Story* (1986).

REGO, WALDELOIR. *Capoeira Angola: Ensaio socio-etnografico* (1968).

REID, CALVIN. "Caught in the Flux." *Transition* (Spring 1995).

REID, IRA DE AUGUSTINE. *The Negro Immigrant: His Background, Characteristics, and Social Adjustment, 1899–1937* (1939).

REIS, JOÃO JOSÉ. *Slave Rebellion in Brazil: The Muslim Uprising of 1835 in Bahia.* Translated by Arthur Brakel (1993).

"Religious Symbolism in African-American Quilts." *Clarion* 14, no. 3, (Summer 1989): 36–43.

*Report of the National Advisory Commission on Civil Disorders* (1968).

RENDER, SYLVIA LYONS. *Charles W. Chesnutt* (1980).

RESWICK, IRMTRAUD. *Traditional Textiles of Tunisia and Related North African Weavings* (1985).

REYNOLDS, MOIRA DAVIDSON. *"Uncle Tom's Cabin" and Mid-Nineteenth Century United States: Pen and Conscience* (1985).

RIBEIRO, RENÉ. *Religião e relações raciais* (1956).

RIBOWSKY, MARK. *Don't Look Back: Satchel Paige and the Shadows of Baseball* (1994).

RICHARDS, LEONARD L. *Gentleman of Property and Standing: Anti-Abolition Mobs in Jacksonian America* (1970).

RICHARDSON, JOE M. *A History of Fisk University, 1865–1946* (1980).

RICHARDSON, MICHAEL, ED. *Refusal of the Shadow: Surrealism and the Caribbean.* Translated by Krzysztof Fijalkowski and Michael Richardson (1996).

RICHMOND, MERLE. *Bid the Vassal Soar: Interpretative Essays on the Life and Poetry of Phillis Wheatley* (ca. 1753–1784) and George Moses Horton (ca. 1797–1883) (1974).

RICH, WILBUR C. *Black Mayors and School Politics: The Failure of Reform in Detroit, Gary, and Newark* (1996).

——. *The New Black Power* (1987).

RILEY, JAMES A. *The Biographical Encyclopedia of the Negro Baseball Leagues* (1994).

——. *Dandy, Day and the Devil* (1987).

RINGGOLD, FAITH. *We Flew Over the Bridge: The Memoirs of Faith Ringgold* (1995).

RISHELL, LYLE. *With A Black Platoon in Combat: A Year in Korea* (1993).

RITCHIE, CARSON. *Rock Art of Africa* (1979).

RITZ, DAVID. *Divided Soul: The Life of Marvin Gaye* (1985).

RIVLIN, BENJAMIN, ED. *Ralph Bunche: The Man and His Times* (1990).

RIVLIN, GARY. *Fire on the Prairie: Chicago's Harold Washington and the Politics of Race* (1993).

ROBERTS, JOHN STORM. *The Latin Tinge: The Impact of Latin American Music on the United States* (1979).

ROBERTS, A. D. "Tippu Tip, Livingstone, and the Chronology of Kazembe." *Azamoa* 2 (1967).

ROBERTS, ANDREW. *A History of Zambia* (1976).

ROBERTS, A. "Nyamwezi Trade." In *Pre-colonial African Trade*, ed. R. Gray and D. Birmingham (1970).

ROBERTS, MARTIN. "'World Music' and the Global Cultural Economy." *Diaspora* 2, no. 2 (1992): 229–41.

ROBERTS, RANDY. *Papa Jack: Jack Johnson and the Era of White Hopes* (1983).

ROBESON, PAUL. *Here I Stand* (1958).

ROBESON, SUSAN. *The Whole World in His Hands: A Pictorial Biography of Paul Robeson* (1981).

ROBINSON, DONALD. *Slavery in the Structure of American Politics, 1765–1820* (1971).

ROBINSON, JACKIE, WITH ALFRED DUCKETT. *I Never Had It Made* (1972).

ROBINSON, JO ANN GIBSON. *The Montgomery Bus Boycott and the Women Who Started It: The Memoir of Jo Ann Robinson* (1987).

ROBINSON, JONTYLE THERESA, AND WENDY GREENHOUSE. *The Art of Archibald J. Motley, Jr.* (1991).

ROBINSON, RAY, AND DAVE ANDERSON. *Sugar Ray* (1969).

ROBINSON, WILLIAM H. *Phillis Wheatley and her Writings* (1984).

RODMAN, SELDEN. *Renaissance in Haiti: Popular Painters in the Black Republic* (1948).

——. *Where Art is Joy: Haitian Art: The First Forty Years* (1988).

RODNEY, WALTER. *A History of the Guyanese Working People, 1881–1905.* (1981).

ROGERS, KIM LACY. *Righteous Lives: Narratives of the New Orleans Civil Rights Movement* (1993).

ROLLIN, FRANK A. *Life and Public Services of Martin R. Delany, Sub-assistant Commissioner, Bureau Relief of Refugees, Freedmen, and of Abandoned Lands, and Late Major 104th U.S. Colored Troops* (1868).

ROLLOCK, BARBARA. *Black Authors and Illustrators of Children's Books* (1988).

ROMAINE, SUZANNE. *Bilingualism* (1989).

RONDÓN, CÉSAR MIGUEL. *El libro de la salsa: Cronica de la m'sica del Caribe urbano* (1980).

RO, RONIN. *Gangsta: Merchandizing the Rhymes of Violence* (1996).

ROSE, AL. *Eubie Blake* (1979).

ROSELLO, MIREILLE. *Littérature et identité créole aux Antilles* (1992).

ROSE, TRICIA. *Black Noise: Rap Music and Black Culture in Contemporary America* (1994).

ROSE, WILLIE LEE, ED. *A Documentary History of Slavery in North America* (1976).

ROSS, B. JOYCE. *J. E. Spingarn and the Rise of the NAACP, 1911–1939* (1972).

ROTH, DAVID. *Sacred Honor: A Biography of Colin Powell* (1993).

ROULHE, NELLIE C. *Work, Play, and Commitment: A History of the First Fifty Years, Jack and Jill of America, Incorporated* (1989).

ROUT, LESLIE B. *The African Experience in Spanish America, 1502 to the Present Day* (1976).

ROVINE, VICTORIA. "Bogolanfini in Bamako: The Biography of a Malian Textile." *African Arts* 30 (1997).

ROWELL, CHARLES H., AND BRUCE WILLIS. "Interview with Afro-Brazilian playwright and poet Luiz Silva Cuti." *Callaloo* 18, no. 4 (Fall 1996): 729–33.

RUEDA NOVOA, ROCÍO. *Zambaje y autonomía: La historia de Esmeraldas siglos XVI-XIX* (1990).

RUEDY, JOHN. *Modern Algeria: The Origins and Development of a Nation* (1992).

RUDWICK, ELLIOTT M. *Race Riot at East St. Louis, July 2, 1917* (1964).

RUFF, SHAWN STEWART. *Go the Way Your Blood Beats: An Anthology of Lesbian and Gay Fiction by African-American Writers* (1996).

RULE, SHEILA. "Fredi Washington, 90, Actress; Broke Ground for Black Artists." *New York Times* (June 30, 1994): D21.

RUSSELL, ROSS. *Bird Lives: The High Life and Hard Times of Charlie (Yardbird) Parker* (1973).

——. *Jazz Style in Kansas City and the Southwest* (1971).

RUSSELL-WOOD, A. J. R. *The Black Man in Slavery and Freedom in Colonial Brazil* (1982).

SACK, KEVIN. "A Dynamic Farewell from a Longtime Rights Leader." *New York Times* (July 29, 1997).

——. "Ex-Charlotte Mayor Earns Helms Rematch." *New York Times* (May 8, 1996): B10.

SAGINI, MASHAK M. *The African and the African American University: A Historical and Sociological Analysis* (1996).

SALEM, NORMA. HABIB *Bourguiba, Islam and the Creation of Tunisia* (1984).

SALZMAN, JACK, DAVID LIONEL SMITH, AND CORNEL WEST, EDS. *Encyclopedia of African-American Culture and History.* 5 vols. (1996).

SAMKANGE, STANLAKE. *What Rhodes Really Said About Africans* (1982).

SAMMONS, JEFFREY T. *Beyond the Ring: The Role of Boxing in American Society* (1988).

SAMMONS, VIVIAN O. *Blacks in Science and Medicine* (1990).

SÁNCHEZ-BOUDY, José. *Diccionario de cubanismos m·s usuales (Como habla el cubano)*. 6 vols. (1978–1992).

SANDERSON, PETER. *Marvel Universe* (1995).

SANDOVAL, ALONSO DE. *De instauranda aethiopum salute - Un tratado sobre la esclavitud*. Translated by Enriqueta Vila Vilar (1987).

SAN MIGUEL, PEDRO. "The Dominican Peasantry and the Market Economy: The Peasants of the Cibao: 1880–1960." Ph.D. diss. Columbia University, 1987.

———. "The Making of a Peasantry: Dominican Agrarian History from the Sixteenth to the Twentieth Century." *Punto y Coma* 2, nos.1 and 2 (1990): 143–62.

SANTINO, JACK. *Miles of Smiles, Years of Struggle: Stories of Black Pullman Porters* (1989).

SANTOS, SYDNEY M. G. DOS. *André Rebouças e seu tempo* (1985).

SARTRE, JEAN-PAUL. "Orphée Noire." *Situations* 3 (1949): 227–86.

SATCHEL, LEROY. *Pitchin' Man: Satchel Paige's Own Story* (1992).

SATER, WILLIAM F. "The Black Experience in Chile." In *Slavery and Race Relations in Latin America*, ed. Robert Brent Toplin (1974).

SAUNDERS, A. C. *A Social History of Black Slaves and Freedmen in Portugal (1441–1555)* (1982).

SAVIANI, DERMEVAL, GERMAN RAMA, NORBERTO LAMARRA, INÉS AGUERRONDO, AND GREGÓRIO WEINBERG. *Desenvolvimento e educação na América Latina* (1987).

SAVOIA, RAFAEL. *Actas del Primer Congreso de Historia del Negro en el Ecuador y Sur de Colombia, Esmeraldas, 14–16 de octubre* (1988).

———, ed. *El Negro en la historia: Raices africanas in la nacionalidad ecuatorana* (1992).

SCARANO, JULITA. *Cotidiano e solidariedade: Vida di·ria da gente de cor nas Minas Gerais, século XVIII* (1994).

SCHAFFER, MATT, AND CHRISTINE COOPER. *Mandinko: The Ethnography of a West African Holy Land* (1980).

SCHARFMAN, RONNIE L. *"Engagement" and the Language of the Subject in the Poetry of Aimé Césaire* (1987).

SCHATZBERG, MICHAEL. *The Dialectics of Oppression in Zaire* (1988).

SCHEADER, CATHERINE. *Shirley Chisholm: Teacher and Congresswoman* (1990).

SCHIEFFELIN, BAMBI, AND RACHELLE DOUCET. "The 'Real' Haitian Creole: Ideology, Metalinguistics, and Orthographic Choices." *American Ethnologist* 21, no. 1 (1994): 176–200.

SCHNEIDER, JOHN J., AND D. STANLEY EITZEN. "Racial Segregation by Professional Football Positions,1960–1985." *Sociology and Social Research* 70, no. 4 (1986): 259–61.

SCHNEIDER, JOHN T. *Dictionary of African Borrowings in Brazilian Portuguese* (1991).

SCHREINER, CLAUS. *Música brasileira: A History of Popular Music and the People of Brazil*. Translated by Mark Weinstein (1993).

SCHUBERT, FRANK. *Black Valor: Buffalo Soldiers and the Medal of Honor, 1870–1898* (1997).

SCHULLER, GUNTHER. *Early Jazz: Its Roots and Musical Development* (1968).

——. *The Swing Era: The Development of Jazz, 1930–1945* (1989).

SCHWARTZMAN, MYRON. *Romare Bearden: His Life and Art* (1990).

SCHWARTZ-BART, SIMONE. *The Bridge of Beyond*. Translated by Barbara Bray. Introduction by Bridget Jones (1982).

SCHWARZ, ROBERTO. *Misplaced Ideas: Essays on Brazilian Culture* (1992).

SCOTT, KENNETH. "The Slave Insurrection in New York in 1712." *New York Historical Society Quarterly* 45 (January 1961).

SECRETAN, THIERRY. *Going into Darkness: Fantastic Coffins from Africa* (1995).

SENGHOR, LÉOPOLD SEDAR. *Liberté*. 5 vols. (1964–1993).

SERAILE, WILLIAM. *Voice of Dissent: Theophilus Gould Steward (1843–1924) and Black America* (1991).

SERELS, M. Mitchell. *A History of the Jews of Tangier in the Nineteenth and Twentieth Centuries* (1991).

SHARP, WILLIAM FREDERICK. *Slavery on the Spanish Frontier: The Colombian ChocÛ, 1680–1810* (1976).

SHANNON, SANDRA G. *The Dramatic Vision of August Wilson* (1995).

SHAW, ARNOLD. *Honkers and Shouters: The Golden Years of Rhythm and Blues* (1978).

SHAW, DONALD L. *Alejo Carpentier* (1985).

SHERMAN, JOAN. *Invisible Poets: Afro-Americans of the Nineteenth Century*. 2d ed. (1989).

SHERMAN, RICHARD B. *The Case of Odell Waller and Virginia Justice, 1940–1942* (1992).

SHIELDS, JOHN C. "Phillis Wheatley." In *African American Writers*, ed. Valerie Smith (1991).

SHOCKLEY, ANN ALLEN. *Afro-American Women Writers, 1746–1933: An Anthology and Critical Guide* (1988).

SHOGAN, ROBERT, AND TOM CRAIG. *The Detroit Race Riot: A Study in Violence* (1964).

SHOMAN, ASSAD. *13 Chapters of a History of Belize* (1994).

SHUCARD, ALAN R. *Countee Cullen* (1984).

*Sierra Leone: Twelve Years of Economic Achievement and Political Consolidation under the APC and Dr. Siaka Stevens, 1968–1980* (1980).

SILL, ROBERT. *David Hammons in the Hood* (1994).

SILVA, J. ROMÃO DA. *Luís Gama e suas poesias satíricas* (1981).

SILVERA, MAKEDA, ED. *The Other Woman: Women of Colour in Contemporary Canadian Literature* (1994).

SILVESTER, PETER. *A Left Hand like God: A History of Boogie-Woogie Piano* (1988).

SIMKINS, CUTHBERT O. *Coltrane: A Musical Biography* (1975).

SIMMONS, DIANE. *Jamaica Kincaid* (1994).

SIMO, ANA MARÍA. *Lydia Cabrera: An Intimate Portrait* (1984).

SIMMS, PETER. *Trouble in Guyana: An Account of People, Personalities, and Politics as They Were in British Guiana* (1966).

SIMPSON, DAVID IAN H. *Marburg and Ebola Virus Infections: A Guide for Their Diagnosis, Management, and Control* (1977).

SIMPSON, GEORGE EATON. *Black Religions in the New World.* (1978).

——. *The Shango Cult in Trinidad* (1965).

SIMS, JANET L. *Marian Anderson: An Annotated Bibliography and Discography* (1981).

SIMS, LOWERY STOKES. *Robert Colescott, A Retrospective 1975–1986* (1987).

SIMS, RUDINE. *Shadow and Substance: Afro-American Experience in Contemporary Children's Fiction* (1982).

SINGER, BARRY. *Black and Blue: The Life and Lyrics of Andy Razaf* (1992).

SINNETTE, ELINOR DES VERNEY. *Arthur Alfonso Schomburg, Black Bibliophile & Collector: A Biography* (1989).

SINNETTE, ELINOR DES VERNEY, W. PAUL COATES, AND THOMAS C. BATTLE, EDS. *Black Bibliophiles and Collectors: Preservers of Black History* (1990).

SITKOFF, HARVARD. *A New Deal for Blacks: The Emergence of Civil Rights as a National Issue*. Vol. I, *The Depression Decade* (1978).

SKIDMORE, THOMAS E. *Black Into White: Race and Nationality in Brazilian Thought* (1974; revised ed., 1993).

SLATER, LES. "What is Mas? What is Carnival? Profiling Carnival and its Origins." *Black Diaspora: A Global Black Magazine* (August 1997).

SLAUGHTER, THOMAS PAUL. *Bloody Dawn: The Christiana Riot and Racial Violence in the Antebellum North* (1991).

SMITH, ANNA DEVEARE. *Fires in the Mirror: Crown Heights, Brooklyn and Other Identities* (1993).

SMITH, BARBARA, ED. *Home Girls: A Black Feminist Anthology* (1983).

SMITH, CHARLES MICHAEL. "Bruce Nugent: Bohemian of the Harlem Renaissance." In *In the Life: A Black Gay Anthology*, ed. Joseph Beam (1986).

SMITH CÓRDOBA, AMIR. *Vida y obra de Candelario Obeso* (1984).

SMITH, IAN DOUGLAS. *The Great Betrayal: The Memoirs of Ian Douglas Smith* (1997).

SMITH-IRVIN, JEANNETTE. *Footsoldiers of the Universal Negro Improvement Association: Their Own Words* (1988).

SMITH, JESSIE CARNEY. *Black Academic Libraries and Research Collections: An Historical Survey* (1977).

——, ed. *Notable Black American Women*. 2 vols. (1992–1996).

SMITH, KEITHLYN B. *No Easy Pushover: A History of the Working People of Antigua and Barbuda, 1836–1994* (1994).

SMITH, KEITHLYN B., AND FERNANDO C. *To Shoot Hard Labour: The Life and Times of Samuel Smith, an Antiguan Workingman, 1877–1982* (1986).

SMITH, ROBERTA. "A Forgotten Black Painter Is Saved from Obscurity." *New York Times* (June 12, 1992): C18.

SMITH, RONNA. "Vida de Adalberto Ortiz." *Cultura: Revista del Banco Central del Ecuador* 6, no. 16 (1983): 99–118.

SMITH, S. CLAY, JR. "Patricia Roberts Harris: A Champion in Pursuit of Excellence." *Howard Law Journal* 29, no. 3 (1986): 437–55.

SMITH, WILLIAM E. "Commandments Without Moses: Abandoning His Principles, Sullivan Wants U. S. Firms to Pull Out." *Time* (June 15, 1987).

SNOWDEN, FRANK M., JR. *Before Color Prejudice: The Ancient View of Blacks* (1983).

——. *Blacks in Antiquity; Ethiopians in the Greco-Roman Experience* (1970).

SOLLORS, WERNER. *Amiri Baraka/LeRoi Jones: The Quest for a "Populist Modernism"* (1978).

——. *Neither Black nor White, Yet Both: Thematic Explorations of Interracial Literature* (1997).

——, ed. *Multilingual America: Transnationalism, Ethnicity, and the Languages of American Literature* (1998).

SOLOW, BARBARA L., ED. *Slavery and the Rise of the Atlantic System* (1991).

SOMJEE, SULTAN. *Material Culture of Kenya* (1993).

SOMMER, DORIS, *Foundational Fictions : The National Romances of Latin America* (1991).

SOTO, SARA. *Magia e historia en los "Cuentos negros": "Por que" y "Ayapa" de Lydia Cabrera* (1988).

SOUTHERN, EILEEN. *The Music of Black Americans: A History* (1983).

SOYINKA, WOLE. *The Burden of Memory, the Muse of Forgiveness* (1999).

——. *Myth, Literature, and the African World* (1976).

——. *The Open Sore of a Continent: A Personal Narrative of the Nigerian Crisis* (1996).

SPELLMAN, A. B. *Black Music: Four Lives* (1970).

SPINNER, THOMAS J., JR. *A Political and Social History of Guyana, 1945–1983* (1984).

SPIVAK, GAYATRI CHAKTAVORTY. *In Other Worlds: Essays in Cultural Politics* (1987).

SPOFFORD, TIM. *Lynch Street: The May 1970 Slayings at Jackson State College* (1988).

STAMPP, KENNETH M. *The Peculiar Institution: Slavery in the Ante-Bellum South* (1956).

STAM, ROBERT. *Tropical Multiculturalism: A Comparative History of Race in Brazilian Cinema and Culture* (1997).

STAM, ROBERT, AND RANDAL JOHNSON. *Brazilian Cinema.* Rev. and exp. ed. (1995).

STANLEY, HENRY MORTON. *In Darkest Africa; or, The Quest, Rescue and Retreat of Emin, Governor of Equatoria* (1890).

——. *Through the Dark Continent; or The Sources of the Nile around the Great Lakes of Equatorial Africa and Down the Livingstone River to the Atlantic Ocean* (1878).

ST. BOURNE, CLAIR. "The African-American Image in American Cinema." *Black Scholar* 21, no.2 (March-May 1990): 12 (8).

STEARNS, MARSHALL, AND JEAN STEARNS. *Jazz Dance: The Story of American Vernacular Dance.* Rev. ed. (1979).

STEIN, JUDITH E., ET AL. *I Tell My Heart: The Art of Horace Pippin* (1993).

STEIN, STEVE J. "Visual Images of the Lower Classes in Early Twentieth-Century Peru: Soccer as a Window to Social Reality." *In Windows on Latin America: Understanding Society through Photographs,* ed. Robert M. Levine (1987).

STEPAN, NANCY. *The Idea of Race in Science* (1982).

STEPHENS, THOMAS M. *Dictionary of Latin American Racial and Ethnic Terminology* (1989).

STEPTO, ROBERT B. "After Modernism, After Hibernation: Michael Harper, Robert Hayden, and Jay Wright." In *Chant of Saints: A Gathering of Afro-American Literature, Art, and Scholarship* (1979).

——. *From Behind the Veil: A Study of Afro-American Narrative* (1979)

STERLING, DOROTHY. *Black Foremothers: Three Lives* (1988).

——. *The Making of an Afro-American: Martin Robison Delany 1812–1885* (1971).

——. *We Are Your Sisters: Black Women in the Nineteenth Century* (1984).

STERN, YVAN. "Interview: Souleymane Cissé." *Unir Cinema* 23–24 (March-June 1986): 44–45.

STEVENSON, BRENDA, ED. *The Journals of Charlotte Forten Grimké* (1988).

STEVENS, PHILLIPS, JR. "Magic" and "Sorcery and Witchcraft." In *Encyclopedia of Cultural Anthropology*, ed. Melvin Ember and David Levinson (1996).

STEVENS, SIAKA. *What Life Has Taught Me* (1984).

STEWART-BAXTER, DERRICK. *Ma Rainey and the Classic Blues Singers* (1970).

STILL, JUDITH ANNE. *William Grant Still: A Bio-bibliography* (1996).

STILL, WILLIAM. *The Underground Railroad: A Record of Facts, Authentic Narratives, Letters, &c., Narrating the Hardships, Hair-breadth Escapes, and Death Struggles of the Slaves in Their Efforts for Freedom, as Related by Themselves and Others or Witnessed By the Author: Together with Sketches of Some of the Largest Stockholders and Most Liberal Aiders and Advisers of the Road* (1872).

STINSON, SULEE JEAN. *The Dawn of Blaxploitation: Sweet Sweetback's Baadasssss Song and its Audience* (1992).

STORY, ROSALYN M. *And So I Sing: African American Divas of Opera and Concert* (1990).

STRAUSS, NEIL. "Curtis Mayfield" (interview). *New York Times* (February 28, 1996).

STRAUS, NOEL. "Dorthy Maynor Berkshire Soloist." *New York Times* (August 10, 1939).

STOWE, HARRIET BEECHER. *Uncle Tom's Cabin: Authoritative Text. Backgrounds and Contexts* (Norton Critical Edition) (1994).

STREICKER, JOEL. "Policing the Boundaries: Race, Class and Gender in Cartagena, Colombia." *American Ethnologist* 22, no. 1 (1995), 54–74.

STUART, CHRIS, AND TILDE STUART. *Africa's Vanishing Wildlife* (1996).

——. *Chris and Tilde Stuart's Field Guide to the Mammals of Southern Africa* (1994).

STUCKEY, STERLING. *Slave Culture: Nationalist Theory and the Foundations of Black America* (1987).

SUGGS, HENRY LEWIS. *P. B. Young, Newspaper-man: Race, Politics, and Journalism in the New South, 1910–1962* (1988).

SULLIVAN, PATRICIA. *Days of Hope: Race and Democracy in the New Deal Era* (1996).

SUMMERVILLE, JAMES. *Educating Black Doctors: A History of Meharry Medical College* (1983).

SUPER, GEORGE LEE, MICHAEL GARDEN, AND NANCY MARSHALL, EDS. *P. H. Polk: Photographs* (1980).

SUTTON, JOHN E. G. *Dar es Salaam: City, Port, and Region* (1970).

SUZIGAN, GERALDO. *Bossa nova: música, política, educação no Brasil* (1990).

SWEETMAN, DAVID. *Women Leaders in African History* (1984).

SWENSON, JOHN. *Stevie Wonder* (1986).

SYLVANDER, CAROLYN WEDIN. *Jessie Redmon Fauset, Black American Writer* (1981).

TARRY, ELLEN. *The Other Toussaint: A Modern Biography of Pierre Toussaint, a Post-Revolutionary Black* (1981).

TATE, CLAUDIA. *Domestic Allegories of Political Desire: The Black Heroine's Text at the Turn of the Century* (1992).

TAYLOR, FRANK. *Alberta Hunter: A Celebration in Blues* (1987).

TAYLOR, PATRICK. *The Narrative of Liberation: Perspectives on Afro-Caribbean Literature, Popular Culture, and Politics* (1989).

TAYLOR, QUINTARD. *The Forging of a Black Community: Seattle's Central District from 1870 through the Civil Rights Era* (1994).

TEIXEIRA, IVAN. *Obras poéticas de Basilio da Gama* (1996).

TENENBAUM, BARBARA A., ED. *Encyclopedia of Latin American History and Culture.* 5 vols. (1996).

"The Ten Most Beautiful Black Women in America (A Wide Range of External and Internal Beauty)." *Ebony* (July 1987).

TERRY, DON. "Hatcher Begins Battle to Regain Spotlight in Gary." *New York Times.* (May 6, 1991): A12.

TERRY, WALLACE, ED. *Bloods: An Oral History of the Vietnam War, by Black Veterans* (1984).

THOBY-MARCELIN, PHILIPPE. *Panorama de l'art Haïtien* (1956).

THOMAS, ANTONY. *Rhodes* (1996).

THOMAS, BETTYE COLLIER. "Harvey Johnson and the Baltimore Mutual United Brother-hood of Liberty, 1885–1910." In *Black Communities and Urban Development in America, 1720–1990: From Reconstruction to the Great Migration, 1877–1917,* ed. Kenneth L. Kusmer. Vol. IV, part 1 (1991).

THOMAS, BROOK. *Plessy v. Ferguson: A Brief History with Documents* (1997).

THOMAS, DAVID S. G. *The Kalahari Environment* (1991).

THOMAS, HUGH. *Cuba: The Pursuit of Freedom* (1971).

THOMPSON, FRANCESCA. "Final Curtain for Anita Bush." *Black World* 23 (July 1974): 60–61.

THOMPSON, LESLIE. *An Autobiography* (1985).

THOMPSON, ROBERT FERRIS. *Flash of the Spirit: African and Afro-American Art and Philosophy* (1983).

——. *Jean-Michel Basquiat* (1985).

THORNTON, J. MILLS III. "Challenge and Response in the Montgomery Bus Boycott of 1955–1956." *Alabama Review* 33 (1980): 163–235.

THORNTON, JOHN. *Africa and Africans in the Making of the Atlantic World: 1400–1800* (1998).

THORPE, EDWARD. *Black Dance* (1990).

THURMAN, HOWARD. *With Head and Heart: The Autobiography of Howard Thurman* (1979).

TIBBLES, ANTHONY, ED. *Transatlantic Slavery: Against Human Dignity* (1994).

TILLERY, TYRONE. *Claude McKay: A Black Poet's Struggle for Identity* (1992).

TIMBERLAKE, LLOYD. *Africa in Crisis: The Causes, the Cures of Environmental Bankruptcy* (1985).

TINGAY, PAUL, AND DOUG SCOTT. *Handy Guide: Victoria Falls* (1996).

Tinhorao, Ramos José. *Os Negros em Portugal: Uma presença silenciosa* (1988).

Tippu Tip. *Maisha ya Hamed bin Muhammed el Murjebi, Yaani Tippu Tip, kwa Maneno Yake Mwenyewe.* Translated by W. H. Whitely (1966).

Tobias, Channing. "Autobiography." In *Thirteen Americans: Their Spiritual Biographies* (1953).

Tomkins, Calvin, "A Sense of Urgency." *New Yorker* (March 1989): 48–74.

Toobin, Jeffrey. *The Run of His Life: The People v. O. J. Simpson* (1996).

Toop, David. *Ocean of Sound: Aether Talk, Ambient Sound, and Imaginary Worlds* (1995).

Toplin, Robert Brent. *The Abolition of Slavery in Brazil* (1972).

Torrence, Ridgely. *The Story of John Hope* (1948).

Toureh, Fanta. *L'imaginaire dans l'úuvre de Simone Schwartz-Bart: Approche d'une mythologie antillaise* (1986).

Toussaint, Auguste. *History of Mauritius* (1977).

Trexler, Harrison. *Slavery in Missouri, 1804–1865* (1914).

Trevisan, João Silverio. *Perverts in Paradise.* Translated by Martin Foreman (1986).

Truth, Sojourner, and Olive Gilbert, *Narrative of Sojourner Truth, a Northern Slave, Emancipated from Bodily Servitude by the State of New York, in 1828* (1850).

Turnbull, Colin M. The Forest People (1961).

Turner, Frederick W. *Remembering Song: Encounters with the New Orleans Jazz Tradition.* Exp. ed. (1994).

Turner, Lorenzo Dow. *Africanisms in the Gullah Dialect* (1949).

Turner, Mary. *From Chattel Slaves to Wage Slaves: The Dynamics of Labour Bargaining in the Americas* (1995).

——. *Slaves and Missionaries: The Disintegration of Jamaican Slave Society* (1982).

Tushnet, Mark V. *The NAACP's Strategy Against Segregated Education, 1925–1950* (1987).

Tuttle, William M., Jr. *Race Riot: Chicago in the Red Summer of 1919* (1970).

——, ed. *W. E. B. Du Bois* (1973).

Tygiel, Jules. *Baseball's Great Experiment: Jackie Robinson and His Legacy* (1983).

Uche, Nena. "Textiles in Nigeria." *African Technology Forum* 7, no. 2 (1994).

Ullman, Michael. *Jazz Lives: Portraits in Words and Pictures* (1980).

Ullman, Victor. *Martin R. Delany: The Beginnings of Black Nationalism* (1971).

*Unesco General History of Africa.* 8 vols. (1981–1993).

Urban, W. J. *Black Scholar: Horace Mann Bond 1904–1972* (1992).

Urquhart, Brian. *Ralph Bunche: An American Life* (1993).

Valdez Aguilar, Rafael. *Sinaloa: Negritud y olvido* (1993).

Van Deburg, William L. *New Day in Babylon: The Black Power Movement and American Culture, 1965–1975* (1992).

Vandercook, John W. *Black Majesty: The Life of Christophe, King of Haiti* (1934).

Van Sertima, Ivan. *Blacks in Science: Ancient and Modern* (1991).

——, ed. *African Presence in Early America* (1987).

——, ed. *African Presence in Early Europe* (1985).

——, ed. *Black Women in Antiquity* (1984).

VAN SERTIMA, IVAN, AND RUNOKO RASHIDI, EDS. *African Presence in Early Asia* (1988).

VANSINA, JAN. *Les anciens royaumes de la savane: Les états des savanes méridionales de l'Afrique centrale des origines à l'occupation coloniale* (1965).

——. *Art History in Africa: An Introduction to Method* (1984).

——. *The Children of Woot: A History of the Kuba Peoples* (1978).

——. *Kingdoms of the Savanna* (1966).

——. *Oral Tradition as History* (1985).

——. *Paths in the Rainforests: Toward a History of Political Tradition in Equatorial Africa* (1990).

VAN TASSEL, DAVID D., AND JOHN J. GRABOWSKI. *Cleveland: A Tradition of Reform* (1986).

——. *The Encyclopedia of Cleveland History* (1987).

VARELA, BEATRIZ. *El español cubano-americano* (1992).

VASQUEZ DE URRUTIA, PATRICIA, ED. *La democracia en blanco y negro: Colombia en los anos ochenta* (1989).

VEDANA, HARDY. *Jazz em Porto Alegre* (1987).

VENET, WENDY HAMMOND. *Neither Ballots Nor Bullets: Women Abolitionists and the Civil War* (1991).

VERBEKEN, AUGUSTE. *Msiri, roi du Garenganze: L' homme rouge du Katanga* (1956).

VERGER, PIERRE. *Bahia Africa Bahia: Fotografias* (1996).

——. *Bahia and the West African Trade, 1549–1851* (1964).

——. *Dieux d'Afrique; Culte des Orishas et Vodouns à l' ancienne côte des esclaves en Afrique et à Bahia, la baie de tous les saints au Brésil.*

——. *Ewe: Le verbe et le pouvoir des plantes chez les Yoruba* (1997).

——. *Flux et reflux de la traite des nègres entre le Golfe de Bénin et Bahia de todos os Santos, du XVIIè au XIXè siècle* (1968).

——. *Orixas: Deuses iorubas na Africa e no Novo Mundo* (1981).

——. *Retratos da Bahia, 1946 a 1952* (1980).

VERGER, PIERRE, AND JORGE AMADO. *Iconografia dos deuses africanos no candomblé da Bahia* (1980).

VÉRIN, PIERRE. *The History of Civilization in North Madagascar.* Translated by David Smith (1986).

VÉRIN, PIERRE, C. P. KOTTACK, AND P. GORLIN. "The glottochronology of Malagasy speech communities." *Oceanic Linguistics* 8 (1970): 26–83.

VERÍSSIMO, INÁCIO JOSÉ. *André Rebouças através de sua auto-biografia* (1939).

VESTAL, STANLEY. *Mountain Men* (1937).

VICKERY, WALTER N. *Alexander Pushkin* (1970).

VINES, ALEX. *Renamo: Terrorism in Mozambique* (1991).

VITIER, CINTIO, AND FINA GARCÍA MARRUZ, EDS. *Flor oculta de poesia cubana* (1978).

——. *Temas martianos* (1981).

VLACH, JOHN MICHAEL. *The Afro-American Tradition in the Decorative Arts* (1978).

VOGEL, ARNO. *A galinha-d'Angola: Iniciacão e identidade na cultura afro-brasileira* (1993).

WADE, PETER. *Blackness and Race Mixture: The Dynamics of Racial Identity in Colombia* (1993).

——. *Race and Ethnicity in Latin America* (1997).

WAGLEY, CHARLES., ED. *Race and Class in Rural Brazil.* 2d ed. (1963).

WAHLMAN, MAUDE SOUTHWELL. *Contemporary African Arts* (1974).

——. *Signs and Symbols: African Images in African-American Quilts* (1993).

WAKHIST, TSI TSI. "Taking the Helm of the NAACP: The Ever-Ready Evers-Williams." *Crisis* 102 (May/June 1995): 14–19.

WALDMAN, GLORIA F. *Luis Rafael Sánchez: Pasión teatral.* (1988).

WALKER, ETHEL PITTS. "The American Negro Theater." In *The Theater of Black Americans,* ed. Errol Hill (1987).

WALKER, GEORGE E. *The Afro-American in New York City, 1827–1860* (1993).

WALKER, JAMES W. ST. G. *The Black Loyalists: The Search for a Promised Land in Nova Scotia and Sierra Leone, 1783–1870* (1992).

WALKER, MELISSA. *Down from the Mountaintop: Black Women's Novels in the Wake of the Civil Rights Movement, 1966–1989* (1991).

WALLS, WILLIAM J. *The African Methodist Episcopal Zion Church: Reality of the Black Church* (1974).

WARD, WILLIAM EDWARD. "Charles Lenox Remond: Black Abolitionist, 1838–1873." Ph.D. diss., Clark University, 1977.

WARE, GILBERT. *William Hastie: Grace Under Pressure* (1984).

WASHINGTON, BOOKER T. *Up From Slavery* (1901).

WASHINGTON, JAMES M. *Conversations with God* (1994).

WATKINS, MEL. *On The Real Side: Laughing, Lying, and Signifying. The Underground Tradition of African-American Humor* (1994).

WATSON, ALAN. *Slave Law in the Americas* (1989).

WATSON, DENTON L. *Lion in the Lobby: Clarence Mitchell, Jr.'s Struggle for the Passage of Civil Rights Laws* (1990).

WATTS, JILL. *God, Harlem U.S.A.: The Father Divine Story* (1992).

WEARE, WALTER B. *Black Business in the New South: A Social History of the North Carolina Mutual Life Insurance Company* (1973).

WEAVER, JOHN DOWNING. *The Brownsville Raid* (1970).

——. *The Senator and the Sharecropper's Son: Exoneration of the Brownsville Soldiers* (1997).

WEAVER, ROBERT C. "The Health Care of Our Cities." *National Medical Association Journal* (January 1968): 42–48.

WEBB, BARBARA J. *Myth and History in Caribbean Fiction: Alejo Carpentier, Wilson Harris, and Edouard Glissant* (1992).

WEBB, LILLIAN ASHCROFT. *About My Father's Business: The Life of Elder Michaux* (1981).

WEINBERG, KENNETH G. *Black Victory: Carl Stokes and the Winning of Cleveland* (1968).

WEINSTEIN, BRIAN. *Eboué* (1972).

WEINSTEIN, NORMAN. *A Night in Tunisia: Imaginings of Africa in Jazz* (1993).

WEISS, NANCY J. *Farewell to the Party of Lincoln: Black Politics in the Age of FDR* (1983).

———. *Whitney M. Young, Jr., and the Struggle for Civil Rights* (1989).

WELLS-BARNETT, IDA B. *On Lynchings: Southern Horrors; A Red Record; Mob Rule in New Orleans* (1969).

WESLEY, CHARLES H. *Charles H. Wesley: The Intellectual Tradition of a Black; Historian*, ed. James L. Conyers, Jr. (1997).

WESLEY, DOROTHY PORTER. "Integration Versus Separatism: William Cooper Nell's Role in the Struggle for Equality." In *Courage and Conscience: Black and White Abolitionists in Boston*, ed. Donald M. Jacobs (1993): 207–24.

WEST, CORNEL. *Beyond Eurocentrism and Multiculturalism* (1993).

———. *Black Theology and Marxist Thought* (1979).

———. *Keeping Faith: Philosophy and Race in America* (1993).

———. *Prophetic Reflections: Notes on Race and Power in America* (1993).

———. *Race Matters* (1993).

WEST, GUIDA. *The National Welfare Rights Movement: The Social Protest of Poor Women* (1981).

"What Martin Luther King Would Do Now about Drugs, Poverty and Black-Jewish Relations: Widow and Associates Tell How He Would Respond to Today's Burning Issues." *Ebony* (January 1991).

WHEAT, ELLEN HARKINS. *Jacob Lawrence, American Painter* (1986).

WHEELER, B. GORDON. *Black California: The History of African-Americans in the Golden State* (1993).

WHITE, ALVIN, "LET ME TELL YOU ABOUT MY LOVE AFFAIR WITH FLORENCE MILLS." *Sepia* 26, no. 11 (November 1977).

WHITE, TIMOTHY. *Catch a Fire: The Life of Bob Marley*. Rev. and enl. ed. (1998).

WHITE, WALTER F. *A Man Called White: The Autobiography of Walter White* (1948; reprint ed., 1995).

———. *Rope and Faggot: A Biography of Judge Lynch* (1929).

WHITFIELD, STEPHEN J. *A Death in the Delta: The Story of Emmett Till* (1988).

WHITING, ALBERT N. *Guardians of the Flame: Historically Black Colleges Yesterday, Today, and Tomorrow* (1991).

WHITMAN, MARK, ED. *Removing a Badge of Slavery: The Record of Brown v. Board of Education* (1993).

WHITTEN, NORMAN. *Black Frontiersmen: A South American Case* (1974).

———, ed. *Cultural Transformations and Ethnicity in Modern Ecuador* (1981).

WICKER, TOM. *A Time to Die* (1975).

WIENER, LEO. *Africa and the Discovery of America*. Vol. I (1920).

WIGG, DAVID. *And Then Forgot to Tell Us Why: A Look at the Campaign Against River Blindness in West Africa* (1993).

WIKRAMANAYAKE, MARINA. *A World in Shadow: The Free Black in Antebellum South Carolina* (1973).

WILKINS, ROY. *Standing Fast: The Autobiography of Roy Wilkins* (1982).

WILLIAMS, ELSIE A. *The Humor of Jackie Moms Mabley: An African American Comedic Tradition* (1995).

WILLIAMS, ERIC. *Capitalism and Slavery* (1944; reprint ed., 1994).

——. *Inward Hunger: The Education of a Prime Minister* (1969).

WILLIAMS, LORNA V. "Mor'a Delgado and the Cuban Slave Narrative." *Modern Language Notes* 108, no. 2 (March 1993): 302–13.

——. *The Representation of Slavery in Cuban Fiction.* (1994).

WILLIAMS, MICHAEL W. *Pan-Africanism: An Annotated Bibliography* (1992).

WILLIAMSON, JANICE. *Sounding Differences: Conversations with Seventeen Canadian Women Writers* (1993).

WILLIAMSON, JOEL. *After Slavery: The Negro in South Carolina During Reconstruction, 1861–1877* (1965; reprint ed., 1990).

——. *The Crucible of Race: Black-White Relations in the American South Since Emancipation* (1984).

——. *New People: Miscegenation and Mulattoes in the United States* (1980).

WILLIAMS, PONTHEOLLA T. *Robert Hayden: A Critical Analysis of His Poetry* (1987).

WILLIAMS, ROGER. *The Bonds: An American Family* (1971).

WILLIS, SUSAN. "Crushed Geraniums: Juan Francisco Manzano and the Language of Slavery." In *The Slave's Narrative*, ed. Charles T. Davis and Henry Louis Gates, Jr. (1985).

——. *Specifying: Black Women Writing the American Experience* (1987).

WILLIS-THOMAS, DEBORAH. *Black Photographers, 1840–1940: An Illustrated Bio-Bibliography* (1985).

——. *An Illustrated Bio-Bibliography of Black Photographers, 1940–1988* (1989).

WILMER, VALERIE. "'Blackamoors' and the British Beat." *In Views on Black American Music*, no. 3 (1985–1988): 60–64.

WILSON, CHARLES REAGAN, AND WILLIAM FERRIS, EDS. *Encyclopedia of Southern Culture* (1989).

WILSON, MARY, WITH PATRICIA ROMANOWSKI AND AHRGUS JULLIARD. *Dreamgirl: My Life as a Supreme* (1986).

WILSON, WILLIAM JULIUS. *The Bridge over the Racial Divide: Rising Inequality and Coalition Politics* (1999).

——. *When Work Disappears: The World of the New Urban Poor* (1996).

WINANT, HOWARD. "Rethinking Race in Brazil." *Journal of Latin American Studies* 24 (1992): 173–92.

WINCH, JULIE. *Philadelphia's Black Elite: Activism, Accommodation, and the Struggle for Autonomy, 1787–1848* (1988).

WINKS, ROBIN W. *The Blacks in Canada: A History* (1997).

WIPPLER, MIGENE GONZÁLEZ. *Santería: The Religion* (1982).

WOIDEK, CARL. *Charlie Parker: His Music and Life* (1996).

WOLFENSTEIN, EUGENE VICTOR. *The Victims of Democracy: Malcolm X and the Black Revolution* (1981).

WOLSELEY, ROLAND E. *The Black Press, U.S.A.* (1990).

WOODBRIDGE, HENSLEY C. "Glossary of Names Found in Colonial Latin America for Crosses Among Indians, Negroes, and Whites." *Journal of the Washington Academy of Sciences* 38 (1948): 353–62.

WOOD, JOE, ED. *Malcolm X: In Our Own Image* (1992).

WOOD, PETER H. *Black Majority: Negroes in Colonial South Carolina from 1670 through the Stono Rebellion* (1974).

WOOD, PETER H., AND KAREN C. C. DALTON. *Winslow Homer's Images of Blacks: The Civil War and Reconstruction Years* (1988).

WOODSON, CARTER G. "The Negroes of Cincinnati Prior to the Civil War." In *Free Blacks in America, 1800–1860*, ed. John Bracey, Jr. August Meier, and Elliot Rudwick (1971).

WOODS, SYLVIA. *Sylvia's Soul Food: Recipes from Harlem's World Famous Restaurant* (1992).

WOODWARD, C. VANN. *Origins of the New South: 1877–1913* (1951).

——. *Reunion and Reaction: The Compromise of 1877 and the End of Reconstruction* (1951; reprint ed. 1991).

——. *The Strange Career of Jim Crow* (1955).

Woolman, David S. *Stars in the Firmament: Tangier Characters, 1660–1960s* (1997).

WORCESTER, KENT. *C. L. R. James and the American Century, 1938–1953* (1980).

WORLD BANK. *Mauritius Country Report* 4 (1988).

WRIGHT, GILES R. *Afro-Americans in New Jersey: A Short History* (1988).

WRIGHT, LEE ALFRED. *Identity, Family, and Folklore in African American Literature* (1995).

WRIGHT, RICHARD R., JR. *The Negro in Pennsylvania, A Study in Economic History* (1969).

WUBBEN, HUBERT H. *Civil War Iowa and the Copperhead Movement* (1980).

WYNES, CHARLES E. *Charles Richard Drew: The Man and the Myth* (1988).

XAVIER, ISMAIL. *Allegories of Under-development: Aesthetics and Politics in Modern Brazilian Cinema* (1997).

YANCEY, DWAYNE. *When Hell Froze Over: The Untold Story of Doug Wilder: A Black Politician's Rise to Power in the South* (1988).

YAU, JOHN. "Please, Wait by the Coatroom: Wifredo Lam in the Museum of Modern Art." *Arts Magazine* 4 (1988): 56–59.

YELLIN, JEAN FAGAN, AND JOHN C. VAN HORNE, EDS. *The Abolitionist Sisterhood: Women's Political Culture in Antebellum America* (1994).

YOHE, KRISTINE A. "Gloria Naylor." In *The Oxford Companion to African American Literature*, ed. James David Hart and Phillip W. Leininger. 6th ed. (1995).

YOUNG, ANDREW. *An Easy Burden: The Civil Rights Movement and the Transformation of America* (1996).

——. *A Way Out of No Way: The Spiritual Memoirs of Andrew Young* (1994).

YOUNG, CRAWFORD. *Politics in the Congo: Decolonization and Independence* (1965).

ZANGRANDO, ROBERT. *The NAACP Crusade Against Lynching, 1909–1950* (1980).

ZENÓN CRUZ, ISABELO. *Narciso descubre su trasero: El negro en la cultura puertorriqueña.* 2d ed. (1975).

ZIELINA, MARIA CARMEN. *La africania en el cuento cubano y puertorriqueño* (1992).

ZINN, HOWARD. *SNCC: The New Abolitionists* (1965).